THE NEW CAMBRIDGE COMPANION TO
# JESUS

*The New Cambridge Companion to Jesus* serves as the most up-to-date guide and resource for understanding Jesus's multifaceted legacy, enduring impact over time and space, and relevance in today's world. Integrating textual, historical, theological, and cultural perspectives, the chapters, specially commissioned for this volume, also offer a fresh and diverse overview of Jesus's significance in contemporary global contexts. Key features include insights into Jesus's life and teachings, his role in different religious traditions, and his influence on art, music, and global cultures. The volume also addresses contemporary issues of poverty, race, and power dynamics, making it especially relevant for today's readers. The Companion offers a diversity of perspectives from which to approach the unique identity and importance of Jesus beyond the 2020s, whether in relation to Christianity's cultural and existential crises in the Americas, its precipitous decline in Western Europe, or its unprecedented growth and proliferation in Africa and Asia.

**Markus Bockmuehl** is the University of Oxford's Dean Ireland's Professor of the Exegesis of Holy Scripture and a fellow of Keble College. He is also a fellow of the Royal Historical Society and currently MacDonald Agape Visiting Professor at the Pontifical University of St. Thomas (Angelicum) in Rome. He is the author or editor of two dozen books and 150 articles.

CAMBRIDGE COMPANIONS TO RELIGION

This is a series of companions to major topics and key figures in theology and religious studies. Each volume contains specially commissioned chapters by international scholars, which provide an accessible and stimulating introduction to the subject for new readers and nonspecialists.

*Other Titles in the Series*

AMERICAN CATHOLICISM Edited by Margaret M. McGuinness and Thomas F. Rzeznik

AMERICAN ISLAM Edited by Juliane Hammer and Omid Safi

AMERICAN JUDAISM Edited by Dana Evan Kaplan

AMERICAN METHODISM Edited by Jason E. Vickers

AMERICAN PROTESTANTISM Edited by Jason E. Vickers and Jennifer Woodruff Tait

ANCIENT MEDITERRANEAN RELIGIONS Edited by Barbette Stanley Spaeth

APOCALYPTIC LITERATURE Edited by Colin McAllister

APOSTOLIC FATHERS Edited by Michael F. Bird and Scott Harrower

AUGUSTINE'S CITY OF GOD Edited by David Vincent Meconi

AUGUSTINE'S "CONFESSIONS" Edited by Tarmo Toom

KARL BARTH Edited by John Webster

THE BIBLE, 2nd edition Edited by Bruce Chilton

THE BIBLE AND LITERATURE Edited by Calum Carmichael

BIBLICAL INTERPRETATION Edited by John Barton

BLACK THEOLOGY Edited by Dwight N. Hopkins and Edward P. Antonio

DIETRICH BONHOEFFER Edited by John de Gruchy

JOHN CALVIN Edited by Donald K. McKim

CHRISTIAN DOCTRINE Edited by Colin Gunton

CHRISTIAN ETHICS Edited by Robin Gill

CHRISTIAN MYSTICISM Edited by Amy Hollywood and Patricia Z. Beckman

CHRISTIAN PHILOSOPHICAL THEOLOGY Edited by Charles Taliaferro and Chad V. Meister

CHRISTIAN POLITICAL THEOLOGY Edited by Craig Hovey and Elizabeth Phillips

CHRISTIANITY AND THE ENVIRONMENT Edited by Alexander J. B. Hampton and Douglas Hedley

THE CISTERIAN ORDER Edited by Mette Birkedal Bruun

CLASSICAL ISLAMIC THEOLOGY Edited by Tim Winter

THE COUNCIL OF NICAEA Edited by Young Richard Kim

JONATHAN EDWARDS Edited by Stephen J. Stein

EVANGELICAL THEOLOGY Edited by Timothy Larsen and Daniel J. Treier

*(continued after index)*

THE NEW CAMBRIDGE COMPANION TO
# JESUS

Edited by

Markus Bockmuehl
*University of Oxford*

Shaftesbury Road, Cambridge CB2 8EA, United Kingdom

One Liberty Plaza, 20th Floor, New York, NY 10006, USA

477 Williamstown Road, Port Melbourne, VIC 3207, Australia

314–321, 3rd Floor, Plot 3, Splendor Forum, Jasola District Centre, New Delhi – 110025, India

103 Penang Road, #05-06/07, Visioncrest Commercial, Singapore 238467

Cambridge University Press is part of Cambridge University Press & Assessment, a department of the University of Cambridge.

We share the University's mission to contribute to society through the pursuit of education, learning and research at the highest international levels of excellence.

www.cambridge.org
Information on this title: www.cambridge.org/9781009233026

DOI: 10.1017/9781009233002

© Cambridge University Press & Assessment 2025

This publication is in copyright. Subject to statutory exception and to the provisions of relevant collective licensing agreements, no reproduction of any part may take place without the written permission of Cambridge University Press & Assessment.

When citing this work, please include a reference to the
DOI 10.1017/9781009233002

First published 2025

Printed in the United Kingdom by CPI Group Ltd, Croydon CR0 4YY

*A catalogue record for this publication is available from the British Library*

*Library of Congress Cataloging-in-Publication Data*
NAMES: Bockmuehl, Markus, editor.
TITLE: The New Cambridge companion to Jesus / edited by Markus Bockmuehl, University of Oxford.
DESCRIPTION: Cambridge, United Kingdom ; New York, NY, USA : Cambridge University Press, 2025. | Series: Cambridge companions to religion | Includes bibliographical references and index.
IDENTIFIERS: LCCN 2024014426 | ISBN 9781009233026 (hardback) | ISBN 9781009233002 (ebook)
SUBJECTS: LCSH: Jesus Christ – Biography. | Jesus Christ – History of doctrines.
CLASSIFICATION: LCC BT301.3 .N485 2025 | DDC 232–dc23/eng/20240708
LC record available at https://lccn.loc.gov/2024014426

ISBN 978-1-009-23302-6 Hardback
ISBN 978-1-009-23299-9 Paperback

Cambridge University Press & Assessment has no responsibility for the persistence or accuracy of URLs for external or third-party internet websites referred to in this publication and does not guarantee that any content on such websites is, or will remain, accurate or appropriate.

Funding for research on Chapter 10 and for a subvention to print images has been received from the European Commission's Horizon 2020 research and innovation programme under Marie Skłodowska-Curie grant agreement no. 891569, "Expanding the Gospel according to Matthew: Continuity and Change in Early Gospel Literature," at the University of Oxford.

# Contents

*List of Contributors* page ix
*Acknowledgements* xi
*A Note on Referencing and Abbreviations* xiii

Introduction  1
MARKUS BOCKMUEHL

## Part I  *Origins*

1 Life and Aims of Jesus  11
   DALE C. ALLISON, JR.

2 Jesus's Religion, Praxis, and Experience of God  26
   LUTZ DOERING

3 Jesus in the Fourfold Gospel  44
   J. TYLER BROWN AND NATHAN EUBANK

4 Paul's Jesus as the Christ  58
   MATTHEW V. NOVENSON

5 The Risen Jesus  72
   MARKUS BOCKMUEHL

6 Jesus and the Triune God  88
   LEWIS AYRES

7 Jesus in the Scriptures of Israel  103
   JENNIE GRILLO

## Part II  *The Diversity of Reception*

8 The Apocryphal Jesus  121
   JACOB A. RODRIGUEZ

9 The Islamic Jesus  137
   NICOLAI SINAI

10   Jesus in Christian Material Culture   154
     JEREMIAH COOGAN

11   Jesus in Art and Music   171
     ROBIN JENSEN AND JEREMY BEGBIE

12   Jesus in the Story of Spirituality and Worship   197
     VOLKER LEPPIN

## Part III   Ethics, Theology, and Critical Scholarship

13   Jesus in Christian Discipleship and Ethics   217
     REBEKAH EKLUND

14   The Body of Jesus in His People   232
     THOMAS JOSEPH WHITE, OP

15   The Church's Jesus in Modern Theology   250
     EMMANUEL DURAND, OP

16   The History of Jesus in Biblical Scholarship   265
     JAMES CARLETON PAGET

## Part IV   The Global Jesus Today

17   The Jewish Jesus in Christian and in Jewish Memory   283
     BARBARA U. MEYER

18   The Racial Jesus   299
     JONATHAN TRAN

19   Jesus, Power, and the Global Poor   313
     CARLOS RAÚL SOSA SILIEZAR AND ARUTHUCKAL
     VARUGHESE JOHN

20   The Asian Faces of Jesus   330
     K. K. YEO

21   Jesus of Africa   346
     DIANE B. STINTON AND VICTOR I. EZIGBO

## Part V   Outlook

22   The Future of Jesus of Nazareth: Yesterday, Today,
     and Tomorrow   365
     C. KAVIN ROWE

   *Bibliography*   379
   *Ancient Sources Index*   400
   *Subject Index*   421

# Contributors

**Dale C. Allison, Jr.,** Princeton Theological Seminary (USA)
**Lewis Ayres,** University of Durham (UK)
**Jeremy Begbie,** Duke University (USA)
**Markus Bockmuehl,** University of Oxford (UK)
**J. Tyler Brown,** University of Oxford (UK)
**James Carleton Paget,** University of Cambridge (UK)
**Jeremiah Coogan,** Jesuit School of Theology, Santa Clara University (USA)
**Lutz Doering,** University of Münster (Germany)
**Emmanuel Durand, OP,** University of Fribourg (Switzerland)
**Rebekah Eklund,** Loyola University Maryland (USA)
**Nathan Eubank,** University of Notre Dame (USA)
**Victor I. Ezigbo,** Bethel University (USA)
**Jennie Grillo,** University of Notre Dame (USA)
**Robin Jensen,** University of Notre Dame (USA)
**Aruthuckal Varughese John,** South Asia Institute of Advanced Christian Studies (India)
**Volker Leppin,** Yale University (USA)
**Barbara U. Meyer,** Tel Aviv University (Israel)
**Matthew V. Novenson,** University of Edinburgh (UK)
**Jacob A. Rodriguez,** Trinity School for Ministry (USA)
**C. Kavin Rowe,** Duke University (USA)
**Carlos Raúl Sosa Siliezar,** Wheaton College (USA)
**Nicolai Sinai,** University of Oxford (UK)
**Diane B. Stinton,** Regent College (Canada)

**Jonathan Tran,** Baylor University (USA)

**Thomas Joseph White, OP,** Pontifical University of St. Thomas (Angelicum) (Italy)

**K. K. Yeo,** Garrett-Evangelical Theological Seminary (USA)

# Acknowledgements

It has been a great privilege to partner with such a distinguished interdisciplinary team of authors from around the world. More than once I marvelled at the willingness of these accomplished colleagues to work with me – not only to accept my invitation to write a minimally footnoted and tediously space-restricted chapter to someone else's design and deadline but to put up with demands for changes and amendments when the job seemed already done. What I have found most humbling of all, however, is the seriousness and dedication to the task on the part of a significant number of fellow authors who faced sharply testing personal circumstances – from multiple long-term health challenges and close family bereavements all the way to revisions and email replies between air-raid alarms in Tel Aviv. I am deeply grateful to them all, including those whose circumstances ultimately did not permit them to complete the task.

On the latter front, I am enormously indebted to friends who inexplicably agreed to abandon all other personal and professional commitments to produce last-minute substitutes for the otherwise certain loss of two crucial chapters. A chapter on 'the sexual and gendered Jesus' unfortunately had to be abandoned. Unlike most other edited volumes like a Festschrift or conference proceedings, Cambridge Companion designs have few optional components or built-in redundancies. Uncompensated withdrawals leave a hole, which an editor must hope that readers and reviewers will forgive or fail to notice.

I am most grateful to the incomparable Beatrice Rehl, who persisted in her multi-year campaign to persuade this volume's reluctant editor to take on a second round of this task – and then patiently, prudently, and practically supported the entire undertaking from start to finish, based on her successful production of several dozen such volumes. Additional thanks are due to Jeremiah Coogan, as well as to the University of Oxford's Faculty of Theology and Religion and the European Research

Council, for supporting this volume's colour supplement pages from residual funds held in the research account of his Marie Skłodowska-Curie Actions fellowship based in Oxford 2020–22.

My colleagues at the University of Oxford kindly supported the two-term sabbatical leave that facilitated most of the editorial work for this volume. Most importantly, I thank my wife Celia and family for the generous encouragement to persist with two periods of research and writing abroad, which turned out to coincide inconveniently with her own unexpected new senior leadership role.

# A Note on Referencing and Abbreviations

References have been kept to an economic minimum. Lists of the most important sources feature in a concluding 'Further Reading' section in each chapter; these and all other entries can be found in the General Bibliography at the end of the book. Abbreviations follow the *SBL Handbook of Style*, 2nd ed. (Collins 2014). Additions include ALD = Aramaic Levi Document (Greenfield, Stone, and Eshel 2004) and CIIP = *Corpus Inscriptionum Iudaeae/Palaestinae* (Ameling and Cotton 2010–23).

# Introduction

MARKUS BOCKMUEHL

As the second quarter of this century dawns, our subject is alive and present to the lived experience of more people around the world than at any time in history. Asian and African readers need no reminder of this reality, even as Western readers do well to ponder it in the supposed twilight years of North Atlantic forms of Christianity, whose extinction the pollsters have been predicting for the later decades of this century.

Globally, by contrast, precipitous decline in Europe and North America has been dwarfed by the growth of new followers of Jesus elsewhere: the overall number has in fact grown by at least half a billion people since the original edition of *The Cambridge Companion to Jesus* was published in 2001. One might go further to note that these additional believers in Asia, Africa, and Latin America may be more numerous than those who lived in Europe or North America at any one time in history. 'The future of the world's most popular religion is African', noted *The Economist* (25 December 2015).

## A NEW CAMBRIDGE COMPANION TO JESUS

These and other cultural tectonic shifts have necessarily altered what historical and contemporary study of Jesus might mean, and a thorough redesign of the Companion has sought to acknowledge the implications of these shifts for introducing Jesus afresh a quarter of a century later. Two chapters (5 and 16) are extensively rewritten and updated from the 2001 predecessor volume; all others are newly commissioned.

The present volume continues the 2001 Companion's conviction that it is impossible to understand Jesus purely as a subject of ancient history. It remains the case that 'history, literature, theology and the dynamic of a living, worldwide religious reality all appropriately impinge on the study of Jesus' (cover). Similarly, the past and the present of Jesus are entangled in such a way that a fully historical understanding of either dimension depends in no small part on the other. The

*New Cambridge Companion to Jesus* likewise retains an interest in both 'The Jesus of History' and 'The History of Jesus': the historic and the contemporary religious reality of Jesus are reciprocally illuminating for any understanding of his abiding global significance today.

At the same time, here we engage energetically with critical developments in scholarship and culture over the past twenty-five years, while widening engagement with the subject matter's footprint and importance in the contemporary world. Themes of contemporary relevance have been thrown into much sharper relief by developments of the last few years. Hotly contested challenges of culture and race, gender and decolonization, along with Christianity's global reorientation from a Western-dominated perspective to a global, primarily Southern and Eastern Jesus, have come into ever sharper relief and generated important new critical questions. Our new table of contents in this volume further accentuates that a 'Companion to Jesus' cannot be a merely 'historical' and 'critical' exercise produced by or for scholars of the ancient Mediterranean. Even from within the scholarly study of the New Testament, twenty-first-century Jesus research has also more explicitly tackled some associated questions of institutional and political power – from imperialism and the Imperial cult to postcolonial, racial, and gender topics. Especially when viewed on a global canvas, at times these intersectional questions about Jesus have been shown to conflict with each other, as in perceptions of Western feminism or gender theory as colonizing.

THE ARGUMENT OF THIS VOLUME

The outline of this volume proceeds in approximately historical fashion, but less than a quarter of its chapters are expressly devoted to the Jesus of history and of the New Testament.

**Origins**
Two opening chapters introduce Jesus as a historical figure deeply rooted in Jewish life, tradition, and Scripture, colouring his identity, law observance, and role as a teacher and healer. This fruitful dialectic of two somewhat different perspectives allows the contours of Jesus's first-century setting to gain in depth, colour, and definition.

Dale C. Allison, Jr.'s overview of the life and aims of Jesus concentrates on his charismatic public ministry, his teachings about the kingdom of God, his role specifically as a messianic figure, and the circumstances leading to his crucifixion. He highlights his itinerant lifestyle, miracles, and eschatological teachings and paints a portrait of him as a transformative figure challenging existing religious and social norms. Jesus engaged in teaching and performing miracles, fostering religious renewal with his conviction that the kingdom of God was emerging through his endeavours. Through his personal authority, he garnered significant support but also incited substantial opposition.

Turning to Jesus's religion, praxis, and experience of God, Lutz Doering draws out more of the everyday aspects of first-century Jewish life and their influence on Jesus's worldview and mission. Here, his experience of the defeat of Satan and the coming kingdom of God is contextualized in his full participation in the routine practices of Jewish life, in synagogue gatherings, in the broader praxis and discussion of Torah and ritual observance, and in his personal relationship to God and of his own vocation. Immersed in Jewish life, Jesus adhered to its customs while interpreting them in the light of God's kingdom. He emphasized a relational Torah approach, valuing love and ethics over ritual precision, and taught about a compassionate God as Father in a transformative message.

From historical reconstruction, the next two chapters address the earliest written accounts of Jesus. Here, we begin with the distinctive characterizations of Jesus in the four New Testament Gospels (J. Tyler Brown and Nathan Eubank). Mark's Jesus emerges as the paradoxically crucified king of Israel, while Matthew places him in the tradition of Moses and David, as the promised prophet like Moses and the shepherd renewing God's covenant with Israel's lost sheep. Luke stresses the role of Jesus as a champion of the poor, fulfilling Israel's redemption. John's Jesus is the eternal Word and the glorified Son who is one with his heavenly Father. This quartet soon emerged as uniquely authoritative among Christian communities, amidst a continuing diversity of narratives about Jesus.

The corpus of Paul's letters partly predates the Gospels but follows them in the canonical order of the New Testament. Matthew V. Novenson notes that here Jesus is most often called 'Christ' or messiah, a term that raises numerous conceptual and linguistic questions. For Paul, to identify Jesus as the Christ means that God has sent him: his mission included to die on the cross and rise from the dead 'for us', to defeat hostile forces, and to restore ultimate rule to God as king.

From here, the continued prominence of Jesus after his crucifixion owes much to his followers' key religious and theological affirmations about his resurrection, his divine identity, and his presence in Israel's Scriptures. These topics occupy the following three chapters.

As the editor's own contribution documents, Christian history and experience ride crucially on the resurrection of Jesus from the dead, a transformative reality that early Christian sources assert consistently but in considerable narrative diversity. In their claim that 'God raised Jesus from the dead', the New Testament writers attest an event in history but also a new reality that transcends the register of available language and analogy.

The resulting questions about the identity of Jesus continued to preoccupy Christian reception for several centuries to come. Lewis Ayres scrutinizes how classical creeds and early councils document this process of understanding Jesus Christ's identity and the redemptive power of the incarnate Word. These formative and foundational formulae came to resonate across the great majority of Christian theological traditions, focusing on the Trinity in the fourth century and more specifically on Christology in debates over the next three centuries. For classical Christian theology, to understand the saving significance of Jesus means to recognize him as that Logos made human and as coequal with the Father and Spirit in the life of God.

Both internally and vis-à-vis Jewish conversation partners, the question of Jesus's presence in the prophetic Scriptures of Israel remained a defining feature of intellectual and religious reflection about him throughout the early centuries. Christian interpretations often assert Jesus's tangible presence in Israel's Scriptures, for example through angelic manifestations. But as Jennie Grillo demonstrates, this stands in contrast to more subtle indications of the pre-incarnate Logos's interactions with Israel, particularly if one takes seriously the New Testament's focus on the novelty of incarnate Logos. A more promising hermeneutical approach has viewed the Old Testament as speaking in a transformed way in the light of Jesus: Scriptural meanings that were once concealed become clear in the light of the cross and resurrection of Jesus.

## The Diversity of Reception
The next five chapters all highlight something of the reception-historical footprint of Jesus – whether literary, religious, material, or artistic. The contributors have curated eclectic but representative soundings from late antiquity to the medieval and early modern periods.

Although the four gospels of Matthew, Mark, Luke, and John soon attained an authoritative prominence in Christian appropriation of the narrative of Jesus, this was by no means the end of gospel writing as a way for Christians to engage with his life and teaching. Jacob A. Rodriguez draws out the diversity of noncanonical gospel traditions. Some of these align with, and others diverge from, the canonical gospels' account of his infancy, ministry, passion, and dialogues. Jesus emerges as a strikingly wise or obstreperous child, a faithful follower or a critic of Jewish law, a philosopher or mythological hero, and occasionally as the opponent of his own apostolic church. Within their social and religious contexts, these characterizations suggest intriguingly complementary or sometimes competing understandings of Jesus, thus enriching our grasp of early Christian heterogeneity and doctrinal evolution.

Beginning in the seventh century, this footprint of the canonical and apocryphal Jesus's reception finds one of its most influential expressions in the Islamic tradition. Nicolai Sinai examines how the Qur'an affirms Jesus as a prophet but not divine, and not the Son of God. Its picture of him develops aspects of Christian tradition about Jesus and Mary, including his miraculous birth, but omits central gospel events such as the passion. It reinterprets his crucifixion as a divine act of rescue from adversaries and affirms his resurrection. Later Islamic traditions developed a portrait of Jesus as an ascetic, emphasizing his humanity and submission to God.

Jeremiah Coogan next traces some of the material aspects of the Christian reception of Jesus, with a particular focus on the early centuries. Jesus's presence and influence were expressed through a variety of textual, visual, and other media, as well as liturgies, relics, and symbols. This material presentation and re-presentation of Jesus was nourished through core Christian theological concepts and practices whose impact has endured from antiquity, underscoring the importance of material forms for engaging both tangible and intangible aspects of the presence of Jesus.

Such materiality also soon found specific development in Christian artistic expression. In their chapter, Robin Jensen and Jeremy Begbie show that alongside the New Testament's continuing normative access to Jesus of Nazareth's person and identity, artists across the centuries have portrayed Jesus through non-textual means – here explored in dialogical fashion through visual art and music.

Often no less material in expression, the story of Jesus in Christian spirituality is the focus of Volker Leppin's discussion. At its heart are practices and experiences focused on the tangible representation and re-enactment of Jesus's presence, taking as their point of departure the key phases of his life, from childhood through his adult ministry to the passion. Identification with Jesus often entails as its foil what Leppin calls 'counter-identification' with others, in the service of personal renewal and deeper commitment to the person and example of Jesus.

## Ethics, Theology, and Critical Scholarship

Four chapters now address the important place of Jesus in Christian doctrinal and moral theology and in modern theological and historical study.

Rebekah Eklund explores the place of Jesus in ethics through the double commandment of love for God and the neighbour, here associated with the imitation of Jesus and concentrated in five distinctive practices: care for the poor, sacramental practices of the Lord's Supper and baptism, prayer (including lament), forgiveness and reconciliation, and self-giving.

Turning next to the continuing place of Jesus in the Christian theology of the church and the sacraments, Thomas Joseph White, OP, begins by noting that Paul already conceives of both the church and the Eucharist as the body of Christ. In trying to give a consistent account of this view, Thomas Aquinas and other medieval theologians developed the idea of the church as the 'mystical body' of Christ, constituted through the Eucharist as the 'true body' of Christ. This medieval conception has continued to shape modern accounts of the church as a sign and instrument of grace for all human beings, who are called to the same communion in the one Christ.

Emmanuel Durand, OP, more specifically attends to modern theology, for which Jesus of Nazareth remains the vital key to understanding Christian faith. His unique relationship with God and the Holy Spirit underwrites his bond with every human being. Scholars continue to wrestle with the way his identity addresses central questions of the Creed, including humanity's capacity for engagement with God, the relationship between individuality and universality, the unity of life and matter, and the place of hope in dealing with the challenges of history. Christ is here seen to be relevant not only to core theological issues but to the lived reality of every believer in the presence of God.

Modern theological study of Jesus has only rarely engaged with modern historical study; so it seemed important to juxtapose them here. Durand's chapter is followed by James Carleton Paget's stocktaking of the story of the historical Jesus in biblical scholarship. Questions considered here include the usefulness of the term 'the historical Jesus', the extent to which the 'Quest' for him can be meaningfully divided into separate periods or chapters of research, and the debilitating problems of often highly particular and incompatible historical methodologies and presuppositions. In the face of these challenges, Carleton Paget counsels greater epistemological modesty.

### The Global Jesus Today

Five chapters now address an eclectic set of questions arising from the global dimensions already noted, each of which has the potential both to enrich and to disrupt the critical priorities of earlier generations.

Barbara U. Meyer notes that Jesus's Jewish identity exercises a fundamental and critical role not just in Christianity's relationship with Judaism today but in fact in its own ongoing account of him. Christian reappropriation of the 'memory' of this Jewish Jesus will help not only to rewrite the history and potential of that relationship but to energize the renewal of Christian exegesis and theology itself.

Jonathan Tran relates the racial challenge of Jesus to the setting of the historical Jesus, refusing to embed alleged tensions between the historical and the racial Jesus, or indeed between the historical Jesus and the Christ of faith. His critique leads him to discern the potential of fresh vitality in the study of history that scholars of race have tended to urge us to distrust.

Turning to the intricate dynamic of Jesus in relation to global structures of power and poverty, Carlos Raúl Sosa Siliezar from Latin America and Aruthuckal Varughese John from India discover a Jesus of the Gospels whose message and example attest to his care for the poor and presence in the life of his people. In so doing, Jesus offers a challenge to unjust social patterns and structures and an account of working in solidarity with the poor.

The Malaysian scholar K. K. Yeo examines Asian presentations of Jesus, examining key missionary and theological developments through the centuries. He notes diversely indigenized profiles of Jesus and the challenges of different social, political, religious, linguistic, and artistic contexts in Asian understandings of Jesus Christ. Jesus's many Asian faces give rise to a tension between the universal and the indigenous church that nevertheless undergirds Asian Christianity's authentic mission.

Finally, since we are about to embark on Christianity's African century, Diane B. Stinton and Victor I. Ezigbo rightly stress that Jesus is not an alien, white, or Western import to Africa: instead, Africa has played a part in his story for 2,000 years. Beginning from a reading of the Acts of the Apostles, the authors examine devotion to Jesus in Africa and African Christology. As in Asia, the church in Africa manifests the universality of Jesus presented in indigenous settings and idioms.

### Outlook

C. Kavin Rowe offers a concluding reflection on the question of where this leaves us in relation to the Future of Jesus. For his followers, Jesus of Nazareth engages and embodies their hope and the fulfilment of creation's purpose. Since the history of Christian reflection finds both his earthly life and his divine identity to be comprehensible only in light of the other, this union has the effect of dynamically linking his and our past, present, and future. Jesus's transformative impact on humanity and history points to the final reconciliation and realization of the Kingdom, both in his historical presence and in his eternal nature.

# Part I
*Origins*

# 1 Life and Aims of Jesus
## DALE C. ALLISON, JR.

Jesus of Nazareth was born in or shortly before 4 BCE, when Herod the Great died. He was executed by order of the Roman State, probably in either 30 or 33 CE. A Galilean Jew, he was a rhetorically gifted teacher adept at composing aphorisms, similes, and parables.[1] He was no less a miracle worker and messianic figure. His chief aim was to promote religious renewal among the Jewish people in anticipation of the kingdom of God, which he believed to be dawning in his ministry. His vision of fundamental change appealed not just to the disaffected but to individuals from different social strata.

Sympathizers remembered him as a commanding, charismatic presence who operated with self-confident authority, worked wonders with a word, and, despite displaying compassion and enjoining love, made radical demands and promulgated rigorous moral standards. Detractors accused him of being allied with evil spirits, breaking the Sabbath, eating and drinking to excess, blaspheming, and befriending unsavory or impious characters.

Jesus appears to have been, before his public ministry, not a peasant or subsistence farmer but an artisan, probably a carpenter (*tektōn*, Mark 6:3; Justin, *Dial.* 88). As such, he likely traveled: Nazareth was too small to require his full-time services. But we know next to nothing about him until his baptism by John the Baptist, which he may have experienced as a prophetic commissioning (Mark 1:9–11). John 3:22–24 reports that Jesus baptized for a time. If so, at some point, perhaps after the Baptist's arrest (Mark 1:14; John 3:24), he discontinued the practice and began his own ministry, with special attention to the ill, the poor, and the marginalized.

Evidently unmarried, Jesus was an itinerant. He had no home but was always a visitor (Matt 8:20 par. Luke 9:58). He frequented Galilean

---

[1] For the methodological issues surrounding sources and criteria of authenticity, see Allison 2010, 1–30; Keith and Le Donne 2012.

villages, whose average population was 200–400. But he also spent considerable time in Capernaum, which had a few thousand residents (Matt 11:23 par. Luke 10:15; Mark 1:21–2:1; 9:33; John 2:12; 6:17, 24, 59). The sources also have him in Judea (Mark 1:4–9; Luke 4:44; John 2:13–3:36), the region of Tyre (Mark 7:24), the area of Caesarea Philippi (Mark 8:27), the Decapolis (Mark 5:20; 7:31), Samaria (Luke 9:52), and "beyond the Jordan" (Mark 10:1; John 1:28–29; 10:40).

Apart from Jerusalem, he seems to have skirted urban centers such as Tiberias and Sepphoris. He is never depicted in an agora or marketplace. Perhaps he was alienated not only from the Herodian dynasty (Luke 13:32) and Roman ways (Mark 10:42–44) but more generally from urban commercialization. The focus of his ministry was, in any case, the rural people of Israel (Matt 10:5–6; Rom 15:8), although he was not hostile to gentiles (Mark 5:1–20; 7:24–30; that early Christians missionized gentiles is unexpected if Jesus dismissed them altogether). He was probably more than once in Jerusalem for festivals, as John's Gospel purports, and he likely met opposition there before his final visit (Mark 3:22; 7:1; John 7:1). The synoptic chronology (i.e. of Matthew, Mark, and Luke), which recounts only a single visit, is compressed.

Jesus was a liminal figure, an outsider who had abandoned ordinary life. He was unallied with established sources of social, economic, or religious authority – he was not scribe, not Pharisee, not priest, not leader of a synagogue – and as his popularity grew, so did the hostility of those who were so allied. Their antagonism is a gauge of his impact. Eventually the opposition of certain Jewish leaders in Jerusalem found common cause with the Roman procurator, and Jesus was arrested and executed. The movement he initiated, despite being centered on and driven by his immediate presence, was not thereby extinguished.

## THE KINGDOM OF GOD AND ESCHATOLOGY

The central theme of Jesus's public proclamation is "the kingdom of God." In summations of his message, it has "come near" (*ēngiken*; Mark 1:14–15; Matt 10:7 par. Luke 10:9). This means it will arrive soon, which is consistent with other sayings (Matt 10:23; Mark 9:1; 13:30; Luke 18:8), as well as with the hope of the early church (Rom 13:11; 1 Thess 1:10; 4:13–18). Such expectation also lines up with Jewish sources in which "kingdom" is both an eschatological reality (Dan 7:14; 4Q246 2 5; 4Q521 2 2:7; Sib. Or. 3:46–48; T. Mos. 10:1) and not far off (Dan 12:6–13; 1 En. 94:6–8; 95:6; 4 Ezra 4:26; 5:45; 8:61; 2 Bar. 85:10).

Jesus's eschatology functioned as a practical theodicy. It did not account for evil but prophesied its demise through a series of radical, divinely worked reversals. The hungry will be full, the sorrowful will laugh, the persecuted will be rewarded (Matt 5:3–12 par. Luke 6:20–23). Many who are first will be last, and the last will be first (Mark 10:31; Gos. Thom. 4). The exalted will be humbled, the humbled exalted (Matt 23:12 par. Luke 14:11; 18:14).

"Kingdom" was Jesus's shorthand for the world that divine intervention would soon remake and transform. People will "enter" and "inherit" it, as Israel once entered and inherited the promised land (Matt 5:20; 7:21; 19:29; 25:34; Mark 9:47; 10:15, 17, 24, 25; Luke 10:25; 23:42; John 3:5). Even if the formulation in Matthew 5:5 – "Blessed are the meek, for they will inherit the earth" – is secondary, it is not misleading. Jesus expected not the destruction and replacement of this world but its renewal, a world in which the promises to Israel would be fulfilled. One may compare 2 Baruch 73, which foresees a world without war, disease, or anxiety, a world full of joy, rest, and gladness, a world in which people will no longer die. Jesus similarly hoped for a radically transfigured world, one in which God's will for earth will be done as it is now in heaven.

While Jesus was not a systematic thinker, the sources suggest a coherent eschatological scenario, a series of closely connected events: a period of great tribulation (Matt 10:34–36 par. Luke 12:51–53; Mark 13:3–23); appearance of the Son of Man (Matt 24:27, 37–39 par. Luke 17:24–30; Mark 13:26; 14:62); resurrection (Matt 12:41–42 par. Luke 11:31–32; Mark 12:18–27; Luke 14:12–14; John 5:28–29); and the last judgment, which will issue in reward in the kingdom for some and punishment in Gehenna for others (Matt 5:12 par. Luke 6:23; Matt 6:19–21 par. Luke 12:33–34; Matt 7:2 par. Luke 6:37; Matt 10:32–33 par. Luke 12:8–9; Mark 12:40; Matt 25:31–46). While these elements appear also in Jewish sources, distinctive of Jesus were his self-identification with the Son of Man (see the section "Self-Conception" later in the chapter) and a link between response to his ministry and judgment (Matt 10:32–33 par. Luke 12:8–9; Matt 11:20–24 par. Luke 10:12–15). Unlike 4 Ezra 7:28–31, the rabbis and perhaps Paul in 1 Corinthians 15:24–28, there is little evidence that Jesus distinguished between a temporary messianic kingdom and an eternal world to come.

In Luke 17:20–21, Jesus says that "the kingdom of God is not coming with things that can be observed; nor will they say, 'Look, here it is!' or 'There it is!' For, in fact, the kingdom of God is among you." Some scholars have held that, if the kingdom was future for Jesus, he is unlikely to have also believed it to be present. For them, either Jesus did not utter Luke 17:21 or it does not signal the kingdom's presence. The saying might mean, for instance: "The kingdom is in your reach, in your power to enter it." But Matthew 12:28 par. Luke 11:20 clearly speaks of the kingdom's presence: "if it is by the Spirit of God that I cast out demons, then the kingdom of God has come upon you." There is little reason to deny that Jesus conceived of the kingdom as coming over time and so both present and future. The kingdom is both present and future for Paul (Rom 14:17; 1 Cor 4:20; 6:9–10; 15:50, 24; Gal 5:21) as well as the synoptic evangelists, and the eschaton does not arrive in a moment but rather over a period of time in Deutero-Isaiah, Jubilees 23, the Apocalypse of Weeks (1 En. 93 + 91:12–17), and the Apocalypse of Abraham. It was the same for Jesus. Something greater than Solomon had already appeared (Matt 12:41–42 par. Luke 11:31–32). Even before the resurrection, people could begin to see what prophets only longed to see (Matt 13:16–17 par. Luke 10:23–24).

If the final overthrow of Satan and all evil belong to Jewish eschatological expectation (Jub. 23:29; 50:5; 4Q300 3; 1 En. 54:4–6; T. Mos. 10:1–3), for Jesus the battle has begun, and the devil is losing. A confident sense of eschatological victory appears not only in Matt 12:28 par. Luke 11:20 but also in Mark 3:27 ("the strong man" has been bound) as well as Luke 10:18, which might reflect a visionary experience: "I watched Satan fall from heaven like a flash of lightning." The healings, too, hold eschatological significance. Jewish texts anticipate that the end time will bring healing (Isa 57:18–19; 58:8; Jer 30:17; Ezek 34:16; Jub. 23:29–30; 1QS 4:6–7), and Matthew 11:4–5 par. Luke 7:22 – "Go and tell John what you hear and see: the blind receive their sight, the lame walk, those with a skin disease are cleansed, the deaf hear, the dead are raised, and the poor have good news brought to them" – through its borrowing of lines from Isaiah (Isa 26:19; 29:18–19; 35:5–6; 42:18; 61:1; cf. 4Q521 2 2:7–13), claims the realization of that expectation. The blessings of the new age have begun to fall on the world. This is why Jesus, actualizing his own beatitude (Luke 6:21), anticipates the eschatological banquet (Isa 25:6–8; Ezek 39:17–20; 1Q28a 2; Matt 8:11 par. Luke 13:29; Mark 14:25) with celebratory meals (Mark 2:18–20).

If the blessings of the end are already becoming manifest, at the same time the tribulation of the latter days (Dan 12:1; Mark 13:3–23; 4 Ezra 6:24; m. Soṭah 9:15) has begun. The citizens of the kingdom suffer violence (Matt 11:12–13 par. Luke 16:16). Persecution and even martyrdom lie ahead (Matt 5:10–12 par. Luke 6:22–23; Matt 10:23; Mark 8:34–35; 13:9–13). It is not yet the era of messianic peace and reconciliation

(Isa 2:4; Mal 4:6) but the time of the sword, and foes are in one's own house (Matt 10:34–36 par. Luke 12:51–53; Gos. Thom. 16). One should pray for deliverance from the time of trial (Matt 6:13 par. Luke 11:4).

According to Mark 1:14–15, the announcement of the kingdom's nearness was coupled with a call to repent (Matt 11:21 par. Luke 10:13; Matt 12:41 par. Luke 11:32; Luke 13:1–5). This association reflects the far-flung belief, grounded in Deuteronomy 4:25–31; 30:1–10, that the return and redemption of scattered Israel at the end of days will coincide with the repentance of God's people (Hos 14:1–3; Joel 2:12–14; Tob 13:5–6; Jub. 1:15, 22–23; 23:26; 4Q398 14–17; T. Mos. 1:18; T. Jud. 23:3–5; T. Dan. 6:4; Philo, *Praem.* 87–98, 162–70). This expectation may explain why the tradition does not reflect imminent expectation alone: Some sayings foresee a span, brief but of unspecified duration, between Jesus's end and the end of status quo history (Mark 2:20; 13:34–35; 14:7, 25; Matt 23:39 par. Luke 13:35; 17:22; 1 Cor 11:24–25). Jesus presumably undertook his work in the hope that he would be heeded. But his reproaches of "this generation" (Matt 12:39–42 par. Luke 11:29–32; Matt 17:17 par. Luke 9:41; Mark 8:38; 9:19) and the woes over Galilean cities (Matt 11:20–24 par. Luke 10:12–15) reveal profound disappointment (cf. Mark 12:1–12). While there is not enough evidence to support the old theory of a Galilean crisis, Jesus likely hoped for a corporate repentance that did not eventuate to his satisfaction; and if he took the promise, "I will return to you," to be contingent on "return to me" (Zech 1:3; Mal 3:7), the possibility of eschatological delay (Hab 2:3–4; 1QpHab 7:10–12) would have been real.

Although Galilee in Jesus's day may have been fairly stable politically, his vision of a restored Israel no doubt stirred up hopes for the end of Roman rule (cf. John 6:15). Some have surmised that he was a revolutionary, like those who rebelled against Rome in the 60s. This would certainly explain why he was crucified with rebellious bandits (Mark 15:27). But the character in the passion narrative is remarkably unaggressive, which accords with the imperatives in Matthew 5:38–48 par. Luke 6:27–36; and Paul's letters, our earliest Christian sources, do not incite violence but feature a savior who is the antithesis of a military leader – humble, meek, mild (2 Cor 10:1; Phil 2:8). We know from Daniel, the Testament of Moses, and 2 Baruch that it was possible to hope for the destruction of an occupying power without calling for violence: One could await divine intervention. Further, although the Baptist was not a violent revolutionary, Josephus reports that Herod Antipas arrested him because he fretted that his preaching would foment political unrest (*Ant.* 18.118). Matters were likely similar with Jesus.

### ETHICS AND TORAH

Jesus's proclamation of the kingdom was deeply ethical and social, and his eschatological expectation added urgency to his demands. Yet the proximity of the end did not of itself generate imperatives. Those came from the Torah and attendant traditions. (Jesus was probably literate. Even if not, his knowledge of Scripture and its interpretation appears to have been considerable.)

Mark 12:28-34 makes the chief duties love of God and neighbor. To conjoin these imperatives from Torah (Deut 6:4-5; Lev 19:18) is to endorse Moses. Indeed, Mark 12:28-34 may assume, as Philo taught, that the decalogue encapsulates all of Torah and falls into two halves, the first enjoining love of God, the second love of neighbor (*Decal.* 19-20, 108-110, 154; *Spec. leg.* 1.1; cf. Rom 13:9). In other words, these two imperatives stand for the entire law. In line with this, Jesus elsewhere affirms the law's abiding validity (Matt 5:18 par. Luke 16:17), endorses Mosaic imperatives (Mark 1:44; 7:21; 10:19; Matt 23:23 par. Luke 11:42), criticizes others for breaking Torah (Mark 7:8-13), and rebuts those who accuse him of acting unlawfully (Mark 2:23-28).

Jesus seemingly was engaged particularly with Leviticus 19, which was so important for Second Temple and rabbinic Judaism. That chapter, in addition to commanding that one not hate but rather love one's neighbor, contains teaching about both retaliation and judging. Picking up on Leviticus 19:18 – "You will not take vengeance or bear a grudge against any of your people" – Matthew 5:38-47 par. Luke 6:27-35 prohibits vengeance and rejects the conventional reciprocity of returning evil for evil. Jesus also endorses the golden rule (Matt 7:12 par. Luke 6:31), which was traditionally associated with Leviticus 19 (Tob 4:14-15; Jub. 36:4; Ep. Arist. 207; Tg. Ps.-J. 19:18; cf. Did. 1:2), and he rewrites Leviticus 19:2, turning "You will be holy, for I the Lord your God am holy" into "Be merciful, just as your Father is merciful" (Luke 6:36). He gives "Love your neighbor" a broad interpretation: It includes enemies (Matt 5:44 par. Luke 6:27; Luke 10:29-37). Provocatively, he amends Leviticus 19:15-17, as though to say: "You have heard that it was said to those of old, 'You shall judge your neighbor.' But I say to you, 'Do not judge'" (Matt 7:1-2 par. Luke 6:37-38).

Tensions between Jesus and the Torah are not confined to Matthew 7:1-2 par. Luke 6:37-38. "Hate your father and mother" (Luke 14:26; cf. Matt 10:37) is formulated over against Exodus 20:12 par. Deuteronomy 5:16: "Honor your father and mother." The prohibition of divorce and remarriage (Matt 5:31–32 par. Luke 16:18; Mark 10:2–12; 1 Cor 7:10–11) does not match what Moses said on the subject (Deut 24:1–4). It is the same with the injunction against swearing in Matthew 5:33–37: Jesus disallows what Moses permitted (Exod 20:7; Lev 19:12).

Jesus's apparently inconsistent attitude to Torah reflects his messianic context. According to Matthew 11:13 par. Luke 16:16, the law and the prophets were until John; since then the good news of the kingdom is preached (Luke) or the kingdom has suffered violence (Matthew). The new has arrived; things are different (Mark 2:21–22). The consummation, when sin will be eradicated, is nigh, and to the extent that the law makes concessions to sin, it is postlapsarian and needs revision. If "from the beginning it was not so" (Matt 19:8), then it should not be so now (Mark 10:2–12). The ideal future becomes the imperative for life in the present.

Jesus's stance vis-à-vis Torah was messianic in another way. The demands he made on behalf of the kingdom surpassed all other demands, including those in Torah. If following him entailed not burying one's father, then that was the requirement. The Babylonian Talmud (b. Yeb. 90b) teaches, with reference to the prophet like Moses of Deuteronomy 18:15, 18: "Come and hear: 'You will listen to him,' even if he tells you to transgress some of the commandments in the Torah, as happened with Elijah on Mount Carmel [in 1 Kings 18 the prophet sacrifices outside the temple], obey him in every respect, in accord with the needs of the hour." Imperatives can conflict, and Jesus, who took himself to be the eschatological prophet like Moses (see the section "Self-Conception"), operated with the conviction that the needs of the eschatological crisis sometimes required exceptional demands.

Although Jesus did not require the same of all (see "Itinerants, Householders, and Discipleship"), he called everyone, in the face of the last judgment, to return to God. This is the broad context for observance of Torah and Jesus's moral teaching. Nowhere do his sayings assume that individuals will be saved by virtue of descent from Abraham. In this Jesus followed the Baptist. The latter insisted that descent from Abraham will not guarantee passing the final judgment (Matt 3:7–10 par. Luke 3:7–9), and he conducted a one-time baptism of repentance for the forgiveness of sins (Mark 1:4). Jesus similarly mandated becoming, in effect, a convert. He called for beginning one's religious life anew, for becoming like a little child (Mark 10:15; John 3:3; Gos. Thom. 22; cf. Paul's idea of a "new creation" [2 Cor 5:17; Gal 6:15] and b. Yeb. 22a and b. Bek. 47a, where the convert to Judaism is "like a new-born child").

### ITINERANTS, HOUSEHOLDERS, AND DISCIPLESHIP

Jesus called some to "become passers-by" (Gos. Thom. 42), to follow him literally by abandoning their ordinary lives to share his itinerant lifestyle (Matt 8:18–22 par. Luke 9:57–62; Mark 1:16–20; 2:13–17). Their dislocation and detachment from ordinary life matched their eschatological orientation: They were not at home in the present.

Jesus was an itinerant largely because he wished to spread his message (Mark 1:38), and this was one reason he called disciples to follow him: They too were to proclaim the kingdom, thereby becoming fishers of people (Mark 1:17). They were to enlarge the scope of his influence (Matt 10:5–16; Mark 6:8–11; Luke 10:1–12). (That they preached what Jesus preached implies that they were already repeating his words before his death. The Jesus tradition began then.)

We do not know how often Jesus and his band were away from hospitable households or how often they ventured beyond day trips and passed the night in the open or how often food and drink were serious issues. But the directive to pray for daily bread (Matt 6:11 par. Luke 11:3) and the counsel to be not anxious about food and clothing (Matt 6:25–34 par. Luke 12:22–32) were heard by people who, because on the road (Mark 1:35; 6:31–35; 8:4; Luke 5:16), must at least on occasion have fretted about such things. (This holds whether or not the Galilean economy in Jesus's day was generally oppressive, a disputed subject.)

From his sympathizers Jesus selected a group of twelve (Mark 3:13–19; Matt 19:28 par. Luke 22:28–30; 1 Cor 15:5). Collectively they were a prophetic sign and eschatological symbol. Representing the twelve tribes of Israel (cf. 1QM 2.1–3), they reflected Jesus's hope for the literal restoration of all Israel, including the lost tribes (cf. Matt 8:11–12 par. Luke 13:28–29; Mark 13:27; Hos 11:11; 2 Macc 1:27; 2:18; Bar. 4:37; 5:5; 1 En. 57:1).

Jesus's entourage included women. There are no call stories for any of them, and it has been argued that his female supporters were all householders, not itinerants. But there was nothing extraordinary about women being out and about – as the Gospels themselves attest – and the proposal goes against Mark 15:40–41 and Luke 8:1–3. It seems likely that at least a few women not only went up with Jesus to Jerusalem for Passover but, earlier on, traveled with him around Galilee. Whether we should call these female coworkers "disciples" is debated. The Gospels do not do so. Given the androcentric focus of the sources, we can say little more except (i) some offered pecuniary support (Luke 8:3); (ii) Jesus is nowhere quoted as making disparaging remarks about women (contrast Sirach 42.14; T. Reub. 5.1; Josephus, *C. Ap.* 2.201; t. Ber. 6.18);

(iii) multiple sayings pair the activity or circumstances of women with the activity or circumstances of men (e.g. Matt 12:41–42 par. Luke 11:31–32; Matt 13:31–33 par. Luke 13:18–21; Luke 4:25–27; 12:45; Luke 15:4–10); and (iv) one of his female followers, Mary of Magdala, appears to have played a key role in the emergence of belief in Jesus's resurrection (Matt 28:9–10; Mark 16:1–8; John 20:14–18).

In addition to those who literally followed him, Jesus had supporters who stayed at home. He did not, despite harsh words about family ties and possessions (Mark 10:17–31; Matt 6:19–21 par. Luke 12:33–34; Luke 6:24–26; 16:1–31; Gos. Thom. 36, 42, 56; etc.), ask everyone to abandon conventional livelihoods or leave home (Matt 24:17–18 par. Luke 17:31–32/Mark 13:15–16; 2:11; 5:19; 8:26; Luke 19:1–10). His critical comments were relative to circumstance. Although he believed that traditional social structures were passing away and were not of chief importance, he decried them not in principle but precisely when they came into conflict with his cause. The harsh words about families reflect occasions when someone turned down Jesus's call to follow him (Mark 10:17–22) or effected familial strife (Matt 10:35–36 = Luke 12:51–53).

## HEALINGS AND MIRACLES

The modern quest for the historical Jesus began with Enlightenment thinkers for whom miracles were impossible. With that negation as their starting point, their task was to uncover the original Jesus behind the credulous overlay. While the quest has grown far beyond that, contemporary historians often adopt reductionistic strategies when elucidating miracles: A story may be due to haggadic invention, to mutation of a memory into legend, or to misperception or misinterpretation of real events. But whatever one's take on miracles, the presence of the latter in the Gospels is not of itself reason to infer that they are late and mostly legendary. Countless reports of extraordinary events, however explained, have come and continue to come from eyewitnesses. It is equally undeniable that some religious charismatics, such as the Roman Catholic Saint Don Bosco (d. 1888) and the Indian guru Sai Baba of Shirdi (d. 1918), have been trailed by numerous astounding claims while alive. It was so with Jesus. Even some opponents conceded that he could do the extraordinary (Matt 12:27 par. Luke 11:19; Mark 3:22–27; cf. Josephus, *Ant.* 18.63).

Jesus appears to have been "the most successful exorcist and healer of his time" (Casey 2010, 107). Distinctive is his unmediated authority. He does not use incantations. Usually he does not even pray. It is as though he has numinous power in himself. Equally notable is the variety: exorcisms, healings of various afflictions, raisings of the dead, and so-called nature miracles (e.g. calming the sea, feeding a multitude, walking on water, changing water into wine). While it is all but impossible to evaluate the historicity of most of the stories, Jesus presumably drew crowds as much or more for his miracles as his teaching. But the two were intimately related, for the former illustrated the latter in at least two ways: They (i) embodied his insistence on loving and serving others, especially the unfortunate and (ii) were testimony to the dawning of eschatological blessings (Matt 11:2–6 par. Luke 7:18–23).

Among the exceptional abilities reported are foreseeing events, perceiving what others think, and knowing from afar what is happening (Matt 12:22–30 par. Luke 11:14–23; Mark 2:1–12; 6:45–52; 9:33–37; 11:1–10; Luke 5:1–11; 6:6–11; 7:36–50; 9:46–48; John 1:35–52; 2:23–25; 4:4–42; etc.). The large number of relevant texts indicates that some who knew him perceived Jesus to be a clairvoyant prophet.

SELF-CONCEPTION

Discussion of Jesus's self-conception has been much affected by theological – as well as anti-theological – interests. Many have desired to bring his ideas as close to later creedal orthodoxy as possible. Others have wished to do the opposite. The truth seems to be that Jesus had an exalted self-perception, which is best understood not in Arian or Athanasian terms but via comparison with divine agents in Second Temple Jewish texts, such as Melchizedek in 11QMelchizedek and the Son of Man in 1 Enoch 37–71.

Much modern scholarship converged on the idea that Jesus took himself to be a prophet, more particularly an eschatological prophet. The sources report that others identified him as such (Matt 21:11, 46; Mark 6:15; 8:28; Luke 7:16, 39; 24:19; John 4:19; 6:14; 7:40, 52; 9:17; Gos. Thom. 52). They also have Jesus observing, with reference to his ministry, that "prophets are not without honour, except in their hometown, and among their own kin, and in their own house" (Mark 6:4; cf. John 4:44; Gos. Thom. 31), as well as avowing, "Today, tomorrow, and the next day I must be on my way, because it is impossible for a prophet to be killed outside of Jerusalem" (Luke 13:33). When one adds that others near his time and place, including John the Baptist, were known as prophets (Matt 11:9 par. Luke 7:26; Josephus, *Bell.* 2.261–63), that Jesus, like some canonical prophets (Jer 16:1–2; Ezek 4:1–17; Hos 1:2–8), evidently engaged in symbolic acts (Mark 3:13–19; 6:30–44; 11:1–10, 12–14, 15–19;

14:22–25), and that the Gospels regularly depict him as a seer (Matt 10:23–25; Mark 8:31; 13:2, 5–37; etc.), the common conclusion follows.

Many have hesitated to attribute to Jesus a larger conception than this. On their view, Jesus proclaimed not himself but the kingdom, and more exalted christological ideas were secondary developments. At least two impulses help account for this traditional judgment. One is the historical conviction that all doctrine, including Christology, evolved over time. If there is distance between Origen and Athanasius, and if there is distance between the Synoptics and John's Gospel, then there must be distance between the historical Jesus and the Synoptics, which means development from the lesser to the greater.

A second impulse has been theological, the concern that if Jesus thought too highly of himself, we cannot think so highly of him: That would be reason to fret about his mental health. But whatever one makes of the psychology, nearly insuperable difficulties beset the verdict that Jesus thought less of himself than he reportedly thought of the Baptist, which was that John was "more than a prophet" (Matt 11:9 par. Luke 7:26).

The earliest sources for the Jesus movement are the authentic letters of Paul. In them Jesus is already God's "Son" (Rom 1:9; Gal 4:4; 1 Cor 1:9; 1 Thess 1:10; etc.), the "Lord" (passim), pre-existent (2 Cor 8:9), and thoroughly allied with God the Father (Rom 1:7–8; 2 Cor 13:13; Gal 1:1, 3; 4:6; etc.). This includes materials that, according to many, are pre-Pauline – the confession in Romans 1:2–4, the Aramaic prayer "Maranatha" (1 Cor 16:22), and the poetic section in Philippians 2:5–11. Paul, then, establishes the early advent of a high Christology. Moreover, while the apostle argues about many things, such as circumcising gentiles and spiritual gifts, he nowhere defends his christological formulations. This implies that those formulations were not idiosyncratic, that his exalted Christology was taken for granted and widespread.

While multiple factors contributed to early high Christology, Jesus's convictions about himself mark the point of origin. Nothing is explained by positing that, soon after Easter, Jesus's admirers, without his help, turned him into someone akin to the Elect One in 1 Enoch 37–71. Rather, positing continuity, which means positing a lofty self-consciousness for Jesus, is the more reasonable path, and it accords with the fact that, in many sayings attributed to him, Jesus is the locus of end-time events. His successful exorcisms inaugurate the end (Matt 12:28 par. Luke 11:20). He is the fulfillment of prophetic texts in Isaiah, especially Isaiah 61 (Matt 5:3–12 par. Luke 6:20–23; Matt 11:2–6 par. Luke 7:18–23; Luke 4:16–21). Those who reject or disobey him will suffer judgment (Matt 7:24–27 par. Luke 6:46–49; Matt 10:32–33 par. Luke 12:8–9; Matt 11:21–24 par. Luke 10:12–15; Mark 8:38). He will, like the figure in Daniel 7:13–14, come on the clouds of heaven (Mark 13:26–27; 14:62). He will sit on a throne (Matt 25:31; Mark 10:35–40; 14:62). The quantity of materials that gives Jesus star billing is sufficiently large as to compel a choice. Either all of this material is misleading, in which case the tradition is so distorted that a skeptical stance seems in order, or at least some of it fairly represents Jesus, in which case he was the center of his own eschatological scenario.

Beyond this generality, Jesus probably conceived of himself as the eschatological prophet like Moses in particular (Deut 18:15, 18; 1QS 9.11; 4Q175). This is, despite the failure of most scholarship to draw the inference, the best explanation for the series of correlations between traditions about him and traditions about Moses. When Jesus claims to cast out demons by "the finger of God," he is like the lawgiver, who also worked wonders by "the finger of God" (Exod 8:19). When, at the Last Supper, Jesus uses the phrase, "my blood of the covenant" (Mark 14:24), he is alluding to Exodus 24:8, where Moses dashes blood on the people and says, "Here is the blood of the covenant that the Lord has made with you in accordance with all these words." When, in Matthew 5:21–48, Jesus sets his words beside and even, at points, seemingly over against Moses, his status vis-à-vis Moses is (as the commentaries prove) inevitably posed. When, in Luke 12:35–38, Jesus implores his hearers, whom he likens to slaves, to "Fasten a belt around your waists (*humōn hai osphues periezōsmenai*) and let your lamps be lit," he is replaying the exodus, which took place at night (Exod 12:42; Tg. Neof., Tg. Ps.-J. and Frag. Tg. [MS Vatican Ebr. 440] on Exod 12:42) and involved Moses commanding the Israelite slaves to gird up their loins (LXX Exod 12:11: *hai osphues humōn periezōsmenai*). When Jesus characterizes his generation as "evil" (Matt 12:39–42 = Luke 11:29–32), "faithless" and "perverse" (Matt 17:17 = Luke 9:41; Mark 9:19), and "adulterous" and "sinful" (Mark 8:38), he is using language associated with the generation in the wilderness, so his day is like Moses's day (Num 32:13; Deut 1:35; 32:20). The present is again like the past when Jesus bids his disciples to pray, "Give us this day our daily bread" (Matt 6:11 par. Luke 11:3), for the phrase recalls Exodus 16, where God "gives" manna, which is called "bread," and which is sent daily or day by day (Exod 16:4–5, 22–30; Luke's *to kath' hēmeran* precisely matches LXX Exod 16:5). These and additional texts, when added together, depict a new Moses in a new exodus.

Jesus also thought himself destined to be Israel's king: (i) The Romans crucified him. The best explanation is that they worried about the unrest attending a popular figure some took to be "king of the Jews" (the inscription above the cross: Mark 15:2, 9, 12, 18, 26; John 18:33, 39; 19:3, 19, 21). That some imagined Jesus to be an insurrectionist with regal pretensions entails that the issue of kingship was there before Easter (cf. John 6:15). (ii) Belief in Jesus's resurrection would not have moved anyone to identify him as Israel's king, as if to turn him into someone he had not been before. On the contrary, the resurrection functioned to vindicate Jesus, which meant vindicating the hopes his followers already had. (iii) If Jesus selected twelve disciples (Mark 3:13–19) to represent the twelve tribes of Israel (Matt 19:28), it is significant that he is not among their number. As the one who chose them, he was rather their leader, which implies his leadership of restored Israel.

(iv) Jesus predicted not only the destruction of Jerusalem's temple but probably claimed that he would build another (Mark 14:58; 15:29; John 2:13–22). This matters because the idea (based on an eschatological reading of 2 Sam 7:13–14) of a Davidic or messianic figure rebuilding the temple was an eschatological motif (cf. Zech 6:12–13; 4QFlorilegium; Sib. Or. 5:422; Tg. on Isa 53:5). (v) Matthew 19:28 par. Luke 22:28–30 (a promise that implicitly includes Judas and is unlikely pure invention) and Mark 10:35–45 (James and John want to sit on Jesus's right and left) envisage thrones for Jesus's disciples. Given that he is their leader, he too must await a throne (Matt 25:31; Mark 14:62). Such expectation must in part lie behind the conviction, which arose quite early, that Jesus is even now seated at God's right hand: Promise had become fulfillment (Acts 2:34–35; 5:31; 7:55–56; Rom 8:34; Col 3:1). (vi) Some Jews anticipated that Israel's eschatological king would be God's son (cf. 4Q174 1.10–13; 4Q246 2.1). This is the likely matrix for the confession of Jesus as God's "Son," a confession that goes back to Christian beginnings. It was there at the beginning because Jesus himself stirred messianic expectations. If he was nonetheless shy of the title "Messiah," that may have been because his status and role were not his to establish: God alone would grant and proclaim those.

By far the most frequent title Jesus uses in the Gospels is "the Son of man." The Greek (*ho huios tou anthrōpou*) is unusual and must derive from Aramaic. Intense debate over the expression, which is rare outside the Gospels, continues unabated. But attempts to eliminate all allusion to Daniel 7:13–14 from the originating tradition fail, as does the proposal that, for Jesus, the Son of man was not himself but an eschatological person nowhere else hinted at in the tradition. Jesus appears to have found himself, or perhaps himself and his followers, in Daniel 7:13–14, in the scene where "one like a son of man" comes on the clouds of heaven and receives everlasting dominion, glory, and kingship.

### CONFLICT AND MARTYRDOM

Beside the formal passion predictions in Mark (8:31; 9.31; 10:33–34), a mass of material purports that Jesus anticipated an untimely death (Allison 2010, 423–33). That he spoke about his own demise is already tradition for Paul (1 Cor 11:23–25). The apostle, moreover, believed that Jesus "did not please himself" (Rom 15:3) but "gave himself for our sins" (Gal 1:4; cf. 2:20), that he humbled himself and became "obedient to the point of death – even death on a cross" (Phil 2:8). These convictions assume that Jesus did not run from death but embraced it as a martyr.

Perhaps Jesus had real premonitions. Or perhaps he began to contemplate death because he saw, in the late stages of his ministry, which way the wind was blowing: It had become plain that conflict with authorities in Jerusalem, both Jewish and Roman, was inevitable. His tradition emphasized the martyrdom of prophets (Matt 23:29–37 par. Luke 11:48–51; 13:34; the Lives of the Prophets), and Herod Antipas had recently beheaded the Baptist. It is also credible that biblical scripts played a role. Before the one like a son of man comes in Daniel 7, the holy ones, who share his destiny (7:14, 18), suffer persecution (7:21). If, furthermore, Jesus found himself in Isaiah 61, he may likewise have read himself into earlier chapters that feature a suffering servant. Mark 10.45 ("give his life as a ransom for many") and 14:24 ("poured out for many") seem to echo Isaiah 53:11–12 ("poured out himself to death," "bore the sin of many").

Jesus might at some point have hoped not to taste death before seeing the kingdom in its fullness (Mark 9:1). If so, we do not know when he came to have second thoughts. It is also possible, if memory informs Mark 14:32–42 (Gethsemane), that his conviction never amounted to certainty. However that may be, he will, given his eschatological expectations, have understood his death to be part of the unprecedented "time of anguish" that would mark the latter days (Dan 12:1).

What precisely triggered Jesus's arrest is unclear. Maybe it was a disturbance in the temple and a prophecy of its destruction that brought things to a head (Mark 11:15–17; 14:58; but the event occurs much earlier in John 2:13–17). Whatever the cause, both Jewish and Roman authorities were involved in the events that led to his crucifixion. According to 1 Thessalonians 2:14–16 (which is not a post-Pauline interpolation), the Jews (or Judeans) "killed both the Lord Jesus and the prophets." Yet in 1 Corinthians 2:8, Paul writes that "the rulers of this age ... crucified the Lord of glory." "The rulers of this age" are or include the Roman authorities. Paul, then, agrees with the Gospels, where Jesus's execution trails actions taken by members of the Sanhedrin and then Pilate (Mark 14:53–65; 15:1–15; John 18:12–19:16). Josephus similarly has both Pilate and "men of the highest standing among us" involved in Jesus's demise (*Ant.* 18.64). While one can detect a tendency in the tradition to lay more blame on the Jews and less on the Romans, the involvement of Jewish authorities cannot be eliminated. Jesus in any case will have appeared, however briefly, before Pilate, just as Jesus son of Ananias appeared before Albinus, and just as James and Simon the sons of Judas the Galilean stood before Tiberius Alexander (Josephus, *Ant.* 20.102; *Bell.* 6.300–309). As Josephus wrote: "Pilate condemned him to the cross" (*Ant.* 18.64).

FURTHER READING

Allison, Dale C., Jr. 2010. *Constructing Jesus: Memory, Imagination, and History*. Grand Rapids: Baker Academic.
Casey, Maurice. 2010. *Jesus of Nazareth: An Independent Historian's Account of His Life and Teaching*. London: T & T Clark.
Destro, Adriana and Mauro Pesce. 2012. *Encounters with Jesus: The Man in His Place and Time*. Minneapolis: Fortress.
Dunn, James D. G. 2003. *Christianity in the Making, Vol. 1: Jesus Remembered*. Grand Rapids: Eerdmans.
Hengel, Martin and Anna Maria Schwemer. 2019. *Jesus and Judaism*. Waco: Baylor University Press.
Keith, Chris and Anthony Le Donne, eds. 2012. *Jesus, Criteria, and the Demise of Authenticity*. London: T & T Clark Continuum.
Meier, John P. 1991–2016. *A Marginal Jew: Rethinking the Historical Jesus*. 5 vols. Anchor Bible Reference Library. New Haven: Yale University Press.
Schröter, Jens and Christine Jacobi, eds. 2022. *The Jesus Handbook*. Grand Rapids: Eerdmans.
Theissen, Gerd and Annette Merz. 1998. *The Historical Jesus: A Comprehensive Guide*. Minneapolis: Fortress.
Wright, N. T. 1996. *Jesus and the Victory of God*. Minneapolis: Fortress.

## 2 Jesus's Religion, Praxis, and Experience of God

LUTZ DOERING

### JESUS'S RELIGIOUS FORMATION

While Jesus's life appears as remarkably transformative in the New Testament Gospels, there is also much to be gained from attending quite specifically to the Jewishness of his religious formation and experience, vision, and hope. Jesus was born into a Jewish family. As "Joseph's son" (Luke 3:23; 4:22; John 1:45; cf. Matt 1:16), he was regarded as a Jew. According to Luke 2:21, he was circumcised on the eighth day (cf. Gen 17:12–14). Jesus grew up in Galilee – according to the Gospels, in Nazareth (Mark 1:9; Matt 2:23; Luke 4:16; etc.). Jews in Galilee had come from either Judea or the Babylonian diaspora from the second century BCE onward. In the first century CE, Jewish religious life in Galilee was rather similar to that in Judea, although due to the distance people would come less frequently in contact with the temple. Being a Jew meant living according to a particular lifestyle shaped by commandments of the Torah, in addition to certain basic convictions about the world and its inhabitants, its origin, and its future. As scholarship during the past forty years has made abundantly clear, Torah observance was not seen as a way to "earn salvation" but rather as a response to the covenant between God and Israel. However, there were differences in the norms for Torah observance (the halakhah) and in worldview across the various elite groups and in the ordinary Jewish population (more on this in the section "Elite Groups ['Sects'] in Relation to Jesus").

Jesus would have participated in the daily routine and meal practice with his parents and siblings, and he would have celebrated the Sabbath and Jewish festivals with his family and relatives. He would have learned about the Torah commandments particularly from his father Joseph (cf. Philo, *Hypoth.* 7.14), who would also have taught him to read and to write in Hebrew (cf. Sir 30:3–4; Jub. 11:16; 47:9; Josephus, *Ag. Ap.* 2.204; T. Levi 13:2; ALD 13:4, 6, 15 [= 88, 90, 98]; Ps.-Philo, LAB 22:5–6), although the extent of literacy among Jews varied. In addition to the family, he would have attended synagogue assemblies in which the Torah was read and interpreted (more on this in the section "Jewish Life as Experienced by Jesus"). Luke 2:41–52 portrays Jesus as accompanying his parents on the pilgrimage to Jerusalem for Passover. According to Matthew 4:1–11, Jesus is well-versed in the Torah, especially on the relation between God and human beings as summarized in words from Deuteronomy (Deut 6:13, 16; 8:3).

### JEWISH LIFE AS EXPERIENCED BY JESUS

What was Jewish life according to the Torah like in the late Second Temple period? Jews both close to Jerusalem and further away would say the *Shema' Israel* ("Hear O Israel"; Deut 6:4–5 and related verses) twice, in the morning when rising and in the evening when going to bed (Josephus, *Ant.* 4.212; see also m. Ber. 1–2), and this prayer was also central for Jesus (Mark 12:29–30 par. Matt 22:37; Luke 10:27). Apart from it, there would have been no obligatory daily prayer for common Jews at the time: The thrice-daily prayer obligatory for all male Jews (the Eighteen Benedictions) is an innovation in response to the destruction of the Jerusalem temple, although voluntary prayer, partly using early forms of the Eighteen Benedictions, was widespread. In some circles, we find the development of daily, Sabbath, and festival prayers (cf. 4Q503–509), although thrice-daily prayers still seem voluntary at the time (see Dan 6:11[Eng. 10]; Ps 55:18[Eng. 17]). In addition, on every Sabbath morning the Jews – men and women, perhaps also children – gathered in the synagogue, mainly for the reading and the interpretation of the Torah (Philo, *Hypoth.* 7.12–13; Josephus, *Ant.* 16.43; *Ag. Ap.* 2.175; Luke 4:16–21, though it is unclear how widespread a reading from the Prophets was at the time). This is confirmed by the Greek Theodotus inscription (*CIIP* 9), from a first-century CE synagogue in Jerusalem, according to which Theodotus, from a family of diaspora Jews, built the synagogue "for the reading of the Law and the teaching of the commandments."

Recent archaeological excavations have brought to light a number of buildings that can be identified as first-century CE synagogues. In addition to the synagogues at Gamla in the Golan, Masada (in secondary use during the first Judean war, 66–70 CE), and Herodium (in secondary use during the first or/and second Judean war, 132–5 CE), as well as the Jerusalem synagogue (not extant) to which the Theodotus inscription belonged, there are two synagogues at Magdala – the first town excavated in which two synagogues were found. There is perhaps also one at Khirbet Qana in Galilee, although the latter might have operated only between 70 and 135 CE. Further, there are synagogues at Qiryat Sefer and Khirbet Umm el-Umdan (both near modern Mode'in) in the Judean Shephelah, and potentially at Khirbet Diab (north of Jerusalem) and Khirbet eṭ-Ṭawani (close to Hebron) in the Judean Mountains (see Doering and Krause 2020). Synagogue buildings and the gatherings in them would thus be a familiar experience for Jesus in Galilee. The main characteristic of these synagogues is benches on three or four sides around an open middle space, suitable for an assembly especially to sit and listen to readings and interpretations and to engage in other communal activity. When Jesus calls up the man with the withered hand in a synagogue on the Sabbath, "Come to the center" (Mark 3:3), this would nicely fit such a building plan. The synagogues also functioned as schools: While children would be taught basic reading and writing skills by their fathers, the sabbatical gatherings led by specialists in Torah reading and interpretation would have contributed to knowledge of the Bible and Jewish laws. Smaller side rooms, as discovered, for example, in the synagogues at Magdala and Gamla, might have served study groups, also during weekdays.

It should be noted that "worship" in Second Temple Judaism was less homogeneous than we might imagine: While ordinary Jews prayed voluntarily and gathered locally for the study of the Torah on the Sabbath, it was in the Jerusalem temple only that a different kind of worship took place: the sacrificial service. This featured the twice-daily burnt offering (morning and afternoon; Num 28:3–9), as well as the burnt offerings for Sabbaths (Num 28:9–10; Matt 12:5) and holidays (Num 28:11–29:39), sin and guilt offerings (Lev 4–5) for certain unintentional offenses, sacrifices at the completion of purification times (cf. Lev 12:6–8; Luke 2:22–24 [following childbirth]; Lev 14:2–32; Mark 1:44 parr. [after skin disease]), as well as votive offerings (Matt 5:23–24) and other ceremonies. This would have been known to ordinary Jews all over the Land of Israel and beyond, though they would have infrequently participated in them, for example, when coming to Jerusalem during pilgrimage festivals (Passover/*Pesaḥ*, Weeks/*Shavuʿot*, and Tabernacles/*Sukkot*). The Mishnah claims (m. Taʿan. 4:2–3) that there was a link between the sacrifices at the temple and Jewish communities across the Land of Israel: the *maʿamadot*, gatherings of ordinary Israelites fasting and reading the creation account at times when their related priestly and Levitical cycles (cf. 1 Chron 24) were offering sacrifices in Jerusalem.

A different link can be seen in one of the Magdala synagogues, discovered in 2009: a stone table featuring, among other things, a relief of the temple menorah together with further temple vessels. Most likely, this was meant to connect the reading and studying activity in the remote synagogue with the sacrificial service in the Jerusalem temple. We shall discuss Jesus's ambivalent attitude toward the temple in a section devoted to this topic later in the chapter.

An important aspect of Jewish law was keeping the Sabbath. Exodus 20:8-11 and Deuteronomy 5:12-15 call for abstention from "labor" (mela'khah) on the Sabbath, although it is unclear what this entails. Other biblical passages add further details, such as the ban on agricultural work (Exod 34:21; Neh 13:15-18), gathering wood (Num 15:26-36), lighting fire (Exod 35:3), doing business (Isa 58:13; Neh 10:32; 13:15-18), carrying loads (Jer 17:19-27; Neh 13:19), walking (longer) ways (Exod 16:29; Isa 18:13), or suggest that meals be prepared on Friday, before the start of Sabbath at dusk (cf. Exod 16:5, regarding the manna). Since the Maccabean period, a concern with human life in danger on the Sabbath is attested, and Jewish groups permitted in various ways the transgression of the Sabbath commandment in order to save human life, both in war, allowing self-defense (see 1 Macc 2:40-41), and in everyday situations, attending to persons in danger (see Luke 14:5; t. Šabb. 15[16]:11-17; Mek. *shabbeta ki tiśśa* 1). This is a theme that recurs in our discussion of Jesus's attitude toward the Sabbath in the section "Jesus's Views on Torah and Halakhah."

Another significant area of the Torah was the dietary laws. Jews basically abstained from consuming unclean animals (the most important of which are specified in Lev 11), whereas cleft-footed animals with divided hoofs and chewing the cud, as well as fowl and fish with fins and scales, were permitted. It is clear that Jesus shared the basic dietary laws (on Mark 7:19, see the comments in the section "Jesus's Views on Torah and Halakhah"). A further, related, area of the law was ritual purity. Thus, events connected with sex, birth, illness, and death render persons temporarily impure, for different periods of time: semen emission and intercourse, for one day (Lev 15:16-18); menstruation, for seven days, and the one touching a menstruant, for one day (Lev 15:19); birth, for up to forty days (for a boy) or up to eighty days (for a girl; Lev 12:2-5); skin disease, for seven days after its disappearance (Lev 13-14); male flux emitters (Lev 15:2-13) and hemorrhaging women (Lev 15:25-28), for seven days after the end of the flux, and the one touching them, for one day; finally, those touching a corpse, for seven days, requiring a special form of cleansing with purification water on the third and seventh day (Num 19). For many of the lesser impurities, immersion in water is required. Since the Hasmonean period, stepped pools used for ritual purification were constructed in the Land of Israel. Such pools, called *miqwa'ot* (the term is rabbinic), would have been a familiar sight for Jesus and his family. In addition, since the time of Herod I, stone vessels of various sizes are attested at places of Jewish settlement all over the Land of Israel, including Galilee; they are plausibly used out of concern for ritual purity, since stone (unlike clay) does not transmit impurity (cf. John 2:6; m. Kelim 10:1). We shall see in the section "Jesus's Views on Torah and Halakhah" that Jesus did not refrain from touching defiling people; this does not imply that he would not have acknowledged their impure status, but the focus of his activity apparently was to cure them and thus help them become pure.

A final area of Torah observance is the separation of firstfruits and tithes. Firstfruits were to be brought to the altar in Jerusalem and given to the priests; according to Nehemiah 10:36, this entailed "all first-fruit of our land and the first-fruits of all fruit of every tree," although later it was understood to relate to the seven species for which the Land of Israel was renowned (according to Deut 8:8, "a land of wheat and barley, of vines and fig trees and pomegranates, a land of olive trees and honey," the latter taken to refer to dates). While fruits were brought in baskets when ripe (Deut 26:1–11), the firstfruits of barley were brought on the day of the *'omer* festival, according to the prevailing (Pharisaic) view, on the day following the first day of Passover (cf. Lev 23:11), whereas the firstfruits of wheat were brought on *Shavu'ot*, seven weeks later, in the form of two loaves of bread (Lev 23:15–17). Vegetable tithe later known as "first tithe" was to be brought from "grain, wine, and oil" (thus Deut 18:23), but texts such as Tobit 1:7 (G$^{II}$, the longer form of the Greek texts) mention also "pomegranate, figs, and other fruit-trees." According to a dominant view, it was given to the Levites, who then had to give a tenth of it to the priests (Num 18:21–28); a minority of sources (for example, Judith 11:13; Jub. 13:25–27) demand that it be directly given to the priests, who were also the recipients of the cattle tithe (Lev 27:32; Tob 1:7 G$^{II}$). Another type, called "second tithe" in Tobit 1:7 for the first time, consists of monetary proceeds that should be spent in Jerusalem (Deut 14:22–27; Jub. 32:10–14). Finally, there is a tithe for poor people (Deut 14:28–29; 26:12–13; Josephus, *Ant.* 4.240; Tob 1:8), the "pauper's tithe" in the diction of the later rabbis, that was given in each third year. Jesus would have been aware that Pharisees, in particular, were concerned with the correct procedures of tithing, and he seems to have accepted their extension of tithing to include different kinds of herbs, though he criticized their concomitant neglect of "justice and love of God" (Luke 11:42 par. Matt 23:23; cf. Luke 18:12), which, as we shall see, is in line with his general stance on the commandments. Jesus's "religion" therefore developed in conversation and debate with the various "sects" of Second Temple Judaism to which we now turn.

### ELITE GROUPS ("SECTS") IN RELATION TO JESUS

Since the Hasmonaean period, several elite groups ("sects") had been formed who represented different social, political, ideological, and theological outlooks. They are the proof that Second Temple Judaism was not uniform but pluriform. This is also important for locating Jesus within Judaism: There was no "normative Judaism," against which other Jews would have appeared as deviants. Rather, we find different varieties of Judaism. This is a term preferable to speaking of "Judaisms" in the plural, because all varieties shared some basic concepts such as the election of Israel, the centrality of the Torah, or the importance of the Jerusalem temple (whether or not they deemed it being run appropriately at the time).

Josephus tells us about the Pharisees, the Sadducees, and the Essenes (*J.W.* 2.119–166; *Ant.* 18.11–22), who were in existence from the Hasmonean period onward and which he presents as different "philosophies." According to Josephus, the Pharisees believed in both fate and the power of the human will; they affirmed the immortality of the soul and resurrection to new life for the good but eternal punishment for the bad. They were distinguished by their accuracy in Torah observance and followed statutes from the tradition of the fathers (*Ant.* 13.297; cf. Mark 7:3, 5; Gal 1:14) in addition to the Pentateuch. As we know from the Gospels, they devoted special attention to keeping the Sabbath (Mark 2:23–3.6 parr.), to ritual purity (Mark 7:3–6), and, as we have seen, to separating the tithes. Nevertheless, their halakhah was adaptable to the requirements of life. The Sadducees drew their support from the priestly aristocracy (*Ant.* 18.17); they were guided only by the "written laws" and rejected additional traditions (*Ant.* 13.297). They denied the resurrection of the dead (Mark 12:18–27 parr.; Acts 23:8), a belief clearly expressed only on the fringes of the Hebrew Scriptures (e.g. Dan 12:2–3; Isa 25:8; 26:19). They also denied divine predestination and attributed everything to human will. Their legal norms (halakhah) were conservative and little adaptable. This they shared with the third sect, the Essenes, a group not mentioned by name in the New

Testament but referred to also by Philo (*Prob.* 75–91; *Hypoth.* 11.1–18) and Pliny the Elder (*Nat.* 5.73). According to Josephus, they attributed everything to divine predestination (*Ant.* 13.172) and affirmed the immortality of the soul (*J.W.* 2.154–158; according to the parallel in Hippolytus, *Haer.* 9.27.1, resurrection). According to the long passage *J.W.* 2.119–161, the Essenes inter alia despised marriage, had their property in common, avoided contact with oil, and wore white robes. Before sunrise, they said their prayers, then focused on work, interrupted by midday and evening meals, preceded by immersion. They did not swear oaths, except when joining the sect, searched the Scriptures, and studied the healing qualities of roots and stones. After three years of probation, applicants were accepted; those guilty of major offenses were expelled. Spitting in the meeting was forbidden, and the Essenes observed the Sabbath with additional scrutiny, avoiding to defecate on this day. Josephus writes that they were divided into four classes depending on the length of their membership, and that they also had a marrying branch. Soon after the discovery of the first Dead Sea Scrolls in 1947, scholars proposed the identification of the group(s) mentioned in these texts with the Essenes. Although the ancient reports about the Essenes are highly stylized, there are a number of significant similarities in the Scrolls, especially with the *yaḥad* as mentioned in the Rule of the Community: a gradual process of admission (1QS 6.13–23), communal meals (6.4–5), common property (1.11–13; 5.1–3; 6.17–20), temporary exclusion and permanent expulsion (6.24–7.25), spitting prohibited in the assembly (7.13), and dualistic statements on predestination (3.13–4.1). On the other hand, some differences remain; thus, there is no text in the Scrolls that prescribes celibacy, although the Community Rule seems to address men only. There are, however, other texts, such as the Damascus Document, that presume marriage and family life. It would be possible to imagine "the Essenes" as comprising different, though related groups. Finally, for the first century CE, Josephus speaks also of a "fourth philosophy" (*Ant.* 18.9, 23), related to the Pharisees but anti-Roman minded; it is usually identified with the Zealots (a term Josephus avoids for the time before the first Judean war). Overall, the Pharisees were the most popular of the sects, but even they did not constitute "normative" Judaism. Many of the Pharisaic practices were shared by the wider population, although most common people did not formally belong to any of the elite groups. Thus, it is fair to say that despite the dominance of the elite groups, most Jews in the Land of Israel were not "sectarian."

Jesus, too, apparently did not belong to any of these elite groups, although he is closest to the Pharisees in his legal outlook. This perhaps explains why they constitute his major discussion partners in the Galilean narratives of the Synoptic Gospels. Like the Pharisees, Jesus is concerned more with the daily life of common Jews, with relations between fellow humans and between humans and God, than with issues concerning the cult. Like Hillel – perhaps a Pharisaic forerunner of the Rabbis – he puts prime emphasis on the Golden Rule as a variant of the love commandment (Matt 7:12; cf. ARN B 26; b. Shab. 31a; cf. also Tob 4:15; Jub. 36:4; Let. Aris. 207; Tg. Ps.-J. Lev 19:18), and like R. Eliezer – often seen as a successor of conservative Pharisees – he deems the love commandment as summarizing the Torah (Mark 12:28–31 parr.; cf. Sifra *qedoshim* parashah 2, pereq 2 [89a Weiss]). Mark imagines a "scribe" – contextually, a Pharisaic scribe, who relished Jesus's rebuttal of the Sadducees' question – to agree on the importance of the double love commandment (Mark 12:32–34). Unlike the Pharisees, though, Jesus is more proactive in his relation toward sinners and marginalized: Rather than relying on his own righteousness and keeping away from sinners and impure persons, as the Gospels claim the Pharisees did (e.g. Mark 2:15–17 parr.; Luke 18:9–14), Jesus is said to have approached sinners and pronounced the forgiveness of sins to them, and he is said to have expelled demons and healed the sick, thereby also terminating the status of defilement (e.g. of lepers [Mark 1:40–44 parr.], of a hemorrhaging woman [Mark 5:25–34 parr.]). Also, Jesus was apparently unwilling to accept the "traditions of the elders" exhibited by the Pharisees (Mark 7:3, 5; cf. vv. 8–9). In this aspect, he was similar to the Sadducees, although he did not share their rejection of the expectation of resurrection (Mark 12:18–27 parr.). What were the reasons for these differences?

## THE KINGDOM OF GOD INAUGURATED

The central element in Jesus's ministry is the notion that the kingdom or the kingship of God (*basileia tou theou*, both the spatial and the dynamic aspect is referenced) has "come near" (Mark 1:15) and is, in fact, already inaugurated (see Matt 13:16–17 par. Luke 10:23–24) while its full realization is still pending (see Matt 6:10 par. Luke 11:2; Mark 9:1; 14:25). The Parable of the Mustard Seed (Mark 4:30–32) contrasts the small beginnings of the kingdom with its great fulfillment. The tradition of the kingdom or kingship of God has its origins in the pre-exilic

Jerusalem temple cult (cf. Isa 6:5, Isaiah's vision of his calling in the temple, "my eyes have seen the king, the Lord of hosts"), where YHWH is addressed as "enthroned on the cherubim" (2 Kings 19:15 par. Isa 37:16) and his inauguration and rule as "king" is celebrated (Ps 47; 93; 96–97; 99). It is continued in the Songs of the Sabbath Sacrifice found at Qumran (4Q400–407; 11Q17) and Masada (Mas 1k), in which God is praised as king in the midst of the host of angels. After the Romans under Pompey intervened in Judea in the contest between Hyrcanus II and Aristobulus II, the delegates of the people "asked not to be ruled by a king, saying that it was the custom of their country to obey the priests of the God who was venerated by them" (Josephus, *Ant.* 14.41; cf. Diod. Sic. 40.2). Thus, they pointed to the model of a "theocracy" (cf. Josephus, *Ag. Ap.* 2.165), in which God's rule is mediated by the priests, while the last Hasmoneans were seen as inept representatives of the priesthood. However, the Romans, in the long term, chose to give the rule to kings (Herod I, later Agrippa I) or to govern the region directly. This provided the context for political expectations of the kingship of God (e.g. among the "fourth philosophy," the Zealots). For Jesus, however, the *basileia* was not to be brought by anti-Roman action. More pertinent was the tradition that God would come to rule in the eschaton when he punishes the kings of the earth (Isa 24:21–22) and after victory over his enemies would be king over all the earth (Zech 14:1–9). Moreover, in the apocalyptic tradition the idea developed that at the end of days God would hold judgment, with punishment of his enemies and reward for the righteous (cf. Dan 7:26; 12:2–3).

Jesus learned from John the Baptist that God's judgment was near and that the present times were a final opportunity for repentance; John proclaimed in the desert "a baptism of repentance for the forgiveness of sins" (Mark 1:4). This does not negate the temple cult with its provision for atonement but considers it insufficient. In particular, John attacked the certainty of salvation that was based on belonging to the descendants of Abraham (Luke 3:7–9 par.): Jews must repent individually. By asking to be baptized by John, Jesus accepted this approach. But whereas John focused on the final opportunity for repentance before the great judgment, Jesus apparently had a defining experience. He witnessed that Satan, the ultimate enemy of God, had been disempowered: "I saw Satan fall like a flash of lightning" (Luke 10:18), and "the strong man" had been "tied up" (see Mark 3:27). With the disempowerment of Satan, the kingship of God was inaugurated and was drawing near. This is the crucial innovation in Jesus's ministry, which puts all other aspects of his activity into perspective.

Jesus experienced himself as a witness to, and an agent of, the inaugurated kingdom of God. Jesus's exorcisms are testimony that, with Satan, also the demons have lost their power and can be cast out: "if it is by the finger of God that I cast out the demons, then the kingdom of God has come to you" (Luke 11:20). In Jesus's healings, too, the advent of the kingdom of God can be experienced, and through Jesus's therapeutic activity God restores human beings to their original, creational wholeness (Matt 11:2–4 par. Luke 7:22–23). Jesus lets his disciples also participate in these healing powers (with some exceptions; see Mark 9:28–29), so that through their therapies also the kingdom of God has come near (Luke 9:1–2; 10:9). Jesus's table fellowship allows a foretaste of the eschatological banquet that is expected in the fully realized kingdom; it is precisely the neglected ones who will be granted a place at the table in the kingdom of God (Luke 13:29 par. Matt 8:11; Luke 14:16–24 par. Matt 22:1–14). The poor, the humble, the hungry, the weeping, and the persecuted are blessed because theirs is the kingdom of God (Luke 6:20–22; Matt 5:3–11). Similarly, Jesus presents children as examples of those who enter the kingdom of God (Mark 10:14–15). Jesus maintains the announcement of God's judgment; but he also offers the opportunity of forgiveness (Mark 2:5–12), and in doing so he turns toward people deemed morally dubious, such as tax collectors and prostitutes, who he says are more likely to enter the kingdom of God than the pious (Matt 21:28–32). In fact, as we shall see, the most characteristic expression Jesus uses for God is "father": In the kingdom of God, the providence of the divine father can be experienced anew (see Matt 6:26, 32), but God is also like a father who takes back the prodigal son (Luke 15:11–32).

## JESUS'S VIEWS ON ISRAEL

The focus of Jesus's ministry was clearly centered on members of the people of Israel. The area of his travel and activity is largely limited to areas of Jewish settlement (the Galilee, see Mark 1:14; Judea and Perea, see Mark 10:1; and here, Jerusalem and environs, see Mark 11:1; etc.). Excursions beyond these areas are few and exceptional: the Decapolis on the other shore of the Sea of Galilee (Mark 5:1–17), the area of Caesarea Philippi (Mark 8:27), and Tyre (Mark 7:24). By calling twelve disciples (Mark 3:14–19), Jesus appears to hint at a renewal of Israel from among the group of his followers. Apparently, Jews from various parts of the Land of Israel followed him (see Mark 3:7–8; Luke 6:17, including Idumea and the coastal region of Syro-Phoenicia).

Nevertheless, Jesus focuses not on a "national" renewal of Israel but on gaining "human beings" or "people" for the kingdom of God (Mark 1:17 par. "fishers of people"). His disciples are called to leave their social contexts and "follow" him, becoming themselves also agents of the inaugurated kingship of God. The toning down of the national aspect may have facilitated Jesus's occasional turning toward non-Jews, which, however, remains the exception and thus confirms the rule: the "Greek" Syro-Phoenician woman (Mark 7:24–29) who had to persuade Jesus to intervene on her daughter's behalf, or the centurion at Capernaum (Matt 8:5–13 par.) who deemed himself unworthy that Jesus come under his roof. It was this occasional – though not principled – openness that allowed later Christian tradition to extend the message of Christ also to non-Jews.

### JESUS'S VIEWS ON TORAH AND HALAKHAH

Jesus seems to have held a particular interpretation of the Torah and legal norms (halakhah) that was similarly shaped by his message of the inaugurated kingdom of God. Unlike what much of scholarship until the end of the twentieth century claimed, he did not attempt to "abolish" or "critique" the Torah. Rather, within the diversity of Second Temple Judaism outlined in this chapter, he criticized certain approaches to the Torah and proposed an interpretation of it that put prime focus on the spirit and the intention of the divine law, and on commandments concerning the relation with fellow human beings and with God, at the expense of ritual minutiae. For some areas of Jewish law, he appears to have propagated the recourse to the primordial institution of the law that can now be recovered in the eschaton (*Urzeit–Endzeit* correlation). Thus, according to Mark 2:27, "the Sabbath was made (*egeneto*, literally, 'has become') for humankind, not humankind for the Sabbath," which points to the primordial institution of the Sabbath for the benefit of human beings. Hence, actions alleviating human need on the Sabbath, such as plucking corn by the hungry, appear to be seen as permissible. Attending to people in need on the Sabbath, Jesus typically healed human beings with severe – albeit not life-threatening – impairments on this day (Mark 3:1–5 parr.; Luke 13:11–13; 14:1–5), apparently justifying this as an extension of "life-saving" (see Mark 3:4 "is it lawful ... to save life or to kill?"), which as such was a widely accepted reason for "overriding" the Sabbath commandment (see the section "Jesus's Religious Formation").

Similarly, in Mark 10:3–6, Jesus contrasts the concession of Moses according to Deuteronomy 24:1 to write a certificate of divorce because of "your hardness of heart" with the primordial joining of one man with one woman (see Gen 1:27; 2:24 quoted in Mark 10:6–8). Thus, in the horizon of the kingdom of God, in which it may be expected that hearts are no longer hardened (cf. Mark 8:17), divorce shall not be pursued (Mark 10:9; cf. Doering 2009). In fact, divorce does not sever the marriage bond of those uniquely joined with one another, like the primordial couple, and those remarrying after divorce commit adultery (Mark 10:11–12; cf. Luke 16:18). Matt 5:32; 19:9 make an exception for divorce in the case of "sexual indecency" (*porneia*), thus representing a view similar to that held the by the School of Shammai (see m. Giṭ. 9.10). While marriage should not be dissolved in the kingdom, it is nevertheless not of ultimate value: Those resurrected from the dead will not marry because they are "like the angels" (Mark 12:25 parr.), and some – including, apparently, Jesus himself – anticipated this in their lives (see Matt 19:12).

With respect to purity, Jesus prioritizes moral over ritual purity: Foods going into a person from outside do not defile the person but evil intentions coming out of the heart do (Mark 7:15, 19a; note again the crucial locus of the "heart"). Moreover, Jesus arguably represents the "older" approach that does not accept the – probably Pharisaic – innovation of handwashing before meals, an obligation meant to prevent the spread of impurity from the hands via liquids onto foods, which would thereby become impure in second degree and render the person consuming them impure (Furstenberg 2008). That Jesus, according to Mark 7:19b, "declared all foods clean" could be (and was later) understood as an abolition of dietary laws. However, in its immediate context, the statement might originally have affirmed the good "biblical" view that contaminated foods do not defile a person from the inside. The Gospels assume that Jesus in other respects paid attention to purification procedures, as in the case of a healed leper (Mark 1:44; Matt 8:4).

The gospel writers perceived Jesus's approach to the Torah as being aptly summarized by the double love commandment, loving "the Lord your God from your whole heart and from your whole soul and from your whole mind and from your whole strength" (thus Mark 12:30; cf. Deut 6:5) and loving "your neighbor as yourself" (Mark 12:31; cf. Lev 19:19; parallels in Matt 22:37–39; Luke 10:27). Although there is no exact earlier example of coupling these two love commandments as the sum of the Torah, we should note that Philo of Alexandria speaks of "two heads high above the innumerable individual laws and doctrines: the regulating of one's conduct towards God by the rules of piety and holiness, and of one's conduct towards men by the rules of humanity and justice" (*Spec.* 2.63; cf. T. Dan 5:3; T. Iss. 5:1–2). As mentioned, Hillel is credited with the use of the Golden Rule in rabbinic texts, and the Golden Rule is also used for phrasing the commandment of loving one's neighbor in Targum Ps.-Jon. Lev 19:19 (cf. also Matt 7:12). In sum, Jesus appears to have centered his Torah interpretation on the love of God and of one's neighbor. The latter is presented in the Gospels as extending beyond the confines of one's worshipping community – hence, including Samaritans (Luke 10:30–37) – and ethnic boundaries – hence, encompassing one's "enemies" (Matt 5:44).

In line with the central role of the double love commandment, Jesus seems to have prioritized the intention of laws and their social dimension, as compared to a formalistic, "outward" observance of laws. At least this is how Matthew presents Jesus's teaching: Not only murder but even being angry with one's brother or sister is what is prohibited by the Sixth (Fifth) Commandment in Jesus's interpretation; not only adultery but even the lustful gaze is targeted by the Seventh (Sixth) Commandment (Matt 5:21–30). It is best not to swear any oaths, which are not mandatory in the Torah, in order to avoid the grave transgression of perjury (Matt 5:33–37). Moreover, it seems that Jesus, as presented by Matthew, opposed the extension of "talionic," retributive thinking to everyday situations and suggested reactions that unsettle the potent opponent: extending the other cheek, stripping full naked by surrendering the coat also when someone demands your undergarment, or overfulfilling the compulsory labor by the "extra mile" (Matt 5:38–42). Again, this is not a "critique" of the Torah but rather its specific interpretation in light of the inaugurated kingdom of God. The strong eschatological urgency of the kingdom also explains the provocative nature of some of Jesus's statements, although these need not be taken as infringing the Torah. Thus, Jesus's radical reply to the one mourning his father, "follow me, and let the dead bury their own dead" (Matt 8:22), does not suggest that the father's corpse should be left unburied but rather that others – provocatively called (spiritually) "dead" – should take care of the burial, a procedure for which there is precedent in the Torah with respect to the high priest and the Nazirite (Lev 21:11–12; Num 6:6), with no evidence that this precedent was abandoned during the Second Temple period.

To be sure, Jesus teaches "as one having authority, and not as their scribes" (Matt 7:29). However, a similar teaching authority is attested in the Dead Sea Scrolls for the one "who teaches righteousness in the last days" (CD-A 6.11) and perhaps already for the Teacher of

Righteousness, on which this expected figure was modeled. Some of the Dead Sea Scrolls clearly expected "the Prophet" as an eschatological figure alongside the royal and the priestly Messiah (4Q175; 1QS 9.11), and it is possible that Jesus was seen, and was to be seen, as "the Prophet like Moses" (Deut 18:15), who would decide Torah in the eschaton.

## JESUS'S ATTITUDE AND EXPECTATION TOWARD THE TEMPLE

Jesus acknowledged the Jerusalem temple in principle (see earlier in the chapter on the advice to the healed leper) but he criticized the way it was run at his time. In this, he was not alone. The Qumran community considered the Jerusalem temple as run by the high priest defiled (see 1QpHab 12.7–9) and viewed itself as an interim "temple of man/men/Adam" (*miqdash adam*; 4Q174 1+2+21 i 6–7), "a foundation of the holy spirit for eternal truth, to atone for the guilt of transgression and the treachery of sin" (1QS 9.3–6; cf. 5.4–7; 8.4–11; 11.7–9). Yet Josephus reports about the Essenes that, while they do not sacrifice, they send gifts to the temple (*Ant.* 18.19). The Jesus tradition features both a temple action and words about the temple. In his temple action (Mark 11:15–17 parr.; John 2:13–16), Jesus symbolically and verbally criticizes the trading with money and sacrificial animals in the temple. This does not necessarily constitute a challenge to the sacrificial system: Money changers and animal traders could well set up their stalls outside the temple. The remark (only in Mark 11:16) that "he would not allow anyone to carry any vessel/implement (*skeuos*) through the temple" might mean that Jesus criticized the profanation of the sacred precinct by carrying ordinary vessels or implements through it (for the prohibition of a short-cut through the temple area see also m. Ber. 9:5; Josephus, *Ag. Ap.* 2.106, 108–9). This seems a rather credible statement in view of Mark's general disinterest in ritual issues: It is unlikely that the disallowance should be limited to *holy* vessels, effectively bringing the sacrificial cult to a halt, which would be too circumstantial a way of expressing such a far-reaching intervention. If this is correct, Jesus's critique can be seen to be in line with the expectation of Zechariah 14:21 ("and there shall no longer be a trader [this is one meaning of *kena'ani*] in the house of the Lord of hosts on that day"), alluded to in John 2:16 ("stop making my father's house a marketplace"). However, this does not mean that Jesus was simply content with a reform of the temple. This is suggested by the sayings about the temple that may have originated in Jesus's preaching: the prediction of the temple destruction (Mark 13:2) and the testimony, albeit explicitly labeled "false" in Mark (perhaps because of the agency ascribed to Jesus himself), "We heard him say, 'I will destroy this temple that is made with hands, and in three days I will build another, not made with hands'" (Mark 14:58; cf. John 2:19). It is likely that underlying these statements is Jesus's expectation that the Herodian temple will soon be replaced by an eschatological temple. Such an expectation is found in a number of Jewish sources: The Qumran *yaḥad* expected its own interim "temple of man/men/Adam" to be followed by an eschatological "temple of YHWH" (4Q174 1+2+21 i 2–7). Earlier in the second century BCE, the book of Jubilees looked forward "until the time of the new creation when the heavens, the earth, and all their creatures will be renewed ..., until the time when the temple of the Lord will be created in Jerusalem on Mt Zion" (Jub. 1:29). Similarly, the Temple Scroll, in divine speech, expected an eschatological temple in the new creation (11QT$^a$ 29.8–10). The Animal Apocalypse, similarly from the second century BCE, anticipated a new, eschatological Jerusalem (1 En. 90.28–29; although it does not specifically mention a temple building). Therefore, Jesus joins other Jews in the expectation of an eschatological temple, although it is unclear how and for when he reckoned with its coming. It is debated whether Jesus indeed used his farewell meal with his disciples (Mark 14:17–25 parr.) in order to institute a new cult in the Lord's Supper, or whether the motifs of "covenant blood" (Mark 14:24 par.; cf. Matt 26:28 "for the forgiveness of sins") or "new covenant in my blood" (Luke 22:20) were not rather the outcome of early Christian reflection on the death of Jesus interpreted as sacrificial death.

### JESUS'S VIEW OF GOD

When Jesus speaks of God, he refers to the God of Israel. He does not proclaim a radically "new" perception of God, although the central notion of the inaugurated *basileia*, with Jesus's experience that his ministry serves a specific role in the latter, has also repercussions for the emphases in Jesus's proclamation of the God of Israel. God is certainly the one God professed in the *Shemaʿ Israel* (Mark 12:29; cf. Deut 6:4). He is the creator of heaven(s) and earth, and of the human beings in creation (see Mark 10:6; cf. Gen 1–2). Moreover, he is also the God who steadily provides for his creation: He "makes his sun rise on the evil and the good" (Matt 5:45), and he continues to care for flowers and sparrows, so that "worry" about the needs of daily life is unnecessary (Matt 6:25–31). Instead, those striving first for the kingdom of God will receive all things they need in their lives (Matt 6:33). In addition, Jesus presents God as the judge who will pronounce judgment on the wicked according to their deeds (see Luke 10:13–15 par.; also Mark 12:28–40). However, compared with John the Baptist, the focus is now on the "good news" of the approaching kingdom of God that is palpable in Jesus's ministry. Jesus thus emphasizes the relationship between the individual and God, as well as the more "universalist" aspects deriving from divine providence, and does not highlight the "national" aspect of God's covenantal relationship with Israel. Nevertheless, as the law interpreted by Jesus is Israel's Torah, he clearly presupposes the covenant also.

Especially notable in Jesus's proclamation of God is his address of God as "father" (which has left a strong footprint in the Jesus tradition, with more than 150 occurrences, always in the mouth of Jesus). It is a way in which Jesus himself addresses God (see Mark 14:36 "*abba*, father"; Luke 10:22 par. "my father") but which he also uses with regard to the disciples (see Matt 6:26, 32 "your heavenly father") and teaches them to use in their prayer (see Luke 11:2 "father" par. Matt 6:9 "our father"). Research in the last decades has shown that *abba* is not a particularly "intimate" or childlike way of addressing the father, and that "my father," despite earlier claims to the contrary, is indeed attested as an address of God in Second Temple Judaism, namely in two – apparently nonsectarian – texts from Qumran, 4Q372 1 16 ("my father and my God") and 4Q460 9 i 6 ("my father and my Lord"), thereby continuing statements like "you are my father," used of God for example at Ps 89:27 (cf. Sir 51:10 Hebrew Ms B, also Syriac). While therefore clearly a potential address of God in Second Temple Judaism (cf. "our father" in rabbinic traditions), the high frequency of the "father" address in the Jesus tradition is conspicuous and suggests a special focus in Jesus's proclamation of God. Subsequently, it facilitated seeing an exclusive proximity between Jesus the Son and God the Father.

## JESUS'S VIEWS OF HIMSELF

Jesus viewed himself as a messenger in words and deed in the service of the inaugurated kingdom of God. As shown in this chapter, he was aware that he participated in God's victory over the (disempowered) forces of evil, that his table fellowship constituted a foretaste of the eschatological banquet, and that his message was part of the restoration of humankind. It is, however, debated what precise role he viewed for himself. In the section "The Kingdom of God Inaugurated," it was suggested that he might have seen himself as an end-time prophet, perhaps along the model of the Prophet like Moses (Deut 18:15). Did he also think about himself in categories of other eschatological figures that were considered in Second Temple Judaism? It is unclear whether the kingdom or kingship of *God* necessarily required a *human* messiah king, and Jesus's actions certainly overlap only in a limited way with what could be expected from a coming king of Davidic lineage (cf. Pss. Sol. 17). The most indicative similarities would be, first, the exorcistic and therapeutic activities ascribed to Solomon (cf. Wis 7:20; *Ant.* 8.45–49; 11Q11 ii 2; T. Sol.) and to some extent to David (cf. 11QPs[a] xxvii 9–10; 11Q11 v 4 – vi 3), and second – if historical – Jesus's entry into Jerusalem on a donkey (Mark 11:1–7; cf. Zech 9:9; Gen 49:11). It is therefore unclear to what extent Jesus himself raised (Davidic) messianic claims, although he apparently evoked such a view of himself in others (see Mark 11:9–10 parr.; the *titulus crucis*, Mark 15:26 parr.; John 19:19). In addition, Jesus's references to the Son of Man, while often sounding as if he referred to another figure, might have been understood to relate to himself (see Mark 14:61–62, although this might show later Christian reflection). His saying about the disciples sitting, alongside the Son of Man, on "twelve thrones" judging the tribes of Israel (Matt 19:28; cf. Luke 22:30) suggests a role for himself in these events, too. Moreover, it is likely that, on his way to Jerusalem, if not earlier, Jesus came to the conclusion that his own death served a certain function in the eschatological events. That he held a farewell meal with his disciples (Mark 14:17–25 parr.; John 13:1–30), during which, according to the Synoptic Gospels and Paul (1 Cor 11:23–25), he reflected on surrendering his life for the community commemorating him, would support this, whereas the account about his prayer in Gethsemane (Mark 14:32–42 parr.) portrays him as coming to accept this role somewhat reluctantly. While violent death in Jerusalem is certainly a fate a Jewish prophet might anticipate (see Luke 13:33–34), and Jesus apparently came to anticipate it, this is, however, not what most of his preaching and actions in Galilee and environs focused on.

### FURTHER READING

Doering, Lutz. 2009. "Marriage and Creation in Mark 10 and CD 4-5." In *Echoes from the Caves: Qumran and the New Testament*, edited by F. García Martínez, 133–63. STDJ 85. Leiden: Brill.

Doering, Lutz and Andrew R. Krause, eds. 2020. *Synagogues in the Hellenistic and Roman Periods: Archaeological Finds, New Methods, New Theories*. Ioudaioi 11. Göttingen: Vandenhoeck & Ruprecht.

Furstenberg, Yair. 2008. "Defilement Penetrating the Body: A New Understanding of Contamination in Mark 7.15." *New Testament Studies* 54: 176–200.
Schröter, Jens and Christine Jacobi, eds. 2022. *The Jesus Handbook*. Grand Rapids: Eerdmans.
Theißen, Gerd and Annette Merz. 2023. *Wer war Jesus? Der erinnerte Jesus in historischer Sicht: Ein Lehrbuch*. Göttingen: Vandenhoeck & Ruprecht. (Revised German version of Theissen, Gerd and Annette Merz. 1998. *The Historical Jesus: A Comprehensive Guide*. Translated by J. Bowden. London: SCM Press.)

# 3 Jesus in the Fourfold Gospel

J. TYLER BROWN AND NATHAN EUBANK

However unremarkable it may seem to readers familiar with the Christian Bible, the fact that the New Testament (NT) begins with four consecutive, different narratives of the life of Jesus presents a challenge to interpreters who wish to perceive the one Jesus within the canonical Four. While not utterly without scriptural precedent,[1] such a repetition of narrative is nevertheless a canonical novelty. To symbolize this fourfold gospel's unified witness to Jesus, the ancient church famously looked to the four angelic creatures of Ezekiel 1:10 and Revelation 4:7. For Irenaeus, who first proposed this symbolic connection, the number of the Gospels could not in fact be any other: Just as surely as there are four zones of the earth and four winds, so the church which is present throughout the world should itself stand upon these four evangelical pillars (*Against Heresies* 3.11.8). This appeal to theological fittingness or proportionality does not, of course, describe in historical terms how these four portraits came to be regarded, amidst the proliferation of Jesus books particularly in the second century, as *the* canonical depictions of Jesus of Nazareth. It does, however, gesture powerfully toward the consequences of their canonization: No single portrait among the Four definitively captures the life of Jesus without reference to the others, but this irreducible plurality exists within a unity bounded by the eventual recognition of the fourfold gospel as a textual object in its own right (see Watson 2013, 13). In this lies the invitation and challenge of the fourfold gospel.

## THE LIFE OF JESUS IN EARLY CHRISTIANITY BEFORE MARK

The earliest canonical portrait, Mark's Gospel, was perhaps not written until the late 60s or early 70s CE, given its preoccupation with

---

[1] Cf. 1–2 Sam and 1–2 Kings with 1–2 Chron; Ex–Num with Deut; the "rewritten Bible" in, e.g., Jubilees; Barton 2001, 177.

the destruction of the Temple (Mark 13). Well before Mark, however, Paul's epistles show early Christian interest in the life of Jesus, for example in his messiahship and descent from David (Rom 1:3); his family (Gal 1:19; 1 Cor 9:5); his character (Phil 2:6–11; 2 Cor 8.9; Rom 15.3); his teaching (1 Cor 7:10–11; Rom 14.14); the tradition of his final meal on the night he was betrayed (1 Cor 11:23–26); and the story of his crucifixion and resurrection (1 Cor 15:3–11). Luke's preface also indicates a widespread interest in Jesus's life preceding the composition of his gospel ("many have undertaken to arrange a narrative (*diēgēsis*)"; 1:1–4). This is sometimes taken to suggest the existence of gospel-like texts that preceded Mark, although this is by no means certain.

## THE JESUS OF MARK

Mark's Gospel is traditionally an interpretation of Peter's preaching about Jesus (Eusebius *His. eccl.* 3.39.15), a claim arguably reaching back to the last decades of the first century and one which is sometimes dismissed too quickly (see, e.g., Bauckham 2017, 202–39). If reliable, it would ground Mark's Gospel within apostolic memory of Jesus. Not only, however, is Mark potentially connected with Petrine memory of Jesus, perhaps in Rome (see 1 Pet 5:13); it may also reflect the influence of Pauline thought (e.g., in its presentation of the paradox of Jesus's crucifixion as Israel's king, or in its approach to matters of Torah in, e.g., 7:19; see, e.g., Marcus 2000). This would be natural if Mark were indeed composed in Rome, given the importance of both apostles' memory in that city, although it is perhaps not entirely incompatible with an Alexandrian or other provenance (see Eusebius *Hist. eccl.* 2.16.1–2). This potential combined influence of two foundational apostles renders particularly significant the fact that Mark is the generative literary form followed by the other canonical gospels, including, as may be an emerging consensus, the Fourth Gospel (see, e.g., Becker et al. 2021). In this way, despite Mark's striking unpopularity in comparison with Matthew and John from the second century until the period of modern biblical scholarship (evident in Mark's relatively slim manuscript transmission, fewer citations, and reduced attention in biblical commentaries), Mark nevertheless makes a definitive impact on all subsequent interpretation of the life of Jesus.

Mark's opening words, "The beginning of the gospel (*euangelion*) of Jesus Christ" (1:1), arguably introduce the whole work, although probably with reference to its content rather than to a literary genre as such.[2] Readers would have known the term "gospel" from early Christian proclamation *about* Jesus (sixty of seventy-six NT uses are in Paul, but it also appears importantly in, e.g., Peter's preaching in Acts 15:4). The term's ultimate source is the Isaianic "proclamation" (*euangelizomai*) of glad tidings to Israel (e.g. Isa 61:1; 52:7) mediated through Jesus's own proclamation of the inbreaking reign of Israel's God (Mark 1:14–15). That inbreaking reign stands as a central reason for and is arguably the ultimate theological horizon of Mark's writing of the good news about Jesus.

Strikingly, Mark gives no account of Jesus's birth but instead briefly narrates his baptism by John (1:9–11) and temptation in the wilderness (1:12–13) before having him burst onto the scene in Galilee conducting, like his namesake Joshua, holy war on death's forces (see, e.g., Thiessen 2020). Jesus proves to be a healer and an exorcist (1:21–34, 40–45). He teaches "with authority and not as the scribes" (1:21, 27) but engages as one obedient to Torah in the back and forth of halakhic debates with Pharisees over fasting, the Sabbath, and purity law (2:18–3:6; 7:1–23). He is also a prophet who can read the thoughts of those around him (2:8). By calling precisely twelve disciples, the rabbi Jesus (9:5; 11:21; 14:45) evokes the promised restoration of Israel's twelve tribes, placing himself at the heart of that renewal (3:13–19). He claims the authority to forgive sins as the "Son of Man" (*ho huios tou anthropou*), a crucial but ambiguous appellation deriving in part from the vision of Daniel 7:13–14 in which a human figure is given dominion over the earth, but one which also can simply mean "human being" (2:10; see, e.g., Bauckham 2023).

Still, Mark's Jesus is a mystery. He teaches in parables designed to conceal (4:12) and commands silence from those whom he heals (e.g. 1:25, 44; 5:43; 7:36; 8:26; but cf. 5:19). This distinctive Markan theme is typically referred to as the "messianic secret" (*das Messiasgeheimnis*), a phrase coined by Wrede in 1901 (English trans. Wrede 1971) to describe his (later discarded) theory that Mark invented this motif to hide the fact that Jesus never referred to himself as the Messiah. However, Jesus's secretiveness in fact plays an integral role within Mark's narrative in that his identity can only become truly clear to human beings after his crucifixion and resurrection from the dead (Goodacre 2021, 86–88; see Mark 14:62; 15:39; 16:7; but cf. 1:24).

This fact is the key to the Gospel's central section, which is bookended by healings of men whose blindness evokes the disciples' lack

---

[2] See also Mark 13:10; 14:9; Matt 24:14; 26:13; but cf. *biblos* ("book") in Matt 1:1 and *diēgēsis* ("narrative") in Luke 1:1.

of spiritual vision (8:22–26; 10:46–52). Although Peter finally confesses the truth about Jesus: "You are the Messiah" (8:29), even he cannot accept its consequences – that Jesus must be rejected by the Jerusalem religious officials, suffer, be killed, and "after three days rise again" (8:31). Even after Jesus's transfiguration, James and John fail to perceive the nature of Jesus's kingship – their request to sit on Jesus's right and left when he enters his kingdom (10:35–45) ironically anticipates their absence when Jesus is crucified with criminals on his right and left, his cross having been carried by a different Simon (15:21, 26–27).

The final days leading up to his death enclose the paradox of the Markan Jesus's identity more clearly than any others. In his celebration of the Passover, Jesus is simply a Galilean Jewish pilgrim, but this pilgrim makes a royal entrance into Jerusalem (11:1–11); prophetically interrupts Temple commerce (11:15–19); arguably suggests his status both as David's Son and his Lord (12:35–37); and places his own body and blood at the center of the Passover meal with his disciples (14:22–25). Finally, standing on trial before the Sanhedrin, he answers publicly the question hanging over the entirety of Mark's Gospel: "Are you the Messiah, the Son of the Blessed One?" "I am," he says, "and 'you will see the Son of Man seated at the right hand of the Power' and 'coming with the clouds of heaven'" (14:62–63; Ps 110:1; Dan 7:13–14). This messianic self-identification definitively breaks the silence of Mark's Jesus. His trial and crucifixion are then shot through with mock-royal imagery deployed by Mark in the proclamation of his paradoxical kingship (e.g. 15:17–20). Mark has Jesus ironically referred to six times as "king," an enthronement-by-crucifixion (15:2, 9, 12, 18, 26, 32). Ironic but by no means sarcastic, the centurion's confession, "Truly this man was the Son of God" (15:39), reflects the epistemological effect of Jesus's kingdom-bringing death.[3]

Furthermore, despite the abrupt closure of Mark's Gospel, in which the female first witnesses of the empty tomb tell no one what they had seen, "because they were afraid" (16:8, ending on an awkward "for" [*gar*]), the end is not pure irony or impenetrable paradox. Mark's early Christian readership knew that Mary Magdalene, Mary, and Salome did not remain silent. Moreover, the "young man in a white robe" at the tomb also comes off as a reliable witness, and he points to Jesus's own by-definition trustworthy predictions of his resurrection and promise to meet Peter and the other disciples in Galilee ("just as he told you"; 16:5–7). Nevertheless, the deficiency of the Markan ending (remedied

---

[3] *Pace*, e.g., Juel 1994, 74.

by the second-century scribal authors of the Longer Ending, featuring a greatest hits collection of resurrection appearances: to Mary Magdalene, to two walking in the country, and to the Eleven, as well as recounting Jesus's ascension and the apostles' successful evangelism; 16:9–20) must surely have been part of the impetus animating the pen of Mark's greatest admirer: the evangelist Matthew.

### THE JESUS OF MATTHEW

Between the Synoptic Gospels, the amount of common material is usually thought to be too extensive – including passages where there is lengthy, verbatim agreement in Greek – to be explained merely by shared oral traditions. It is also easier to explain Matthew and Luke as developments of Mark rather than the other way around. Some 90 percent of Mark is taken up into Matthew, which might conceivably indicate that the Matthean evangelist intended to replace Mark entirely (as in any case almost occurred, as noted briefly in the previous section). Alternatively, Matthew may represent a revision and localization of Mark's Roman-oriented gospel for Matthew's Syrian Jewish-Christian audience, written perhaps not long after Mark.

Unlike Mark, Matthew recounts the genealogical descent of Jesus from David and Abraham (through Joseph) (1:1–17), grounding him emphatically within Jewish messianic expectations. Matthew narrates the birth of Jesus (who is so named because he will "save his people from their sins"; 1:21) in Bethlehem from the virgin Mary and places upon him the further name "Emmanuel," or "God with us" (1:23; cf. Isa 7:14). This theme of Jesus as the embodiment of God's presence forms an *inclusio* together with the assurance of Jesus's abiding presence with his disciples "to the end of the age" in the Gospel's last verse (28:20; cf. 18:20; Bockmuehl 2022, 3–7). That royal presence comes immediately to the attention of King Herod, whose massacre of infant boys around Bethlehem in the attempt to destroy the child Jesus aligns him with the Pharaoh of the exodus (2:16–18; Exod 1:22). This scenario sets up the characterization of Jesus in terms of a Moses/exodus typology that trades in contrasts as well as comparison. For example, *Joseph* is warned in a *dream* to take the child to Egypt, where he is raised until the death of the king seeking his life, fulfilling Hosea 11:1: "out of Egypt I have called my Son" (2:13–15, 19–23; cf. Exod 2–4; see further, Allison 1993, 140–69).

The Sermon on the Mount (Matt 5–7) may expand on this typology: Moses received the Law for Israel atop Sinai – Jesus issues the eschatological interpretation of the Law from a mountain. "Do not think that I have come to abolish the Law or the Prophets; I have come not to abolish but to fulfill" (5:17). To "fulfill" (*pleroō*) in Matthew, despite regular protests to the contrary, does not mean to "replace" but instead to bring to a fullness, including in the so-called antitheses (5:21-48; see also e.g.,1:22-23; 2:14-15). There can be no abrogation of Torah, down to the letter, for Matthew's Jesus (5:18-19).

This is evident particularly in the dispute between Jesus and some Pharisees and scribes about handwashing, in which Matthew redacts Mark to limit the discussion only to the halakhic question of whether unwashed hands transmit uncleanness to food (Matt 15:1-20; cf. Mark 7:19). Furthermore, Matthew's Jesus affirms the present and, in principle, abiding validity of the Temple sacrifices (5:23) and the priesthood (12:5), and he engages in fierce halakhic debate with Pharisees and scribes over what counts as the "weightier matters of the Law" (e.g. 23:23) without any suggestion of its obsolescence. Moreover, Jesus's prophetic interruption of Temple commerce is not a rejection of that house of prayer itself, any more than the judgment of corrupt tenants is a rejection of the beloved vineyard, Israel (21:12-17, 33-44; see also Isa 5:1-7; Jer 7:1-15). For this reason, the Jesus of Matthew may perhaps be better described as the Prophet-like-Moses (see the echo of Deut 18:15, "Hear him!" (*akouete autou*) in Matt 17:5, with Moses and Elijah present) rather than simply as the "New Moses," lest the latter be misunderstood to suggest a replacement theology repugnant to central Matthean concerns.

Through this Moses typology, Matthew presents Jesus the Jewish teacher. This is also a Markan theme, but Matthew reports a far greater and more structured amount of Jesus's teaching. Moreover, Jesus's parables in Matthew are not explicitly designed to conceal but instead to train scribes for the kingdom of heaven (13:51-52). Teaching is itself central to the apostolic mission to the nations (28:20), which presumably includes teaching the Messiah's commandments to gentile converts who are themselves understood to have become part of Israel or perhaps indeed to become Jewish (note the limitation of the apostolic mission to "the towns of Israel until the Son of Man comes"; 10:23).

Matthew's Jesus is also equally characterized as the messianic Son of David who heals, significantly expanding the Markan presentation of this motif (e.g. Matt 9:27; 12:23; 20:30-31 \\ Mark 10:47-48; cf. Matt 1:1-17). This shepherding role is also more clearly passed on to the *ekklēsia* ("assembly"), a crucial term for Matthew rooted in Israel's assembling at Sinai (e.g. Deut 9:10; from Heb *qahal*) and one with overtones of

Israel's eschatological restoration (cf., e.g., 1QSa 2.4). Peter is given "the keys of the kingdom of heaven" to "bind" and "loose," most likely indicating his supreme teaching authority within this assembly (Matt 16:16–19; Davies and Allison 2004, 629, 638–40). However, that authority clearly resides also in the *ekklēsia* itself and not merely with the chief apostle (18:15–20).

Despite containing elements with a history of pernicious anti-Jewish interpretation (e.g. 27:24–25; but see Sider-Hamilton 2017, 181–228), the death of Jesus in Matthew is presented as a renewal of the one covenant of Israel with God (see "my blood of *the* covenant"; 26:28; Exod 24:8). Furthermore, although the Matthean Jesus's fierce internecine polemic with the Pharisees (itself likely a function of Matthew's more explicitly Jewish social location) is reflected in this gospel's passion narrative (21:25; 27:62–66), Jesus's arrest comes in fact at the order of the ruling class of Sadducees and chief priests (26:47). The strikingly apocalyptic, even cosmic note Matthew adds after Jesus's death regarding the earthquake and the resurrection of Jerusalem's buried saints further emphasizes the significance of Jesus's death as Israel's king and *for* Israel as a covenant renewal (27:51–53).

In light of these events, and by contrast with Mark, the confession of Matthew's centurion and those with him is indisputably a genuine acclamation of praise (27:54). Matthew's risen Jesus also does not fail to satisfy with resurrection appearances both to the two Marys at the empty tomb (28:9–10) and again on a mountain to the Eleven in Galilee. The Matthean Jesus who there commissions his disciples to teach and to baptize includes his own name in the Triune baptismal formula, claims to have been given "all authority in heaven and on earth" (cf. Dan 7:13–14), and promises his enduring presence even in his physical absence (28:16–20; cf. 1:23). In this, Matthew's Christology is, if not explicitly higher than Mark's, at least more explicitly articulated.

### THE JESUS OF LUKE

Luke's changes to Mark are conspicuously similar to Matthew's, a fact that lies at the heart of the Synoptic problem. The two-source hypothesis holds that, in addition to Mark, Matthew and Luke used a common source containing sayings of Jesus, Q (from German *Quelle*, meaning "source"), that explains their extensive overlap (see, e.g., Robinson et al. 2000). Others believe that Luke used both Mark and Matthew (see, e.g., Goodacre 2002). Luke also presents a further consideration for analysis of the fourfold gospel in his composition of a sequel, the Acts of the Apostles, which many regard as the second volume of a single work, "Luke-Acts." The ancient church, however, tended to receive Luke (written ca. 70–100 CE) as part of the fourfold gospel and Acts (written perhaps shortly after Luke) as a distinct work. In any case, we are concerned here with Jesus in the fourfold gospel, so Luke will be the primary focus.

Luke's Gospel opens in the Jerusalem Temple with the priestly service of Zechariah, father of John the Baptizer, as it will close with the apostles' worship in that same Jerusalem Temple (24:52–53). The births of John and Jesus are narrated with a rich allusiveness to Israel's Scriptures, not least in the appearance of Gabriel in the annunciation to Mary (1:26–38; cf. Dan 8–9) and in Mary's Magnificat (1:46–55; cf. Hannah's song in 1 Sam 2:1–10). The focus is on God's redemption of Israel signaled by the birth of Jesus, born to the "house of his child David" (1:70) and circumcised on the eighth day (2:21). At his dedication to the Lord, the righteous elder Simeon memorably encapsulates the significance of Jesus's birth: "For my eyes have seen your salvation, which you have prepared in the presence of all peoples, a light for revelation to the gentiles and for glory to your people Israel" (2:30–32). This dialectic, the salvation of gentiles for the glory of Israel, plays a crucial role in the Acts of the Apostles, but already in Luke's Gospel it is a prominent motif (e.g. 4:25–27; 7:1–10; 11:29–32).

Programmatically, Luke's Jesus announces in the synagogue that he is anointed with the Spirit of the Lord "to bring good news to the poor ... to proclaim release to the captives and recovery of sight to the blind, to set free those who are oppressed, to proclaim the year of the Lord's favor" (4:18–19; reading from the Isaiah scroll at 61:1–2). Themes here of liberation and jubilee (see Lev 25:10) provide a scriptural interpretative frame for Jesus's prophetic championing of the poor, a motif already evident in the Magnificat but also famously in the difference between the Matthean versus Lukan first beatitude. In Matthew, Jesus says, "Blessed are the poor in spirit" (5:3), but in Luke he says simply, "Blessed are the poor" (6:20). In Matthew, Jesus will preside over a final judgment with a generous but fair evaluation of one's deeds, specifically in relation to "the least of these brothers and sisters of mine," probably the poor and needy within the *ekklēsia* (25:40). Slightly in contrast, Luke's Jesus articulates a sweeping eschatological reversal of fortunes in which "all who exalt themselves will be humbled, and those who humble themselves will be exalted" (14:11; 18:14; see also, e.g., 16:19–31; 18:15–17).

The generous response of Zacchaeus (19:1–10), implicitly contrasted with that of the rich ruler (18:18–30), is a paradigmatic example of a righteous response to this imminent eschatological justice. This contrast may also be reflected in the ruler's confused addressing of Jesus as "Good Teacher," simultaneously playing fast and loose with the divine Goodness and inadequately addressing the Lord of Luke (18:18–19), compared with Zacchaeus's fitting address of Jesus as "Lord" (*kyrie*; 19:8).[4] Luke in fact consistently identifies Jesus as "the Lord" (*ho kyrios*), as in the angelic announcement to the shepherds that "to you is born this day in the city of David a Savior, who is Christ the Lord" (2:10). The mother of Jesus plays a particularly exalted theological role for Luke in this regard: Mary is the mother of Elizabeth's "Lord" (1:43), but Mary's "Lord" is clearly the God of Israel (1:47; see Rowe 2006, 34–55). Further to this point, women in Luke are not only among the lowly whom the Lord raises up (1:52) or to whom he extends welcome and forgiveness (7:36–50) – they are also among those who care for Jesus in his own poverty (8:2–3; 23:55–24:1) and who first announce his resurrection (24:10).

The teaching material in Luke is more widely dispersed than in Matthew and, thus, perhaps receives less obvious emphasis. However, parables such as the Good Samaritan (10:25–37) and the Prodigal Son (15:11–32) are in fact uniquely Lukan material contained within his distinctive travel narrative (9:51–19:44), which places Jesus's teaching and actions in the context of his journey to Jerusalem. The intense focus on Jerusalem in this section (9:51; 13:31–35; 19:41–44), along with the Gospel's opening and closing in the holy city (noted earlier in this section), stresses its importance to Jesus. Jerusalem will, significantly, continue as the base of operations in Acts even as the gospel travels to the ends of the earth (e.g. Acts 1–7, 15, 21).

Luke's Jesus is thus a prophet and a teacher, but Jesus's words also define his profile in another Lukan context: Whereas in Mark and Matthew Jesus expresses only a scriptural cry of Godforsakenness from the cross (Mark 15:34 \\ Matt 27:47; Ps 22:1), in Luke Jesus remains in control throughout. He pities the mourning women of Jerusalem over himself (23:28–31); forgives his crucifiers (23:34);[5] promises a place in Paradise with himself to one of his repentant co-crucified (23:43); and entrusts his spirit serenely to God (23:46; cf. Ps 31:5). Finally, the risen

---

[4] Note the narrator's naming of Jesus as "the Lord" (*ho kyrios*) immediately prior; 19:7; see Rowe 2006, 147.

[5] This verse is textually uncertain, but if original may be a significant witness against the claim that Jesus's death in Luke is not atoning. Cf. "forgiveness" here with 24:47. See further Wilson 2016, 114–18.

Jesus of Luke features in the most artistically sensitive of the synoptic resurrection appearances, walking with Cleopas and another disciple toward Emmaus as a familiar stranger whose self-referential scriptural interpretation rekindles the embers of hope (24:25–27, 32) and whose breaking of the (eucharistic) bread opens the disciples' eyes to his true identity (24:30–31). This emphasis on scriptural fulfillment is repeated in Jesus's final instructions to the Eleven (24:44–49). In an important chain link with Acts, Luke's Jesus then ascends to heaven before their eyes (24:50–53).

## THE JESUS OF JOHN

Written most likely after the Synoptics in the late first century (although its priority has occasionally been suggested), John's Gospel launches instantly into the stratosphere, reaching into the eternity of the divine Word that was "in the beginning" (*en archē*), and was "with God" (*pros ton theon*), and "was God" (*theos ēn*) (1:1).[6] This lofty beginning, which like Mark entirely omits any narrative of Jesus's birth, forms a pair of bookends with Thomas's exclamation of praise: "My Lord and my God!" (*ho kyrios mou kai ho theos mou*; 20:28). Thus the stated purpose of the Fourth Gospel, "that you may believe that Jesus is the Messiah, the Son of God, and that through believing you may have life in his name" (20:21), is heard in an elevated context, one in which "Son of God" resonates in both a messianic and a uniquely filial register, as expressed in the Prologue (1:14; 18) and throughout the body of the Gospel (e.g. 5:17–28; 10:38; 14:8–14; 17:1–5, 11). In John, the Sonship of Jesus is defining of the Fatherhood of God, and vice versa, even if the Son remains subordinate to the Father within their union (e.g. 10:25–30).

"[T]he Word became flesh and dwelt (*skēnoō*; cf. Sir 24:8) among us, and we have seen his glory (*doxa*), the glory as of a father's only son" (1:14). In addition to the importance of this verse for all subsequent Christian theology, it might well summarize the whole of the Fourth Gospel. John emphasizes this revelation of the glory of God in the flesh by audaciously moving forward Jesus's Temple action from its synoptic location during the week of Jesus's passion to 2:13–22, very early in the Gospel. (This is the first of several Jewish festivals during which John has Jesus in Jerusalem; e.g., Tabernacles in 7:1–52; Hanukkah in 10:22–39. John's narration of Jesus's participation in these festivals arguably

---

[6] Cf., e.g., Wis 18:15–16; Sir 24:8; 1 Enoch 41:1–2; see, e.g., Loader 2018.

displays the most extensive religious and geographical knowledge of Jerusalem among the Gospels.) Jesus's prediction of his raising up the destroyed Temple, presented ambiguously in Mark and Matthew as false testimony against Jesus (Mark 14:58 \\ Matt 26:60–61), is here unambiguously spoken with reference to his own body as temple (2:19–21).

Those in the Temple had demanded a sign of Jesus's authority, and unlike in the Synoptics the Jesus of John obligingly performs no less than seven "signs" (*sēmeia*) that reveal his "glory" (2:11). Each sign functions as an iconographic presentation of Jesus, and the seventh, the raising of Lazarus, is the precipitating incident of Jesus's arrest and crucifixion (11:45–53). Along the way, John's elevation of the synoptic presentation of Jesus is particularly evident in the celebrated drumbeat of "I am" (*egō eimi*) sayings, expressed both in the absolute (e.g., 4:26; 6:20; 8:24; 18:5, 6, 8) and in the predicate nominative (e.g., "I am the bread of life"; 6:35; "I am the light of the world"; 8:12). However, almost everything in the "I am" sayings is anticipated in the Synoptics (e.g., Mark 6:50; 14:62; Anderson 2011, 168–69). Nevertheless, the comparative forthrightness of John's Jesus corresponds to the already-present eschatology of this gospel: "The hour is coming and now is" for true, spiritual worship (4:23) and even the resurrection of the dead (5:25).

However, this foregrounding of Jesus's divine as well as messianic (e.g. 6:15) identity should not be allowed to obscure the deep structural similarity between John and Mark (which John probably knew), not only in their shared baptism-to-cross/resurrection narrative but also in the Johannine equivalent of Mark's "messianic secret": as in the Jesus of John's propensity for hiding (7:10–11); the unbelief of the crowds despite the signs (12:36–37); and the disciples' failure to understand Jesus's (divine) identity until after his resurrection (2:22) or "glorification" (12:16; Goodacre 2021, 86–88). That glorification occurs, in John's profound extension of Mark, in the "lifting up" (*hypsoō*) of the Son of Man on the cross (3:14; 12:32) during his "hour" (12:27). John achieves an astonishing scriptural articulation of this paradox by fusing Isaiah's Temple vision, in which the Lord God is "on high" (*hypsēlos*) and fills the Temple with his "glory" (*doxa*) (6:1 LXX), with the fourth Servant Song, in which the suffering Servant is "lifted up" (*hypsoō*) and "glorified" (*doxazō*) (Isa 52:13 LXX). "Isaiah said this because he saw his glory and spoke about him" (John 12:38–41; Frey 2018, 245–47).

On the one hand, Jesus is "the Lamb of God who takes away the sin of the world" (1:29), crucified, probably, on the day before Passover as the lambs were being slaughtered (see 13:1; 18:28). (Jesus's glorification in his death may slightly overshadow this sin-removing element – "eternal life" is available in John simply through knowing Jesus; e.g. 3:16; 17:3; but cf. 1 John 2:2). On the other hand, Jesus dominates in his passion: unhesitatingly embracing his "hour" (12:27; cf. Mark 14:35–36); bowling over the arresting guards with a word (18:5–6); and carrying his own cross (19:17; cf. Mark 15:21). "No one takes [my life] from me ... I have power to lay it down, and I have power to take it up again" (10:18). Only in self-imposed weakness does Jesus from the cross arrange for the Beloved Disciple to care for his mother (19:26–27), declare his thirst to fulfill Scripture (19:28–29; Ps 69:21), and finish his task with his head bowed (19:30). In this Johannine paradox there is potential for a recognition of the divine glory as coextensive with the divine love (3:16; 13:34–35; 15:13).

Nevertheless, the resurrection of Jesus is not an afterthought, and the disciples do not expect it as a matter of course, including Mary Magdalene, for whom even an angel will not do in place of her Lord (20:13; cf. the fearful state of the Eleven in 20:19 and Thomas's initial disbelief in 20:25). Mary's mistaken identification of Jesus as the gardener famously may say more than she knows, in that Jesus appears to be a new Adam in a new creation (see 18:1; 19:5, 34, 41; 20:15). As promised (e.g. in 14:16 regarding "another Paraclete"), Jesus breathes the Spirit into the disciples (20:22) to prepare for his departure (a worrying concern for Jesus's disciples in John 14–16). Finally, and cathartically for readers of the fourfold gospel, the appendix in John's final chapter reconciles Peter thoroughly with Jesus before our eyes (21:15–19).

## THE RECEPTION OF THE FOURFOLD GOSPEL

How then did this fourfold gospel canon come to be? There are two caricatures, appearing in both popular and scholarly guises, which vie for our attention: The first, which appeals to the conspiracy-minded and makes for sensational fiction, holds that fourth-century (or indeed late second-century) bishops simply chose their preferred gospels. The second, unthinkingly traditionalist view holds that the canonical Four were always the unquestioned, authoritative witnesses to Jesus and that the noncanonical gospels were from the start patently heretical deviations from a canonical norm. Both of these extremes contain, of course, elements of the truth. Christian bishops did sometimes suppress other gospels, as in Serapion's famous opposition to the use of the Gospel of Peter at Rhossus in the late second century (Eusebius *Hist. eccl.* 6.12.1–6), and from around that time the proto-canonical Four were indeed increasingly secure and backed by ecclesiastical authority.

On the other hand, however, the canonical Four are the oldest surviving gospels, and none of the extant other gospels ever seriously threatened to become canonical.

Furthermore, "[k]nown portions of one or more of the subsequently canonical gospels were ... cited as 'the gospel' before *any* of the extant noncanonical gospels were composed" (e.g. Didache 8.2 [Matt 6:9–13]; 2 Clement 8:5 [Luke 16:10–11]; Bockmuehl 2017, 6). Justin (by ca. 150–65 CE) knows the individual writings themselves as "Gospels" (*euangelia*; *1 Apol.* 66.3), and he refers to "memoirs collected by the apostles and those who followed them" (*Dial* 103.8). This might suggest at least two by apostles (Matthew and John) and two by apostolic followers (Mark and Luke). Furthermore, while the attribution of Matthew to the apostle is particularly difficult to accept, the case for the proto-canonical gospels' anonymity has been shown to be weaker than previously supposed and the traditional authorial attributions to be both early and stable (Gathercole 2018, 470–76; see also Hengel 1985). Nevertheless, it is not until Irenaeus (or possibly the Muratorian Fragment, depending on its dating) that a leading Christian figure explicitly limits the canonical scope to the familiar Four (*Against Heresies* 3.11.8; ca. 180–90 CE). Moreover, as Jacob A. Rodriguez's chapter in this volume demonstrates, quite a few noncanonical gospels continued to flourish long after the consensus of a canonical fourfold gospel definitively emerged (e.g. Protevangelium of James, Gospel of Thomas, Marcion's Gospel, Tatian's Diatessaron). Nevertheless, the noncanonical gospels are, in the end, epiphenomenal upon the proto-canonical Four.

## CONCLUSION

What does it, therefore, mean to receive this fourfold witness to the one Jesus? Approaches to this challenge range between two polarities at the ends of a spectrum: At one end, historical and theological differences between the Gospels are viewed as an embarrassment to be downplayed or harmonized. Such a model, however, arguably violates the integrity of each evangelist's witness. At the other end, these historical and theological differences are seized upon as generative *in themselves* of spiritual truth while any quest for a historical Jesus behind the gospel texts is repudiated.[7] However, this approach arguably severs the relationship between the historical Jesus and his canonical reception.

---

[7] Cf. Watson 2013, 550. Whether, as Watson asserts (542–52), this is an accurate interpretation of Origen's hermeneutic is a matter of debate; cf. Mulder 2019, 169.

A more fruitful path may be represented by an "apostolic conference" model that seeks to respect the catholicity of the NT witness without pressing for exact agreement in every particular, instead focusing on what is held in common (Caird 1994, 1–26). Such an approach might adopt the Markan blueprint shared by all four canonical gospels, from Jesus's baptism by John to his crucifixion and resurrection, as a starting point for identifying their common *kerygma* (message). Because the distinctive contributions of each gospel are registered as individual voices in a shared conversation about the one Jesus, this approach can hold together tensions and complexities within Jesus's historical impact on his followers, such as that reflected in the contrast between the crucified and Godforsaken Jesus of Matthew and Mark and the crucified and self-controlled Lord of Luke and John. In this way, there is an embrace of the historical Jesus as the very same person who is dialogically received and proclaimed in the fourfold gospel.

### FURTHER READING

Allison, Dale C. 2013. *The New Moses: A Matthean Typology*. Eugene: Wipf & Stock.

Bauckham, Richard. 2017. *Jesus and the Eyewitnesses: The Gospels as Eyewitness Testimony*. 2nd ed. Grand Rapids: Eerdmans.

Becker, Eve-Marie, Helen K. Bond, and Catrin H. Williams, eds. 2021. *John's Transformation of Mark*. London: T & T Clark.

Bockmuehl, Markus. 2022. "Being Emmanuel: Matthew's Ever-Present Jesus?" *NTS* 68: 1–12.

Frey, Jörg. 2018. *The Glory of the Crucified One: Theology and Christology in the Fourth Gospel*. Translated by Wayne Coppins and Christoph Heilig. The Baylor-Mohr Siebeck Studies in Early Christianity Series. Waco: Baylor University Press.

Gathercole, Simon. 2022. *The Gospel and the Gospels: Christian Proclamation and Early Jesus Books*. Grand Rapids: Eerdmans.

Hengel, Martin. 2000. *The Four Gospels and the One Gospel of Jesus Christ: An Investigation of the Collection and Origin of the Canonical Gospels*. London: SCM.

Rowe, C. Kavin. 2006. *Early Narrative Christology: The Lord in the Gospel of Luke*. BZNW 139. Berlin: Walter de Gruyter.

Thiessen, Matthew. 2020. *Jesus and the Forces of Death: The Gospels' Portrayal of Ritual Impurity within First-Century Judaism*. Grand Rapids: Baker Academic.

Watson, Francis. 2013. *Gospel Writing: A Canonical Perspective*. Grand Rapids: Eerdmans.

## 4 Paul's Jesus as the Christ

MATTHEW V. NOVENSON

As it happens, our earliest extant evidence of any kind for Jesus of Nazareth is a small corpus of letters written by an almost exact contemporary, a diaspora Jewish writer named Paul,[1] who probably never met Jesus before Jesus's death but who claimed to have met him *after* his death. As a consequence of this unusual meeting, Paul became convinced that Jesus was the messiah, sent by God to liberate Israel, the gentiles, and the cosmos itself from their sin and misery. The means of this liberation was the resurrection of the dead, and the proof of it was the fact that Jesus himself had been raised from the dead by God, triggering the final redemption of all things. Paul took it to be his own God-given task to hurry around the northern shore of the Mediterranean Sea, from Judea to Spain, announcing this news to gentiles, so that they might survive the day of God's wrath and join with Israel in entering into the kingdom of God (Fredriksen 2017). The extant letters of Paul are communications that he sent, during his travels, to small assemblies of gentiles-in-Christ dotted across Asia Minor, Macedonia, Achaia, and Italy. On almost every page of every letter, Paul writes about the glorified Jesus, whom he calls the *christos*: Christ, messiah, or anointed (Novenson 2012).

### CHRIST MEANS MESSIAH

Just here lies a very interesting story from the history of modern biblical criticism. The Greek word *christos* is a verbal adjective derived from the verb *chriō*, meaning to anoint, rub, or smear something (especially oil) on something or someone. *Christos* thus literally means "anointed," and as a substantive, which is how it often appears, "an anointed person." In ancient Greek language generally, this is an intelligible but

---

[1] Throughout, all translations of the letters of Paul and other ancient sources are my own unless otherwise noted.

bizarre idiom, because human beings are not normally anointed or smeared (except perhaps athletes in the gymnasium, though the word is not normally used of them). In ancient Hebrew, however, the idiom does make good sense, because ancient Israelites had a custom of anointing (Hebrew *mashaḥ*) certain functionaries – especially kings and priests – with oil as a means of consecrating them to their respective offices. A person thus anointed (*mashaḥ*) could be called a *mashiaḥ*, or anointed person. (And from this, via Latin, we get modern words like English messiah, German *Messias*, and French *messie*.) When, in the third to second centuries BCE, the Jewish holy books were translated from Hebrew into Greek, the title *mashiaḥ* was consistently glossed with its near equivalency *christos*. Most ancient Greek speakers would not use the word *christos* of a person, but Jewish Greek speakers did, following the custom of their Hebrew-speaking forebears (Novenson 2017).

Enter Paul, a Greek-speaking Jew of the eastern diaspora. (Where, exactly, is uncertain; Paul's later biographer Luke thinks that he was from southeastern Asia Minor, but Paul himself never says). In his letters, Paul writes some 260-odd times of a *christos*, "anointed person," which, had he been writing in Hebrew, would have been *mashiaḥ*, or messiah. These 260-odd instances of the word *christos* are, in fact, the most from any single ancient writer, Jewish, Christian, Greek, Roman, or otherwise. Statistically speaking, then, one might have thought that Paul should count as first-order evidence of Jewish messianism in the Greek-speaking diaspora. And yet, for complicated reasons having to do with ideological agendas in modern New Testament scholarship, a more than century-long academic consensus used to say that Paul did *not* think of Jesus as the messiah, even if the writers of all the other books in the canonical New Testament did. According to this consensus, when Paul calls Jesus the *christos*, he means it as a proper name ("Christ"), not a title ("the messiah"). The most popular form of this hypothesis argued that, because Paul was apostle to the *gentiles*, he rejected Jewish categories like messiah in favor of Hellenistic or other gentile-friendly alternatives (on this history of scholarship, see Novenson 2012, 12–33).

That popular argument was always quite weak, but in theory it was trying to explain several notable features of how Paul actually writes the word *christos* in his letters, which differ in some ways from how some other ancient authors write the word (Kramer 1966; Dahl 1991, 15–26). First, Paul always writes *christos* as if its referent is the person Jesus, not as an office or role ("the messiah") the particular incumbent of which is an open question. Second, and relatedly, Paul never writes a sentence of the form "Jesus is the *christos*"; that is, he never formally predicates it of Jesus, as, for instance, Mark, Matthew, Luke, and John all do (Mark 8:29; 14:61–62; Matt 16:16; 26:63–64; Luke 9:20; 22:67; Acts 2:36, 17:3; John 4:25-26, 20:31). (I say never, but 1 Cor 2:2 is a possible exception, depending how we construe the syntax, which could be: "I resolved to know nothing among you except *that Jesus is the Christ*, and that he was crucified." And Phil 2:11 could be another.) Third, when Paul writes *christos*, he never follows it with a qualifying noun in the genitive, as in well-known phrases like "the Lord's anointed" or "the messiah of Israel." Fourth, Paul very often writes *christos* without the Greek article *ho*, equivalent to the English definite article "the."

Many twentieth-century interpreters took these four grammatical features to suggest that, for Paul, *christos* was effectively a second name for Jesus, not the title "messiah" that it was in other Jewish Greek texts. But as recent research has tended to bear out, this inference was a *non sequitur*, and in fact false (Wright 1991; Jipp 2015). All the features of the way Paul writes the word *christos* match the way ancient authors wrote (what classicists who study Greek names call) honorifics: words like Augustus, Epiphanes, Bar Kokhba, and so on, which were used of certain high-status persons in lieu of their proper names and their titles of office. Thus, for instance, Caesar's name was Caesar, his title emperor (Latin *imperator*), and his honorific Augustus ("venerable"); Antiochus IV's name was Antiochus, his title king (Greek *basileus*), and his honorific Epiphanes ("illustrious"); and so on. In the same way, Paul writes Jesus's name as Jesus, his title as lord (Greek *kurios*), and his honorific as messiah (Greek *christos*) (see further Novenson 2012, 64–97). The upshot of all this is that Paul does *not*, contrary to the old scholarly consensus, deny or forget the messiahship of Jesus. He assumes it (thus rightly Hewitt 2020; Bühner 2021).

### GOD SENT HIS SON

But messiahs come in many different forms and do many different things, so the interesting question about any particular text is how exactly it understands its messiah to function. In the case of the letters of Paul, we can trace several key moments in the career of the messiah Jesus, the first of which is his being sent by his father, namely God. One succinct statement of this Pauline idea comes in Galatians 4: "When we were infants, we were enslaved under the elements of the cosmos. But when the fulness of time came, God sent his son, born of a woman, born under the law, so that he might redeem those under the law, so that we might receive adoption" (Gal 4:3–5). Paul here assumes a kind of cosmic timeline, an age of enslavement under the elements followed by a new order in which humans become free sons of God. The mechanism for transition from the one to the other is the sending of the messiah. In order for mortal humans ("born of a woman, born under the law") to enter their glorified state, God must first send the messiah to share their condition ("born of a woman, born under the law") and to ransom them out of it. Why exactly this is necessary goes unstated; for Paul, it has the status of a first principle (Sanders 1977).

But if the appearing of the messiah Jesus can be characterized as a divine sending, we might well wonder where, if anywhere, he was before he was sent. Paul says very little by way of answer to this question, but in one passage, at least, he seems to assume that the messiah enjoyed a kind of divine life before his human life: "Christ Jesus existed in the shape of God, but did not consider it plunder to be equal to God; rather, he emptied himself, assuming the shape of a slave, coming in the likeness of humans; and being found in form as a human he humiliated himself" (Phil 2:5–8). This passage is less clear than we might like about a number of details. It does not even attempt to answer the question – so important to late ancient Christian theology – of the precise ontological relation between God the father and Christ the son. Nor does it share the Gospel of John's more famous idiom of "incarnation," en-flesh-ment, speaking instead of Christ's god-form and human-form, respectively. Crucially, however, Paul in Philippians 2 does assume that the messiah, before he appeared on the human stage, was hidden away with God, an idea that a number of other ancient Jewish texts also share (Bühner 2021, 23–64).

When he does appear on the human stage, "born of a woman," it is important for Paul that the messiah is born to a family descended from the ancient Judahite king David. He needs to be, and is, not just an Israelite in general but a Davidide in particular, a rightful heir to the office of messiah (McCaulley 2019). (Ancient Jewish texts disagree among themselves over what counts as a "rightful" genealogy of a messiah; see Novenson 2017, 65–113. But Paul, with many others, expects a Davidic pedigree.) Thus Paul writes that Jesus "came from the seed of David according to the flesh, and was appointed son of God in power according to the spirit of holiness from the resurrection of the dead" (Rom 1:3–4). Later in the same letter, Paul quotes an oracle of the ancient prophet Isaiah as referring to Jesus: "The root of Jesse shall come, even he who rises to rule the gentiles; in him the gentiles shall hope" (Rom 15:12 citing Isa 11:10). In the scriptural story of the kings, Jesse was the father of king David (1 Sam 16–17); thus the "root of Jesse" is the latter-day descendant of David whom God will one day raise up. (Paul probably associates God *raising* Jesus from the dead with the biblical idea of God *raising up* the messiah in the fulness of time.) What is more, in the Greek version of Isaiah 11 that Paul cites, this root of Jesse "rises to rule the gentiles." Paul reckons that this prophecy is coming to pass in his, Paul's, own apostolic work in Asia, Macedonia, Achaia, and beyond: Paul is announcing the Jewish messiah to gentiles, and they (the gentiles) are obeying him (the messiah) by swearing their trust or allegiance (Greek *pistis*, "faith") to him in baptism. Thus Paul's own day-to-day experience confirms him in his conviction that Jesus is indeed the messiah.

One final Pauline text about "God sending his son" begins to help us see why Paul locates so much of Jesus's messianic vocation in his death and resurrection, about which we will have more to say. Again in his Letter to the Romans, Paul writes,

> As for the inability of the law, namely, that it was weakened through the flesh – God, by sending his son in the likeness of the flesh of sin, and for sin, condemned sin in the flesh, in order that the upright act of the law might be fulfilled in us who walk not according to the flesh but according to the pneuma. (Rom 8:3–4)

Here, as in Phil 2, God sends his son in the *form* or *likeness* of the people whom he comes to ransom; the messiah assimilates to their miserable condition, described here in terms of "flesh" and "sin" and elsewhere in terms of "death." God "condemns sin in the flesh" in order to bring about a new kind of life, one that lies beyond sin, flesh, and death but is only accessible by going *through* death, not around it. Which brings us to the next moment in the Jesus's messianic career.

### DYING FOR OTHERS

It is a truism that many, even most of the texts collected in the New Testament focus more on Jesus's death than on his life. But if Martin Kähler could call the Gospels "passion narratives with extended introductions" (Kähler 1964, 80), then the letters of Paul are, if anything, even more singularly focused on the death of Jesus (and his resurrection and postmortem life). It is clear that Paul knew more than a little about the life and teachings of Jesus (e.g. his instruction on divorce in 1 Cor 7:10–11 and on the ritual thanksgiving meal in 1 Cor 11:23–26; and other possible allusions in Rom 14:14; 2 Cor 8:9; 1 Thess 2:15; 4:2), but in his letters Paul is mostly uninterested in relating any of this. He claims to be, and in fact he is, preoccupied with "the *crucified* messiah" (1 Cor 1:23; 2:2; Gal 3:1; 6:14). But how, exactly, the crucifixion of the messiah functions as a divine gift (*charis*, often translated "grace") to Israel and to the world is a famous puzzle, one often discussed under the Christian theological rubric of "the atonement," which rubric unfortunately hinders as well as helps our effort to understand Paul's view on this question (Stowers 1994, 1–41, 194–226).

One of the most influential accounts, in Western Christian theology, at least, says that the death of Jesus somehow effects forgiveness of sins. On this account, sins are the problem, forgiveness the solution, and the death of Jesus the mechanism that achieves that solution. There are several problems with this account, but in regard to the letters of Paul, the chief problem is that Paul almost never mentions forgiveness of sins and never connects it to the death of Jesus. Paul's one mention of forgiveness comes in Romans 4, where he quotes the psalm that says, "Blessed are they whose lawless acts are forgiven, whose sins are covered; blessed is the man to whom the Lord will not reckon sin" (Ps 32:1–2). Paul takes this verse to describe an experience that he calls "having righteousness reckoned without works of the law," which is a wonderful thing that God can do for people, did for Abraham the patriarch long ago, and now does for people-in-Christ, but not – judging from Paul's letters – through any mechanism where Christ dying is the *condition* for God forgiving (otherwise God could not have done it in the case of Abraham). Once Paul says that "the messiah died for our sins" (1 Cor 15:3), once that "he gave himself for our sins" (Gal 1:4), and once that "he was handed over for our [moral] lapses" (Rom 4:25). Interpreters have happily filled in the blanks and taken these texts to mean that, by Paul's lights, Jesus died *to forgive sins*, but there is no positive warrant for filling in the blanks in this way.

Paul does say that Christ died *for sins*, but far more frequently he says that Christ died *for people*. (Hence we should probably understand the former claim in light of the latter: Christ dies for sins in the sense that he dies for people beset by sins.) "Christ died for us" (1 Thess 5:10; Rom 5:8). Any other person in the Christ-assembly is "your brother for whom Christ died" (Rom 14:15). Paul sometimes emphasizes the unworthiness of the beneficiaries of this death-for-others: "Christ died for the impious" (Rom 5:6). He attributes the gift sometimes to Jesus's own volition, sometimes to the will of God. "He [Christ] gave himself for our sins" (Gal 1:4), but also "God handed over his son for us all" (Rom 8:32). As this latter quote illustrates, the "us" for whom Christ died are sometimes said to be, simply, everyone. "One died for all people; therefore all people died" (2 Cor 5:14). And again, "He [Christ] died for all people" (2 Cor 5:15). Indeed, in one telling passage, Paul explains Jesus's voluntary death as a strategy for gathering up all people – the dead as well as the living – under his, Jesus's, messianic rule: "Christ died and then lived so that he might be lord of both the dead and the living" (Rom 14:9). And in another passage, as a strategy for getting people out of the age of sin and death and into another, far better state: "He gave himself for our sins so as to take us out of the present evil age" (Gal 1:4).

If we press the question how, exactly, Christ's death can be *for people*, the clearest answer Paul gives – which is admittedly still a rather mysterious one, though it does make good sense of all the texts quoted in this chapter – is that Christ dies *for* people by dying *with* people (Schweitzer 1931, 101–40; Hewitt 2020). Thus Paul speaks frequently about how people-in-Christ have actually *died with* Christ: "We died with Christ" (Rom 6:8); "I have been crucified with Christ" (Gal 2:20); and so on. The reason Paul regards this as a happy outcome, which it may not appear at first glance, is that to die with Christ is also to come out the other side with him: to share his kind of sinless, undying life. But according to Paul's logic, there is no way of attaining that blessed state otherwise than by dying. And this, arguably, suggests an interpretation of "Christ dying for sins." As Paul puts it in another telling passage, "The person who has died has been rightwised away from sin" (Rom 6:7). In other words, all those who die with Christ in baptism are translated into a mode of existence beyond sin. Christ died for their sins in the sense that his death put an end to their sins. (Thus Paul can figure the death of Christ in 1 Cor 5:7 as the death of the Passover lamb – as a number of early Christian texts also do – because the Passover sacrifice marks liberation from enslavement.) It often used to be said in Jewish-Christian polemics that the Jewish messiah is a mortal human, while the Christian messiah is a god (on these polemics see Novenson 2017, 187–216). But for Paul (who is arguably both Jewish and Christian, depending on how exactly we define those terms), the messiah emphatically is a mortal human – he has to be, otherwise he could not die for others – even if, after his resurrection, he becomes something very much like a god.

## THE RESURRECTION OF THE DEAD

Writing a generation after Paul, at the end of the first century CE, the anonymous author of the Jewish apocalypse 4 Ezra paints his own scene of the messiah dying for his people:

> My son the messiah shall be revealed with those who are with him, and those who remain shall rejoice 400 years. And after these years my son the messiah shall die, and all who draw human breath. And the world shall be turned back to primeval silence for seven days, as it was at the first beginnings, so that no one shall be left. And after seven days the world, which is not yet awake, shall be roused, and that which is corruptible shall perish. And the earth shall give up those who are asleep in it. (4 Ezra 7:28–32; Latin version trans. Metzger in Charlesworth, *Old Testament Pseudepigrapha*)

The messiah of 4 Ezra does not rise from the dead, but his death does trigger the general resurrection ("the earth shall give up those who are asleep in it") and the re-creation of the cosmos ("the world, which is not yet awake, shall be roused"). Which is very close, indeed, to what Paul says about the messiah Jesus. There are two key differences: For Paul, the messiah himself must rise from the dead in order to bring all the dead with him. And for Paul, this is not a vision of what will one day come to pass but an event of very recent memory. Paul knows that Jesus has risen from the dead because, he says, he has seen him with his own eyes on at least one occasion, perhaps more than one (Gal 1:12, 16; 2:2; 2 Cor 12:1). And Paul reasons similarly to 4 Ezra: If the messiah has come, died, and risen, then the resurrection of the dead and the re-creation of the cosmos are at hand. Already by the late first century, Christian theology would make peace with deferring the eschaton to a more distant future, but Paul, being an almost exact contemporary of Jesus, does not do so; for him, the resurrection is now (Schweitzer 1931, 52–100).

This issue comes to the fore in one of the texts we noted earlier in the chapter. Recall that Jesus, according to Paul, "came from the seed of David according to the flesh, and was appointed son of God in power according to the spirit of holiness from the resurrection of the dead" (Rom 1:3–4). Jesus's coming from the seed of David makes him *eligible for the office* of messiah. But the achievement that actually *establishes* him as messiah ("son of God in power") is the resurrection of the dead. Not "*his* resurrection *from* the dead" – a common mistranslation of this verse – but "the resurrection of the dead," as Augustine rightly insists in his commentary on Romans (Fredriksen 2017). That is, Jesus's rising from the dead is not a one-off event happening out of due time but the beginning of the general resurrection. All the righteous are about to – and Jesus himself currently does – live an undying, glorified, postmortem kind of life. Not *in spite of* but *because of* Jesus's death, he, Jesus, now relates to Paul as an immediate, personal, divine presence: "He is at the right hand of God interceding for us" (Rom 8:34); "I live by trust in the son of God who loves me" (Gal 2:20); and so on.

What is more, this helps to explain why Paul thinks that he can address gentiles-in-Christ in his letters as if they were somehow already participating in the moral life of the resurrection, because, by Paul's lights, they are. Admittedly, Paul does not say, as one deutero-Pauline writer does, that people-in-Christ have already been raised from the dead and ascended to heaven (Eph 2:6: "[God] raised us together and seated us together in the heavens in Christ Jesus"). But Paul does say that people-in-Christ are semi-resurrected, as it were – "revivified," in the helpful idiom of Boakye (2017) – already imbued with the same divine pneuma (commonly translated "spirit") that the risen Christ himself has or is but also still temporarily possessed of mortal bodies of flesh (as the risen Christ is no longer). They are still, therefore, "weighed down" by this body of flesh (2 Cor 5:4) but also genuinely capable of transcending it, of living into the undying life of the resurrection that they will very soon enjoy fully. It is in this sense that "our commonwealth is in the heavens" (Phil 3:20) and "the Jerusalem above is our mother [city]" (Gal 4:26). Which is why, for instance, Paul holds out celibacy as a virtue (1 Cor 7): not simply for a principled asceticism or pragmatism but because he thinks that the sexless life of the resurrection is accessible now for those who have the divine pneuma in sufficient measure.

By the same token, the messiah's role in effecting the resurrection of the dead goes a long way toward explaining Paul's famously complicated discourse about the law of Moses, that is, the Torah or Pentateuch (Schweitzer 1931, 177–204). This discourse is often said to be impenetrable or even incoherent, but in fact, in light of the premises noted, it makes a certain clear sense. Paul takes for granted (what is in fact the case) that the law of Moses legislates for mortals, people who sin and die, and therefore have use of a system that regulates sin and impurity and ensures ritual access to God. Paul concedes that, for such people, the law of Moses is actually a model system (Gal 3:19, 24). But he also thinks that people-in-Christ, because they are already full of the life-making pneuma of the risen Jesus, are actually no longer mere mortals. They are *pneumatikoi*, pneumatic humans, people who have begun to live the same undying life that the risen Jesus lives, and are, to just that extent, beyond the jurisdiction of the law. In short, all of Paul's difficult sayings about the law of Moses follow from his conviction that the messiah has in fact come and effected the resurrection of the dead.

### PUTTING ENEMIES UNDER HIS FEET

Paul's messiah is not only like the messiah in 4 Ezra 7 who dies in order to bring about new creation. He is also like the messiah in Psalms of Solomon 17 who fights battles and subdues enemies on God's behalf. The messiah Jesus is, in short, a warrior (Fredriksen 2017). "He puts enemies under his feet" (1 Cor 15:25). We have already seen one important example of this: He compels "the obedience of trust among all the gentiles" (Rom 1:5; 16:26). *Pistis*, often translated "faith," but perhaps better "trust," "loyalty," or "allegiance," is Paul's technical term for the ideal response to the announcement of the messiah. As in the Psalms of Solomon – or, for that matter, the much older biblical royal psalms – the nations, or gentiles, pledge their trust or allegiance to the Israelite king messiah. They "bow the knee" (Paul's idiom, Phil 2:10), a gesture of surrender and obeisance, and they acknowledge him as their *kurios*, lord or master. It is no accident, then, that Paul characterizes his own vocation as "the embassy to the gentiles" (Gal 2:8; Rom 1:5), a mission of divine diplomacy meant to bring about their voluntary surrender and thus avert a more violent day of wrath (Novenson 2012, 156–60).

Gentiles, as Paul sees it, live in a natural state of hostility toward God (Rom 1:18–32). But not so Israel, who have the ancestors, the promises, the covenants, the temple worship, and indeed the messiah himself (Rom 9:4–5). At the moment when Paul writes his Letter to the Romans, however, he concedes that Israel is, temporarily, "hostile in regard to the announcement" (Rom 11:28), that is, to Paul's announcement that the crucified and risen Jesus is the messiah. Paul knows that most of his co-ethnics do not believe that announcement to be true, but he cannot bring himself to countenance either (1) that he himself might be wrong about Jesus or (2) that God will fail to deliver Israel safely into the kingdom of God. Romans 9–11, therefore, is a virtuoso explanation of how God must, mysteriously, have willed Israel's current hostility to Paul's announcement precisely in order to make more time and space for gentiles to come in, lest they be lost. Most Jewish messiahs down the centuries have tended to have majority Jewish followings, but already in Paul's lifetime the messianic movement around Jesus was proving an exception. The Jewish messiah had appeared, but his constituency was turning out to be more gentile than Jewish. Later Christian writers would rationalize this in supersessionist terms, but it does not occur to Paul to do so. For him, God has temporarily hardened Jewish hearts so that the messiah has time to put still more gentiles under his feet (Stowers 1994, 213–26).

But it is not only human beings who must be put under the messiah's feet; it is also superhuman beings (Schweitzer 1931). Paul speaks repeatedly in his letters about certain beings – gods, lords, angels, daemons, rulers, powers, elements – that might threaten to foil the final victory of people-in-Christ but will surely not succeed in doing so. "I am confident that neither death nor life nor angels nor rulers nor present things nor future things nor powers nor height nor depth nor any other creature will be able to part us from the love of God which is in Christ Jesus our lord" (Rom 8:38–39). The reason that these superhuman powers cannot succeed in thwarting the righteous is, first, because Christ is putting all of these unruly powers under his feet (1 Cor 15:25) – making them obedient even as he makes gentile humans obedient – and, second, because Christ's life-making pneuma actually elevates people-in-Christ up the cosmic scale of glory so that they themselves are superior to the powers (e.g. 1 Cor 6:3, where people-in-Christ sit in judgment over angels).

Paul says little about the identity of these superhuman powers, but there is a plausible argument that they, too, are gentile. That is, that the anonymous gods, lords, angels, rulers, powers, and so on, are, within Paul's Jewish cosmology, actually the gods or angels of the nations (Fredriksen 2017, 77–93). There is a long tradition in ancient Jewish cosmology, going back at least as far as Deuteronomy, of interpreting the gods of other nations (Marduk, Isis, Zeus, et al.) as angels deputized by God to oversee the affairs of their respective nations: divine regional managers, so to speak. In the Greek version of Deuteronomy that Paul would have read, it says, "When the Most High divided the nations, when he scattered the sons of Adam, he set the boundaries of the nations according to the number of the angels of God" (Deut 32:8 LXX). In keeping with this tradition, the book of Daniel knows of national angels overseeing at least Persia, Greece, and Judea (Dan 10). Meanwhile Paul, for his part, traverses gentile nations recruiting their people to pledge allegiance to the Jewish God and his messiah. Paul worries about angels, rulers, and powers trying to stand in his way, trying to prevent gentile humans from pledging allegiance to Christ. Quite plausibly, then, the angels, rulers, and powers that he has in mind are these divine regional managers. Feeling threatened by the defection of "their" people, they lash out at Paul. Not to worry, however, because the messiah is busy putting all these powers under his feet.

## THE KINGSHIP OF GOD

As we have seen, Paul's messiah enjoyed a form of divine life ("existing in the shape of God," Phil 2:6) even before he was sent by his father, but as a prize for his voluntary death God rewards him even more highly: "God exalted him higher still, and gave him the name that is above every name, so that at the name of Jesus every knee might bow, whether of heavenly or earthly or chthonic beings, and every tongue confess that Jesus Christ is lord, to the glory of God the father" (Phil 2:9–11). This passage contains in a nutshell the puzzle of Jesus's uniquely exalted status, which has been both a premise and a problem for Christian theology (Bühner 2021). Jesus is exalted above every other being in the cosmos save one: God the father. God goes so far as to grant him to bear "the name" – which almost certainly means the ineffable divine name – but even here Jesus remains the name-bearing messiah, and God remains the father. All knees bow to Jesus, but all glory goes to God the father. Paul vaunts Jesus above every created thing in the cosmos (Rom 8:38–39), but he never calls Jesus God (contrast John 1:1). (Romans 9:5 is a possible exception to this claim but not an actual exception, in my view.) For Paul, the father is rightly called God, and the son/messiah is rightly called lord (1 Cor 8:6).

This, then, makes sense of the scene Paul sketches in 1 Corinthians 15 of the final resolution of all things.

> Then comes the end, when he hands over the kingship to the God and father, when he nullifies ever rule and every authority and power. For he must reign [or: be king] until such time as he puts all the enemies under his feet. The last enemy to be nullified is death. For *he subjected everything under his feet* [Ps 8:6]. When it says that *everything* was subjected, that obviously excludes the one who subjected everything to him. But when everything is subjected to him, then the son himself will be subjected to the one who subjected everything to him, that God may be all in everything. (1 Cor 15:24–28)

Here, remarkably, the messiah's mission ends with his own "being subjected" to his father after he has done the work of putting everything else in the cosmos under his feet. He must reign (*basileuō*, serve as king) until he has brought all powers in the cosmos to heel, at which point he hands over the kingship (*basileia*) to God the father. The final clause – "that God may be all in everything" – might mean to point to a state of affairs in which all that exists is taken back up into God, from whom it came in the first place (cf. Rom 11:36: "All things proceed out of ... and resolve into God"). If that is what it means, then the very notion of kingship or reign might seem to us not to be apt, since the distinction between God and all things would have been mended (an idea familiar to some strands of Eastern Christian theology, less so Western).

However that may be, elsewhere, too, Paul refers to this final, blessed state of affairs as the *basileia tou theou*, the kingship or kingdom of God. And the hope of human beings is to inherit it. "God calls you into his own kingdom and splendour" (1 Thess 2:12). Certain characteristics, however, can disqualify humans from inheriting the kingdom of God. Moral deficiency, for one: "The unrighteous will not inherit the kingdom of God" (1 Cor 6:9–10); "People who practice such [wicked] things will not inherit the kingdom of God" (Gal 5:21). But also physical deficiency: "Flesh and blood cannot inherit the kingdom of God, nor does perishability inherit the imperishable" (1 Cor 15:50). That is to say, in order to inherit the kingdom of God, humans have to undergo a physical metamorphosis, from a body of flesh to a body of pneuma, which is precisely the point of resurrection. What exactly this kingdom is like Paul does not say in any detail, but he does hint in a few places: "The kingdom of God is not in speech but in power" (1 Cor 4:20); "The kingdom of God is not food and drink, but righteousness, peace, and joy in the holy pneuma" (Rom 14:17). It is, in short, the mode of life enjoyed by God and by the risen Christ but now made accessible to human beings, the newborn children of God.

CONCLUSION

Ironically in light of the history of research mentioned at the beginning of this chapter, the one thing we *do* know about Jesus in the letters of Paul is that he is the messiah (as was rightly recognized by Schweitzer 1931; Davies 1948; Wright 1991). Paul everywhere refers to him as such, and his particular functions coincide at many points with other figures from the history of Jewish messianism. In particular, he is the son of God, sent by his father, dies for others, effects the resurrection of the dead, puts enemies under his feet, and hands over the kingship to God. Indeed, there are points at which the letters of Paul stand in tension with the later Christian tradition that canonized them precisely because Jesus is for Paul, as he was not for some later Christians, the messiah. Whether modern Christianity can or should reclaim that oldest apostolic confession of Jesus as messiah is an interesting and a complicated question. Be that as it may, without it we cannot hope to understand the history of Jesus, Paul, the other apostles, and the ancient Judaism of which they were all part.

## FURTHER READING

Boakye, Andrew K. 2017. *Death and Life: Resurrection, Restoration, and Rectification in Paul's Letter to the Galatians*. Eugene: Pickwick.

Bühner, Ruben A. 2021. *Messianic High Christology: New Testament Variants of Second Temple Judaism*. Waco: Baylor University Press.

Dahl, Nils Alstrup. 1991. *Jesus the Christ: The Historical Origins of Christological Doctrine*. Edited by Donald H. Juel. Minneapolis: Fortress.

Davies, W. D. 1948. *Paul and Rabbinic Judaism: Some Rabbinic Elements in Pauline Theology*. London: SPCK.

Fredriksen, Paula. 2017. *Paul, the Pagans' Apostle*. New Haven: Yale University Press.

Hewitt, J. Thomas. 2020. *Messiah and Scripture: Paul's "In Christ" Idiom in Its Ancient Jewish Context*. WUNT 2:522. Tübingen: Mohr Siebeck.

Jipp, Joshua W. 2015. *Christ Is King: Paul's Royal Ideology*. Minneapolis: Fortress.

Kähler, Martin. 1964. *The So-Called Historical Jesus and the Historic, Biblical Christ*. Translated by Carl E. Braaten. Philadelphia: Fortress.

Kramer, Werner R. 1966. *Christ, Lord, Son of God*. Translated by B. Hardy. SBT 50. London: SCM.

McCaulley, Esau. 2019. *Sharing in the Son's Inheritance: Davidic Messianism and Paul's Worldwide Interpretation of the Abrahamic Land Promise in Galatians*. LNTS 608. London: T & T Clark.

Novenson, Matthew V. 2012. *Christ among the Messiahs: Christ Language in Paul and Messiah Language in Ancient Judaism*. Oxford: Oxford University Press.

Novenson, Matthew V. 2017. *The Grammar of Messianism: An Ancient Jewish Political Idiom and Its Users*. Oxford: Oxford University Press.

Sanders, E. P. 1977. *Paul and Palestinian Judaism*. Philadelphia: Fortress.

Schweitzer, Albert. 1931. *The Mysticism of Paul the Apostle*. Translated by W. Montgomery. London: A&C Black.

Stowers, Stanley K. 1994. *A Rereading of Romans: Justice, Jews, and Gentiles*. New Haven: Yale University Press.

Wright, N. T. 1991. *The Climax of the Covenant: Christ and the Law in Pauline Theology*. Edinburgh: T & T Clark.

## 5 The Risen Jesus
MARKUS BOCKMUEHL

'God raised Jesus from the dead.' Our knowledge of Jesus of Nazareth and his impact on history depends almost uniquely on his followers' conviction about an event after his execution: inexplicably and yet unmistakably, Jesus was experienced as visibly present and alive in personal encounters with his disciples soon after his death and burial. Without that conviction, affirmed explicitly by virtually all extant early Christian sources and contested by none, we would almost certainly know nothing about Jesus at all.

Within at most fifteen years of the crucifixion, the resurrection of Jesus was deeply embedded not just in the original Palestinian Jewish communities of his followers but in Paul's new missionary outreach to the gentile world of Asia Minor and Greece (1 Thess 1:10; 4:14; Gal 1:1), based on a shared tradition inherited from Judean believers in the very first years of the Christian movement: Jesus died and was buried, but was 'raised on the third day' and then seen by Peter (Cephas), his inner circle of twelve disciples, a larger group of 500 followers, then by his brother James and by all the apostles together – and ultimately by Paul himself (1 Cor 15:3–8). Paul insists, in fact, that this reality is indispensable to the very possibility of Christian faith: 'if Christ has not been raised, your faith is futile' (1 Cor 15:17, 19, 32).

Rudolf Bultmann (1884–1976), the last century's most famous New Testament critic, fully recognized the logical force of that argument as much as he found it distastefully 'dangerous' – *'fatal'*, indeed. In his view, Paul's 'attempt to make the resurrection of Jesus credible as an objective historical fact' shows he failed to understand what Bultmann understood: no historical fact could possibly bear in any way on a resurrection from the dead (Bultmann 1948, 48; trans. Bultmann 1953, 39).

By the turn of the present century, scholarly literature on the 'historical Jesus' had comfortably embraced a studied neglect of his resurrection. Some easily dismissed its relevance on the strength of their (historically implausible) conviction that Jesus's Jewish cadaver must have been tossed into a public lime-pit or devoured by birds and stray dogs (so, e.g., Crossan 1994, 127, 154). But even the more methodologically prudent and circumspect 'historical Jesus' questers tended to sideline or avoid the resurrection – typically on the pretext that it is reducible to a question of 'faith' or of 'theology', about which no self-respecting 'historian' could possibly have anything to say (e.g. Meier 1991–2016, 1:13).

To be sure, quite what 'resurrection' might mean is never clearly defined in our early sources, with interpretations varying appreciably. And unlike some later, noncanonical accounts like the Gospel of Peter, the New Testament writings do not attempt to narrate or describe this event itself.

'History' and 'myth', truth and rhetoric, experience and interpretation all converge in any serious attempt to make sense of the early Christians' extraordinary, unprecedented, and complex claim about Jesus. It does not lend itself to one-dimensional explanations, whether in terms of 'miracle', 'myth', 'metaphor', or for that matter of 'history'. Such category mistakes are also not helped by slam-dunk rationalism of either the apologetic or the sceptical variety: nuanced historical inquiry simply cannot deliver straightforward 'evidence', either 'that God raised Jesus from the dead' or 'that God did no such thing' (Allison 2021, 3).

Resurrections are not meaningfully subject to scholarly judgements about causes and effects, let alone about historical probabilities. It may (Allison 2021) or may not be useful to contextualize the gospel accounts in relation to historic or contemporary experiences of the paranormal. For all the mystery and complexity of that alleged third day after the crucifixion, however, it is a matter of historical record that *something* happened – something decisive and far-reaching in the experience of the first Christians which shaped the course of world history to an extent unlike any event before or since. This footprint of Jesus is thus open to historical inquiry and of the utmost importance for any historical understanding (cf. Wright 2003, 1–31).

Only outcomes ultimately allow the mass of brute facts to become interpretable as history: only they make it possible to distinguish the salient from the trivial. As a mere humanitarian sage and cultural dissident, Jesus would have remained insignificant, scarcely mentioned or more likely ignored by contemporary historians (cf. Josephus, *Ant.* 18.63–64; 20.200) – and unlikely ever to be available as a meaningful subject of historical interest. Absent the unexpected resurrection of Jesus, even his disciples could only lament failed messianic hopes (Luke 24:21); faced with the event, they went on to attest nothing less than 'a new birth into a living hope through the resurrection of Jesus Christ from the dead' (1 Pet 1:3). However one proceeds in the end to interpret the historical or theological significance of this claim and its underlying experiences, it stands at the very heart of any properly 'historical' assessment of Jesus of Nazareth.

COMPLEX SOURCES

Given their evident importance to authors and audiences alike, the Easter stories are marked by a striking degree of diversity and tension. The four gospels embed their cognate affirmation in brief narrative accounts that do agree on a few key features: after his public execution on a Roman cross, Jesus is buried in the tomb of the Sanhedrin member Joseph of Arimathea. Two days later (counting inclusively: 'on the third day' or 'after three days'), this evidently identifiable tomb is found empty by women disciples including Mary Magdalene. Quite what happens then, however, appears a jumble of excited claims and counter-claims in each of the four gospels, which seems impossible to reduce to an orderly narrative.

### Mark

Mark's is the briefest and most primitive form of the narrative, particularly in its earliest extant form (16:1–8). Mary Magdalene and two others find the tomb open and come across only 'a young man in a white robe', who asks them to tell the disciples that Jesus has been raised and will meet them in Galilee. The earliest text ends abruptly with the women saying 'nothing to anyone' and fleeing in fear (16:8); Mark's Greek syntax famously reinforces that abruptness by the striking staccato of concluding on the particle *gar* ('for'). Although Mark consistently anticipates both the resurrection of Jesus and the (angelic) instruction to meet him in Galilee (8:31; 9:9, 31; 10:34; 14:28), no such encounter is narrated in the earliest form of his text (unlike in the early second-century appendix at 16:9–20).

Twentieth-century commentators liked to speculate about this problem by invoking either a supposedly lost original ending of the Gospel or, conversely, Mark's generation of existential drama by projecting the unfulfilled angelic promise of encounter into the reader's present. And yet, the very insistence of those predictions presupposes their fulfilment: the narrative would instantly collapse if, as some scholars have argued, readers either knew or suspected that the promised encounter of 16:8 had never transpired.

Even a Markan text ending at 16:8 (which as such is not attested prior to the fourth century) implies a reader who already knows a narrative resembling that of Matthew 28 – or for that matter of Mark 16:9–20, composed a generation later, which became the most successful and ultimately canonical ending of this gospel. Drawing loosely on accounts in the other canonical gospels, it supplies resurrection appearances first to Mary Magdalene (who *does* inform the disciples), then to two disciples 'walking into the country', and finally before his ascension to 'the Eleven' (i.e. minus Judas Iscariot) 'as they were having dinner'.

## Matthew

Matthew's own, still rather economic account is the New Testament text that comes closest to narrating the resurrection itself (28:2–3): an angel descends from heaven in the midst of an earthquake to roll back the stone and sit on it. On seeing the empty tomb and being instructed to inform the disciples as in Mark, the two Marys encounter Jesus in person before going on to tell the disciples 'with fear and great joy' (28:8) – thus becoming 'apostles of the apostles', as later Christian writers put it (e.g. Jerome *Comm. Soph.* preface). Following a brief apologetic interlude on the Jewish chief priests bribing the Roman guard at the tomb to remain silent (28:11–15), the risen Jesus does in fact appear to the eleven remaining disciples on a mountain in Galilee to commission them and promise his continuing presence.

## Luke

The Third Evangelist provides the fullest and most concrete narrative of encounters with the risen Jesus exclusively in and around Jerusalem, mapped explicitly onto Jesus's messianic fulfilment of Scripture. Once again it is his female Galilean followers who become the 'apostles of the apostles', even though their Easter witness is at first dismissed by men (24:11). Subsequent experiences involve Peter (24:12, 24), Cleopas and another disciple on the way to Emmaus (24:13–33), and finally 'the Eleven' and their friends, with whom Jesus eats and with whom he goes to the Mount of Olives before 'he withdrew from them and was carried up into heaven' (24:51).

## Acts

Luke's second volume interprets and complements his earlier account. Here, the period of Jesus's pre-ascension appearances presents 'many convincing proofs' of his resurrection during a period of not one but forty days (1:3), again explicitly confined to Jerusalem. Developing what is elsewhere described as Jesus's exaltation to heaven, the ascension becomes for Luke an event envisaged in strikingly spatial terms: Jesus is 'lifted up' bodily in front of his disciples, then taken out of their sight by a cloud (1:9). The inner circle of twelve apostles and witnesses of the resurrection is restored with the selection of Matthias (1:21–26). While for Luke the ascension pauses all further earthly encounters with the risen Christ until his return (1:11), Paul's encounter with Jesus on the Damascus Road is described three times in terms of an individually granted 'heavenly vision' (26:19; cf. 9:3–7; 22:6–10; 26:12–18). One subsequent ecstatic vision in the Temple grants Paul to hear and 'see Jesus' (22:18).

### John

The Fourth Gospel has Peter and the Beloved Disciple racing to the tomb at Mary Magdalene's news and finding in it only the folded gravecloths – enough for the Beloved Disciple to 'see and believe' (20:8). Mary meanwhile, lingering by the tomb, meets the risen Jesus whom she initially mistakes for a gardener and who forbids her to touch him (20:17). Appearing later through closed doors to ten of the disciples to commission and empower them with the Holy Spirit, Jesus returns a week later to overcome the doubts of the previously absent Thomas, who unlike Mary is invited to touch his wounded side. An additional resurrection appearance at the Sea of Galilee involves a miraculous catch of fish and a meal, during which Jesus rehabilitates Simon Peter and appoints him as pastor of his flock (21:1–23).

### Paul

Part of Paul's own formative instruction which he then transmitted to new believers at Corinth, our earliest attested sequence (1 Cor 15:3–7) makes no explicit mention of the tomb or of women as the first to discover it. It features appearances to Cephas (i.e. Peter) and 'the Twelve' (i.e. presumably including Matthias) but uniquely also to James, to 'five hundred' believers at once, to 'all the apostles' – and ultimately to Paul himself: Paul 'saw' Jesus as no one after him did (1 Cor 9:1; 'last of all', 15:8) and received a distinctive apostolic 'revelation' of Jesus (Gal. 1:16).

### MAKING SENSE OF CONFLICTING TRADITIONS

These and similar considerations have seemed to many critics to subvert the credibility of the sources in a jumble of contradictions about such matters as the times and locations of the appearances, the named individuals involved, and the accessibility of Jesus in the body or form in which he appears. Attempts to integrate and harmonize a single narrative have certainly not been lacking, but none has gained widespread acceptance. Sceptical interpreters through the ages have assured each other that the phenomena are reducible to individual and group hallucinations or visions, suggesting either that the earliest tradition had no knowledge of an empty (if indeed any) tomb or else that empty tombs were of course hardly out of the ordinary in antiquity. On this account, once tomb and appearance stories had begun to accumulate, each new feature was developed in response to the immediate apologetic and pastoral needs of the evangelist's respective community.

Such reductionist 'nothing but' accounts may flatter scholarly prejudice but rarely do justice to historical realities. For Paul, for example, the argument of 1 Corinthians 15:3–7 explicitly reproduces as authoritative a catechesis received from apostolic communities in Judaea, long before his arrival in Corinth in the year 50/51. This, however, is to endorse his dependence on a normative tradition that evidently trumps his preferred declaration of an apostolic pedigree directly authorized and at least equivalent to that of the Jerusalem apostles (e.g. Gal 1:11–19, 2:1–10; 1 Cor 3:22–4:1; 2 Cor 11:5, 22–23). Unlike all four of the evangelists, Paul does not explicitly mention an empty tomb. And yet, to affirm it alongside a resurrection would for a Jew be tautologous: the fact that the body of Jesus was 'buried' leaves no room for any form of it to remain in the tomb (cf. Wright 2003, 321). Throughout the chapter, it is a non-negotiable pillar of Paul's interpretation that resurrection life is fundamentally 'bodily' (15:35–58).

The New Testament documents do assert a consensus on the truth and significance of the resurrection witness (note 1 Cor 15:11). The continuing narrative mayhem of the various accounts, even four or five decades after the event, may itself bear eloquent testimony to the force of this consensus. 'Calculated deception should have produced greater unanimity. Instead, there seem to have been competitors: "I saw him first!" "No! I did"' (Sanders 1993, 280). The surprising but undeniable convergence of these competing convictions in the Easter affirmations suggests a generative event of irreducibly colossal magnitude (cf. Hoskyns and Davey 1981, 282–84). A similar dynamic may be at work in the question of whether it was Peter (1 Cor 15:5) or rather, as in all four gospels, Mary Magdalene and the women disciples who first witnessed the resurrection and thus became 'apostles of the apostles'.

### EVIDENCE AND TESTIMONY

The Easter narratives point to an event in historical time and space and yet which is not straightforwardly ordered and sequenced within historical time and space. This intrinsic polyvalence requires further comment. Luke, John, and Paul are particularly committed to the factual nature of the resurrection, established by 'convincing proofs' (so Acts 1:4). At no point, however, do these early Christian sources treat the resurrection witness as 'evidence that demands a verdict' – or even in the positive conviction that 'no other explanation could or would do' to explain an empty tomb and appearances (Wright 2003, 717).

Even on a comprehensively sympathetic reading, the 'facts' are far from self-interpreting. We know of many empty first-century tombs, other messiahs who died a violent death, and many crucified men (some of whose skeletons, like Yohanan at Jerusalem's Giv'at ha-Mivtar, have turned up with a nail still stuck through their ankles). Ancient tomb robbery was a thriving industry; and as both Matthew (28:13) and John (20:13) already knew, an empty tomb can be interpreted in a variety of other ways – not all of them self-evidently absurd.

None of the New Testament authors claim to be eyewitnesses. The risen Jesus repeatedly proves difficult or ambiguous to identify, even for close followers (Matt 28:17; Luke 24:16; John 20:14–15, 21:4); Mark's longer ending even speaks of him appearing 'in another form' (16:12). As a result, any synoptic reading of the different sources may leave us with considerable bewilderment about who saw what, where, when, and how. The Easter encounters repeatedly occasion both faith and doubt even in the very people who saw the risen Jesus and worshipped him (e.g. Matt 28:17, 'but they hesitated' (my translation)).

Documentary archives and public records might well certify a crucifixion but could not do so for a resurrection. Although the firm conviction of the early Christians certainly claims to be factual, it depends not on forensic 'evidence' but on a reliable tradition authenticated by apostolic eyewitness. As the Peter of Acts puts it, God granted Jesus to appear 'not to all the people, but to us who were chosen by God as witnesses, and who ate and drank with him after he rose from the dead' (10:41). It is the apostles, and only they, who are able and indeed 'commanded' to serve as guarantors of the resurrection tradition (10:42; cf. Acts 1:22, 25; 1 Cor 9:1; John 19:35; 21:24; 1 John 1:1–3).

What is 'doubting' (*apistos*) about the Fourth Gospel's Thomas is not his desire for facts but his emphatic refusal to trust the apostolic testimony: 'unless [I see and touch him], I will not believe' (John 20:25, 27, 29).

(Even then, of course, he does not abandon the community of faith – and so is present to encounter Jesus the second time round.)

The apostolic writers, then, did not attempt to mount some sort of watertight 'proof' of the resurrection. But they evidently did find themselves confronted with a series of diversely experienced encounters that required interpretation and appropriation in profoundly theological terms. Their conclusions were reached not on the basis of a rationally unassailable or psychologically comfortable case (to James and Paul, at least, it manifestly was not) but because the Jesus they encountered was emphatically alive and present calling and committing them to his mission. As commentators have noted since antiquity, the resurrection encounters almost invariably have a converting and energizing effect on those who were until that point doubtful, demoralized, or opposed, and would have remained so without them (e.g. Chrysostom *Hom. 1 Cor.* 4.4 on 1:25, PG 61:36; cf. further Atkins 2019).

This reality of a transformative encounter with the present Jesus best accounts for the talk of 'resurrection'. The New Testament resurrection accounts are not literary constructs but rather 'derive ultimately from people's real experiences, however curious' (Allison 2021, 345). Getting to grips with such inexplicable and yet undeniable events would inevitably distend the available language and categories of explanation to breaking point.

## THE LANGUAGE OF 'RESURRECTION'

But why would the early witnesses resort to the rather distinctive Jewish language of 'resurrection' in describing the Easter experiences? The walking dead getting up from their coffins were, after all, an uncommon but repeatedly attested phenomenon until the advent of modern medicine. Jesus, too, was credited with returning newly dead people to life at Capernaum, Nain, and Bethany (Mark 5:35–41 parr.; Luke 7:11–16; John 11:38–44). Even the gospels report some of his Jewish contemporaries believing that prophets recent or ancient might be 'raised from the dead' and walk among the living (Mark 6:14–16; 8:28; 9:12 parr.; cf., e.g., 2 Macc 15:13–16; b. *B. Meṣ.* 59b). Moses and Elijah were believed to have been assumed bodily to heaven rather than buried; both attended later Jewish teachers from Rabbi Akiva in the second century to Shabbetai Tzvi in the seventeenth. Greco-Roman stories, too, are familiar with the motifs of finding unexpectedly empty tombs whose occupants subsequently reappear alive and well (e.g. Chariton's probably second-century novel *Chaireas and Callirhoë*, bk. 3). Various historical heroes posthumously appeared to their followers, underwent apotheosis, and even became the subjects of new and thriving cults (examples range from Roman emperors to philosophical figures like Apollonius of Tyana).

Beginning no later than the second century, Celsus and other critics of Christianity began to make the most of such apparent analogies (e.g. Origen, *C. Cels.* 2.55–58). Regardless of their polemical intent or critical merit, several of these parallels clearly document the extent to which popular Jewish and Greco-Roman cultural typologies would render intelligible the reception as well as the propagation of a resurrected and ascended Jesus.

That said, none of these cases concerns someone publicly crucified as a common criminal. More importantly, none parallels the specifically Jewish apocalyptic connotation of the claim that the Easter events mark the 'resurrection' as God's victory at the beginning of a new creation – an idea consonant with Jewish interpretation of prophetic books like Isaiah, Hosea, Ezekiel, and Daniel (cf. further Levenson 2006). In both Judaism and Hellenism, the mere apparition or exaltation of a dead hero was perfectly conceivable without entailing either a bodily resurrection or the idea that God had thereby inaugurated the life of the world to come.

Precisely the assurance of resurrection, however, is in the New Testament taken to authenticate Jesus as the messianic Son of David (Acts 2:31–36; 13:34–37; Rom 1:3–4; 2 Tim 2:8; Rev 22:16): God has raised, exalted, and established him as the Son of God empowered by the Spirit (e.g. Rom 1:4; Phil 2:19–10; Matt 28:18). The raising of Jesus functions as the onset, the analogous 'firstfruits', of the comprehensive, general resurrection (1 Cor 15:20, 23; cf., e.g., Matt 27:52–53; Rev 1:5). And thus the perishable, 'natural' (*psychikon*) body of this world is here contrasted with the immortal, 'spiritual' (*pneumatikon*) one (15:42, 44) of the world to come. To belong to this risen Lord is to share in 'indescribable and glorious joy' (1 Pet 1:8; cf. Luke 24:52; John 20:20), expectantly looking to participate in 'the power of his resurrection' (Phil 3:10–11). It was this decisiveness of the Easter events that understandably made their interpretation so highly charged: 'We know that Christ, being raised from the dead, will never die again; death no longer has dominion over him' (Rom 6:9).

If nothing else, such hyperbolic theological language shows that the assertion of Jesus's resurrection does in fact depart in important respects from all known contemporary typologies for empty tombs, apparitions, and apotheoses. The ancients knew full well that a *ghost* 'does not have flesh and bones' (Luke 24:39) and does not eat or drink but that a *resuscitated body* might easily have and do all those things. And yet, neither of these perfectly familiar and acceptable tropes is invoked by any of the diverse New Testament witnesses.

This intense cultural idiosyncrasy of the resurrection claim is well worth underlining: insofar as this is history, it is history with a heavy Palestinian Jewish accent. Matthew's Roman guards (27:62–66; 28:4), if they were indeed at the tomb and if they saw anything, would not and could not have described this in the apocalyptic language of 'resurrection' – be they adherents of the cult of the emperor, of Mithras, or even of Isis. Paul is later plausibly described as struggling to make himself understood by philosophers in Athens (Acts 17:18, 32), and Christianity's ancient intellectual critics returned to the supposed absurdity of this theme again and again (e.g. Celsus in Origen *C. Cels.* 5.14; 6.29). Neither, of course, would 'resurrection' be a natural point of reference for their supposed Sadducean paymasters, who are plausibly described as plotting to nip any populist hocus-pocus well and truly in the bud (Matt 27:62–66; 28:4, 11–15; cf. Acts 23:6–8).

In the context of first-century Pharisaic and apocalyptic Judaism, however, 'resurrection' was the only available terminology to name this otherwise unprecedented experience. Unparalleled events occasioned a unique language – in principle no less striking in the first century than in the twenty-first (cf. already Mark 9:10). For all its inalienable cultural idiosyncrasy, the angelic announcement that 'He is not here, for he has been raised' (Matt 28:6) encapsulates the only possible way in which Jewish followers of Jesus could explain the confusingly diverse and yet convergent experiences of both absence and presence that followed his crucifixion.

Had those experiences been either purely visionary or straightforwardly material in nature, Palestinian Judaism had plenty of narrative and conceptual devices to signal that fact, as other texts did. Certain Jewish visionary features do surface in the narratives and may indeed gain in poignancy from their Passover setting. But the plain sense of all the appearance accounts is nevertheless that the risen Jesus was encountered and seen, not 'visualized', as personally present.

Conventional categories, indeed, rapidly appear to founder on the reality that is being described, 'immanent' and 'transcendent' features often starkly clashing or juxtaposed. It is precisely Thomas's anatomically tactile Jesus who can be described as having entered, just a moment earlier, through locked doors (John 20:26)! Although evidently unanticipated by those who went on to embrace it, the only available category big enough to fit the reality turned out to be the eschatological affirmation of resurrection at the hands of the living God of Israel: 'This Jesus God raised up' (Acts 2:32).

The Christian language of 'resurrection' finds its origin in the circumstances of a specific time, place, and culture: those of first-century Jerusalem. It was Jerusalem's religious conflicts, political machinations, and colonial occupation which made Jesus a victim of juridical persecution as well as Roman torture and crucifixion. And it was in this city that he was first seen as risen from the dead – at once Jerusalem's victim and the vanquisher of Jerusalem's oppression (cf. Williams 1982, 7–28).

### HISTORY AND A RESURRECTED JESUS

We return, then, to the problem with which we began. There are good reasons to interpret the resurrection as a theological affirmation rooted in historical fact – at a minimum, in the discovery of an empty tomb followed by variously described encounters with its occupant. Regardless of the precise view one may take on the phenomenology of this foundational event, its historicity was quite evidently the logical and psychological precondition for any sort of continued 'Christian' existence. Without it, our sources would be silent: there could have been no abiding interest in either Jesus of Nazareth or the exalted Christ of faith. On this point the history of Christianity firmly holds together the bodily identity of Jesus of Nazareth with that of the risen and ascended Christ.

This point casts serious doubt on the romanticism of attempts, from Ernest Renan's in 1863 to the present day, to salvage something noble and admirable out of the plundered remains of an unresurrected Jesus. In that regard, the Pauline reasoning of 1 Corinthians entails a remarkably contemporary and sober realism: no resurrection, no Jesus.

> If Christ has not been raised, your faith is futile, and you are still in your sins. Then those also who have died in Christ have perished. If for this life only we have hoped in Christ, we are of all people most to be pitied.... If the dead are not raised, 'Let us eat and drink, for tomorrow we die'. (1 Cor 15:17–19, 32)

Far from being able to set aside a matter outside his or her purview, then, the conscientious historian of Jesus – precisely qua historian – is necessarily entangled in a matter of historical and more than historical consequence.

This entanglement is further reinforced by the extent to which a doctrine of resurrection appears to have been an important component of Jesus of Nazareth's own eschatology, rooted in his interpretation of Scripture, a connection that is not lost on the evangelists themselves. All four of them explicitly relate the meaning of the resurrection to the teachings of Jesus. This is perhaps most powerfully evident in Jesus's so-called passion predictions, which in virtually every case include an explicit reference to resurrection (Mark 8:31, 9:31, 10:34 parr.; cf. also Mark 9:9; 12:10–11; 13:26; 14:25, 28; Matt 12:40, 27:63; Luke 24:6–7, 46; John 2:20–22; 11:25).

Although at one time fashionably dismissed as late fabrications for the reassurance of doubting Christian minds, their pattern of righteous suffering and vindication is in contemporary scholarship more commonly linked to an ancient and well-documented tradition of Second Temple Judaism grounded in texts like Genesis 22, Job, Jonah, the righteous servant in Isaiah 53, the vindicated Son of Man in Daniel 7, the murdered firstborn of the house of David in Zechariah 12:10–13:1, and Psalms like 22, 69, and 118. Echoed widely throughout the gospels and in Jewish sources (e.g. Wisd 2; 2 Macc 6–7; 4 Macc 6, 17; 4Q225; cf. b. Ber. 56b; b. Sukk. 52a; Pirqe R. El. 31; cf. Yal. 575, 581 on Zech), this Jewish tradition evokes a pattern of the innocent sufferer's trust in God's faithfulness finding approval and assurance of ultimate vindication – not just for himself but for all his people. Even the well-attested but much-queried trope that such vindication was to take place 'on the third day according to the Scriptures' (1 Cor 15:3; Mark 8:31; 10:34 etc.) may well find its basis in reflection on texts like Hosea 6:2, which the Targum explicitly applies to the general resurrection (cf. also Matt 12:40 with Jonah 1:17 [=2:1 MT/LXX]).

Another example of Jesus of Nazareth's concern for the resurrection is his refutation of the sceptical Sadducees, in good Pharisaic fashion demonstrating the resurrection on the basis of the Torah (cf. m. Sanh. 10.1). Here, interestingly, the state of the resurrected is said to be 'like angels in heaven' (Mark 12:25). Although we should not perhaps overinterpret the implied phenomenology of his dig at apparently angel-denying opponents (Acts 23:8), Jesus's statement may bear out the New Testament's repeated placement of his resurrection, ascension, and return in the company of angels.

We may add, finally, that the Last Supper tradition offers further confirmation of this link in Jesus's mind. He connects his present suffering 'for many' with his future resurrection most strikingly in the Nazirite vow he takes on the eve of his arrest: 'Truly I tell you, I will never again drink of the fruit of the vine until that day when I drink it new in the kingdom of God' (Mark 14:25 parr.).

In other words, the apostolic Easter experiences actually converge with a recurrent theme in the ministry of Jesus himself, which makes the resurrection an important key to understanding the aspirations as well as the demise of the historical Jesus, in his own view and in that of his followers. Even before Easter, Jesus seems to have implied that his own violent death would need to be interpreted back to front, as it were. He cast his fate deliberately within the scriptural framework of suffering and vindication. In that context, his death at the hands of his enemies could only be understood in the light of what would happen – or fail to happen – afterwards.

Significantly, his followers continued to give dramatic expression to that correlation in their continued meal fellowship, meeting specifically 'on the first day of the week', the day of the resurrection, to commemorate Jesus's Last Supper and death and to participate in his presence in bread and wine (see, e.g., Acts 20:7; 1 Cor 16:2; Did. 14.1; 1 Cor 10:16; 11:23–27; Justin *1 Apol.* 65–67).

## RESURRECTION AND ASCENSION, PRESENCE AND PAROUSIA

Whatever happened to the risen Jesus? Only Luke narrates a visible, space-time ascension of Jesus to heaven, as we saw. But in fact all the early witnesses imply only a limited period of appearances – even if some, perhaps to accommodate Paul, later extended this from Luke's forty days to eighteen months (Irenaeus *Haer.* 1.3.2, 30.14; Apocryphon of James). And they consistently connect his resurrection with his exaltation to God's heavenly glory and power.

The resurrection thus entails a Jesus who is alive as well as exalted, both here and not-here, present both to the world and to the majesty of God, in heaven yet near and coming. His presence is bodily, personal, and continuous with Jesus of Nazareth, though not now visible and tangible until his Parousia, his coming in glory: his resurrected bodily ascension to heaven underwrites his coming from heaven in that same resurrected body (Acts 1:11). Although raised from the dead, he still bears the scars of his sacrifice in the crucifixion – a point deployed apologetically in the gospels (Luke 24:39; John 20:25–28) but perhaps also christologically of the heavenly Lamb 'standing as if it had been slaughtered' (Rev 5:6) – his woundedness, it seems, is not eliminated but glorified (a perspective that has found an evocative but theologically challenging application to disability studies: e.g. Brock 2019; more critically, Moss 2019).

Although expressed quite diversely, a comparable striking bodily and spatial dialectic recurs across the range of early Christian writings. The end of the appearances and the present hiddenness of Jesus matter no less than his nearness and real presence in time and space.

That real presence in turn is multiply mediated through the Spirit of God. This mediation occurs 'sacramentally', above all in eucharistic remembrance of his death and in baptism 'into' his death and resurrection (a reality of new creation whose conception ranges from the believer's identifying with Christ's crucifixion for the intended purpose of participating in resurrection life, to a present incorporation into death, resurrection, and even exaltation with him: Rom 6:4, 8, 11; Phil 3:10–12; Col 3:1–4; Eph 2:5–6). Mediation of the risen Jesus's presence also occurs in his body that is the church (its mission and teaching, its service of the poor, its worship and fellowship and judgement) as well as in the body of his apostle, in Jesus's word and authority, and even in apostolic writings about him. Some believers are granted one or more direct encounters with a post-ascension vision or voice of Jesus – beginning with the apostle Paul himself. Far from an attempt to compensate for a Christology of absence, as is sometimes claimed, the ascension of the risen Jesus instead inaugurates 'the new, definitive, and insuppressible form of his presence ... working through the power of his Spirit' (Benedict XVI 2009).

## MYTH OR METAPHOR?

This strikingly integrative function of the resurrection of Jesus is consistently echoed and appropriated in the New Testament and patristic writings. Paul knew the crucifixion to be 'a stumbling block to Jews and foolishness to the Greeks' (1 Cor 1:23) – and without the resurrection, faith is therefore futile. Precisely because of it, however, the cross can and does assume the redemptive significance that apparently already begins to be envisaged for it in Jesus's own teaching (e.g. Mark 10:45; 14:22–24 and parallels). Even the earliest traditions already stress the resurrection's integral role in vindicating the purpose of his life and death, confirming him as Son of God 'with power' and validating the crucifixion 'for our sins' by being raised 'for our justification' (Rom 1:3–4; 4:25). Christians, like their critics, were well aware that Jesus's crucifixion and resurrection stand and fall together: without the latter, the former would remain a pointless moral void, a failure; there would be nothing of consequence for believers to believe (1 Cor 15:17–19, 32).

Whether or not one deems that early Christian reasoning persuasive, it is important to recognize it for what it is: an attempt to do interpretative justice to Jesus of Nazareth within the first-century world that he himself inhabited, and to identify the implications for his followers' life and faith. 'God raised Jesus from the dead' has consequences: 'what we can know historically about Christ's resurrection must not be abstracted from the question of what we can hope from it, and what we have to do in its name' (Moltmann 1996, 80).

The resurrection is indeed a kind of religious metaphor, as is sometimes rather too blithely asserted – but its function is quite the opposite of conventional religious metaphors. From Plato's Cave to C. S. Lewis's Narnia, such metaphors employ the literal and familiar to speak (one hopes truthfully) of an otherworldly reality. The New Testament witness to the resurrection of Jesus, by contrast, finds only an eschatological reality adequate to describe a historical one, and only transcendent language sufficient to capture a bodily event. Heaven is no longer a metaphor of earthly bliss, or the world to come a pleasant postscript to mortality. Instead, Easter claims a newly redeemed earthly reality as a metaphor of heaven and transforms mortal life into the vestibule of paradise. Along similar lines, the resurrection resembles a myth turned inside out: for the pagan apologist Sallustius, the genius of the ancient myths is that 'these things never happened, but always are' (*On the Gods and the World*, 1). By contrast, Christian writers like Justin, Clement, and Eusebius saw the myths and philosophies of antiquity as vaguely adumbrated hopes and truths that in the incarnation and resurrection of Jesus came to real embodied fruition.

The resurrection inaugurates the defining historical, moral, and ecological reality that is the 'new creation' (O'Donovan 1994). The risen and ascended body of Jesus sanctifies and will transform the bodies of all who belong to him: he will turn their humiliation and 'bondage to decay' into the freedom of divine glory, in the process destroying death itself (Rom 8:21–3; Phil 3:21; 1 Cor 15:26). This cosmic reach of the New Testament's Easter message is dramatically captured in the classic Orthodox Easter icons: the risen Jesus, ascending to heaven, extends his hand to raise up the awaking dead.

'God raised Jesus from the dead' marks the liminal point at which the identity of Jesus is confirmed ('with power', as Romans 1: 4 puts it). It affirms not an earthly 'coming back to life' (resuscitation) but his bodily inauguration of the life of God's sovereign new creation of the world, being exalted in his human body as the pioneer of its heavenly and permanent redemption. For any narrowly self-styled 'historical criticism' intent on bracketing it out, the resurrection must inevitably remain a historical reality that is both awkward and unsatisfactory. Had we no knowledge of it, study of Jesus would be neither interesting nor, given the concomitant absence of sources, remotely possible. Yet the resurrection is *historical* in the sense of being located at a moment in the past that has a before and after, which was experienced and attested by other historical human beings, and whose proximate and more distant effects are utterly instrumental to the course of history. And yet, it also constitutes a transcendent reality which 'inexorably changes the register' of the available experiential and linguistic range of analogy (Williams 1996, 91).

## FURTHER READING

Alkier, Stefan. 2013. *The Reality of the Resurrection: The New Testament Witness*. Translated by L. A. Huizenga. Waco: Baylor University Press.
Allison, Dale C. 2021. *The Resurrection of Jesus*. London: T & T Clark.
Bryan, Christopher. 2011. *The Resurrection of the Messiah*. New York: Oxford University Press.
Elledge, C. D. 2017. *Resurrection of the Dead in Early Judaism, 200 BCE–CE 200*. Oxford: Oxford University Press.
Farrow, Douglas. 2011. *Ascension Theology*. London: T & T Clark.
Habermas, Gary R. 2021. *Risen Indeed: A Historical Investigation into the Resurrection of Jesus*. Ashland: Lexham Press.
Levenson, Jon D. 2006. *Resurrection and the Restoration of Israel: The Ultimate Victory of the God of Life*. New Haven: Yale University Press.
Levering, Matthew. 2019. *Did Jesus Rise from the Dead? Historical and Theological Reflections*. Oxford: Oxford University Press.
Licona, Mike. 2010. *The Resurrection of Jesus: A New Historiographical Approach*. Downers Grove: IVP Academic/Apollos.
Setzer, Claudia. 2004. *Resurrection of the Body in Early Judaism and Early Christianity: Doctrine, Community, and Self-Definition*. Leiden: Brill.
Williams, Rowan. 1982. *Resurrection: Interpreting the Easter Gospel*. London: Darton, Longman & Todd.
Wright, N. T. 2003. *The Resurrection of the Son of God*. London: SPCK.

# 6 Jesus and the Triune God
LEWIS AYRES

Most Christian traditions owe their fundamental visions of creation and salvation to the creedal and conciliar traditions of the early church, not only the Catholic, Orthodox and Oriental Orthodox traditions but also those traditions stemming from the sixteenth-century reformations. For all of these traditions, we can only understand who Jesus Christ was by thinking of him and his work in the context of Trinitarian belief. Although these communions would put the matter in a variety of different ways, the matrix of Trinitarian and christological belief which evolved in the patristic period is not understood by them primarily as a supplement to the Scriptures but as a drawing out and formulating of Scripture's meaning and depths.

For many Protestant traditions the Scriptures, as the authoritative witness to the Word spoken in the world, will still be understood as the norm within which creedal formulations should be interpreted. For some less creedal groups, such as the Baptist or Wesleyan/Methodist traditions, principles that owe a great deal to the early creeds have always been taken as particularly suitable guides to the meaning of Scripture. Within the Catholic and Orthodox traditions, the apostolic preaching ordered by the work of Christ and the Spirit is seen to have resulted both in a written Scripture and in the life of the church where that Scripture is proclaimed and understood. The creedal teaching of the church is thus not to be envisaged over against Scripture so much as an integral part of a unified tradition that is Scripture's natural home. Just as the 'New' Testament is a divinely inspired reading of the Old, so the church's teaching tradition is an inspired drawing out of Scripture's depths – even given the coincident insistence that Scripture holds a unique place as revealed.

Given all of this, if we are to understand how Christ is perceived in the context of classical Trinitarian theology, we can do little better than consider how the doctrinal conflicts of the early church shaped a vision of Christ (for a short and elegant introduction, see Wilken 2003). Those conflicts are often divided into two, the Trinitarian controversies of the fourth century (those which often used to be called the 'Arian' controversy) and the christological controversies that beset the Christian world from the fifth to the seventh century. From one perspective this division is helpful, if for no other reason than that the christological controversies of later centuries occurred among those who shared Nicene Trinitarian beliefs. But from another perspective this division is unhelpful because both phases of this controversy concerned overlapping questions that deeply shape how one envisages the character of salvation and the identity of Christ.

## NICENE TRINITARIAN THEOLOGY

The story of the fourth-century controversies has been told many times and scholars are constantly struggling to find new and more adequate ways to draw together the evidence we have. For our purposes only the most cursory narratives will suffice (for more, see Ayres 2004; for a selection of texts, see Radde-Gallwitz 2017). A conflict arose in Alexandria involving a priest called Arius. This controversy spread across the eastern Mediterranean and eventually the emperor Constantine called a council of bishops to Nicaea in 325. Those bishops produced a short creed which described the Son as born 'from the essence of the Father' and as 'consubstantial with' (*homoousios*) the Father. Exactly what they meant by those terms is not clear (although we do know that the terms were intended to exclude Arius!), but it is clear that Nicaea was the beginning and not the end of a controversy. The controversy that had erupted around Arius brought to the surface debates that had rumbled on since the second century about how Christians should speak of the Word, Wisdom or Son of God that was in Christ. It was only in the last decades of the fourth century that anything like a resolution to this conflict was found as new formulations of Trinitarian faith emerged.

The controversy that broke out in the early fourth century concerned the status of the Word or Son or Wisdom. The earliest Christians adapted a wide range of existing Jewish terminologies and passages from the Hebrew Bible to speak of a reality that existed alongside or in the divine: the divine name, glory, wisdom, word, the angel of the Lord, alongside the visions of Daniel and Ezekiel. These terminologies offered multiple resources for thought and multiple ways of understanding the relationship between God and what was in Christ. Already in the first century, in some of the documents that would be incorporated into the canonical New Testament, the tendency of Christians to attribute divine titles to Christ is clear.

In the first couple of centuries of the Christian era we see a number of styles of talking about who was in Christ, and questions of monotheism and divine generation are already central. In the first place, Christians understood themselves to believe in the one God who was the source of all: in a common second-century phrase, in a God who enclosed everything but was enclosed by nothing. However the Word or Son was to be envisaged, monotheism was non-negotiable. Some figures approached this problem by finding ways to speak of the Son's generation from the Father as a Word once thought and now expressed, or light from light. Others explored ways of speaking that more directly presented the Son as a distinct lesser being, identifying the Son as unique and yet within the context of monotheism. Different traditions of thought were able to appeal to different scriptural resources to articulate their positions.

In the early fourth century, Arius taught that the Son was a unique but distinct reality appearing before time as we know it and for the purpose of creation. The true God does not act directly in the world but sends the Son or Word. Arius's bishop, Alexander of Alexandria, on the other hand, while still in some sense treating the Son as an intermediary between the Father and the World, saw the Father–Son relationship as eternal. If God is eternally Father, then he eternally has a Son. Various terminologies and analogies were marshalled to present the Son as born from the Father, and yet without a division of divinity, as distinct but in a unique relationship of origin. Arguing along these lines offered a vision of God's immediate presence in the world that pointed forward to the basic assumptions of what would become classical Trinitarian orthodoxy. But these two positions were not simply those of individuals; both could find supporters throughout the Christian world, and although there are not simply two groups involved here, we are able (with caution) to talk about different family groupings among the many ways of approaching this problem. Over the sixty years following Nicaea this controversy raged, the various traditions involved also gradually evolving.

From the early 360s, we see emerging a set of basic principles that would constitute the basis for the theological vision that has since been known as Nicene, although a number of its key principles were not stated by those present at Nicaea many years before. The Council of Constantinople in 381 reiterated the faith of Nicaea along with a creed that is probably a revision of the original, but it is these broader principles that were the context within which the participants at the 381 council thought their creed should be understood – and which provided the context for understanding who Christ was.

What then are the marks of this later Nicene theology? Four basic principles stand out. First, God is one simple power, glory, majesty, essence, rule, Godhead and nature. It is important to note that this list contains a variety of terms, each of which had its own resonances. Of particular importance is that which comes first, power. This was a term with a rich metaphysical history, and it emphasised that God must be one reality or nature, because every nature showed its own power (just as it is intrinsic to fire to give off heat). The same term also helped to reinforce the belief that Christians believed in one God – Trinitarian theology does not work against Christians being monotheists – it is rather the form that Christian monotheism takes.

Second, there are three persons. And again, while in Greek the term *hypostasis* becomes central (and in Latin *persona*), originally all sorts of terms were acceptable; what mattered was that the three persons were irreducible. The clearly *Trinitarian* statement that there are *three* is a consequence of the later stages of the fourth-century controversies when the status of the Spirit also came under question. Nicene theologians such as Athanasius of Alexandria, Basil of Caesarea and Didymus the Blind were key figures in articulating why and how Christians should speak of the Spirit as coequal with Father and Son. As we shall see, doing so was of considerable significance for how Nicene theology speaks about the identity and work of Christ.

Third, each of the three is the fullness of what it is to be God – Son and Spirit were not only fully God in conjunction with the other two. To say this would have meant that each lacked something of the fullness of divinity. Instead, each divine person is fully God *and* is fully God with the other two. This is a seeming paradox for us because there are no realities in the created order with these characteristics. As each of the three is fully God, what is it that distinguishes them? It is their relations of origin. In other words, the Son is in all things the same as the Father except insofar as he is begotten and is eternally from the Father; the Spirit is eternally in a particular relationship to Father and Son and it is only this that distinguishes the Spirit. In different forms this principle emerges in Latin- and Greek-speaking theology, and it further serves to emphasise the coequality of the three.

Fourth, the three persons operate inseparably; in every action of one person, the other two are acting. Thus although we say, correctly, that the Son alone became incarnate, we must also confess that in the Son becoming incarnate the Father and the Spirit are also at work.

This perspective on every action is of great importance when we consider the sending of the Son and his death and resurrection. It forces us to fight against simple accounts of, say, the Father acting on the Son (or giving up the Son), and which present the Son as a passive agent.

While we may seem to have strayed some way from talking directly about Christ, Nicene Trinitarian theology provides the fundamental context for understanding and interpreting Christ's life, ministry and death, as well as the events of the resurrection, ascension and continuing action of Christ in the creation. Perhaps the most important consequence is that Son and Spirit are not seen as mediatorial beings operating between a distant God and the created order; and thus Christ, as the Incarnate Word, simply *is* God active in the world.

There is much more to be said here, and to start that discussion I will take an illustration. Let us look briefly at Augustine's understanding of the Eucharist and hence the church in a famous passage of his *The City of God*. He begins here by commenting on the nature of true sacrifice:

> [Since] true sacrifices are works of mercy shown to ourselves or to our neighbours and done with reference to God, and since works of mercy have no other object than to set us free from misery and to make us blessed, and since this cannot be done other than through that good of which it is said, 'it is good for me to draw near to the city of God': it surely follows that the whole of the redeemed city – that is the congregation and fellowship of the saints – is offered to God as a universal sacrifice for us through the great high priest who, in his passion, offered even himself for us in the form of a servant, so that we might be the body of so great a head ... This is the sacrifice of Christians: 'we being many, are one body in Christ'. And this also, as the faithful know, is the sacrifice which the Church continually celebrates in the sacrament of the altar, by which she demonstrates that she herself is offered in the offering that she makes to God. (*City of God* 10.6; Dyson 1998, 399–400)

True sacrifices are works of mercy performed with reference to God, and they are performed by drawing near to the city of God – by which Augustine refers to growth in love and contemplation of God. But how do we draw near to God? We do so, for Augustine, because we are drawn *into* Christ and thus offered to the Father. Elsewhere in his corpus Augustine explains that, as he ascends to the Father, Christ draws us into himself and 'animates' his body through the gift of the Spirit. Christ is a complex reality, both one person with us and yet also the head who goes on before the body. But note that Christ can draw us into himself such that we are mysteriously one person with him only because he possesses as his own the full power of divinity. The Spirit is also the fullness of God immediately and intimately present with those drawn into Christ. Thus, in the background to the theology laid out in this passage is an account of the inseparable operation of Son and Spirit as fully God present to us and transforming us.

When Augustine speaks in this passage about Christ offering both himself to God *and* offering the church that is because Christians are in Christ. In the Eucharist, then, we both truly receive Christ, for Augustine, and we receive (as he says elsewhere) 'what we are' (because we are in Christ). It is because Augustine sees Christ and the Spirit as fully God that he is able to present this eucharistic account of our being drawn into the exchange of love in the Trinity. Indeed, we should note how this picture, while it focuses on the Eucharist, covers an understanding of Christ's sacrifice in the widest sense. Because Augustine reads the New Testament's accounts of Christ dying for humanity in the light of his Nicene Trinitarian theology, he emphasises the mystery of the event as an inner-Trinitarian exchange. Christ is not purely sent by the Father at a distance; the Son also sends himself and is never somehow separate from the Father or the Spirit. For Augustine, the Spirit is God and is Love – he takes literally 1 John 4.16's statement that God is Love – and so Christians love through the presence of the Spirit, God, within them. One need not follow all of Augustine's particular vision to see that classical Trinitarian theology has significant consequences for how one understands the events of Christ's death and resurrection, as well as the life of the church. At the very least, but a vital 'least', placing those events in the context of Trinitarian theology forces the theologian to examine carefully where mystery must attend simply because we speak of divine power and of the inseparability of the divine persons. Here, for example, Christ's unity with us is a mystery and results in expressions that can seem paradoxical, because Word and Spirit operate with divine power to draw us into Christ's person.

As I noted, not all theologians of the period paralleled Augustine's striking vision; he shows us just one version of the ways in which understanding Christ as the (fully divine) Word made flesh enabled an account of Christians' participation in Christ. Another is found in the way that a number of theologians made use of the principle that God became human, that humans might become God – a theology often summed up by the terms *theosis* or deification. Such theologies are able to present Christ as the means by which humanity is transformed because he is God present with us. The same theologies are able to present the work of the Spirit as incorporating us into Christ, or as 'deifying' because the Spirit is now understood as the immediate presence of God with us. At the same time, reflection on the existence of all things in Christ – as the one through whom all things were created – meshes with reflection on Christ as the one who restores creation. In both cases, new firmly Nicene visions of creation are possible in which the created order exists in the immediate presence of God. It is because Son (or Word or Wisdom) and Spirit share the divine nature and divine power that they transcend all the conditions of temporality and materiality that are so inescapable for us, and this can be immediately present to us. All of this flows from the clarities of Nicene Trinitarian theology.

ONE AND THE SAME LORD

It is time now to look to the controversies of the period after the fifth century that focus directly on the constitution of Christ's person. In the early fifth century a controversy arose between Cyril, bishop of Alexandria, and Nestorius, originally from Antioch and now bishop of Constantinople (see Daley 2018; Williams 2018). The controversy began over whether it was appropriate to accord Mary the title of *Theotokos* – 'God-Bearer' or 'Mother of God' – but both parties knew that this concerned fundamental questions about the person of Christ. This controversy shows us two figures both assuming the principles of a late fourth-century Trinitarian theology and trying to work out some of its implications for how we understand Christ. Nestorius insists very strongly on the transcendence of the Word, coequal with Father and Spirit, and because of this he tends to separate Christ's humanity from his divinity. For Nestorius, what is born is the humanity of Christ, not his divinity, and hence Mary could appropriately be termed *Christotokos* – bearer of Christ – but not *Theotokos*. When Nestorius tries to explain what happens on the cross, he uses language that separates the humanity and the divinity starkly:

> [T]he incarnate God did not die; he raised up the one in whom he was incarnate. He stooped down to raise up what had collapsed, but he did not fall ... if you want to lift up someone who is lying down, do you not touch body with body and, by joining yourself to the other person, lift up the hurt one...? (Nestorius, *First Sermon against the Theotokos*; Norris 1980, 125)

The language that Nestorius uses here speaks *as if* we are discussing two realities – to his opponents it easily sounds as if he means two *persons* – and the analogy he offers does not help, speaking as it does of one person picking up another. That Nestorius's commitment to Nicene Trinitarian theology is an important part of the background can be seen when, just a few lines later, he quotes Hebrews 1.3's 'the Son is the radiance of his glory' to describe Christ as coequal with the Father and hence sharing the Father's eternity. This text had been much debated in the fourth century and used to promote Nicene theology. Because of it – and John 1.1–3 – Nestorius tells us that we are preserved from misinterpreting Philippians 2.5–7 and thinking that the Word truly changed from being to not being in the form of God. Nicene Trinitarian theology thus drives Nestorius to distinguish quite sharply the human from the divine in Christ. In fairness we must note that after he had been deposed and was in exile, Nestorius wrote at length trying to show that he had not intended the strong separation of which he had been accused; but his emphasis, at least, is clear.

Cyril of Alexandria, on the other hand, holds to a Trinitarian theology equally Nicene, but he sees the character of divine action rather differently. It is *because* the Son works with the full power of divinity that he can take to himself a human reality in true unity. He writes, for example, as follows:

> [Speaking of the Nicene creed] ... these doctrines we too must follow, taking note of the Word of God's 'being incarnate' and 'being made man.' We do not mean that the nature of the Word was changed and made flesh, or, on the other hand, that he was transformed into a complete man consisting of body and soul, but instead we affirm this: that the Word substantially united to himself flesh endowed with life and reason, in a manner mysterious and incomprehensible ... and that though the natures joined together to form a real unity are different, one and the same Christ and Son comes from them. (*Second Letter to Nestorius*, 3; Wickham 1983, 5–7)

> We confess that the very Son begotten of God the Father, Only-Begotten God, impassible though he is in his own nature, has (as the Bible says) suffered in flesh for our sake and that he was in the crucified body claiming the sufferings of his flesh as his own impassibly. By nature Life and personally the Resurrection though he exists and is, 'by God's grace,' he tasted 'death for every person' in surrendering his body to it ... we confess his return to life from the dead and his ascension into heaven when we perform in

Church the unbloody service, when we approach the sacramental gifts and are hallowed participants in the holy flesh and precious body of Christ ... [receiving] the personal, truly vitalizing flesh of God the Word himself. (*Third Letter to Nestorius*, 6–7; Wickham 1983, 21–23)

These two quotations take us to the heart of Cyril's vision, a vision which in its essentials became the teaching of the Christian church in both East and West until the Reformation and in many cases beyond. In the first passage Cyril emphasises that, no, the Word does not and cannot change; yet the Word of God takes to himself 'flesh endowed with life' – the phrasing of the Word taking to himself is vital here because it emphasises that the incarnate Christ is the result of an action of the Word and that the subject in the incarnate Christ – the centre of his personality if you will – is not a product of the union, but the Word. Were we to have met Christ in first-century Galilee we would have met the Word with his flesh. Now this mysterious union that does not involve the Word changing is 'mysterious and incomprehensible'; we can say what it is not and a few things about it, yes, but it is a unique union and escapes our comprehension. Cyril's account so far is one dependent on Trinitarian theology, on a conception of the Word as coeternal with Father and Spirit, and as operating with the power of God.

In the second passage we see a little of how this shapes his account of Christ's work. While the Word does not in a fundamental sense suffer, he does in a mysterious way suffer 'in his flesh.' Notice how different Cyril's patterns of speech are from those of Nestorius: Cyril does not allow us a hint of two 'persons'; rather, through the mysterious union between Word and his flesh (notice the possessive pronoun), the Word *does* suffer, but in his flesh. It is that transformed flesh, moreover, that becomes central to our salvation. When Cyril goes on to mention the Eucharist he speaks of us participating *in* the flesh of Christ which has become 'life-giving'. And thus, through the union that the Word brings about, the flesh becomes the means of our salvation. Every bit as much as Nestorius, Cyril is shaping an account of Christ and Christ's work that is founded in Nicene Trinitarian theology.

It is because of his divine status that the Word acts in and transforms his humanity into the vehicle of our redemption – that to which we are united in the church and that which we consume in the Eucharist. In the incarnation we encounter the Word, as he often states, with his 'life-giving flesh'. Thus Cyril sees Nicene Trinitarian theology as enabling and indeed demanding a vision of Christ as the immediate presence of the creating and redeeming Word in his flesh. In many ways the controversies that follow on for the next two centuries result in a reassertion of Cyril's central insight, amplified by a denser meditation on how we envisage the union between humanity and the Word.

Ultimately a council met at Chalcedon near Constantinople in 451 and drew up a statement of faith:

> Therefore, following the saintly fathers, we all with one voice teach the confession of one and the same Son, our Lord Jesus Christ; the same perfect in divinity and perfect in humanity, the same truly God and truly man, of a rational soul and a body; consubstantial (*homoousios*) with the Father as regards his divinity, and the same consubstantial (*homoousios*) with us as regards his humanity; like us in all things except for sin; begotten before the ages from the Father as regards his divinity, and in the last days the same for us and for our salvation from Mary, the virgin God bearer (*Theotokos*), as regards his humanity; one and the same Christ, Son, Lord, only-begotten, acknowledged in two natures (*physeis*) which undergo no confusion, no change, no division, no separation; at no point was the difference between the natures taken away through the union, but rather the property of both natures is preserved and comes together into a single person (*prosopon*) and a single subsistent being (*hypostasis*); he is not parted or divided into two persons (*prosopa*), but is one and the same only-begotten Son, God, Word, Lord Jesus Christ. (Tanner 1990, 86)

The first thing to note is the rather obvious parallelism: Christ is both one with us as human *and* one with the Father. The seeming paradox of Christ's being is, once again, heightened by Nicene theology because Jesus is not *like* God; he simply is one with the Father even as he is one with humanity. The fourfold expression – no confusion, no change, no division, no separation – carefully parallels two terms that emphasise the truth of the union and two that emphasise the irreducibility of the two natures. The goal is to highlight the mysterious paradox of this unique union.

But alongside this parallelism we also see a strong insistence on the fact that we speak of one character in the story of the Word's double birth. 'One and the same' Lord is born both in eternity and from Mary. And here we come again to a vital question for all classical Christology: who is the subject in Christ? Were we to meet and speak with Jesus would we be meeting with one who is the *result* of a union between the divine Word and a human being? In other words is the subject to whom we are speaking the result of the union and thus technically neither the human nature nor the Word of God? If one focuses on the use of 'one and the same' in Chalcedon's definition then the answer is a resounding no; the one with whom we would meet and speak *is* the Word with his flesh. Such an answer once again presses us to see the Incarnate Christ in a Trinitarian perspective and to recognise the immediacy with which God creates and saves. But if we concentrate on Chalcedon's paralleling of divine and human it can seem as if the unity of character is being undermined. It can seem as if the unity that results in Christ's flesh being transformed is not yet taken sufficiently seriously. And it was precisely such a perception that led many to reject Chalcedon and led to much significant controversy in the centuries that followed.

In a chapter of this size, once again, I will not try to tell the story in any detail. Rather, I will briefly consider two moments in that story that were decisive in shaping classical Christology's account of Christ in a Trinitarian context. The first moment is the first half of the sixth century. This period saw a number of attempts by Chalcedonians to find formulae of faith that would entice the opponents of Chalcedon into union. These ultimately failed, leading to the establishment of the non-Chalcedonian Christian communions (the 'Oriental Orthodox' of whom the largest remaining group are the Copts of Egypt), but they also led to an important clarification of the Chalcedonian tradition. One easy way of accessing this tradition is through attending to a work written by (or least one whose writing was supervised by) the emperor Justinian and published as the *Edict on the Right Faith* in 551. Justinian supports Chalcedon, but his emphasis is on Christ as the Incarnate Word in a form that directly echoes Cyril's language:

> [W]e do not accept that God the Word who worked miracles is someone other than the Christ who suffered, but we profess one and the same Jesus Christ our Lord, the Word of God incarnate and made man, and that his are both the miracles and the sufferings that he underwent voluntarily in the flesh. For neither did some man give himself for us, but the Word himself gave his own body for us, so that our faith and hope should not be in the humanity, but that we should place our faith in God the Word himself. (*Edict*, Price 2012, 130–31)

Christ is the Word with his flesh, and because the flesh is his we attribute to him the miracles and the suffering. For Justinian, imagining Christ in this way is fundamental if we are to be directed appropriately towards the God who has saved. That aspect of Chalcedon's definition which insists primarily on a balance between natures and on each having its own 'activity' is here encompassed by the prior insistence on the Word as the constant subject of all Christ's actions. It is this focus that becomes a foundation for the later tradition's interpretation of Chalcedon at least up until the Reformation.

The second moment I will consider here is the final phase of the christological controversies, which took place over the half-century between ca. 630 and 680. The great division among Christians in the eastern half of the Christian world was still that between Chalcedonians and anti-Chalcedonians (termed by their enemies 'monophysites'), and some still sought paths towards reunification. One path explored was to argue that, as a result of the union, we might speak of Christ as having one activity or energy, and later one will.

The principle that a distinct reality operates with its own activity or energy was rooted in a number of ancient philosophical traditions, and it had a comprehensibility that appealed even to those without deep philosophical learning. And thus, if we confess that Christ is truly one thing, then surely we can say that he has one activity or energy? But to the opponents of this position there was a fundamental mistake here, and once again while this may seem a rather obscure point, it gets to the heart of what it is to think about Jesus in a Trinitarian perspective.

Chalcedon certainly insisted on the unity of Christ's person, but it did so via a series of paradoxical statements, *because* that unity is of a form that we cannot comprehend. Divinity and humanity do not mix in the manner in which two created realities might, and the unity brought about by divine action can be both a true unity and yet one that lies beyond our comprehension. In the attempt to emphasise Christ's unity the assertion of a unitary activity in Christ pushed too far towards making the mystery of his unity comprehensible. But, of course, to deny that there is one activity leads us quite naturally to ask how we might comprehend there being more than one activity in a single person! This question bites particularly hard when we come to the question of Christ's wills.

The teaching that Christ had only one will followed directly on the arguments about his activity and it seemed to many a way of emphasising the unity of Christ in a way that might provide a formula for the unification of Christians. 'Will' seemed an important category and perhaps easier to discuss. And yet, here, the problems were in fact compounded rather than eased because they affect not only how we consider the union – how far can we imagine that union – but also how we think about Christ's human nature: if Christ had only one will, was it a human will or a divine? Now 'will' is a short word but one that encompasses many meanings. From one point of view when we speak of 'my will' we speak of a faculty most evident in my choices: I demonstrate that I am an individual with a will by choosing this rather than that. But from another point of view we may speak of will as something more like a fundamental desire. Thus, we may say that human beings have a natural will or desire for self-preservation. In this sense we are not talking about conscious choice but about a constitutive feature of each individual human being. All of these different senses of the term were available to Greek authors and come to play in this controversy. Quite naturally, when theologians began to focus on the question of Christ's will they were drawn to explore the interpretation of scriptural texts that seem directly pertinent, and one of the most hotly contested was Matthew 26:39, where Jesus, praying in the garden of Gethsemane, says, 'My Father, if it be possible, let this cup pass from me; nevertheless, not as I will, but as you will.'

One of the architects of the position established as christological orthodoxy at the Third Council of Constantinople in 680–81 was Maximus the Confessor (who was, by that point, dead). Leaping straight into his reading of Jesus's prayer in Gethsemane will take us to the heart of this final plank in classical theology's Trinitarian vision of Christ. Maximus argues, first, that Christ does not have the 'gnomic' will that we have as fallen human beings, a will that chooses between possibilities. Rather Christ's human nature has a 'natural' human will for such things as self-preservation. In the Gethsemane scene we see Christ give expression to his human will when he says 'Let this cup pass from me', but we can see that this human will, unencumbered by the problems that stem from fallenness, constantly gives itself up to the divine will, and thus Christ also prays 'but not my will ...'. Christ's person in no way sees a competitive relationship between two wills, but a perfect human natural will, sustained by Word and Spirit, gives itself constantly up to the Word with whom it is united. The Constantinopolitan Council of 680 offers a short statement which lacks some of Maximus's subtlety but which follows the same basic argument. What we might term the Chalcedonian principle is followed; as with Christ's two natures, Christ's two wills 'undergo no division, no change, no partition, no confusion'. And, even as this is true, the basic Cyrilline principle is also stated (and Cyril himself is specifically invoked), that the Word is the subject of all that occurs in Christ: 'believing our Lord Jesus Christ, even after his incarnation, to be one of the Holy Trinity and our true God ... the two natural wills and principles of action meet in correspondence [in his one *hypostasis*] for the salvation of the human race' (Tanner 1990: 129–30).

CONCLUSION

Like the Trinitarian debates that preceded them, the christological debates can be daunting when they are encountered for the first time. And yet, once we grasp their overall story and arc it is possible to see that they are fundamentally about articulating how we should understand Jesus in the context of Nicene Trinitarian theology. That theology demands of us that we recognise Christ as the Incarnate Word, as the Word with his flesh, that in Christ God is directly present to us. At the same time, we are called to recognise that the mysterious union that constitutes Christ is that; because it is brought about by divine power it is a priori incomprehensible to us. As theologians, our job is to say what can be said, especially in aid of identifying where the mystery rests and why, and to police our imaginations from saying too much. In undertaking this sometimes astringent task we are always drawing ourselves back to the fundamental principles of Trinitarian theology.

There are a number of ways in which the christological debates I have described left questions open and where a longer essay might trace centuries of subsequent discussion (for an excellent introduction to medieval Western debates and their continued utility, see White 2015). Exactly how to conceive of Christ's humanity as a real individual example of humanity and yet as being without its own personality except in the Word was a topic much discussed in the latter phase of the christological controversies and throughout subsequent centuries. Of more immediate relevance to Trinitarian theology, the role of the Spirit in the incarnate Christ is a topic much discussed but about which creeds and conciliar definitions say little. The bare principle that the Spirit is at work in the Word assuming flesh and in Christ's ministry, death and resurrection is clear, but the tradition offers a wide variety of paths for exploring how this is so. But finally, note that we have already discussed the importance of the Spirit's role in the context of the relationship of Christians to the risen Christ. I briefly explored the example of Augustine's ecclesiology to show one way in which classical Trinitarian theology sees Christ's salvific mission as only comprehensible by seeing Christians as drawn into Christ by the work of the Spirit. There are, then, questions left open by the early doctrinal definitions, and there are paths for thought shaped by them, but the fundamental framework is one which insists that Jesus Christ is only truly comprehended in Trinitarian perspective.

## FURTHER READING

Ayres, Lewis. 2004. *Nicaea and Its Legacy*. Oxford: Oxford University Press.
Daley, Brian E. 2018. *God Visible: Patristic Christology Reconsidered*. Oxford: Oxford University Press.
DelCogliano, Mark. 2022. *Christ: Through the Nestorian Controversy*. The Cambridge Edition of Early Christian Writings 3. Cambridge: Cambridge University Press.
Dyson, R. W., ed. 1998. *Augustine: The City of God Against the Pagans*. Cambridge Texts in the History of Political Thought. Cambridge: Cambridge University Press.
Norris, Richard A. 1980. *The Christological Controversy*. Philadelphia: Fortress.
Price, Richard. 2012. *The Acts of the Council of Constantinople of 553*. Liverpool: Liverpool University Press.
Radde-Gallwitz, Andrew, ed. 2017. *God*. The Cambridge Edition of Early Christian Writings 1. Cambridge: Cambridge University Press.
Tanner, Norman P., ed. 1990. *Decrees of the Ecumenical Councils*. 2 vols. Washington, DC: Georgetown University Press.
White, Thomas Joseph. 2015. *The Incarnate Lord: A Thomistic Study in Christology*. Washington, DC: Catholic University of America Press.
Wickham, Lionel R., ed. 1983. *Cyril of Alexandria: Select Letters*. Oxford Early Christian Texts. Oxford: Clarendon Press.
Wilken, Robert Louis. 2003. *The Spirit of Early Christian Thought: Seeking the Face of God*. New Haven: Yale University Press.
Williams, Rowan. 2018. *Christ the Heart of Creation*. London: Bloomsbury Continuum.

# 7 Jesus in the Scriptures of Israel

JENNIE GRILLO

The idea that Jesus could be in Israel's Scriptures will strike different audiences as either impossible or necessary, and perhaps both. On the one hand, to speak of Jesus *within* the Scriptures of Israel seems to violate historical possibility and a natural sense of justice that sees these writings as belonging properly to pre-Christian Judaism. On the other hand, the universal Christian practice from the earliest times has been to do exactly that, so that speaking of Jesus in the Scriptures of Israel is an utterly naturalized habit of Christian orthodoxy and piety. This chapter examines possible theological rationales for that habit which seek to address the legitimate historical and inter-religious questions. I consider and reject one widespread justification, but I propose a different traditional explanation which, I suggest, does justice both to the logic of Christian belief and to the real and ongoing character of these writings as Jewish Scripture.

Many readers have found Jesus within Israel's Scriptures in a strong ontological sense, in the anthropomorphic theophanies or angelophanies of the Old Testament. In the angel of the burning bush or the fourth figure in the fiery furnace of Daniel, Jesus was identified by scholars of another generation like Ernst Wilhelm Hengstenberg (1836–9, esp. 107–23) or Wilhelm Vischer (1949).[1] For example, Vischer writes of Jacob's nighttime fight with a mysterious figure in Genesis 32:

> And now we are able with Luther to say, 'without the slightest contradiction this man was not an angel, but our Lord Jesus Christ ... He was well known to the holy patriarchs, for He often appeared to them and spoke with them. Therefore He showed Himself to the

---

[1] For more recent examples, see Venard 2015 and especially scholars influenced by the Theophaneia School such as Pentiuc 2021, 76–83. Bogdan Bucur has traced the early roots of this kind of reading behind Justin Martyr and on into the conciliar era and in Byzantine hymnography, offering a nuanced examination of the interpretive issues, e.g. Bucur 2018.

fathers in such form as would indicate that He would sometime dwell with us on earth in the flesh and in human form'. Jesus Christ is therefore the undeclared name of this man. (Vischer 1949, 1:153)

## JESUS IN PLAIN SIGHT IN ISRAEL'S SCRIPTURES: A DISAGREEMENT

Should we follow this pattern of seeing Jesus's real presence at these particular points within Israel's Scriptures? The problem is that 'Jesus', and arguably also 'Christ', is an identity contingent upon historical existence at a particular time and place which is not the time and place of the Old Testament text. To use the label 'Jesus of Nazareth' identifies a man from Roman Palestine (even if also infinitely onwards), who has a point of origin in time and space, in the womb of Mary. He is therefore not among the cast of characters available to the Old Testament writers. This point is made in a classic essay of Kavin Rowe's, going back to the strictures of James Barr on Vischer's project:

> to have Jesus parading about during the time of the Old Testament is to dehistoricize the scandalous claim of the incarnation captured explicitly in the biblical *egeneto* ('became') of John 1:14 (such a move could also lead to an anti-Judaism wherein Jesus' Jewishness ceases to be important in any substantive way). (Rowe 2002, 298)

So when Paul speaks of 'Christ Jesus' who 'emptied himself ... being born in human likeness' (Phil 2:5–7, *NRSV*), then that historically situated identity 'Christ Jesus' is used retrospectively to speak of a continuous person at a time before the later-assumed identity applied, much as I might say, 'My husband broke his arm three times as a child', though when he broke his arm he was not my husband. But strictly speaking, 'Jesus Christ' is an identity not yet applicable in Old Testament times.

Before leaving this possibility behind, we might ask whether these theophanies remain relatable to Jesus in any way at all. Minimally, we could say that they show that in the biblical witness the God of Israel meets humans in the appearance of a human like them, and that human shape and speech, even plurality of persons, seem to be natural to God. The encounter of the disciples with Jesus on the Emmaus road in Luke 24 feels familiar because it echoes Genesis 18: this is not the first time God has appeared as a traveller who arrives with no tracks and joins his followers as they walk and eat, in a body that looks like theirs but is in fact not like theirs, and then is suddenly gone. This would be a history-of-religions approach which, in Christopher Seitz's words, undertakes 'to show that the God of Israel ... is related to the world and the covenanted Israel in ways that find religious correlation with the later views of Christian faith, when it comes to the Doctrine of the Trinity' (Seitz 2011, 29).[2]

But more maximally, we could say that the figure in the furnace or in the burning bush is the pre-incarnate Word: the connection to the incarnate Jesus would then be not just one of analogy or affinity of presentation but actually of continuous personhood. 'Jesus of Nazareth' may name the first-century Jew of the incarnation, but if that man is continuous with – is the same person as – the pre-incarnate Word, then it might become possible to say that we do see him in those theophanic appearances. But here the arc of the two testaments imposes a little caution. It is not only that Jesus is not incarnate before the incarnation but more broadly he is not really around at all. That absence is signalled in much of the language with which the New Testament refers to the pre-existent Son: language like descending from heaven (Rom 10:6–7, 1 Cor 15:47), giving up riches (2 Cor 8:9), being sent forth from the Father (Gal 4:4), visiting from on high (Luke 1:78), the name Immanuel as a *new* state of affairs, before which he was not 'with us' (Matt 1:23). Those terms speak of a pre-existent Christ who is not in the world: not only not incarnate but also somewhere else altogether. It is an apt summary of all this language when the Nicene Creed has 'for our salvation he *came down from heaven*'. Most of the New Testament texts which do talk about the activity of the pre-incarnate Son, and relate it to God's self-presentation in the Old Testament, tend to cluster around the events of creation (1 Cor 8:6, Col 1:16–17, Heb 1:2, 10, John 1:1–3). But after that engagement in the work of creating, the activity of the Word in the world is more diffuse, less visible.

Following Jesus's own identification of himself with Wisdom (Matt 11:29; cf. Sir 1:56; Deutsch 1990), the most natural place to see the pre-incarnate Logos in the Old Testament is in the figure of Wisdom – that is, as a presence which is immanent but always just behind the scenes.[3] Wisdom, too, has her home in heaven (Wis 9:9–10, 17; Sir 24:1–2, 4–5),

---

[2] Seitz finds this approach overcareful and unpersuasive, though it has much to commend it as exemplified in the work of Benedict Viviano on the Trinity in the Old Testament (Viviano 1998) or the work of Michael Wyschogrod (1993) and Benjamin Sommer (2009) comparing God's modes of presence in the Hebrew Bible with the idea of incarnation.

[3] For a full exposition of this idea see Boyarin 2001, though he sees the Logos also in front of and not only behind the scenes.

and when she is sent forth from there into the world, she is everywhere more than somewhere, filling the world and pervading all things (Wis 1:7; 7:24; 8:1). Images express this quiet omnipresence: Wisdom is a mist covering the earth (Sir 24:3), a liquid poured out on every living thing (Sir 1:10), a fragrance emanating out from Jerusalem (Sir 24:15), a voice permeating the streets of the city (Prov 8:2–3); she is behind and above the contingencies of history (Wis 8:8; Prov 8:15–16), ministering or simply resting in the inmost recess of tabernacle or temple (Sir 24:10–11). She is always just out of reach, elusive, above all to be sought (Sir 3:12; 6:27; Job 28). Even where Wisdom's action in history is maximally specified, it is not in particular personal appearances but as an invisible sustaining hand: preserving Adam, steering Noah, keeping Abraham blameless, guiding Jacob, staying with Joseph (Wis 10). In passages like these, the God who dwells among the Israelites (Exod 29:45) and walks about in the midst of their camp (Deut 23:15) is encountered as a personal Logos subsisting and acting in ways which extend that divine presence in the world.

From all this, the pre-incarnate Logos in the Old Testament seems more like the inner workings of a clock than like the cuckoo that keeps popping out of it. I will come back to the presence of Jesus in Daniel 3 and all those angelomorphic theophanies by another route, but for now a preliminary conclusion might be that picking out potential appearances of Jesus in plain sight in the text of the Hebrew Scriptures is a mistake both because it mutes the subtle witness of the pre-incarnate Word and because it short-circuits a hermeneutical process which the New Testament and a great deal of later Christian reflection actually lay out for us. I turn to that hermeneutical process now.

### JESUS INVISIBLE THEN VISIBLE IN ISRAEL'S SCRIPTURES: A PROPOSAL

When we ask about Jesus in the Scriptures of Israel, we are probably asking not only about the status of alleged appearances like that in the fiery furnace; rather, we confront the question of whether Israel's Scriptures can be said to speak of Jesus, to refer to him. In this chapter, the answer I explore to that question is 'no and yes': before Jesus's death and resurrection, no, they do not, or at least not intelligibly; and after Jesus's death and resurrection, yes, they do, comprehensively. This is not an original proposal but a widely attested traditional position. Here is its formulation by the Pontifical Biblical Commission in the 1993 document *On the Interpretation of the Bible in the Church*:

> The paschal event, the death and resurrection of Jesus, has established a radically new historical context, which sheds fresh light upon ancient texts and causes them to undergo a change in meaning. (Béchard 2002, 281)

That phrase 'causes them to undergo a change in meaning' is the central idea to this way of thinking: put otherwise in that document, the death and resurrection of Jesus 'gives a meaning to the Scriptures' which is called 'a new determination of meaning' and contrasted with what the document calls 'the proper meaning of the Old Testament' (Béchard 2002, 262). That is, after the Easter events there is a meaning within Israel's Scriptures – and it is really a feature of those texts, not a reading practice performed upon them but a meaning *in there* – which was not perceptible there before but is truly there now. The same idea is captured in the formulation of the Second Vatican Council's constitution *Dei verbum* that 'the books of the Old Testament ... acquire and show forth their full meaning in the New Testament' (*DV* 16).

In the language used to express this idea there is a spectrum in the degree to which the post-Jesus meaning is wholly new: there in *Dei verbum* 'acquire' sounds completely new, whereas 'show forth' sounds like it was already there but not lying on the surface. And that range between a hidden meaning and a meaning newly introduced is present all across different formulations of this view, in church documents and much wider afield in scholarship and in the New Testament itself. Henri de Lubac positions himself at one end of the spectrum in saying that 'the act of redemption is not a key which by unlocking the Old Testament reveals a meaning already present in it. This act in some sort creates the meaning' (de Lubac 1950, 100). Raymond Brown in his early work *The Sensus Plenior of Sacred Scripture* is more or less at the other end: 'Further revelation makes clear a sense that was already there; it does not create a new one' (Brown 1955, 125); the *sensus plenior* 'is seen to exist in the words of a biblical text (or group of texts, or even a whole book) when they are studied in the light of further revelation' (Brown 1955, 92).

But it may be possible to see these two ways of thinking as not quite so opposite as those formulations make them: de Lubac does say that, in a somewhat ideal sense only, the later meaning is already there, but 'It is only for God, from the eternal point of view, that the Old Testament contains the New already in a mystery ... so that if, to suppose an impossibility, Christ had not come, no man confronted with the sacred text would have the right to go beyond its literal meaning' (de Lubac 1950, 100). He captures this paradox of the presence but invisibility of Christ in the Old Testament by using the image of the transfiguration: 'Moses and Elias are transfigured only in the glory of Thabor' (de Lubac 1950: 100). That is, without a supernatural revelatory event, Moses and Elijah would not be associated with the glorified Christ; it takes a transfiguration to show the Old Testament in this light.[4] Transfiguration as an image suggests the appearance of a meaning that is at one and the same time inherent and completely new, just as Jesus's transfiguration shows something real but not humanly perceptible. The important thing seems to be that the later uncovering of the meaning present in the original text has something cataclysmic, apocalyptic about it – not a simple growth in understanding but a decisive unveiling with an element of surprise great enough that to speak of the creation of new meaning is a warranted level of rhetoric. So in contrast to the view that sees Jesus already there wrestling with Jacob or appearing to Abraham, Jesus is *not* there in the plain sense of Israel's Scriptures; but the upheaval of his death and resurrection reconfigures reality and discloses a set of connections whereby the lines triangulated between elements of Israel's Scriptures now newly converge on Jesus and speak of him.

It is important to add that precisely because those connections do have a logical coherence we cannot say that it was totally impossible to identify Jesus as their meeting point before the Easter event. It is a major claim of the New Testament and early Christianity that Jesus fits into the outline of the various messianic figures in the Old Testament – royal, prophetic, priestly, servant, and so on. That legible set of expectations means that John's disciples are apparently able to answer their own question 'Are you the one who is to come?' on the basis of recollected images from their Scriptures (Matt 11:2–6; Luke 7:18–23); it also means that Jesus can be presented as rebuking his hearers for failing to make a connection that was possible ('If you believed Moses, you would believe me, because he wrote about me', John 5:46); and of course this will become a major strand of early Christian apologetic. But at the same time, there is throughout the New Testament a stress on the sudden thunderbolt of an insight that is new. We might think of language like the veil over the inherent glory of Moses and the old covenant in 2 Corinthians 3, removed in Christ; or the repeated language in the Pauline letters of revealed mystery, such as the phrasing at the end of Romans about the revelation of the mystery kept secret for long ages

---

[4] For a parallel use of transfiguration, see Brown 1955, 49.

but now manifested 'through the prophetic writings' (Rom 16:25; cf. Eph 3:5) – here we see both the hiddenness of this mystery and Israel's Scriptures as its eventual revealed locus. A phrase from an early essay of John Barton captures the tension of these perspectives: 'Christianity both accepts Israel's theological system as a coherent whole, and completes it in a way which is unforeseeable, but natural once you have seen it' (Barton 1976, 265).

### LATENT MEANING AS A SCRIPTURAL PHENOMENON

Is the understanding outlined here an explanatory model imposed upon the Bible or does it derive from the Bible? My suggestion is that we do find adumbrated within the Hebrew Scriptures the idea that God's written word works this way; and within the New Testament, too, we find the view that this is what has in fact happened. An extended example concerns the book of Isaiah, which is in large measure structured around the idea of originally closed or incomprehensible revelation which at a later date becomes open or comprehensible. As is well known, that unfolds across the book as follows: the prophet Isaiah, at a midpoint in his prophetic career, receives his famous commission to speak incomprehensible words to an audience that is to be rendered blind and deaf, in the hardening saying of chapter 6:

> Go and say to this people:
>     'Keep listening, but do not comprehend;
>     keep looking, but do not understand.'
> Make the mind of this people dull,
>     and stop their ears,
>     and shut their eyes,
> so that they may not look with their eyes
>     and listen with their ears
> and comprehend with their minds
>     and turn and be healed. (Isa 6:9–10)

Within the collection of narrative materials scattered throughout chapters 6–9, the prophet's message is not heard and not seen in exactly this way by people and king, and that means that the presently incomprehensible message must instead be written down for a future time. So in 8:16 we hear what seems to be the prophet's voice in this little first-person narrative say, 'Bind up the testimony, seal up the teaching among my disciples ... See, I and the children whom the LORD has given me are signs and portents in Israel from the LORD of hosts.' We are left with an impenetrable teaching – *torah* here – persisting as a written residue. In at least two more places the book of Isaiah uses again the motif of writing which preserves for the future a message which is incomprehensible in the present: in 30:8 Isaiah is told, 'Go now, write it before them on a tablet, and inscribe it in a book, so that it may be for the time to come as a witness forever' (30:9–10). And in the much later 29:11–12, 'the vision of all this' is a sealed book which cannot be read. There is, then, a repeating motif which pictures the words of the prophet, incomprehensible to his original audience of contemporaries, as written down and sealed for a future time of unsealing and understanding (Blenkinsopp 2006).

This anticipation of the opening of the sealed teaching gives rise to a great deal of later interpretation within the corpus of Isaiah, in the listening and comprehensibly speaking new prophet of chapter 50 (vv. 4–9) and chapter 40 (v. 9) (Williamson 1994: 94–115), and also outside the book of Isaiah, in Daniel and at Qumran. All this is well known about the book of Isaiah; my suggestion is that it is a rather precise parallel to the view I have suggested about the workings of Scripture. There is the idea of an incomprehensible, hidden content to the prophetic word, and the particular written character of that literary deposit means that later rereading can uncover hidden meaning, can open the sealed book. And of course the book of Isaiah is relevant not only as a parallel but as a datum in the argument made by the New Testament: several writers take up material from Isaiah to explain their own standpoint, characterizing the witness to Jesus in Israel's Scriptures as once closed and incomprehensible but now made plain by the paschal events.

Matthew's Gospel offers us a way of seeing the hiddenness of Israel's Scriptures in Isaiah's terms. In Matthew 13:10, Jesus uses Isaiah 6's language of hearing but not understanding, looking but not seeing to frame his own use of parables. But just as in Isaiah, what is not comprehensible is nevertheless meant to be made plain by revelation: this is clearest in the saying at the end of the parables in Matthew 13:34–35:

> This was to fulfill what had been spoken through the prophet:
> 'I will open my mouth to speak in parables;
> I will proclaim what has been hidden from the foundation of the world.'

This citation from Psalm 78 exactly captures that dynamic of ancient, hidden sayings now performing effective revelation. Some textual witnesses specify 'the prophet' here as Isaiah, and attributing this psalm to Isaiah perfectly sums up the Isaianic process taking place within Matthew. The signal example of those who have their eyes opened to the hidden meanings of the Scriptures are of course the disciples: they are made able to see and hear, in an explicit reversal of Isaiah's hardening saying (Matt 13:16). And later, in Matthew's telling of the scene at Caesarea Philippi in chapter 16, the piece of christological scriptural interpretation which Peter has just performed by saying that Jesus is the Messiah is described again in language of impossible understanding divinely given. Peter has arrived at this understanding of the Scriptures by revelation in the present ('flesh and blood has not revealed this to you, but my Father in heaven', 16:17), and when Jesus elucidates Peter's insight further, he does so distinctively from Scripture: 'Jesus began to *show* his disciples that he must go to Jerusalem and undergo great suffering' (Matt 16:21), in contrast to just 'teach' in Mark 8:31 – 'teach' needs no source, but 'show' gestures to a scriptural source. So the revelation of the Messiah is a process of scriptural interpretation, but only as Scripture is divinely opened up. In all of this, scriptural revelation is seen to have a hidden content whose exposure is a divine act, and this is not only a parallel process to the unfolding of written Scripture within the book of Isaiah but understood as an instantiation of the closedness and opening of the book of Isaiah in the present. As Joseph Blenkinsopp put it, speaking of Matthew's use of Isaiah generally: 'The event or circumstance in the life of Jesus therefore, in some way, activates for the first time a meaning or reference latent in a text written centuries earlier' (Blenkinsopp 2006, 151).

And we could add to this numerous examples from elsewhere in the New Testament. The Gospel of John includes several statements that have exactly the same structure whereby the paschal events make the underlying sense of the Scriptures newly visible, such as John 12:16: 'His disciples did not understand these things at first; but when Jesus was glorified, then they remembered that these things had been written of him and had been done to him' – here the post-resurrection context is necessary to understand the Scripture (see also John 2:22, 20:8–9). Or for Luke, the risen Jesus on the Emmaus road needs to open hearts and minds to understand the Scriptures: whatever he says here about himself in the Scriptures is only perceptible by supernatural action performed on the reader. None of this, of course, is to say that Israel's Scriptures are wholly or even largely obscure, or to deny that they perform effective revelation entirely on their own. Rather, there is an unlooked-for surplus beyond the already clear meaning: it is this one thing, rather than everything, that had been hidden and is now brought to light.

## JESUS IN ISRAEL'S SCRIPTURES: SCOPE AND EXPECTATIONS

What might be some advantages of this way of seeing Jesus in Israel's Scriptures? This view seems to distinguish adequately between ontology – claims about the eternity of the Word – and the particular voice of the Scriptures, rather than pushing all the ontological claims into the Scriptures in a way which seems destructive of the Old Testament in its givenness. Perhaps similarly, this view may avoid obliterating Israel's Scriptures by preserving some distance from them. To say that the Old Testament *speaks of* Jesus is not quite the same as to say Jesus is *in it*: concepts like testifying, speaking about, foreshadowing, preparation, typology, even predictive prophecy, all depend on a gap and on the preservation of the separate identity of the earlier voice. Rather than saying that Jesus 'is' the manna in the desert, Jesus's own words in John 6:49–50 depend upon the disjunction – *unlike* the ancestors who ate and still died, whoever eats *this* bread will live forever.

In turn, on this view it is not correct to say that Jesus's Jewish contemporaries ought to have recognized him from the Scriptures: in fact, if we follow Matthew's use of Isaiah then recognizing Jesus from the Scriptures is humanly impossible, rather than to be expected. The Pontifical Biblical Commission's document *The Jewish People and Their Sacred Scriptures in the Christian Bible* puts it this way: 'Like ... the process of photographic development, the person of Jesus and the events concerning him now appear in the Scriptures with a fullness of meaning that could not be hitherto perceived' (para 64). Origen himself says that 'Before the coming of Christ, the Law and the prophets *did not contain* the proclamation which belongs to the definition of the gospel since he who explained the mysteries in them had not yet come. But since the Savior has come ... he has made all things gospel, as it were' (*Commentary on John* 1.33; Heine 1989, 40). Thus the rebuke of the risen Jesus to the disciples on the Emmaus road, 'Oh, how foolish you are, and how slow of heart to believe all that the prophets have declared' (Luke 24:25) is not generalizable but only a post-resurrection perspective: it is just at that moment that the disciples have the final piece of the jigsaw which makes it possible to slot all the others into place. The critique depends upon the full understanding of the paschal mystery and the backward light it casts. And that process is actually understood as an ongoing one, not a completed one: *Dei verbum* uses the language of constant advancing towards the fullness of divine truth stored up in the mystery of faith, as the words of God are brought to completion as the centuries go by (8), and 'The meaning of the sacred writings is more profoundly understood' (24); so this is not a totalizing claim to a final delimiting of meaning.

Also, and perhaps paradoxically, this view is more satisfyingly comprehensive than the approach of Hengstenberg, Vischer and others. The problem with the habit of identifying Christ in those angelic theophanies is that it claims both too much and too little. It claims too much because it rides roughshod over the nature of Scripture and tries to push ontology into the text; but it also claims too little, in saying that it is *unusually* or even *only* here that we see Christ in the Old Testament, like a few flashes of lightning. But the language of 'everything written about me in the law of Moses, the prophets and the psalms' (Luke 24:44), or de Lubac's image of the transfiguration of the Scriptures, suggests rather than identifying Jesus in a few places in a primary sense an openness to seeing him everywhere in this secondary sense: with hindsight, Jesus in Luke 24 'interpreted to them the things about himself in *all* the scriptures' (Luke 24:27). And of course that will include too those angelic theophanies: on this view, it is possible to join in with the hymns of Romanos or the commentary of Hippolytus which do see Jesus in the fiery furnace – but as part of a long catena of examples spanning the Old Testament, suggesting that this is an overall strategy of second reading rather than an isolated sighting.

Finally, it may be worth saying that the view I have sketched out still makes a real claim about the nature of the Scriptures. Part of the polemical urgency in some claims for Jesus as the plain-sense predicate of the Old Testament derives from the fair criticism that there can be a certain unreality to a figural or typological way of seeing Jesus in Israel's Scriptures.[5] Figural interpretation risks being reducible to a reading practice or a language game, in which these texts do not actually speak of Christ but we agree to read them as if they did, so that they simply furnish a symbolic vocabulary for things we want to say on other grounds. Instead, the view suggested here can undergird the practice of figural reading with a rationale which is more than convention: it makes the claim that the newly perceptible meaning is there latent in the texts themselves. As in the old fourfold paradigm, the spiritual senses beyond the literal (allegorical, moral and anagogical) are senses *of Scripture*.

---

[5] See Venard 2015, 23–24, 29; though this worry is already addressed by Auerbach 1984, 30–35.

### THREE EXAMPLES: DAVID, MOSES, SUSANNA

How might we, in the time after the paschal events, read Israel's Scriptures with the expectation that they have acquired a new or previously hidden sense but without erasing or overwriting what was there already? One of the signal ways that Christian readers have seen Christ in all the Scriptures is in the figure of Israel's king, or individual kings, pre-eminently David. Does reading Israel's kings through the filter of Jesus have to be a reading that displaces or talks over the particular voice of the Old Testament? Certainly when a popular nineteenth-century hymn hails Jesus as 'Great David's greater son' that does displace David's actual greater son in the books of Kings or in Psalm 72, who of course is Solomon. But displacing Solomon so that we only remember David and subsume future kingship under the banner of David is a move that some biblical writers themselves already make: 'Great David's greater son' might actually be a perfect description of the Chronicler's Josiah. This is a different identification to Jesus but the same way of distilling and redirecting Israelite kingship away from its course in the earlier historical books into a pattern like Ezekiel's where all later kings are simply David (Ezek 37:24).

Differently, seeing Christ in Israel's kings also picks up on the way that much kingship ideology in the Old Testament is ideal or unreal, and that shortfall is itself often carried over into Christian uses rather than solved. When that hymn continues with the line 'He shall come down like showers upon the fruitful earth', we are presented with a royal image of a very different, almost mystical kind, recalling the idyll of Psalm 72: 'May he [Solomon] be like rain that falls on the mown grass, like showers that water the earth; in his days may righteousness flourish and peace abound until the moon is no more' (Ps 72:6–7; cf. Prov 16:15; 2 Sam 23:3–4). So much of what contributes most to seeing Christ in the kings of Israel's Scriptures is like this vision of kingship: romantic, idealized, unreal. In fact Israel's Scriptures sometimes project kingship onto an eschatological future paradise, as in Isaiah 9 or Isaiah 11: perhaps the most evocative way of putting this in the book of Isaiah is the oracle of chapter 33, 'Your eyes will see the king in his beauty; they will behold a land that stretches far away' (33:17), and here human kingship is attenuated to the point where it dissolves into the kingship of God (33:22).

But the point is *not* that whereas these Old Testament pictures of kingship are unrealized or ideal ones the New Testament then fills in the gap and answers this lack. For one thing, this unrealized aspect is a point of similarity and not a point of difference between Old Testament thinking about kingship and its adaptation to the kingship of Jesus. When Advent lectionaries pick up those oracles from the book of Isaiah and make them speak about Jesus, the point is not one of fulfilment but of shared positioning in front of an as yet unfulfilled ideal future – these oracles when applied to Jesus in Advent work to set the eschatological horizon of Christian hopes too, so that a deferred, future fulfilment is a point of commonality with the original context of the oracles, not a point of difference.

It is also worth considering what the 'gap' or 'lack' picture of Old Testament kingship can do within Christology: the gap is not one which is plugged by Jesus but rather carried over into Christian thinking. When David, barefoot, goes weeping up the Mount of Olives in 2 Samuel 15:30, a Christian reader will see Jesus here in this icon of humiliated and defeated kingship; it is not that fixing David's abjection would turn him into Jesus. Seeing Jesus in the deposed and exiled kings of Israel's Scriptures does not here mean construing the relationship as one of inverse and obverse; rather, the relationship is one of likeness and continuity.

My second example is Moses. If we were to read the Old Testament narratives of Moses's life looking for what concerns Jesus in all the Scriptures, we might follow the lead of Matthew's infancy narrative to see in the infant Moses the infant Jesus, likewise hunted by a tyrant who wants to kill him. But this connection does more than set up a pattern of prophecy and fulfilment: allowing Moses's infancy narrative to refract Christ's offers us a fuller affective dimension. We encounter a baby boy crying, around him a swirl of maternal care and loss; there is nursing the child and giving up the child, and a partial dislocation of natural motherhood; then a long hidden life before the time comes to step onto the stage of public ministry. Here too likeness rather than inferiority does a lot of the work in a christological reading of Moses. Moses is a source of authority, even of glory for Jesus: the presence of Moses is part of what builds the glorification of Jesus at the Transfiguration. Jesus's unearthly brightness on the mountain makes sense by making him *like* Moses on Mount Sinai, and if this episode in the Synoptic Gospels makes a claim about Jesus's divine identity it does so via Moses: Moses's shining face reflected the terrible radiance expected of an ancient Near Eastern god, including the God of Israel. So when the New Testament writers present Jesus as a Moses-like figure they draw Jesus into the circle of the glory and authority of Moses, even if they ultimately draw him to the centre of that circle.

One final example might be Susanna, the heroine of that story of attempted rape and divinely ordained deliverance in the Greek Additions to Daniel. The New Testament does not take up Susanna as an obvious way to see Christ in Israel's Scriptures. And yet at her trial, Susanna stands in dignified silence in front of two false witnesses, as her accusers lay hands on her and strip off her clothes with a crowd of onlookers gazing at her as she is condemned to death. That tableau has looked to many interpreters like Jesus before Pilate, likewise the mute object of a shaming gaze, so that the *Ecce homo* reenacts the earlier scene. Looking at Susanna and listening to her silence is for the reader of the gospels like a mirror image of the mocking and the display of Christ. We could perhaps take Susanna as an instance of Gerard Manley Hopkins's famous line 'Christ plays in ten thousand places – lovely in limbs, and lovely in eyes not his', and it is also impossible not to wonder whether with that word 'playing' Hopkins is gesturing to a female figure earlier still, the co-creator in Proverbs 8 who plays alongside God and who offers another image to later christological readers. Talk of 'play' shades off into what mid-twentieth-century Catholic hermeneutics called 'accommodation' – not the usual theological sense of accommodation but a precise term for the practice of using Scripture as a language for meanings *not* contained within it, a thesaurus for Christian speech. Perhaps talk of Christ playing in the loveliness of Susanna is accommodation, on that definition, rather than a real sense of Israel's Scriptures – but indulging that kind of reading, Brown writes: 'After all, in the Scriptures we are in our Father's house where the children are permitted to play' (Brown 1955, 28).

Seeing Jesus in Israel's Scriptures, then, is a matter of hindsight rather than first sight, but the New Testament and the Christian tradition insist that this hindsight is a true perception, grounded not in a hermeneutical method but in a claim about what has taken place in the death and resurrection of Jesus. Instead of isolated sightings, this kind of second reading sees Jesus throughout all the Scriptures, in a pursuit of understanding that resists closure.

### FURTHER READING

Benoit, Pierre. 1982. "Préexistence et incarnation." In *Exégèse et théologie*, vol. 4, 11–61. Paris: Éditions du Cerf.
Daniélou, Jean. 1960. *From Shadows to Reality: Studies in Biblical Typology of the Fathers*. Translated by Dom Wulstan Hibberd. London: Burns & Oates.
Dawson, John David. 2001. *Christian Figural Reading and the Fashioning of Identity*. Berkeley: University of California Press.

De Lubac, Henri. 2007. *History and Spirit: The Understanding of Scripture According to Origen*. Translated by Anne Englund Nash. San Francisco, CA: Ignatius.

Hays, Richard B. 1989. *Echoes of Scripture in the Letters of Paul*. New Haven: Yale University Press.

Hays, Richard B. 2016. *Echoes of Scripture in the Gospels*. Waco: Baylor University Press.

Henze, Matthias and David Lincicum, eds. 2023. *Israel's Scriptures in Early Christian Writings: The Use of the Old Testament in the New*. Grand Rapids: Eerdmans.

Witte, Markus. 2013. *Jesus Christus im Alten Testament: eine biblisch-theologische Skizze*. Vienna: Lit Verlag.

Wyschogrod, Michael. 1983. *The Body of Faith: God and the People of Israel*. New York: Seabury.

Young, Frances M. 1997. *Biblical Exegesis and the Formation of Christian Culture*. Cambridge: Cambridge University Press.

**Part II**

*The Diversity of Reception*

# 8 The Apocryphal Jesus
## JACOB A. RODRIGUEZ

Jesus of Nazareth inspired manifold receptions in the centuries following his climactic death, the most influential of which are preserved in the gospels that came to be recognized as canonical. These gospels came to dominate the religious imagination of the early Jesus movement, arguably coalescing into a fourfold collection by the midpoint of the second century.

Nevertheless, other significant trajectories of Jesus reception emerged in the second century – some gathered momentum into late antiquity and the medieval era, while others all but disappeared as fragments buried in history. The present chapter focuses on the portraits displayed in these extracanonical traditions. The Jesus of these traditions is perhaps appropriately termed the "Apocryphal Jesus" – hidden, that is, either by deliberate esotericism in the traditions (e.g. the Gospel of Thomas) or by the accidents of history (e.g. numerous Jesus fragments lost in an ancient landfill site in Oxyrhynchus).

### THE APOCRYPHAL JESUS AND THE CANONICAL GOSPELS

Our point of departure must be to define the sources, commonly known as the apocryphal gospels, a collection of about eighty diverse texts from early Christianity. They offer a unique glimpse into the varied ways early Christians engaged with the story and teachings of Jesus. These texts, which emerged in a period when the New Testament canon was not yet formalized, reveal the multifaceted nature of early Christian thought and practice. Second-century Christianity was not yet bounded by clear New Testament canonical limits. Instead, it witnessed a dynamic proliferation of gospel literature, which we may think of as "Jesus books." This creative phase also saw the development of various gospel harmonies and fragments, many of which survive only in parts.

Gospel writing in the early Christian context can be understood as the process of transforming oral and written traditions about Jesus into textual narratives. This practice likely began with the assembly of sayings and narratives predating the Gospel of Mark, the earliest canonical gospel. Extending the definition, gospel writing continued into late antiquity, expanding into an anthology of Jesus books that evolved well beyond the bounds of the canonical texts. Amidst this literary fecundity, a significant development was the early preference for the four-gospel collection comprising Matthew, Mark, Luke, and John. It is important to note that this preference emerged alongside an ongoing production of new Jesus books, a phenomenon reflecting both literary continuity and theological exploration within early Christianity.

The first-century gospels appear to have exercised a remarkable informal influence over the form and content of their successors. Despite being less widely copied than the others, the Gospel of Mark, in particular, initiated a new form of literary expression for the Jesus tradition by blending written biography with elements of oral transmission. This ground-breaking (and it seems genre-defining) approach led subsequent gospel writers, including the authors of Matthew, Luke, and John, to emulate and expand upon Mark's narrative framework. Second-century gospels similarly relied upon this Markan framework either overtly or implicitly, often focusing on specific aspects of Jesus's life, such as his infancy or post-resurrection appearances. Even texts focusing on dialogue or sayings typically presuppose some such underlying narrative. True, some ended up diverging significantly from their predecessors or indeed from the prototype, but none appears to have been written with the intention of replacing the canonical gospels. These texts, despite their diversity, were epiphenomenal to the established outline and substance of the earlier gospels.

The numerous second-century gospels manifested in various forms, each contributing uniquely to the expanding corpus of Jesus literature. These included infancy gospels, like the Protevangelium of James and the Infancy Gospel of Thomas. Ministry gospels, albeit fragmentary, presented narratives from Jesus's public ministry.[1] Passion gospels, such as the Gospel of Peter, focused on the events of Jesus's crucifixion and its aftermath. Additionally, dialogue gospels, such as the Sophia of Jesus Christ, the Epistula Apostolorum, and the Gospel of Mary, offered imaginative explorations of Jesus's interactions with his disciples, typically set after his resurrection. Finally, two influential second-century Jesus books – Marcion's Euangelion

---

[1] Many of these are extant only in papyrus fragments; e.g. P.Oxy. 210; P.Oxy. 840; P.Oxy. 1224; P.Oxy. 4009; P.Oxy. 5072; P. Mert. II.51; cf. Bernhard 2006.

and Tatian's Diatessaron – attempted to reduce this pluriformity of Jesus books to uniformity, the former by trimming down a version of Luke's Gospel and the latter by combining all four canonical gospels into a harmonious narrative.

### JESUS IN APOCRYPHAL MEMORY

The epiphenomenal nature of the apocryphal gospels, and their relative distance from the world of first-century Palestine, has caused recent scholarship to question their value in reconstructing the historical Jesus. Nevertheless, scholars also recognize that apocryphal Jesus traditions are still immensely valuable for understanding how various early Christian groups shaped their identity through the process of remembering Jesus. In this sense, the communal memory of Jesus was not so much an exercise in historical accuracy as a way of negotiating the contemporary concerns of a group as it related to a past that was anchored in the person of Jesus.[2] In the second century – a century that has been accurately described as a "laboratory" for Christian identity formation – various sectors within the Jesus movement responded differently to sociocultural currents.[3] How should Jesus followers understand their identity vis-à-vis the tragic, consequential outcomes of the Jewish revolts under the reigns of Trajan (115–17 CE) and Hadrian (132–35 CE)? To what extent could Jesus's teachings compete with the leading philosophies of the second century (e.g. Stoicism and Middle Platonism), and could Jesus even be considered a respectable philosopher? Do the parochial Jesus traditions of the earliest (canonical) gospels adequately address the ancient pursuit of transcendence? And what should Christians make of the many lacunae in Jesus's biography – his parentage, childhood, and post-resurrection appearances? These, and many other questions, spurred Christians on to elaborate, restage, refashion, and at times even subvert, the Jesus traditions of the canonical gospels. Some engaged first-century gospels as a foundation to be developed, others ventured into speculative recreations of the Jesus tradition that bore little resemblance to memories anchored in first-century Roman Palestine. Although these developments vary in their correspondence to earliest apostolic tradition, they all reflect a vibrant reception of the man from Nazareth, and they proffer numerous portraits of Jesus

---

[2] For recent advances in the social memory approach to Jesus studies, see Butticaz 2020.
[3] Cf. Markschies 1998.

as the object of diverse religious devotion. We will briefly elaborate on several of these portraits, based on a representative sample of Jesus books from a broad spectrum of theological affinities.

## APOCRYPHAL PORTRAITS OF JESUS

### Jesus the Child

Any observant reader (whether ancient or modern) of the canonical gospels would notice that they are remarkably taciturn regarding Jesus's childhood. This lacuna was ripe for literary innovation in the second century and following centuries – not least given the Greco-Roman trope valuing childhood exploits of great figures. Immensely popular and influential from antiquity to the medieval period, the Protevangelium of James relates the origins of Jesus's earthly family, with particular focus on Mary and Joseph as righteous Hebrews waiting expectantly for the salvation of Israel. While Jesus is a nearly invisible character (the narrative ends shortly after his birth), this Jesus book introduces aspects of Jesus's identity that became mainstream in Christian tradition, for example that Jesus's "brothers" were half-brothers, sons of Joseph's previous wife, and that his mother maintained perpetual virginity after his birth. Another detail in the Protevangelium of James, that Jesus was born in a cave rather than a stable, is corroborated by other early Christian testimony within geographic proximity to Jesus's traditional birthplace, raising the possibility that it is a genuine historical datum.[4] We should hasten to add that the Protevangelium of James is in no real sense "apocryphal": It was never hidden by authorial design, ecclesial dogma, or historical accident. Rather, it was well received among many traditions within historic Christianity and often read alongside the canonical gospels – as indeed it continues to shape liturgical texts and hymnography associated with Marian Feasts in the Eastern churches. It is, however, regularly treated alongside apocryphal gospels by modern scholars since it contributes extracanonical traditions about Jesus.

The Infancy Gospel of Thomas, resembling the picaresque with its episodic form, focuses on Jesus's childhood experiences from ages five to twelve. It paints a picture of a rather mischievous and, at times, petulant Jesus. At the outset of the narrative, Joseph reprimands Jesus for crafting sparrows with clay on the Sabbath, and Jesus responds by

---

[4] Cf. the testimony of Justin Martyr (*Dial.* 78), Origen (*Cels.* 1.51), and Jerome (*Epist.* 46.11; 58.3; 108.10).

clapping his hands and turning them into live sparrows that immediately fly away. The Infancy Gospel of Thomas also contains a noteworthy episode in which Jesus, aware of his own pre-existence, talks back to his teacher and shows him the true meaning of "alpha" and "beta" (Inf. Gos. Thom. 6). This same episode makes a cameo in the proto-orthodox Epistula Apostolorum (Ep. Apos. 4.1–2), and Irenaeus mentions that he has found it in a spurious gospel used by the heretical sect known as the Marcosians (Adv. Haer. 1.20.1). The multiple attestation of this episode suggests that it had considerable currency among second-century Christians of various stripes. The textual tradition of the Infancy Gospel of Thomas strongly indicates it was a rolling corpus with less stability than other Jesus books, and so a memorable childhood episode like this one would easily find its way into this collection. The Infancy Gospel of Thomas enjoyed a wide, even if controversial, reception among various Christian groups well into the medieval era, and its footprint can even be found in Islamic sources (e.g. the Qur'an 3:49; 5:110).

The composition and reception histories of the Protevangelium of James and the Infancy Gospel of Thomas demonstrate well the relationship of the apocryphal Jesus to the canonical Jesus. Apocryphal and noncanonical Jesus books fill lacunae in the canonical gospel narrative by developing nascent themes (e.g. Jesus's precocious interactions with teachers and parents in Luke 2:41–50) in novel directions (e.g. Jesus as a pettish boy flaunting his divine powers in the Infancy Gospel of Thomas). The apocryphal construction of the boy Jesus is an expression of Jesus memory in its own right, but it is nonetheless inextricably linked to the canonical memory of Jesus.

### The Supersessionist Jesus

As we mentioned in the section "Jesus in Apocryphal Memory," Christian self-definition in the second century could not avoid the tumultuous events of the Jewish revolts in 115–17 CE and 132–34 CE. In many respects, second-century Christians used the momentum of Jewish national tragedy to propel themselves onto a more prominent stage within the drama of Greco-Roman religious affairs.

The tendency to invalidate the Jewish Scriptures with the advent of the new teaching of Jesus is readily apparent in several apocryphal Jesus books. In the Gospel according to Thomas, logion 52, the disciples ask Jesus if the "twenty-four prophets" who "spoke in Israel" spoke about him. Jesus seems to deride the testimony of the Israelite prophets (twenty-four probably symbolizing the books of the majority canon of

Jewish Scriptures), replying, "You have neglected the living one in front of you ... and spoken of the dead."[5] Similarly, in the second-century Sethian Gnostic work the Apocryphon of John, Jesus explicitly contradicts Moses and his writings no less than four times.[6] To a lesser extent, the Gospel of Peter separates the ministry of Jesus from the Scriptures of Israel. In the substantial fragment that remains extant in the Akhmim Codex, the Jewish Scriptures are fulfilled only in a negative sense: The Jews' Scriptures seal their own condemnation. There is no positive sense in which Jesus's death and resurrection fulfill the Scriptures of Israel. In fact, Jesus's death before sunset is shown to be in direct contradiction with a regulation laid down in the Law (cf. Deut 21:23). Indeed, the narrative voice distances the implied author from the Scriptures of Israel, saying that they were written "for them [the Jews]."[7] Even more extensive in its de-Judaizing of the canonical tradition, Marcion's Euangelion consistently omits portions of its Lukan counterpart that locate Jesus's life and ministry as a fulfillment of the Jewish Scriptures.[8]

A more pernicious tendency among apocryphal Jesus traditions is to dispossess the Jews of their place in the economy of salvation (this they share with a regrettably large swathe of the proto-orthodox reception of the canonical Jesus). The narrator of the Gospel of Peter distances himself not only from the Jewish Scriptures but also from the Jewish people, and he transfers the actions of Pilate and the Roman soldiers – the mockery, torture, and crucifixion of Jesus – exclusively to the Jews. The narrative voice of the Gospel of Peter pronounces judgment on the Jews to a greater extent than any of the canonical narrators: "And so they [the Jews] brought everything to fulfillment, heaping upon themselves the full measure of their sins."[9] The Jesus of the Gospel of Thomas disparages circumcision, a central cultural institution of the Jews (logion 53).[10] Jesus, in the Gospel of Judas, mockingly laughs at the disciples for praying to their god, and then he declares, "Truly, [I] say to you, no generation of the people in your midst can

---

[5] Trans. Gathercole 2021, 58.
[6] Ap. John 61.19–21; 70.22; 71.3; 77.6 (the versification here refers to the folio and line numbers).
[7] On the lack of positive fulfillment of Scripture in Gos. Pet., see Gathercole 2022, 315–25.
[8] In his authoritative text of Marcion's Euangelion, Roth 2015 identifies (among many others) the following passages as omitted by Marcion: Luke 1–2; 3:21–4:13; 9:31; 11:30–32; 18:31–33; 20:9–17, 37–38; 21:21–22; 22:35–38.
[9] Gos. Pet. 5.17; trans. Gathercole 2021, 209.
[10] Gos. Thom. 53; in the canonical gospels, circumcision is never disparaged (Luke 1:59; 2:21; John 7:22–23).

know me."[11] Israel's god is depicted as a demonic creator-spirit named Saklas, and the twelve tribes of Israel are said to be servants of this evil demiurge.[12] The Jesus painted in these apocryphal accounts is a far cry from one who is the hope for the "consolation of Israel" (Luke 2:25), the "rising of many in Israel" (Luke 2:34), or the "redemption of Jerusalem" (Luke 2:38).

It is hotly debated to what extent the canonical Jesus already allows for a supersessionist reading of his teachings. Though the present author would argue that the canonical gospels do not in themselves exhibit supersessionist intention, the reception of their traditions by both proto-orthodox and apocryphal authors from the second century onward make it undeniable that they do harbor supersessionist potential. It is precisely this potential that many apocryphal gospels and Jesus books exploit, to the detriment of Jesus's own historical grounding in the story of Israel and his mission to the children of Abraham.

### The Torah-Observant Jesus

The supersessionist portrait of Jesus was not the only strategy for negotiating the Jesus movement's relationship to the Scriptures of Israel and the fate of the Jewish people. In addition to the anti-Marcionite writings of proto-orthodox church fathers who affirm the enduring validity of the Jewish Scriptures, apocryphal fragments remain of early Christian memory of Jesus not as an abolisher of the Torah or the Prophets but rather as their faithful observer and fulfiller.

The Torah-observant Jesus teaches the importance of obedience to the Law and the Prophets. In the Gospel according to the Hebrews, Jesus commands the rich man seeking salvation to "do what the Law and the Prophets say," and to do so by caring for his "many brothers, fellow sons of Abraham, who are clothed in dung, dying from hunger."[13] The Diatessaron at several points gives an even more Torah-affirming version of Jesus's teaching than the Synoptic parallels. For example, the Matthean Jesus commands the cleansed leper to "show yourself to the priests and offer the gift that Moses commanded" (Matt 8:4). The Diatessaron, on the other hand, probably had Jesus say: "show yourself to the priests and fulfill the law."[14] And where Matthew 19:16 has the rich man ask, "What good deed must I do to

---

[11] Gos. Judas 34; trans. Gathercole 2021, 195.
[12] Gos. Judas 18.
[13] Gos. Heb. fr. 12; trans. Gathercole 2021, 166.
[14] This is the most plausible reconstruction of the Diatessaron at this point, taken from Ephrem the Syrian's wording in *Commentary on the Gospel* 12.21, 23.

inherit eternal life?," the Diatessaron situates this discussion of Torah with language more closely resembling the parallel in Leviticus (18:5): "What shall I do to live?"[15]

The Torah-observant Jesus not only teaches his hearers to keep the Law; he also embodies the vindication of the hopes of a Torah-faithful Israel. The author of the Protevangelium of James goes to great lengths to demonstrate how Jesus was born into a pious Jewish family who by all accounts lived as faithful Israelites. Jesus's mother, Mary, is a virgin who was brought up in the Temple, where she served as a seamstress who wove the curtain for the Holy Place (Prot. Jas. 7–10). Her undefiled virginity, even after conceiving Jesus, is vindicated by the high priest's test for purity (Prot. Jas. 16). When Jesus is born, a Hebrew midwife witnesses the miraculous event and declares that "salvation has come to Israel" (Prot. Jas. 19). Jesus's earthly history is situated squarely within a narrative of Israel faithfully keeping Torah and waiting for the promises of God to come to fruition.

Finally, the Torah-observant Jesus practices what he preaches. The early Gospel fragment P.Oxy. 840 (the text of which dates somewhere in the second to fourth centuries CE) contains a debate between Jesus and a Pharisaic chief priest named Levi. Although Jesus disagrees with Levi about the meaning of ritual cleansings, his own defense includes the claim that he only looked upon the sacred vessels of the Temple after washing ceremonially in the pool of David.

The memory of Jesus as a Torah-observant Jew of course goes back to canonical gospel traditions. Jesus's famous statement in Matthew says as much: "I did not come to abolish the Law or the Prophets, but rather to fulfill them" (Matt 5:17). Similarly, Luke recounts Jesus's circumcision on the eighth day "according to the Law of Moses" (Luke 2:22) and "as it is written in the Law of the Lord" (2:23). The Johannine Jesus likewise keeps the most important Jewish feasts. Even the Markan Jesus, who appears at first glance to abolish the laws against unclean foods (Mark 7:1–23), is never said to break them himself.[16] Given the propensity of many early Christians to minimize Jesus's Jewishness, it is noteworthy that certain apocryphal traditions about Jesus work in the opposite direction.

### The Literate, "Bookish" Jesus

The question of Jesus's literacy (or lack thereof) became a salient aspect of the communal memory of Jesus in the second century and

---

[15] Cf. Ephrem, *Commentary on the Gospel* 15.1.
[16] Cf. Thiessen 2020, 187–96.

continued to garner imaginative recollection in late antiquity. In the second century, as Christianity began to consolidate its systems of belief around a new collection of apostolic writings to parallel the Jewish Scriptures, the historical person of Jesus came to be seen as intimately concerned with the production of apostolic books. In the second-century Apocryphon of James, the risen Jesus appears to the twelve disciples as they are writing down his teachings in books (Ap. Jas. 2.5–20). Jesus pulls James aside along with Peter to give them exclusive access to special revelation; in plausibly Valentinian fashion, salvation is revealed to the initiated few. Another second-century apocryphal Jesus book, the Epistula Apostolorum, employs the theme of apostolic textualization in the service of proto-orthodoxy. In the Epistula, the risen Jesus endorses the collective apostolic enterprise of textualizing the gospel, a written testimony that the apostles distribute to the churches of the north, south, east, and west (Ep. Apos. 1–2; 31). Though the theology of the Epistula and the Apocryphon of James are probably at odds, their shared use of a textualizing memory of Jesus attests to the rhetorical power of a "bookish" Jesus in the second-century apocryphal milieu.

In the apocryphal tradition, Jesus not only supports the inscripturation of his teaching; he is also fully literate, able to read and to write. It is likely that the early followers of Marcion believed that Jesus wrote the whole gospel (which, in their system, was Marcion's own Euangelion). We can infer this from the fourth-century Dialogue of Adamantius, where the Marcionite teachers Megethius and Marcus say as much.[17] Around this same period, Aphrahat, the Persian church father writing in Syriac, attributes the written gospel tradition to Jesus himself.[18]

Dating even earlier (probably to the third century), Jesus's correspondence with Abgar purports to preserve letters written and exchanged between Jesus and the Mesopotamian king Abgar.[19] Abgar initiates the correspondence, telling Jesus how he has heard of his mighty acts of healing and asking him to come and heal his own affliction. Jesus replies, using language from John's Gospel, blessing Abgar for believing even without seeing, and promising to send one of his disciples after his ascension to heal Abgar.

---

[17] Adamantius, *Dialogue* 1.8; 2.13–14.
[18] Aphrahat, *Demonstrations* 4.10; 8.3; 14.9; 21.1; 23.1; 25.53; cf. Baarda 2019, 14.
[19] Eusebius preserves the apocryphal Epistles of Christ and Abgar in *Hist. eccl.* 1.13.11–22.

Arguably the earliest tradition of Jesus's scribal literacy is the independent episode of Jesus defending and forgiving the woman caught in adultery, commonly known as the Pericope Adulterae (see John 7:53–8.11).[20] Some scholars argue that this episode first appeared in a third-century version of the Gospel according to the Hebrews and in the fourth century was eventually interpolated into some Greek and Latin copies of John.[21] In the version extant in most of the later Johannine manuscript tradition, Jesus is depicted as writing on the ground, demonstrating his authority over the scribes and perhaps alluding to his authorship of the Law of Moses.

As with the Torah-observant characterization of Jesus, the literate Jesus makes his first appearance in the canonical gospels, though it is mostly implied. In Jesus's disputes with the scribes, he frequently makes the rhetorical appeal, "have you never read?" and then goes on to quote a relevant portion of the Law or Prophets.[22] In Mark 12:26, Jesus even makes reference to the location in the Torah scroll where one would find the passage he is citing (in this case, Exod 3:6). Luke 4:16–20 explicitly corroborates the memory of Jesus as, at the very least, a semiliterate rabbi. The literary potential of a literate Jesus comes to fruition in apocryphal portraits of Jesus the scribe.

### Jesus the Philosopher

In the writings of the second-century apologists, one can identify a concerted effort made by Christians to portray Jesus as a reputable philosopher, rather than a mere sophist, and his teachings as a way of life superior to the popular philosophical schools of that era. The portrait of Jesus as a philosopher is also promulgated in several apocryphal gospels.

Recent Thomasine scholarship has identified the structure of the 114 logia in the Gospel according to Thomas as a gnomological anthology – a collection of sayings of a wise sage compiled by a philosophical school.[23] Thomas finds a notable parallel in the Didaskalikos of Alcinous, a late first- or early second-century epitome of sayings from Plato's *Timaeus* and *Parmenides*. Alcinous reworked and rearranged citations from each of these philosophical works for a school setting. In the same way, Thomas collects and arranges 114 sayings of Jesus so that a school of readers can remember well the teachings of their

---

[20] Cf. Keith 2009.
[21] Cf. Knust and Wasserman 2018.
[22] Cf. Wright 2017, 121–52.
[23] Kloppenborg 2014.

founding philosopher. In many of these sayings, the synoptic tradition is de-historicized and reworked into a more Platonizing frame, with particular focus on the philosophical pursuit of knowledge.

Like the gnomological anthology, the dialogue format of several other apocryphal works (e.g. the Questions of Bartholomew, the Apocryphon of James, and the Dialogue of the Savior) lends itself to a philosophical presentation of Jesus's teaching. In the Sophia of Jesus Christ, the risen Jesus positions himself as the greatest philosopher, exposing the disagreements among lesser philosophers regarding the "ordering of the world and its movement." Jesus in the Gospel of Mary is just as philosophical. In this second-century dialogue gospel, Jesus expounds upon such classical philosophical themes as "the Good," "nature," "matter," "form," and "desire." One scholar has described the Gospel of Mary's characterization of Jesus's teaching as an effort to "explain the relevance of Jesus' Jewish gospel in the context of contemporary [second-century] mainstream philosophy."[24]

The idea that Jesus was a philosopher was not an invention of the second century. The Gospel according to John arguably recasts the Jesus tradition as a philosopher's biography. As George van Kooten notes, the Johannine evangelist brings the Greeks into proximity with Jesus (John 7:35; 12:20), depicts Jesus as a philosopher walking up and down in a stoa of the Temple, and quite plausibly transforms the classical motif of the *erastai* by referring to himself as the student whom Jesus loved with divine rather than erotic love.[25] The apocryphal Jesus as philosopher is therefore a further development of a canonical theme.

### Jesus the Mythographer

The most respected philosophers of Greco-Roman antiquity were also mythographers in their own right, and so it should come as no surprise that some early Christians – who most likely viewed Jesus as such a teacher – would reconstruct the memories of their charismatic founder as an explainer of myths. The religious imagination of the ancient Mediterranean (whether in its Greco-Roman or Egyptian forms) also contributed to this portrayal of Jesus.

In the Gospel of Judas, a Sethian Gnostic text, Jesus speaks to Judas in private, in the days before his crucifixion. He reveals the transcendent monad, the "Great Invisible Spirit" (Gos. Judas 47), who initiates emanations and successive differentiations known as "aeons." With

---

[24] de Boer 2010, 338.
[25] Cf. van Kooten 2019, 282–357.

each emanation, the aeons become farther removed from the Great Invisible Spirit (Gos. Judas 47–49), and they eventually spawn a corrupted cosmos consisting of an upper realm (Gos. Judas 50), and a lower realm, also known as Hades/chaos (Gos. Judas 51). In the lower realm, twelve demonic figures emerge and create Adam and Eve, who are allotted a temporary mortal existence. Adam and Eve are thus perceived to live in a cosmos created and governed by demonic forces, bound by their fleshly mortality. Jesus appears to reveal, in secret to Judas, salvation through esoteric knowledge of the aeons. Jesus's own self-disclosure is one of a spiritual being temporarily resident in a body that would soon be crucified. Similar versions of the Sethian Gnostic myth are revealed through Jesus's teaching in the Apocryphon of John. In the Gospel of the Egyptians, an even more complicated mythology and cosmogony is revealed through the esoteric teaching of the primordial Seth, who clothed himself in the human Jesus.[26]

Discoursing on primeval history is not entirely foreign to the canonical Jesus. In Mark 10:6–9 (cf. Matt 19:4–6), Jesus appeals to the Jewish story of creation as foundational for human origins and teleology. And the Johannine Jesus goes so far as claiming pre-existence "before Abraham was born" (John 8:58). While we can locate the origins of this portrait in the canonical gospels, the apocryphal Jesus becomes a much more imaginative mythographer, taking on the language and fascinations of Egyptian and Greco-Roman cosmologies.

**Jesus the Harrower of Hell**
The relationship of Jesus's death and resurrection to those who had died before his first advent was a topic that fascinated Christians of the second century onward. Perhaps this fascination was motivated by a desire to make sense of the status of the patriarchs and prophets in the Christian movement. Or perhaps it was a way in which early Christians told their stories in forms more familiar to Greco-Roman or Egyptian mythologies of the underworld. Whatever the motivation may be, beginning in the second century, apocryphal Jesus books develop the motif of Jesus's "harrowing" of Hell.

In the Gospel of Peter, at the scene of the resurrection, a walking, talking cross comes out of the tomb, and a voice from the heavens asks the cross if it has preached to "those who are asleep." The cross, probably an epiphanic symbolic token of the risen Christ, declares

---

[26] To this list of mythographic accounts of Jesus, one could also add the Sophia of Jesus Christ and the First Apocalypse of James, among others.

emphatically, "Yes!" Thus, the harrowing of Hell is summarized in a mere sentence in the Gospel of Peter. However, this tradition is developed in great detail in the Questions of Bartholomew and even more so in a recension of the Gospel of Nicodemus.

Although the canonical gospels are silent about Jesus's activity in the realm of the dead,[27] early Christian reflection took a keen interest in the motif of Jesus's harrowing of Hell.[28] Indeed, Jesus's descent to the dead made it into the *regula fidei* in the second century. It makes sense, then, that Jesus books written in the era in which this teaching was more widespread would situate it within their narratives.

**The Anti-Apostolic Jesus**
Many of the aforementioned apocryphal portraits of Jesus are more or less grounded in themes found in the earliest strata of apostolic memory of Jesus. Some of these portraits develop in trajectories that become untethered from early apostolic tradition, but they nevertheless maintain traces of indebtedness to the foundational documents of the Jesus tradition. Other portraits of Jesus, on the other hand, actively subvert the Jesus of apostolic memory. Three examples suffice to demonstrate this phenomenon: the Gospels of Thomas and Judas and the Gospel of the Egyptians.

In the Gospel according to Thomas, Jesus's secret teachings revealed to Thomas simultaneously presuppose the religious currency of the canonical synoptic tradition, and they also subvert it in favor of the higher, esoteric teaching solely preserved by a pseudepigraphical Thomas. Thus, the Jesus of Thomas gives more than a hint of a critique against the apostolic collective, especially Simon Peter and Matthew (see esp. logion 13). The Gospel of Mary gives an equally critical portrayal of Peter (Gos. Mary 17–19). To an even greater extent than Thomas and Mary, the Gospel of Judas criticizes the apostolic collective through the mouth of Jesus – and a mocking mouth at that. Jesus mocks the apostolic Eucharist, accuses the disciples of sexual deviancy, and labels their god as a demonic spirit. This Jesus is the antithesis of the Messiah of the proto-orthodox kerygma. Similarly, the primordial "Great Seth," who speaks as the author of the Gospel of the Egyptians and claims to have inhabited the human Jesus, derides "the apostles and

---

[27] With the possible exception of Jesus's being "in the heart of the earth for three days" in Matthew 12:40.
[28] Cf. The *Shepherd of Hermas* 9.16.5, Justin Martyr (*Dial.* 72.4), Irenaeus (*Adv. Haer.* 4.33.1, 12), Tertullian (*De anima* 55), and perhaps the first-century precursors in 1 Peter 3:19; 4:6.

the preachers" for not understanding the truth of Seth's revelation.[29] In the case of the Gospel of Judas and the Gospel of the Egyptians, the anti-apostolic Jesus is most likely the product of Sethian Gnostic groups seeking to differentiate themselves from the proto-orthodox.

It is worth mentioning that the anti-apostolic Jesus is actually a minority report within apocryphal Jesus traditions. Many apocryphal Jesus books presuppose the religious currency or theological authority of the canonical gospels, and some even appeal to the authority of the apostolic collective. One such text, already mentioned in this chapter, is the Epistula Apostolorum. By all accounts, it champions a proto-orthodox apologia for Jesus Christ, foretold by prophets, crucified under Pontius Pilate, risen in the flesh, and proclaimed by the apostles. Based on the testimony of the Epistula, we might even speak of a final portrait of the apocryphal Jesus: the apostolic Jesus. This is the Jesus of the canonical gospels, and many depictions of Jesus in the apocryphal tradition are but developments of this archetype. As such, they demonstrate that the apostolic portrait of Jesus held the most gravitas in the early Jesus movement as it matured into the Nicene faith.

## THE APOCRYPHAL JESUS IN JEWISH AND MUSLIM RECEPTION

Before concluding our chapter on the apocryphal Jesus, we must briefly mention the significant trajectories of reception in Jewish and Muslim literature. In the late second century there emerged a Jewish "anti-Gospel," a series of Jewish traditions employed by the second-century philosopher Celsus in opposition to the Christian faith. These traditions survive in fragments quoted by Origen in his response to Celsus, *Against Celsus*. They sought to discredit the historical claims of early apostolic memory, and they were later codified in the medieval Jewish *Toledoth Yeshu*, a polemical narrative of the life of Jesus roughly resembling the Gospel of Matthew. This polemical anti-Gospel was widely circulated and alleged that Jesus was the illegitimate child of Mary and a Roman soldier named Pandera.[30] Similar polemic can be found in the Talmud's account that Jesus was stoned and hanged on Passover Eve for being a "sorcerer" (*mesit*) who led the people astray.[31]

---

[29] Gos. Eg. folio 68.
[30] See the essays in Schäfer 2011.
[31] *b.Sanh.* 43a; Schäfer 2007 argues that this tradition is the product of fifth-century polemics, but Instone-Brewer 2011 dates it to the first century.

The early Muslim reception of Jesus picked up traditions found in Christian apocrypha, such as the Qur'an's retelling of Jesus's childhood miracle of the clay birds. The late medieval (or early modern) Gospel of Barnabas harmonizes the fourfold gospel while promoting the docetic teaching that Jesus did not die on the cross but was mistaken for a lookalike, namely Judas.[32] The Jesus of the Gospel of Barnabas uses John the Baptist's language to foretell the coming of Muhammad, the one whose sandals he is not worthy to untie.[33]

## CONCLUSION

In the present chapter, we have focused mostly on apocryphal portraits of Jesus as they emerged in the Jesus books of the second to fourth centuries – and we have surveyed only a representative sample. The apocryphal Jesus continued to take shape into the medieval Christian as well as the early Islamic eras, with Christians of many cultural-linguistic locations composing scores of other New Testament apocrypha – a development richly documented in the recent burgeoning of translations, editions, introductions, and commentaries on various New Testament apocrypha.[34]

All in all, the apocryphal portraits mentioned in this chapter reflect the broad spectrum of early Christian engagement with Jesus's memory. They highlight the variety of interpretations and appropriations of the gospel narrative, showing a process of theological exploration and experimentation. These memories, mostly preserved in the apocryphal gospels, illustrate the evolving understanding of Jesus's identity and teachings, contributing to the development of Christian doctrine and practice. Although diverse and sometimes controversial, apocryphal Jesus books largely function as complements to the canonical tradition. Among other things, they document early Christian processes of defining faith and doctrine, and while they often diverge in focus and interpretation, they collectively contribute to a deeper understanding of the early Christian engagement with the figure of Jesus Christ. The first

---

[32] With 222 chapters, the Gospel of Barnabas is not included in any recent anthologies of Christian apocrypha, but the 1907 translation by Ragg and Ragg is available open access online.

[33] Cf. Bockmuehl 2017, 132. See Nicolai Sinai's chapter in the present volume for a substantial introduction to the Islamic Jesus.

[34] See especially the volumes edited by Burke and Landau in the Further Reading section in this chapter, as well as the recent single-volume collections by Ehrman and Pleše 2011 and Gathercole 2021.

two centuries of the Jesus movement witnessed the solidification of the four canonical gospels as a collective cornerstone for Christian communities across the Mediterranean. At the same time, the "Apocryphal Jesus" – portrayed in various forms across sundry other ancient Jesus books – reflects a vibrant and exploratory phase in the Christian theological and literary tradition, and an important bridge to the reception of Jesus in late antiquity and the Middle Ages.

### FURTHER READING

Bockmuehl, Markus. 2017. *Ancient Apocryphal Gospels*. Louisville: Westminster John Knox.

Burke, Tony and Brent Landau, eds. 2016–2023. *New Testament Apocrypha: More Noncanonical Scriptures*. 3 vols. Grand Rapids: Eerdmans.

Ehrman, Bart D. and Zlatko Pleše. 2011. *The Apocryphal Gospels: Texts and Translations*. Oxford: Oxford University Press.

Gathercole, Simon. 2021. *The Apocryphal Gospels*. New York: Penguin.

Gathercole, Simon. 2022. *The Gospel and the Gospels: Christian Proclamation and Early Jesus Books*. Grand Rapids: Eerdmans.

Rodriguez, Jacob A. 2023. *Combining Gospels in Early Christianity: The One, the Many, and the Fourfold*. Tübingen: Mohr Siebeck.

Schröter, Jens, Tobias Nicklas, and Joseph Verheyden, eds. 2019. *Gospels and Gospel Reception in the Second Century: Experiments in Reception*. Berlin: De Gruyter.

Watson, Francis. 2022. *What Is a Gospel?* Grand Rapids: Eerdmans.

Watson, Francis and Sarah Parkhouse. 2018. *Connecting Gospels: Beyond the Canonical/Noncanonical Divide*. Oxford: Oxford University Press.

## 9 The Islamic Jesus
NICOLAI SINAI

While the Islamic tradition recognizes Jesus as a divinely authorized emissary, it denies his divinity and casts him as a 'messenger to the Israelites' (Q 3:49), thus stripping him of a properly universal salvific role in God's dealings with humankind at large. Such a role instead devolves upon Muhammad, regarded as God's final prophet who, from an Islamic perspective, represents the ecumenical opening-up of God's prophetic interaction with humans beyond the ethnically particular limits of Israelite prophecy. A considerable range of utterances and narratives that Christians associate with Jesus have resonances in Islamic literature, illustrating how Muslims participated in the variegated stream of interpretive responses to and construals of Jesus. The present chapter begins by reviewing the portrayals of Jesus and Mary in the Qur'an and then moves on to survey, in an inevitably superficial manner, post-Qur'anic Arabic and Persian sources up until the thirteenth century CE.[1]

### JESUS IN THE QUR'AN: GENERAL REMARKS AND OVERVIEW

Before delving into a more detailed examination of the Qur'anic material about Jesus, it is useful to make some general observations. First, the Qur'anic presentation of Jesus, like that of other biblical figures, is highly selective when set against the background of the antecedent biblical tradition: while the Islamic scripture adopts and rearticulates a certain number of biblical or post-biblical motifs, some prominent gospel episodes – including the Three Magi, the Sermon on the Mount, the feeding of the multitude, and the passion narrative – are completely absent from Qur'anic pronouncements about Jesus. Indeed, in line with the Qur'an's general tendency to employ personal names only

---

[1] Specifically on Sufi texts, see in more detail Morrissey in press.

sparingly, there are no Qur'anic references to such biblically familiar characters as Mary's husband Joseph, Herod, or individual disciples, who instead figure only as a collective block (Q 3:52, 5:111–12, 61:14). Rather, the only individuals named in connection with Jesus are his mother Mary, Mary's father (who in Q 3:35 and 66:12 is identified as 'Imrān rather than, as the Christian tradition would have it, Joachim), Zechariah, and the latter's son John (who is not given his customary Christian cognomen 'the Baptist').

Secondly, various features of the Qur'anic Jesus parallel the Qur'anic depiction of other messengers, including Muhammad himself.[2] For example, in Q 61:14 the Qur'an's contemporary adherents, the community of 'believers' around Muhammad, are called upon to be God's militant 'helpers' just as Jesus's disciples had declared themselves to be Jesus's 'helpers' in the face of the unbelief of their Israelite compatriots. What is arguably the climactic situation in the ministry of the Qur'anic Jesus, a *kairos*-like moment requiring Jesus's audience to make a committed decision between belief and unbelief, thus anticipates the situation of Muhammad and his followers. Such parallelism among Qur'anic prophets is rooted in the Islamic scripture's general tendency to assimilate the career and experiences of different prophets and messengers: even though their basic historical distinctness and their entrenched association with certain specific events (e.g. Noah and the Deluge, Moses and the Exodus) is respected, Qur'anic prophetology is rooted in the assumption that God's emissaries throughout history have the same basic task – namely, to remind forgetful and wavering humans of God's existence, power, and moral demands – and are therefore apt to face similar rejection.

Thirdly, Jesus stands apart from other Qur'anic prophets and messengers insofar as he attracts polemical comments about his status and role that explicitly reject an alternative (namely, Christian) understanding of Jesus as divine and as God's son (e.g. Q 19:34–40, 5:17.72.116–17).[3] This reflects the prominence of Christianity and christological controversies in the Qur'an's wider late antique context of emergence. Jesus is expressly quoted as disavowing his own veneration as a divine being (Q 5:116–17) and instead is consistently depicted as having maintained to his audience that God is 'my and your [plural] Lord', who alone merits worship (Q 3:51, 5:72.117, 19:36,

---

[2] See, e.g., Robinson 1991, 36–38; Robinson 2003, 17; Khalidi 2001, 10–11, 15.
[3] See Khalidi 2001, 12.

43:64). Such statements are of course rooted in the Qur'an's stringent monotheism and its condemnation of the human penchant for blurring the boundary between creator and creation by 'associating' (*ashraka*) God with other beings, whether these be the pagan deities worshipped by contemporary Meccans or indeed Christ. As has often been noted, the Qur'an's denial of Jesus's divine sonship is almost certainly the reason why Jesus is so frequently given the genealogical tag 'son of Mary', which forms an implicit contrast with his Christian status as the son of God (e.g. Q 2:87.253, 3:45, 4:157.171).

The Qur'an contains two extended treatments of Jesus and Mary, found in Surah 3 (vv. 33–63) and Surah 19 (vv. 16–40). These two passages, examined in more detail in the following section, revolve around Jesus's annunciation to Mary and his miraculous conception without a human father – a noteworthy Qur'anic concurrence with Christian tradition, yet one that from the Qur'anic vantage point does not entail or indicate Jesus's divine sonship, only the fact that Jesus was, like Adam, brought into being by the creative fiat of an omnipotent divine creator (Q 3:59). The prominence of Mary in these two narratives, as well as the complete absence of Joseph, has given rise to a rich literature exploring how the Qur'an's portrayal of Mary valorizes a feminine figure, undercuts patriarchal norms, or can even be seen to destabilize binary constructions of gender altogether.[4] Other important statements about Jesus occur in Surah 5, which lists some of Jesus's miracles and recounts how God granted the request of Jesus's disciples that God send down to them a banquet table (Q 5:110–18), perhaps a Qur'anic reconfiguration of aspects of the Last Supper and the feeding of the multitude. The concluding verse of Surah 61, Q 61:14, depicts Jesus's confrontation with unbelieving Israelites and provides a more elaborate parallel to a verse in Surah 3's outlook on Jesus's adult ministry (Q 3:52). Further Qur'anic material about Jesus will be referenced at the appropriate places in what follows.

The two extended Jesus-and-Mary pericopes in Surahs 3 and 19 display considerable overlap in wording and narrative detail, as illustrated by Mary's astonished response to the annunciation of Jesus's birth in Q 3:47 and 19:20. At the same time, the two pericopes also comprise separate content – for example, Mary's delivery of her son, which is only recounted in Surah 19 – and show distinctive characteristics and emphases. For instance, Surah 19 has Mary receive the

---

[4] See Ali 2017 with many further references.

annunciation of Jesus's birth from God's 'spirit', who in this context is a quasi-angelic figure presenting himself in human form (Q 19:17) and evidently corresponds to the angel Gabriel in Luke 1:26–38. In Surah 3, however, Mary is accosted not by an individual 'spirit' but rather by 'the angels' in the plural (Q 3:45), just like Zechariah earlier in the same pericope (Q 3:39).[5]

To give a further illustration of the relationship between the Jesus-and-Mary narratives in Surahs 3 and 19, both closely link the figure of Jesus to John (the Baptist) and the latter's father Zechariah, in keeping with Luke 1 and the Christian tradition in general (while toning down the standard Christian casting of John as a lesser forerunner of Jesus).[6] Yet the narrative organization of both Qur'anic passages is quite distinct. Surah 19 presents the annunciation and birth of John and of Jesus as formally self-contained episodes that are placed back-to-back in a larger narrative cycle (vv. 2–15 on Zechariah and John, vv. 16–40 on Mary and Jesus). This is not dissimilar to the way in which Luke 1 first reports the foretelling of the birth of John (vv. 5–25) and then that of Jesus (vv. 26–38). By contrast, Surah 3 fuses the two stories into an overarching narrative sweep. An important commonality, in any case, is that neither Surah 3 nor Surah 19 shows a particular interest in Jesus's adult life, which is only treated in the form of a rather perfunctory flash-forward in Q 3:48–57 and virtually absent from Surah 19.

When placed against the customary distinction between two stages of the Qur'an's genesis, an earlier Meccan and a later Medinan one, the only Meccan passage among the material reviewed so far is Surah 19. Assuming the tenability of a linear chronology of Qur'anic passages (which is not uncontroversial in current scholarship), we may therefore view Q 3:33–63 as a secondary retelling of Q 19:2–40. While reprising the annunciations of John and Jesus from Surah 19, Surah 3 bookends them with a prequel narrating the birth of Mary herself, at the one end, and a concise overview of Jesus's later ministry up until his departure from the world, at the other end (Q 3:55). The phenomenon of secondary retelling that is exemplified by the Jesus-and-Mary pericopes in Surahs 19 and 3 is not uncommon for Qur'anic narrative.

---

[5] Both Zechariah and Mary are also depicted as conversing with a singular interlocutor ("he said") and using the address "O my Lord," implying that they are speaking to God himself, presumably via angelic intermediaries (Q 3:40.47).

[6] But see Q 3:39.

## THE LIVES OF MARY AND JESUS ACCORDING TO THE QUR'AN

As just noted, the Medinan Surah 3 commences its extended pericope on Jesus and Mary by relaying the circumstances of the latter's birth: Mary's mother, identified as 'the wife of 'Imrān', dedicates the child growing in her womb to God (Q 3:35). This child subsequently turns out to be a daughter, who is named Mary (Q 3:36). Mary is then assigned to the care of Zechariah, who visits her in the Israelite sanctuary and is surprised to find her miraculously well provisioned with food, which Mary credits to God (Q 3:37). Perhaps because he is inspired by this display of God's munificence, Zechariah petitions God for progeny of his own (Q 3:38; cf. Q 19:2–6) and is told by the angels that his plea will be granted in the form of a son called John (Q 3:39). As in Surah 19, Zechariah is incredulous at this promise, given that his wife is old and barren, and asks for a confirmatory 'sign'. In consequence, Zechariah is struck with muteness for three days, forcing him to communicate by gestures (Q 3:40–41; cf. Q 19:8–11). Unlike the corresponding biblical verse, Luke 1:20, the Qur'an does not cast Zechariah's muteness as a penalty for his incredulity but simply as a miraculous corroboration of God's ability to transcend and transform the ordinary course of things. (In the Bible, Zechariah is also mute for much longer.) The narrative then shifts back to Mary, who is told by 'the angels' that God has 'chosen' her 'above the women of the world' (Q 3:42; cf. Luke 1:42) and that she, too, will bear a son, to be called 'the Messiah (al-masīḥ) Jesus, son of Mary' (Q 3:45). Both Surah 3 and Surah 19 cite Mary's objection that 'no man has touched me' (Q 3:47, 19:20), and Surah 3 has her angelic interlocutor explain that 'when God decides on something, he merely says to it, "Be," and it is' (Q 3:47). The Qur'an's endorsement of Jesus's virginal conception is therefore clear, even if Mary's impregnation with Jesus is explicitly reported only in Q 19:22. Elsewhere, the Qur'an's divine voice explains that Mary 'guarded her chastity and we breathed our spirit into her' (Q 21:91; cf. Q 66:12), just as God breathed his spirit into Adam (Q 15:29, 32:9, 38:72). If one defensibly construes Q 21:91 and 66:12 to indicate a certain degree of ontological affinity between God and Jesus, it is an affinity that is not peculiar to Jesus but rather encompasses all humans via their ancestor Adam (though the figure of Jesus might perhaps be seen as a peculiar heightening of this general affinity).

Surah 3's annunciation scene ends with a summary of the principal feats and miracles performed by Mary's son, just as the Lukan Gabriel similarly follows up the annunciation with a prediction of Jesus's future prominence (Luke 1:32–33). Thus, Jesus will speak in the cradle (Q 3:46); he will, with God's permission, breathe life into birds from clay; and he will cure the sick and resurrect the dead (Q 3:49; cf. Q 5:110). The Qur'an moreover underlines Jesus's continuity with the Mosaic law rather than his abrogation of it: according to Q 3:50, Jesus will 'confirm what precedes him of the Torah' (cf. Q 5:46 and 61:6), although he will also 'make lawful' a number of things previously forbidden.

As several cross-references have already indicated, Zechariah's plea for progeny and his subsequent muteness as well as the annunciation of Jesus's birth to Mary, all of which Surah 3 reprises from Surah 19, have obvious biblical counterparts in Luke 1. The remainder of the storyline just summarized from Surah 3, however, closely parallels an important extrabiblical text, the Protoevangelium of James, which begins with a very similar, though much more detailed, account of the birth and childhood of Mary. Such conspicuous engagement with narrative traditions from the Protoevangelium is largely confined to the Medinan retelling of Mary's story in Surah 3 and accounts for most of the latter's separate content in comparison with Surah 19, even if Jesus's miraculous vivification of birds from clay, mentioned in Q 3:49 (cf. 5:110), intersects instead with a scene in the Infancy Gospel of Thomas 2.

Surah 3 not only presents additional material about Mary and Jesus compared to the earlier Surah 19 but also shows certain omissions. Specifically, since Surah 3 segues directly from the annunciation scene to a catalogue of Jesus's future accomplishments, it skips (though does not negate) the climax of the Jesus-and-Mary narrative in Surah 19: having conceived Jesus, Mary withdraws to a desolate place, where she gives birth, without there being any clue in the text that Joseph might have been in attendance (Q 19:22–23). In the midst of her solitary labour, alone in the wilderness and presumably at her most vulnerable, Mary cries out in despair (Q 19:23), upon which she is comforted by a voice calling to her 'from underneath her' and directing her to a nearby stream and palm tree that will fortify her (Q 19:24–26). This voice, one infers, is in fact the infant Jesus speaking, who Q 3:46 predicts will 'speak to people from the cradle' (cf. Q 5:110). After delivering her son, Mary returns to her people, and in a dramatic standoff they accuse her of fornication when they see the unwed mother reappear with a newborn child (Q 19:27–28). Mary's detractors, however, are thoroughly rebuffed when the infant Jesus again demonstrates his miraculous ability to speak (Q 19:29–33). The entire sequence drives home how God delivers and vindicates righteous believers who find themselves isolated from or threatened by their contemporaries, a message also very much in evidence in Surah 19's Abraham pericope (Q 19:41–50). But the infant Jesus's address also stresses that he is nothing more than a 'servant of God' (Q 19:30), a rejection of Christian claims that is made even more explicit in a concluding commentary (Q 19:34–40), probably a secondary addition.

A striking feature of Surah 19's nativity scene is the fact that the latter shows no overlap with the canonical accounts of the birth of Jesus in Matthew and Luke, despite the fact that the annunciation of Jesus conveyed to Mary in both Q 19:17–21 and 3:45–47 does have considerable affinity with Luke 1:26–38. Instead of the familiar Bethlehem setting of the Christian nativity, we saw that the Qur'an depicts Mary as giving birth to Jesus in solitude and as being nourished by a nearby stream and palm tree. The Qur'anic narrative here telescopes the nativity with a miracle that the Christian tradition places at a later moment in the life of the infant Jesus, during the flight of the Holy Family to Egypt. The scene is best known from the Latin Gospel of Pseudo-Matthew 20, but this rendition is reliant on older sources.[7] Surah 19's displacement of the palm tree miracle and its utilization as an alternative nativity scene may well be original to the Qur'an. The likely rationale of this narrative telescoping would have been to craft a nativity scene that throws into relief what was just observed to be a general message of the narratives in Surah 19: that God will miraculously aid the pious, however desperate their plight. The combined nativity-cum-palm-tree scene from Surah 19 arguably underscores this point far more concisely than a lengthy rehearsal of standard Christian traditions around Jesus's birth and childhood in their established narrative order, with a host of additional *dramatis personae* (Joseph, the Magi, Herod), might have done.

As already intimated, the Qur'an is fairly vague about later stages of Jesus's life. Apart from the various miracles already alluded to and the confrontation between Jesus's disciples and unbelieving Israelites in Q 3:52 and 61:14, the most noteworthy Qur'anic statement about Jesus's adult ministry is an apparent denial of his death by crucifixion in Q 4:157 that has given rise to considerable interpretive debate.[8] The verse occurs in the context of a list of polemical accusations against the 'scripture-owners', which here seem to intend the Israelites in

---

[7] See Shoemaker 2003, 18–21.
[8] E.g. Lawson 2009, Reynolds 2009, and Mourad 2011.

particular. These opponents are inter alia said to have broken God's covenant and killed his prophets (Q 4:155), two tropes of Christian anti-Judaism. The opponents are then further taken to task for claiming, 'We have killed the Messiah (*al-masīḥ*) Jesus, son of Mary, God's messenger', to which the Qur'an's divine voice responds that 'they did not kill him nor crucify him; rather, it was made to appear to them thus (*shubbiha lahum*)' (Q 4:157). As the following verse goes on to assert, what really transpired is that God 'raised' Jesus 'up to himself' (Q 4:158). This statement pertinently connects to a verse from the summary of Jesus's adult ministry in Surah 3: 'And [recall] when God said, "O Jesus, I am taking you from life (*mutawaffīka*) and am raising you up to me and am cleansing you of the repudiators and am setting those who follow you above the repudiators until the day of resurrection"' (Q 3:55).

In the post-Qur'anic tradition, Q 4:157 spawned stories according to which the victim of the crucifixion was not Jesus but somebody else whom God had 'caused to look similar' (Arabic *shabbaha*, the verb employed in Q 4:157) to Jesus.[9] Such post-Qur'anic traditions likely draw on ancient Gnostic ideas to the effect that Simon of Cyrene was crucified instead of Jesus (cf. already Irenaeus, *Haer*. 1.24.4 and related affirmations at Nag Hammadi). It is uncertain that the Qur'an itself is endorsing such a substitutionist account of the crucifixion, since it does not explicitly refer to anyone taking Jesus's place. Rather, the Qur'an's main concern is to highlight that Jesus, a divinely appointed messenger, did not fall victim to his opponents: as Suleiman Mourad has written, 'the crucifixion of Jesus does not represent a defeat of God'.[10] After all, the Qur'an takes for granted that God will not forsake his messengers but will instead vindicate and deliver them in the face of their unbelieving enemies (e.g. Q 10:103, 40:51).[11] In keeping with this governing assumption, the alleged vaunt by the Israelites that they killed Jesus, 'God's messenger', cited in Q 4:157, is bound to be Qur'anically objectionable.

Does this mean, though, that Jesus did not really die? Not necessarily: especially in view of Q 3:55, cited immediately before the preceding paragraph, the Qur'an may well be accepting Jesus's demise,

---

[9] See, e.g., Brinner 2002, 671.
[10] Mourad 2011, 356.
[11] An attentive reader will wonder whether this claim is not refuted by the reference to Jewish prophet-killing in Q 4:155. However, the Qur'an frequently seems to make a distinction between prophets (singular *nabiyy*) and messengers (singular *rasūl*), though Jesus and some other figures are accorded both titles. The premise of divine deliverance is primarily associated with messengers, not with prophets.

but with the crucial caveat that his death was not caused by his persecutors but rather was God's way of shielding Jesus from the machinations of his foes. Hence, Jesus's departure from life, his ascension or 'lifting-up towards' God, did presumably not involve suffering and humiliation; yet it may well have involved a terminal cessation of Jesus's vital functions. In this regard, Jesus's eventual fate would be similar to that of committed believers who are killed in battle, as per Q 3:169: 'Do not consider those killed on God's path as dead. They are rather alive in God's presence, receiving provision' (similarly Q 2:154).[12] Perhaps, then, Jesus did indeed die, though not as a consequence of the actions of his opponents, and was subsequently resurrected and raised up into God's presence ahead of the general resurrection of the dead. That Jesus's elevation into God's proximity did include his bodily demise is in fact strongly suggested by the general Qur'anic principle that 'everyone shall taste death' (Q 3:185, 21:35, 29:57), as well as by Q 19:33, where Jesus himself alludes to the day of his death and his subsequent resurrection.[13]

The line of interpretation just developed is compatible with the standard Christian idea that Jesus was indeed nailed to a cross and buried but subsequently revealed himself to be alive (again). In fact, one might go so far as to consider rendering the segment 'they did not kill him nor crucify him' (wa-mā qatalūhu wa-mā ṣalabūhu) from Q 4:157 as '*they* did not kill him by crucifying him'[14] or '*they* did not kill him and end his life on the cross'. Where the preceding interpretation of Q 4:157 nonetheless diverges quite substantially from mainstream Christianity is in attaching no salvific importance to the crucifixion: the event was not a vicarious sacrifice of Jesus on behalf of humanity but simply a convenient means by which God removed Jesus from his persecutors, just as God reportedly protected Abraham from being burnt alive (Q 21:69).[15]

The Qur'an applies a certain number of epithets and characterizations to Jesus that call for comment. While Jesus is repeatedly called *al-masīḥ*, an Arabization of 'Messiah' (Q 3:45, 4:157.171.172,

---

[12] See Robinson 2003, 18 and 19, and Mourad 2011, 354.
[13] It is sometimes argued that Q 4:159 entails that Jesus's death lies in the eschatological future rather than in the past, in accordance with a widespread post-Qur'anic opinion. However, there is an alternative interpretation that avoids this inference (Robinson 1991, 78–89; Reynolds 2009, 247–48).
[14] Thus Mourad 2011, 354 (though without the italics).
[15] In the case of Abraham, of course, this almost certainly did not entail a cessation of his vital functions, and the Qur'an reports on subsequent events from Abraham's life.

5:17.72.75, 9:30.31), the Islamic scripture seems to be using the expression merely as an established honorific that is to all intents and purposes part of Jesus's personal name, just as 'Christ' might behave in theologically uninformed English usage. One verse, Q 4:171, furthermore describes Jesus as 'God's messenger and his word, which he cast upon Mary, and his spirit'. Here, the reference to Jesus as God's 'word' (cf. also Q 3:39.45) might remind Christian readers of the concept of a pre-existent *logos* as put forward in John 1. However, the Qur'anic meaning of the expression is far more likely to be connected to the idea that Jesus's conception was effected by God's creative fiat (Q 3:47.59), and perhaps also to Jesus's miraculous ability to speak 'from the cradle' (Q 3:46). Finally, when Q 4:171 calls Jesus God's 'spirit' (literally, 'a spirit from him'), this reflects the insufflation of God's spirit into Mary according to Q 21:91 and Q 66:12 (see earlier in this section) as well as statements to the effect that God fortified Jesus with 'the holy spirit' (Q 2:87.253, 5:110). Fortification by God's spirit, it should be noted, is not limited to Jesus but also reported of the Qur'anic community of believers (Q 58:22). It is important, therefore, not to be misled by superficial resemblances between Qur'anic and established Christian nomenclature and to remain alert to the Qur'an's semantic specificity.

## JESUS IN POST-QUR'ANIC ISLAM: A COMPOSITE CHARACTER PROFILE

Images of Jesus in post-Qur'anic Islam build upon and flesh out the Qur'anic material just reviewed, which leaves significant gaps. As with other biblical figures, the early Islamic tradition amplifies Qur'anic statements about Jesus by recourse to select Christian (or, in other cases, Jewish) elements. For instance, the chapter on Zechariah, John, Mary, and Jesus that is found in a well-known work on prophetic history by al-Thaʿlabī (d. 1035 CE) collates a host of extra-Qur'anic traditions presenting the reader with characters like Joseph, Herod, Lazarus, Simon, Judas, and Mary Magdalene.[16] On occasion, the evident reliance on Christian lore is made explicit by formulations such as 'Christian scholars have said that...' or 'I asked one of the monks'.[17] To adduce one specific example, al-Thaʿlabī cites a retelling of the Last Supper and the crucifixion, attributed to the early traditionist Wahb ibn

---

[16] Brinner 2002, 622–80.
[17] Brinner 2002, 636 and 641.

Munabbih (d. 728 CE?), which is replete with specific New Testament detail, such as the struggle of Jesus's disciples to remain awake, Peter's repeated denial of being connected to Jesus, thirty silver coins, and thorns.[18] At the same time, the passage contends that the victim of the crucifixion was not Jesus but Judas, in line with a prevalent interpretation of Q 4:157 that had emerged by the mid-700s. The narrative thus exhibits an artful attempt to reconcile Qur'anic data with extra-Qur'anic Christian material.[19]

While al-Thaʿlabī arranges his material in a linear and quasi-biographical sequence, Islamic literature also preserves a very large quantity of biographically decontextualized stories about and logia attributed to Jesus, many of which have been collected and translated by Tarif Khalidi.[20] Much of this material presents Jesus as an exponent of asceticism and world-renunciation (zuhd), an image of Jesus that is found as early as the compilations of miscellaneous renunciant traditions by ʿAbdallāh ibn al-Mubārak (d. 797 CE) and Aḥmad ibn Ḥanbal (d. 855 CE). The ascetic dimension of Jesus is well illustrated by an anecdote according to which he cast away even his cup and his comb when observing someone else combing his hair with his fingers and another person drinking with his hands cupped (Khalidi 2001, no. 222; Schimmel 2018, 31). The narration harks back to a similar anecdote that Diogenes Laertius recounts of his namesake, the Cynic philosopher Diogenes, in *Lives of Eminent Philosophers* 6.2.37. Pushing Jesus's voluntary poverty yet further, Abū Bakr ibn Abī al-Dunyā (d. 894 CE) and various later writers, including the Persian poets Sanāʾī (d. ca. 1130 CE) and ʿAṭṭār (d. 1220 CE), recount that Jesus abandoned even the stone on which he was resting his head when mocked by Satan for being satisfied with it (Khalidi 2001, no. 119; Nurbakhsh 2012, 76–78; Schimmel 2018, 35–36). The story is a distant relative of Jesus's temptation by Satan in the New Testament (e.g. Matt 4:1–11), which has additional Islamic parallels.[21] But what is most notable is, again, the ascetic slant that this particular version of an encounter between Jesus and Satan imposes on the character of Jesus. Further ascetic traits reported of Jesus are his meagre possessions, his garments of coarse wool, and his homelessness.[22]

[18] Brinner 2002, 670–71.
[19] Andrae 1987, 26.
[20] Khalidi 2001.
[21] For other encounters between Jesus and Satan, see Khalidi 2001, nos 34 (closest to the Gospel story), 206, 240, 278, 281, 285, 292, 300.
[22] E.g. Khalidi 2001, nos 60, 76–78, 110, 136, 220, 302.

In keeping with his austere lifestyle, the Islamic Jesus is frequently invoked in a didactic capacity, by observing and discoursing on the treachery and ephemerality of the world. One report, preserved by Abū Bakr ibn Abī al-Dunyā and again elaborated in the poetry of ʿAṭṭār, describes Jesus's allegorical vision of the world in the form of a toothless hag decked out with adornments who has slain all of her previous husbands (Khalidi 2001, no. 106; Schimmel 2018, 49–50). Another tale, once again with an early attestation in Abū Bakr ibn Abī al-Dunyā, shows Jesus in the company of a man unable to admit having stolen a loaf of bread, culminating in a Sergio Leone–style finale in which Jesus's companion and two equally rapacious passers-by end up murdering one another for the sake of a treasure of gold that Jesus had created from earth and sand. 'This is the world; beware of it!', Jesus remarks when passing the three corpses (Khalidi 2001, no. 108).

The degree to which Jesus is here depicted as a mere observer failing to have any transformative impact on his fellow traveller and without any redemptive ambitions vis-à-vis 'the world' is particularly intriguing when compared to his Christian incarnation. Even stories with a happier ending can cast Jesus as an observer providing retrospective commentary on initially puzzling turns of events rather than as himself being a catalyst of human change and repentance (Khalidi 2001, nos 144–45). Nonetheless, the Islamic Jesus does have features that are highly redolent of the Jesus of the Gospels, such as calling for humility and mercy, condemning ostentation, offering both of his cheeks to be slapped, requiting insults with blessings, and washing the feet of his disciples.[23] In time, Sufism-affiliated authors like al-Ghazālī (d. 1111) came to augment Jesus's austere and renunciant personality in early Islamic sources with more mystical themes of loving immersion in, and experiential knowledge of, God.[24]

It is pertinent to observe that Jesus's commitment to an ascetic or renunciant lifestyle is not at all suggested by what the Qur'an has to say about him but rather is rooted in the importance of ascetic currents in early post-Qur'anic Islam, an archaic religious orientation that was eventually co-opted into the Sufi tradition with its more mystical stress on the possibility of experiential communion with God.[25] Why did this early Islamic ascetic mood come to attach

---

[23] E.g. Khalidi 2001, nos 3, 4, 9, 29, 56, 66, 80, 100, 269; see also Andrae 1987, 17; Nurbakhsh 2012, 105–6; Schimmel 2018, 52.
[24] See Morrissey in press. Examples are Khalidi 2001, nos 209, 224, 225, 227, 238, 244.
[25] See generally Melchert 2020.

itself specifically to the figure of Jesus? One facilitating factor may have been the biblical Jesus's itinerant lifestyle, which is also foregrounded as a principal trait of his Muslim avatar (e.g. Khalidi 2001, no. 135) and became enshrined in the etymological construct that Jesus's title *al-masīḥ* is to be derived from the Arabic verb *sāḥa*, 'to wander, to roam'. Another factor may have been the likely historical link between early Muslim renunciant piety, on the one hand, and Christian hermits and monks, on the other.[26] It appears that the austere piety modelled by Christian eremites and monks was projected onto Christianity's eponym.

The logia that Islamic texts attribute to Jesus show an unmistakable imprint of Muslim concerns and preoccupations, including traditions in which Jesus interprets or cites the Qur'an or serves as a conduit of divine predictions of Islam, similar to Q 61:6.[27] Nonetheless, the material also stands in recognizable continuity with the Jesus of the Gospels. As Khalidi notes, a significant number of Jesus logia are constructed around a Gospel core or adopt identifiably New Testament phraseology.[28] Thus, Jesus addresses his listeners as the 'salt of the earth', remarks that birds do not reap or plough, predicts the destruction of the Jerusalem Temple, insists that 'each day brings with it his own sustenance', and contrasts Moses's prohibition of adultery and false oaths with his own more far-reaching prohibition of even contemplating adultery or swearing by God at all (Khalidi 2001, nos 7, 15, 71, 78, 190). One report parenthetically notes Jesus's fondness for the formula 'Truly I say to you...' (Khalidi 2001, no. 51; cf. no. 31). A particularly fertile motif for Islamic reimaginations of Jesus seems to have been his New Testament confrontation with the Pharisees, which inspired sayings that are critical of scholars who teach for gain, disseminate erroneous views, are conceited, or fail to practice what they preach.[29]

The Islamic Jesus is, moreover, associated with multiple resurrection stories.[30] Yet unlike their Gospel counterparts (e.g. the Lazarus story in John 11:1-44), quite a few of these narratives feature Jesus

---

[26] Andrae 1987, 7-32; Melchert 2020, 14-16.
[27] See Khalidi 2001, nos 9 (on Q 18:30), 52 (on a frequent Qur'anic verse-closer found, e.g., in Q 2:38), 53 (relating to Q 19:15.33), 87 and 271 (predictions of Islam).
[28] Khalidi 2001, 33-34.
[29] See Khalidi 2001, nos 16-17, 43, 67-68, 92-94, 117, 122, 132, 196, 199, 201-3, 213, 260, 268, 276, 285, 293, 299.
[30] In addition to the following references, see Khalidi 2001, nos 50, 59, 252, as well as Schimmel 2018, 54-56, 69-79, and Nurbakhsh 2012, 114-17.

interrogating dead persons or skulls about their life, the circumstances of their death, or their fate in the afterlife, without subsequently bringing them back to life for good.[31] In one case, Jesus expressly refuses to let a resurrected father continue to live, seeing that 'he no longer has any means of subsistence' (Khalidi 2001, no. 247). In another story, however, an inmate of hell is allowed to remain alive, spends twelve years worshipping God, and thus redeems herself (Khalidi 2001, no. 186). That resurrection can be an emphatically mixed blessing is exemplified by an anecdote in which a believing woman is resurrected at the behest of her widower but then proceeds to elope with a prince, causing her to die as an unbeliever (Khalidi 2001, no. 284). As in some other tales, Jesus here appears as a detached observer of human folly and of the multifarious temptations that the world holds in store.

Sometimes, though not always, the resurrection stories just surveyed make it explicit that the one effecting the resurrection is not Jesus himself but rather God or that Jesus resurrects the person in question only with God's permission and aid (e.g. Khalidi 2001, nos 23, 113, 186, 198, 252). This is in keeping with the fact that the Qur'an, too, underscores that Jesus's miracles were only possible with God's permission (Q 3:49, 5:110). Traditions foregrounding that the true agent of resurrection is God rather than Jesus tie in with a pervasive stress on Jesus's humanity and limitations. For example, Jesus is depicted as being ignorant of the time of the eschatological hour or as crying out in anguish when the hour is mentioned in his presence (Khalidi 2001, nos 5–6, 38). In one of his encounters with Satan, Jesus professes that he does not know whether God 'will save me or not' (Khalidi 2001, no. 34), thus casting Jesus in the same position as other renunciants who were consumed by terror at the danger of damnation. In fact, in one logion Jesus expresses the hope that a pious 'friend of God' will intercede for his sins (Nurbakhsh 2012, 127). Other traditions portray Jesus as having been distracted from immersion in God by the thought of bread, occasioning the veiled rebuke of an old 'friend of God', and as less meritorious than John (Khalidi 2001, nos 124, 209; cf. nos 39 and 239).[32] One utterance has Jesus affirm expressly that 'the world existed and I was not in it' (Khalidi 2001, no. 111), thus precluding his identification with the pre-existent divine *logos* evoked in John 1. Perhaps the

---

[31] Khalidi 2002, nos 23, 113, 198, 234, 248, 252. See also Nurbakhsh 2012, 119–21, and Schimmel 2018, 71–73.

[32] For an opposite assessment, by Rūmī, see Schimmel 2018, 41. According to Khalidi 2001, no. 53, God "recognized the merit of them both."

most memorable expression of this concern to highlight that Jesus too was beset by a degree of imperfection is an anecdote popular in later Persian poets like Sanā'ī, 'Aṭṭār, and Rūmī (d. 1273 CE): When Jesus was lifted up to God, he was found to have carried a needle with him, indicating that even the paradigmatic renunciant Jesus did not manage to shed all worldly ties (Schimmel 2018, 92–95). Owing to this minor infraction, it is said, Jesus was not permitted to dwell with God himself but resides only in the fourth heaven.

A final dimension of the post-Qur'anic Islamic Jesus is his apocalyptic role in an Islamicized version of his second coming.[33] Jesus, believed to have been continuously alive after his rescue from the crucifixion, will return at the end of times to kill a false messiah called the Dajjāl ('Deceiver'), 'break crosses and kill swine', espouse Islam, and finally die, thereby ushering in the end of the world. While Sunnis sometimes found Jesus a convenient means of counterbalancing Shi'ite portrayals of the alternative messianic figure of the Mahdī or 'Rightly Guided One', a wide-ranging study has found that Jesus's role in Muslim apocalyptic scenarios was likely early and reduced over time.[34] Like Jesus's asceticism, Jesus's role in the events leading up to the end of the world has little support in the Qur'an. One verse, Q 4:159, does admittedly announce that on the day of judgement Jesus will serve as a 'witness against' the 'scripture-owners' (i.e. Jews and Christians), but an equivalent role will be played by other messengers (e.g. Q 4:41).[35]

## CONCLUDING REMARKS

Neither the Qur'anic nor the post-Qur'anic Islamic Jesus is a metaphysical reality, an object of complex theological speculation like his Christian counterpart. Rather, in the Qur'an Jesus is principally prominent as the infant son of Mary, a 'servant of God', whose virginal conception and miracle-working illustrate God's power and gracious engagement with humankind but whose status is grievously misconstrued by his professed Christian followers. Post-Qur'anic Islam, meanwhile, casts Jesus as an ascetic, an authoritative moral teacher, and a protagonist in the apocalyptic drama. Jesus's humanity and subordination to God are

---

[33] Jeffery 1951; Cook 2002, 93–109, 172–77.
[34] Cook 2002, 173, 212–13, 323–24. See also Reynolds 2009, 250–51.
[35] Robinson 1991, 87. Another oft-quoted prooftext for Jesus's eschatological role, Q 43:61, is not conclusive. See Robinson 1991, 90–93, and Reynolds 2009, 248–49.

often underscored, which contributes to a general impression that Jesus does not exercise miraculous or salvific powers in his own right.

The preceding glimpses at Islamic construals of Jesus allow us to isolate, with all due caution, the kernel of what one might call an Islamic Christology, in the sense of a principled doctrinal stance on Jesus: his life, teaching, and actions tend to be valorized as manifesting divine agency or exemplary human piety, as far as this is compatible with the fundamental Islamic premise that Jesus must not be ontologically assimilated to God any more than other creatures. Historically, this is an understanding of Jesus that may be viewed as due to a critical reception of Christian lore and doctrine from the vantage point afforded by the adamant monotheism that forms the Qur'an's doctrinal centrepiece. Thus understood, Islamic Christology is a secondary response to mainstream (i.e. Pauline and Nicaean) Christianity.

It is true that writers from John Toland (d. 1722) to the contemporary Turkish author Mustafa Akyol have suggested that what the Qur'an has to say about Jesus resembles, and may even be historically continuous with, certain early Christian views of Jesus that have been subsumed under the label 'Jewish Christianity'.[36] To the present author at least, such a Jewish-Christian genealogy of the Qur'anic Jesus seems unlikely on a number of well-rehearsed counts (such as the lack of any attestation for a survival until the seventh century CE of forms of Christianity that are describable as 'Jewish Christianity', however defined). And yet the Qur'an's prophetic and non-divine Christology, which nonetheless accepts Jesus's virgin birth and his ascension to God, and perhaps even his death on the cross, may be viewed as a fundamentally coherent and theologically stimulating alternative to mainstream Christianity's view of Christ as a divine saviour, wherever one ultimately ends up pledging confessional allegiance (if any).

FURTHER READING

Akyol, Mustafa. 2017. *The Islamic Jesus: How the King of the Jews Became a Prophet of the Muslims*. New York: St. Martin's Press.

Ali, Kecia. 2017. "Destabilizing Gender, Reproducing Maternity: Mary in the Qur'ān." *Journal of the International Qur'anic Studies Association* 2: 89–109.

Andrae, Tor. 1987. *In the Garden of Myrtles: Studies in Early Islamic Mysticism*. Translated by Birgitta Sharpe. Albany: State University of New York Press.

---

[36] Akyol 2017.

Brinner, William M. (trans.). 2002. ʿArāʾis al-Majālis fī Qiṣaṣ al-Anbiyāʾ *or "Lives of the Prophets" as Recounted by Abū Isḥāq Aḥmad ibn Muḥammad ibn Ibrāhīm al-Thaʿlabī*. Leiden: Brill.
Cook, David. 2002. *Studies in Muslim Apocalyptic*. Princeton: Darwin Press.
Jeffery, Arthur. 1951. "The Descent of Jesus in Muhammadan Eschatology." In *The Joy of Study: Papers on New Testament and Related Subjects Presented to Honor Frederick Clifton Grant*, edited by Sherman E. Johnson, 107–26. New York: Macmillan.
Khalidi, Tarif. 2001. *The Muslim Jesus: Sayings and Stories in Islamic Literature*. Cambridge, MA: Harvard University Press.
Lawson, Todd. 2009. *The Crucifixion and the Qur'an*. London: Oneworld.
Melchert, Christoph. 2020. *Before Sufism: Early Islamic Renunciant Piety*. Berlin: De Gruyter.
Morrissey, Fitzroy. In press. "Jesus in Islamic Mysticism." In *Son of Mary: Jesus in Muslim Tradition*, edited by Stephen R. Burge. Atlanta: SBL Press.
Mourad, Suleiman A. 2011. "Does the Qurʾān Deny or Assert Jesus's Crucifixion and Death?" In *New Perspectives on the Qurʾān: The Qurʾān in Its Historical Context 2*, edited by Gabriel S. Reynolds, 349–57. Abingdon: Routledge.
Nurbakhsh, Javad. 2012. *Jesus in the Eyes of the Sufis*. New York: Khaniqahi Nimatullahi Publications (originally published 1983).
Reynolds, Gabriel S. 2009. "The Muslim Jesus: Dead or Alive?" *Bulletin of the School of Oriental and African Studies* 72.2: 237–58.
Robinson, Neal. 1991. *Christ in Islam and Christianity*. Albany: State University of New York Press.
Robinson, Neal. 2003. "Jesus." In *Encyclopaedia of the Qurʾān*, edited by Jane Dammen McAuliffe, vol. 3, 7–21. Leiden: Brill.
Schimmel, Annemarie. 2018. *Jesus und Maria in der islamischen Mystik*. [Xanten]: Chalice Verlag (originally published Munich: Kösel Verlag, 1996).
Shoemaker, Stephen J. 2003. "Christmas in the Qurʾān: The Qurʾānic Account of Jesus' Nativity and Palestinian Local Tradition." *Jerusalem Studies in Arabic and Islam* 28: 11–39.

## 10 Jesus in Christian Material Culture
JEREMIAH COOGAN

From the early Jesus movement onward, Christians have experienced the presence and power of Jesus mediated through material objects. Through texts, visual depictions, and other objects, Christians both *represent* (depict) and *re-present* (make present) Jesus in their own contexts. This chapter offers a series of soundings of these dynamics, focusing especially on evidence from the first five centuries CE that reflects the presence and power of Jesus in the materiality of text, liturgy, relic, and symbol. These early Christian theologies and practices continue to reverberate in later historical periods, across cultural contexts and social locations.

I begin with the fictional correspondence between Jesus and Abgar V of Edessa. The variegated ways that people from antiquity onward have used this correspondence illuminate themes in Jesus's material reception that extend to other texts and artifacts. I then survey varied ways in which early Christians understood gospel texts as manifesting Jesus's presence and power in material form. The theologies and practices surrounding sacraments and relics similarly reflect the twin dynamics of *representation* and *re-presentation*. This in turn invites consideration of the rich symbolic vocabularies, instantiated in varied material objects, through which Jesus is remembered and reimagined. I conclude with a discussion of how these phenomena reflect a capacious theological dialectic of Jesus's presence and absence.

### JESUS AND ABGAR

Writing early in the fourth century, the bishop and historian Eusebius of Caesarea (ca. 260–339/40 CE) recounts a story about Abgar V, ruler of Edessa (present-day Urfa in Türkiye). Abgar's "body was being wracked by a fearsome ailment that could not be cured by any human power" (*Hist. eccl.* 1.13.2, trans. Schott). Having heard of Jesus's marvelous deeds, Abgar dispatches messengers entreating Jesus to come heal him. Yet Jesus is reluctant to interrupt his ministry in Galilee and Judea for a journey to Mesopotamia. As Eusebius writes, "Jesus ... did not answer the supplicant's request at that time, but rather deemed him worthy of a personal letter and undertook to send one of his disciples to cure the disease and to offer salvation both to him and to all who belonged to him" (*Hist. eccl.* 1.13.3, trans. Schott).[1] In subsequent centuries, this "personal letter" took on a vibrant life of its own as an object instantiating Jesus's presence and power. The history of the Abgar correspondence thus illuminates several central dynamics in the material reception of Jesus.

For Eusebius, the Abgar correspondence connects Christian literary history to Jesus himself. Eusebius claims that he has found and translated the autographs of Abgar's letter and Jesus's response preserved in Edessa's archives (*Hist. eccl.* 1.13.5, 22; cf. Egeria, *Itin.* 17.1). The assertion of a verifiable material record advances Eusebius's bibliographic history of early Christianity, with its focus on books and documents, real and imagined. Nor is Eusebius the only one to appeal to ancient manuscripts to support claims about Jesus. Justin of Rome (d. ca. 165), for example, appeals to the archived *acta* of Pilate (*1 Apol.* 35.9; 48.3), while even in the twenty-first century, manuscript discoveries are deployed as sources for new revelations about Jesus's life and message (Jacobs 2023).

The Abgar correspondence exhibits remarkable vitality beyond Eusebius's history. From the fourth century onward, people used Jesus's letter to ward off disease, injury, and other malevolent forces. (We observe the same dynamics for gospel amulets, discussed later in this chapter.) At least twenty-two Greek and Coptic artifacts from late ancient Egypt preserve forms of the Abgar correspondence, written variously on wood, ostraca, papyrus, parchment, and limestone. It also appears in inscriptions from Mesopotamia, Anatolia, and the Aegean. As J. Gregory Given (2016) demonstrates, these artifacts adapt the Abgar correspondence as the specific circumstances demand.

One such object is a small papyrus amulet excavated in Egypt and dated between the seventh and ninth centuries CE, known as P. Mich. inv. 6213 (Wilfong and Sullivan 2005) (Figure 1). The extant Coptic text includes the following conclusion to Jesus's letter to Abgar:

---

[1] We observe resonances with gospel narratives in which Jesus heals from a distance with a word (Matthew 8:5–13 // Luke 7:1–10) or with the healing properties of fabric that had touched Paul in Acts (19:12).

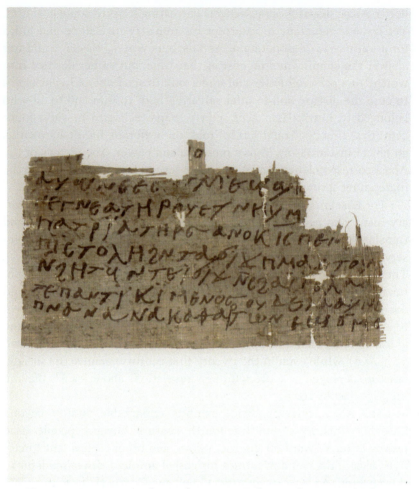

Figure 1 Papyrus amulet with correspondence of Jesus and Abgar in Sahidic Coptic (seventh to ninth centuries CE). P. Mich. inv. 6213 verso, University of Michigan Library, Ann Arbor, Michigan. Photo: Used with permission.

They will hear it to the end of the world, and the generations who will come after you in your whole country. It is I, Jesus, who have written this letter with my hand. [As for] the place where one will affix this manuscript, no power of the adversary, nor any activity of the unclean spirit will be able to come near that place forever.[2]

---

[2] This translation follows Wilfong and Sullivan 2005, 113, including their reconstructions of the text.

In contrast to Eusebius's version, this amulet emphasizes that the text has been written by Jesus himself and asserts the efficacy of the written object to counteract the power of unclean spirits. It is not primarily an object to be read but an object of physical power. The text written by Jesus's own hand – and apparently even a copy of it – has the power to heal ailments and ward off disease. Several late ancient amulets containing the Abgar correspondence exhibit patterns of damage that result from being worn or carried until the physical writing surface wore out (e.g. P. Vind. K 08636, fifth century CE). This use continues. Even in eighteenth- and nineteenth-century England, people reportedly used framed copies of this text to defend against harm (Given 2016).

Transformations of the Abgar narrative introduce a further aspect of Jesus's material reception. The late fourth- or early fifth-century Syriac text known as the Teaching of Addai expands the story. Ḥanan, one of Abgar's messengers, paints a portrait of Jesus to bring back to Edessa (Doctr. Add. 6.1–2). This is the earliest attestation of the *Mandylion* portrait, an icon that was kept in Edessa until it was translated to

Figure 2 Triptych with the *Mandylion*. Russian (1637 CE). Inv. no. 1975.87, Metropolitan Museum of Art, New York, New York. Photo: Public domain.

Constantinople in 944 CE. Later developments of the tradition maintain that the image was created by the imprint of Jesus's face onto the cloth as an *acheiropoiēton*, an image "not made by human hands." This iconography continues to be used for divine assistance and protection, as in the seventeenth-century Muscovite icon shown as Figure 2 (Metropolitan Museum of Art, inv. no. 1975.87).

## MATERIAL TEXTS

As the history of the Abgar correspondence reveals, the material text can manifest Jesus's power and presence. His handwritten trace or visual form is materialized through amulets, inscriptions, icons, and other objects. Nor is the Abgar legend the only context in which we see the idea of Jesus powerfully acting or even physically present in textual form. These dynamics attend textual objects in varied media, from amulets on scraps and single sheets, to miniature codices, to large-format books. Just as the theological significance of these objects exceeds their textual content, scriptural theologies and practices are not limited to readers or intellectuals. As John Lowden writes, "as the cross is an image of Christ, so is the gospel book" (Lowden 2007, 28). The theological conviction that the gospel book manifests the presence of Jesus himself illuminates early Christian practices and conflicts, and continues to influence Christian scriptural theologies and practices today.

Widespread preference for the codex is a distinctive feature of early Christian book culture. The preference for this particular material form of the book – a format with a spine and pages, often associated in the Roman Mediterranean with workaday texts and non-elite reading – is part of how the book-as-object marked Christian identity (Hurtado 2006, 43–93). The codex and graphic conventions such as *nomina sacra* (discussed in the section "Signs and Symbols") are the oldest attested elements of a Christian material culture. The significance of the book as a symbol of identity is best understood in a broader context in which the Christian sacred book, especially the gospel codex, was understood as embodying divine speech and even the presence of Jesus the divine *logos* (cf. John 1:1). Keith (2020) has argued that early Christian reading events articulated the gospel book as a physical embodiment of the kerygmatic message and an iconic representation of Jesus's presence. The gospel book represented, even re-presented, both its theological content *and* the person it proclaimed, Jesus Christ. The practice of bringing the gospel book into the congregation for liturgical reading, symbolizing the affirmation that "the Word became flesh and lived among us" (John 1:14), offers a dynamic expression of this scriptural theology. The symbolic alignment of Christ with the book is reflected in the Pantocrator at the eastern end of many churches from late antiquity onward, where Christ is often shown holding a codex (Watson 2007, 481).

This theological significance of the gospel book extends beyond the emergent fourfold gospel of Matthew, Mark, Luke, and John. Varied early Christian movements imagined Jesus as manifested or even embodied in the book. The second-century thinker Valentinus and his followers embraced theologies of the book in which Jesus was imagined as scripturally embodied in textual artifacts; in the Gospel of Truth (NHC I 3), Jesus is crucified in the form of the book (Gos. Truth 20.21–39; Kreps 2022). Moreover, as the Abgar correspondence reminds us, Jesus's textual presence extends beyond the "book" to other written artifacts. The significance of these reading events and these textual objects is intertwined with how early Christians understood and experienced the presence and power of Jesus.

Early Christians used texts about Jesus as objects of power (Coogan 2018). Both gospel books and other textual objects might be employed to repel evil or provide healing. The second- or third-century Acts of Andrew describes a woman using "the gospel" to repel sexual assault: "Trophima in the brothel prayed continually, and had the gospel on her bosom, and no one could approach her" (Acts Andr. epitome 23). In fourth-century Antioch, John Chrysostom (ca. 347–407 CE) refers to gospel books placed on thresholds of houses to repel harm (Hom. Jo. 32). Augustine of Hippo (354–430 CE) complains that congregants use the Gospel according to John as a cure for fever (Tract. Ev. Jo. 7.12.2). While Augustine objects, he acknowledges the gospel's efficacy as an object of healing power. The fifth-century Acts of Barnabas imagine that apostle using the Gospel according to Matthew to heal someone (Acts Barn. 15). This power extends beyond physical protection and healing. Epiphanius of Salamis (d. 403) describes the spiritually transformative power of the book as an object: "The mere sight of these books renders us less inclined to sin and incites us to believe more firmly in righteousness" (*The Sayings of the Desert Fathers*, Epiphanius 8 (trans. Ward 1975); cf. Acts Andr. epitome 23, 28).

Powerful texts about Jesus could be worn or carried. Both literary evidence and physical artifacts reflect the use of miniature codices, books small enough to wear or carry. Chrysostom mentions women who wear gospels around their necks (*Hom. Matt.* 72.2; *Adv. Iud.* 8), perhaps paralleling the example of Trophima from the Acts of Andrew. These practices were not limited to the canonical gospels or to books. Amulets on papyrus, parchment, and ostraca – from the ornate to the inexpensive – excerpt and adapt texts about Jesus (De Bruyn and Dijkstra 2011). Many combine multiple texts. At least seven Greek and Coptic amulets from late ancient Egypt use opening lines (*incipits*) from gospel books. As Joseph Sanzo argues, these *incipits* represent a whole text in just a few lines (Sanzo 2014). As early as Origen of Alexandria, Christian thinkers argue that stories about Jesus are effective in healing (*Cels.* 1.6). It is thus no surprise that we find amulets containing short narratives (*historiolae*) about Jesus. In addition to the Abgar narrative, we find narratives familiar from the canonical gospels, often shortened and adapted.[3] Amulets may combine text and image, as in the example of a small sixth- or seventh-century intaglio amulet on hematite (Figure 3: Metropolitan Museum of Art 17.190.491). The amulet creatively rewrites Jesus's healing of the woman with a hemorrhage (cf. Mark 5:25–34; Luke 8:43–48). The front depicts the woman kneeling before Jesus; the back depicts the woman standing in prayer. These apotropaic and therapeutic practices reflect the use of textual objects to access Jesus's power and presence.

The power of "gospel" texts might also be deployed in other ways. Christians from late antiquity onward used gospel books for book divination (bibliomancy). In the fifth century, Augustine grudgingly concedes that this practice is preferable to consulting daemons (*Ep.* 55.20). As in bibliomantic practices using Homer or Vergil, a questioner (perhaps assisted by an expert) would open the gospel text to a random page and use the emergent passage as the response to their inquiry. Traces of such divinatory uses are visible in manuscripts. Several manuscripts of John are equipped with "interpretations" (*hermēneiai*) that deploy gospel text for oracular purposes; this phenomenon is attested in Greek, Latin, Syriac, Coptic, Armenian, and Georgian manuscripts from late antiquity and the Middle Ages (Metzger 1988). One such example is P. CtYBR inv. 4641, a fifth- to seventh-century Coptic codex of John (Jones 2014). Less frequently, *hermēneiai* accompany other gospels (e.g. Mark in the fifth-century Greek–Latin bilingual Codex Bezae). Other divinatory texts echo the category "gospel" without offering a

---

[3] Examples: Matt 4:23–24 (P. Oxy. 1077, sixth-century); Matt 27:62–64 + 28:2–5 (P. Oxy. 4406, fifth/sixth century); a reference to the healing of Peter's mother-in-law (P. Mon. Epiph. 591, seventh century); Matt 11:25–30 (*SO* 24 [1945]: 121–40, fourth century).

Figure 3 Intaglio amulet on hematite, depicting Jesus and woman with hemorrhage (sixth or seventh century CE). Inv. no. 17.190.491, Metropolitan Museum of Art, New York, New York.
Photo: Public domain.

gospel text in any traditional sense. For example, a sixth-century divinatory book in Sahidic Coptic strikingly titles itself the "Gospel of the Lots of Mary" (Cambridge, Sackler Museum, inv. 1984.669; ed. Luijendijk 2014). As with other divinatory gospel texts, the questioner can open to a random page in search of guidance, yet this manuscript consists *only* of the divinatory content. These bibliomantic uses of the gospel reflect how Christians (and perhaps others) used material texts to appeal to Jesus for guidance.

The gospel codex as a physical manifestation of Jesus's presence and power is not only a feature of "popular" religion but also plays a role in legal practices and ecclesial conflicts. In the early fourth century CE, Jesus's physical presence in the (gospel) book becomes a potent site of conflict. Starting in 303 CE, Diocletian and his co-emperors decreed the destruction of Christian books. This unprecedented legal measure suggests that the books were understood by Roman authorities as powerful objects in the same legal category as books of divination or incantations, that is, as objects of "magical" power (Coogan 2022: 309–12). The imperial edicts thus parallel the emergent Christian theologies of the sacred book attested in other sources.

Fourth- and fifth-century conflicts over the "handing over" (*traditio*) of Christian sacred books illuminate these emergent theologies. In North Africa, the church was divided over the correct response to *traditores*, those who had betrayed the sacred books. The Donatist bishop Petilian (fl. ca. 400 CE) draws a parallel between Judas's betrayal of the incarnate divine Word and the more recent betrayal of the inscribed divine word under persecution (*apud* Augustine, *C. litt. Petil.* 3.32.72; cf. 2.11.25; Coogan 2018, 383–84). This "iconic relationship between sacred text and divine Word" is most clearly visible for the gospels, which form the center of these polemics (Coogan 2018, 384). The argument depends on the idea that the gospel book embodies Jesus himself; by surrendering the sacred text, *traditores* participate in Judas's crime. In this argument, Petilian echoes another Roman legal paradigm, in which the destruction of an author's books enacts a textual execution of the author (Howley 2017; Coogan 2018). Destruction of gospel texts is understood as violence against Jesus's own body (Keith 2021). Crucially, Augustine's response to Petilian does not challenge the idea that Jesus is powerfully present through the gospel text. Where Augustine and Petilian diverge is that Augustine understands the presence of Jesus to be manifested not simply (or only) in the gospel codex but rather insofar as the divine Word speaks when the gospels are proclaimed in liturgy (Coogan 2018: 386–87). It is the Christian reading event that makes Jesus present. Despite their sharp polemics and real disagreements, Petilian and Augustine agree that Jesus is made present (*re-presented*) through the gospel book. These fourth- and fifth-century controversies over the destruction of Christian scripture reflect the same impulse to understand Jesus in and as the book that we observed in the Gospel of Truth.

Other ecclesial and juridical contexts reflect the power of the gospel book as a manifestation of Jesus's presence. As surveyed by Caroline Humfress, gospel books in late antiquity possessed a "preeminent status" as representations of Jesus's authority, an authority that was deployed in the context of legal proceedings (Humfress 2007, 150–51). The fifth-century historian Sozomen describes the use of the gospel book to confirm an oath (*Hist. eccl.* 6.30.10–11). According to the sixth-century *Codex* of Justinian (3.1.14.1), one should not begin a trial "until sacred scriptures are deposited before the judicial seat." To recognize contemporary resonances, we need only recall the political-*cum*-theological power implied by placing one's hand on a Bible to swear an oath in the courtroom or when assuming public office.

Ecclesial authorities deployed the iconic power of the gospel book in similar ways. Written accounts and iconographic depictions of the First Council of Ephesus (431 CE) emphasize the gospel codex as authority and witness for the proceedings. A ninth-century Byzantine miniature, for example, shows the gospel codex and the emperor Theodosius II enthroned side by side (Watson 2007, 481). The prominent placement of a gospel book is also reported for the councils of Nicaea (325 CE) and Chalcedon (451 CE) (Humfress 2007, 151). These ritual gestures invoke divine presence, enabling political and ecclesial officials to appropriate divine authority. Such gestures parallel the production of monumental scriptural codices, especially massive and ornate gospel books. These are objects to be displayed, admired, and revered just as much as they are objects to be read; their cost and physical size emphasize their significance as material objects, physical representations of the divine Word (Lowden 2007).

The material reception of Jesus in book culture is refracted across a wide range of artifacts and practices, from diminutive amulets to monumental codices, from book-burning to the enthronement of the gospel codex. Yet the common thread is a conviction that the Jesus's presence and power are manifested and mediated through textual objects. These late ancient theologies of the written gospel as a material re-presentation of Jesus continue to flourish and develop in subsequent historical periods.

## SACRAMENTS AND RELICS

In our discussion of gospels and other texts about Jesus, we observed theologies and practices in which textual objects both *represent* (depict) and *re-present* (make present) Jesus Christ. These twin dynamics also emerge in approaches to sacraments and relics. As in the scriptural theologies discussed earlier in this chapter, these early receptions of Jesus resonate across later historical periods and cultural contexts.

Eucharistic presence is a vital part of Jesus's material reception from antiquity until the present, as Christians encounter the living Jesus through bread and wine. As Ann Astell writes, describing medieval eucharistic piety, "eating the Eucharist was thus simultaneously to 'see' Christ and to 'touch' this vision, to reach out for it, and to embody it virtuously" (Astell 2006, 14). The significance assigned to the eucharistic elements is refracted through embodied practices and material artifacts that express the conviction that Jesus is powerfully present in the cup and host. Inchoate expressions of the idea that the eucharistic bread and wine materially represent Jesus or even make him tangibly present appear already in the writings that would become the Christian New Testament (Matt 26:26; Mark 14:22; Luke 22:19; John 6:35, 48, 51, 55; 1 Cor 11:24). By the early second century, Ignatius of Antioch can describe the bread as the "medicine of immortality," through which one can "live in Jesus Christ forever" (*Eph.* 20:2). From antiquity onward, people have appealed to the powerful presence of Jesus by using the eucharistic bread as an apotropaic or therapeutic object – although such practices have been condemned by various ecclesiastical authorities (Maraschi 2017).

Eucharistic practice exerts a powerful influence on other aspects of Christian material culture as well. Altars, tabernacles, and church architecture (e.g. Eastern orientation, cruciform design) give material form to eucharistic theologies. Patens, chalices, pyxides, and other eucharistic vessels themselves come to represent the embodied presence of Jesus. The enormous cultural significance of the holy grail, the chalice from the Last Supper – in religious imagination, visual art, and literary elaboration – offers just one example. Eucharistic practice and piety, in which the cup and host materially represent or make present Jesus, intersect with scriptural theologies. The same charges of *traditio* (betrayal) that accompanied handing over the sacred books in the fourth-century persecution were also brought against those who surrendered liturgical vessels (e.g. Optatus of Milevis, *App.* 1, ed. SC 413: 306–7; cf. Coogan 2018, 384). Just as the divine Word/word was enfleshed, quite literally, in the parchment of the gospel codex, so also the flesh of divine Word was offered in the eucharistic meal. To hand over either the gospel or the vessels containing the eucharistic body was, then, to betray Jesus himself. The ongoing entanglement of Jesus's scriptural and eucharistic embodiment is reflected in the overlapping visual vocabularies used in the construction and decoration of late ancient and medieval gospel books and sacramental pyxides (Lowden 2007) (Figure 4).

Relics are another dimension of the material reception of Jesus, providing further opportunities for the tangible re-presentation of his saving power. The *Mandylion* portrait is one striking example. Starting in the late fourth century, historians and homilists begin to narrate the discovery (*inventio*) of the true cross in Jerusalem by Helena Augusta, mother of Constantine I (e.g. Ambrose, *Ob. Theo.* 46–48; Chrysostom, *Hom. Jo.* 75.1 (PG 59: 461); Rufinus, *Hist. eccl.* 10.7–8; cf. Hillner 2022, 231–34). This legendary event, emphasizing the growing importance of the cross as a symbol of Christian identity, is further refracted in icons and other visual depictions. By the end of the fourth century, fragments of the "true cross" are scattered around the Mediterranean; over time, these would often be preserved in ornate reliquaries that share the same visual vocabularies as gospel books and sacramental pyxides. These relics prompt their own material traces, both through the construction of reliquaries (or entire churches) and also through robust iconographic reception of *inventio* narratives (Jensen 2017). The relationship between relics and icons has frequently prompted theological reflection and conflict centered precisely on the tension between representation and presence (Jensen 2023).

Other relics of Jesus's life, especially of his passion, continue to emerge throughout late antiquity and beyond, providing further opportunities for imagined connection between Jesus's own material existence and the present reality of those viewing and venerating these objects. Relics of Jesus's life could be sites of authority or conflict, deployed as sources of authority for theological claims or for the significance of a church or see. As Andrew Jacobs has explored, moreover, late ancient debates about Jesus's foreskin – and occasional claims to possess this piece of his flesh – offered the material impetus for debates about Jesus's ethnicity and the nature of his embodiment (Jacobs 2012).

Arguably, the most significant relic of Jesus's life is the "Holy Land" itself. While Helena's claim to have discovered a wooden cross in Jerusalem is dubious, what is clear is her pilgrimage to the (real or

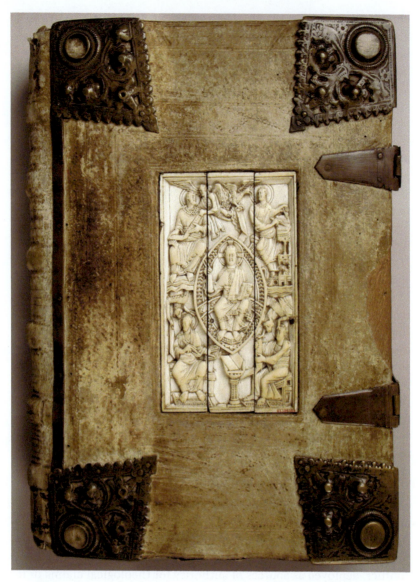

Figure 4 Ivory book cover with Christ and the four evangelists (eleventh century CE). Inv. no. 41.100.168, Metropolitan Museum of Art, New York, New York. Photo: Public domain.

imagined) sites of Jesus's life and her role as patron for the construction of churches and shrines on these sites, most notably the Church of the Holy Sepulchre. Christian theologies of space, land, and pilgrimage engage the physical geography of (Late) Roman Palestine as a kind of installation-space relic for Jesus's life and death. This is visible already in the writings of Eusebius and Jerome and is even more evident in how pilgrims (such as Egeria or the Piacenza Pilgrim) from the fourth century onward describe their encounters with space, scripture, and Jesus himself (Leyerle 1996).

Yet if the "Holy Land" is itself a large-scale relic, it is refracted into a thousand smaller material receptions of Jesus. Pilgrims carry away flasks of water from the Jordan, *ampulae* of olive oil from Galilee and Gethsemane, and various other physical objects. Materiality affords a sense of tangible connection with Jesus's own human life in Galilee, Samaria, and Judea. The built environment of churches and pilgrimage routes facilitates such practices of travel and imagination; one can walk the steps of Jesus on the medieval *Via Dolorosa* or remember the nativity in Bethlehem (right alongside Jerome). Pilgrimage narratives and descriptions of the "holy places" (e.g. Adomnán of Iona's seventh-century work *De locis sanctis*) assert a physical connection with distant sacred space and an opportunity to navigate the texts in a readerly pilgrimage (O'Loughlin 2007). These logics continue right into the present for Christians from many different theological traditions.

SIGNS AND SYMBOLS

Jesus is remembered and reimagined through a capacious range of symbolic vocabularies, instantiated in manifold material artifacts. Here, I focus on three sets of early examples: *nomina sacra*, the staurogram and the cross, and the chi-rho. *Nomina sacra* ("sacred names") are a distinctive feature of Christian manuscripts in Greek, Latin, Coptic, Armenian, and other languages. The graphic convention marks a number of theologically significant words, including Jesus (ἰησοῦς), Christ (χριστός), son (υἱός), God (θεός), Lord (κύριος), savior (σωτήρ), and cross (σταυρός). Instead of writing out the full word, scribes would abbreviate by using a few letters with a line written above. The exact set of words written as *nomina sacra* and the abbreviated forms used vary between manuscripts. While the system is not limited to Jesus's name, this scribal practice reflects a reverence for Jesus's name alongside the divine name. Hurtado has argued that "the initial impulse was christological" and that the system attests "early Christian reverence shown to the name of Jesus" (Hurtado 1998, 671–72). While first attested in manuscripts, *nomina sacra* become a widespread feature of Christian art, inscriptions, and iconography.

The chi-rho (☧) is a symbol formed by superimposing the Greek letters chi (Χ) and rho (Ρ), the first two letters of the word "Christ" (ΧΡΙΣΤΟΣ, *christos*). It is attested as a Christian symbol starting in the fourth century CE, where it is associated especially (although unreliably) with Constantine's victory at the Battle of the Milvian Bridge (312 CE). It is imagined as a symbol that conveys divine favor or power, presumably but ambiguously from the Christian God. The symbol becomes a key part of Constantinian imperial iconography, appearing on coins and inscriptions. It also appears in Christian burial contexts, church architecture, and manuscripts. The staurogram (⳨) is a graphic convention reflected in Christian manuscripts as early as the late second or early third century (e.g. 𝔓66). When writing the words "cross" (σταυρός) and "crucifixion" (σταυρόω), the Greek letters tau (Τ) and rho (Ρ) are superimposed to form a cross. The tau is the crossbeam, while the rho is the vertical shaft and perhaps also depicts the head of a suspended human form. This graphic convention highlights the significance of Jesus's crucifixion and, as in the case of *nomina sacra*, attests the interweaving of Christian textual practices and theology.

Starting in the late second or early third century, the cross is attested as a symbol of Christian identity in other contexts as well. A second- or third-century CE graffito mockingly depicts Jesus's crucifixion (Harley-McGowan 2020). The text reads "Alexamenos worships (his) god," while the crucified god is depicted as a donkey-headed human. The early third-century Christian writers Minucius Felix (*Oct.* 9; 29) and Tertullian (*Apol.* 16; *Cor.* 3) likewise attest the cross as a Christian symbol. Tertullian mentions the practice of tracing the shape on one's forehead (*Cor.* 3) – perhaps to mark identity, to express devotion, or to appeal for divine assistance, or even all three. Starting in the fourth century, Christians increasingly incorporate crucifixion imagery into religious iconography. Yet while the cross is now the dominant symbol of Christian identity, it did not have the same predominance in the first several Christian centuries, when a wider range of symbols were regularly used in visual art, popular piety, and theological argument (Jensen 2017).

CONCLUSION: PRESENCE AND ABSENCE

In this chapter, we have observed the ways in which the reception of Jesus in Christian material culture reflects an expansive theological dialectic of Jesus's presence and absence. From the gospel codex to the sites of the "Holy Land," from the eucharistic elements to scratched graffiti and inked symbols, Christians have found the material reception of Jesus a way to negotiate this tension.

The tug-of-war between presence and absence is visible already in the writings that would become the New Testament, themselves among the earliest material artifacts of the Jesus tradition. At the conclusion of Mark's Gospel, the young man at the empty tomb gives the women a message for Peter and the other disciples: Jesus "is going ahead of you to Galilee; there you will see him" (Mark 16:7). For Mark's disciples, as for Mark's readers, Jesus is absent. This raises the question: "Where is Jesus now?" The Johannine Jesus is likewise absent ("I am ascending to my father...," John 20:17), although the Paraclete is present to act on Jesus's behalf (e.g. John 16:7). Matthew concludes his gospel with Jesus's mountaintop promise that "I am with you every day, even to the end of the age" (Matt 28:20). Yet this is explained only partly by the earlier promise that "where two or three are gathered in my name, I am there in their midst" (Matt 18:20). In what sense is Jesus present? In what sense absent? How can one encounter Jesus now?

Our opening example, the Abgar correspondence, encapsulates and responds to this tension. In its many divergent forms, the correspondence envisions a situation where Jesus and Abgar are separated by a wide geographic distance and, in fact, never meet face-to-face. Yet although Jesus is absent, he is nonetheless powerfully present in text or image, letter or portrait. This presence is undoubtedly partial, yet remains efficacious – to cure disease, to ward off harm, to defend against enemies. Some material receptions of Jesus tend toward *representation*, the depiction of an absent Jesus; others tend toward *re-presentation*, the efficacious manifestation of Jesus's presence, power, even embodiment.

### FURTHER READING

Coogan, Jeremiah. 2018. "Divine Truth, Presence, and Power: Christian Books in Roman North Africa." *Journal of Late Antiquity* 11: 375–95.

Coogan, Jeremiah. 2022. "Misusing Books: Material Texts and Lived Religion in the Roman Mediterranean." *Religion in the Roman Empire* 8: 301–16.

Given, J. Gregory. 2016. "Utility and Variance in Late Antique Witnesses to the Abgar-Jesus Correspondence." *Archiv für Religionsgeschichte* 17: 187–222.

Harley-McGowan, Felicity. 2020. "The Alexamenos Graffito." In *The Reception of Jesus in the First Three Centuries: Volume Three: From Celsus to the Catacombs: Visual, Liturgical, and Non-Christian Receptions of Jesus in the Second and Third Centuries CE*, edited by Chris Keith, Helen K. Bond, Christine Jacobi, and Jens Schröter, 105–40. London: T&T Clark.

Hillner, Julia. 2022. *Helena Augusta: Mother of the Empire*. Oxford: Oxford University Press.
Hurtado, Larry W. 2006. *The Earliest Christian Artifacts: Manuscripts and Christian Origins*. Grand Rapids: Eerdmans.
Jacobs, Andrew. 2023. *Gospel Thrillers: Conspiracy, Fiction, and the Vulnerable Bible*. Cambridge: Cambridge University Press.
Jensen, Robin M. 2017. *The Cross: History, Art, and Controversy*. Cambridge, MA: Harvard University Press.
Jensen, Robin M. 2023. "Icons as Relics, Relics as Icons." In *Interacting with Saints in the Late Antique and Medieval Worlds*, ed. Robert Wiśniewski, Raymond Van Dam, and Bryan Ward-Perkins, 17–45. Turnhout: Brepols.
Keith, Chris. 2020. *The Gospel as Manuscript: An Early History of the Jesus Tradition as Material Artifact*. Oxford: Oxford University Press.
Klingshirn, William E. and Linda Safran, eds. 2007. *The Early Christian Book*. Washington, DC: Catholic University of America Press.
Kreps, Anne Starr. 2022. *The Crucified Book: Sacred Writing in the Age of Valentinus*. Philadelphia: University of Pennsylvania Press.
Leyerle, Blake. 1996. "Landscape as Cartography in Early Christian Pilgrim Narratives." *Journal of Early Christian Studies* 64: 119–43.
Maraschi, Andrea. 2017. "Sympathy for the Lord: The Host and Elements of Sympathetic Magic in Late Medieval Exempla." *Journal of Medieval Religious Cultures* 43: 209–30.

# 11 Jesus in Art and Music

ROBIN JENSEN AND JEREMY BEGBIE

This chapter explores five distinct ways that artists portrayed Jesus over the centuries: as Shepherd, Victor, Lover, Innocent Victim, and King of kings. Each of these themes is illustrated through selected examples of pictorial art and musical compositions. The selections include artworks from the earliest Christian era to the present time and, while a mere handful among an almost infinite number of possible choices, offer insights into how their composers expressed – and the faithful encountered – the person and story of Jesus visually and aurally. In these works, viewers and audiences would have come to understand the many dimensions of Christ's person and work sensorially: his caretaking love, his triumph, his innocent humility, and his transcendent power.

JESUS AS SHEPHERD

## In Visual Art

*Protector and Guide: The One Who Brings Us Safely Home*
The image of the Good Shepherd – a rustic, beardless youth, wearing a short tunic and high laced boots and carrying a ram or lamb over his shoulder – is prominent in Christian art through the centuries. He clutches the animal's four feet with one hand and holds a bucket of milk or a staff in the other. The Shepherd was especially common in early Christian iconography, appearing in both Roman catacomb painting (Figure 5) and early relief carving. Set in a simple, pastoral landscape, he usually is accompanied by one or more sheep. A pouch strung over his shoulders probably held stones to ward off predators.

In Christian art, the image is usually understood to represent Christ, but only in a symbolic sense. As such, the shepherd figure alludes to the biblical caretaking shepherds who represented the caretaking Lord. He is the one who brings the thirsty to water and guides the dying safely through the valley of death (see Ps 23) or who seeks

*171*

Figure 5 *The Good Shepherd*, from the Catacomb of Callixtus, Crypt of Lucina, Rome. From G. Wilpert, *Roma Sotteranea: Le Pitture delle Catacombe Romane*, vol. 2 (1903), Tav. 66.2.

the lost sheep and brings it home (Matt 18:10–14). The prophet Isaiah portrays God as tending his flock like a shepherd, gathering the lambs and carrying them gently in his bosom (Isa 40:11). Thus, Jesus's self-identification as the Good Shepherd is not meant to be taken literally but as a way to convey his willingness to lay down his life for those who recognize and respond to his voice (John 10:11–18). Scripture regularly reminds the reader that sheep need guidance. A flock without a shepherd can go astray and become the prey of wild beasts (Ezek 34:5; Matt 9:35–38).

Notwithstanding the shepherd's obvious connections with scriptural imagery, its portrayal in early Christian art had an ancient precedent in Greco-Roman mythological iconography as the figure of Hermes, the ram-bearer who was also the one who conveyed the souls of the dead safely into the next world. Perhaps this was one reason that it was adopted and became an especially favorite image for funerary decoration in the first centuries.

Despite its early popularity, by the late fourth century the shepherd figure gradually gave way to other pictorial subjects. Although it never completely disappeared, the shepherd began to appear as an older and bearded figure, dressed in a longer robe, and often among a whole flock in a widely expanded natural setting. In one particularly lavish fifth-century mosaic in Ravenna, the shepherd appears more regal than rustic; he wields a slender gold and gemmed cross rather than a pastoral staff. In more recent times, the shepherd is often more sentimentally depicted gazing tenderly at the young lamb he carries in his arm (Figure 6; see Verkerk 2020). By contrast to this portrayal of the shepherd as a gentle but mature male, in the early twentieth century the artist Henry Ossawa Tanner rendered the shepherd as a young boy standing in a barren landscape among his flock (Figure 7). His clothing, the traditional costume of Palestinian shepherds of Tanner's time, as well as the setting were likely inspired by the artist's travels to the Holy Land. He too gazes affectionately down at a tiny lamb in his left hand; a ewe nuzzles the hem of his garment. However, because the artist emphasizes the shepherd's youth, and even by using a cool palette (pale blue and purple hues), he renders him almost more vulnerable than his flock.

## In Music
*Promise and Fulfillment: "He Shall Feed His Flock"*
Among composers and performers, the imagery of shepherding, and of Jesus as shepherd, has been no less beloved. Along with a multitude of hymns and songs, many of them drawing on Psalm 23, it has been taken up in large-scale works, by far the best-known example appearing in *Messiah* by the Baroque composer George Frideric Handel (1685–1759).

Although others have often combined Old and New Testament texts to render Christ in music, Handel does so with a rare and profound skill, employing some of music's most distinctive techniques. Indeed, *Messiah* taken as a whole presents us with an unprecedented integration of prophecy and fulfillment, weaving a huge variety of texts – all of

Figure 6 Bernhard Plockhorst, *Jesus as the Good Shepherd*, ca. 1889, Wikimedia Creative Commons (location of the original painting unknown).

Figure 7 Henry Ossawa Tanner, *The Good Shepherd*, 1917, oil on canvas, 65 × 81 cm. Crystal Bridges Museum of American Art, Bentonville, Arkansas, 2019.5. Photography by Edward C. Robison III. Used with permission of the Museum.

them biblical – into a compelling unity. We are led on a musical journey from Old Testament prophecy, the incarnation, passion, and resurrection of Christ through to the final triumph of the church and the climactic redemption of the end times. Although a good deal of the credit must go to the compiler and arranger of the texts, Charles Jennens (1700–73), it is Handel's genius to make us believe they all belong together.

Handel's mastery is perhaps nowhere clearer than when he combines Old and New Testament verses in the alto aria "He Shall Feed His Flock." Two texts are set, the first picking up on the shepherd imagery in Isaiah 40:11, "He shall feed his flock," the second from Matthew 11:28–29, here rendered as "Come unto Him ye that are heavy laden, and He will give you rest." (The change from "me" to "Him" is consistent with Jennens's concern throughout *Messiah* to portray Jesus as the one who is *now* honored and worshipped. Unlike

J. S. Bach's settings of the passion narratives, we hear nothing of the inner feelings and struggles of the man Jesus; the focus is resolutely on Christ's divine authority.)

Handel was a master of contrast – of modes (major and minor), rhythms, moods – but what is especially striking about this piece is its consistency and stability. We are not led from one contrasting key to another, the rhythm is constant, the mood unfailingly comforting – as befits both texts – with no flourishes or musical asides. The continuity of old and new is thus never in doubt. Moreover, a rhythmic pattern underlies the entire aria, a pattern associated by this time with rural life and landscapes and widely used when shepherding was in view. The Matthew text is thus given the gentle, caring connotations of shepherding: It is the Shepherd who offers rest and relief to the heavily laden.

But Handel's master stroke is to have identical music for each text yet elevating us from F major for the Isaiah text to the higher B flat major for the Matthew verse. This is the kind of transformation music is supremely well equipped to make, and here it aptly evokes the dramatic shift from old to new creation.

### JESUS AS VICTOR

#### In Music

*Victory in Humiliation: "Es ist vollbracht"*
Music has frequently been used to celebrate victory: Trumpet fanfares and drum rolls have accompanied military triumphs for centuries. But what if a victory is won through a shameful death? If visual artists have had their imaginations stretched here, so have musicians. The challenge becomes especially acute if one is faced with John's Gospel, where triumph is enacted in what would seem to be the very converse of victory, the crucifixion of a naked man. The Fourth Gospel portrays the crucifixion as Jesus' "lifting up," the King's enthronement, the Son's glorification. Here God's victory is revealed in pathetic degradation, splendor in ignominy. This theme became crucial for Martin Luther: Divine glory is focused in a repugnant, threatening, and puzzling death. And it is a theme the German Lutheran J. S. Bach (1685–1750) presents unforgettably in an aria at the heart of his *St John Passion*, rendering Jesus's climactic cry "Es ist vollbracht" (It is finished!) (John 19:30).

Placed at the structural center of the *Passion*, this alto aria opens with a winding, haunting theme played by the viola da gamba, a precursor to the cello. Appearing only at this point in the *St John Passion*, the da gamba has a highly distinctive timbre – thin and reedy – being associated with French Baroque court music, and thus with royalty and wealth. The "dotted style" rhythms it plays here were likewise typical of this genre. Here, however, this music is marked "molto adagio" (very slow), and most of the notes are smoothly linked – quite uncharacteristic of the French style. Its phrases sigh and fall, limping and often halting. The atmosphere is unmistakably one of lament; indeed, the melody alone could well be heard as evoking the sighs of a dying man. Kingly majesty dwells in intense sorrow. As Michael Marissen puts it: "As Bach's music has it, then, Jesus' majesty is 'hidden' in its opposite" (Marissen 1998, 19).

In due course, the alto enters, picking up and varying the da gamba's theme:

It is finished!
O hope for ev'ry ailing spirit!
The night of grief
Is now its final hours counting.

But without any warning, in the midst of this sighing and dying comes a stunning eruption: "Judah's hero triumphs with power and ends the strife," the alto sings, with strings, bassoon, and continuo furiously playing in a *stile concitato* ("excited style," with fast-repeated notes) borrowed from the Italian Baroque. The connotations now are of military success; B minor lament has turned to D major, a key commonly linked in Baroque music with victory. The falling, exhaling of the da gamba is answered by soaring, battle-like fanfares. The forces of darkness have met their defeat at the cross; Christ has set the captives free.

No less suddenly, the music comes to a dramatic halt on a diminished chord, the most unstable chord in Bach's armory, and resolves back into the lamenting of the da gamba, prefacing the alto's final "It is finished." Now, however, the lament is heard with the unmistakable echoes of conquest ringing in the memory.

### In Visual Art
*Death Crowned with Glory: The Folly of the Cross and the Power of God*

Depictions of Christ's passion appear relatively late in Christian iconography. Perhaps the first appears on one of four sides of a small ivory box, dated to the 420s. The box, probably from a Roman workshop, is a fine example of early fifth-century ivory carving. All four panel sides display unprecedented scenes of Jesus's trial, crucifixion, resurrection, and post-resurrection appearance to his apostles, but the

Figure 8 *Crucifixion and Judas's Suicide*, Ivory plaque, ca. 420–30, northern Italy or Rome. Photo credit: @ The Trustees of the British Museum.

image on the third shows Christ upright and still robustly alive on the cross (Figure 8). His expression is serene rather than anguished; his open eyes directly engage the viewer. The nails in his hands or the wound on his side are not bleeding; his body neither sags nor twists in agony. On the right, the centurion looks up in awe; the Virgin and the Beloved Disciple stand stoically on the left. By contrast to Christ's living and vigorous physique, Judas's suspended corpse hangs in shame.

By comparison to later crucifixion scenes, the oldest images rarely show Christ's suffering or death. Rather, as in this ivory, they portray him as awake, aware, and alive. He is not a victim but a victor, the winner of the battle over sin, death, and the devil. Such depictions conform to how early Christian theologians understood Christ's self-sacrifice as a conquest that tricked or trapped Satan and opened the gates of Hell. It was not a vicarious acceptance of punishment that humans owed to God for their sins but an act that brought life out of death and triumph from defeat.

Christ's voluntary and heroic death is expressed in Rome's Basilica of San Clemente, in its eleventh-century mosaic apse (Figure 9). Although

Figure 9 *Christ as the Tree of Life*. Apse mosaic, Basilica of San Clemente, Rome, ca. 1130s. Photo: Author.

the central crucifix shows Christ's head inclining and his eyes evidently closed as if to say, "it is finished," his body remains upright and his arms extend as if offering an embrace. The Virgin and the Beloved Disciple stand passively and even pensively on either side of him. Marvelously, the cross, dotted with twelve white doves to represent the apostles, rises from the midst of a huge acanthus plant, bursting like a tree of life. Its curling tendrils spread across the rest of the space and enclose birds, animals, baskets of fruit, and humans in the acts of herding and harvesting. The gold background intensifies the visual expression of glory. At the apex of the mosaic, God's hand holds out a crown of victory to Christ, the symbol of his triumph. At the bottom of the scene, two stags drink from the four rivers of Paradise, a reference both to Psalm 42 and to the Edenic garden. Just above them, a smaller deer consumes a serpent, perhaps alluding to an ancient belief that deer eat venomous snakes but here also a reminder that, by the cross's victory, the serpent of Genesis is ultimately destroyed.

A different visualization of Christ's victory over death shows him trampling on a serpent and a lion, referring to the text of Psalm 91, verse 13, "You shall tread on the lion and the adder, the young lion and the serpent you will trample under foot." Christian imagery often

Figure 10 *Christ as Heroic Warrior*. Stuttgart Psalter, Cod. bib. facs. quart.132 b. fol. 23, 107v (Psalm 91:13), ca. 820–30, Württembergische Landesbibliothek. Photo: Wikimedia creative commons.

renders this to suggest Christ's defeat of Satan. A famous sixth-century mosaic version of this appears in the Archiepiscopal Chapel of Ravenna in which Christ, dressed as a Roman soldier, stomps on the heads of a lion and a snake. Similarly, in this medieval image from the Stuttgart Psalter (Figure 10), Christ, wearing chainmail and a helmet, thrusts a cross like a lance into the mouth of a coiling serpent and plants his feet firmly on the serpent's body as well as the head of a crouching lion.

JESUS AS LOVER

**In Visual Art**
*As Christ Loved the Church That She Might Be Holy*
Medieval pictorial depictions of Christ embracing a female figure emerged to express the idea of Christ as a lover, either of the church or of the human soul. Typically, these images show Christ as a bridegroom (*sponsus*) embracing his bride (*sponsa*) and often are accompanied by the opening line from the biblical Song of Songs, "Let him kiss me with the kisses of his mouth" (*Osculetur me osculo oris sui*). For example, in a fifteenth-century manuscript now in the National Library of the Netherlands at the Hague (Figure 11), Christ has his

Figure 11 *The Heavenly Bridegroom and His Bride*, illumination from the Song of Songs, ca. 1130. The Hague, KB 76 E 7 fol. 122r (Bible Moralisée). Used with permission of the National Library of the Netherlands.

arms around a woman wearing a crown and a long red dress. They stand in front of a blue tapestry and on the tiled floor of an interior chamber, appointed to suggest, perhaps, an ecclesial setting. Beneath their image the first lines of the Song are introduced with an ornately decorated initial O.

Medieval manuscripts of the Song of Songs often include similar illuminations, some of them dating to the early twelfth century. The female figure is usually interpreted as a personification of the church (Ecclesia) but sometimes extended to also suggest the Virgin Mary. From the twelfth century onward, the theme of Christ as lover became especially popular in writings like those of Bernard of Clairvaux, William of St.-Thierry, and Henry Suso, as well as the mystical visions of such women religious as Hadewijch of Brabant or Mechthild of Magdeburg. Yet, no later than the third century, in the allegorical exegesis of Origen of Alexandria, the Song was interpreted as celebrating the desire of the soul for union with the Divine Word (see King 2005).

The idea of mystical marriage also occurred in legends about women saints, most notably in the story of Catherine of Alexandria who, according to tradition, received a wedding ring from the infant Christ. Although the earliest documentary evidence for the legend dates to the early fourteenth century, the subject became especially prominent in the fifteenth and sixteenth. The usual presentation of the event shows St. Catherine, kneeling before the Virgin Mary who holds the Christ child on her lap. The infant leans out of his mother's arms to place a wedding ring on St. Catherine's finger.

A different representation of Christ as tender lover portrays the Beloved Disciple (John the Evangelist) in an almost intimate connection to Christ. Based on his identification as the disciple whom Jesus loved and who reclined on his breast at the Last Supper (John 13:23 and 19:26), medieval artists often rendered the figure of John as a long-haired and beardless youth, resting his head on Jesus's chest (Figure 12). In many examples, Jesus's and John's right hands are joined to suggest their unique bond.

A particularly didactic image of Christ as lover is seen in a fifteenth-century German woodcut print, now in the National Gallery in Washington, DC. Christ, still tied to his cross and holding the bundle of sticks from his flagellation, pulls a rope tied around the waist of a monk who offers his heart to him (Figure 13). The explanatory texts, printed on scrolls within the image, record the words Jesus says to the monk, "Son, give me your heart, I do not remit the punishment of the

Figure 12 *Christ and St. John the Evangelist*, 1300–20, artist unknown, Germany, Swabia, near Bodensee. Cleveland Museum of Art, purchase from the J. H. Wade Fund 1928.753 (open access).

one that I hold dear," along with the monk's response: "O Lord, this I want. I desire it, for this reason you should pull me." Below a small demon tries to tempt the monk with a bag of money, while an angel in the upper right corner admonishes him: "Think of the last days, then you will never sin."

Figure 13 *Jesus Attracting the Faithful to Heart* (1480–90), artist unknown. German woodcut, Rosenwald Collection, National Gallery of Art, Washington, DC (open access).

## In Music

*Songs of the Heart: "To Be Alone with You"*

That there is some special link between music and sexual desire has been a perennial theme in almost every culture, a link corroborated in a large body of contemporary psychological research. It is hardly surprising, then, that many hymn and song writers have been attracted to the strands of Christian erotic piety we find appearing in visual art and not flinched at giving them pointed musical expression. In the last fifty years or so, this is especially so in that stream of evangelical congregational music known as "contemporary praise and worship," where the theme of Jesus as lover has often played a key part, whether subliminally or overtly.

Many are highly suspicious of all such language in the context of worship, readily pointing to the hazards of projecting inappropriate features of earthly love on to the divine, and of falling into a kind of adolescent self-indulgence all too redolent of a clinging possessiveness. Others are less squeamish and quite prepared to employ the imagery of Jesus as lover, provided it is supported biblically and that it appears in contexts that have sufficient checks and balances to offset its obvious dangers.

The American singer and highly successful songwriter Sufjan Stevens (1975–) stands to one side of the contemporary worship stream – indeed, he is often highly critical of it, and in any case his output rarely includes material for a congregational singing. But his music has proved immensely popular in Christian circles of all stripes. Although a committed believer, he distances himself from the label "Christian artist," preferring to approach theological themes obliquely, retelling biblical stories and addressing pressing cultural concerns: such as consumerism, social media addiction, and political polarization.

In several interviews, he speaks about his liking for blending the topics of spirituality and sexuality. A prime example is one of his best-known songs from his album *Seven Swans* (2004) – "To be Alone with You."

> I'd swim across Lake Michigan
> I'd sell my shoes
> I'd give my body to be back again
> In the rest of the room
>
> To be alone with you ...
>
> You gave your body to the lonely
> They took your clothes
> You gave up a wife and a family
> You gave your ghost
>
> To be alone with me. ...
>
> You went up on a tree ...
>
> To be alone with me ...
>
> I've never known a man who loved me

The sense of erotic intimacy here is accentuated by the simplicity of the musical arrangement and its sense of gentle enticement, borne along by Stevens's breathless, almost whispering delivery.

To whom is this expression of desire addressed? Undoubtedly, a Christian will struggle hard *not* to read these lines without thinking of Jesus. The christological allusions seem almost blatant at times: "sacred space," the "tree," "They took your clothes / You gave up a wife and a family," "gave your ghost"; and the album taken as a whole is predominantly concerned with Christian themes. On the other hand, to insist the song is exclusively "about" Jesus would be to overpress a point. Jesus is not actually named; all this could be addressed to an earthly lover. Indeed, as a swathe of online commentary has confirmed, it is unclear whether Stevens is speaking to a this-worldly lover or to Jesus. And a further ambiguity crops up in the last line: Is this a male lover? Perhaps the greatest value of a song like this is to remind us that love of Jesus/God and erotic love for another human are by no means as neatly separable as some might like to think.

### JESUS AS INNOCENT VICTIM

**In Music**

*The Guiltless One:* St Luke Passion

Luke the Evangelist is especially well known for his distinctive accent on Christ's innocence: In his gospel, we are left in no doubt that Jesus went willingly to crucifixion for sins he did not commit. When Jesus is facing Pilate, Mark's Gospel makes no mention of Jesus's guilt or innocence, but Luke (who knows and uses Mark) has Pilate declaring Jesus's innocence three times to the angry crowd (23:4, 14, 22). Herod likewise believes Jesus is undeserving of the death penalty (23:15). One of the criminals executed next to Jesus, guilty by his own admission, insists Jesus has done nothing wrong (23:14). And the gentile centurion at the foot of the cross proclaims Jesus not as the Son of God (as in Mark's Gospel) but as "a righteous man" (23:47). Even so, it should be noted, Jesus is not portrayed as a hapless and helpless casualty of the evil machinations of corrupt power but as faithful, the Righteous One, oriented resolutely to his Father's will, dying in accordance with God's promise to rescue those who *are* indeed mired in guilt.

In 2013, a fresh work by the Scottish composer James MacMillan (1959–) received its first performance in the Royal Concertgebouw in Amsterdam – his *St Luke Passion.* And "fresh" is the operative word, for it turned out to be strikingly original in a number of respects, and not least in its rendering of Jesus's innocence.

Most of the *Passion* consists, as we might expect, of a setting of chapters 22 and 23 of Luke's Gospel, covering the period from the Last Supper to Jesus's death and burial. Taking just over an hour to perform, it is scored for a standard-sized orchestra and two choirs. But when it comes to portraying Jesus, MacMillan departs from all standard procedures. One of the crucial matters any composer faces in setting a passion text is how to mark Jesus out from the other characters in the passion drama. Bach in his *St Matthew Passion* famously surrounds Christ with a "halo" of strings whenever he sings. In his earlier *St John Passion,* MacMillan gave the part to a bass, and since Christ is the only soloist in this work, the contrast between Jesus and the other vocalists (two choirs) is especially sharp. However, here in the *St Luke Passion,*

MacMillan gives Jesus's words to a children's choir, who sing either in unison or in three parts (in triads or polyphony, the Trinitarian allusion being quite deliberate). MacMillan writes: "Any Passion that casts Christ as a soloist immediately makes him take human form as an adult male, whereas I wanted to examine his otherness, sanctity, and mystery."[1] The comment certainly makes sense (although the Christ of John's Gospel would perhaps be a more obvious candidate for otherness, sanctity, and mystery). What the children's choir will perhaps more likely connote for many is innocence, something MacMillan hints was also intended.[2]

This unswerving steadiness is vividly conveyed by the relative calmness of the music given to the children's choir. The writing is generally richly tonal or semitonal (i.e. clearly in stable keys), highly consonant, radiating warmth of a kind rarely present elsewhere in the work – indeed, the music for this choir is often juxtaposed dramatically with the extreme dissonance that MacMillan typically employs to connote the evil forces that drove Jesus to his death. Summarizing Luke's perspective, Walter Moberly writes: "How are the powers of evil overcome? By a positive goodness which trusts unswervingly in God, repays hatred with love, and is a channel for the mighty power of God to flow through" (Moberly 1988, 38). And that, many commentators on his *Passion* seem to agree, is just what MacMillan has turned into sound.

**In Visual Art**
*He Did No Violence and There Was No Deceit in His Mouth*
Depictions of Christ standing before Pilate appear early in Christian pictorial art and remain a popular subject through the ages. In many of these, Christ stands in near profile, his head bowed, his eyes looking downward rather than directly at Pilate, who turns his gaze away from Christ as he washes his hands, as if unable to confront the innocent one whom he will allow to be condemned to death (Figure 14). In a dramatic, early sixteenth-century painting by Jacopo Tintoretto, the tall Christ's luminous white robe reflects the light coming in from a window to the right and makes his body into a light source itself. By contrast, Pilate's retreat into the shadows suggests his cravenness. In the foreground, an old secretary bends over a ledger, recording the

---

[1] MacMillan 2014.
[2] "Employing a children's choir grants a measure of innocence to Christ as the sacrificial lamb" (MacMillan 2014).

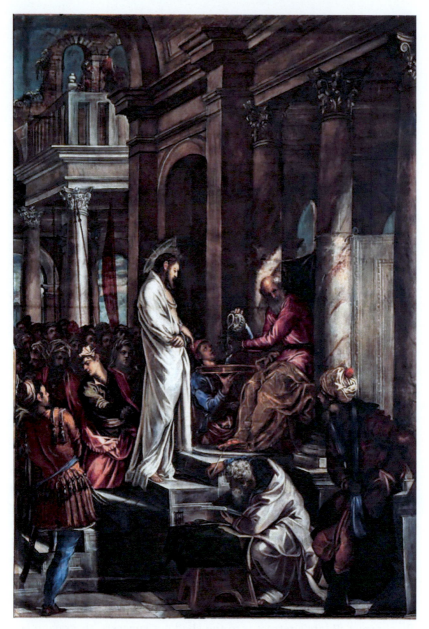

Figure 14 Jacopo Tintoretto, *Christ before Pilate*, 1566–7, oil on canvas, 380 × 515 cm. Scuola Grande di San Rocco, Venice. Open access (Creative Commons License).

Figure 15 Francisco de Zurbarán, *Agnus Dei (Lamb of God)*, ca. 1635–1640. Oil on canvas, (36 × 52 cm); the San Diego Museum of Art: Gift of Anna R. and Amy Putnam, 1847.36. Used with permission of the Museum.

exchange between the judge and the accused. In the background, the gathered crowd stubbornly demands that the governor play his part and order the execution. A swooning female on Christ's left must be Pilate's wife, who tried to warn her husband to "have nothing to do with that righteous man for I have suffered much over him today in a dream" (Matt 27:19).

The idea of Jesus as the sacrificial lamb is literally rendered in depictions of an actual lamb, bound and ready for the ritual slaughter (Figure 15).[3] The lamb is sometimes shown as wounded and bleeding into a eucharistic chalice but sometimes standing upon the rock of Paradise and surrounded by saints and apostles. This is the *agnus dei*, who takes away the sins of the world (John 1:29), a reference to the unblemished lamb sacrificed at Passover that recalls the Israelites' escape from Egypt (Exod 12:1–28). Paul already refers to Christ as the paschal lamb (1 Cor 5:7) and in the book of Revelation describes the Lamb, slain but worthy, whose blood was the ransom for the people of God (Rev 5:9–10).

---

[3] In 692 the eastern Council of Trullo, canon 82, condemned the use of the Lamb as a figure for Christ, insisting the Savior should be depicted in human form only.

A different portrayal of Jesus as an innocent shows him patiently suffering the brutality and scorn from the soldiers who crown him with a wreath of thorns. Jesus's expression in many of these images is one of sorrow but also of resignation, as if he pities those who mistreat him. He shows no anger or even judgment, rather his expression seems to foreshadow the words he will say from the cross in Luke's Gospel, "Father, forgive them for they know not what they do" (Luke 23:34). In a fifteenth-century German altarpiece, Jesus's passivity and silence

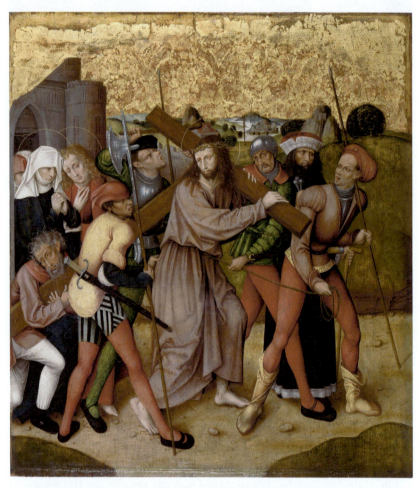

Figure 16 Altarpiece (detail) with the *Passion of Christ: Way to Calvary*. German (artist unknown), ca. 1480–95. Oil on panel with gold leaf, 120 × 9 × 328 cm. Walters Art Museum, Baltimore, acquired by Henry Walters before 1909. Open access, permission of the Museum.

also evoke the silence of the suffering servant in Isaiah – oppressed and afflicted – yet, like the sheep led to slaughter, he does not open his mouth to protest or to condemn those who persecute him (Figure 16) (Isa 53:7, see Acts 8:32). Jesus also becomes the archetype of the noble martyr who refuses to return injustice in kind but rather takes the role of the one who meets corrupt power or human wickedness with nonviolence and offers healing rather than hatred or retribution. The faithful are exhorted to emulate his example, to bless those who curse them, to love their enemies, and to pray for their persecutors (Matt 5:44). Like Christ in these images, who does not revile in return, Christians should endure pain and spiteful treatment (see 1 Pet 1:19–24). In contrast to the understanding of crucifixion as punishing an innocent (divine) victim for human sin, this presentation conveys the message that divine mercy and love can overcome cruelty and abuse.

### JESUS AS KING AND LORD OF LORDS

#### In Visual Art
*God Exalted Him to the Highest Place and Gave Him the Name Above Every Name*

The early fifth-century Roman Basilica of Santa Pudenziana, the oldest surviving mosaic apse in a Christian church, displays an almost unprecedented depiction of a darkly bearded Christ seated on a gemmed throne, wearing a golden robe with purple stripes and surrounded by his twelve apostles (Figure 17). Christ holds an open book, displaying the legend *Dominus Conservator Ecclesiae Pudenzianae* (the Lord is the Preserver of the Church of Pudenziana). In the background, a gem-studded gold cross rises from a rocky mount, behind a walled city. The mount depicts Golgotha, but four creatures in the sunrise sky surrounding the cross indicate that the city most likely represents the *New* Jerusalem, the city described in the book of Revelation, chapter 21. Thus, this image portrays Jesus at his return, the one who comes again in glory (see Matt 19:28).

Almost as far different from Christ as the caretaking Good Shepherd as possible, this Christ is ruler of the Cosmos, reigning from Heaven. It calls to mind the texts of Revelation 11:15, "The kingdom of the world has become the kingdom of our Lord and of his Christ, and he shall reign for ever and ever," and 17:14, "the Lamb will conquer for he is Lord of lords and King of kings." Yet it also echoes other Scripture passages, including Psalm 103:19, "The Lord has established his throne in the heavens and his kingdom

Figure 17 *Christ Enthroned*. Apse mosaic, Basilica of Santa Pudenziana, Rome, ca. 405. Photo: Author.

rules over all"; the text of Ephesians 1:17–21, "The God of our Lord Jesus Christ ... made him sit at his right hand in the heavenly places, far above all rule and authority and power and dominion and above every name that is named, not only in this age but in the that which is to come"; and the petition of 1 Peter 5:11, "To him be the dominion for ever and ever."

The icon of Christ as King or Christ in majesty became prominent in both Eastern and Western art from the early Middle Ages to the present day. It was not intended to authorize any earthly, mortal ruler as the special agent of God but rather to proclaim that the only true sovereign of the world is Christ himself. In Eastern Christian iconography it is specifically identified as the image of Christ the *Pantocrator*, the all-powerful Lord. In this Russian icon (Figure 18), as in the mosaic at Santa Pudenziana, he holds a book, here a codex of the Scriptures, to suggest his roles as teacher and judge as well as universal Lord.

A different image of Christ as King illustrates his entry to Jerusalem, as recorded in the New Testament Gospels (see Matt 21:1–11 and parallels). The story explicitly portrays this event as an imperial adventus – an emperor's ceremonial arrival into a city.

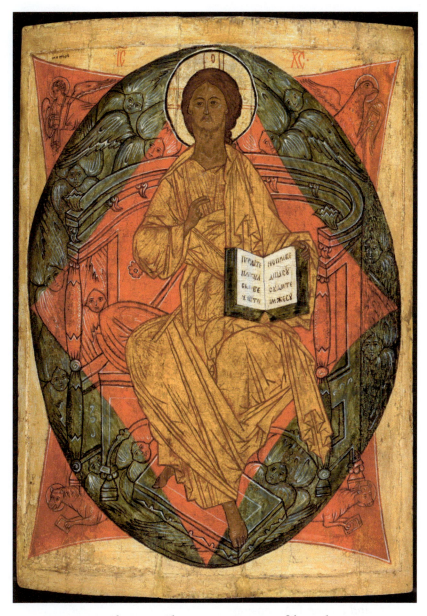

Figure 18 *Christ in Glory*, icon, Russian, fifteenth century. Tempura on wood, 107 × 78.4 cm. Metropolitan Museum of Art, New York, gift of George R. Hann, 1944. Open Access, permission of the Museum.

Figure 19 Pietro Lorenzetti, *Christ's Entry into Jerusalem*, fresco, Lower Church, San Francesco, Assisi, 1310–19. Photo credit Alfredo Dagli Orti/Art Resource, New York.

However, while a secular ruler would arrive mounted on a horse or in a chariot, Jesus rides a humbler animal – a donkey.[4] The episode is colorfully captured in an early fourteenth-century work by the Sienese artist Pietro Lorenzetti, in the Lower Church of San Francesco at Assisi (Figure 19). Here Christ wears a richly embroidered purple cloak and is greeted by an outpouring mass of citizens, carrying palm branches and spreading garments on the road to create a "red carpet" welcome.

### In Music
*Joy and Prayer:* L'Ascension

Arguably the most distinguished and influential French composer of his generation, and certainly the most overtly theological, Olivier Messiaen (1908–92) stands as a colossus of twentieth-century music. Through a vast output spanning some six decades, and covering an

[4] Jensen 2015, esp. 24–33.

astonishing variety of instruments and voices, he deployed a sophisticated musical toolbox that would catch the attention of his modernist and avant-garde contemporaries, and yet serve a focused, Catholic imagination of the world under the Lordship of Christ. Virtually all his pieces display some form of explicit Christian intent or reference. The driving force of his work was never in doubt: "The first idea that I wished to express – and the most important, because it stands above them all – is the existence of the truths of the Catholic faith" (Samuel 1976, 2). It is especially appropriate that we should be considering Messiaen in a chapter on Jesus in visual art and music: Like many, he saw colors in his mind's eye when he heard music, even going as far as describing his musical language as a "theological rainbow."

*L'Ascension* (1932–3) comprises a group of four pieces for large orchestra that Messiaen later arranged for organ and which explore the theme of Jesus's kingly ascension. Although the music employs a wide variety of modernist techniques he had developed by this time, the overall mood or ethos is consistently positive. In this, he stands apart from currents in theology that read the ascension in primarily negative terms, as concerning Christ's absence or withdrawal. Messiaen puts the accent firmly where the biblical texts put it: on Jesus's exaltation to the right hand of the Father as enthroned King and Lord, and on the heavenly intercession which this exaltation inaugurates.

So it is no accident that the movement that stands out from the others is the third, heralded by fanfares: "Alleluias on the Trumpets, Alleluias on the Cymbals. 'The Lord is gone up with the sound of a trumpet, O clap your hands all ye people; shout unto God with the voice of triumph.'" With its lilting syncopation and regular rhythm, there are clear allusions to (especially Baroque) dance forms. When Messiaen arranged the work for organ, he judged what he had written for orchestra was unsuitable and substituted a no less energetic and exuberant movement, complete with an ecstatic toccata, entitled *Transports de joie d'une âme devant la gloire du Christ qui est la sienne* (Outbursts of Joy from a Soul before the Glory of Christ Which Is Its Own Glory).

Throughout his career, Messiaen was fascinated by music's engagement with time, and especially the way in which eternity could be evoked by composing music in which the "arrow of time" that marks so much of our lives and provides the momentum that energizes Western music is deliberately resisted. This, he believed, could bring a foretaste of eternal life with God. There is something of this diminishing of forward motion in the opening movement of *L'Ascension*,

*Majesté du Christ demandant sa gloire à son Père* (The Majesty of Christ Praying That His Father Should glorify Him). The second piece, *Alléluias sereins d'une âme qui désire le ciel* (Serene Alleluias of a Soul That Longs for Heaven), also conjures up a sense of near-stasis, not least through having the main theme stripped of any harmony that could push it forwards. But it is in the final movement, *Prière du Christ montant vers son Père* (Prayer of Christ Ascending towards His Father), that Messiaen's evocation of the ascended Christ's transcendence over time is most compellingly conveyed. Christ prays to his Father, yet outside this world's time. The extremely slow tempo unhindered by bar lines and meter, the repeated rising phrases fanning out into full silences, the rich and lush harmony bathing the listener in assurance – all these combine to produce a theological "painting in sound" that has rarely been equaled.

### FURTHER READING

Begbie, Jeremy S. 2007. *Resounding Truth: Christian Wisdom in the World of Music*. Grand Rapids: Baker.

Begbie, Jeremy S. 2020. "Making the Familiar Unfamiliar: Macmillan's *St Luke Passion*." In *James Macmillan Studies*, edited by George Parsons and Robert Sholl, 111–28. Cambridge: Cambridge University Press.

Butt, John. 2011. "George Frederic Handel and *The Messiah*." In *The Oxford Handbook of the Reception History of the Bible*, edited by Michael Lieb, Emma Mason, and Jonathan Roberts, 294–306. Oxford: Oxford University Press.

Coakley, Sarah. 2013. *God, Sexuality and the Self: An Essay "on the Trinity"*. Cambridge: Cambridge University Press.

Freeman, Jennifer Awes. 2022. *The Good Shepherd*. Waco: Baylor University Press.

Harries, Richard. 2004. *The Passion in Art*. London: Routledge.

Horner, Al. 2020. "'I Have a Sense of Urgency': Sufjan Stevens Wakes from the American Dream." *The Guardian*, September 25. www.theguardian.com/music/2020/sep/25/sufjan-stevens-interview-the-ascension

Jensen, Robin M. 2017. *The Cross: History, Art, and Controversy*. Cambridge, MA: Harvard University Press.

Loewe, Andreas. 2014. *Johann Sebastian Bach's St John Passion (BWV 245): A Theological Commentary*. Leiden: Brill.

MacMillan, James. 2014. "Interview about *St Luke Passion*." Boosey & Hawkes. www.boosey.com/cr/news/James-MacMillan-interview-about-new-St-Luke-Passion/100345.

Muir, Carolyn Diskant. 2013. *Saintly Bridge and Bridegrooms*. Turnhout: Brepols.

Shenton, Andrew. 2010. *Messiaen the Theologian*. Farnham: Ashgate.

Viladesau, Richard. 2020. *The Wisdom and Power of the Cross: The Passion of Christ in Theology and the Arts*. Oxford: Oxford University Press.

## 12 Jesus in the Story of Spirituality and Worship
VOLKER LEPPIN

Christianity is marked by the absence of its founding figure Jesus Christ. As Michel de Certeau has articulated from the standpoint of cultural theory:

> In the Christian tradition, an initial privation of body goes on producing institutions and discourses that are the effects of and substitutes for that absence: multiple ecclesiastical bodies, doctrinal bodies, and so on. How can a body be made from the word? This question raises the other haunting question of an impossible mourning: 'Where art thou?' (de Certeau 1995, 81).

Christianity has supplied a multitude of answers to this question, far exceeding what a brief chapter like this one can fully present. In a certain sense, all Christian spirituality and worship is concerned with making the absent Jesus present, either by his mere "being here-or-there" like in the sacraments, which we call representation, or by acting and imitating him, which we call reenactment. Both have been employed to the extent that another famous quote is also true. Jaroslav Pelikan writes:

> Regardless of what anyone may personally think or believe about him, Jesus of Nazareth has been the dominant figure in the history of Western culture for almost twenty centuries (Pelikan 1987, 1).

This chapter can, therefore, only compile a few excerpts from the extraordinarily vast and comprehensive narrative of praise and devotion that has been created through the diverse forms of yearning for Jesus's presence in Christian life. The selected sources and examples may carry a Latin-oriented bias but will at least open a window to other traditions.

*The Imitation of Christ* by Thomas à Kempis (1380–1471) is one of the bestselling books of all time. Its title encapsulates the essence of what has motivated Christians across the ages: to follow in the footsteps of their founding figure as the disciples had done before them. Today, this may resonate as a call to moral action, and indeed, it does encourage this aspect to a certain degree. However, to incorporate Jesus into Christian life transcends mere ethical conduct and encompasses something more profound, as we aim to show in the following examples.

This chapter is an attempt to illustrate Jesus's impact on Christian life throughout the history of the church in a number of telling examples. Rather than following a strict chronological order, this overview will be structured around the significant stages of Jesus's life. Thus, we will think about the veneration of Jesus as a child, as a grown man, and, finally, as the one who suffered passion on the cross. Through each of these stages the concept of identification will play a major role, whether in the believer's affirmative identification with Jesus himself or in the counter-identification with those who either loved him or fell short of acknowledging him as the Messiah and ultimately sinned against him. In the concluding section, we explore how the interplay between affirmative identification with Jesus and counter-identification with others created a tension that has served as a call for self-improvement, guiding individuals to align their lives with the example set by Jesus.

### NURSING THE CHILD

While the Gospels of Matthew and Luke provided their readers with accounts of the birth of Jesus, later authors would add stories about his childhood. Some noncanonical or "apocryphal" gospels, such as the Infancy Gospel of Thomas, which contains some material from the second century, introduced childhood stories of Jesus portraying him as a child marked by extraordinary miraculous power, albeit exercised in a somewhat puerile manner. For instance, one anecdote tells of how little Jesus with his friends formed birds from clay on a Sabbath day. When an older Jew chided them for doing artisan work on a Sabbath, Jesus blew breath into the clay figures, making them fly away. We might read stories like this on the one hand as proof of Christ's power, and, on the other hand, as a way to fill the gap the Gospels had left in their account of the earthly human life of Jesus. The desire for a complete biography continued to be fulfilled by similarly imaginative infancy stories, such as the fifth- or sixth-century Syriac/Arabic Infancy Gospel. Nevertheless, the canonical depictions of Jesus's early years, including the stories about the prophets Simeon and Anna, held the utmost importance because they linked the New Testament to the Old and gave narrative expression to the Christian conviction of Jesus's being the Messiah promised in the Hebrew Bible.

Jesus's birth from the Virgin Mary came to be regarded as the most important feature of his early life. However, this was not the case from the beginning. The Gospel of Mark stands without it, and while Easter seems to have been celebrated quite early, there was no clarity about the exact day of Jesus's birth in the first centuries. It seems as though the day of his baptism was initially of more importance, and different groups – in particular Gnostic ones – celebrated the day of Christ's epiphany through baptism, which might have interfered with the adoptionist interpretation of God's calling Jesus his son during baptism. Epiphany was also increasingly linked to the story of the nativity, as we can see in the celebration of the feast of "Holy Epiphany of the Nativity of Christ" on January 6 in Jerusalem and Constantinople by the early fourth century. While some scholars of liturgy see the finally decisive date of December 25 as rooted in symbolism of the third century, historians of religion tend to highlight its emergence from religious syncretism. The first mention of this date as a Christian feast appears in a calendar of 354 CE, which on the one hand marks it as the birth of Christ but elsewhere identifies the same date as the apparent birthday of Sol Invictus, the sun god central to Roman religion, whose cult had previously also been promoted during the reign of Constantine the Great (305–37). This might indicate that the day of Jesus's birth was overshadowed by the Roman concept of Christ as the glorious sovereign over heaven and earth, even if this thesis cannot be taken for granted.

Even so, Jesus's childhood had not been forgotten; instead, veneration of Mary was premised on the stories of her son's early years. This can be seen in another apocryphal gospel, the Gospel (Protoevangelium) of James, which narrated Mary's life from her youth to the time of Jesus's birth. Written in the second century, it likely contains the oldest depiction of Mary nursing the child at her breast. We should note that Mariology, in its proper meaning, is not solely about Mary but rather is also about Jesus, although we cannot delve into the full development of Mariology here. Nevertheless, the Council of Ephesus officially proclaimed her to be the Mother of God in 431, entwining her story with that of her son through the centuries, enriching the narrative of Jesus in Christian spirituality with numerous Mariological legends. Throughout the ages, Mary's virginity remained a prominent focus, seen as the fulfillment of Isaiah's prophecy in Isaiah 7:14.

Leaving behind the particular topic of Mary's veneration, the Christmas scene connects the story of mother and son with a central focus on the infant. These images portray the future impact of the child, emphasizing at once his vulnerability and his potency. The presence of shepherds at the manger signified that the gospel was intended to save all human beings, irrespective of their social status, while increasingly through time the depiction of the magi or kings symbolized the totality of humanity in several respects. The kings were often depicted as representing three stages of life and inhabitants of the three known parts of the Earth – Africa, Asia, and Europe – as Bede had it in his commentary on Matthew (PL 92,13A). Some depictions even include a black person at the manger, which can be seen as a statement that the gospel welcomes all people and races. However, this inclusive interpretation may have been sidelined or suppressed over the centuries to come.

The manger as well as the images of Christ as an infant and toddler served as sources of inspiration for spirituality during the Middle Ages in several ways. Celano's *Vita* attributes the invention of the nativity scene to Francis of Assisi (d. 1226), which is partly true. While he did not create a Christmas crib with figures and a tree, as modern middle-class piety would have it, his biographer Thomas of Celano recounts a significant event in 1223 when the saint arranged for a manger to act as an altar during a Christmas Mass in Greccio. According to Celano, Francis aimed to make the story of Jesus visible to the people's physical eyes (1 Cel 84:8). In later times, Jesus the child was not only visible but touchable as well. Nuns cherished the image of Jesus as a child by having Jesus dolls, nurturing and spiritually growing him through their care. Mystics, particularly women mystics, identified themselves with the Virgin Mary, bearing the child Jesus within their souls as a symbol of profound spiritual birth. Mystical theologians such as Meister Eckhart (d. 1329) and Johannes Tauler (d. 1361) taught about the birth of God within the soul, identifying themselves with the virgin bearing the child. Here we find an example of what has been identified above as the positive aspect of counter-identification, where individuals devote their love to Jesus Christ.

Through late medieval mysticism we can gain insight into certain aspects of Jesus-centered spirituality in early modern Christianity. When the Lutheran pastor Paul Gerhardt (1607–76) authored the hymn "Ich steh an deiner Krippen hier" (I Stand before Thy Manger Fair), he merged the acts of venerating and identifying with the child, particularly when the singer prays in the 14th stanza: "So laß mich doch dein kripplein seyn" (Let me thus be your little manger).

In a deeper sense, Christ the baby made incarnation visible and thus exemplified the encounter of the human and divine nature in Jesus Christ. Medieval liturgy already knew of the *admirabile* or *sacrum commercium*, the admirable or holy exchange between creator and created. What the Council of Chalcedon put into dogmatic words was celebrated here in praise of the divine through the human. In this example, we see common ground between traditional and modern confessions. Little wonder, then, that the idea of exchange remained dominant in modern Protestant thought as well, as seen in hymns such as "Lobt Gott Ihr Christen alle gleich" (Praise God, Ye Christians One and All) by the Lutheran cantor Niklaus Herman (d. 1561). Even if both Lutherans and Reformed Christians were drawn primarily to a spirituality focusing on the cross and Good Friday, they cherished the profound piety of Christmas, with Johann Sebastian Bach's (1685–1750) *Christmas Oratorio* or the first part of Handel's (1685–1759) *Messiah*.

While Bach's music embodied a mystical approach to Jesus the Child, this was not the only way to venerate him between the Middle Ages and modern expressions of piety. There was also a tendency, beginning in the late Middle Ages, to humanize the story of Jesus Christ. Painters loved to depict Jesus as part of his family's fold, with different family images. For example, the grouping of Anna with Mary and the child showed him as a part of three successive generations. The motif of Holy Kinship began to widen family ties until even uncles, aunts, and cousins were included in the depictions. This humanized portrayal, based on the biblical narrative, depicted Jesus and his family as mirrors of civic families in late medieval cities, emphasizing his connection to human society, even if the halo might have shown that he was more than our neighbor in the street.

Having this in mind, some complaints about the modern secularization of Christmas can perhaps be put into a broader context. The story of Jesus the child – human as he was – was inspired by, implied, and perhaps even emphasized a greater connection to worldly values than a strongly theological interpretation of incarnation might want to admit. Christmas rituals became orientated toward family and children as early as in Reformation times, when Christmas, at least in the wake of the Lutheran Reformation, became the feast of giving instead of Saint Nicholas Day. Still, it took time for Christmas to be seen as a family celebration rather than a religious event. Friedrich Schleiermacher already shows awareness of this, though, when writing his *Die Weihnachtsfeier* (*Christmas Celebration*) in 1806. The small booklet shows an attempt to uncover a deeper religious sense within middle-class Christmas celebrations. However, Schleiermacher's efforts might not have been entirely successful, as the figure of Santa Claus, which has little or no connection with Jesus or his namesake Saint Nicholas, now dominates the perception of Christmas, seemingly displacing Jesus from his own birthday celebration.

### LOVING THE MAN

Undoubtedly, the image of a baby in the manger has evoked profound feelings of love. But maternal love was not the only kind expressed by Christians throughout history. A deeply erotic love for Jesus has also been a significant aspect of Christian spirituality, providing a female role model for the believer's relationship with Jesus Christ. Biblical roots for this concept can be traced back to the Hebrew Bible, where the Song of Songs, with its erotic tone, sparked discussions about an allegorical representation of the love between the soul and Jesus Christ, as seen in the writings of Origen (d. 254). Bernard of Clairvaux (d. 1153) further developed this idea of spiritual love in his comprehensive sermons on the Song of Songs, interpreting the bride in this biblical book as the soul and the bridegroom as Jesus. Drawing from his noble upbringing, Bernard employed the language of courtly songs and novels, thus blurring the lines between spiritual love and corporal eroticism. As in the later examples of Meister Eckhart and Johannes Tauler, Bernard adopted a female role model, that of the loving bride, to illustrate what he, the male author, understood in terms of spiritual encounter. Through this imagery, he contributed to the growing portrayal of Jesus as an extraordinary lover who would open the way to salvation through carnal love, at least metaphorically.

In the centuries that followed, the concept of bridal mysticism spread among both religious and semi-religious women, particularly among Beguines, who from the early thirteenth century lived in small, ascetic, self-governing communities that were not formally affiliated with an established order. Whether or not they were constituted within the established religious orders, these communities favored the flourishing of a literary genre that developed a metaphorical approach to theology, and which arguably served as a profound biblical alternative to the more concept-oriented Scholastic discourse of the time. A significant aspect of this literary genre was the portrayal of Jesus as the lover who embraces the mystics, kisses them, and draws intimately close to them, evoking a profound resonance with the effects of sexual encounter.

The erotic dimension is prominently highlighted in the writings of the mystics and in accounts of their lives. In the *Vita Lutgardis* (thirteenth century), we find an explicit juxtaposition between Christ as lover and earthly lovers. After Lutgard, only by the help of God, avoids fornication with a noble young man, she not only turns to Jesus Christ but does so in a scene reminiscent of a young couple's courtship: While sitting somewhere, she sees Jesus in his earthly form, who partially removes his garment, even if only to show her his side wound as the well of all salvation (*De Lutgarde Virgine* 1.2). Furthermore, in a later vision she sees her savior hanging on the cross, who takes his arm from the beam, places it around her neck, and presses her mouth to his side wound for a kiss (*De Lutgarde Virgine* 1.2). Bernard had praised the kiss of the mouth in his sermons, yet Lutgard goes even further, for the side wound is closer to the heart of the beloved than the mouth. Nevertheless, Lutgard is not alone in expressing this sort of intimacy with Christ. Mechthild of Magdeburg (1207–82) describes, in *The Flowing Light of the Godhead*, how soul and bridegroom enter a small chamber, with the soul undressing herself until she is naked. Both lovers come so close that the soul can state, "nothing can be between you and me" (1.44).

At first glance, the earthly Jesus appears to overshadow everything just mentioned. Yet both the writers and recipients of these accounts agreed that what takes place in this dimension of love is not earthly but visionary, spiritual, and ecstatic, even if described in carnal language. Metaphorical descriptions, whether based on real visionary experience or not, enhance the understanding of Jesus as the savior who becomes the individual lover and dispenser of grace to all. These provocative forms of expression, bursting with spiritual and theological impact, depict Jesus as drawing as close to the believer as any person can since sexual intercourse is viewed as the closest form of encounter between human beings.

Even in the biblical text, there are hints that underpin the interplay of eroticism and spiritual love. Through the merging of different biblical passages and legends, one follower of Jesus came to be particularly associated with erotic love and sexuality: Mary Magdalene. In the early church, she was seen as the woman who "has shown great love" (Luke 7:47). Because of Luke's description of this woman as sinful (7:37), readers drew the (textually erroneous) conclusion that "shown great love" referred to sexuality and carnal love. In hybrid traditions, Mary Magdalene was also identified with Martha's sister – also called Mary – who, according to Luke 10:38–42, adored Jesus by sitting at his feet when he visited them both. While Martha, who was busy preparing the meal, chastised Mary for her inaction, Jesus praised Mary for having chosen the better part. Emphasizing contemplation over action, she was an example for many female religious women in the Middle Ages who, in their meditation, adored Jesus Christ as she had done: in love and desire.

The concept of Jesus the Beloved was not restricted to the Middle Ages. Catholic mystics like Teresa of Avila (1515–82) continued to explore this idea, and it would be a misconception to assume that the Reformation brought an end to it. For example, one painting depicts the Lutheran countess Aemilie Juliane of Schwarzburg-Rudolstadt (1637–1706), an influential hymn writer, with her lover Jesus Christ in a garland of roses. Texts of Lutheran orthodoxy, such as Johann Arndt's (1555–1621) *Paradiesgärtlein* (*Garden of Paradise*), which was attached to Bernardine mysticism, also contributed to the genre of bridal mysticism, as did certain compositions by Johann Sebastian Bach.

As love took on a bodily dimension, Jesus's body became a part of the veneration of the Son of God. This could manifest through devotion to his side wound, such as the (so-called "Moravian") Herrnhut Brethren cherishing the *Seitenhöhlchen* (little side hole) in the eighteenth century, or the vision received by the French Salesian nun Margareta Maria Alacoque (1647–90) in 1675, where she saw Jesus's pierced heart and received his promise of love for humanity. Devotion to the Sacred Heart became one of the most significant ways to venerate Jesus in modern spirituality. Although the idea of Jesus as the Beloved may have faded in modernity, the memory has not been completely abandoned. In the late nineteenth century, the iconic Sacré Cœur Basilica was constructed atop the Montmartre summit in Paris. The less spiritual and far more carnal aspect of the love story between Jesus and Mary Magdalene even found its place at the poet's desk in the twentieth century, with the Greek writer Nikos Kazantzakis's (1883–1957) 1955 novel *The Last Temptation*. In this work, instead of dying on the cross, Jesus remains alive and spends his time with Mary Magdalene as his wife. While the book and the subsequent Scorsese movie adaptation undoubtedly stirred controversy, they nevertheless exemplify a more recent manifestation of a long-standing perception of Jesus as fully human, including his sexuality.

## THE DEATH OF JESUS AS A SACRAMENT AND AN EXAMPLE

In *De Trinitate* 4.3, Augustine of Hippo (354–430) reflected on Jesus Christ demonstrating human resurrection *in sacramento et exemplo*, as sacrament and example, meaning that human resurrection would be both an effect and an emulation of Christ's resurrection. He easily applied this conceptual coupling to Jesus's death as well, which has been the core event relating Christian spirituality to its founding figure over the centuries.

**Physical Presence and Representation**
Christ's death as a sacrament and example was not only a spiritual reality. It also bore a physical representation, which can be observed in piety relating to his death, just as much as that relating to his life. As stated at the beginning of this chapter, in the words of Michel de Certeau, through resurrection a "privation" of Jesus's body happened, an "absence," which meant that none of his physical remains could have been preserved. Nevertheless, even in his bodily absence, believers were able to find a physical reminder of Jesus in the places where he had lived and suffered. Pilgrimage to the Holy Land became a common practice among Christians. Indeed, the geography common to every biblical account made it possible to follow in the footsteps of Jesus. And despite changes to Jerusalem's topography over the centuries, pilgrims could still find the locations mentioned in the Bible, often marked by church buildings. The Church of the Holy Sepulchre was one of the most important pilgrimage sites, constructed under Emperor Constantine in the fourth century and later rebuilt during the Crusades, which – by contemporary definition – were essentially armed pilgrimages, even if as an afterthought they were part of European expansion.

Pilgrimage was not solely about seeking indulgences or calculating time in purgatory, as some reformed and modern critics have suggested. Instead, it was a deeper spiritual experience where Jesus found representation in geography and architecture. Late medieval authors believed that Jesus's virtue was transmitted from his resurrected body through sites in which he had been present. Nevertheless, pilgrimage was ultimately not accessible to all due to both economic constraints and the challenges posed by long-time Muslim rule in the region.

As a result, representations and reenactments of the events and places in which Jesus had been present began to be established in Europe. In the Middle Ages, the Holy Sepulchre was replicated in several locations. As early as 940, Bishop Konrad of Constance (934–75) erected a replica of the rotunda covering the Holy Sepulchre in Jerusalem. Templar Knights would typically follow this style of round building, as can be seen in Laon, London, and elsewhere. Whenever this kind of building was erected, Jesus's tomb found a place of representation.

Often, representation could turn into reenactment, further drawing the believer into active participation through all of their senses. In many cases, a replica of the Holy Sepulchre served as a stage for liturgical plays, particularly during the holy week of Easter. In an ideal liturgical play, the crucifix would be taken from the altar and buried in the Holy Sepulchre on Good Friday. After three days, it would be returned to the altar, and, while the tomb lay empty, the resurrected Jesus Christ would be presented to the congregation. Such plays were a serious and integral part of worship, leading to debates about who could be authorized to play Jesus, a task usually only admitted to a priest.

We might wonder if and when this genre of religious drama turned secular. In fact, as early as the late Middle Ages, the performance of passion plays had moved from the interior of churches to public venues such as marketplaces and other civic venues. However, while to modern sensibilities this may appear to be a form of secularization, late medieval urban society should not be understood as secularized. The primary motivation for such a move was to proclaim the Gospel and to foster public belief and trust in God. These plays showcased more elaborate poetical skills than their liturgical counterparts. We might see them as a genre of transition within a long process. Early modern drama about Jesus was clearly intended to be spiritual in nature. While contemporary theater is less focused on Jesus than it was compared to medieval times, we cannot easily define its dramatic representation of Jesus as completely secularized. Furthermore, as debates around the display of anti-Semitism in Mel Gibson's *Passion of the Christ* indicate, contemporary art is not so far from our remote predecessors who often openly discriminated against Jews in their dramatic accounts of Jesus's death.

The desire to make Christ tangible also led to the cult of bodily relics of his presence. While the theology of Christ's resurrection reinforced the physical experience that "He is not here" (Matt 28:6), religious creativity found ways to mediate this through relics associated with Jesus. The most important contact relic was the cross itself, believed to have been found by Constantine's mother Helena in Jerusalem, who brought it to Europe. For centuries, the holy cross was venerated only in fragments distributed across the then-known world. Even the smallest wooden part was considered to contain Jesus's salvific suffering.

Fabrics were also revered as relics, such as the seamless robe of Jesus preserved in Trier, which attracted pilgrimages from the late Middle Ages. Another significant relic, even closer to Jesus, is the veil of Veronica, a piece of fabric said to bear the image of Jesus's face as he pressed it to the cloth during the passion. To a certain degree this relic, preserved in the Latin church, served to replace the *mandylion*, which had been venerated in the Byzantine church but was lost during the Fourth Crusade. Both relics brought believers closer to an imagined visual appearance of Jesus. By merging Platonic ontology, which posits a particular presence of the imaged in the image, with faith in the miraculous ways God chooses to meet humans, both images relate the beholder directly to Jesus himself. By means of divine power, his earthly features could be seen in their transition from life to death.

The veil relic could not be multiplied in the same manner as the cross because, in this case, dividing the original (which was kept hidden from public view and only periodically exhibited) would have destroyed it. Therefore, the relic had to be multiplied through replication rather than division. Any replica would bear the likeness of the original, leading to a significant number of paintings depicting the veil in Europe. This, in turn, shaped the prevailing idea of what Jesus looked like, an image that continues to endure to this day. The Shroud of Turin, which came into preservation in Turin no earlier than 1578, has, unlike the veil, been a subject of debate since people first claimed it bore an imprint of Jesus's body. Such debates indicate that the medieval church was not complacent about the origin and authenticity of its relics. Indeed, they knew of doubt, even if they took for granted the authenticity of some holy objects that to the modern mind would be doubtful.

Faith extended beyond contact relics. Just because Christ's body was gone did not mean that absolutely nothing of his physical body had been preserved. The cult of relics, while respecting the intangibility of his resurrected body, came to focus on the imagination of reproducible parts of Jesus's body like hair or fingernails. Jesus's blood shed during the crucifixion was one of the most common relics, often associated with miracles. Other relics were linked to Jesus's childhood, such as his primary teeth or foreskin.

As strange as some of these relics may seem to modern sensibilities, any instance indicates a spiritual desire for an impression of what was seen to be the real historical Jesus. This sense of Jesus's historical personage was not of course the same as what a modern scientific approach would call the historical Jesus. The de-emphasis on this major part of traditional spirituality in post-Enlightenment research may lead its results to exist in tension with this direct, immediate, and often intimate relation to Jesus.

## Liturgical Reenactment and Representation

While the Eucharist is the most prominent representation of Christ, any extended evaluation of the subject would lead us deeper into the doctrine of the sacrament than necessary for this overview. On the other hand, we cannot entirely overlook the significance of the eucharistic liturgy, which serves as the most pronounced staging of a scene from Jesus's life.

As early as the Gospels and Paul's first letter to the Corinthians, the Lord's Supper is exactly what its name implies: a meal conducted "in remembrance of me." Regardless of its definition, the person presiding over the meal sits in Jesus's place, and the performance of the liturgy follows the events reported in the Bible to have taken place during Maundy Thursday. The congregation, assembled around the table of the Lord, reenacts the very last evening he spent with his disciples. The essence of that moment of institution and communion, for believers, becomes true for the entire service.

Liturgically, Christian believers followed the life of Jesus, as guided by teachings like those of Cyril of Jerusalem (313–86), in whose *Catechetical Lectures* the Church of the Holy Sepulchre is used as the stage to convey the passion of Christ and prepare catechumens for baptism. Similarly, medieval commentaries depict the Holy Mass as a reflection of Jesus's life. Ideally, the Holy Mass would be a reflection of Jesus's life, allowing the congregation to partake in their founder's experiences. However, the intended immediate representation of Jesus was not always accomplished. The reenactment was of necessity guided by one person, who naturally assumed the role of representing him. Thus, a vicarious system was introduced, in which the priest served as a mediator and could be seen as the vicar of Christ.

Despite this inclination to a hierarchical understanding of the church established in the Middle Ages, the idea of representing Jesus's life persisted. As mentioned earlier regarding passion plays, every feast of the church related to periods or events in Jesus's life made space for reenactments that aimed to make Christ present. Famously, in late medieval palm processions, a wooden figure of Jesus riding on a donkey would accompany the processing crowd of believers. And on Ascension Day, a figure of Jesus would be drawn up to the ceiling of the church building and disappear through a hole, creating a dramatic staging of Jesus's life.

Early modern confessional culture, particularly in Catholic areas, continued to uphold this idea of visual representation, while the Protestant Reformation, even more in its Calvinist branch than in its

Lutheran parts, distanced itself from this visual culture and emphasized the presence of Jesus more through the word. When Luther argued that the Bible mainly focused on *Christus pro nobis* (Christ for us), he made Jesus present in an audible and – to a certain degree – cognitive way, in contrast to the visual reenactment in plays. However, he still shared the idea that liturgy was nothing other than the representation and, through proclaimed word, reenactment of Jesus Christ.

Through various transformations, evangelical piety, particularly since the Great Awakening in the eighteenth century, has preserved this idea of the verbal presence of Christ. In twentieth- and twenty-first-century global Christianity, there is a deep-hearted Jesus piety, where worship is seen as a way of listening to Jesus's personal call.

### Following the Example

Hearing Jesus's call directly often resonates more with an understanding of him as example rather than solely as sacrament, as was prevalent in the medieval Mass and Luther's sacramental understanding of the effective word. However, viewing Jesus as an example is again deeply rooted in Christian spirituality, especially concerning his salvific death. In early Christianity, one of the primary ways to follow his example was to follow him into martyrdom. The acts of early Christian martyrs read like verbal replicas of the trial of Christ. When facing Roman authorities, the martyrs acted as Jesus had before Pontius Pilate. More than in any other case we have dealt with up to now, this is a clear example of identification rather than counter-identification, as the martyrs identified strongly with Jesus, despite not being allowed to do so openly.

It is noteworthy that while the martyrs identified with Jesus, they also upheld certain distinctions between themselves and Christ. For instance, traditions of Peter being crucified upside down, and Andrew on an X-shaped cross, demonstrate Christian attempts to preserve the distinctiveness of Jesus in their strong identification with him. Jesus became present within the martyrs regardless of whether they were male or female, as exemplified by the case of Blandina, a female martyr who upon her death in 177 was seen by others as the crucified Christ himself, according to Eusebius (*Hist. eccl.* 5.1.41).

Even after the victory of Christendom in the Roman Empire and the medieval world marked the virtual end of martyrdom, the passion of Christ continued to be present in various ways. A notable example is found in a letter announcing the death of Francis of Assisi (1181/2–1226), where the order general Elias of Cortona described the saint's body as bearing the stigmata of Jesus Christ. While this report may raise questions of historical accuracy, Franciscans saw this event as a literal fulfillment of Galatians 6:17. According to early reports, Francis had been marked by the five wounds of Jesus shortly before he died, signifying his identification as an *alter Christus*, a second Christ. This level of identification with Jesus was considered the highest, although it would not be limited to Francis alone, as the example of Catherine of Siena (1347–80) and popular Catholic belief even into the nineteenth and twentieth centuries show.

When Lutgard (mentioned earlier in the chapter) felt a vein bursting close to her heart (*Vita Lutgardis* 2.25), or when she reddened like blood through a vision of Christ (*Vita Lutgardis* 2.23), these experiences reveal, despite attempts by her biographers to downplay this impression, an undeniable identification with Christ. On the other hand, many female saints, such as Elizabeth of Hungary (1207–31), preferred a counter-identification, taking on the role of Jesus's servant. According to Matthew 25, Jesus identified with the poor and sick whom Elisabeth cared for. This counter-identification also mediated the presence of Jesus to the world of believers.

In the Middle Ages, the central concept of relating to Jesus in the way of identification or counter-identification was compassion. Some individuals, like the Dominican monk Henry Suso, sought to imitate Jesus in visionary experiences. Henry undertook a visionary walk through his monastery, ending in his being nailed to the cross. Others focused on identifying with Jesus's mother, Mary, as seen in the widespread literary form of *planctus Mariae*, where the faithful were invited to mourn on Mary's behalf since, having ascended to heaven, she was no longer able to feel pain. Or, to take another example, the Pietà, a late medieval sculptural motif, depicted a tearful Mary holding her deceased son on her lap, further emphasizing the theme of compassion in spirituality.

However, some treatises introduced a surprising aspect of counter-identification. A late medieval treatise meditating on the crucifixion conveyed the idea that each person was responsible for Jesus's death: "Vnd du arme creatur ein vrsach gewesen bist seines sterbens" (And you, poor creature, have been the reason for his dying).[1] This had the effect of personalizing the theological idea of human sin being resolved through Jesus Christ: Even centuries after Golgotha, the believer should see themselves as liable for Jesus's death. Modern

---

[1] Geiler von Kaysersberg 1516, D 5ʳ.

Protestantism continued this theme of late medieval counter-identification by critiquing compassion piety and highlighting the sinful individual's guilt in relation to Jesus's death. Thus, the aim was not merely to follow in Jesus's steps but to understand one's own sinful state by suffering in counter-identification.

Nonetheless, both types of piety, affirmative identification and counter-identification, were deeply rooted in late medieval spirituality. Both sought to find meaning in the suffering of Jesus for Christians' self-knowledge as sinners and the path to salvation through Christ. Jesuit spiritual praxis, such as the *Spiritual Exercises*, emphasized following the way of Jesus to passion and the cross. Ultimately, the shaping of Jesus spirituality in identification and counter-identification has endured in and evolved into modern Christianity.

### JESUS'S SENDING INTO THE WORLD

In modernity, the approach to thinking about Jesus has shifted toward ethical imitation, focusing on following the example of Jesus Christ in action and practice. Even if this approach is held in suspicion by some who regard it as a modernization of the Gospel, it is in fact rooted in biblical traditions. For example, the call in Matthew 28 to baptize, preach, and spread Jesus's mission among people is accomplished through the efforts of human beings.

Through the centuries, the call to adjust the virtues of life to the example of Jesus was heard. While the twelfth-century apostolic movement (*vita apostolica*) was named after the disciples, its adherents clearly wanted to follow Jesus himself, specifically in poverty and humility. The same is true of the Franciscan movement, whose father, as mentioned, was identified with Jesus by stigmatization. One compelling reason to believe in his identification was his genuine commitment to align his life and the lives of others with the call of Jesus to embrace poverty.

In modernity, this idea continued not only in the now "confessional" Catholic mendicant orders but also among some "Anabaptists" and so-called "Spiritualists," who – in the wake of the Reformation – tried to orient their lives toward the primitive church and the life of Jesus Christ. The Son of Man who "has nowhere to lay his head" became the model for these movements characterized by their critique of hegemonic society and its convenience. Following Christ above all else entailed a separation from what is common in this world.

In the face of Cromwell's revolt, the Royalist Anglican writer Jeremy Taylor (1613–67) in his *The Great Exemplar* presented the practical impact of Jesus's life on Christians. This kind of ethical interpretation became the overarching identity of Christianity during the Enlightenment, as theologians saw Jesus's message as the epitome of reasonable human ethics. Deistic approaches, too, following medieval predecessors, used Jesus and his impact to critique the church. Even Kant's *Religion within the Boundaries of Mere Reason* can be seen as a product of this ethical understanding of Jesus, although Kant was inclined to minimize religious language. In his time, Protestant preachers, along with some Catholics who embraced Enlightenment ideals, emphasized the concept of the Christian life as one guided by the principles of the Sermon on the Mount, following in the footsteps of Jesus.

Over the past two centuries, the ethical dimension has played a predominant role in how Christians, as well as their less religious contemporaries, perceive Jesus. The ecumenical movement united the communities gathered in the World Council of Churches in the Conciliar Process for Justice, Peace and the Preservation of Creation in the 1980s. This exemplifies the way in which Western Christianity's particular emphasis on ethics has extended to other traditions, including Orthodoxy, which in previous centuries may have shown less interest in the human aspects of Jesus.

In the nineteenth century, novelists such as Leo Tolstoy (1828–1910) and Fyodor Dostoevsky (1821–81) developed a profound interest in Jesus's earthly life as a measure and exemplar for human communities. This resonated with the different forms of Jesus-orientated ethics in the Western world. For Thomas Jefferson (1743–1826), who compiled biblical passages for *The Life and Morals of Jesus of Nazareth* (known today as *The Jefferson Bible*), Jesus's religious ideas served as the foundation for republican commitment.

In later generations, the focus shifted toward the social impact of the Gospel, as seen in the adoption of socialist ideas in various parts of Christianity since the nineteenth century. The civil rights movement also adopted Jesus's life as a means to improve this world. Martin Luther King Jr. explicitly connected his commitment to Jesus's call, stating, "I heard the voice of Jesus saying still to fight on."[2] As a consequence of viewing Jesus as supportive of social movements, the traditional depiction of Jesus as a white man, prevalent in the Western church over the

[2] King 1998, 78.

centuries, has been rightfully questioned. In recent decades, a more diverse image of Jesus has emerged, bringing to light perspectives that have been concealed under the veil of Veronica for centuries.

FURTHER READING

Blum, Edward J. and Paul Harvey. 2014. *The Color of Christ: The Son of God and the Saga of Race in America*. Chapel Hill: University of North Carolina Press.

Bynum, Caroline Walker. 1984. *Jesus as Mother: Studies in the Spirituality of the High Middle Ages*. Berkeley: University of California Press.

Certeau, Michel de. 1995. *The Mystic Fable, Vol. 1: The Sixteenth and Seventeenth Centuries*. Translated by Michael B. Smith. Chicago: University of Chicago Press.

Connelly, Mark. 2012. *Christmas: A History*. London: Tauris.

Leppin, Volker. 2023. *Medieval Spirituality: An Introduction*. Baylor: University Press.

Pelikan, Jaroslav. 1987. *Jesus through the Centuries: His Place in the History of Culture*. New York: Perennial Library.

Rittgers, Ronald. 2012. *The Reformation of Suffering: Pastoral Theology and Lay Piety in Late Medieval and Early Modern Germany*. New York: Oxford University Press.

**Part III**
*Ethics, Theology, and Critical Scholarship*

## 13 Jesus in Christian Discipleship and Ethics
REBEKAH EKLUND

"Follow me," Jesus said; and for two millennia, many have endeavored to do so. Because Jesus also said, "Take up your cross and follow me," Christians have long understood discipleship, that is, following Jesus, to be a life both obedient to Jesus's teaching and patterned on the shape of Jesus's own life, especially his death and resurrection. For this reason, Christian discipleship is sometimes referred to as the way of the cross. While this varies from context to context, surely some commonalities should make such a life recognizable, not only in belief but also in practice.

When Jesus gave his final instructions to his disciples, he commissioned them to go and make other disciples, baptizing them into the new community of people gathered around the teachings of their risen Lord (Matt 28:18–20; Acts 1:8). This chapter focuses on five practices that derive directly from Jesus's teaching and life: (1) care for the poor and needy, including the contested practice of seeing Christ in the poor; (2) the sacramental practices of the Lord's Supper and baptism; (3) prayer; (4) forgiveness, reconciliation, and peacemaking; and (5) self-giving or *kenōsis*. Jesus described the double love commandment for God and neighbor as the sum of all the law and the prophets (Matt 22:36–40), and the practices in this chapter also flow from those twin imperatives. All five overlap and intertwine; none can be neatly separated from the others, or from a host of other important Christian practices, such as evangelism and worship.

### CARE FOR THE POOR

Jesus's teaching consistently highlights the spiritual perils of wealth and exhorts both divestment and generosity, two practices that became deeply embedded in Christianity. Indeed, one of the marks of the early Christian movement was a commitment to sharing possessions so that nobody was in need (Acts 2:44–45; 4:32–35). In imitation of Jesus's healing ministry and in obedience to Jesus's teaching, early Christians were marked by their commitment to caring for the needy and the sick.

This commitment endured even while it adapted to fit new cultural and political contexts. After the conversion of Constantine, almsgiving became institutionalized in the church in a new way. Churches became the primary, and sometimes only, institution that provided aid to the needy. For example, Christians founded orphanages and hospitals and centers for food distribution. In the modern era, such aid to the needy has continued, though unease with traditional almsgiving as paternalistic and counterproductive has given rise to alternative models, which tend to focus less on giving money and more on empowering communities, as with the Christian Community Development Association (CCDA), founded by John Perkins in 1989. Another alternative is found in the "intentional communities" that began popping up in a variety of contexts in the mid twentieth century and which orient around the practice of "being with" (i.e. sharing life and resources with) the poor or marginalized. Examples include Taizé; the Bruderhof communities; Jesus People USA in Chicago; and the Catholic Worker Movement. A smaller iteration within American Protestantism is new monasticism, which is diverse and loosely defined. In general, its practitioners aim to resist Western individualism and materialism. While it remains small, it birthed a number of individual houses where a group of people pool resources and share life together.

Another iteration of caring for the poor by sharing life with them focuses not on material poverty but on the vulnerability of profound intellectual disability. Various organizations aim to treat people with disabilities with dignity and respect as persons in need of friendship and companionship. It is not at all clear if people with disabilities ought to fall under the rubric of care for the needy or sick. For some, people with disabilities are the marginalized or excluded who call out for welcome and full inclusion in the life and ministry of the church. For others, people with disabilities are akin to the sick who long for Jesus's healing power. In each approach, Jesus's teaching and actions provide a template.

### Jesus in Disability Ethics

Disability ethics include a wide range of relatively distinct areas, including a variety of physical disabilities, neurological difference like autism, and intellectual disability. People who have disabilities and those who advocate for them do not always agree on how to approach these issues or even what terminology to use. One key question is whether disability is construed as illness or as identity, as an impediment to flourishing or simply a different way of being. The gospel narratives pose a challenge to the latter approach.

All four gospels agree that Jesus was a healer of all kinds of maladies, including what we would today call disabilities. People who cannot see, walk, or hear flocked to Jesus for healing. Not only did Jesus heal them; he declared that their new abilities to see, walk, and hear were a sign of God's in-breaking kingdom (Luke 4:18–19; 7:18–22). Hans Reinders summarizes the dilemma: Where one reader who is blind might feel alienated from the gospel healing stories for their depictions of blindness as a problem to be solved (or as a metaphor for spiritual ignorance), another reader who is blind might take comfort in the power of Jesus to heal and might continue to pray for their own healing or for deliverance from their condition (Reinders 2008, 330–32).

Among the healing stories, the man born blind receives special attention, since Jesus uses the occasion to break the association his disciples seem to have made between sin and disability. Reinders notes, "Christian people in our own culture often see disabled people in that same negative light, whether they are aware of it or not" (Reinders 2008, 327). John 9 thus entails Jesus's rejection of the tendency to view people with disabilities as lesser, even if it remains in other ways a straightforward healing narrative.

Jesus's resurrected body – raised with its wounds – is another focal point. Amos Yong, for example, describes the nail marks in Jesus's risen body as marks of Jesus's "impairment" and notes that these marks are redeemed but not erased. For Yong, this does not mean that Jesus's risen body is disabled but that Jesus, in his incarnation and in his resurrection, enters into the experience of disability and empathizes with it (Yong 2011, 126–28). Nancy Eiesland takes this logic one step further. As a person who lives with a disability, Eiesland is concerned to develop a liberatory theology of disability, one that envisions "a God who is for us" (i.e. for people with disabilities) and a corresponding vision of a church that is likewise for people with disabilities (Eiesland 1994, 90). She argues that the body of Jesus is raised with disabilities: The nail marks in his hands and feet (Luke 24:36–43 and John 20:24–28) constitute a physical disability, and his "disfigured side" (from the wound of the sword, John 20:27) is a "hidden" disability (Eiesland 1994, 101). Thus Jesus – and, by Trinitarian logic, God – is disabled.

For Yong, as for Eiesland, Jesus's risen and wounded body suggests an eschatological vision of "the redemption rather than the elimination of disabilities" (Yong 2011, 132). Does this mean that people with disabilities will likewise continue to bear the "wounds" of their disabilities in their resurrected bodies? Those who say yes (like Eiesland) emphasize the continuity of identity: If a person who never walked in this life is "healed" and has the ability to walk in the next life, will they be the same person? For Eiesland, the answer is no; therefore, she argues that her disability will not be eliminated in the next life but will no longer be an impediment to flourishing. Others insist that a resurrected life entails perfect wholeness, which for them means the healing of their physical or mental disabilities.

This debate surfaces a valuable truth. Early Christians like Macrina and her brother Gregory of Nyssa wrestled with the tension between transformation and continuity in the nature of the resurrected life. Gregory recognized that if we were utterly remade, we would no longer be ourselves, in all our uniqueness; in that case, he asked, "Then what is the resurrection to me, if instead of me some other person will return to life?" (Gregory of Nyssa, *De anima et resurrectione* PG 46:140c). At the same time, he argued that to be raised simply as we are would be an "endless misfortune" (Gregory of Nyssa, *De anima et resurrectione* PG 46:137c). Macrina's interpretation of 1 Corinthians 15:35–49 provided the solution, midway between these two problems: The seeds of our current frail and fallible bodies will flower into "greater magnificence" (Gregory of Nyssa, *De anima et resurrectione* PG 46:153c).[1]

From a Christian perspective, surely whatever marks of the Fall we bear in our bodies, whatever hinders us from wholeness in this life, will be no more in the next; but just as surely, whatever makes us fundamentally who we are will endure even while it is redeemed and transformed. If the analogy to Christ's risen body holds true (Luke 24:31, 36–42; John 20:14–17, 19–20, 24–28; 21:4, 7, 12), people will bear the scars of their struggles in the next life but none of the pain. However God brings about their wholeness, Christians trust that the body with which people are raised will be imperishable, glorious, powerful, and (paradoxically) spiritual (*pneumatikon*) (1 Cor 15:42–44).

Finally, disability ethics raise important questions about the nature of Christian discipleship, especially in relation to people with intellectual disabilities. Scholars like John Swinton, Grant Macaskill, and Brian Brock urge churches to view people with autism or intellectual disabilities not as objects of care but as disciples. Discipleship programs in churches sometimes focus on learning Scripture or doctrine, which

[1] Author's translations.

might not be options in such cases. How much intellectual capacity is needed to be a disciple? How might definitions of following Jesus include those with severe mental illness, autism, or profound intellectual disabilities? Such questions remind us that Jesus welcomed the weak of the world into the kingdom ahead of the strong. Christians have long believed that the poor (broadly conceived) and the marginalized show something of who Jesus is and reveal the upside-down nature of God's reign.

### Seeing Christ in the Poor

Although Jesus himself was, in some ways, one of the poor, it is the parable of the sheep and the goats that gives rise to the notion that Jesus is revealed in all the poor (Matt 25:31–46). The parable turns the tables and asks Jesus's listeners to consider the *helped*, and not the *helper*, the Christ-figure. Christ is found in the hungry, the thirsty, the traveling stranger, the unclothed, the sick, and the prisoner. The moral force of the parable seems clear; an eternal reward awaits those who show mercy and give concrete aid to the needy. For centuries, preachers like Ambrose of Milan and John Chrysostom used Matthew 25 to exhort their congregations toward greater mercy and generosity to the poor. More recently, advocates (including Pope Francis) have invoked the imperative to welcome the stranger in debates over the ethical treatment of immigrants, migrants, and refugees. Still, some questions remain.

One is whether to focus on giving aid to "one of the least of these" (*heni toutōn tōn elachistōn*) in general (as in Matt 25:45) or to "one of the least of these brothers and sisters of mine" (*heni toutōn tōn adelfōn mou tōn elachistōn*) (as in Matt 25:40). To many readers, the former suggests any person in need, whereas the latter implies a disciple or follower of Christ, since Jesus elsewhere in Matthew refers to his disciples as his brothers (12:49; 23:8) and to fellow Christians as brothers (Matt 5:22–24; 18:15–22). If "one of these little ones" (*hena tōn mikrōn toutōn*) is a parallel phrase, the association is further strengthened (Matt 10:42; 18:6). The parable, then, would be less about mercy to any person in need (an imperative already laid out elsewhere in the gospel) and more about the reward that awaits those who help a Christian or apostle in need. Immediately following this parable, the plot to have Jesus killed is put in motion, and Jesus himself enacts several of the categories in the parable (thirst, nakedness, imprisonment). Perhaps the parable then also functions as a foreshadowing of the passion and the suffering that his disciples will likewise endure on the way of the cross. Nonetheless,

Matthew 25 has created the enduring motif of Christ as a poor stranger arriving at the door, asking for hospitality or food, and it has occasioned extraordinary acts of mercy and generosity. To give to such a person is giving directly to Christ.

For Sarah Coakley, the capacity to see Christ in the poor is closely linked to what she calls "the capacity for graced recognition of the identity of the risen Jesus" (Coakley 2008, 310–11). During Jesus's resurrection appearances, he is, mysteriously, difficult to recognize. This implies that recognizing the risen Jesus (whether in the breaking of bread or in the faces of the poor) requires "a profound epistemic transformation" wrought by the Spirit, a sharpening of our senses (Coakley 2008, 313). This transformation is brought about by a set of Christian practices, including contemplation and meditation, the sacraments, and the acts of mercy named in Matthew 25 (Coakley 2008, 315–17).

The point of learning to see Christ in the poor is obviously not to make an ontological identification between the two; the poor are not to be worshipped or venerated as Christ. Instead, the identification is a functional, evocative one. Perhaps our senses require cleansing because we are prone to see God in the majestic and powerful, rather than in the ugly and weak. Jesus's insistence that we can find him in the needy can function not only to prompt us toward mercy but to make us look harder for the image of God in those we might otherwise wish to avoid.

Liberation theology takes this logic one step further. For many Latin American theologians, the Christ one sees in the poor is specifically the crucified Christ. The Jesuit Ignacio Ellacuría was first to write about the people of El Salvador as a crucified people, and the phrase was subsequently picked up by others, including Jon Sobrino and Leonardo Boff. Sobrino uses the term in part as a plea to Christians in the North to hear the cries of the South (Sobrino 1994, vii–viii). Like Ellacuría, he associates all the poor and oppressed of the world with the suffering and crucified Christ. This world, Sobrino writes, "is one gigantic cross for millions of innocent people who die at the hands of executioners" (Sobrino 1994, 4).

This way of construing the poor goes a step beyond Matthew 25's call to see Christ in the poor, and a step even beyond the Lukan beatitude "blessed are the poor" (Luke 6:20), even though both texts pave the way. Sobrino insists that "the crucified people are the actualization of Christ crucified, the true servant of [the LORD]" (Sobrino 1994, 51). The purpose of the analogy is not contemplation of the redemptive suffering of the poor; it is the alleviation of their suffering. Mercy is necessary but insufficient if not accompanied by justice, through the reordering of unjust social structures that trap people in poverty and place them on their crosses in the first place. Sobrino's plea is for the world to remove people from their crosses – and to stop crucifying them at all.

The analogy, of course, collapses at just this point. Jesus did not need to be removed from his cross; he voluntarily took it up (and thereby, in Christian teaching, accomplished God's salvation). Unlike Jesus, the crucified people today do not willingly take on suffering. Nonetheless, the plea remains urgent for Christians in the global North to wake up to the suffering of the least of these their brothers and sisters. I think of Augustine's principle: Even if an interpretation is not what the original author intended, it is not invalid if it leads to greater love of God and neighbor (Augustine, *De doctrina Christiana* 1.36.40–41).

### SACRAMENTAL PRACTICES

If Matthew 25 suggests that Jesus's ongoing presence manifests in the bodies of the needy, Jesus's instructions at the Last Supper point to his enduring presence in the bread and wine of the Eucharist. In Luke's account, Jesus tells his disciples, "Do this in remembrance of me" (Luke 22:19b); reenacting the meal became a key Christian practice relatively soon after his death and resurrection (1 Cor 11:23–26). Paul's discussion of the Lord's Supper in 1 Corinthians 11 reveals not only its central place within Christian tradition but also its ethical import. Paul expressed his outrage that Christians in Corinth were using the Lord's Supper to sow division rather than to actualize unity. Richer Christians were humiliating their poorer brothers and sisters in the way that they performed the meal, thus (in Paul's view) invalidating the sacrament altogether (1 Cor 11:17–22, 27–34). They were eating their own suppers, not the Lord's Supper (1 Cor 11:20–21).

Paul's analysis implies that eating the Lord's Supper ought to shape Christians to be a certain kind of people (united across class lines, for example) but that *merely* eating the Lord's Supper is insufficient if not accompanied by other practices (generosity, hospitality, solidarity). For Paul, the Corinthians' way of eating does not invalidate the real presence of Christ in the bread and wine, the two elements of the Lord's Supper or Eucharist, but means that Christ is present as judge (1 Cor 11:29–30). Paul could have invoked the prophets, who insisted that God rejects the prayers and sacrifices of a people who simultaneously commit injustices (Amos 5:21–24; Isa 58:3–10). Eating the Lord's Supper in memory of Jesus cannot be separated from other aspects of following Jesus, such as care for the hungry.

Like the Eucharist, baptism is one of the earliest and most formational Christian practices. According to the gospels, Jesus himself never baptized anyone. Instead, he was baptized by his cousin John, for whom baptizing was so central to his ministry that he comes to be known as John the Baptist. In Matthew's Gospel, the risen Christ commissions his followers to "make disciples of all nations, baptizing them in the name of the Father and of the Son and of the Holy Spirit" (Matt 28:19). Christian baptism retains John the Baptist's emphasis on the cleansing of sin and functions as a rite of initiation into the church, while it also takes on a deeper theological significance. The apostle Paul describes baptism as a form of dying and rising with Christ (Rom 6:3–4), which is perhaps most vividly displayed in the practice of full immersion baptism. The new believer is plunged beneath the water, signifying their death to sin and their old self, and raised up out of the water, signifying their resurrection to new life in Christ, a life of discipleship. For Paul, those who have been baptized are now "clothed ... with Christ," so that "there is no longer Jew or Greek; there is no longer slave or free; there is no longer male and female, for all of you are one in Christ Jesus" (Gal 3:27–28). This unity in Christ does not erase differences or individual identities but subordinates them to the new life of discipleship.

### PRAYER

Just as Jesus took almsgiving for granted as a practice of faith (Matt 6:2), so he also assumed prayer and fasting as normative (Matt 6:5–7, 16–18). These three practices, taken together, constitute the heart of Jewish piety and ethics in the first century and point us back to the unity of the commandments to love God and neighbor. Jewish and Christian traditions both consider almsgiving as a form of giving back to God, as much as it is a form of giving to the needy neighbor. They likewise see prayer and fasting as reorienting one away from the self and toward God and neighbor.

While Jesus gave instructions concerning each of these practices, his lengthiest and most detailed instructions concern prayer. Jesus himself withdrew to secluded places to spend time in prayer, a practice noted especially in Luke's Gospel (Luke 5:16; 6:12), meaning that the regular practice of prayer is one form of the imitation of Christ. Particularly in Gethsemane and while on the cross, Jesus's prayers are laments, which suggests that lament may also be a form of imitating Jesus. At the least, it commends lament as a Christian practice modeled on Jesus's own practice in times of struggle and distress.

Christians also pray in obedience to Jesus's instruction. Indeed, when Jesus issues one of his most direct and detailed instructions to his disciples (a rather rare event, given his propensity to teach in parables), it is about how to pray (Matt 6:9; Luke 11:2; see also Luke 11:9, 18:1). The Lord's Prayer, as it came to be known, stands at the heart of the Matthean Sermon on the Mount, placing it directly at the center of a collection of Jesus's ethical teachings. This should encourage us to think of prayer as an ethical act and to consider how prayer might undergird and enable the other ethical actions laid out in the Sermon. Similarly, it reminds us that the power of the Holy Spirit and the presence of the risen Jesus (Matt 28:20) are essential to a Christ-shaped life.

The prayer is framed at beginning and end with eschatological petitions for God's kingdom to arrive and for deliverance from *peirasmos* (Matt 6:13a; Luke 11:4b), a time of trial or testing sometimes associated with the turbulent birthing of the new age. Even after Jesus's resurrection, Christian prayer continues to take place in an eschatological context, in the time when the new age has begun to dawn but before its full arrival.

Tucked into the middle of the eschatological petitions is a practical ethical instruction about forgiveness. A petition for divine forgiveness ("forgive us") comes with a condition: "as we also have forgiven our debtors" (Matt 6:12) or "for we ourselves forgive everyone indebted to us" (Luke 11:4). As Allen Verhey notes, this instruction has both spiritual and economic ramifications: "To pray this prayer is to want to be part of the economy of mercy and the society of forgiveness that is like the kingdom of God" (Verhey 2002, 268). Just in case the equation was not clear, in Matthew's account Jesus spells it out: "For if you forgive others their trespasses, your heavenly Father will also forgive you, but if you do not forgive others, neither will your Father forgive your trespasses" (Matt 6:14–15). Owing to this and other texts (such as Jesus asking the Father to forgive even his crucifiers in Luke 23:34), forgiveness has become a central Christian hallmark.

FORGIVENESS AND RECONCILIATION

While the imperative to forgive is clear, the practice is not simple. Is forgiveness mandated only for those who repent, as Luke suggests but Matthew does not (Matt 18:21–22; Luke 17:3–4)? The act of forgiveness may or may not include reconciliation or the forging of a new relationship. Acts of violence, ranging from terrorist attacks to domestic violence, pose sharp challenges to the Christian commitment to forgiveness. Must the abused forgive their abusers, or the oppressed forgive their oppressors? The model of Jesus, who forgave even those who betrayed and crucified him, presses the Christian tradition always toward forgiveness. Simultaneously, Jesus issued scathing condemnations of those who failed to use their power to provide justice and show mercy to those under their care. A Christian might forgive their abuser by willing their good and renouncing the right to harm them in return but might also demand justice from God (as in the parable of the widow and the unjust judge [Luke 18:1–8]). Forgiveness does not mean allowing the abuser to continue their abuse; rather it demands that we bring to the forefront the relationship between forgiveness, accountability, and justice – a conversation that merits much greater attention than this chapter can give.

Another growing area is restorative justice, an alternative to retributive justice that focuses on repairing the harm done to a community rather than simply punishing the offender. Advocates argue that biblical models of justice, unlike most modern systems of criminal justice, concentrate on restoration and reconciliation, rather than retribution.

### Peacebuilding

Inasmuch as forgiveness means renouncing the right to return evil for evil, it is closely related to nonviolence. The Christian commitment to nonviolence derives from Jesus's teaching, especially the Sermon on the Mount (Matt 5:9, 38–48), and Jesus's willing acceptance of death, including his refusal to fight back or resist when arrested. For pacifists, Jesus's teachings on nonviolence are binding, nonnegotiable, and apply to all Christians today. Other scholars argue that Jesus's ethic of non-retaliation was intended for a short interim period in first-century Galilee but has no place in modern geopolitics. For just war advocates, force must sometimes be used to protect the vulnerable, fulfilling the command to love the neighbor. While pacifism and just war remain important positions in Christian ethics, in recent decades some Christian ethicists have developed an alternative approach. This third way is alternatively called just peace, just peacemaking, or peacebuilding.

Peacebuilding is not interested in the question of whether force is ever allowed or under what circumstances force can be used. It asks an entirely different and broader set of questions. Before a conflict begins, what can we do to make peace more possible and war or violence less likely? This might include just and sustainable economic development. At a more local scale, it might involve people known as "violence interrupters," who seek to defuse conflicts before they turn violent. In the midst of a conflict, peacebuilding asks, what can we do in order to bring about peace? This might include nonviolent direct action, diplomatic negotiation, independent initiatives designed to de-escalate a conflict, and taking responsibility for wrongdoing. And in the aftermath of a conflict, how can a society be rebuilt in a way that not only restores it to peace and wholeness but seeks to minimize the possibility that violence will break out again?

For long-time advocate Glen Stassen, just peacemaking is a manifestation of incarnational discipleship. Along with a group of other Christian scholars, he crafted a set of ten just peacemaking practices, each of which is linked with specific verses from the Sermon on the Mount (Stassen 2012, 196–214). The practices concentrate their energies on international peacemaking, both in terms of deterrence and in terms of ending conflicts once they begin.

Another advocate is Lisa Sowle Cahill, who calls her approach peacebuilding. Like Stassen, she focuses on the transformation of social structures. Cahill writes, "Like pacifists, peacebuilders take their primary inspiration from the life and teaching of Jesus, but they especially stress the fact that he inaugurates God's reign and renews all creation, making it possible to transform social injustices" (Cahill 2019, 1). Unlike pacifists, Cahill and some other peacebuilding advocates typically accept a measure of force as a necessary aspect of justice for the disenfranchised.

### SELF-GIVING

This brings us to the final theme: self-giving, or what is sometimes called the practice of *kenōsis*, a Greek word that means self-emptying and derives from Paul's letter to the Philippians, which describes Christ as one who, "though he existed in the form of God, did not regard equality with God as something to be grasped, but emptied himself, taking the form of a slave, assuming human likeness" (Phil 2:5–6). *Kenōsis* involves renunciation of privilege and power in exchange for service and love. It also returns us to the theme with which I began: the way of the cross. Michael Gorman uses the term "cruciformity" as a shorthand for "conformity to the crucified Christ" or, more specifically, "sacrificial, ... self-giving, ... status-renouncing" love (Gorman 2021, 4, 173).

Like the other practices in this chapter, self-giving love derives both from Jesus's teaching and from Jesus's own life. When Jesus exhorted his disciples to serve rather than to be served, he enacted this lesson by kneeling to wash their feet (John 13:3–17). Along with the footwashing, the other central text is Philippians 2, which directly encourages Christians to imitate Jesus in the way that he "emptied himself" (*heauton ekenōsen*) (Phil 2:7). "Let the same mind be in you ...," urges Paul (Phil 2:5).

This is perhaps the hardest practice to pin down in concrete terms. Peacemaking is hard work, but I think we generally know what the end goal is. The challenge is how to get there. But what does self-giving look like in action, in a particular human life, in a specific social context? How do aspects of social identity like class, gender, and race come into play? Renunciation of power or status depends at least in part on how much power or status one has (or does not have) to begin with.

Critics of the emphasis on self-giving love point out that it seems to focus on those who have power or privilege to renounce, while having less to say to those without power. Advocates like Gorman insist that cruciformity is a practice available to all regardless of social status (Gorman 2021, 394–97). In addition, the term cruciformity has a particular limitation, since it appears to point only to Christ's crucifixion and not also to his resurrection, even though the concept itself intends to encompass both.

When it comes to gender, feminist theologians have long debated whether an ethic of self-giving is harmful for women or if it can be incorporated into a feminist ethic of discipleship. Some have critiqued self-giving love as an ethic that is commended by men but practiced by women. Others have sought to re-narrate its meaning and function. Sarah Coakley, for example, interprets *kenōsis* not as self-emptying but as a form of dependence on God that applies equally to women and to men. For her, *kenōsis* is "power in vulnerability" – a space, enabled by contemplative prayer, "in which non-coercive divine power manifests itself" (Coakley 1996, 84). Thus *kenōsis* is equally available to both male and female disciples, as it is a stance toward God rather than toward others. Anna Selak suggests that Anna Mercedes's definition of *kenōsis* as "power for," which emphasizes action on behalf of others, could serve as a more active or outward-facing supplement to Coakley's approach (Selak 2017, 545).

Selak also points out that most approaches to kenotic imitation neglect the second half of the pattern: the exaltation. She proposes that *kenōsis* thus entails self-emptying *and* filling by God, in ways that involve spiritual transformation and take shape in just action. We cannot imitate Christ's self-giving exactly; we are not called to die on our own crosses. Instead, "The human analogue is a fullness of the spirit of God that can overflow, thus bringing about the Reign of God that is already but not yet" (Selak 2017, 546). This returns us to the eschatological theme of the Lord's Prayer, making both prayer and *kenōsis* practices for this tensive space where we dwell between the now and the not yet.

Liberationist scholars and practitioners from the global church who take up the ethical implications of self-giving offer similar critiques and revisions. For example, the African theologian Mercy Amba Oduyoye, like Coakley and other white feminists, does not reject *kenōsis* altogether. Instead, she writes, "What African women reject is the combination of cross and sacrifice laid on them by people who have no intention of walking those paths themselves" (Oduyoye 2010, 179). They do not need to take up suffering; they already suffer. Jesus is the liberator who did not impose suffering but who overcame "life-denying forces," who made a bent-over woman stand up straight, who healed a woman with a constant flow of blood, and who gave a dead son back to a grieving widow (Amoah and Oduyoye 1989, 43, 174).

When Virginia Fabella shares reflections from Filipino and Korean women, she discusses how these women equate Jesus's passion with their own suffering, in ways that echo the motif of the "crucified peoples." Filipino women, she writes, "are today the Christ disfigured in his passion." In some ways, she says, this is an unwitting or passive *imitatio Christi*, but in other ways it becomes active, as when Filipino women "have taken up the struggle on behalf of their sisters and of the rest of the suffering poor" (Fabella 1989, 110). This helpfully creates a distinction between involuntary imitation of Christ's suffering and voluntary acceptance of suffering as a form of costly discipleship.

All these examples suggest that self-giving love is best seen as a practice embodied in a community rather than only by an individual – where those with power choose to yield to those without, where those who have always knelt learn to stand, and where those who have always stood learn to kneel (Winner 2011, 273–75).

## CONCLUSION

Imitation of Jesus is a communal endeavor, not fundamentally a solitary one. At the end of the Gospel of Matthew, when the risen Christ commissions his disciples, his final words are "remember, I am with you always, to the end of the age" (Matt 28:20). Empowered by the ongoing presence of the risen Christ, this community of disciples orients itself around the double love commandment. Grounded in prayer (the love of God), the cross-shaped community turns outward in self-giving love to a broken and needy world (the love of neighbor).

Perhaps most of all, imitation of Jesus is a way of life that rejects the world's measures of success (power, wealth, privilege) in favor of what looks to the world like weakness and foolishness (humility, renunciation, love to the undeserving) (1 Cor 1:18). The way of Jesus is a downward trajectory, in his crucifixion, which means self-giving and identification with the poor and needy; but it is also an upward one, in his resurrection and ascension, which signifies new life and freedom in Christ, the abundant life offered by the gospel, a renewed vision, and joy in the morning after a long night of sorrow. Taken together, cross and resurrection are the shape of discipleship.

### FURTHER READING

Amoah, Elizabeth and Mercy Amba Oduyoye. 1989. "The Christ for African Women." In *With Passion and Compassion: Third World Women Doing Theology*, edited by Virginia Fabella and Mercy Amba Oduyoye, 35–46. Maryknoll: Orbis.

Cahill, Lisa Sowle. 2019. *Blessed Are the Peacemakers: Just War, Pacifism, and Peacebuilding*. Minneapolis: Fortress Press.

Coakley, Sarah. 1996. "Kenosis and Subversion: On the Repression of 'Vulnerability' in Christian Feminist Writing." In *Swallowing a Fishbone? Feminist Theologians Debate Christianity*, edited by Daphne Hampson, 82–111. London: SPCK.

Coakley, Sarah. 2008. "The Identity of the Risen Jesus: Finding Jesus Christ in the Poor." In *Seeking the Identity of Jesus: A Pilgrimage*, edited by Beverly Roberts Gaventa and Richard B. Hays, 301–22. Grand Rapids: Eerdmans.

Eiesland, Nancy L. 1994. *The Disabled God: Toward a Liberatory Theology of Disability*. Nashville: Abingdon Press.

Fabella, Virginia. 1989. "A Common Methodology for Diverse Christologies?" In *With Passion and Compassion: Third World Women Doing Theology*, edited by Virginia Fabella and Mercy Amba Oduyoye, 108–17. Maryknoll: Orbis.

Gorman, Michael J. 2021. *Cruciformity: Paul's Narrative Spirituality of the Cross*, 20th anniversary ed. Grand Rapids: Eerdmans.

Oduyoye, Mercy Amba. 2010. "Jesus Christ." In *Hope Abundant: Third World and Indigenous Women's Theology*, edited by Kwok Pui-lan, 167–85. Maryknoll: Orbis Books.

Reinders, Hans. 2008. *Receiving the Gift of Friendship: Profound Disability, Theological Anthropology, and Ethics*. Grand Rapids: Eerdmans.

Selak, Annie. 2017. "Orthodoxy, Orthopraxis, and Orthopathy: Evaluating the Feminist Kenosis Debate." *Modern Theology* 33: 529–48.

Sobrino, Jon. 1994. *Principle of Mercy: Taking the Crucified People from the Cross.* Maryknoll: Orbis.

Stassen, Glen. 2012. *A Thicker Jesus: Incarnational Discipleship in a Secular Age.* Louisville: Westminster John Knox.

Verhey, Allen. 2002. *Remembering Jesus: Christian Community, Scripture, and the Moral Life.* Grand Rapids: Eerdmans.

Winner, Lauren F. 2011. "Interceding: Standing, Kneeling, and Gender." In *The Blackwell Companion to Christian Ethics*, 2nd ed., edited by Stanley Hauerwas and Samuel Wells, 264–76. Malden: Wiley-Blackwell.

Yong, Amos. 2011. *The Bible, Disability, and the Church: A New Vision of the People of God.* Grand Rapids: Eerdmans.

## 14 The Body of Jesus in His People
THOMAS JOSEPH WHITE, OP

The early Christian movement gave rise to a highly original conception of the presence of God in human history. Primitive Christian authors claimed that God himself has taken on a human nature in Jesus of Nazareth, a man who is one with the Lord of Israel. This idea of the "incarnation" of God in an individual human nature is novel when considered against the backdrop of Second Temple Judaism. Israelite prophetic authors had claimed that God the Creator reveals his identity to Israel in a distinctive way. There are even ideas in their writings of the glory of God becoming manifest to and within the people of Israel. However, members of the early Christian movement, themselves predominantly Jewish, claimed that the God of Israel had become human to redeem the human race and had been crucified and resurrected in his human nature. Indeed, the earliest Christians clearly worshipped Christ as Lord and God, and in this sense initiated the kind of intellectual and religious practices that would eventually give rise to the fifth-century Chalcedonian declaration of Christ as true God and true man.

At the same time, they also simultaneously affirmed something else about the church of Christ that is no less startling. Various New Testament authors affirm that human beings themselves are now being incorporated by grace into a new form of participation in the life of God (eternal life). On this view, human beings have no sufficient access to the inner life and essence of God by their own natural power. Instead, they can encounter God as Father, Son, and Holy Spirit by grace alone. They do so not only individually but above all in a collective way, in the visible church, which was instituted by Christ in his earthly life and after the resurrection, in the sending forth of the Holy Spirit upon the apostles.

We can note as a point of fact that this historically novel Christian claim is clearly not pantheistic or monistic, as if human beings are always, already united with God in the depths of their beings and simply need enlightenment so as to become better aware of this fact. Nor is it, on the other side, characterized by the mere affirmation of radical divine transcendence and the apophatic incomprehensibility of God, who is distinct from his creation, and who remains always inaccessible, imperfectly represented by diverse and partially incompatible religious traditions. Christianity acknowledges the transcendence and hiddenness of the Creator but insists also on the gratuitous gift of intimacy with God and knowledge of God's own inner life by a new divine initiative.

In what follows I explore this idea of the church as the body of Christ, a collective participation in the presence and life of God. I do so not diachronically by analysis of the "development of doctrines" from the New Testament to patristic, medieval, Reformation era, and modern authors, though I avert to historical sources. Instead, I treat the topic thematically or systematically, using the theology of Thomas Aquinas principally as a guide, while also making use of a series of historical, pre-medieval, and modern references and while also taking into account a variety of ecumenical considerations.

As a Catholic theologian I advert to two concepts throughout this chapter, that of "mystery" and that of the "mystical body." When Catholic theologians speak of a "mystery" of faith, they mean to indicate something that cannot be grasped merely by natural reason but that is revealed to us by grace. Further, a mystery is inherently intelligible but also difficult for us to understand due to its perfection, and inexhaustible in intelligibility due to its depth and splendor. The "mysteries" of the Holy Trinity and of the Incarnation, for example, are realities we can know of, contemplate, and progressively understand by cooperating with the grace of faith. They cast light on all other realities as the highest and most intrinsically intelligible of all things. Meanwhile, the notion of the church as the "mystical body" of Christ is an idea developed in medieval Catholic theology (as I will come to) to designate baptized Christians as participants by grace in the life of Christ and in the divine nature. Traditionally the collective life of the church is denoted as the "mystical body" of Christ to distinguish the church from the resurrected body of Christ and his real presence in the Eucharist. In this way of thinking, the latter presence, the "true body" of Christ present in the Eucharist, is the source of the life of the church as the "mystical body" of Christ. It is mystical because, while the church is not Christ, Christ is communicating the life of grace to human beings in the church, which we can understand only imperfectly, even as we participate in the process.

I will proceed, then, by considering four main ideas briefly: the church as the *mystical* body of Christ in classical Christian thought, the *sacramental* sources of Christian life, the *eucharistic* body of Christ in the church and its spiritual fruits, and the inclusive political and cosmic implications of a eucharistic ecclesiology.

## THE CHURCH AS THE MYSTICAL BODY OF CHRIST

The Pauline notion of the church as the body of Christ is articulated principally in 1 Corinthians 10:16–17; 12:12–27, Romans 6:3–4, and 12:4–6, and finds echoes in other passages of the New Testament, such as Colossians 1:18, 24; 2:19; 3:15 and Ephesians 1:10, 22–23; 2:16; 3:6; 4:4, 12, 15–16, 25; 5:23, 30. We are told in these passages that in Christian baptism the Holy Spirit incorporates believers into the body of Christ. Christ is the head of the church, and there are diverse members in Christ's body, who have distinct gifts and roles. By grace, we can dwell "in" Christ as we might dwell by grace in God and in the collective life of a transcendent person. Meanwhile, in the celebration of the Eucharist, the church communes in the body and blood of Christ himself. The resurrected and glorified Christ is remaking all things in view of their eschatological reconstitution, and this new life is somehow meant to affect all of the cosmos.

The idea of the church as the body of Christ underwent development in the fourth and fifth centuries, particularly in the Latin West, in the face of the Donatist schism and the Arian crisis. The idea is promoted in various ways by figures like Hilary, Ambrose, and Augustine and was subject to especially important thematic reflection in the work of the latter. On Augustine's view, Christian baptism incorporates a person by grace into the ecclesial body of Christ, which is one, apostolic, and universal.[1] This incorporation implies an inward configuration to Christ, by participation in the grace of his headship, or his "capital" grace. Insofar as Christ is God and Lord, he is one in substance with the Father and the Holy Spirit. Insofar as he is human, he is a recipient and source of grace for all of humanity.[2] Thus union with Christ as man, in virtue of the grace of baptism, has

---

[1] Augustine, *On Baptism against the Donatists*, 1.1, 19; *The Trinity*, 2. 30.
[2] Augustine, *The Trinity*, 4.12–19.

for its final end or purpose, communion with the divinity of Christ, and by extension, with the mystery of the Father, Son, and Holy Spirit.[3] Therefore the church is the visible locus of communion with the Holy Trinity, through the medium of the humanity of Christ, and this participation occurs by means of sacramental incorporation into the life of Christ and his grace.

### Aquinas on the Grace of Christ

In the thirteenth century, Thomas Aquinas took up the Augustinian notion of grace and the headship of Christ. He reflected in a systematic way on the essence of grace and its origination in Christ, correlating his analysis with an Eastern patristic theme inherited from John of Damascus (660 to ca. 750), that of the humanity of Christ as the "instrument" of his divine person. John, following previous Byzantine theological authors, had argued that the humanity of Christ united to the divine person of the Word functions as a living instrument, in his human mind and heart, to actively intend and will what the eternal Father wills, in unity with the Son and the Holy Spirit. Consequently, when God the Holy Trinity communicates grace to the world, God does so in and with the concordant human intention and desire of the man Jesus Christ in his resurrected life.[4] We can break down Aquinas's understanding of the head–body relationship of Christ and the church by considering three successive ideas.

First, on Aquinas's view, grace is a mysterious gift of God that transforms human beings from within. It does not give them a new nature so as to change what they are essentially as rational animals, as if baptism communicated a new species of human personhood. Rather, grace communicates to the human soul a new supernatural quality, received from God into the essence of the soul.[5] This property then blossoms in this life principally within the twin spiritual faculties of intellect and will, by inclining them toward supernatural intellectual knowledge of God (in faith) and supernatural volitional union with God (by hope and charity).[6] This inward inclination of the person toward union with God is accompanied by "infused" moral virtue (the grace of Christian

---

[3] Augustine, *Tractates on the Gospel of John*, 21, 8; *City of God*, 9.15; 17; 10.20; 11.2.
[4] John Damascene, *Exposition of the Orthodox Faith*, 3.13–19.
[5] Aquinas, *Summa theologiae* (ST), 1–2, q. 110, a. 2. The *Summa* is made up of four parts. ST 1 is on Trinity and creation; ST 1–2 is on human actions, law, and grace; ST 2–2 is on virtues and vices; ST 3 is on Christ and the sacraments.
[6] Aquinas, ST 1–2, q. 110, a. 3.

prudence, justice, fortitude, and temperance) and the gifts of the Holy Spirit.[7] The life of grace is already an initial participation in the eternal life of God, as it inclines the human soul toward union with God after death and individual judgment in the "beatific vision," that is to say, the immediate intuitive knowledge of the essence of God.[8] In the world to come, the body of the human being and the psychosomatic subjectivity of the human person will also be affected and transformed by the grace of God after the pattern of the resurrection of Christ.[9] Human beings are thus progressively transformed by grace into a participation in the life of God.

Second, this life of grace is given principally and in its fullness by the Holy Trinity to the human soul of Christ, which is the human soul of the eternal Word made human. Jesus as man has within himself a plenitude of grace that moves him from within, in all his acts of understanding and volition, to think freely and will harmoniously in accord with the divine will.[10] This is true both in his earthly life and in his resurrected state. His human activity as man in both these states is not only entirely authentic in its integrity and freedom but also takes place in synergy with his divine activity.[11] The Holy Spirit fills his human nature with grace and moves him inwardly as head of the church, so that he freely intends to communicate grace to all human beings, who receive grace in light of his meritorious life, passion, and resurrection.[12] In all this, the humanity of Christ is the living instrument of the divinity, so that his human nature and his earthly life among us are the human image and revelation of his uncreated life as the Son of God with the Father and the Holy Spirit.[13]

Third, according to Aquinas, the grace of Christ is universal in extension, reaching back historically and diachronically to the first human beings, and reaching out synchronically to all human beings who come into existence. Grace is christological in origin (given either in anticipation before or subsequently in light of the merits of the human life of Christ). It is ecclesial in orientation, as it inclines all human beings inwardly toward the universal visible life of the

---

[7] Aquinas, ST 1-2, qq. 62; 63; 68.
[8] Aquinas, ST 1, q. 12.
[9] Aquinas, ST 3, q. 69, aa. 3-4.
[10] Aquinas, ST 3, q. 7.
[11] Aquinas, ST 3, q. 18.
[12] Aquinas, ST 3, q. 8, aa. 1-3, 5-6.
[13] Aquinas, ST 3, q. 19.

church, the gathering of all human societies and persons into visible and sacramental communion with God.[14] Against any notion of restricted atonement theology, Aquinas reasons that if Christ died for all persons (1 John 2:1–2), then the grace of God must be offered to all persons, in a variety of ways, including in non-sacramental forms both now and in the time prior to Christ.[15] However, this grace is also always already oriented toward the visible and invisible communion of the visible church in its sacramental dimensions.[16] Taking inspiration from Aristotle's notion of the human person as a singular hylomorphic (form and matter) substance composed of both body and spiritual soul, Aquinas posits that the human person is itself already a kind of sacramental anticipation of the life of grace: a visible sign of the inward work of grace in the world. Thus human cultures develop what he calls "sacraments of the natural law" by which they anticipate in the life of grace, in gestures and in ritual form, the fullness of ecclesial life that comes into being in the visible, sacramental regime of the apostolic church instituted by Christ.[17]

## Sacramental Sources of Christian Life

New Testament authors convey the idea that the grace of Christ is received from the sacraments, initially through Christian baptism and in a particular way in virtue of the Eucharist (John 3:5; 6:53–55; 1 Cor 10:16–17; 12:13). Medieval Western theologians sought to understand this process through an analysis of what they took to be the seven sacraments instituted by Christ and the apostles in the founding epoch of the church. So understood, the seven sacraments are diverse, coordinated signs in and through which God communicates a participation in the grace of Christ. The various sacraments have diverse effects that are distinct but organically and spiritually related to one another. The medievals typically followed Peter Lombard in distinguishing three dimensions proper to each sacrament, so as to explain its proper effect. The *sacramentum tantum* (sign itself) consists in spoken words (the form of the sacrament), accompanied by a physical action or the use of a physical substance (the matter, construed broadly where "matter" denotes that through which the sign

---

[14] Aquinas, ST 3, q. 8, a. 1; 2–2, q. 2, aa. 5–9.
[15] Aquinas, ST 3, q. 8, a. 3.
[16] Aquinas, ST 3, q. 73, a. 3; q. 79, a. 1.
[17] Aquinas, *Commentary on the Sentences*, 4, d. 1, q. 2, a. 6, sol. 3; ST 1–2, q. 98, a. 5, ad 3; q. 103, a. 1.

is conveyed). The *res et sacramentum* (the reality of grace in the sign) is the first and the irreversible ontological effect of the sacrament, which is given irrespectively of the sanctity of the recipient, and which is irreversible in effect. The *res tantum* (ultimate reality itself) is the final effect of the sacrament in the order of sanctifying grace, which depends for its reception and continued existence upon the conditions of the recipient, especially in his or her free cooperation with the grace of God.

It helps to provide an example. In the case of baptism, Aquinas takes the *sacramentum tantum* to consist in water poured over the head (the gesture or matter of the sacrament) accompanied by the baptismal formula that invokes the name of the Trinity (the vocal sign or form of the sacrament). The *res et sacramentum* is the irreversible ontological effect, which Aquinas takes to be the character of baptism, a spiritual mark imprinted on the soul that provides a permanent disposition to the reception of other sacraments in the Christian life, and that is given in an unrepeatable fashion, so that even if one forsakes the Christian faith after baptism, any return to the church does not require repetition of baptism prior to reception of future sacraments. This inward disposition is meant to dispose one, however, to live effectively in the life of sanctifying grace. The *res tantum* of baptism is precisely this: the communication of sanctifying grace that remedies the effects of original sin by constituting the human person into a state of friendship with God in the life of faith, hope, and charity, infused moral virtues, and the gifts of the Holy Spirit.[18] This life is then sustained and nurtured by the other sacraments, though it can be lost or forsaken through neglect or free defection from the Christian life. Sanctifying grace also incorporates a person into the one body of Christ, with Christ as the mystical head of the human person, and with other baptized Christians as co-constituted members of Christ's visible body.

Other sacraments follow a similar pattern of interpretation, which can be understood from a schematic presentation in this table.[19]

---

[18] Aquinas, ST 3, q. 66, a. 1.
[19] For textual foundations for the table, see Aquinas, ST 3, q. 66, a. 1; q. 72; q. 73, a. 6; q. 84, a. 1; *Commentary on the Sentences* 4, d. 23, q. 1, aa. 1–2; 4, d. 24, q. 1, a. 1; 4, d. 26, q. 2, aa. 1–3.

| SACRAMENT | Sacramentum tantum | Res et sacramentum | Res tantum |
|---|---|---|---|
| Baptism | Water poured on the head while saying the Trinitarian formula | The character (permanent disposition) of baptism | Sanctifying grace (inclination to acts of the theological virtues, infused moral virtues, disposition to receive gifts of the Holy Spirit) |
| Confirmation | Anointing of the head with oil, accompanied by the words of the bishop | The character (permanent disposition) of confirmation | The grace of fortitude to bear witness to Christ publicly with integrity and courage |
| Eucharist | Bread and wine and the words of consecration | The real presence of the true body and blood of Christ | The grace of the church, the mystical body of Christ, fruit of communion in the body and blood of Christ |
| Matrimony | The consent of the baptized couple, who intend Christian marriage, materialized in consummated marital love | The indissoluble bond of marriage | The grace of Christian marriage; sanctification of the couple through shared mutual friendship, sacrifice, and the Christian education of their children |

| SACRAMENT | Sacramentum tantum | Res et sacramentum | Res tantum |
|---|---|---|---|
| Holy orders | The laying on of hands by a bishop and the invocation of the Holy Spirit | The character (permanent disposition) of holy orders, in one of the threefold gradations of bishop, presbyter, or deacon | The sanctifying grace communicated to the minister in the engagement of his ministerial activity |
| Sacramental penance and reconciliation | The confession of sins by the penitent, and the words of pardon pronounced by the bishop or a delegated priest | The grace of true contrition of sins in the mind and heart of the penitent | Reconciliation with God and the church |
| Anointing of the sick | The anointing with oil of the hands and head accompanied by the prayer of the church invoking the aid of the Holy Spirit | The forgiveness of venial sins | The sanctifying grace of spiritually fruitful union with Christ in suffering and death |

One might wonder from this list whether there is an intrinsic and spiritually organic order to the seven sacraments, so understood. Aquinas understands the order with reference to four key ideas: foundations for the Christian life, anthropological states of life that require the help of sanctification, remedies for defects, and the summit and perfection of the Christian life.[20] Baptism and confirmation pertain to the first category. They are foundational sacraments in that they provide the recipient with incorporation into the body of Christ, by way of character and sanctifying grace, so as to convey a living disposition to grow in spiritual union with Christ in a life of public discipleship. Matrimony and holy orders pertain to distinct states of life, as they provide supernatural grace to assist in the sanctification of natural marriage and family life, or the service of the ecclesial community through ordained ministry, which provides sacramental life and pastoral care to others. (Meanwhile, on this view, religious life is made possible by living out baptismal grace in a distinct way, through the evangelical counsels of poverty, chastity, and obedience, as the free embrace of a radicalized form of baptized existence.) Sacramental penance and the anointing of the sick are sacraments that remedy defects of soul (penance) or body and soul (anointing) and act to forgive sins and reorient the penitent toward eternal life, even amidst adverse circumstances. Finally, the Eucharist is in a category of its own, as the sacrament toward which all the others are oriented. The Eucharist is unique because only in this sacrament is Christ present not only as one who acts instrumentally by his virtual power (by an operational presence) but also substantially.[21] Therefore, there is something eschatologically ultimate about the Eucharist, and all other sacraments are ordered toward it, so that their celebration has its most ultimate realization in the complementary and coordinated celebration of the Eucharist.

Of course, the viewpoint depicted briefly here represents the normative Catholic view but is not adequately representative of the equivalent views found in Eastern Orthodox and Eastern Oriental (non-Chalcedonian) churches. These latter churches hold to a view of the sacramental mysteries that is very similar to that of the Catholic church regarding the seven sacraments, as evidenced in recent ecumenical statements.[22] However, they understand the organic order of these

---

[20] Aquinas, ST 3, q. 65, aa. 1–2.
[21] Aquinas, ST 3, q. 65, a. 3.
[22] See, for example, the Catholic–Eastern Orthodox *Uniatism, Method of Union of the Past; and the Present Search for Full Communion*, Balamand (Lebanon), June 23, 1993, and the *Joint International Commission for the Theological Dialogue between*

sacraments within a larger liturgical context of symbolic acts, wherein less distinction need be drawn between these particular seven sources of grace and other liturgical and religious aspects of the Christian life. Reformed Christian traditions issued from figures like Luther, Zwingli, and Calvin, meanwhile, dispute the apostolic origins of five of the sacraments, and maintain the need only for Christian baptism and the Lord's Supper. Their interpretations of these sacraments differ from those presented in this chapter and their views also differ sometimes significantly from those of one another, especially regarding the Eucharist. Without pretending here to provide a substantive introduction to Protestant notions of sacramentality, we can note in passing two important ideas common to these traditions.

First, the Reformers had in common the concern to mitigate the influence of what they considered to be an excessive Catholic and Orthodox theology of sacramental mediations that was built, on their view, on an accretion of man-made artificial customs that are not of apostolic origin. Second, however, they believed that the sacraments of baptism and the Lord's Supper were means instituted by Christ for the communication of grace. Calvin does not hesitate to call sacraments "instruments" of grace and maintains the distinction between the *sacramentum tantum, res et sacramentum*, and *res tantum* inherited from Lombard, even if he interprets the content of the sacraments differently from Roman Catholic theologians.[23] The upshot of these ideas is that there remains, even in the midst of the important differences between Catholics and Protestants, an important utility of reference to the common sources of medieval theology that inspired each, including the schemas regarding the threefold dimensionality of the sacraments, which influenced both early modern Catholics and Protestants in diverse ways. The knowledge of this traditional shared influence can assist in robust future ecumenical conversations regarding convergent and distinct but relational convictions regarding the church as the mystical body of Christ. Far from being an impasse to ecumenical conversation regarding the life of the church and the sacraments, the knowledge of the medieval analysis of

---

the Roman Catholic Church and the Orthodox Church, from Ravenna, October 8–14, 2007; and the Catholic-Oriental Orthodox, *The Sacraments in the Life of the Church*, Joint International Commission for Theological Dialogue Between the Catholic Church and the Oriental Orthodox Churches, June 23, 2022. These documents are available at the Vatican Dicastery for the Promotion of the Unity of Christians, www.christianunity.va/.

[23] Calvin, *Institutes of the Christian Religion*, 4.14.12–16; 4.17.1.

the threefold dimensionality of the sacraments is essential for understanding historically and thematically both where Protestant and Catholic traditions diverge as well as where they converge.

## THE EUCHARISTIC BODY OF CHRIST IN THE CHURCH AND ITS SPIRITUAL FRUITS

It is interesting within this context to consider the theology of the "three bodies" of Christ, as it developed in the mature period of high medieval theological reflection. Augustine in his *City of God* and other texts explored the idea that the Eucharist as the presence of the body and blood of Christ received in holy communion has for its effect the communicating of a participation in grace so as to make the church the body of Christ. This idea led to reflection among ninth-century Augustinians, such as Amalarius of Metz, on the relation of three notions of the body of Christ: the living resurrected body of the Lord, his eucharistic body and blood, and the church as the body of Christ. What is the relation between these three realities, each denoted as "the body of Christ"? Theologians of the period undertook reflections on the symbolism of the Mass to decipher how the imagery contained therein referred back to the historical mysteries of the life of Christ (his incarnation, death, and resurrection, depicted in the elements of bread and wine) and forward to the mystery of the church, so that the Eucharist itself should be understood to convey symbolically and effectively to the church a real participation in the corporate life of Christ and its spiritual benefits.[24] This vibrant and diversified process of theological reflection was subject to a kind of internal crisis, however, in the eleventh century when Berengar of Tours interpreted the Eucharist itself in primarily spiritual terms, understanding it as an outward sign of an inward grace, not unlike the other six sacraments. For this reason, in 1215 bishops at the Fourth Lateran Council solemnly affirmed the doctrine of transubstantiation (substantial conversion) stating that in the mass, when the words of consecration are said over the bread and wine by a validly ordained priest, they become the body and blood of Christ.

Aquinas sets out to resolve the theological question of the ontological relation of the three bodies. He notes that the resurrected body of Christ is not contiguous or spatially present within the current cosmos as we experience it but that, in his glorified state, Christ can act upon

---

[24] See the study of de Lubac 2006.

our world and render himself present to it by the power of God.[25] His eschatological human nature is not thus wholly "outside" of the physical universe but is present to it in a distinct and novel state of being. In the Eucharist the resurrected Christ is rendered present in a sacramental mode, so that what were formerly bread and wine truly become the body and blood of the glorified Christ.[26] However, the ontological properties (accidents) of bread and wine remain, such as the quantity and qualities of bread and wine. The living Christ is present ontologically in the accidents without newly accruing their properties to himself.[27] These properties no longer subsist in a substance, then, since they are no longer bread and wine, but are not accrued to the glorified body of Christ either. He is present in them as long as they remain, prior to consumption by the church or corruption by external elements.[28] In this way, the church can live in the mysterious and real presence of Christ in the Eucharist, but what the church and her membership do to the sacramental species (when they consume and digest them) does not alter the ontological reality and state of the glorified Christ.[29] He subsists under the signs of bread and wine, where he can be worshipped and so that the church can commune with him. The true body on the altar is thus identical with the glorified body of Christ, present in a mysterious way, without any alteration of the heavenly status of the glorified Christ.

How then should we understand the mystical body of the church? Aquinas associates the true body of Christ present in the Eucharist with the *res et sacramentum* and the mystical body of the church with the *res tantum* of the Eucharist.[30] In other words, the Eucharist by its proper effect of grace produces the living communion of the church. The Eucharist renders effective the living communion of the church in charity. It symbolizes this communion in three ways: first as food and drink, or nourishment of the spiritual life in charity; secondly as sacrifice, since the double consecration of the body and then the blood separately symbolizes the separation of the body and blood of Christ in the passion. The benefits of the passion are communicated to the faithful by reverent reception of the body and blood. Third, it symbolizes ecclesial unity since all eat from one paten and drink from

[25] Aquinas, ST 3, q. 56, a. 1; q. 57, aa. 4–5.
[26] Aquinas, ST 3, q. 75, a. 4 and 8.
[27] Aquinas, ST 3, q. 75, a. 5; q. 77, a. 1.
[28] Aquinas, ST 3, q. 77, a. 4.
[29] Aquinas, ST 3, q. 76, a. 5–6.
[30] See on what follows in this paragraph, Aquinas, ST 3, q. 79, a. 1.

one chalice (cf. 1 Cor 10:16–17), and so the Eucharist effectuates the corporate unity of the mystical body. In all of these ways the Eucharist realizes sacramentally what it signifies.

By his striking affirmation that the Eucharist effectuates the mystical body of the visible Catholic church, Aquinas suggests overtly that in some way all grace that is given in history whether before or after the time of Christ has an inclusive ecclesiological finality: Grace orients all human beings in history inwardly toward one catholic communion that is both visible and invisible, animated by a common participation in the life of Christ. All who participate in his grace are joined with one another, however implicitly, in a common knowledge of the mystery of the Holy Trinity, and in common bonds of divine charity. This ecclesiological vision has eschatological consequences. Even in the life of heaven, then, there is a visible mediation of grace, since the humanity of Christ will forever play an instrumental, mediating role in its communication, even as this christological grace allows the human community to enjoy the vision of God, the Trinity, immediately in itself.[31] In this sense, there will be a sublimation of all previous sacramental life into a higher order of christological presence, rather than a sheer discontinuation of visible mediations. Furthermore, the bodily life of human persons is an essential part of God's creation and is truly redeemed by Christ. This bodily life of the human community is to be reconstituted within the resurrected order, present in the eschatological church, as Christ's extended mystical body.

### POLITICAL AND COSMIC IMPLICATIONS OF A EUCHARISTIC ECCLESIOLOGY

In modern Catholic theology, the notion of the church as the mystical body of Christ has played a key role in thinking about the unity of the human race. The eucharistic theology mentioned in this chapter has also played a role in understanding the political and cosmic dimensions of Christology. The Second Vatican Council documents *Lumen gentium* and *Gaudium et spes*, for example, make use of the Thomistic notion of the universal headship of Christ in order to think about a twofold truth. On the one side, because Christ is the universal redeemer of humanity in virtue of his incarnation, passion, and resurrection, so all human beings are related to him in the order of

---

[31] Aquinas ST 3, q. 22, a. 5.

grace, which is offered in some way to all.[32] The scandal of particularity proper to the Christian claim that he is the unique mediator of salvation implies also the notion of his universal importance: that grace is offered by Christ to all persons. On the other side, this means all human beings are related in some way to the visible church, which contains the plenitude of the means of salvation, including the seven sacraments identified in Catholic teaching.[33] The church then is said to be herself "like a sacrament or as a sign and instrument" of God.[34] She is the indication that God intends to redeem humanity and unite the human race to himself effectively, in Christ, and in a common eucharistic communion.

This idea of the christological mediation of all salvation and of the ecclesiological finality of all salvation within the corporate body of Christ might seem to exclude the possibility of respectful consideration of any role in human history for non-Catholic forms of Christianity or for other human religious traditions. However, the view indicated in Catholic doctrine (especially in *Lumen gentium*, 14–16) proposes a contrary vision, in which all the baptized and the ecclesial traditions that they participate in can contribute positively to a collective life in Christ and are thus related in some way to the one eucharistic communion that takes on a plenary manifestation and visibility in the Catholic church.[35] Ecumenism then is a process of discernment of a deeper ground of unity shared already in Christ that can intensify and expand. Other non-Christian religious traditions, meanwhile, may be related to Christianity historically as potentially grace-initiated indications of the human drive to discover and find union with the transcendent mystery that is at the origin of existence.[36] Christian engagement with non-Christian religions then can seek a common ground for points of unity and ethical cooperation, based in the belief that the grace of Christ is present and active in the whole of humanity.

There are political ramifications to this idea as well. Traditional Catholic theology maintains that even apart from divine revelation

---

[32] The Second Vatican Council, Pastoral Constitution on the Church in the Modern World, *Gaudium et spes*, no. 22.
[33] The Second Vatican Council, Dogmatic Constitution on the Church, *Lumen gentium*, no. 13–16.
[34] *Lumen gentium*, no. 1.
[35] *Lumen gentium*, no. 15; and the Second Vatican Council Decree on Ecumenism, *Unitatis redintegratio*.
[36] *Lumen gentium*, no. 16, and the Second Vatican Council Declaration on the Church to Non-Christian Religions, *Nostra aetate*.

there are genuine resources within human philosophical traditions for a universal humanism, one that is metaphysically realistic and ethical in kind. It is based on a study of human nature, the dignity of human personhood, and a reasonable ethical analysis of social justice and the common good of human beings. The universality of the notion of Christ's mystical body, however, adds a specifically Christian note to this idea of a universal humanism. Understood in light of the doctrine of Christ's mystical body, one can perceive that every human being is made in the image of God, principally in virtue of the personal capacities of understanding and deliberate love.[37] Each person is one who Christ seeks to redeem. Thus also each human being can be subject to the charity of Christ, as a fruit of eucharistic communion, and this charity is exhibited in Christian friendship, justice, and mercy, shown to all persons and not only those who are visible members of the body of Christ by baptism.

This christological humanism is also a bulwark against any form of racism or colonial inegalitarianism that would deny dignity and human rights to particular individuals or subgroups within the larger framework of society.[38] It offers Christian believers distinctively supernatural motivations against totalitarian forms of government that would reduce the meaning and scope of human freedom to the realm of the immanent political life of the state or social polity. Because the human person is called to a transcendent life in God, he or she therefore cannot be instrumentalized for ultimate ends that are merely political, however noble they may be. This is true not only of individuals but also of collective cultures, subsidiary institutions (such as universities or families), and political states, which all have a dignity of their own and cannot be manipulated for purely political ends.[39]

At the same time, this very idea of a universal calling of all human beings and collective social groups to a union with God by grace, in Christ, provides a decisive motivation for the protection of religious freedom in those who choose not to be religious, since their conscience and freedom of religious decision-making is something sacred, marked by the dignity of those who must seek and embrace the truth freely.[40] This "negative" freedom from religiosity of a tyrannical kind also has a collective form, since families or societies that wish to preserve their

---

[37] See *Gaudium et spes*, no. 12, 24, 68.
[38] *Gaudium et spes*, no. 26, 29.
[39] *Gaudium et spes*, no. 19, 25, 43.
[40] See the Second Vatican Council Declaration on Religious Freedom, *Dignitatis humanae*.

freedom from religious coercion of any kind also retain their dignity as free, truth-seeking beings. The sacramental order cannot be dissociated from these various concerns, as it requires the protection of the free engagement and truth-seeking of every human person for its genuine acceptance and ethically profound celebration.

Finally, eucharistic ecclesiology offers one resources for thinking about the cosmic implications of the resurrection of Christ. If Christ in his resurrected glory is already present in a mysterious way, in the Eucharist and within the life of the church, then the "end of the world" is already happening. The Eucharist is a discrete but genuine proleptic sign of the future of humanity and the cosmos, fully transformed by the grace of God. Modern Christian theology of the creation posits the ethical importance for all human beings of a just ecological respect of the earth, so that it is protected as an environment for past and future life, and so that it is respected ontologically as a reflection of the hidden splendor of God. Analogously, a Christology of the mystical body posits creation as the place of the eventual redemption of the physical world, of its living forms, and of the human person in particular, in both body and soul. In light of the resurrection and the eucharistic presence of Christ in the church, we must affirm that God is committed to the preservation and eschatological transformation of the physical cosmos, which is deserving of human respect. This is already made evident in the body of the Virgin Mary who was the genuine mother of God, and in the resurrected flesh of the Son of God, present in the liturgical and sacramental life of the church. Christ, then, is the omega point of creation, the final immanent term and exemplar toward which all things are oriented, and who is already present sacramentally among us in the church. In him, we might say that a second big bang, a new creation, is happening. However, this truth provides us with warrant and responsibility to take seriously, for specifically religious and Christian reasons, the ontological dignity and respect due to the physical creation and the interdependent natural life forms that make human life in this universe possible.

## CONCLUSION

We might conclude by simply noting both the persistent continuity and the dynamic vigor down through time of the Christian idea of the church as the corporate body of Christ. This notion of the body of Jesus in his people, of the mystical body of Christ, is one that has had and that continues to have a marvelous fruitfulness in Christian history, in common ecclesial life, and in theological and spiritual reflection. The idea invites us to take account, perhaps with new eyes, of the uniqueness of Christianity as a movement that proposes a novel sense of the presence of God in history. "For God was in Christ reconciling the world to himself" (2 Cor 5:19). "Unless you eat the flesh of the Son of man and drink his blood, you have no life in you" (John 6:53). These strange and even offensive words seem to point us to a central truth of the Christian religion that St. Augustine underscored already long ago, that Jesus Christ as the head and the church as his body are but one mystical person, the whole Christ.[41]

### FURTHER READING

Aquinas, Thomas. 1947. *Summa Theologica*. Translated by Dominicans of the English Province. 3 vols. New York: Benziger.
Bettenson, Henry Scowcroft, ed. 1984. *Augustine: City of God*. London: Penguin.
Calvin, Jean. 1960. *Institutes of the Christian Religion*. 2 vols. Philadelphia: Westminster Press.
De Lubac, Henri. 2006. *Corpus Mysticum: The Eucharist and the Church in the Middle Ages*. Translated by Gemma Simmonds. Edited by Laurence Paul Hemming and Susan Frank Parsons. Faith in Reason. Notre Dame: University of Notre Dame Press.
Emery, Gilles. 2004. "The Ecclesial Fruit of the Eucharist in St. Thomas Aquinas." *Nova et vetera* 2: 43–60.
Flannery, Austin, ed. 2004. *Vatican Council II: The Conciliar and Post-Conciliar Documents*. Northport: Costello.
Tillard, Jean Marie Roger. 1967. *The Eucharist; Pasch of God's People*. Translated by D. L. Wienk. Staten Island: Alba House.

---

[41] "Marvel, be glad, we are made Christ. For if He is the head, we are the members: the whole man is He and we." Augustine, *Tractate on the Gospel of John*, 21.8. [Trans. J. Gibb, *Nicene and Post-Nicene Fathers*, Vol. 7, ed. P. Schaff (Buffalo, NY: Christian Literature Publishing Co., 1888).]

## 15 The Church's Jesus in Modern Theology
EMMANUEL DURAND, OP

The Christologies elaborated within various Christian denominations in the last forty years bear witness to a major effort to incorporate the results of new research on the historical Jesus, especially with respect to the Third Quest focused on the Jewishness of Jesus. A failure to address this dimension would have amounted to a return to a form of docetism. The traces of Jesus's humanity are prerequisites or materials for history. In order for a history to be written, however, a certain interest must exist, a method must be adopted and a narrative developed. History-writing is not a purely objective undertaking, and some divergence among historians' portraits of Jesus is to be expected. Nevertheless, history, as a discipline, is a necessary counterpart to Christology, enabling us to vividly preserve the strangeness of Jesus in his historical context and to shield him from simplistic or erroneous appropriations. At the same time, now that the efforts of historians have borne fruit, it appears that a merely historical characterisation of Jesus has no binding force for believers, especially if it is severed from religious narratives and collective memory (Lohfink 2012).

In certain respects, the narrative analysis of the Gospels and the focus on narrativity in Christology are a response to this shortcoming of historical methodology. In a story, the initial situation is characterised by a certain lack, and the characters are driven by transformational actions. The reader thus discovers resources that allow him or her to be addressed and to undergo a reconfiguration in his or her own situations of impasse or lack (Lovinfosse and Durand 2021). She or he is addressed by Christ and offered the opportunity to enter into conformity with Christ. Nonetheless, while such a narrative approach to the Gospels is inspiring, it does not exhaust the literary genres of biblical witness (Ricoeur 2001). Prophetic proclamations and the transmission of wisdom must also find their place within a systematic Christology.

Once the significance of historical portraits of Jesus for the reality of the proclamation of faith had been acknowledged, other issues took priority. The first of these, in my view, is that of the prophetic and systematic relevance of Christ Jesus: What is the illuminating power of the Christ of faith in the contemporary world and contemporary culture? Is the Christ of the Christian tradition real enough to sustain discipleship in a context as fragmented as ours?

One of the ways in which theologians are responding to this challenge is by meticulously demonstrating that Christ stands at the heart of a new intelligibility, not merely of the other central mysteries of the faith but also of the cosmos, the human being, culture and politics. At present, numerous theologians are working to build bridges between the church fathers and contemporary issues, such as the autonomy of the created order, the plasticity of human nature, resistance to totalitarianism, the ecological crisis, the challenge of hope and so on. This represents a new and fruitful stage in the theology of christological renewal.

Through the 'ressourcement' trend, a return to the patristic sources has revealed that this corpus exhibits an abundance of value – not merely normative but also heuristic (Beeley 2012; Daley 2018). A similar movement is currently working to renew systematic Christology by means of an ingenious rereading of biblical sources. These authors are especially attentive to the intertextuality between the books and episodes that make up the Christian Bible (Volf and McAnnally-Linz 2022).

From a Roman Catholic perspective, to place Christ once again at the centre of a constellation of delicate and even burning questions is to apply, in a modernised form, the order or hierarchy of truths. As laid out at the Second Vatican Council in the context of ecumenical dialogue, this theological principle places Christ – the Word made flesh and the paschal Christ – at the heart of the entire edifice of the Christian faith. Starting from the centre of this faith, we must advance step by step in the doctrinal dialogue between denominations (Vatican Council II, *Unitatis Redintegratio*, no. 11). Several present-day Christologies go further by applying this principle to a reflection that transcends the strict limits of the *Credo*, thus enabling the Christian faith to engage with other spheres of contemporary life in the world. Nonetheless, Christ's relationship with the Father and the Holy Spirit remains primordial and decisive when it comes to understanding the person of the Christ as the focal point of the illumination of faith. There can be no balanced Christocentrism that does not presuppose the doctrine of the Trinity (Webster 2015).

## JESUS, THE TRINITY AND ATONEMENT

According to the Christian faith, the identity of Jesus of Nazareth is made manifest through his connection to the Father who sends him, to the Holy Spirit whose coming he promises and to all the people he has come to save. Jesus's identity is thus seen to be relational: in his very being, Jesus stands in relation to the Father and to the Holy Spirit, while through his mission, he also stands in relation to all human beings, the beneficiaries of his offer of salvation.

**The Relationships That Make the Being of Christ Jesus Unique**
The relationship of Jesus to the Father and to the Holy Spirit is laid out in the doctrine of the Trinity: the Father, the Son and the Holy Spirit constitute a single God when it comes to their substance (*ousia*), while representing distinct relational subjects when it comes to their individual persons (*hypostasis*). In his singular humanity, Jesus is the Messiah or Christ, the Anointed par excellence, because he has received from God the Anointing of the Holy Spirit (2 Cor 1:21–22; Acts 10:38). As a unique ontological subject, Jesus is the person of the eternal Son of God who takes on a singular, concrete human nature. The being and mission of Jesus can only be understood through the prism of the doctrine of the Trinity, even if only the outlines of this doctrine are sketched in the New Testament.

The nature of Jesus's relationship to all human beings is spelled out in the belief in his incarnation and the doctrine of redemption. The Son takes on a concrete and mortal humanity, capable of suffering, which is bound together with that of all other human beings. In his human existence, the Son is confronted with a refusal to believe, a trial, a violent passion and an ignominious death. However, in virtue of God's design and the charity of the human Christ, this final event is redemptive for the whole of humanity touched by sin and death.

**Salvation in Christ: Theology, Liturgy, Existence**
How precisely the cross and resurrection of Jesus bring about salvation remains a matter of debate both between and within Christian denominations. The Melkite theologian Khaled Anatolios has recently made a strong proposal from an ecumenical perspective (Anatolios 2020). It is often said that salvation is one of the central mysteries of the Christian faith and that it has given rise to numerous theological models, not only in patristic times but also in the present day. According to Anatolios, however, the conciliar declarations about the Trinity and Christ take up and transmit a true and non-arbitrary dogma of salvation that is revealed to be more fundamental than the various theological models that have competed with or succeeded one other.

Anatolios's proposal is informed by two fundamental theses: (i) 'Christ saves us by fulfilling humanity's original vocation to participate, from the position of the Son, in the mutual glorification of the persons of the divine Trinity'; (ii) 'Christ saves us by vicariously repenting for humanity's sinful rejection of humanity's doxological vocation and its violation and distortion of divine glory' (Anatolios 2020, 32). To capture these two theses in a succinct formulation, we can say that Anatolios understands Christ's salvific work as a form of *doxological contrition* or *vicarious worship and repentance*. He is careful to show how the representative aspect of this soteriology differs from liberation theology, the theory of mimetic violence and the theory of penal substitution, all three of which are fiercely debated in Western theology.

The cornerstone of Anatolios's argument is the Byzantine liturgy of Lent, the Easter Triduum, Ascension and Pentecost. As he sees it, theology loses its vitality when it is severed from the liturgy, the supreme location of the experience of salvation: theology and liturgy must illuminate each other, just as the *lex credendi* and the *lex orandi* do. This approach is distinctive of a new orientation in Christology from a confessional perspective: the communal practice of faith is the living organ of the tradition of Christ. The Easter liturgy provides the terrain upon which systematic Christology can develop in a coherent and relevant way.

At the same time, the liturgy of salvation must not be cut off from experiences of salvation. Instead, we should juxtapose the liturgy, as a celebration of Easter, with the anticipated experience of salvation among individuals today awaiting sacramental or eschatological confirmation. Otherwise, the liturgy risks coming across as hollow and remaining external to the truth of the grace that gushes forth from the Easter event.

Let us take an example from the Gospel of Luke. When Jesus Christ addresses Zacchaeus and invites himself into his home, he affirms that 'salvation' (*sōteria*) has come upon his house (Luke 19:1–10). Astonishingly, however, he does not require that this salvation be completed or confirmed by a sacrifice at the Temple. Here, sacrificing is made unnecessary by the subsequent conversion of Zacchaeus, since he undertakes to make amends for his errors through abundant generosity towards the poor and his victims. In theological terms, Zacchaeus offers genuine 'satisfaction'. The normal – admittedly temporary – mediation of the Temple liturgy is surpassed here by the exercise of charity in relation to Christ himself.

Believers gain access to Christ the Saviour primarily by listening to his word and celebrating his passion and resurrection. The liturgy is a supremely instructive and objectifying form of mediation. The sacraments connect human beings to the salvific act of Christ. However, the scope and relevance of salvation clearly extend beyond the liturgical experience. Let us not forget that Jesus of Nazareth was a layman under Jewish law and that the salvation he instituted was not subordinated to Temple liturgies. On the contrary, it was enacted in an impure and off-putting way, outside the city, seemingly at the greatest possible remove from liturgical sacrality (Vanhoye 2022, 19). Experiences of 'ordinary' (i.e. not yet final) salvation involving extensive mediation – such as onerous fraternity, uncomfortable hospitality, selfless service, boundless forgiveness, heroic fidelity, a life dedicated to others, abandonment at the moment of death – are probably a concrete sign of the actual possibility offered to many individuals to partake, through the Spirit of Christ, of the paschal mystery (Vatican Council II, *Gaudium et Spes*, no. 22).

## CHRIST AND THE HUMAN CONDITION

Faith in the incarnation of the Word presupposes the capacity of human nature to unite with God. Conversely, the fact that the Word took on a concrete and singular humanity sheds light on the human condition in all its scope and variety. Flesh in the biblical sense refers to the human condition in its intrinsic fragility (Isa 40:6; John 1:14), which is de facto exacerbated by the sin of the world. By 'human nature', I mean the constitutive and unifying principle of our common humanity, while by 'human condition' I mean the complexity and variety of the concrete modalities of human existence. In what follows, we will consider: (i) the openness of human nature to God, (ii) the absence of competition between the human and the divine and (iii) the coming together of the singular and the universal in Christ.

According to the common doctrine of the orthodox faith, which derives from the councils of the fourth and fifth centuries, the term 'incarnation' refers to the birth of the Word of God, as a person, in the flesh born of a Jewish woman. Although Jesus himself never sinned, he took on the flesh of sinners, with all the passions, temptations and frailties common to it (John of Damascus, *De fide orthodoxa*, 64 [SC 540; MPG III, 20]). The Son of God and the son of Mary are one and the same person. There is a single subject of existence and action: the eternal Word who took on a concrete humanity within time. Moreover, this humanity was created in the very act of being united with the Word, meaning that the humanity of Jesus in no way precedes its union with the Word. Jesus of Nazareth is the unique person of the eternal Word, which is present and active in our common flesh.

### The Openness of Human Nature to God

Human nature did not need to be transformed, corrected or augmented in order to be united with the eternal Word. It was created in such a way as to be capable of union with God; it was created by the Word and for the Word. For believers, union with God is achieved by means of transformative grace and acts of charity. As for Christ Jesus, union with the Word is given in his being and an abundance of grace flows from him. In Jesus, human nature did not first need to receive transformative grace before it could be united with God. The incarnation reveals that human nature is inherently open to God, notwithstanding the sin that affects it in our case.

Christ reveals what God intended human nature to be (Tanner 2010, 24). First of all, human nature is directed towards fellowship and union with God. This transformation does not involve a fusion of the human and the divine, or the loss of what makes us human, but is instead a union free from confusion. In our case, deification requires salvation from the sin of the world and from our own personal faults. Deification is accomplished through the cross and the resurrection. Christ achieves 'doxological contrition' for the benefit of all human beings (Anatolios 2020). However, the incarnation of the Word in the common flesh of sinners reveals that, in its constitution, human nature remains receptive to union and open to God.

The openness of human nature to God has two implications, whose importance can clearly be seen today: (i) human nature is plastic and (ii) it is not easily defined. There is a long tradition of arguing that human nature is the most plastic of all natures: this was notably the position of Gregory of Nyssa, Pico della Mirandola and Blaise Pascal. Kathryn Tanner has reinvigorated this line of thought in a postmodern context, and her argument deserves attention (Tanner 2010, 39–57). Like all creatures, humans are receptive to their surroundings. The human soul is responsive to the beings and forms that make it grow. This is a consequence of free choice, and as a result the soul can attach itself to higher goods that elevate it or to lesser goods that weigh it down. In Greek anthropology, 'a particular man is characterised according to the impression produced in his soul by the objects of his choice' (Clement of Alexandria, *Stromata* 4.23.150). The human soul is fundamentally drawn towards the unlimited goodness of God. This is why human nature is the most plastic of all natures: it pursues *by free choice* an indefinite, *unlimited* goodness that is diffracted in all created goods. From this results an infinite number of individual paths. The impossibility of giving a restrictive definition of human nature is the consequence of its abundance, of its being drawn towards God, whose goodness is not circumscribed by any specific form. This is confirmed in the Gospels by the 'many faces of being called' (Lohfink 2012, 86–99).

## The Absence of Competition between the Human and the Divine

The incarnation also reveals the absence of rivalry between the human and the divine. The otherness of God does not imply any contrariety between immanence and transcendence. Because he is radically different from all created things, without being the first of a kind or series, God is present in the most intimate way to all his creatures. The fact that God is present or that he acts within the sphere of human intimacy in no way detracts from created being and human agency. This correct conception of God's transcendence is presupposed by Christology and finds its confirmation in Christ, as Rowan Williams has forcefully argued in recent years.

According to Williams, an orthodox Christology of the incarnation is what allows us to check the correctness of the theological articulation between the infinite and the finite, between divine action and human action (Williams 2018). These are not comparable or rival magnitudes within the physical world, which could be combined or set against each other, because they do not at all exist in the same register or category. One and the same created effect can proceed wholly from the divine and wholly from the human, according to two incommensurable yet articulated causes (Thomas Aquinas, *Summa contra Gentiles*, 3.70). When it comes to Christ, there is no form of competition, contrariety, accumulation or incompatibility between the divine and human. In support of his argument, Williams invokes the Christology of Thomas Aquinas. Although it may seem strange to some modern minds, Williams understands the doctrine of Christ's unique being – which is the very being (*esse*) of the divine person of the Word – as the guarantee of a Christology that is metaphysically adequate to the mystery of the incarnation.

Through the concrete modalities of Jesus's life, including his self-emptying, the Word truly delivered himself to the world. According to the Christian faith, the divine 'hypostasis' or 'person' of Christ Jesus did not occlude his concrete humanity and history. On the contrary, the fact that Christ's human nature belongs to the very being of the Word ('enhypostasis') makes it possible to accept his human history, with all its weight and meaning, as the truth of creation and salvation (see Barth 1956, par. 59).

## The Coincidence of the Singular and the Universal

In Christ, the false opposition between the singular and the universal is overcome. The singularity of a human being consists of more than his or her individual particularities, such as ancestry, measurements, gender, profession, life history and so on. Instead, human singularity presupposes these particularities and unifies them. When these particularities are taken on by a subject, they interact with one another to produce a unique countenance. Singularity is thus the unique configuration of an original personality, including both its basic traits and its unfolding over time. According to the philosophical tradition of humanism, some individuals enhance their singularity more than others through the breadth of their curiosity, experiences and friendships. Exploring various states of the human condition results in a greater openness to others through the communication of singularities (Magnard 2009). The most common example of this is friendship based on immediate sympathy, a mutual recognition devoid of preconditions.

Such is the paradox of human singularity: the more developed a human being's singularity, the more capable she or he is of entering into a relationship with other singularities. An orientation towards the universal is not the opposite of singularity but rather its relational property. The more fully my singularity asserts itself, the more capable I am of entertaining a range of different affinities. The greatest degree of human singularity is thus potentially marked by a hitherto unseen capacity to be everything for everyone, to be directed towards everyone. Yet this is the most fundamental definition of the universal: the one-for-all. Such a situation tends to emerge when a singular being develops an affinity with a large number of other singular subjects of diverse kinds. At the same time, a singular human being who is oriented towards everyone, and thus potentially universal, would provoke irritation, rejection and even murderous exasperation in certain individuals, because her or his capacity for interaction would be too vigorous, too engaged, too disconcerting. The ability of a singular being to cultivate affinities thus brings with it provocation and confrontation.

We reach here the crux of my argument: thanks to its multifaceted richness, a high degree of human singularity confers on an individual an extraordinary capacity to relate to and to address others. However, this potential is actualised not only in sympathy but also in confrontation. In the Christian faith, the ideal figure I have just sketched is de facto embodied by Jesus of Nazareth: in his time and since, he has addressed people in a unique way on the basis of his singularity as a universal man (Durand 2018).

## CHRIST AND PHYSICAL CREATION

In the context of the ecological crisis, Christ's relationship to both living beings and matter has been questioned in a new and innovative way, drawing support from the patristic tradition. The New Testament makes clear in various ways that the salvation brought about by Christ has far-reaching repercussions: its effects are not limited to the transformation of human beings, even if they are the ones concerned in the first instance. This way of looking at things raises a question about the foundation laid down by the incarnation of the Son of God. To what extent did he take on the emergence of life and the components of matter? To what extent is Christ connected to other forms of life and existence? What is the ultimate scope of the recapitulation and transfiguration of the universe in Christ? Against the backdrop of the ecological crisis, essays on biblical and patristic hermeneutics have made significant contributions to the construction of an eco-theology. One creative development in Christology deserves particular attention, namely the 'Deep Incarnation' movement.

### Proclaiming a Christ with Far-Reaching Salvific Implications

Several gospel accounts mention the sovereignty of Jesus of Nazareth over both wild animals (Mark 1:13) and the physical elements (Mark 4:39). The death of Jesus also had immediate repercussions for the physical, human world (Matt 27:51–54). Other New Testament texts project Christ's salvific action onto the whole of creation, whether in terms of liberation (Rom 8:21), reconciliation (Col 1:20), recapitulation (Eph 1:22) or adoration (Rev 5:13). How, then, can we account for the relationship of solidarity and integration between Christ and physical creation in its full expanse?

In the Jewish apocalyptic traditions that form the backdrop to the New Testament, the whole of creation partakes indirectly of the hope of salvation, because it is marked by the consequences of sin, whether this is seen as human or angelic (Hahne 2006). However, the solidarity between Christ Jesus and physical creation has remained largely unacknowledged in the Western tradition, although several Eastern church fathers understood human beings and their created environment to share a common destiny, in conformity with God's design (Blowers 2013).

### The Working Hypothesis of Deep Incarnation

The incarnation of the Logos should be thought of both extensionally (scope) and intensionally (depth) (Gregersen 2015). In taking on human flesh as Jesus of Nazareth, the Logos not only adopted his concrete humanity and passion-exaltation, connecting with all human beings on their own terrain, but also bound himself to the material conditions of the whole of created reality, to all forms of biological life and to the painful experiences of all sentient creatures. This relationship with non-human creatures is not simply a reflection of God's intention but also a product of the concrete reality of incarnation under the basic conditions of existence in the material world. Deep Incarnation thus extends to the whole of cosmic reality and all forms of life the well-known soteriological principle: 'what has not been assumed has not been healed, but it is what has been united to God that has been saved' (Gregory Nazianzen, *Letter* 101). In opposition to Apollinarius, Gregory applied this principle to the human condition in its entirety, while the advocates of Deep Incarnation extend it to the complete nexus of cosmic and living realities – an interdependence that is, in certain ways, partially taken on by the Logos through his specifically human incarnation.

Originally, Deep Incarnation affirmed itself as an intuition inspired by Martin Luther's 'theology of the Cross', one capable of absorbing the lost lives, selection, predation and suffering associated with biological evolution. The cross of Christ is the 'icon' or 'sacrament' – depending on the specific author and Christian denomination – of God's presence to every creature that suffers violence. While we do not know the ultimate how, the promise of healing and transfiguration contained in Christ's resurrection extends to every living being that falls to the ground and dies.

Current approaches to Deep Incarnation strive to anchor this innovative Christology earlier in the Christian tradition, tracing it all the way back to Irenaeus of Lyon and Athanasius of Alexandria (Edwards 2019). Two theses endorsed by Irenaeus are of fundamental importance here: first, 'the only perspective from which the beginning of creation can be understood is that of the end, the Word of the Cross, and the final transformation of all things in Christ' (Edwards 2019, 35; Irenaeus, *Adversus haereses*, 1.22.3). Second, 'the Word who was crucified in the form of a cross, is the Word who was already imprinted on all dimensions of creation. The whole creation is cruciform' (Edwards 2019, 40; Irenaeus, *Demonstration*, 34). Not only does physical creation in its entirety bear witness to God, since it is fashioned jointly by the Word and the Holy Spirit, but, from the very beginning, the development of biological life bears within itself a trace of the paschal mystery. The crucified and glorified Christ draws the whole of creation towards its final recapitulation. It is also possible, incidentally, to identify an affinity between the theology of Irenaeus and that of Paul with respect to the ultimate destiny of material creation.

Ultimately, Deep Incarnation draws on the model of the *Totus Christus*. According to this doctrine, as formulated by Augustine, the total Christ undergoes growth, because in his full form he unifies successive states. He fundamentally remains one and the same subject of existence, while becoming ever more inclusive. The same, unique Christ is pre-existent, undergoes incarnation, is abased, dies and then comes back to life, before finally being exalted in Heaven. In virtue of his incarnation, he is the head of all humanity, whose nature he shares. In virtue of his glorification, he gives life to all the members of his body, especially those passing through the tribulations of this present life. According to Deep Incarnation, the paradigm of salvific inclusion not only applies to the progressive assimilation of the elect into the body of the paschal Christ but also entails a differentiated integration of all flesh and all material creatures into Christ the man, in conformity with the mode and receptivity proper to each created form of existence (Gregersen 2015, 20–21). Although human beings, and therefore Christ, can be seen as a 'microcosm' encompassing all the degrees of being or integrated stages of emergence, the solidarity of the human Christ with humanity as a whole is of a different nature than his connection with plants and minerals (Bauckham 2015, 37–45). In drawing attention to the cosmic implications of incarnation and salvation, we must be careful to avoid making the concept of incarnation so malleable that its meaning becomes unclear.

### CHRIST AND HOPE

In the last twenty years, we have been repeatedly caught off guard by unforeseen crises that have impacted us on the collective level. These disconcerting surprises have laid bare our inability to avoid situations of rupture: we have been unable to foresee them despite our belief that our techno-scientific rationality would protect us. By contrast, theological hope is a crucial mode of orientation that helps us to live when faced with the loss of our ideas about the future. Hope is the sense of the possibility of the good, which ought to be received as a gift (Dalferth 2016). In the midst of adversity and obscurity, we generally no longer hope for this or that particular outcome but rather for something unexpected to surprise us. Hope of this kind entails facing up to what remains closed or impossible for us. We exercise theological hope when we remain open in wilful expectation, receptive to being surprised by the good. Christ himself underwent such a labour of hope for the sake of others.

### Jesus's Hopeful Outlook on Others

During his public ministry, Jesus had a uniquely hopeful way of looking at people and situations. Where anyone else might have seen a mere tired crowd, he saw the people of God lacking a shepherd (Mark 6:34). While the disciples admired the stones of the Temple and the donations made by the wealthy, he fixed his gaze on an inconspicuous widow and the extraordinary significance of the two coins she gave (Luke 21:1–4). Where everyone else saw a sinner embroiled in crooked dealings, he saw a man capable of rising up if called (Mark 2:14). Where Simon the Pharisee saw a public sinner, he recognised a woman capable of being forgiven (Luke 7:36–50). Jesus's gaze is no mere natural gaze. Rather, he contemplates the possibilities of grace, discerning what is still in embryonic form. His gaze is the gaze of the Envoy. As a result of his keen missionary awareness, Jesus is able to discern that the reign of God is coming, because it has already been proffered by God in full. As a result of being fully absorbed by his mission, Jesus views all situations in terms of (potential or actual) openness and closedness towards God. Jesus takes seriously the jubilee year of grace (Luke 4:19). It is an auspicious time: everything has been made available by God in order to convert his people. Salvation lies close at hand, within the grasp of faith. Nothing is lacking on God's side. Delay, avoidance and refusal come from men, not God (Lohfink 2012, 24–39). Jesus sees the coming of the Kingdom, although it still lies beyond the ken of natural judgement. He hoped for the conversion of his people and the salvation of humanity (Thomas Aquinas, *Sup. Psalmos*, ps. 15, no. 1; ps. 30, no. 1). But did he also hope for something for himself in this life?

### Trial: Becoming a Principle of Salvation for All

At a certain point in his ministry, Jesus was most probably confronted with the loss of his initial understanding about the salvation of his people as the reign of God. While they themselves were able to accept the word and deeds of God's reign and thus be brought together, refusal and rejection gradually gained the upper hand among the leaders of the people, the chief priests and the scribes. Subsequently, salvation would take a confrontational path, one that had to contend with closed-mindedness, rejection, manipulation, violence and hatred. Before arriving at his passion, Jesus was compelled to experience a share of mourning and acceptance, as a well as a certain reorientation with regard to how the offer of salvation could be realised (Rahner 1992, 228–63).

There is only one moment where Jesus hopes for salvation for himself. In Gethsemane, he asks his Father to save him from his looming violent death: 'My Father, if it is possible, let this cup pass from me'

(Matt 26:39a). This is the last temptation: avoidance. As we read, we are used to moving directly on to Jesus's assent in the next half-verse. However, Matthew indicates that the first part of Jesus's prayer in Gethsemane lasted about an hour. For Jesus, in that moment, the process of passing through temptation and surrendering to the Father's will had a duration and represented genuine toil (Lovinfosse and Durand 2021, 185–95). The outcome was not a given: 'Yet not what I want, but what you want' (Matt 26:39b). This labour of assenting was even repeated a second (Matt 26:42) and then a third time (Matt 26:44).

The Epistle to the Hebrews gives a more pitiful version of Jesus's struggle to assent. With a loud cry and in tears, Jesus begs the Father to save him from death (Heb 5:7). The author of the letter comments: 'and he was heard because of his reverent submission' (Heb 5:7). Yet Jesus was not spared a violent death. His prayer was answered not with reference to its immediate object, namely being spared, but in accordance with the intention of his life as a whole: 'he became the source of eternal salvation for all who obey him' (Heb 5:9). It is by consenting to lose his life, rather than saving it, that Jesus becomes the Saviour in act, in accordance with his mission (see Aquinas, *Super Heb.* 5:7, ed. Marietti, 1953, nos. 255–57). The renunciation of what he had momentarily hoped to attain for himself – being spared death – gives full weight to the hope he brings for others. This comes with a price: Jesus immerses himself in pure hope, stripped of his initial ideas about salvation, in order to learn, in his human condition, about the filial relationship in its purest state (Heb 5:8). In this way, he goes ahead of his disciples and opens a way for them.

Having been glorified and entered the Holy of Holies as a scout, Jesus grounds a new hope for all his disciples. When the high priest entered the Holy of Holies once a year, no one was allowed to follow him (Lev. 16:17). Jesus, by contrast, has entered the sanctuary for eternity, and we are all invited to follow him. We can now present ourselves confidently before the Throne of Grace (Heb 4:14–16; 7:23–27; 10:19–22). Hope is not only grounded in the promise of the faithful God but is also anchored in Heaven in the glorified Christ (Heb 6:18–20). Through the accomplishment of his mission and his exaltation at the Father's right hand, Jesus Christ has given believers a qualitatively new form of hope.

### Anticipation of the Parousia and the Order of Charity

The parousia – the coming of Christ in glory as Lord – is the ultimate hope of Christians. Jesus announces it soberly in Mark 13. In response to a disciple's astonishment at the splendour of the Temple, Jesus affirms: not one stone will be left on another. He then exits the Temple for good and goes to sit on the Mount of Olives. There, he speaks of the signs announcing the second coming of the Son of Man – signs from every age that show that this world is crumbling. It is out of balance and passing away. He then refers to the great tribulation of Jerusalem, a desecration of what is holiest for Jewish believers. However, the key point is what comes next: the arrival of the Son of Man is preceded by a deconstruction of physical creation, in particular the heavenly lights and the cosmic powers (Mark 13:24–25; Gen 1:14–19). God undoes what he established on the fourth day of creation. Only he is able to do this. To what end? The de-creation takes place in order to allow the power and brilliance of the Son of Man to manifest. The cosmic powers give way to the ultimate power of the Son. The brightness of the stars give way to the ultimate glory of the Son. He gathers the elect from every corner of the world and is himself the seat of the final world. For all believers, the new frame of reference is astonishing: 'Heaven and earth will pass away, but my words will not pass away' (Mark 13:31).

Jesus's eschatological discourse in Mark 13 is bookended by two disconcerting gestures made by women: the poor widow who gives all she has to live on (Mark 12:44) and the unknown woman from Bethany who anoints Jesus's head (Mark 14:3). These two women touch on the one thing that is truly definitive – concrete gestures of charity – while the disciples look at the stones or discuss the amazing amount of donations. Wherever the gospel is proclaimed, people remember the poor, unnoticed widow in the Temple and the nameless woman in Bethany (Mark 13:9). Their memory is eternal.

To put these two women's gestures in context from a theological perspective, we can have recourse to the three orders of reality evoked by Blaise Pascal (*Fragments*, ed. Brunschvicg, no. 793). The cosmos astonishes us and dizzies us with its beauty and excess. In time and space, we are overawed by a form of infinity. Yet even the most minuscule achievement of the human spirit completely surpasses the order of the cosmos. A young child composing a poem is more admirable than the play of galaxies. However, we must not stop there, for the smallest act of charity surpasses the greatest achievements of the human spirit. It belongs to the order of the definitive. Yet it is precisely at this level that the gestures of the two women that frame the eschatological discourse are situated.

## CONCLUSION

As proclaimed by the churches, Jesus of Nazareth is the key to unlocking the depth and breadth of the Christian faith. Jesus's relations to God and to the Holy Spirit ground his potential relation to every human being. As a consequence of his identity, to be unveiled in theology, Christ also illuminates a whole set of questions at the frontier of the Creed: among others, the openness of human nature to God, the relationship between the human and the divine, the paradox of the singular and the universal, the unity of matter and life, the challenge of hope among historical ordeals. Christ offers a new understanding, not only of the core issues of the Christian faith but also of the present moment of each believer and of what is truly definitive facing God.

## FURTHER READING

Anatolios, Khaled. 2020. *Deification through the Cross: An Eastern Christian Theology of Salvation*. Grand Rapids: Eerdmans.
Durand, Emmanuel. 2018. *Jésus contemporain: Christologie brève et actuelle*. Paris: Cerf.
Edwards, Denis. 2019. *Deep Incarnation: God's Redemptive Suffering with Creatures*. Maryknoll: Orbis.
Gaventa, Beverly Roberts and Richard B. Hays, eds. 2008. *Seeking the Identity of Jesus: A Pilgrimage*. Grand Rapids: Eerdmans.
Gregersen, Niels Henrik, ed. 2015. *Incarnation: On the Scope and Depth of Christology*. Minneapolis: Fortress.
Lohfink, Gerhard. 2012. *Jesus of Nazareth: What He Wanted, Who He Was*. Collegeville: Liturgical Press.
Lovinfosse, M. de and Emmanuel Durand. 2021. *Naître et devenir: La vie conversante de Jésus selon Matthieu*. Paris: Cerf.
Tanner, Kathryn. 2010. *Christ the Key*. Cambridge: Cambridge University Press.
Volf, Miroslav and Ryan McAnnally-Linz. 2022. *The Home of God: A Brief Story of Everything*. Grand Rapids: Brazos Press.
Williams, Rowan. 2018. *Christ the Heart of Creation*. London: Bloomsbury Continuum.

## 16 The History of Jesus in Biblical Scholarship
JAMES CARLETON PAGET

Albert Schweitzer published the most influential account of the scholarly quest for the Jesus of history (1905; 2nd ed. 1913). This book, whose German title was mistranslated as *The Quest of the Historical Jesus*, created an arresting but strikingly subjective narrative, which made his own solution to the problem appear as the natural end of the story.[1] This Alsatian scholar represents, in an exaggerated form, the difficulties of writing a historiography of the subject of this chapter.

In what follows I shall write a narrative, too. Inevitably, it will be impressionistic. My aims will be more prosaic than Schweitzer's, namely to give a sense of some of the main fault lines in the history of research, highlighting continuities and discontinuities, and asking questions about progress in study and the extent to which the study has a meaningful future.

### A NARRATIVE: THE PROBLEM OF DEFINITION AND A BEGINNING

Any narrative of the 'Quest' immediately confronts two interconnected questions. The first relates to the definition of the term 'historical Jesus'. To many this figure is the Jesus reconstructable on the basis of historical methods, however understood, with whatever remains left over irrelevant. To others it is the Jesus who lived in history, with historical methods deemed helpful but not the exclusive arbiters of what is accepted as 'authentic'. To still others, it is little more than an unattainable construct, a positivistic delusion, best forgotten about. Such definitions encroach on where to begin any narrative about the subject. Schweitzer, reflecting the first definition, began with Hermann Samuel Reimarus's essay 'On the Aims of Jesus and His Followers', published posthumously in 1778. He did so partly because he thought that the

---

[1] See Giambrone 2022.

roots of historical Jesus research lay in anti-dogmatism, which he saw as a motivating factor in Reimarus's account, and partly because he regarded the latter as exemplifying characteristics of what he took to be a 'good' account of Jesus's life. Schweitzer's choice continues to be contested, though it still retains some supporters.[2]

## FROM ANTIQUITY TO THE ENLIGHTENMENT

If, however, one perceives the Quest in terms of an interest in the figure of Jesus as he lived and died (to some extent the second definition), then arguably it was evident from a very early stage.[3] The presence of the Gospels in the New Testament canon is proof of this, however we perceive their authors' concern for historical accuracy or understand the genre of their texts. This concern is similarly exemplified in some of the so-called apocryphal gospels with their desire to fill in gaps in the canonical gospels' narrative of Jesus's life, or give alternative, more definitive accounts. More abstractly, a comparable concern is evident in most Christians' opposition to docetism, a lurking presence from earliest times. That opposition received verbal expression in a variety of definitions of Jesus's person, culminating in Chalcedon, though here an interest in Jesus's life is overshadowed by a concern with his nature (Brown and Evans 2022, 1:92–100).

Absent from the above is evidence of critical engagement with the Gospels as reliable witnesses to Jesus's life. Antiquity hints at such engagement. Papias's comments about the haphazard order of Mark's Gospel (*Hist. eccl.* 3.39.15) imply some critical engagement. Tatian's synthesising account in his Diatessaron can be seen as a response to the discrepancies between the Gospels, as can the creation of Eusebius's so-called canons. If 'critical', however, denotes 'doubting' or 'negative', then this is evidenced from the second century. Examples of such engagement include the pagan Celsus's polemical interpretation of the canonical accounts of Jesus's birth, death, resurrection, miracles and teaching, and his revisionist account of Jesus's life, preserved in Origen's *Against Celsus* (Wilken 1984, 108–12), as well as the third-century Porphyry's even more fragmentarily preserved attack upon the Gospels' historical integrity. The latter especially emphasised the disharmony between the Gospels and was keen to reveal the unreliability of the disciples'

---

[2] On this see Birch 2018. *The Jesus Handbook* (Schröter and Jacobi 2022) begins with 'Antiquity'.
[3] See Brown and Evans 2022, 3–62.

witness to Jesus. Augustine's lengthy *De consensu evangelistarum* was partly a response to Porphyry's criticisms (Wilken 1984, 144–47).

In medieval Christian Europe less interest was shown in defending or attacking the Gospels from a historical perspective.[4] The *Toledoth Yeshu*, a satirical and polemical retelling of the story of Jesus written by Jews, existing in multiple forms, is thought by some to have originated in this period, though it elicited no straightforward refutation. Continuing a tradition found in the apocryphal gospels, some Christians concentrated on elaborating the content of the Gospels in poetry and prose, mainly for the purposes of Christian instruction;[5] and many gospel harmonies were produced. The Renaissance's growing concern with linguistic and textual study, classically exemplified in Lorenzo Valla's study of the Vulgate, Erasmus's edition of the Greek New Testament and an ever-increasing interest in Hebraica, offered initial stimuli to the more technical study of biblical documents. Similar concern emerges in the Reformers' interest in the writing of biblical harmonies, now with the innovative use of parallel columns (Mercator 1592), which allowed the reader better to evaluate both the discrepancies between the gospel accounts and the proposed solutions of the harmonists.

The increased interest in Hebraica, especially in rabbinical commentaries and other ancient Jewish writings, also produced a growing sense of the importance of such works for the study of the Gospels. Sebastian Münster, for instance, who was Professor of Hebrew and Theology at the University of Basle from 1528 to 1553, wrote a commentary on Matthew's Gospel (1537) which assumed that the world from which Jesus emerged was best understood as Jewish and so justified use of such rabbinical texts. While Münster and others did not question the historicity of the Gospels, their work assumed the historically contextualised nature of Jesus and his followers.

From this same period, significance has been attached to aspects of the so-called Radical Reformation, especially in the growth of anti-Trinitarianism and forms of Unitarianism.[6] The individuals associated with these movements, like Servetus (1511–53), while placing an emphasis on Jesus as human and hence implying certain things about his identity, did not question the veracity of Scripture. They simply argued that 'an anti-trinitarian Christology represented a more accurate reading of the Gospels' (Birch 2018, 30).

---

[4] See Pals 1982, 6–7. Also see Schröter and Jacobi 2022, 24–25.
[5] See Pals 1982, 7.
[6] See Brown and Evans 2022, 123–26.

It is probably in the seventeenth century that the major seeds of the modern study of the historical Jesus are found. Different factors account for this. Some have to do with a growing conviction among a minority of Christians that the Bible's witness to truth could not be sustained by an appeal to revelation but rather to reason. Anything that smacked of the miraculous or the particular was suspect. The growth of scepticism informed this together with an increasing sense of the importance of scientific explanation; and further stimulus may have come from a deep discontent with established religion caused by the wars of the mid seventeenth century.

Out of this atmosphere emerged the English deists, including John Toland (1670–1722), Anthony Collins (1676–1729), Thomas Woolston (1670–1731) and Matthew Tindal (1655–1733). They influenced thinking both in Germany and in the United States. While these individuals never produced lives of Jesus and rarely indulged in source or literary criticism, they sowed the seeds of much subsequent historical Jesus research in their conviction that the Jesus of the Gospels who performed miracles, rose from the dead and was central to the subject of Old Testament revelation was a figment of the imagination and was to be replaced by a Jesus who preached a warm-hearted, universal morality (Brown 1984, 36–55, esp. 50–55, see also 183–235; Brown and Evans 2022, 1:184–235). Lingering beneath these ideas and a theme often associated with the seventeenth and eighteenth centuries, but rooted in antiquity, is the idea of 'religious imposture', namely that deceit lay at the root of some religions (Birch 2018, 36–41).

Against this background, Reimarus's essay on the aims of Jesus and his disciples should not be viewed as the novelty Schweitzer claimed it to be. Reimarus (1694–1768) was familiar with the work of the English deists, had travelled in England and had access to a library full of their writings. For Reimarus, central to Jesus's ministry was the preaching of the kingdom of God, a kingdom which, when viewed in an appropriately Jewish context, was political in character. Jesus had messianic pretensions and saw himself as a future king of this new kingdom. His failure to bring this into being in a revolution led to his death, and it was only thanks to his disciples, who turned him into a universal saviour due to return in glory, that Christianity came into being. Many of the assumptions reflected in Reimarus's essay (a scepticism about the possibility of miracle; a rejection of the view that Jesus could be seen as in some sense a fulfilment of Scripture; an accompanying tendency to see him in purely human terms and to emphasise the moral nature of his message; the claim that his views differed from those of his followers; and a robustly sceptical view of the resurrection) were witnessed elsewhere and in that sense his work could be considered as synthetic (Birch 2018, 46). What marks him out is that 'he went beyond the English Deists in developing a comprehensive alternative account of the origins of Christianity' (Brown and Evans 2022, 221–23).

## THE NINETEENTH AND EARLY TWENTIETH CENTURIES

The posthumous publication of this and other essays inspired fierce responses. Johann Salomo Semler (1725–91), while accepting the imperfect character of the Gospels' witness to Christ, challenged Reimarus's view of Jesus and especially his attribution to Jesus of a 'this-worldly' view of the kingdom of God. It was Gotthold Ephraim Lessing (1729–81) who published Reimarus's *Fragments*; and although critical of aspects of his reconstruction, he endorsed Reimarus's essentially human view of Jesus, describing John's Christology as without historical basis (Brown 1984, 16–29). Others, like Heinrich Eberhard Paulus (1761–1851), sought to soften the impact of Reimarus by arguing for the veracity of the accounts of the miracles of Jesus, contending that they gave evidence of natural events which had been falsely but sincerely understood as miraculous. Friedrich Schleiermacher (1768–1834), more on theoretical than historical grounds, sought to defend a form of orthodox Christology by concentrating upon Jesus's God-consciousness as the key to presenting a Christology acceptable to the modern age.

Semler, Paulus and Schleiermacher represented mediating theologies, in which a variety of truces were negotiated between scientific study (*Wissenschaft*) on the one hand and traditional belief (*Glaube*) on the other. Such negotiations seemed to be terminated by David Friedrich Strauss's (1808–74) *Life of Jesus Critically Examined*, whose first edition was published in 1835. For Strauss, gospel criticism had reached an impasse. While rejecting the supernaturalist defences of the Gospels, he also attacked those like Paulus who sought to explain the miracles naturalistically, and like Schleiermacher who argued for a Christology which he thought was philosophically meaningless. For Strauss, the Gospels were dominated by an idea, namely the messianic identity of Jesus, and the disciples' acceptance of the truth of this idea had led them unconsciously to voice that conviction by constructing what Strauss saw as mythological stories about Jesus. What emerged after Strauss had done his work was a messianic pretender who bore no relationship to his dogmatic successor (see Strauss 1972: 296). Strauss's Hegelian attempt to derive something theologically positive from this account was unacceptable to mediating theologians, let alone the orthodox: he offered an idea, the God-man, which pointed to a possibility realisable in all humans but bore no substantive relationship to the figure who had by chance been its originator.

Strauss's book, which sparked a remarkable controversy, was notable not only for the thoroughgoing way it went about presenting its case but also for its total rejection of John's Gospel as a historical source. Perhaps more importantly, Strauss made it clear that scholarship and faith were at daggers drawn.

Those who followed Strauss adopted a variety of approaches. Some embraced a form of Straussian scepticism.[7] Others were less pessimistic and wrote lives of Jesus that were humanistic in content and sought to recreate Jesus's mental and social outlook.[8] Still others turned their attention to an examination of the Gospels themselves, either to identify their tendencies and give them their place in a preconceived understanding of the development of Christianity or to try and establish the literary relationship between them.[9] By the 1860s one could begin to talk about an emerging consensus on this matter in which Mark was seen as the first gospel – and to some, therefore, as the most historically reliable text for reconstructing the life of Jesus.

A group of scholars with liberal theological inclinations emerged during this period. Reflecting the German idealist tradition, their accounts of Jesus's life emphasised his teaching (Hurth 1988, 93–94). Underpinning all of this was a type of historical metaphysics that saw history as the realm in which God revealed himself and human personality as the ultimate domain of revelation (Kloppenborg 2022, 51–52). The tendency in such writing was to emphasise the universal in Jesus's ministry and to see him as a figure whose essential nature stood in contrast to the Jewish culture from which he came, which at best appeared as a husk. Adolf von Harnack's (1851–1930) popular lectures, given in Berlin in 1900, *The Essence of Christianity*, expressed some of these assumptions.

The idea, however, that the work of these theological liberals constituted an agreed consensus is wrong. British and American scholars, for a variety of reasons, though less influential than their German contemporaries,[10] could be seen to resist the broadly sceptical attitude

---

[7] See Bauer 1851–52, who denied the existence of Jesus.
[8] See Renan 1863 and the discussion of its importance in Pals 1982, 32–39.
[9] Note esp. Ferdinand Christian Baur's introduction of the idea of *Tendenzkritik*. See Bauspiess 2017, 185–89.
[10] For explanations as to why this was the case see Pals 1982, 125–63.

to the Gospels' content, exemplified in aspects of German scholarship; and they were more willing to argue for the compatibility of Christian orthodox claims and historical research.[11] In Germany itself, Harnack and Bousset came under heavy attack from German Jewish scholars who objected to the way in which they treated Judaism in their discussions,[12] arguing instead that all aspects of Jesus's life betrayed his Jewish identity. Johannes Weiss (1863–1914) indirectly developed these arguments by insisting that Jesus's proclamation of the kingdom should be understood in a clearly material and Jewish sense as an expectation that God would act directly on behalf of his people in the immediate future (Weiss 1971). Weiss's thesis contradicted the commonly held view, associated especially with his father-in-law Albrecht Ritschl (1822–89), that Jesus's understanding of the kingdom of God was ethical in content. His conclusions were vigorously adopted by Albert Schweitzer, first in a short publication of 1901 and then in his *Quest* of 1906 (2nd ed., 1913), where he arranged the history of research in such a way as to appear its natural end point, maintaining that a proper view of the historiography left one with a position that was either absolutely sceptical, here referring to William Wrede's important work of 1901 on the messianic secret, which strongly questioned the historical value of the first written gospel, or absolutely eschatological. More significant was the alienating picture Schweitzer drew of Jesus ('He will be to our age an enigma and a stranger', Schweitzer 2000: 479). More than Weiss, Schweitzer articulated the difficulty which a historical/eschatological view of Jesus presented to a readership keen to appropriate his 'personality' for their time, not least the authors of the texts Schweitzer called the liberal lives, whose views he attacked but partially reflected.[13]

Some pushed back against the idea of the historical Jesus. It was argued that Jesus did not exist at all, a position which had been espoused probably in the eighteenth century but came to prominence in the first decade of the twentieth.[14] This could seem like a natural conclusion arising out of the overwhelming scepticism of some about the historical

[11] Pals 1982. He notes that some British scholars did write more sceptical lives, but these accounts were normally derivative and rarely influential in the way that their more conservative alternatives were.
[12] For Jewish critics of early twentieth-century Protestant representations of Judaism and Jesus as a Jew, see Wiese 2004, 159–215, here citing in particular the work of, inter alios, Moritz Güdemann, Leo Baeck, and Fritz Perles.
[13] In the end Schweitzer's own appropriation of Jesus bears the hallmarks of a liberal hermeneutic as he invokes the eternal relevance of Jesus's will.
[14] Meggitt 2019. See works by John M. Robertson and Arthur Drews, discussed by Weaver 1999, 49–62. Drews's book caused a very public controversy.

value of the Gospels. If, as Otto Schmiedel claimed, only ten sayings in the gospel tradition went back to Jesus, then there was a sense in which he might as well not have existed. Others undermined the quest from a theological angle. Martin Kähler (1835–1912) argued that the Gospels did not consciously distinguish the preached Jesus from the historical one, making the sifting of fact from fancy a subjective task, and its end result a fifth gospel that had more to do with the interpreter than the truth. Rudolf Bultmann (1884–1976) took up elements of Kähler's view in his own form-critical studies of the Gospels. Clear that the kerygmatic or proclaimed Jesus was primary in the concerns of the church, he argued that the Synoptic Gospels consisted of individual pericopes, which more often than not in their present form addressed the concerns of the developing church and betrayed little interest in Jesus as he lived in Palestine. This led to his oft-quoted but sometimes misunderstood claim that 'we can know almost nothing about the life and personality of Christ' (Bultmann 1934, 8), which to some seemed the natural consequence of form criticism.

### From 1940 to the So-Called Third Quest

Bultmann's views, which reflected a theological atmosphere in German-speaking lands, exemplified in the neo-orthodoxy of Karl Barth, were not universally accepted; and those who claim that, inspired by the assumptions of form criticism, this was an era of 'No Quest' have failed to take account of the situation in Anglophonic lands in particular, where greater confidence in the gospel accounts prevailed and where lives of Jesus continued to be written.[15] The view that an article by Ernst Käsemann, written in 1953, which argued that historical knowledge about Jesus was essential and requisite, marked the beginning of a 'new quest' has been overdone perhaps because Käsemann was Bultmann's student, so that within a circumscribed context the claims of his essay appeared striking.[16]

A feature of the so-called new quest (a tepid and theologically informed engagement with the historical Jesus, which was critical of Bultmann's scepticism but reflected it at the same time – those who accepted Käsemann's objections to Bultmann, including Käsemann himself, hardly set about detailed reconstructions of Jesus's life), now largely

---

[15] See Weaver 1999. Allison 2005 lists many books written about Jesus in the 1920s, 1930s and 1940s.
[16] See Allison 2005.

discredited as a self-contained period of study,[17] was the appearance of detailed discussion of criteria for the establishment of historically reliable material in the Gospels. Such criteria, implicitly or explicitly, had always existed; but now the pursuit of the subject was more self-conscious.[18] Significant amongst them were the criteria of embarrassment (e.g. of more developed Christian beliefs), multiple attestation and double dissimilarity. The last of these asserted that a statement attributed to Jesus in the Gospels is genuine if it has no parallels either in the Judaism from which Jesus hailed or in subsequent Christian traditions. This criterion summarised two contested tendencies in the developing tradition of historical Jesus research. The first was a scepticism about the extent to which the church and Jesus were in any kind of continuity. Even before Reimarus, the view that the church misrepresented the 'real' Jesus existed (note what we have said about the theory of imposture). The second tendency lay in the view that genuine traditions about Jesus would be marked by what distinguished him from the Judaism out of which he emerged. This reflected the view, already mentioned, that what was important about Jesus's personality was what stood in contrast to Judaism. That assumption reached its sad crescendo in the claim that Jesus was not an ethnic Jew at all, which was argued for especially in the Nazi period by Gerhard Kittel and Walter Grundmann in particular.[19]

Assumptions associated with dissimilarity were seriously modified from the late 1970s in a period sometimes given the title 'Third Quest', following N. T. Wright. Quoting Joseph Klausner almost sixty years before, E. P. Sanders argued in 1984 that a good solution to the problem of the historical Jesus needed to show how Jesus lived totally within Judaism but was the origin of a movement which separated from it.[20] Wright, operating with different assumptions from Sanders, could voice similar convictions in his influential publication of 1996. Books which invoked Jesus's Jewish identity proliferated in the period and the criterion of dissimilarity was especially criticised. Apparent affirmation of Jesus's Jewish character led to a return, admittedly in different forms, to a vision of Jesus as influenced heavily by eschatology and a tendency to play down presentations of him as an opponent of Jewish law. Dissimilarity was modified by the criterion of plausibility, which

---

[17] See, for instance the appearance of books by Oscar Cullmann, Ferdinand Hahn and Reginald H. Fuller, all of which would not comport to a 'new quest' definition.
[18] Perrin 1967.
[19] See Heschel 2008 for detailed discussion.
[20] Sanders 1985, 3.

claimed that accounts of Jesus's ministry should make sense within his own Jewish setting. Elements of this approach were stimulated by the discovery of the Dead Sea Scrolls and their ongoing publication, though the extent to which the Holocaust was influential has been exaggerated in accounts of this apparent shift in attitude.[21]

The move to an apparently more conservative view of the gospel tradition, thought by some to be a characteristic of the Third Quest, was questioned by the Jesus Seminar, with its highly sceptical view of the gospel tradition and its strong alignment to a Jesus compatible with a reconstructed Q tradition and sections of the apocryphal gospels, including the Gospel of Thomas. The seminar was founded in 1985, reached public prominence in the United States in the 1990s, but had come to be seen as a spent force in the early 2000s and was dissolved in 2006 on the death of its founder, Robert Funk.[22]

The Third Quest was associated with other characteristics, including a commitment to a so-called non-theological approach. For some, however, it is an unhelpful and artificial construction. It is allied to a periodisation of Jesus research which no longer seems sustainable, assuming some kind of a break from what preceded, when the era betrays more continuities with the latter;[23] it can seem triumphalist, reflecting what Allison has called "chronological snobbery";[24] and it appears deceptively homogenising where in truth the field of historical Jesus studies remains as disparate as it ever did.

## SINCE 2000

The subject of historical Jesus studies seems as lively as ever if weight of publication is considered. A recent bibliography demonstrates this;[25] and the proliferation of handbooks and new dictionaries indicates a

---

[21] See Crossley 2013 for relevant literature. He attributes more significance to international events like the Six Day War showing that the Holocaust proliferated as a topic of discussion in the United States after 1967.

[22] Meier 1999, 459, places the Jesus Seminar within the Third Quest whereas Wright puts it in the New Quest (Wright 1996, 28–82).

[23] The issue of Jesus's Jewish identity is an example. Note how, from an earlier period, Weiss and Schweitzer reflect a Jewish Jesus, how Jewish scholars critical of Protestant representations of Judaism at the beginning of the twentieth century emphasized Jesus's Jewish origins. Other significant authors who emphasized Jesus's Jewish origins before the 'Third Quest' include Klausner as well as Vermes 1973. Allison 2005 is right to note an intensification of interest but right to reject a temporal break into a Third Quest on this basis.

[24] See Allison 2005, 14.

[25] Massey 2023, 76, notes 1,200 publications since 2000.

persistent need to update.[26] During the same period a new journal, *The Journal for the Study of the Historical Jesus*, has appeared, even a brief review of whose pages shows the diverse character of study and the difficulty of discerning patterns.

Scholars have become more concerned with the back story of the Quest. This can manifest itself in meta-criticism of the subject revealing, for instance, the way that issues such as nationalism have affected the way the subject has been studied.[27] This approach is consistent with the work of liberation or feminist theologians, who for some time have revealed problematic assumptions underlying conventional historical approaches (Schüssler Fiorenza 2000). Similarly beholden to a meta-critical analysis are attempts to argue for a more self-consciously theological approach, a movement away from the metaphysics, as one scholar has it, of secularism, to a differently conceived metaphysics, or one that takes more seriously the relationship between systematic theology and historical study.[28] The latter reflects tendencies in study since Kähler, which to some are unappealing but to others understandable.

Another feature of more recent work has been the perfervid questioning of the criteria, not only on technical grounds (such concerns preceded this period)[29] but on the basis of a critique of the assumptions undergirding them, namely a desire to get back behind the texts to a Jesus who is somehow independent of the texts of which he is a part – an aim, it is claimed, which is impossible. Much of what is written in this context is dependent upon more recent engagement with ideas about memory and in particular social memory, as this has been developed by Jan Assmann. Here the idea that all recording of the past 'is woven into the fabric of the present',[30] and so all history is remembered history, has led to the view that the aim of historical Jesus studies is to explain imaginatively the origins of the Gospels rather than seeing them as allowing access to a reconstructable reality behind them.[31] Others, citing similar work on the frailty of human memory, have invoked the idea of gist, emphasising the identification of recurrent themes (what Allison has termed 'recurrent attestation') in the Gospels and elucidating these against the Judaism of which Jesus was a part and the church

---

[26] See Holmen and Porter 2011; and Schröter and Jacobi 2022.
[27] See Moxnes 2011.
[28] See Rowlands 2023; Giambrone 2022.
[29] See Hooker 1971.
[30] Bond 2020, xviii, quoting Assmann.
[31] For further discussion with a short bibliography see Schröter 2022, 108–20.

which emerged from him.[32] In this context there is a reconceived sense of being able to create a portrait of Jesus rather than simply the social reality which created the text. Such conclusions have been opposed and the appeal of that opposition can be seen in the success of Richard Bauckham's (2006; 2nd ed., 2017) book on Jesus and the eyewitnesses, which takes a more conservative view of the issue of memory and the transmission of tradition, itself emerging from earlier work on memory by Scandinavian scholars such as Birger Gerhardsson.

Emphasis on memory has led to more interest in the idea of reception. The latter is partially invoked to make the interpreter aware of the tradition of interpretation through which they view the historical Jesus as well as the way in which the originating events of the Jesus tradition have acted as catalysts for multiple interpretations. The way reception relates directly to the issue of historical reconstruction is less clear, with some seeking to distinguish between effects and reception.[33]

Jesus's place within Judaism continues to exercise critics. Some emphasise the extent to which this discussion constitutes an advance on earlier periods of discussion.[34] Others question this view,[35] arguing, as already noted, that Judaism has always been a part of the discussion.[36] Others question the agenda behind the debate, arguing that it is often freighted by a set of Christian assumptions in which Jesus is often portrayed as transcending or going beyond or intensifying Judaism.[37] The difficulty lies in the fact that many of those who study the historical Jesus are Christians and see Jesus as a universal figure, transcending issues of race and context, though some have sought to show how the issue of Jesus's ethnic specificity is compatible with a conventional Christian theology. Also contributory is the view already alluded to, that any good solution to the problem of the historical Jesus should situate him within Judaism and explain why the movement associated with him became a separate entity. This could be said to encourage the phenomenon James Crossley and others criticise, namely a focus on the originality of Jesus.

---

[32] Allison 2010, 1–30.
[33] See Schröter and Jacobi 2022, 487–89. Also Bond 2020.
[34] See Evans 2006 as an example of a much-repeated nostrum.
[35] See Crossley 2013, 109, n. 1, for relevant bibliography.
[36] See Bermejo Rubio 2009.
[37] Crossley 2013, 116. He characterizes this Jesus as 'a Jewish, but not that Jewish Jesus' (117).

Jesus's social setting continues to be a matter of dispute. Some of these discussions have focused on Galilee and the economic and political circumstances of that client kingdom. Others have posited a rebellious Jesus, whose attitude to violence is at best ambivalent. Still others have moved towards a more marxisant interpretation in which Jesus the individual agent of change is played down and his membership, albeit a significant one, of a rural protest movement has come to be seen as more important.[38] This is a debate that has a long pedigree, going back to Reimarus himself and to Albert Kalthoff in the early twentieth century.

In terms of sources, the view that the Gospels best conform to *bioi* (biographies) continues to garner support with some notable contrary voices. The importance of such a conclusion for questions relating to historicity is disputed, however.[39] The hypothesis of a sayings source 'Q' can no longer be regarded as an unstoppable 'juggernaut', with works demanding its abandonment proving influential.[40] The view that apocryphal gospels present material both independent of the Synoptics and historically reliable is in decline when compared with its heyday in the 1980s and 1990s. A growth in interest in John's Gospel as a historical source for Jesus has witnessed a revival, with some talking in this connection about a 'Fourth Quest', but it has not attracted significant support.

Archaeological discoveries pertinent to historical Jesus research have occasionally intruded into public life but rarely are they directly relevant; and if they are, their relevance is disputed or they are thought to be hoaxes.[41] Excavations of pre-70 synagogues in Galilee have supported the previously disputed view that the Galilee of Jesus's time contained synagogues. One thinks of the synagogues at Tel Rekhesh, at Wadi Hamam and at Magdala with its famous stone, a city whose excavations, not yet fully absorbed, potentially elucidate life around the Sea of Galilee at the time of Jesus (Bauckham 2018).

Finally, it is worth noting the ongoing shift of influence in the discussion of the subject from German-speaking lands to Anglophonic ones, in particular the United States. That is not to say that German scholars do not continue to play a part, but the era in which the latter initiated and dominated the debates to which English-speaking scholars largely responded has disappeared.

---

[38] Crossley and Myles 2023.
[39] Bond 2020.
[40] See Goodacre 2002.
[41] See esp. the ossuaries discovered at the Talpiot tomb and the so-called James ossuary.

## PROGRESS?

It is tempting to think that one's own time is marked by striking sagacity. This is foolhardy, for, if anything, a review of this kind reveals the instability of any conclusions arrived at within the field as well as the continuities which exist between different eras of research, further undercutting a tendency to periodise that history.

Some persist, however, in arguing for progress. They locate this in the Jesus and Judaism debate, where both the more recent intensification of the discussion and the manner in which it has been conducted when compared to a previous era seem striking.[42] But where precisely do we locate progress in this discussion? Is the progress moral or historical, especially when the conclusions are so various? Indeed, should the subject even be problematised in the way it often is? Others might argue that there is more information than there once was; but even if that were true, questions remain about how such 'new' information should be digested. Progress in the humanities is more difficult to gauge than it is in the so-called hard sciences; and so trying to quantify progress in the 'quest' can seem futile.

Against this background, some see the field as stagnant and demand 'The Next Quest for the Historical Jesus'.[43] In such a revisionist agenda the emphasis will be upon social histories of scholarship; a less individualised view of Jesus, seen in in an abandonment of the 'backward-looking' idea of Jesus as a 'great man' of history with more emphasis being placed upon him as a part of a movement based in agrarian Galilee; upon an abandonment of the criteria with greater emphasis on explaining why certain traditions about Jesus ended up in the Gospels; upon a newly conceived vision of the Jewishness of Jesus with an emphasis upon what it meant to be Jewish in the ancient world rather than an obsessive concern on 'who was and who was not a proper Jew'; and upon class, slavery, ethnicity, gender and sexuality and reception history. It is difficult to know how many will assent to this vision of the Quest or what it will look like. Some will see it as too pessimistic, regretting its movement away from a focus on Jesus who is an agent to an emphasis on the setting and the movement that produced the Gospels. Others, by contrast, will see this as a realistic and fresh vision. Such diversity will reflect the variant groups who study the subject.

---

[42] Evans 2006.
[43] See *JSHJ* 19 (2021) 'Editorial', 261.

It is difficult, then, to point to any clear consensus in the study of the Quest, even as this relates to what its subject of study should be. Scholars pursue the subject for different reasons and with variant aims in sight, not least because their assumptions differ considerably. The canonical gospel writers presented narratives of Jesus's life, which, except for Mark, included resurrection accounts; but with some notable exceptions, many participants in a quest of the historical Jesus avoid discussion of the post-crucifixion Jesus; and yet without the latter, no discussion of Jesus's life would be merited. Such a paradox, often justified by reference to the secular assumptions of any historical research, may seem strange to some, not least a public who continue to show interest in the figure of Jesus from a variety of perspectives, which often do not chime with the concerns of the scholarly guild.[44] For many different audiences, including, of course, the polychrome Christian community, the historical Jesus remains actual and alive; and they ensure, to some extent, the perennial interest in the subject. Conclusions, as this review has shown, are inevitably provisional and should be taken to encourage an appropriate modesty among scholars intent upon pursuing the 'Quest'.

## FURTHER READING

Allison, Dale C. 2010. *Constructing Jesus: Memory, Imagination, and History*. Grand Rapids: Baker Academic.
Bauckham, Richard. 2017. *Jesus and the Eyewitnesses*. 2nd ed. Grand Rapids: Eerdmans.
Bermejo-Rubio, Fernando 2009. 'The Fiction of the "Three Quests": An Argument for Dismantling a Dubious Historiographical Paradigm.' *JSHJ* 7: 211–53.
Brown, Colin, with Craig A. Evans. 2022. *A History of the Quests for the Historical Jesus*. 2 vols. Grand Rapids: Zondervan Academic.
Käsemann, Ernst. 1964. 'The Problem of the Historical Jesus.' In *Essays on New Testament Themes*, 15–47. London: SCM.
Keith, Chris and Anthony Le Donne, eds. 2013. *Jesus, Criteria, and the Demise of Authenticity*. London: T&T Clark.
Keith, Chris et al., eds. 2020. *The Reception of Jesus in the First Three Centuries*. 3 vols. London: T & T Clark.

---

[44] As an example, when Simon Gathercole published an article in *The Guardian* on 14 April 2017 (Good Friday) refuting the idea of Jesus's non-existence, it generated well over a million views in four days. For discussion of the need to respond to interest in this matter, see Meggitt 2019 in critique of scholars who dismiss the debate as unworthy of their attention.

Meggitt, Justin. 2023. "Putting the Apocalyptic Jesus to the Sword: Why Were Jesus's Disciples Armed?" *JSNT* 45: 371–404.

Pals, Daniel L. 1982. *The Victorian Lives of Jesus*. San Antonio: Trinity University Press.

Sanders, E. P. 1985. *Jesus and Judaism*. London: SCM/Fortress.

Schröter, Jens and Christine Jacobi. 2022. *The Jesus Handbook*. Eerdmans: Grand Rapids.

Schüssler-Fiorenza, Elisabeth. 2000. *Jesus and the Politics of Interpretation*. New York: Continuum.

Schweitzer, Albert. 2000. *The Quest of the Historical Jesus*. London: SCM.

Theissen, Gerd and Merz, Annette. 1998. *The Historical Jesus: A Comprehensive Guide*. London: SCM.

Weaver, Walter. 1999. *The Historical Jesus in the Twentieth Century: 1900–1950*. Harrisburg: Trinity Press International.

**Part IV**
*The Global Jesus Today*

## 17 The Jewish Jesus in Christian and in Jewish Memory

BARBARA U. MEYER

Christians and Jews have always known that Jesus was Jewish. At the same time, historians continue to study Jesus within Second Temple Judaism and theologians discover new meanings to his being Jewish. Especially since the age of the Enlightenment, Jewish and Christian Bible scholars have reminded each other of Jesus's Jewish belonging, with varying objectives. The contemporary history of remembering Jesus's Jewishness offers a fascinating angle from which to study Christian–Jewish relations up through the present. Jewish scholars since the seventeenth century have highlighted this memory in order to deflect anti-Semitism and to criticize gospel exegesis projecting Christian superiority. It took several centuries until Christians began to understand this criticism as a helpful corrective to their own scholarship. Only recently have Christian scholars begun to understand the memory of Jesus's Jewishness as a significant resource for rethinking historical research, exegetical methodology, and even dogmatic discourse.

### HISTORY AND MEMORY IN HISTORICAL JESUS RESEARCH

Calling the deep knowledge of Jesus's Jewishness "memory" helps to distinguish it from history and thus to clarify its prospects and capacities. By no means is this memory meant to undermine the search for historical truth. In fact, with both Historical Jesus research and New Testament exegesis, the opposite has proved true: Memory has facilitated critical analysis of a body of historical research that understood itself as scientific but often fell into the anachronistic traps of reconstructing history according to later outcomes. One key example is the emergence of Christianity as a religion distinguished from Judaism. This eventual historical emergence cannot serve as an argument for Jesus himself having transcended, let alone rejected, his Jewish heritage during his lifetime. Here, more accurate memory has helped scientific research to cut through layers of ahistorical readings. Thus, the memory of the Jewish Jesus has become a critical tool not only in the search for the Historical Jesus but also for rewriting the history of Jewish–Christian relations, and especially the so-called parting of the ways, the emergence of Judaism and Christianity as distinct religions that occurred over centuries.

### THE JEWISH JESUS AS A TEXTUAL MEMORY

Christian as well as Jewish scholars know of Jesus the Jew from the New Testament, mainly from the texts of the four gospels. Some Christian and most Jewish scholars are also acquainted with the much later rabbinic polemic texts summarized as the *Toledot Yeshu* tradition that attests to an intra-Jewish transmitted knowledge of Jesus's Jewishness. As numerous exegetes have pointed out, the four gospels' portraits of Jesus are themselves the product of memory. The gospels' texts are based on Jewish oral transmission, as the words of Jesus were first remembered by his contemporary Jewish followers. While some of Jesus's words, sayings, or even parables may have been reliably transmitted, their compositions are the memory work of editors and redactors belonging to the early communities of Jesus followers in the 70s and 80s of the first century. Their knowledge of the Jewish Jesus is fresh: His being Jewish is neither explicitly mentioned nor explained because it is taken for granted. It is not denied or argued about, not requiring either defense or explanation. Instead, his Jewishness is expressed in his sayings, the topics of dialogues, settings of parables, biblical quotes, and intertextuality. All later Christian memories of Jesus the Jew rely on the gospel texts, and reminders of Jesus's Jewishness will go back to these early memories when the entirety of the Jesus story was Jewish: Jesus himself, his family, friends, and first followers. Thus, from a textual perspective, the Christian memory of the Jewish Jesus is inherently bound to Jewish memory. Historically, almost all of Jesus's ethnic, cultural, and religious surrounding was Jewish – but ethnicity, culture, and religion have proven inadequate historical categories. With regard to the term "Jewish," I suggest a text-based approach to describe the scope of its meaning in relation to Jesus and his people: "Jewish" at Jesus's time means to know key narrative and legal texts of the Torah and the prophets, to inhabit central stories, to practice core commandments, and to continue their transmission. This text-based description, not definition, of Judaism is recognizable up until the present, while by no means limiting potential expressions of Jewishness (Meyer 2020).

The historical fact of Jesus's Jewishness is transmitted textually, and New Testament texts are not composed with the intention of providing factual evidence. The category of memory provides a framework to discuss a text-based fact with a complex interpretational tradition. Methodologically, memory offers a perspective that takes both history and textual transmission into account.

**When the Text Does Not Say "the Jewish Jesus"**
The Jewishness of Jesus is a textual memory rarely made explicit: Jesus is almost never described with the adjective "Jewish," nor does any gospel text ever speak of "Jesus, the Jew." Instead, the Synoptic Gospels introduce Jesus as a Jew by telling his story in the textual horizon of the Pentateuch, the Prophets, and the Psalms, and in the historical setting of the late Second Temple period. The Gospels name major sects and professions of Second Temple Judaism, the Sadducees and the Pharisees, scribes and lawyers, without additionally describing those as Jewish. But in the gospel setting everybody is Jewish unless otherwise explicitly stated, as for example in the case of the Canaanite woman (Matt 15:21–28 par. Mark 7:24–30). Adding to the confusion, and eventually fueling anti-Semitism, the term "Jews" is mentioned for the alleged opponents of Jesus in the passion narrative, mainly in its latest version in the Gospel according to John. The combination of making explicit the Jewishness of Jesus's opponents while mostly taking for granted the Jewishness of Jesus himself and of his followers led to a toxic Christian interpretational tradition. The twofold distorted documentation has produced a venomous retention of animosity toward Jews, in which opposition to Jesus is recalled as Jewish while his own Jewishness is only implied and thus clouded. Textually, this process of blurring Jesus's Jewishness by explicitly introducing his opponents as Jews begins in the passion narrative of the New Testament text itself.

**The Memory of Jesus and the Pharisees**
The other major placeholders for Jewishness in the gospel texts are the Pharisees. The Christian interpretational history of the name of this sect will be triple-twisted. The New Testament name for this segment of Second Temple Judaism is historically accurate. But in the Christian interpretational tradition, the word "Pharisees" will become a derogatory epithet rather than simply the name of a group. In many gospel dialogues, the Pharisees are depicted as malevolent interlocutors of Jesus. An additional negative attribution, hypocrisy, also takes root already in gospel texts. It came to be the main connotation for a metaphorical use of the word "Pharisees" in a number of Western languages.

Remarkably, in a decidedly non-Christian context such as Israeli academia, students are not aware of the negative coloration of the term. In contrast, the Pharisees, as the dominant sect to continue and revitalize Jewish life after the destruction of the Second Temple, are credited with the foundation of rabbinic Judaism. In this perspective, the Pharisees are the Jews who serve as a bridge between the Jew Jesus and Jews today. In Second Temple Judaism as well as in the New Testament texts, both Jesus and the Pharisees are clearly Jewish but not explicitly named as Jewish. In terms of memory studies, my thesis is that in the Christian interpretational tradition, the Pharisees' and Jesus's Jewishness will fade or intensify in inverse correlation to each other. While Jesus's Jewishness will often be diminished exegetically, Pharisees will eventually stand for Jews who remain Jews. The Pharisees of the gospel narrative do not join the Jesus group, and Christian readers of the New Testament text will not identify with them. Anachronistic readings of disputes between Jesus and the Pharisees will attribute a "Christian" ethics to Jesus and "Jewish" jurisprudence to the Pharisees.

Here, too, rarely noting Jesus as Jewish in the New Testament text enables a strange twist of Jesus's Jewishness being blurred while another contemporaneous group becomes emblematic of an undiminished Jewishness. We will see how the Jewish counter-memory of Jesus as a Pharisee will play a powerful role in the Jewish–Christian dynamics of remembering the Jewish Jesus.

### The Synoptic Memory of the Jewish Jesus

The most striking indicator for Jesus's Jewishness in the New Testament is his quoting of scriptural legal texts. A synoptic account of Jesus being asked about the most important commandment illustrates how Jesus's belonging to Judaism is expressed, even if he is not called "the Jew Jesus." In the earliest gospel, Mark, Jesus introduces his answer to the question about the greatest commandment with "Hear, O Israel: the Lord our God, the Lord is one" (Mark 12:29; cf. Deut 6:4) – the core Jewish confessional expression until today. In Matthew's synoptic parallel to this episode, Jesus answers the same question by pointing to the God of Israel and identifying Israel as the people commanded to love God. But here in Matthew, as in Luke, both redacted about a decade later than Mark, the words "Hear, O Israel" are dropped. Saying "Hear, O Israel" – in Hebrew *Shma Israel* – unmistakably situates Jesus at the heart of Judaism. The *Shma* is clearly the most striking placeholder for Jesus's Jewishness in the gospel texts, and one may speculate that it was even too striking for the redactor of the Gospel according to Matthew!

## Recalling the Jewish Jesus in the Reformation, the Enlightenment, and the Jewish Reform Movement

At major intersections of European intellectual history, Jews and Christians would employ reminders of the Jewish Jesus, with contrasting objectives. For instance, Christians recall Jesus's Jewishness so as to claim his transcending of it, while Jews do so to demonstrate his historic immersion within Judaism. In European movements for Jewish emancipation, Jesus the Jew served to underscore the validity of Judaism as a respectable religion. As religious rights and diversities were freshly debated in the Protestant Reformation, the Age of Enlightenment, and the Jewish Reform movement, the Jewishness of Jesus became a barometer for Jews' civil rights.

Although the Gospels do not explicitly call Jesus a Jew, the New Testament texts and the Bible as a whole have historically served as the main reminder of Jesus's Jewishness. Thus it is not surprising that a major call to remember Jesus's Jewishness occurred with the Reformation's turn to Scripture. Luther's 1523 sermon "That Jesus Christ Was Born a Jew" was, of course, mainly a missionary effort. The word "born" signals that Jesus's Jewishness was original but could be discontinued or otherwise diminished. Luther's talking of Jesus as a Jew was meant as a missionary gesture toward contemporaneous Jews whom Luther depicted as members of Jesus's family "according to the flesh." Sixteenth-century German Jewry understood this gesture, and in 1537 Josel of Rosheim, the leader of German Jewry, turned to Luther for support against a looming expulsion from Saxony. It would have suited Luther's approach of 1523 to help, but he chose not to. A decade after his unsuccessful attempt to missionize the Jews through persuasion, his stance had changed to pure hostility. Targeting Jews for proselytizing would intensify among later Protestant theologians, both institutionally and individually. The connection between missionary aggression against Jews and awareness of Jesus's Jewishness is an important reminder that the memory of the Jewish Jesus in itself does not offer an automatic prophylactic against Christian anti-Judaism and assertions of spiritual superiority.

Long after the Reformation, the memory of the Jewish Jesus would intensify in the Age of Enlightenment. Christian scholars of the Enlightenment era favored a version of Jesus the ethical teacher over Christ the divine savior. The Jewish Enlightenment philosopher Moses Mendelssohn (1729–86) went a step further: He had a clear understanding of Jesus as observant of Jewish law as early as 1783. In his classic book *Jerusalem, or On Religious Power and Judaism*, he wrote:

Jesus of Nazareth was never heard to say that he had come to release the House of Jacob from the law. Indeed, he said, in express words, rather the opposite; and, what is still more, he himself did the opposite. Jesus of Nazareth himself observed not only the law of Moses but also the ordinances of the rabbis; and whatever seems to contradict this in the speeches and acts ascribed to him appears to do so only at first glance. Closely examined, everything is in complete agreement not only with Scripture, but also with the tradition. If he came to remedy entrenched hypocrisy and sanctimoniousness, he surely would not have given the first example of sanctimoniousness and authorized, by example, a law which should be abrogated and abolished. Rather, the rabbinic principle evidently shines forth from his entire conduct as well as the conduct of his disciples in the early period. *He who is not born into the law need not bind himself to the law; but he who is born into the law must live according to the law, and die according to the law.* If his followers, in later times, thought differently and believed they could release from the law also those Jews who accepted their teaching, this surely happened without his authority.[1]

This late eighteenth-century scholarly analysis of Jesus's observance is remarkable. Mendelssohn notes that Jesus's legal praxis is in compliance with Scripture as well as the rabbinic tradition that began during his lifetime but was committed to writing only about 200 years later in the Mishnah, the first canonization of rabbinic texts and the foundation of the much later Talmud. Almost 200 years after Mendelssohn, David Flusser, an observant Jew and Israeli professor of early Christianity and Second Temple Judaism, affirmed Jesus's observance of contemporaneous Jewish law in detail. The chapter "Law" – translated as "Torah" in the Hebrew translation that appeared only in 2009 – stands at the center of his path-breaking book entitled *Jesus* (Flusser 2001). Mendelssohn had been taken seriously as a philosopher and even labeled the "German Socrates" by his contemporaries, but his analysis of New Testament sources was broadly ignored by the Christian academic world. On the whole, the exegetical insight of Jesus's observance would reach Christian theologians and historians only after a Jewish scholar of New Testament had actually become a university professor, which first happened at the Hebrew University in Jerusalem in the 1960s.

How Jesus's Jewishness is remembered serves as the matrix of Susannah Heschel's intellectual history of nineteenth-century Jewish

---

[1] Mendelssohn 1983, 134 (emphasis in original).

scholarship, *Abraham Geiger and the Jewish Jesus* (Heschel 1998). Her magnum opus about the innovative and erudite Jewish scholar Abraham Geiger (1810–74) cuts through the dynamics of Jewish and Christian religious argumentation at a vital crossroads for Jewish religious renewal. Like Mendelssohn, Geiger's scholarship did not focus on Christianity. Despite his impressive academic writings about rabbinic literature, alongside his extraordinary expertise on the Qur'an and the New Testament, as a Jew he was excluded from obtaining a university professorship. He was a trained rabbi and among the founders of Reform Judaism, eventually holding a post at the Rabbinical College in Berlin. Heschel reports on the outsized anger of Christian scholars about Geiger's scholarship on Jesus's rootedness and immersion in Judaism. Geiger suggested that Jesus belonged to the sect of the Pharisees, a view that would be echoed by a number of Jewish scholars in the twentieth century and continue to be debated in twenty-first-century interreligious historical research (Sievers and Levine 2021). In the nineteenth century, Christian support for the Jewish contextualization of Jesus was rare. Heschel notes the excessive outrage of the Christian Old Testament theologian Franz Delitzsch when Geiger compared Jesus to the famous contemporaneous Jewish sage Hillel. Of course, nineteenth-century Christian exegetes did not agree with Jesus's identification as a Pharisee, whose negative depiction in the Gospels they had thoroughly internalized. But Hillel, traditionally juxtaposed to the "stricter" school of Shamai, stands for kindness. Hillel is the sage who according to Jewish lore epitomized the Torah as loving one's neighbor, and on American college campuses today "Hillel" serves as the name of the students' association that welcomes all Jewish denominations. The anger expressed by Delitzsch and others points to a long-held Christian conviction, that of Jesus's historical uniqueness. It took until the end of the twentieth century to dismantle this approach as ahistorical. In a sharp analysis, the New Testament scholar E. P. Sanders showed that the term "uniqueness" typically implies a claim of superiority. Sanders reminded fellow Christian scholars that the uniqueness of Jesus Christ for Christians is a matter of faith that need not and should not be built on some singular saying of the Historical Jesus (Sanders 1990). It is in fact remarkable that it was not a systematic theologian who made this point but a Christian scholar of the New Testament and the Mishnah. I have myself added to this insight that, from a Christian dogmatic standpoint, validating uniqueness in Jesus's sayings may promote what the church fathers called "dynamism," that is, the view that Jesus became the Son of God on account of his special spiritual powers – rather than having always been the Son of God, which is the patristic view that became dogma (Meyer 2020).

As distinct from Mendelssohn, Geiger openly engaged in a critique of Christianity. Today, many Christian historians would agree with his contextualization of Jesus within Second Temple Judaism. From Jesus's not having, in Geiger's view, said anything original, Geiger concluded that the Christian religion itself lacks originality. This conclusion, however, brings him methodologically close to the opposite Christian anachronistic stance of trying to root the newness of Christianity in the historical Jesus's newness.

### SIDE EFFECTS OF JESUS'S JEWISHNESS DIMINISHED

Biblical scholars from Luther to Delitzsch did not hesitate to call Jesus Jewish. But his Jewishness, in their view, would be in one way or another transcended. A certain "lessening" of Jesus's Jewishness has persisted in Christian New Testament exegesis and the Historical Jesus research until today, with two major lines of argumentation: Jesus's Jewishness is implicitly diminished by describing Jesus as not compliant with Jewish law or else as unique – with his uniqueness not mainly defined by his Jewish heritage. Christian scholars have maintained Jesus's deviance from Jewish law and reinforced his historical uniqueness until the end of the twentieth century. In contrast, Jewish scholars have argued that Jesus complied with contemporaneous Jewish law and often hypothesized his closeness to one or another specific Jewish group, such as the school of Hillel, the Pharisees or more particularly, Second Temple Hasidim.

The claim of Jesus's diminished Jewishness was perpetuated even through the most recent phase of Historical Jesus research, called the "Third Quest," that began in the 1980s. Despite the major effort of Third Quest scholars to contextualize Jesus within Second Temple Judaism, some scholars continued to situate Jesus at the 'margins' of Judaism, with John P. Meier even choosing the title *A Marginal Jew* for his multivolume work (Meier 1991–2016). Yet, in historical perspective, a general situating of Jesus as "marginally Jewish" is not convincing. As an overall declaration, or as the title of a series of books, it sounds like a predicament rather than the result of historical and exegetical research. "Marginally Jewish" as a conclusive attribute hints at a certain lessening of Jewish identity. Situating Jesus at the margins of Judaism builds on an unconvincingly fixed concept of Second Temple Judaism. To claim both that there was one central Judaism and that this central Judaism did not include Jesus seems more like a construct than a conclusion based on historical research. A methodological alternative is presented by Markus Bockmuehl, who seeks to situate Jesus within various halakhic discussions (Bockmuehl 2003).

It is important to note here that a deviant legal opinion does not make a Jew less Jewish. Historically, it is possible that Jesus held a specific legal opinion on a certain matter. That everybody else held the opposite view seems much less probable. If it could be shown that Jesus's various legal opinions fit into a certain halakhic approach, he would fit into the halakhic Judaism of the period no matter how that approach is described. His Jewishness – like Jewishness today – does not intensify or lessen with the adoption of certain legal opinions. Instead, it is expressed by asking halakhic questions and participating in the discussion.

### IMAGINING A JEWISH RECLAMATION OF JESUS

At the beginning of the twentieth century, Christian scholars still focused on the question of the authenticity of certain sayings of Jesus and rarely referred to Jewish scholarship on Jesus. Among Jewish scholars, however, a fresh and lively discussion began about the prospects of a Jewish reclamation of Jesus. In 1924, Joseph Klausner published in Jerusalem the first academic study about Jesus in Hebrew. Written at the same time, but only recently brought to academic attention by Zeev Harvey, is an early text by the great Harvard scholar of religion Harry Austryn Wolfson (1887–1974), one of the first scholars of Jewish Studies to hold an endowed chair at Harvard. Wolfson imagines Jesus as one of the sages, whose real belonging to the Second Temple Jewish world could only be properly recognized in a situation of Jewish cultural autonomy:

> [W]ith the revival of Jewish culture and Jewish learning under free and unhampered conditions in a Jewish environment, painstaking Jewish scholars, in an effort to reorganize and to reclassify our literary treasures, will come to compile anthologies of the wise sayings and inspire teaching of our ancients, they will include among them the sermons and parables of Jesus the Nazarene, the Galilean.

Wolfson focuses on a Jewish reclamation of texts, of sayings transmitted as Jesus's words:

> The readers of those anthologies will pass on from Talmudic and Midrashic selections to those of the Gospels without being conscious of any difference, except of such individual differences as

mark the sayings of men. The sayings of Jesus together with the sayings of other rabbis will win their way into the speech of the people, will become blended and interwoven.

Harvey shows that Wolfson's approach is extraordinary in that he neither criticizes nor praises Jesus. He simply states that his sayings should be recognized as belonging to the Jewish text tradition. There is no comment on Jesus's ethics, as with Joseph Klausner. Most remarkably, and one may add, prophetically, Wolfson imagines Jesus's restoration to the panoply of Jewish thinkers, with neither reproach nor applause, within a context of restored Jewish sovereignty.

Christian scholars, contemporaries of Wolfson, continued to be concerned with Jesus's historicity, the reality of his actual historical existence. In the mid-twentieth century, the debate about Jesus's historicity peaked with a theological statement: The Lutheran New Testament scholar Rudolf Bultmann asserted that what mattered was not if Jesus had actually lived but only that he had been sent by God. This view was meant to project both scientific and religious commitment but was in fact neither historically nor dogmatically adequate. Bultmann's approach resembled docetism, the notion that Jesus had not been a full human being and thus did not really suffer, which was judged a heresy by the church fathers.

In contrast, none of the modern Jewish scholars of Jesus were concerned about his historicity. Geza Vermes and Shmuel Safrai posited that the Hasidim of the Second Temple period were itinerant preachers in the Galilee, without property and with recognized abilities to perform miracles. Since there had been others like him, there was no need to doubt the historicity of Jesus. The Christian theologian Friedrich-Wilhelm Marquardt pointed at this paradox of Jewish scholars expressing greater confidence than Christians regarding the actual historical existence of Jesus (Marquardt 1990). The Pharisees, and especially the Second Temple Hasidim, made Jesus historically imaginable, but Christian scholars did not share this imagination. This changed in the last third of the twentieth century, with Israeli scholarship of Jesus, and with Christian scholars beginning to take Jewish New Testament research seriously. In an extraordinary twist, Jesus's embeddedness in Judaism became the cornerstone of subsequent Historical Jesus research.

### JESUS'S JEWISHNESS IN SYSTEMATIC THEOLOGY

Christian theological reflection upon Jesus's Jewishness began at roughly the same time but long remained at the margins of christological discourse. The Anglican theologian Paul van Buren was among the few systematic theologians to allow Jesus's Jewishness to challenge Christian thought traditions. In line with the title of his Christology, *Christ in Context*, van Buren mostly referred to Jesus as Christ, or Jesus Christ. But it is especially in connection with Jesus's death that van Buren speaks of the Jewish Jesus: "His life was a Jewish life, lived as one of his people. His death was an all-too-typically Jewish death of the time: he was killed by Gentiles. When he died, there was one less Jew in the world."[2] Jesus's Jewish death then becomes important in Paul van Buren's writing about the Shoah – here named "Auschwitz" as was common for critical post-Shoah writing in the late 1980s, consciously avoiding the term "Holocaust" that originated in a language of sacrifice:

> We shall learn to speak of Auschwitz from the perspective of the cross, then, by first learning to speak of the cross from the perspective of Auschwitz. A rule that would appear essential to govern our language in this area is that the death of one Jew, no matter whom or what he was in God's purposes, should not be spoken of as to lessen the significance and the pain of the death of any human being, least of all that of six million other Jews.[3]

Jesus's Jewishness here facilitates a rethinking of redemptive suffering. Notably, van Buren's memory rule is formulated only negatively and does not prescribe a certain or specific interpretation of Jewish suffering as appropriate. But it is the memory of Jesus's Jewishness that leads van Buren to recontextualize the symbol of the cross as a "Jewish death." This recontextualization then helps us to rethink theologies of the cross as no longer immune to Jewish memories of death. I have myself developed a Christian approach to Jesus's Jewish suffering building on Levinas's notion of the Other's suffering (Meyer 2020).

James Cone, the late systematic theologian and one of the leading scholars of Black Theology, found a connection between Jesus's Jewishness and his Blackness: "He *is* black because he *was* Jewish."[4] Cone explicitly affirms the Jewishness of Jesus and draws a line and even a logical link between Jesus's being Jewish and being Black. Theologians of marginalized groups often speak about Jesus's identity by adding themselves to his core group of reference. Jesus's care for the poor is central in classic South American liberation theology, and his healing of women has been emphasized in feminist theologies.

---

[2] Van Buren 1988, 74.
[3] Van Buren 1988, 165.
[4] Cone 1997, 123 (emphasis in original).

But the contemporary Christian confirmation of Jesus's Jewishness is not based on identification. Rather, when Christians of no Jewish background confess Jesus the Jew, they enter the realm of alterity (Meyer 2020). This challenge of otherness is at work whenever Jesus *is* Jewish. Christological reasoning that provides the language for the ongoing connection between Jesus of Nazareth and the Christ of faith will maintain that Jesus Christ is Jewish and will always be Jewish.

Theologically, the Jewishness of Jesus points to the God who sent Jesus, who is, according to the Christian creed, the God of the Bible and creator of the world. Thus Cone rightly points out that Jesus's Blackness does not cancel his Jewishness. Cone did, however, create a temporal hierarchy between them. There is no reason why Christians today could not affirm that he *is* Black and he was, is, and will be Jewish.

The emphasis on Jesus's historical Jewishness does not effectively undo Christian supersessionism, the fallacious idea that Christianity replaced Judaism. This underscores the specifically Christian responsibility to consider Jesus's Jewish identity as a matter not only of the past but also of the present, as Christians do not regard Jesus as of the past alone. But only twenty-first-century Christologies would explore Jesus's present Jewishness.

## THE JEWISH JESUS IN ECUMENICAL CHRISTIAN MEMORY

The search for the Historical Jesus was long dominated by Protestant scholars. Since the Second Vatican Council, the Catholic Church has become invested in opposing anti-Semitism and affirming Judaism. Nevertheless, the text of the famous declaration *Nostra Aetate* does not use the words "Jew" or "Jewish" for Jesus! But a recent official interpretation of *Nostra Aetate*, the Vatican document *The Gifts and the Calling of God are Irrevocable* (2015), offers a clear formulation with regard to the Jewishness of Jesus: "Jesus was a Jew, was at home in the Jewish tradition of his time, and was decisively shaped by this religious milieu." Jesus's Jewishness is comprehensively detailed: "Fully and completely human, a Jew of his time, descendant of Abraham, son of David, shaped by the whole tradition of Israel, heir of the prophets, Jesus stands in continuity with his people and its history."

The Catholic theologian Hans Hermann Henrix finds traces of Jesus's Jewishness in the Chalcedonian creed, specifically in the name of Jesus's mother Miriam who is mentioned there (Henrix 2011). The Lutheran theologian Kayko Driedger Hesslein offers an in-depth inquiry into Jesus's Jewishness in the Chalcedonian Two Natures Doctrine, which she interprets through the concepts of binationality and multiple belongings (Driedger Hesslein 2015). For the most part, in Christian memory the Jewishness of Jesus has been considered as qualifying his humanity. It is only in these twenty-first-century Christologies that the Jewishness of Jesus Christ is also remembered with regard to his divinity. This has opened a new challenge for Christian systematic theology that can no longer leave the Jewish Jesus to Historical Jesus research alone. "While God has no religion, the God of Israel is determined by the partners in covenant … both the humanness and the godliness of the Son are qualified by Jesus's Jewishness, his membership in the covenant of Israel" (Meyer 2011).

## RECENT SCHOLARSHIP AND NEW DIRECTIONS

The history of Jewish and Christian memories of the Jewish Jesus has an extraordinary potential for reformulating Christian–Jewish relations. But it is only with the premise that Christianity has not superseded Judaism and is not spiritually superior that the memory of Jesus the Jew can function as a critical memory. Scholarly discourse about the memory of the Jewish Jesus has never been independent of researchers' academic contexts and their cultural backgrounds. Scholars knowledgeable of rabbinic literature were able to read New Testament texts within a broader frame of reference. Since the turn of the twenty-first century, the lines of religious affiliation and Second Temple literacy have become blurred. Jewish specialists in New Testament exegesis like Amy-Jill Levine converse with Christian experts of the Mishnah like E. P. Sanders. These blurred lines have sharpened the memory of the Jewish Jesus in an unprecedented manner. A most recent example for path-breaking interreligious research is a voluminous study about *The Pharisees*, edited by Joseph Sievers and Amy-Jill Levine. Paula Fredriksen's observations in that book regarding Jesus's practice of wearing *"tsitsit"* provide a striking example for the precision of research that relies on a wide range of contemporaneous sources.

By the first century CE, for example, Deuteronomy 6:4–5, now the opening verses of the Shema, were enacted by wearing *tefillin* (Greek "phylacteries"). Numbers 15:37–41 (the Shema's closing section) mandated the wearing of *tsitsit* (Greek *kraspedon*, "fringe") intended to help wearers recall the commandments. The Synoptic Jesus wears *kraspeda* (e.g. Mark 6:56; Matt 9:20), but apparently his were shorter than those of the Pharisees, and he thought that his followers should not use *tefillin* as broad as those of the Pharisees (Matt 23:5). Did Paul wear *kraspeda*? He nowhere says, so we cannot know. But unless we construct Jesus as essentially Pharisaic – one possible explanation for the Gospels' impression of their near-constant arguments – it would seem that wearing *tsitsit* was a pious practice not limited to Pharisees.[5]

In the twenty-first century, the search for the Jewish Jesus has also diversified. Now some Christian scholars confirm that Jesus lived according to Torah, and Jewish scholars see unique features in his teachings. A small but growing number of Christian theologians have embraced the memory of the Jewish Jesus as their own memory. No longer would all Jewish New Testament scholars predictably view Jesus as observant, nor would Christian exegetes generally doubt Jesus's compliance with contemporaneous Jewish law. Jesus's observance and his legal opinions have become a topic of extensive, detailed, and nuanced analysis (Bockmuehl 2003).

At the same time, memory, while not a critical methodology in and of itself, has proven a promising source of self-criticism when negotiated with the memory of others. In interreligious academic settings, diverse memories have advanced exegetical and historical research. Methodologically, this happened not by simply adding more voices to the discourse but also by increasing the body of texts to be considered. As the works of Paula Fredriksen and Annette Yoshiko Reed show, the study of a rich variety of texts refines the questions and leads to nuanced answers. But it also hones memories over against anachronistic views long internalized by believers and scholars alike, such as claiming uniqueness for the historical Jesus instead of the church's Christ. How to remember the Jewish Jesus without limiting possible understandings of Jewishness remains a challenge for both Jewish and Christian scholars.

Jewish New Testament exegesis continues to offer important insights in the understanding of the Gospels. The Jewishness of Jesus continues to serve as the key memory to correct harmful misunderstandings of core gospel texts like the parables. As Amy-Jill Levine notes in her remarkable study of Jesus's parables, *Short Stories*, contextualization is key to recovering their meaning and fending off misunderstandings. "The message of Jesus and the meaning of the parables need to be heard in their original context, and that context cannot serve as

---

[5] Fredriksen 2021, 122.

an artificial and negative foil to make Jesus look original or countercultural in cases where he is not."[6]

The memory of the Jewish Jesus here leads to historical clarification as well as responsible interpretation that is aware of anti-Jewish pitfalls. Levine's Jewish Jesus helps her many Christian students to situate New Testament texts in a world they may be unfamiliar with, as well as develop an interreligious exegetical competence. The New Testament texts are based on recollections transmitted by Jesus's first followers who were Jewish. They told the story of Jesus in various ways, interconnected with major narratives and legal traditions from the Pentateuch and the Prophets. Thus, in a textual perspective, the Christian memory of the Jewish Jesus is inherently bound to Jewish memory.

In interpretational tradition, the memory of Jesus's Jewishness gets lost and is retrieved according to the memory of Jesus's compliance with the commandments of Second Temple Judaism. This implies a great challenge for today's Christians since the memory of the Jewish Jesus enfolds the memory of a Jewishly observant Jesus. While Jewish observance in the Second Temple period is not the same as today, there are commandments that connect Jesus's time with the present, such as the Sabbath. At the same time, Christians belonging to the main churches and denominations do not follow such characteristically Jewish practices as circumcision and kashrut. In this regard, today's Christians are further away from Jesus than Jews. This clearly presents a challenge to followers of Jesus who cherish his closeness, and it might be the reason for a long exegetical tradition of a Jesus perceived as distanced from law. How then can Christians reconcile their own distance from Jewish legal traditions with Jesus's rootedness in Second Temple Judaism? Christian theologians here need to welcome the thought of alterity to christological reasoning (Meyer 2020). Christians today can be faithful followers of Jesus without following in all his footsteps. This difference need not be experienced as a painful distance but as a theological opportunity to learn otherness that does not need to be assimilated. In this future memory, Jesus will be a Jew whose Jewishness will not be diminished. The unassimilated Jewish Jesus need not lessen the Christian belief in Jesus Christ as sent by God, the unique Son. Instead, the memory of the Jewish Jesus can underscore both a deep connection between Judaism and Christianity and an affirmation of difference. Christians who embraced the Jewish memory of Jesus would not diminish their Christianity. Instead, Jewish memories can facilitate recognition of an unassimilated

[6] Levine 2014, 25.

Jesus and help Christians to reacquaint themselves with a Jesus faithful to Torah and Israel as the same Jesus Christ they have always known.

## FURTHER READING

Bockmuehl, Markus. 2003. *Jewish Law in Gentile Churches: Halakhah and the Beginning of Christian Public Ethics*. Grand Rapids: Baker Academic.

Cone, James. 1997. *God of the Oppressed*. Rev. ed. Maryknoll: Orbis.

Driedger Hesslein, Kayko. 2015. *Dual Citizenship: Two-Natures Christologies and the Jewish Jesus*. Bloomsbury: T&T Clark.

Flusser, David. 2001. *Jesus*. 3rd ed. Jerusalem: Hebrew University Magnes Press.

Fredriksen, Paula. 2021. "Paul, the Perfectly Righteous Pharisee." In *The Pharisees*, edited by Joseph Sievers and Amy-Jill Levine, 112–35. Grand Rapids: Eerdmans.

Harvey, Warren Zev. 2012. "Harry Austryn Wolfson on the Jews' Reclamation of Jesus." In *Jesus Among the Jews: Representation and Thought*, edited by Neta Stahl, 152–58. New York: Routledge.

Henrix, Hans Hermann. 2011. "The Son of God Became Human as a Jew: Implications of the Jewishness of Jesus for Christology." In *Christ Jesus and the Jewish People Today: New Explorations of Theological Interrelationships*, edited by Philip A. Cunningham et al., 114–43. Grand Rapids: Eerdmans.

Heschel, Susannah. 1998. *Abraham Geiger and the Jewish Jesus*. Chicago: University of Chicago Press.

Levine, Amy-Jill. 2014. *Short Stories by Jesus: The Enigmatic Parables of a Controversial Rabbi*. New York: Harper Collins.

Marquardt, Friedrich-Wilhelm. 1990. *Das christliche Bekenntnis zu Jesus, dem Juden. Eine Christologie*. Vol. 1. Munich: Kaiser.

Meier, John P. 1991–2016. *A Marginal Jew: Rethinking the Historical Jesus*. Vols. 1–5. New Haven: Yale University Press.

Mendelssohn, Moses. 1983. *Jerusalem, or On Religious Power and Judaism*. Translated by A. Arkush. Hanover: Brandeis University Press.

Meyer, Barbara U. 2011. "The Dogmatic Significance of Christ Being Jewish." In *Christ Jesus and the Jewish People Today: New Explorations of Theological Interrelationships*, edited by Philip A. Cunningham et al., 144–56. Grand Rapids: Eerdmans.

Meyer, Barbara U. 2020. *Jesus the Jew in Christian Memory: Theological and Philosophical Explorations*. Cambridge: Cambridge University Press.

Sanders, E. P. 1990. *The Question of Uniqueness in the Teaching of Jesus*. London: University of London Press.

Sievers, Joseph and Amy-Jill Levine, eds. 2021. *The Pharisees*. Grand Rapids: Eerdmans.

Van Buren, Paul M. 1988. *A Theology of the Jewish-Christian Reality, Part III: Christ in Context*. San Francisco: Harper & Row.

Wolfson, Harry Austryn. 1973. "How the Jews Will Reclaim Jesus." Introduction to Joseph Jacobs, *Jesus as Others Saw Him*. New York: Arno Press.

# 18 The Racial Jesus

JONATHAN TRAN

Beginning his two-volume history of Asian Christianity, Samuel Hugh Moffett tells us, in case we forgot or somehow never knew, that Jesus was born, lived, and died in what is now called Asia, a fact Moffett emphasizes by referring to Jesus and his disciples as "Asian" (Moffett 1998–2005, 1:3). Pope John Paul II went further in emphasizing Jesus's Asian identity, making not only a historical and geographical point but also a seemingly racial one, quoting Scripture (as if not to put too fine a point on it) in order to say in his apostolic exhortation "In 'the fullness of time' (Gal 4:4), God sent his only-begotten Son, Jesus Christ the Savior, who took flesh as an Asian!" (Committee on Migration 2001). The Korean artist Kim Ki-chang in the 1950s painted a thirty-scene Life of Jesus series that portrayed a characteristically Asian Jesus set against a characteristically Asian backdrop. Objecting to a "progressive whitenization" of European "pointed-nose" Christianity, the American Taiwanese theologian C. S. Song pointed to "the flat-nosed Christ" (Song 1982, 3).

What is happening with these histories, exhortations, images, and gestures, not so much *in* them but *through* them, indeed *because of* them? What work do they do? What is sought in reminding us that Jesus lived and died in Asia, in emphasizing his Asian "flesh" with its darker features, almond-shaped eyes, and flat nose, in casting Christ as Asian? What drives the desire to racialize Jesus, to seek after a racial Jesus?

In the following, I address these questions by offering an account of the racial Jesus, along the way using examples to show what racializing Jesus *does*. Indeed, it is by examining how the examples work – with advocates of the racial Jesus in each case speaking for themselves – that I arrive at the account. I then assess the racial Jesus, and examples thereof, by considering objections and counter-objections, which takes us down the road of seeing how the racial Jesus gets judged by the historical Jesus, and how the racial Jesus finally gives rest to the search for the historical Jesus, "throwing away the ladder" of its secular history.

## QUEST FOR THE RACIAL JESUS

In the late 1960s, St. Cecilia Roman Catholic Church in Detroit, Michigan commissioned a mural for the massive dome atop its sanctuary. A violent race riot had just torn the city apart, leaving hundreds of people arrested, injured, or dead. As if memorializing the uprising and the unbearable conditions that led to it, a twenty-four-foot Black Jesus, painted in the majestic style of a religious icon, would come to adorn the sanctuary dome. The backlash came quickly, with hate mail pouring in and objections piling up as soon as the public found out. The controversy only proved the point, according to St. Cecilia's Father Raymond Ellis. The very anti-Blackness that made it difficult for white people to picture Jesus as Black also made their vitriolic response unsurprising. Anti-Blackness necessitated, according to Father Ellis, positive portrayals of Blackness, and in this case Black beauty, Black majesty, and especially Black divinity. Father Ellis considered it right and natural for his parishioners, almost all of whom were Black, to see Christ as one of them, as someone who could identify with them in their Blackness: "We paint Christ as a black man to express our faith that He lives in the black man and the black man lives in Him" (Poinsett 1969, 171). The mural portrayed how Jesus, rather than abhor them because of their Blackness, belonged to them in their Blackness, and they to him in *his* Blackness (Poinsett 1969, 171).

St. Cecilia's Black Jesus soon after appeared on the cover of the popular American magazine *Ebony*, coming under the story "The Quest for a Black Christ," which made obvious reference to the famous "quest for the historical Jesus." The story later turned to Albert Cleage, a minister at another Detroit church reeling from the riots. In the story, Cleage discusses his book *The Black Messiah*: "When I say that Jesus was black, that Jesus was the black Messiah, I am not saying, 'Wouldn't it be nice if Jesus was black?' or 'Let's pretend that Jesus was black' or 'It's necessary psychologically for us to believe that Jesus was black.' I'm saying that Jesus WAS black" (Poinsett 1969, 176). Cleage was referring to a point in his book where he wrote:

> [T]he historic truth is finally beginning to emerge – that Jesus was the non-white leader of a non-white people struggling for national liberation against the rule of a white nation, Rome. The intermingling of the races in Africa and the Mediterranean area is an established fact. The Nation Israel was a mixture of Chaldeans, Egyptians, Midianites, Ethiopians, Kushites, Babylonians and other dark peoples, all of whom were already mixed with the black people of Central Africa. (Cleage 1968, 3)

In the *Ebony* piece, Cleage presents his own "historical Jesus" and offers what he considers a more truthful and therefore unsettling Christology, where Jesus does not die a meek "lamb of God" gloriously atoning for our sins. Cleage thinks that triumphalist gospel is a characteristically white story underwriting a characteristically white supremacy. Rather, Jesus rose up against oppression as a "revolutionary black leader, a member of the Zealots, the activist group that spurred the succession of rebellions against Rome" seeking to "free Israel's black Jews from oppression and bondage, dying, not for eternal salvation of the individual, but for the rebirth of the lost Black nation" in order to establish "the kingdom of God on earth" over against white oppressors (Poinsett 1969, 176). There is no resurrection for Cleage's Black messiah, just like there is no Trinitarian origin story. There is only the stuff of oppression, empires, and uprisings. Jesus's story bears eternal consequence only in the sense that it speaks to the universal nature of oppression and the equally universal struggle for freedom. Cleage blames Paul and white theology for transforming the Black messiah into a white savior, swapping the revolutionary details of Jesus's life for a mythic legend that only wealthy whites could consider good news. The *pièce de résistance* for Cleage: "White Christians have known this all along, but they wouldn't dare tell us" (Pointsett 1969, 174).

The Detroit riots also marked a turning point for the young theologian James Hal Cone. The riots followed decades of death-dealing racial inequality and injustice in Detroit, and Cone could stay quiet no longer, embarking then on a remarkable theological career as the founder of Black liberation theology. Cone responded to the vitriol surrounding the Black Jesus by commenting: "it is not difficult to see that much of the present negative reaction of white theologians to the Black Christ is due almost exclusively to their whiteness, a cultural fact that determines their theological inquiry, thereby making it almost impossible for them to relate positively to anything black" (Cone 1997, 123). Like Cleage, Cone likens the refusal of the Black Jesus to a refusal Jesus himself faced long ago: "It is particularly similar to the religious leaders' attitude toward Jesus in first-century Palestine when he freely associated with the poor and outcasts and declared that the Kingdom of God is for those called 'sinners' and not for priests and theologians or any of the self designated righteous people" (Cone 1997, 123). Also like Cleage, Cone rejects the notion that the Black Jesus arose as a figment of "psychological disposition" and instead "arises from a faithful examination of Christology's sources (Scripture, tradition and social existence)" (Cone 1997, 122). Cone speaks of Jesus's symbolic and literal

Blackness. Symbolically, "He is black because he was a Jew. The affirmation of the Black Christ can be understood when the significance of his past Jewishness is related dialectically to the significance of his present blackness" (Cone 1997, 123). Literally, "he truly becomes One with the oppressed blacks, taking their suffering as his suffering and revealing that he is found in the history of our struggle, the story of our pain, and the rhythm of our bodies" (Cone 1997, 125). Given Jesus's symbolic Jewish Blackness and his identification with literal Black suffering, there is no need, Cone thinks, to account for Jesus's Blackness the way Cleage does. Doing so only delimits Jesus's ability to identify with all oppressed people, powerfully embodied in but not limited to the suffering and uplift of Black people. While Cone does not see evidence to establish Cleage's Black messiah, he does comment against its detractors: "I perhaps would respect the integrity of their objections to the Black Christ on scholarly grounds, if they applied the same vigorous logic to Christ's whiteness" (Cone 1997, 123).

Kelly Brown Douglas's *The Black Christ* traces the Black Jesus to the early beginnings of Black life in America: "During slavery the Black Christ emerged in contradistinction to the oppression of the White Christ. The White Christ was the center of slaveholding Christianity, while the Black Christ was the center of slave Christianity" (Douglas 1994, 10). Thus, one finds the Black Christ long before St. Cecilia and Cleage commissioned their murals and pronounced "Jesus WAS black": "The Black Christ characteristically (1) reflected an intimate relationship between Jesus and the slaves, (2) radicalized the slaves to fight for their freedom, and (3) illuminated the contradiction between Christianity and the cruelty of slavery" (Douglas 1994, 20). While skin color had been used to racially justify oppression and facilitate its dominative conditions, those racialized as "Black" (and its cognates) reverse engineered the meaning of race to code for God's privileged place among them: "The actual pigmentation of Christ was addressed as Black people began to overtly and consciously connect the fact of their biological givens, especially their skin color, with their oppressive social condition" (Douglas 1994, 30). And, crucially, with Black uplift:

> The strength of the Black Christ is that it embraces Black people in their Blackness. It avows not only what it means to be physically Black, but also Black experience, heritage, and culture. It fosters a sense of self-esteem and pride in Black people as they come to understand that who they are is not abhorred, but valued by the divine being. They are able to see themselves in Christ. (Douglas 1994, 84)

Hence, Douglas says, "a proper understanding of the Black Christ ought to refer to both Christ's physical appearance and to Christ's relationship to the Black freedom struggle ... to call Christ 'Black' suggests something about both Christ's appearance and actions" (Douglas 1994, 5).

Reflecting on the quest for the Black Jesus, Anthony Reddie writes: "The concept of Jesus being one of us (a central concept of the incarnation) remains the key theological theme by which all people have sought to identify with him and he with us in our particular context" (Reddie 2016, 290). For this reason, "A development of a black Jesus has been a central locus to the intellectual development of black theology"; "it is not simply the black identification with Jesus that is crucial, perhaps of greater importance is his identification with black people" (Reddie 2016, 290).

Racializing Jesus takes concepts of identity and belonging and applies them to Jesus Christ, a way of saying, "We're with him," or more so, as Reddie notes, "He's with us." Race here becomes the middle term between Jesus and us insofar as he is Black and we are Black, race serving as the principle of identification, how we identify with Jesus and how he identifies with us. We are identified together, and we belong together because we are Black. We may have everything else in common or nothing else in common, but we have this in common. Hence, identification is the key and it is made by historical analogy.

The payoff of racializing Jesus comes not only in identifying us with Jesus using Blackness as the middle term but additionally in Jesus identifying with God and therefore identifying us with God through Jesus himself as the middle term. This is why Reddie brings up the incarnation, which holds that in Christ there is shared identity between humanity and God. Through Christ, God identifies with humanity, just as through Christ humanity identifies with God, in both cases Jesus – as fully human and fully God, according to creedal definitions of the incarnation – serving as the middle term between the two in a complex analogical relation. Racializing Jesus then follows a logic that involves two pairs each connected by a middle term, race connecting us and Jesus and Jesus connecting humanity and God. The racialized Jesus (e.g. the Black Jesus) brings the two pairs together (the Black Jesus combining the two middle terms, race and Jesus, into a single middle term) through a transitive logic: Inasmuch as Black humanity is identified with the Black Jesus as Black and Jesus is identified with God as God, Black humanity is identified with God. The means by which Black humanity relates to God is through Black Jesus. Through Black Jesus, Black humanity has a share in God. By participating with Black Jesus, Black humanity participates with God. Black Jesus avails God to Black humanity. In each case, the inverse also applies: Black Jesus avails Black humanity to God; by participating with Black Jesus, God participates with Black humanity; through Black Jesus, God has a share in Black humanity; the means by which God relates to Black humanity is through Black Jesus. Such is the payoff of seeing Jesus as Black, of racializing Christ, of analogizing race and pursuing the racial Jesus.

The quest for the racial Jesus is for Cleage and Cone more a recovery or reclamation project than a project of reconstruction or reimagining. They have not concocted the racial Jesus for the "psychological" benefit of politically or personally identifying with him. Rather, they present Jesus as Black because they believe he was Black. Indeed, it is those who deny Jesus's Blackness, they think, that distort history. Cleage and Cone see themselves recovering and reclaiming the racial Jesus in order to prove, in the face of the distortions, the legitimacy of their racial identification. They seek not just a Christ of faith but also the Jesus of history. Consider here another example. The biblical scholar Ahn Byung-Mu champions "the Minjung Jesus" not so that poor, alienated, oppressed Koreans can psychologically identify with him regardless of whether or not the analogy is factually warranted. Instead, the Minjung identify with Jesus because Jesus is like them – poor, alienated, oppressed (Byung-Mu 1983). The analogy hangs on a historical likeness. Accordingly does Ahn say, "Jesus is Minjung and Minjung is Jesus" (Byung-Mu 2019, 23). It is only by "dehistoricizing" Jesus and the biblical record that one's Christ of faith distorts "the historical fact" of the Minjung Jesus; "the *kerygma* being silent about the Jesus Event ... caused distortions of the event" (Byung-Mu 2013, 34, 35).

The move of analogically identifying with Jesus, so crucial for the racial Jesus according to Douglas and Reddie, finds its basis in historical fact, according to Cleage, Cone, and Ahn. This claim to history allows them to believe that they base their political programs and personal projects on how things are, not how they might be – in reality, not fantasy. This felt need to historically license the identification anticipates both objections and counter-objections to the racial Jesus. Yet, as we will see, it also puts advocates of the racial Jesus in the odd position of reprising a mode of thought they have reason to abandon.

## VALORIZING THE RACIAL JESUS AND THE HISTORICAL JESUS

Objections to the racial Jesus follow an expected route, presuming a familiar distinction between a Jesus of history and a Christ of faith. This distinction arose early in the search for the historical Jesus and initiated and determined how the search would proceed, making its driving force an Enlightenment historiography that launched the search in the first place. The modern search begins with the European Enlightenment's disenchantment of theological reason, a philosophical skepticism which opens Christian Scripture to scrutiny consistent with any text claiming historical meaning. Historicizing texts like Scripture did not so much render them God-less as much as presume them so, making secular history, as I shall call this mode of thought, a-theological rather than anti-theological (where the latter entails an argument and the former presumes one). Such skepticism shows, for instance, that the miracles canonically attributed to Jesus are more likely the stuff of faith than fact, something that occurs in belief, not history, which now serves as the ground of judgment (in technical terms, setting the terms of Scripture's verification or falsification after having already shoehorned matters into a rigid empiricism). What emerges from historicizing the Gospels is a distinction – sometimes called a "ditch" – between what history proves about Jesus (the Jesus of history) and what Christian faith believes about Christ (the Christ of faith). Valorizing the two sets up conditions by which the Jesus of history entitles belief in the Christ of faith, where theological judgment is made to answer to the Enlightenment's secularizing impulse. The search's strong distinction between history and faith comes to a head with the startling suggestion that, for confessing Christians, only the Christ of faith matters.

Objections to the racial Jesus presume this distinction between history and faith and valorize the Jesus of history against the racial Jesus's Christ of faith (see Siker 2007). These objections believe that the racial Jesus must be subjected to secular history's skepticism, first presupposing the distinction between the Jesus of history and the Christ of faith and then locating the racial Jesus on the Christ-of-faith side of the ledger, something to be believed rather than proven. Any insistence on bringing the racial Jesus's Christ of faith across the ditch – for example, that "Jesus WAS black" or lived and died in Asia – requires checking it against secular history. Such scrutiny would show that, for instance, contemporary conceptions of race can only be applied to the New Testament anachronistically, that whatever the Gospels mean by race (e.g. Mark 7:26's *genos*) or whatever they are doing in relating Jesus as "Samaritan" (John 8:48–52), "Galilean" (Luke 22:59), "Jewish" (John 19:19), and "Egyptian" (Matt 2:15) remains a far cry from what race means in those contemporary uses seeking to identify through analogy the racial Jesus with the historical Jesus. The historical Jesus existed long before "race" would come to take on the meaning the racial Jesus attributes to Jesus, at a time that could not anticipate the need to racialize Jesus much less claim him as Black or Asian. The historical Jesus is, according to the objection, pre-racial. "Jesus WAS black" is not so much wrong as empty, and the Asian Jesus proves so factually uncontroversial that claiming as much says more about the claim than about Jesus. If anything, the racial Jesus returns us to the search's startling suggestion that the Christ of faith has nothing and needs nothing to do with the Jesus of history. The point of the "Christ of faith" was never proof but belief, and if the kerygmatic racial Christ can inspire and enable certain political programs and personal projects, so be it. Just do not confuse the racial Jesus's Christ of faith with the Jesus of history, the objection admonishes, for to do so is to effectively make Jesus in one's racial image, to impose race where race does not belong – to, as the objection goes, play the race card.

The objection to the objection also follows a (by now) familiar route (see Schüssler Fiorenza 1997; Rivera 2009; Buell 2010; Park 2017). The counter-objection initially presumes the Jesus of history/Christ of faith distinction but then takes a radical turn (though not all the way, as we will see). It starts by pointing out the utter convenience of the fact that those who came up with the search for the historical Jesus also determine its course, that those authoring the distinction also get to govern the criteria of its assessment. That is, European Enlightenment thinkers – which is to say, according to the regular ad hominem critique, white men – both initiated the search for the historical Jesus and determined how it would go, resulting in a search that unsurprisingly ended where it began, one that neatly divides between the Jesus of history and Christ of faith. And not only that. Distinguishing between the two in a way that removes any trace of faith from the Jesus of history formally resembles how European men imagined themselves as white, as a race devoid of color, a race removed of any trace of race. They made themselves raceless and white by imagining Jesus as raceless and white; more likely, they imagined Jesus as raceless and white by projecting their purported whiteness on to him, all in a thinly veiled attempt to underwrite unmistakably white political programs and personal projects (see Blum and Harvey 2012, 7–24). Apparently, it was not only explicit advocates of the racial Jesus who make God in their own image, not only Albert Cleage and the C. S. Song who play the race card. The counter-objection credits explicit advocates of the racial Jesus – those who speak of, say, "Black Jesus" rather than just "Jesus" – for both acknowledging the role of race in their reconstructions and thematizing the acknowledgment as itself theoretically important (using, for example, memory rather than history as a reconstructive frame of reference; see Allison 2010).

The counter-objection takes a radical turn when it shifts its attention to the Enlightenment itself, showing how its disenchantment of theological reason depends on an undisclosed enchantment of secular history. This typically postmodern critique of Enlightenment reason then combines with the ad hominem argument about whiteness, and together issue in a radical (though again, momentary) departure from the Jesus of history/Christ of faith distinction. The search for the historical Jesus turns out to be, according to the counter-objection's radical turn, something of a search and destroy mission, a further instance of an expansionist colonial logic that sought to put the world, including its Christ of faith, under the careful watch of the white gaze. It comes as no surprise, then, that the search ends up marginalizing the racial Jesus while leaving in place a de facto white Jesus standardized by the likes of Warner Sallman's blond-haired, blue-eyed *Head of Christ* portrait painting reproduced a billion times over (McFarlan 2020).

## THROWING AWAY THE LADDER OF SECULAR HISTORY

Just as soon as advocates of the racial Jesus mount their counter-objection, they "chicken out," refusing to "throw away the ladder" on the secular history underwriting both the objection and the counter-objection. Cora Diamond develops the philosophical idea of chickening out and throwing away the ladder in relationship to a view she attributes to Ludwig Wittgenstein. According to Diamond, Wittgenstein believes that philosophy cannot, despite what philosophers often think, be about the task of searching out "the logical form of reality." She sees certain Wittgensteinians adopting this view but failing to go all the way with Wittgenstein, oddly abandoning the search while keeping it going. Diamond thinks searching out "reality" proves useful until it doesn't, and once it does not, one ought to "throw away the ladder." Crucially for Diamond, one needs to search to realize the search's limits; once one has learned what can be learned, including the ladder's limits, it is time to give it up. This is what Diamond means by philosophically throwing away the ladder, what she thinks philosophy comes to under Wittgenstein's tutelage. Again, she sees how Wittgensteinians come to realize the limits of searching out reality but keep returning to it, as if unable to let it go, instead chickening out once they realize that throwing away the ladder entails giving up such notions as "features of reality" that keep in play the very "logical form of reality" they thought to abandon. "What counts as not chickening out is then this, roughly: to throw the ladder away is, among other things, to throw away in the end the attempt to take seriously the language of 'features of reality'" (Diamond 1988, 7).

Something like a theological version of "chickening out" is going on with advocates of the racial Jesus, a similar refusal to "throw away the ladder" on modes of thought that block the racial Jesus from coming to its own conclusions. Recall that the point of the search's strong distinction between history and faith is not to describe in good faith different ways one can relate to Jesus (through history or faith) but rather to prioritize in bad faith the Jesus of history over the Christ of faith, including racial Christs of faith. The objection comes in bad faith, and the counter-objection calls this out by implicating how its secular pretensions lead to what C. S. Song (encountered earlier in this chapter) called a "progressive whitenization." But just as soon as it dismisses secular history for these reasons, the counter-objection calls on it again, oddly in order to legitimize its identifications – feeling that it needs secular history's version of the historical Jesus to makes its case – giving new life to the very thing weaponized against the racial Jesus.

This leads to two problems. The first I mention in passing since I develop it elsewhere (Tran 2022). Prosecuting the case against the objection's bad faith but failing to throw away the ladder on its secular history and progressive whitenization destines the counter-objection to replacing secular history with race as the ground of judgment, pivoting from making theological claims dependent upon modern secularism to making them dependent upon postmodern secularism and its, quoting Shawn Kelley's *Racializing Jesus*, "racialized and essentialized views of identity, human collectivity, and creativity" (Kelley 2002, 224). One scheme makes *history* the arbiter of human action; the other gives *race* that role. Both bank on the enchantments of their age, the first an enchantment of secular reason that prizes empiricism (and its skeptical doubts) and the second an enchantment of ascriptive identity (and its ensuing culture wars) that prizes political programs *as* personal projects, finally giving into the ad hominem thrust that just is race thinking – and likely as a reaction to the excesses of secular reason. All of this becomes evident by observing that once the counter-objection has prosecuted its case against secular reason, the only thing left standing is the racial Jesus, as if the goal of the racial Jesus's counter-objection all along was securing race as the final arbiter. Using race over against reason to arbitrate matters ends up investing race with extraordinary explanatory power, which proves terribly ironic given anti-racism's efforts at destabilizing race's power to explain anything at all.

Discussing the second problem moves in a different direction. Consider again the objection to the racial Jesus. In "Historicizing a Racialized Jesus," Jeffrey Siker raises the familiar concerns about suspicious reconstructions, asserted parallels, and historical fiction, all the nervous energy about anachronism the objection concerns itself with. But then Siker unexpectedly asks, "I wonder if it can actually be any other way, or if it should be any other way" (Siker 2007, 51). Siker's sentiment here brings to mind the literary critic Toril Moi's rhetorical question, "'Socially constructed' as opposed to what?" (Moi 2017, 55). Anachronism as opposed to what? Racialized as opposed to what? Each concern comes with unexamined premises that gain enchanted status when normalized in the Jesus of history/Christ of faith distinction and routinized by rehearsing the objections and counter-objections akin to what Stanley Cavell calls "the recital of skeptical doubt" (Cavell 1979, 420).

To be sure, the skepticism is brought in for the sake of licensing the identification central to the racial Jesus. As we saw with our examples, identification is the key work done by racializing Jesus, where the identification follows a transitive logic tying us to Jesus through race and to God through the racial Jesus. Yet none of that work requires licensing, at least not of the kind secular history both demands and monopolizes. We identify with Jesus because we identify with Jesus. As Cavell says, "nothing" including history "is deeper than the fact, or the extent, of agreement itself" (Cavell 1979, 32). There needs to be nothing deeper than the fact or extent of the agreement internal to identification, no further ground on which to base faith than in how one scripturally finds Jesus. Asked why they identify with Jesus, Christians answer, "To whom else can we go? He has the words of eternal life" (John 6:68, NRSV). Pressing them further turns up some version of, quoting Wittgenstein, "That's just what we do." Pressed yet again, they do not know what to say, thinking the concerns confused or perverse, saying only "Our spade is turned" (Wittgenstein 2009, §217). When Wittgenstein later says, "To use a word without justification does not mean to use it without right" (Wittgenstein 2009, §289), one remembers *The Asian Jesus*'s Michael Amaladoss, who speaks of "my right as an Indian and an Asian to speak of Jesus in my own language and culture and their symbols and images" (Amaladoss 2006, 7). This is what we do.

Throwing away the ladder on secular history does not mean throwing away the Jesus of history, only a certain version of it, one put forth in bad faith in order to valorize history against faith. Indeed, part of what the bad-faith distinction accomplishes is the suggestion that questioning the historical Jesus means throwing away the historical Jesus, suggesting that there is only one way of construing the Jesus of history, and that secular history has a monopoly on it, that secular history in its secularity alone is entitled to the Jesus of history. Seeking legitimacy by handing itself over to a historiography weaponized against it means putting the racial Jesus – and its identifying work – under the thumb of a secular history it knows not to trust.

How else might the historical Jesus come to us if not by secular history? Consider comments by Francis Watson in the original *Cambridge Companion to Jesus*: "The traditions about Jesus that underlie the gospels were developed in the context of the early Christian acknowledgement that what takes place in Jesus is God's definitive and unsurpassable action, and the free creativity with which these traditions were shaped is the expression of that acknowledgement" (Watson 2001, 165). Watson formulates an account whereby the early Christians saw God's action in Christ as the ground of history. This acknowledgment freed them from answering to considerations other than what they believed to be God's "definitive and unsurpassable" action in Christ. This account refuses the strong distinction between history and faith and the distinction's bad-faith objection that Christian faith proceeds without warrant, resigning belief to the far side of history.

Watson goes on: "It is precisely in the material that is most problematic to the secular histories (for examples, the birth and resurrection stories) that this acknowledgment of the true scope and significance of the event of Jesus' life is most clearly manifested" (Watson 2001, 165). Those early Christians Watson mentions arrive at their historical Jesus and thereby their Christian historiography by viewing history through the very thing secular history (and its resignations) prohibits – a full doctrine of God (what Christians call "Christology"), which entails reading Christ's incarnation through the doctrines of divine simplicity and eternality and both as entailments of confessing God as Trinity, where creatures exist in the gratuity of God's infinite life, the surfeit of unending love between Father, Son, and Holy Spirit that spills over into creation, making history the theater of divine activity. Holding one's Christ of faith accountable to history involves checking one's interpretation of events against God's definitive and unsurpassable action as the true ground of history, shifting from secular history's "representational economy" where God cannot exist to what the early Christians called "divine economy" where God necessarily has to, thereby changing what is meant by history insofar as history takes place and is redeemed in Christ (Blanton 2007, 5). The early Christians, Watson thinks, help us out of our confusions about Jesus precisely by calling us to Jesus (see Rowe 2022). Such is the freedom and creativity of theological judgment, the lightness of tradition, the ease of Christology, which allows Christians to shake off the nervous energy driving secular history (Matt 11:30).

Notice that nothing about what Watson says precludes the racial Jesus, but only certain defenses of it. Neither does anything about throwing away the ladder throw away the historical Jesus, for as Watson says, "To be Christian is, among other things, to *care* about the way that Jesus is represented" (Watson 2001, 157, emphasis in original). Or, as Wittgenstein says for his own reasons, "Not empiricism and yet realism in philosophy, that is the hardest thing" (Wittgenstein 1991, 325). What throwing away the ladder does do is refuse the sway a certain historical Jesus had on us, one where secular history is thought to entitle Christian faith, including its identifications, programs, and projects. God grounds judgment about God. Only from the perspective of God's definitive and unsurpassable action can one see the true scope and significance of the event of Jesus's life and alas lean into the freedom and creativity of throwing away the ladder. What counts as not chickening out, returning to Diamond, is then this: to throw away in the end the felt need to license identifications or to take seriously the entitlements of secular history; and in freedom and creativity to allow the racial Jesus to give rest to the search for the historical Jesus.

FURTHER READING

Appiah, Anthony. 1992. *In My Father's House: Africa in the Philosophy of Culture*. Oxford: Oxford University Press.
Blum, Edward J. and Paul Harvey. 2012. *The Color of Christ: The Son of God and the Saga of Race in America*. Chapel Hill: University of North Carolina Press.
Byung-Mu, Ahn. 1983. "Jesus and the Minjung in the Gospel of Mark." In *Minjung Theology: People as the Subjects of History*, edited by The Commission on Theological Concerns of the Christian Conference of Asia, 138–52. London: Zed Press.
Cone, James H. 1997. *God of the Oppressed*. Rev. ed. Maryknoll: Orbis.
Diamond, Cora. 1988. "Throwing Away the Ladder." *Philosophy* 63.243: 5–27.
Douglas, Kelly Brown. 1994. *The Black Christ*. Maryknoll: Orbis.
Gilroy, Paul. 1993. *The Black Atlantic: Modernity and Double Consciousness*. Cambridge, MA: Harvard University Press.
Kelley, Shawn. 2002. *Racializing Jesus: Race, Ideology, and the Formation of Modern Biblical Scholarship*. London: Routledge.
Park, Wongi. 2017. "The Black Jesus, the Mestizo Jesus, and the Historical Jesus." *Biblical Interpretation* 25: 190–205.

Poinsett, Alex. 1969. "The Quest for a Black Christ." *Ebony* 24.2: 170–78.

Reddie, Anthony G. 2016. "The Quest for a Radical Black Jesus: An Antidote to Imperial Mission Christianity." In *Albert Cleage Jr. and the Black Madonna and Child*, edited by Jawanza Eric Clark, 285–300. New York: Palgrave Macmillan.

Siker, Jeffrey. 2007. "Historicizing a Racialized Jesus: Case Studies in the 'Black Christ,' the 'Mestizo Christ,' and White Critique." *Biblical Interpretation* 15: 26–53.

Sugirtharajah, R. S. 2018. *Jesus in Asia*. Cambridge, MA: Harvard University Press.

Tran, Jonathan. 2022. *Asian Americans and the Spirit of Racial Capitalism*. Oxford: Oxford University Press.

## 19 Jesus, Power, and the Global Poor
CARLOS RAÚL SOSA SILIEZAR
AND ARUTHUCKAL VARUGHESE JOHN

There clearly has been progress in the eradication of poverty, with many hundreds of millions of people lifted out of poverty over the last half-century in China, India, Southeast Asia, and elsewhere. Five decades ago, the number of children who died as a result of poverty before reaching the age of five approached 20 million. By 2010, this toll had diminished by 60 percent to 7.6 million deaths. Despite this progress, according to a 2015 United Nations estimate, "10% of the world (or 734 million) lived on less than $1.90 a day."

Often, poverty results from a complex web of interrelated factors. Those caught in the web suffer from the depravity of those who take advantage of them and impersonal systems of societal arrangement that reinforce their social location. However, Jesus, as portrayed in the Gospels and present in the life of the church, offers a direct challenge to this dehumanizing paradigm by demonstrating his solidarity with the poor and opposition to all systems and people that afflict them. Jesus stands as liberator and savior of all those oppressed by sin, spiritual powers, and socioeconomic structures. This is evidenced in his earthly ministry and his presence in the church. While we may "always have the poor" with us (Mark 14:7) due to human corruption and the complexity of impoverishment, the Gospels provide a striking testimony for and guide to the essential work of solidarity with the poor.

### UNDERSTANDING THE DYNAMICS OF POVERTY

Our understanding of poverty in the present day comes with inherent limitations in that even the most accurate statistics and concepts fail to capture the real experiences of people. A modern understanding of poverty is characterized in terms of deficit – a lack of material, such as access to nutrition, sanitation, health care, housing, or skill for employment. Since this viewpoint concentrates on individuals as the locus of deprivation, the solution involves compensation and supply of these lacking elements. In a sense, this approach dehumanizes the poor who tend to appropriate an identity with an inherent sense of deficit often inadvertently conveyed by the donors who assume a messiah complex.

Assessing poverty using relational indicators helps us move beyond merely recognizing material deprivations by elucidating the underlying factors of poverty in relational terms – whether along caste, tribal, or gender fault lines. Using a relational framework of "status-honor" to understand the "poor" in Luke–Acts, Joel Green writes, "status-honor is a measure of social standing that embraces wealth, but also other factors, including access to education, family heritage, ethnicity, vocation, religious purity, and gender. In the Greaco-Roman world, then, poverty is too narrowly defined when understood solely in economic terms" (Green 1994, 65). Similarly, examining the scarcity of clean drinking water in the contemporary South Asian context through a relational lens reveals the disparities along gender and caste divisions. It becomes evident that lower caste women are barred from accessing village wells, and the economic consequences of caste-based discriminations perpetuate their impoverishment. It also reveals the fact that there are rich/poor divisions within contexts that are generally deemed socioeconomically poor.

Amartya Sen, Sabina Alkire, and others see poverty beyond the economic lens to address the problem in a multidimensional way. Sen's work *Development as Freedom* (2000) shifted the approach from purely economic markers of lack of resources or income to human freedom and capabilities. The Capability Approach (Alkire 2005) emphasizes the need to enable agency by involving the poor in decision-making processes to alleviate poverty. Thus, Sen argues that poverty "may be deemed to represent the level at which a person can not only meet nutritional requirements, etc., but also achieve adequate participation in communal activities" (Sen 1983, 167).

Viewing poverty through the lens of "absolute deprivation" perceives it as an inability to attain a specific socioeconomic benchmark. In contrast, "relative deprivation" defines poverty in connection with the circumstances of others' living conditions. While the former regards development and growth as potential solutions to poverty, the latter perspective tends to address it by advocating for the redistribution of wealth. Frequently, these perspectives are deeply entrenched and tend to create political divisions within societies that align broadly with capitalist and socialist ideologies.

Despite the fact that modernization and the profit-centered capitalist drive have had devastating consequences in forcing migration and the disruption of ecological balance, the United Nations 2023 report states, "the share of the world's workers living in extreme poverty fell by half over the last decade: from 14.3 percent in 2010 to 7.1 percent in 2019."[1] The United Nations looks at the Human Development Index (HDI) that includes life expectancy at birth, education, and per capita income as indicators of poverty reduction. "In 1950 life expectancy in developing countries was forty years; by 1990 it had increased to sixty-three years" (World Bank 1993, 1). Modernization and its improvements in health care advancements have resulted in a remarkable increase in life expectancy at birth and a decline in child mortality, especially in the less developed regions of the world.

Despite abundant access to resources and ostensible lack of poverty, the Western world is grappling with issues such as homelessness, drug addiction, and single-parent households at an escalating rate. When examining the extreme violence perpetrated by young people in the inner cities of America, John Dilulio offers a diagnosis of the problem as "moral poverty," which stems from children growing up in environments without the presence of "loving, capable, responsible parents ... It is the poverty of growing up surrounded by deviant, delinquent and criminal adults" (Dilulio 1995, 25).

Our understanding of poverty in the present day should also take into account that, in the latter half of the twentieth century, many regions in the global South, despite being drenched in poverty, held the belief that gaining political independence from their colonial oppressors would herald an era characterized by peace and prosperity. The postcolonial perspective often attributes challenges in the majority world, particularly focusing on the persistence of corruption in the global South, as a continuation of distinct corruptions from the colonial era. For instance, the manipulation of electoral processes by authoritarian rulers could be argued to be influenced by the behaviors of their colonial predecessors. This phenomenon is increasingly becoming conspicuous in multiple nations, whether through the "big man" complex among certain African rulers or the presence of authoritarian regimes in various South Asian, Southeast Asian, and Latin American contexts.

Reality is, however, more complex. Despite the attainment of self-government and political liberty, the complexities of internal crisis resulted in the tragic assassination of Mahatma Gandhi in India and the passing of Kwame Nkrumah, a Ghanaian champion of freedom, while in

---

[1] See, "Peace, Dignity and Equality on a Healthy Planet," *United Nations: Global Issues*, www.un.org/en/global-issues/ending-poverty.

exile. While colonial empires may have intensified tribal divisions, it is important to note that injustices and pervasive corruption existed within cultures long before the advent of colonial powers. Tribal conflicts in African settings and caste-based discriminations in South Asian contexts have favored specific tribes and communities while marginalizing others.

The New Testament, and in particular the Gospels, complexifies one-dimensional understandings of poverty by identifying spiritual oppression as a relevant factor. On the one hand, the Synoptic Gospels attribute spiritual oppression to demonic powers. Various narratives of exorcism include an unclean spirit who tried to destroy a boy, casting him into fire and into water (Mark 9:17, 22); demons that led a man to live among the tombs and to cut himself with stones (Luke 8:26–33); and Satan oppressing a woman who was bent over for eighteen years (Luke 13:16). On the other hand, Jesus restores many people oppressed by demons and casts out the unclean spirits with his word (Matt 8:16). These powerful acts of liberation signaled that he is the Messiah (Matt 11:5), that the Spirit of the Lord was upon him (Luke 4:18–19), and that God's kingdom had arrived (Matt 12:25–28). While the Synoptic Gospels offer a wholistic vision of poverty that includes spiritual dimensions, they also present Jesus as God's liberator who confronts earthly powers and authoritatively destroys spiritual oppression. For the reader of the Gospel of Matthew, for example, Jesus's ministry among the oppressed and the marginalized is the unmistakable evidence that he is God's savior: "'Are you the one who is to come, or shall we look for another?' ... Jesus answered them, 'Go and tell John what you hear and see: ... the poor have good news preached to them'" (Matt 11:3–5).

## JESUS'S CONCERN FOR THE POOR IN THE CANONICAL GOSPELS

Having provided a few introductory comments about different understandings of the complex dynamics of poverty, we now turn to the canonical sources, especially the Gospels, to demonstrate that Jesus had a radical and relevant approach to challenges of wealth and power. Long before the writing of the Gospels, Israel's Scriptures emphasize the prominence of the poor in God's kingdom. God has a clear concern for the poor through the command to provide for the needy in Israel (Deut 15:11). In Leviticus, the landowning farmers are instructed to purposefully leave behind grain for the poor to gather (19:9–10). The Prophets fervently denounce the rich for oppressing the poor (Isa 58:6–7; Amos 2:7; 8:5–6). Proverbs warns against exploiting the poor simply "because they are poor" (22:22). The Scriptures of Israel, across eras and genres, vehemently warn against oppressing the poor lest one face God's judgment.

The canonical gospels unanimously emphasize the relevance of Jesus to the problem of poverty. The context of his ministry, his interactions with the rich and the poor, and his teachings show God's identification with the poor through a preferential treatment of those marginalized within a society.

Socioeconomic poverty and lack of political power are the very contexts of Jesus's birth, earthly ministry, and post-resurrection mission through the apostles. Caesar Augustus's politically motivated decree forced Joseph and Mary to abandon their home in Galilee and travel to Bethlehem, where Jesus was born in a humble manger (Luke 2:1-7). In his irrational thirst for power, King Herod terrorized Bethlehem, causing Joseph and his family to seek refuge in Egypt, a foreign territory (Matt 2:13, 16). When Jesus began his ministry in the region of Galilee, he was criticized for coming from the tiny and recent settlement of Nazareth (John 1:46). Jesus announced the good news of God's kingdom in Galilee, the social and religious periphery of Jewish society. After his resurrection, the angel tells Mary and Mary Magdalene that Jesus "is going before you to Galilee" (Matt 28:7), and the risen Christ himself asks his disciples to tell his brothers "to go to Galilee, and there they will see me" (Matt 28:10). The risen Lord encounters his followers in the same place where he first proclaimed that he was anointed to proclaim good news to the poor, in Galilee (see Luke 4:16).

Jesus's radical approach to challenges of wealth and power is clearly seen in his interactions with people during his earthly ministry. The canonical gospels include stories of Jesus interacting positively with those who are materially rich but marginalized on other grounds (e.g. the spiritually poor) and engaging specific people who were not materially poor (e.g. Luke 19:1-10). However, his ministry toward people who had access to financial resources often carried a strong call to repentance that placed demands on their love and use of money. Luke, in particular, portrays Jesus as proclaiming that he was anointed to announce good news for the sick, the marginalized, the poor, and the oppressed (Luke 4:18-21). This proclamation represents one of the most powerful rhetorical expressions regarding his ministry toward the impoverished. This emphasis is also evident in the other Synoptic Gospels. Matthew and Mark describe Jesus cleansing lepers, restoring the sight of the blind, and casting out demons from people, even from a man who lived in the country of the Gerasenes (Mark 5:1-20).

During his earthly ministry, Jesus demonstrated that he came to empower the poor. First, to the poor came the signs of God's kingdom. These signs, such as Jesus's healing of the sick, accompanied his preaching of the good news (Matt 4:23–25; 8:16; 9:35; 10:7–8; 11:5; 15:29–31). Those who were healed often exemplify faith (Mark 5:34; Matt 9:22; 15:27–28) because, in contrast to the elites, they understood the authority of Jesus and appropriated his healing power. Second, the poor are portrayed in the Gospels as the privileged recipients of divine revelation. The only disciples who witness the transfiguration of Jesus and the manifestation of Moses and Elijah on a high mountain were the three fishermen (Matt 17:1–3; cf. 4:18–22). Last, Jesus emphasized his close association with the poor in his eschatological discourse before the Last Supper. Jesus told his disciples that those who feed the hungry, give water to the thirsty, embrace the stranger, clothe the naked, care for the sick, and visit prisoners are serving the King himself (Matt 25:34–36). The reward for those who serve the poor is nothing short of gaining access to God's kingdom and enjoyment of eternal life (Matt 25:46).

In addition to his interaction with people during this earthly ministry, Jesus's teachings further support his relevance to the problem of poverty. Jesus shows, on the one hand, that his followers should privilege the poor in the missionary agenda of the church and, on the other hand, that they should avoid pursuing wealth for selfish purposes and instead use resources to serve the outcast. Although Jesus taught his disciples to pay the temple tax and the royal tax to Caesar (Matt 17:24–27; 22:15–22), his life was an example of resistance to pursuing and using wealth, authority, and power for self-glorification. The beginning of Jesus's earthly ministry is preceded by his time in the desert where the devil offered Jesus all kingdoms of the world, their authority, and glory. Jesus immediately rejected Satan's temptation, asserting his exclusive service to the Lord (Luke 4:5–8; Matt 4:8–10). Jesus also refused to use violence to demonstrate the power of his kingdom. Instead, Jesus is subjected to mockery, physical punishment, and death. In his conversation with Pilate before his crucifixion, Jesus tells the Roman ruler that if his kingdom were of this world, his servants would fight to save his life (John 18:36).

Jesus's teaching also highlights that rather than the elites receiving favored treatment, the poor are the privileged recipients of God's revelation. Jesus blesses the poor and the hungry, promising them satisfaction of their needs and entrance into God's kingdom (Luke 6:20–21). God reveals through other lowly characters an upside-down vision of reality.

For example, Mary's song proclaims that God will exalt the humble and will bring down the mighty from their thrones (Luke 1:46–55).

The teachings of Jesus also encourage readers to avoid power and wealth for selfish purposes. He prohibited his disciples to lay up for themselves treasures on earth (Matt 6:19), or acquiring gold, silver, or copper while fulfilling their missionary duties (Matt 10:9). Jesus even challenged rich people to sell everything they had and give the money to the poor (Matt 19:21). More positively, Jesus asks his disciples to live a life of generosity in a world where poverty will be a persistent reality (Matt 26:11). He taught to give to the needy in secret (Matt 6:2–4), to serve others instead of trying to be the greatest (Luke 9:46–48; Matt 23:11), and to show compassion and liberality to people from diverse ethnic backgrounds (Luke 10:25–37). Above all, Jesus's disciples should distinguish themselves by seeking and promoting justice, unlike the self-righteous religious leaders: "But woe to you Pharisees! ... For you ... neglect justice and the love of God. These you ought to have done" (Luke 11:42).

Although Jesus plainly beckons his disciples to side with the poor in this world, all four gospels suggest that the pervasive problems of injustice, marginalization, poverty, and violence will only have an eschatological solution. Jesus blessed the poor and those who seek justice, promising them of their inheritance in the kingdom of heaven (Luke 6:20–21; Matt 5:6). For those renouncing material possessions in this world to follow him, Jesus promises eternal rewards (Matt 19:29). Despite the ubiquitous problem of poverty, Jesus warns of eschatological judgment to remediate this injustice and predicts that the unrepentant rich will hunger (Luke 6:25; cf. 1:53). While intervening in an inheritance dispute, Jesus told the parable of the rich fool who lost his soul by accumulating wealth instead of sharing his resources (Luke 12:13–21). In his interaction with a rich ruler, Jesus asserted that it is very difficult for a wealthy person to enter the kingdom of God (Luke 18:18–30). In the Gospels, the poor are empowered through Jesus privileging them in his ministry, his clear call to his disciples to seek justice, and the eschatological hope that he will intervene to reward the oppressed and punish those who have used power and wealth for self-glorification.

### JESUS, THE CHURCH, AND EMPOWERMENT: HOPE AND DIGNITY FOR THE POOR

From the earliest generation of his disciples to the present day, there has been a consistent embrace of Jesus's radical approach to the challenges of wealth and power. Although some have attempted to use Jesus to legitimize the use of power to oppress others, countless generations of Christians have resisted the temptation to use power to justify the oppression of God's creation for personal gain. Instead, they have prophetically served the poor and denounced the brutality of systems and policies that undermine the flourishing of all human beings.

Christians past and present have addressed the problem of poverty by appealing to Jesus. Ever since the earliest generations of Christianity, Jesus has been appropriated through both withdrawal and engagement, action and contemplation, principled quietism and zealous political engagement – sometimes simultaneously. The focus of this section, however, is on how Christians who are represented in global organizations have engaged with the problem of poverty by appealing to Jesus in the canonical gospels. This, in turn, will demonstrate the abiding global significance of Jesus today.

Following the example of Jesus as found in the canonical gospels, the global church in its multiple forms has developed various theological responses to the problem of poverty. The Lausanne Covenant, one of the most influential documents in the Protestant church worldwide, included a section entitled "Christian Social Responsibility." According to the document, Christian discipleship to Jesus Christ provides the basis for the affirmation that "evangelism and sociopolitical involvement are both part of our Christian duty" and the conviction that evangelism implies "a message of judgment upon every form of alienation, oppression and discrimination" (Stott 1975, 25). Additionally, Vatican Council II remains the most important Roman Catholic effort to bring traditional Christianity to consider the new global challenges. The dogmatic constitution *Lumen gentium* asserts that the church stands in solidarity with the poor because Jesus also suffered affliction, weakness, and poverty. The foundation of that theological statement is the conviction that poverty and persecution shaped Jesus's work of salvation.

Guided by the integral connection between poverty, wealth, and ecology (PWE), the World Council of Churches (WCC), following the 2006 Porto Alegre assembly, initiated the PWE program. The WCC statement on *Just Finance and an Economy of Life* called for a democratic system "grounded on a framework of common values: honesty, social justice, human dignity, mutual accountability and ecological sustainability." It obligated the "participation for all in decision-making processes that impact lives, [and provides] for people's basic needs through just livelihoods" (Mshana and Peralta 2015, 9).

At a regional level, the Episcopal Conferences (Spanish acronym, CELAM) and the Congresses on Evangelism (Spanish acronym, CLADE) have articulated Christology to engage the problem of global injustice. In 1979, leaders from *evangélicas* churches (Protestant communities with a strong conviction that the Gospel transforms individuals and societies) spread across Latin America gathered to address relevant issues. One of the main papers delivered at the Congress was entitled "Christ and the Antichrist in Proclamation," authored by René Padilla of Argentina and Valdir Steuernagel from Brazil. They highlighted that the antichrist is active in the world operating through political, economic, and social powers. Therefore, they concluded, the church should resemble Jesus's earthly ministry. Most recently, in 2012, the final declaration of leaders from *evangélicas* churches began with this statement of discipleship: "Faced with false, commercialized, esoteric, and spiritualized images that allude to religious conceptions of Jesus, we recognize the urgent need to follow Jesus fully in his path of life" (Fernandes et al., 2013). The document encourages disciples of Jesus to find biblical answers to pressing human needs in Latin America.

For Latin American Roman Catholics, the Episcopal Conference in Medellín in 1968 privileges the presentation of Jesus as *liberator*. Jesus is savior in the sense that he *liberates* human beings from all sorts of oppression, including hunger, injustice, and misery. Bishops in Medellín also insisted that Jesus is present and active in current history. In light of this theological reality, the church maintains a strong hope and mobilizes on behalf of the liberation of the poor (*praxis*). The most recent Episcopal Conference published a conclusive document that includes references to the resurrection of Jesus to shape the mission of the church. It states that communities of faith in the region should privilege a discourse of abundant life in a region where millions endure the daily specter of suffering and death.

Acknowledging its ethical responsibility to alleviate poverty, the church has actively undertaken substantial social charity efforts. In 2007, approximately 60 percent of all nongovernmental organizations (NGOs) affiliated with the United Nations were linked to Christian organizations. The nineteenth century saw the emergence of international Christian NGOs, both Protestant (YMCA in 1844) and Catholic (Caritas in 1897), which in the later decades led the social action in many of the poorest parts of the world. Christian NGOs worked to provide clean drinking water in the form of tube wells and lavatories to households to prevent waterborne diseases. Yet, despite these concerted efforts, the United Nations International Children's Emergency

Fund (UNICEF) and the World Health Organization's (WHO) *State of the World's Sanitation Report* (2020) record that "over half the world's population, 4.2 billion people, use sanitation services that leave human waste untreated, threatening human and environmental health" (UNICEF and WHO 2020, 11).

The work of rescue and rehabilitation of bonded laborers has been undertaken by several NGOs. While most nations are signatories of global charters and agreements containing legislation against bonded slavery and similar social evils, cultural biases and entrenched social customs persist, perpetuating oppression of the poor. The NGOs find themselves in no position to change cultures and societies that have internalized oppressive structures. Given these challenges, any lasting change in social thinking requires collaboration with local governments. The success rates of rescue and rehabilitation by the NGOs significantly improve when government officials and the law enforcement agencies are co-opted for the process. Significant progress also requires engaging cultural and social understanding in the transformational work. However, such engagements by the NGOs are sometimes challenged by local governments as imposing foreign standards in local cultures – a case in point would be the Asian Values Discourse, which tends to see the very concept of "Human Rights" as a Western construct and antithetical to "Asian Values." In such scenarios, it becomes essential for development practitioners to leverage local values that align with the mission of societal liberation.

In South Asia, as in other parts of the world, local governments have picked up work that earlier was mostly undertaken by NGOs. Tremendous strides have been made by the Indian government to provide 105 million toilets to households, serving more than 500 million people in the first five years of implementing the Swachh Bharat Mission of making India open defecation free (ODF). Similarly, the Indian government initiated the Har Ghar Jal (Water for Every Household) scheme in 2019 to provide water to every household. According to the WHO June 2023 report, with universal access to clean drinking water in the country "almost 14 million DALYS (Disability adjusted life years) from the diarrhoeal disease are estimated to be averted, resulting in estimated cost savings of up to USD 101 billion."[2] While such projects garner popular support and inform voting patterns that influence political participation in poverty alleviation, affirmative actions that provide privileges and quotas for poor communities are more challenging as they tend to

---

[2] As quoted in *Business Standard*, June 9, 2023; see https://bit.ly/WHO23.

tip the fine balance of power in the society. The relative peace between ethnic communities in many parts of the world is easily disturbed with one community aspiring to a larger piece of the pie in the distribution of resources. Collaborative participation between NGOs and local governments is pivotal, given the fine balance required in the distribution.

Overall, NGOs find that it is more effective to collaborate and work alongside local governments to transform communities. From the very beginning, the International Justice Mission (IJM), for instance, has been engaged in rescue and rehabilitation work among bonded laborers in South Asia and has collaborated with various government bodies, including policymakers, law enforcement agencies, and rehabilitation institutions. The very nature of rescuing bonded laborers from powerful business enterprises, often with connections to political power, has necessitated the active participation of government agencies. This calls for substantial investment in drives to make government agencies aware of the problem and draw them into participating in the rescue and rehabilitation of bonded laborers. In short, collaborative efforts tend to bring better outcomes.

While these examples effectively illustrate witnessing in the name of Jesus, one may also observe that gospel proclamation as a component of the Christian mission has come under criticism in the past decades, leading to what Lamin Sanneh describes as the "Western guilt complex." By assessing certain Western missionaries and their motives, this attitude tends to conflate all Christian mission engagement with a form of Western imperialism or another "mischief of the white race in the rest of the world" (Sanneh 1987). Consequently, there is a withdrawal from proclamation, often leaving Christian mission merely as a form of social service. Yet any lasting transformation necessitates interventions that extend beyond the sociopolitical sphere, also encompassing ideological shifts and reforms in belief systems. As Walter Wink writes, "The church has no more important task than to expose these delusional assumptions as the Dragon's game" (Wink 1992, 96).

## CONFRONTING POVERTY'S COMPLEXITIES: SYSTEMIC FORCES AND CULTURAL HURDLES

Jesus's radical and relevant approach to challenges of wealth and power is not limited to his example and teachings in his interactions with individuals in the first century or his appropriation by Christian global institutions in modern times. The Gospels' portrayal of Jesus challenging systemic forces and structural oppression has the potential to make a significant difference to contemporary systemic problems and enduring power structures that have solidified over time.

Combating the challenges of poverty within modern contexts is a complex task since they frequently stem from systemic issues and deeply ingrained attitudes that sustain the oppression of the impoverished. Specifically, there are at least three contemporary challenges where attention to Jesus's example can make a significant difference. The first is in the area of resistance from the privileged sections of society. In the current context, developmental work that NGOs undertake in poverty-stricken regions tends to garner resistance from the privileged sections of society. The following story, observed by one of the authors of this chapter, vividly depicts the intricacies of a systemic problem. Reverend John and his wife Susamma were social workers among the silk farm laborers in a remote region in South Asia. Initially, the laborers with whom they worked regularly spent their meager wage for their day's labor on toddy (a local alcoholic drink) on their way back home from work, resulting in regular physical and emotional violence against their wives and children. With little money to provide for their families, they were caught in a cycle of economic misery and were given to alcoholism purportedly to forget their misery. John helped them procure a bank loan, resulting in each family owning a hand-operated silk yarning wheel. The local production of silk yarn within households swiftly ushered in prosperity for these families. Simultaneously, they witnessed the transformation of lives and freedom from alcoholism through church attendance that further led to an increase in the families' income. With increased financial stability, the former laborers could now provide their families with adequate nutrition and clothing, and even send their children to nearby schools, resulting in their collective upward social mobility. However, the wealthy landlords who owned the silk farms were not happy with this transformation. They not only faced the absence of inexpensive labor but also found themselves to some extent in competition with the former laborers who had now transitioned. Fueled by their loss of control over the labor force, the landlords resorted to bribing the police to apprehend the men, alleging that they were disturbing their established cultural and customary norms due to the laborers' adoption of Christianity.

In Acts 16:16–24, we encounter a similar episode when Paul heals an enslaved girl with the spirit of divination. Luke lets us in on the real reason for why Paul and Silas were subject to unjust imprisonment. She had "brought her owners a great deal of money by fortune-telling" (Acts 16:16), and "when her owners saw that their hope of making money was gone, they seized Paul and Silas and dragged them into the marketplace before the authorities" (Acts 16:19). Far more than cultural offense attributed to "foreign customs," the enslavers were perturbed by the economic repercussions that resulted from the healing of the clairvoyant.

The above story in Acts not only illustrates the challenges that the Gospel might encounter in missionary interventions involving cultural interactions but also underscores the economic underpinnings of social structures that exploit the poor, entwining them within oppressive religious and cultural frameworks. The exploitative social structure additionally provides the wealthy with the ability to "oppress" and to drag the poor "into the courts" (James 2:6). Consequently, in many cultures, the rich, whose interests are served by the poor, assume a sense of entitlement and control over the poor and trap them in an unending cycle of subservience.

The New Testament writings can also offer more than examples that illustrate the systemic challenge of resistance from the privileged sections of society. The portrayal of Jesus in the Gospels confronting power structures should influence contemporary Christians in global contexts where injustice is pervasive. As noted earlier in the chapter, the world that Jesus enters with his incarnation is deeply affected by poverty. The Synoptic Gospels offer several examples of Jesus interacting with people located on the margins of society. Their social situation was the result of complex factors, exacerbated by oppressive systems of power and specific religious and political authorities. Some religious leaders often neglected the needs of people (Mark 6:34). Specifically, Jesus denounces the teachers of the law who "like[d] to walk around in flowing robes and be greeted with respect in the marketplaces and have the most important seats in the synagogues and the places of honor at banquets" and prophetically accuses them of devouring widows' houses and making lengthy prayers for a show (Mark 12:38–40). Yet it is important not to interpret Jesus's strong criticism of religious leaders as an indictment against the synagogue. He regularly visited these places of communal gathering, reading Scripture and teaching about God's kingdom in that setting (Mark 1:21; Luke 4:42–44).

John the Baptist also confronted power structures and, consequently, suffered at the hands of political authorities. Jesus contrasts John with people "dressed in fine clothes" who live in "kings' palaces" (Matt 11:8). The Gospel of Matthew portrays the Baptist as a person without political authority who came from the wilderness (Matt 3:1). For John's prophetic witness against the illegal marriage of Herod to Herodias, the wife of Herod's brother Philip, Herod arrests and imprisons him. However, Herodias, discontent with the mere arrest of John, uses her own daughter to manipulate the tetrarch into giving her John the Baptist's head on a platter. Thus, Herod and Herodias execute the prophet from God (Matt 14:1–8). John stands as a witness not only to political rulers but also to religious authorities. His humble attire, clothes made of camel's hair and a leather belt around his waist (Matt 3:4), contrasts with his powerful words against Matthew's Pharisees and Sadducees: "You brood of vipers! ... The axe is already at the root of the trees, and every tree that does not produce good fruit will be cut down and thrown into the fire" (Matt 3:10).

The second contemporary challenge has to do with systemic economic issues that lead to poverty. Jesus's powerful call to repentance to the rich offers an alternative scenario. Even in cases where overt oppression of the poor by the rich is not apparent, systemic economic issues seem to plague a substantial portion of farming households, constituting nearly 50 percent of the population in India. As reported by Samrat Sharma and Piyush Aggrawal, the "average agricultural household in India ... has debt equivalent to 60 percent of their annual income" (Sharma and Aggrawal 2021). Apart from natural calamities like droughts and floods, unfavorable trade conditions have driven farmers to bankruptcy and financial debt. The convergence of financial hardships intensifying family issues has propelled numerous farmers to resort to the drastic measure of suicide. In recent times, farmer suicides in the Indian context have reached alarming levels. The National Crime Records Bureau (NCRB) reported more than 17,000 farmers committing suicide between 2018 and 2020.

The oppression that many people experienced in occupied Judea, Galilee, and Samaria was not restricted to imperial injustice. Rich people with some political power also took advantage of an oppressive system to obtain personal financial gain. Tax collectors often stole money from people, taking far more money than the taxes they owed. The encounter of Jesus with Zacchaeus illustrates this point. Zacchaeus was a chief tax collector explicitly described as "rich" (Luke 19:1). People in Jericho referred to him as a "sinner" because it is probable that he had defrauded them, causing their impoverishment (Luke 19:7). Yet his encounter with Jesus prompts a promise of repentance: "If I have defrauded anyone of anything, I restore it fourfold" (Luke 19:8). It is likely that Zacchaeus is representative of other rich people mentioned in the gospel accounts who obtained their wealth by taking advantage of the poor. Jesus calls on the rich ruler to sell his possessions and distribute to the poor (Luke 18:22) and the rich man who refused to share his food with the poor is contrasted with Lazarus, a poor man covered with sores and living among the dogs (Luke 16:19–22).

The third contemporary challenge to gospel change is the opposition posed by sociocultural and religious beliefs. The new vision of reality and Jesus's clear call to radical service and generosity offer concrete hope of liberation for the poor who suffer oppression and the potential salvation of the wealthy who misuse their power for oppression.

Sociocultural and religious beliefs wield significant influence in the trajectory of economic development. As the Argentinian sociologist and historian Mariano Grondona argues, "The paradox of economic development is that economic values are not enough to ensure it ... The values accepted or neglected by a nation fall within the cultural field. We may thus say that economic development is a cultural process" (Grondona 2000, 46). Predicated on this, he makes the claim that cultures may be distinguished as "resiliently progress-prone" and "persistently progress-resistant."

One of the religious and cultural beliefs prevalent in many societies that tend to reinforce the lack of agency in the individual is fatalism. Fatalism, as a cultural belief, significantly contributes to the trapping of individuals within cycles of adversity and is often far more insidious than mere material deprivation. For instance, the doctrine of karma that is common in South Asia is a belief that one's past life determines one's present and future. Insofar as it is understood in a deterministic manner, it construes one's current condition as a direct consequence of one's previous actions. This perspective implies a sense of helplessness, as individuals perceive their present suffering as predetermined and inevitable. The individual perceives themself as too insignificant to challenge the cosmic forces of karma and alter or improve their plight. The lasting nature of poverty within communities arrested by a web of conceptual deceptions can be addressed only by replacing those false narratives with truth.

As the doctrine of karma illustrates, one of the pivotal aspects of poverty is a sense of powerlessness that manifests as a deficiency in both freedom and agency. This can be observed across social frameworks, spanning from exclusion in community decision-making processes to the outright obliteration of agency, as evidenced by instances such as human trafficking. Those who stand to benefit from the oppressive structures tend to view the poor as inherently of less value and undeserving of anything better, often tagging the poor with terms such as "unintelligent" or "lazy." These beliefs are quickly internalized by the poor, leading them to believe that their circumstances are somehow justified. In this way, the poor find themselves entrenched within socioeconomic structures that keep them in bondage, and in many cases enslaved as bonded laborers. Whether it is the illegal practice of bonded labor in the brick kilns of India or the global sex trafficking of mostly young girls from poorer countries for prostitution or the migrant workers of South Asia in the Middle East, poverty is at the very root of slavery. The cycle follows a familiar pattern: Individuals are enticed with upfront monetary offers, drawing them away from their homes with the prospect of employment and financial independence. However, upon reaching their intended workplace, they discover themselves trapped as bonded laborers, stripped of their passports, and facing insurmountable challenges in repaying the advance, as their employers manipulate the situation to their advantage.

CONCLUSION

The present chapter has highlighted the abiding global significance of Jesus today in matters related to power and poverty. Jesus's radical approach to the challenges of wealth and power has made a significant impact on modern Christian witness. Without the abundant New Testament testimony from his life and teachings, it is highly plausible that those who have employed Jesus's name to justify oppression would have prevailed. Although many Christian institutions and churches today are committed to learn from those in the margins, serve those who are oppressed, and show solidarity with the poor, the work of the church is still unfinished. The complexity of contemporary power dynamics serves as an invitation to the modern followers of Jesus to seek justice while awaiting the eschatological solution to evil in the world.

FURTHER READING

Dilulio, John, Jr. 1995. "The Coming of the Super-Predators." *The Weekly Standard*, November 27.

Fernandes, Clemir et al. 2013. "CLADE V Pastoral Letter: Final Declaration of CLADE V." *Journal of Latin American Theology* 8.1: 75–79.

Green, Joel B. 1994. "Good News to Whom?" In *Jesus of Nazareth: Lord and Christ*, edited by Joel B. Green and Max Turner, 59–74. Grand Rapids: Eerdmans.

Grondona, Mariano. 2000. "A Cultural Typology of Economic Development." In *Culture Matters: How Values Shape Human Progress*, edited by Lawrence E. Harrison and Samuel P. Huntington, 44–55. New York: Basic Books.

Mshana, Rogate R. and Athena Peralta. 2015. *Economy of Life: Linking Poverty, Wealth and Ecology*. Geneva: World Council of Churches.
Sanneh, Lamin. 1987. "Christian Missions and the Western Guilt Complex." *The Christian Century*, April 8: 331–34.
Sen, Amartya. 1983. "Poor, Relatively Speaking." *Oxford Economic Papers* 35: 153–69.
Sen, Amartya. 2000. *Development as Freedom*. New Delhi: Oxford University Press.
Sharma, Samrat and Piyush Aggrawal. 2021. "Income and Debt Account of Indian Farmers: Explained." *India Today*, November 20.
Stott, John. 1975. *The Lausanne Covenant: Exposition and Commentary*. Minneapolis: World Wide Publications.
Wink, Walter. 1992. *Engaging the Powers: Discernment and Resistance in a World of Domination*. Minnesota: Fortress Press.

# 20 The Asian Faces of Jesus

K. K. YEO

Jesus and his early followers were Galilean and Judean in the (Roman-occupied) Palestine of West Asia – the "Middle East" or "Near East" from a European perspective. Being a large and iridescent continent, Asia has no singular culture, no common language, and no homogeneous identity. Asian theologies today are culturally diverse, indigenized, and profoundly catholic, thus manifesting an Asian Jesus whose face is expansively hybrid and kaleidoscopically radiant. This chapter embarks on a short cross-cultural journey in Asia, sketching Jesus in broad brushstrokes with a rich palette on an expansive canvas. This aerial view highlights modern East and South Asian Christologies, resplendent at times with the symbiotically related biblical images of Jesus in the Mediterranean landscape.

"Face" as *prosōpon* (mask, person) connotes identity, portrait, icon, and "visage" (Lévinas 1979). Face has its associative meaning of "enfacement" (identity) and "revelation" (presence) – just as "the appearance (*eidos*) of Jesus' countenance (*prosōpon*)" (Luke 9:29) manifests an indelible icon of Jesus. The following macro themes and basic forms of our perceptions of Jesus in Asia take cues from Jesus's own question to his first followers in Caesarea Philippi, "Who do you say that I am?" (Matt 16:15; Mark 8:29; Luke 9:20):[1] (1) The first section discusses the way Asian raw material (language, culture, artform) is used to express ("say") Jesus; (2) the second section paints the way Asians ("you") cast the salvific work of Jesus in context; (3) the third section delineates the relationship between the Christ who is believed and who is the identifier ("who") for his followers in Asia; and (4) the last section concludes with an Asian christological hermeneutic that aims to be dialogical and biblical in its global understanding of Jesus Christ ("I am").

Asian churches have neither monolithic nor linear propagation. In the first century the "apostle to Asia," St. Thomas, brought the gospel

---

[1] All Bible texts are from NRSV, unless otherwise indicated.

of Jesus to South India, which is evidenced by early Christian tradition such as the Syriac Acts of Thomas and King Gundaphar of India who was "identified by some as the patron of St. Thomas" (Moffett 1998–2005, 1:15; cf. 1:24–63). During the apostolic period, the apostles St. Bartholomew and St. Thaddeus preached Christ in Armenia, which became the first Christian nation in the fourth century. Another line of propagation is the modern Protestant missionary movement and global (and a few local) Pentecostal initiatives that presented Christ to Asia in Bible translation, education and literacy development, social services, and spiritual revivals – such as William Carey (1761–1834) and Amy Carmichael (1867–1951) to India; Henry Martin (1781–1812) to India and Persia; Adoniram Judson (1788–1850) to Burma; Robert Morrison (1782–1834) and Hudson Taylor (1832–1905) to China (see Moffett 1998–2005, vol. 2); and Azusa Street's Apostolic Faith's missionaries (G. E. Berg and Robert F. Cook) to central India (Kerala and Tamil Nadu) in the early 1900s (see Anderson and Tang 2005). Beyond the dissemination of Greek and Latin Christologies from Euro-American Catholic and Protestant churches in East and South Asia, the Church of the East serves the gospel mission of God throughout Asia.

## TRANSLATION AND EXPRESSION OF THE INDIGENIZED FACES OF JESUS

The indigenized faces of Jesus in Asia do radiate common features within the perspectives of the global church. Indigenous raw material, such as language, culture, arts, and religion in Asia, serve as tropes to name and refine the enfacement of Jesus. Depending on the degree of indigenization in the translation and expression of the Palestinian Jesus, Asian faces of Jesus Christ range from "stranger" or even "barbarian" to friend and natural Asian person.

### Indigenized and "Inreligionized" Jesus

The Syrian Church of the East in the first few centuries translated the gospel message from Aramaic/Syriac and Greek in Galilee and Damascus (Acts 9:1–6), Antioch (Acts 11:19–26), and Mesopotamia to other languages in Persia (Iran), Armenia, India, Mongolia, and other places in Asia. Syrian merchants and scholar-missionaries came to China in the early Tang dynasty (618–907 CE). The Syrian monk Alopen (ca. 600–50) was commissioned to translate the "true sutra" of the Church of the East for the Chinese Imperial Library. A document dated 781 CE titled *Sutra of Veneration* lists some biblical book titles in Chinese translation and expresses the Trinity as the "three persons" (*sans shen*) united in the one body of the "mysterious person the royal Father Aloha [Elohim, God] ... the responding person the royal Son *Mishihe* [Messiah, Christ] ... the witnessing person Rûḥâ d̠-Qûd̠šâ [the Spirit of Holiness]" (Liu 2021, 241).

The invaluable *Jingjiao Bei*/Stele (the so-called Nestorian Tablet, a misnomer in the sense that Jingjiao Christology is not Nestorian) contains the christological expression "hid his majesty and assumed a human being" – similar to the perspective of the Antiochene school in Syria on *logos-anthropos* Christology (the eternal Word assumes the human Jesus). Both the Syriac church and the Chinese *Jingjiao* affirm the distinctive natures of divinity and humanity of Christ while holding their union in one person of Christ (hypostatic union; cf. John 17:5).

The *Jingjiao* Stele indicates an inculturation that involves "inreligionization" (the Sri Lankan Jesuit priest Aloysius Pieris's term), as carved on the stele are two dragons holding a pearl, a cross (not a crucifix) that surmounts a lotus (the emblem for Buddhism), and a cloud (the emblem for Daoism or Islam). Asian religious symbols and scriptures become the mediating raw material for Asian biblical Christologies. This is at one level similar to the way Paul would quote extrabiblical material (in Acts 17:28; 1 Cor 15:33; Tit 1:12) – although not for his *christological* formulations, thus raising the question of whether and how to use cultural material in Christologies.

Another example of inreligionization comes from the Spanish Jesuit missionary Jerome Xavier (great-nephew of Saint Francis Xavier), who retold the story of Jesus in his *Mirʾāt al-quds* (Mirror of Holiness) with the intention to convert the Mughal court (India) of Emperor Akbar and his son, Jahangir, to the Catholic faith (Sugirtharajah 2018, 12–16).

### Buddho-Daoist Jesus

Asia is the birthplace of Zoroaster, Gautama Buddha, Jesus, and Mani, and their teachings are primarily ways of life – out of such wisdom and ethics come the metaphysical ruminations of philosophies. Asian theologians readily use the Bible and Theravada Buddhism (the *Sila*) to construct Christology based on right thought (theology), right speech (teaching), and right action (living).

The Buddho-Daoist Christ was the only permitted appearance in a centralized Tang Chinese empire where "foreign religions" were banned (in 845 CE) and Buddhism and Daoism were the approved, legitimate ones. The Chinese *Jingjiao* then expresses the Tri-unity as the "three persons" (*san shen* in Chinese), using a loanword from Buddhist Sanskrit, "*Trikāya*," the three bodies of Buddha; these are "the *Dharmakāya* (*fashen* in Chinese), the truth-body, unlimited and unfathomable; *Saṃbhogakāya* (*paoshen*), the enjoyment body, blissful and bright; and the *Nirmāṇakāya* (*yingshen*), the response body, compassionate and visible" (Liu 2021, 241). Another example of direct inreligionized translation is "the cloak (*himation*) of Jesus" (Luke 8:44) rendered as *jiasha* (Sanskrit *kāṣāya*), a dress commonly worn by Buddhist monks to this day.

### Jesus the Sage, Jesus the Teacher, and Jesus the "Barbarian"

Similar to the Matthean Jesus, the Asian Jesus has been highly regarded as the authoritative teacher (Matt 7:28–29, 8:5–13, 10:1, 28:18). Catholic missionaries sought to persuade the elite and intelligentsia to follow Christ. Many of them, such as Giulio Aleni (1582–1649), translated the Vulgate's term *Dominus* for Jesus (i.e. "Lord"; e.g. John 4:11) into the Confucianist term *zunzhe*, literally "honorable one," depicting Jesus to be a morally perfect savior and sage. Matteo Ricci (1552–1610) turned to a Confucian Christ in his *The True Meaning of the Lord of Heaven*. Ricci imprinted moral-spiritual Confucian teaching on Jesus's portrait and dimmed the light on "proclaiming Christ crucified" (1 Cor 1:23, 2:2), whereas both Franciscans and Dominicans have been more explicit in their preaching of Jesus's crucifixion in Asia. Ricci's image of Jesus is of one who dresses like himself – in the silk robes of the literati; while the Japanese Jesus is dressed in a kimono, and the Indian Jesus in the saffron robe worn by Hindu holy sages called *sadhus*. In the Asian learning traditions, the followers of Jesus are "God-taught" (1 Thess 4:9) to love one another and inherit eternal life.

In the Pakistani and Indian context, Raymundo Panikkar projects Jesus's perfect union with God as parallel to the idea of perfect self-realization in Hinduism (Panikkar 1964). Mahatma Gandhi (1869–1948) drew much inspiration from the Hindu and Jainist traditions, as well as Jesus's teachings, especially the Sermon on the Mount, casting Jesus as a morally perfect teacher. Imitating Jesus, Gandhi's *satyagraha* (the search for truth) and *ahimsa* (nonviolence) would empower the Indian people for national independence.

Such an amicable, exemplary Jesus has not always been popular in Asia. Anti-Christian edicts in Japan since the sixteenth century, until they were lifted in 1873, rejected Jesus as a perceived European foreigner and "aggressor." Large numbers of anti-Christian treatises from Confucian and Buddhist apologists and critics were published in seventeenth-century China, viewing Jesus as a "barbarian" or "foreign demon" (*yanggui*) who posed serious threats to Chinese civilization.

The "rites controversy" in many Asian countries that practice ancestral veneration, Shinto shrine worship, shamanistic rituals, or traditional rites of Indigenous cultures has projected the propaganda that Jesus and his followers are not welcome in Asia. Some Asians have reproached the incommensurability of Jesus's perfection and his crucifixion as a criminal. Others have impugned God's justice in appointing his Son Jesus to appear first to the "chosen people" of Israel, while ignoring other peoples. In parts of Asia even today, the Christian faith is considered an "evil cult" (*xiejiao*) and Jesus's friends imprisoned or murdered as "heretics," their church buildings demolished, and uplifted crosses dismantled.

### Vernacular Christology

The Asian expression of Jesus and the translation of the biblical God have been contested. There is no sacred language, and to incarnate God-in-Jesus in-linguistically all vernaculars are used to name the previously "unknown" God and Jesus (Acts 17) in Asia. The Islamic government in Malaysia once prohibited Christians from using the pre-Islamic Arabic word "Allah" to translate God in their Bible, despite the fact that the Qur'an and Islamic tradition do regard Jesus ('*Īsā*) as a Muslim. Similarly, the Burmese Buddhist monk Ashin Agga Dhamma condemned Christians using "Pali words such as *Phaya* (god), *Thawara* (eternal), *Thama* (truth)" (Li 2014, 312) in their Bible.

However, in the cross-cultural and interreligious Indonesian context, J. B. Banawiratma has long explored the dialogue between Javanese culture and biblical Christology in order to form and transform local communities (Banawiratma 1998, 366). Other theologians, mentioned in the intercultural work of A. A. Yewangoe, affirm the dialogical naming of the biblical God and Jesus as *Iho*, the supreme divinity exalted by Maoris in New Zealand; "*Panda nyura ngara, panda peka tamu*" (the one whose name cannot be spoken), the supreme divinity in Sumba, Indonesia; "*Uis Neno Mnanu*" (the Lord of Heaven) in Timor; and *Debata*, who is "*Ompu Tuan Mula Jadi na Bolon*" (the One who is great and strong, the Origin of all that is) of the Batak Toba tribe in Sumatra (Yewangoe 2003: 94–95).

The first Protestant Chinese Bible, *Shen-tian Sheng-shu* (literally, "God Heaven Holy Book") was the ecumenical effort of Robert Morrison, William Milne (1785–1822), and Chinese contributors including Li Shi-gong, Yun Kwan-ming, and Chen Lao-yi. Likewise, the Chinese Union Bible was an ecumenical effort, reflected in its cross-linguistic translation. For example, it translates *agapē* and *logos* respectively into *ren* (benevolence, in its Confucianist meaning) and *dao*, thus signifying the Chinese Jesus as Love and Word. The Greek word *logos* in the Gospel of John is rendered as *dao* in Chinese, a Daoist term that has rich meanings of eternal principle, practical wisdom, and eloquent speech. Jesus as *Dao* means he is (1) the Creator of the cosmos, (2) personified Wisdom, and (3) the self-proclaimed "I am" or "I will be what I will be" of Exodus 3:14, the rhetorical-*Dao* God who speaks order from chaos, meaning from void.

These vernacular faces of Jesus not only fulfill cultural ideals, expressing biblical concepts in Chinese understanding, but also use biblical messages to reread Chinese cultures. Bible translation has inculturated the good news of Jesus; it has also contributed to the linguistic development of many Asian nations and people groups (dialects). Bible translators edited dictionaries, such as Robert Morrison's *A Dictionary of the Chinese Language* (1815), Affonso Gonsalvez's *Chinese–Portuguese Dictionary* (1836), Vial Paul's *Dictionnaire Français–Lolo, Dialecte Gni* (1909), and Judson's *Burmese–English Dictionary* (1921). Biblical vocabulary and syntax, such as the Chinese Union Bible's, were even adopted in the development of a national language (*Guoyu*).

## INTERPRETATION AND THE SAVING WORK OF JESUS IN ASIAN CONTEXTS

Asia's massive and multilayered life situations have numerous problems – problems also found in other continents and faced by the global church – including poverty and war, natural disaster and population displacement, colonialism and dictatorship, migration and exile, human trafficking and piracy. The salvific work of Jesus requires his followers in Asia to interpret Jesus in the dynamic intersection of faith and life context.

The Welsh Baptist missionary Timothy Richard (1845–1919) practiced his integration approach to reach Chinese elites *and* grassroots communities and to work in famine relief *and* preaching the gospel. Many Pentecostals in Asia are "'Evangelical' in theology, ... believing in a personal ... salvation, ... 'living a holy life'" (Anderson and Tang 2005, 2). Yet recent adherents such as the Yoido Full Gospel Church in Korea and the Jesus Is Lord movement in the Philippines not only have learned from their Latin American siblings about salvation from social and political systems but also demonstrate that liberation theology's "preferential option for the poor" can be fulfilled by the poor's "preferential option for the Spirit" (Chestnut 2003).

### Christ the King on Earth and in Heaven

In the New Testament, Jesus is asked, "Are you the Messiah, the Son of God?" (Matt 26:63; Mark 14:61; Luke 22:67). In Mark 15:26, "The inscription of the charge against him read, 'The King of the Jews'" (see also Matt 27:37; Luke 23:38; John 19:19). Against the Pax Romana context of conquest, the Gospels portray Jesus the king riding on a donkey (Matt 21:1–11; Mark 11:1–11, Luke 19:28–44; John 12:12–19 in relation to 1 Kings 1:33; Zech 9:9–10) for peace, a king who did not save himself (e.g. by coming down from the cross) but saved others (Matt 27:39–42; Mark 15:29–32; Luke 23:35–37) in service to them: "for the Son of Man came not to be served but to serve, and to give his life as a ransom for many" (Mark 10:45). In the Asian context, where tribal, religious, political, and racial conflicts are disturbingly common, Gani Wiyono sees Javanese Jesus to be the *Ratu Adil*, the Just King in Indonesia – although, besides the biblical witness, he also uses Javanese religious wisdom, which speaks of the Just King who will usher a messianic hope of cosmic, spiritual, and social liberation from sin, poverty, and injustice (Wiyono 1999).

During the Qing dynasty (1721–1911), China went through violent changes, especially wars within (warlords) and without (trade conflicts with foreign nations). Hong Xiuquan's (1814–64) self-claim to be Christ's younger brother turned the Jesus-the-King message into a psychotic "gospel." He initiated the Taiping Rebellion (1850–64) to exorcise the Manchu "demons" and foreign "aggressors" from China, but in the end failed to set up a Christian millenarian theocracy on earth. Partly because of this eerie historical memory, later independent family churches, such as Christian Assembly (Little Flock, founded by Watchman Nee [1903–72] in 1922) and Christian Tabernacle (founded by Wang Mingdao [1900–91]) in China committed themselves to love Christ *only*. By contrast, Wu Leiquan (1870–1944) argued for a socialist kingdom and a Jesus of idealism (perfect personhood) and materialism (justice and peace to the world), and the Three-Self *Patriotic* Movement (TSPM) did not find any discrepancy between loving Christ *and* their socialist country.

Can a Christian church adopt a state ideology to support Christian identity *and* social harmony? Is praying politically subversive? And what does it mean that "Jesus is Lord"? Acts 17 narrates the Thessalonian crowd charging Paul and Silas for contradicting the decree of Caesar, "saying that there is another king named Jesus" (17:7). Paul was preaching neither about insurrection nor about subversion of the Roman Empire, but as Roman audiences did then, so Chinese crowds or governments can today perceive the faith of "Jesus as Lord" as a threat to the existing political power. Wang Yi (b. 1973), the pastor of the Qiuyu (Early Rain) Church who preached Jesus as Lord, was sentenced to nine years in prison for "inciting subversion of state power" (Nation and Tseng 2022, 234). Christians in Hong Kong are navigating similarly treacherous waters regarding biblical faith clashing with the politicized perception of such faith as treason, such as in the Umbrella Movement or Occupy Central with Love and Peace that protest the will of the Chinese Communist rule in Hong Kong. The current agreement in Vatican–China relations on the appointment of Chinese bishops and the placement of the portrait of the Chinese Communist Party's general secretary Xi Jinping in liturgical spaces of TSPM churches sharpen the question of whether a "sinicized Jesus" has threatened to dethrone Christ as Lord and King.

Asia's Jesus as King highlights Jesus's liberation of his followers from oppressive or totalitarian systems in Asia. Because of the Korean economic and politically oppressive system, *minjung* (the masses) theology (pioneered by the theologians Ahn Byung-mu and Suh Nam Dong) strongly accentuates Jesus the Liberator. By the same token, M. M. Thomas (1916–96) and Stanley Samartha (1920–2001) in India championed a Christology of revolution (Küster 2001, chap. 7). Akin to two sides of the same coin, the revolutionary work of Jesus does coexist with his mystical work in the lives of many Asian followers of Jesus.

**Jesus the In-Between, the Mystery**

Diasporic migration and refugeeism are the new normal in the Asian way of life. Thus, Christian life in Asia is analogous to living with Jesus with nomadic consciousness, in exile and migration, in marginality and liminality. Adoniram Judson, a Baptist US missionary known for his Burmese Bible translation (with the significant help of the Burmese scholar U Shwe Ngong), wrote of his experience of God as "a great Unknown ... I find Him not" (Moffett 1998–2005, 2:334 n.34). In the context of the East Asian worlds of meditation and the quest for supernatural bliss, the mystical understanding of Jesus has enabled Jesus's followers there to pursue salvation in Orthodox divinization (*theosis*), intertwined with the Daoist soteriology of "becoming immortals" (*chengxian*), or the Buddhist Jesus of attaining Buddha-nature (*tathāgatagarbha*).

Yin-yang language has become widely used as a metaphor for an assimilated Christology among Asian theologians (e.g. Jung Young Lee, K. K. Yeo), that is, a Christology that is fully biblical *and* fully inculturated in Asia, like the two natures in the one person of Christ. Facile God-talk with "either-or" grammar may be accessible and popular, but it is not enduring in an Asia that prefers nuances. Asian Christologies favor Ignatius of Antioch's Christology of silence: "through his [Jesus's] speech he may act and by his silence he may be known" (Ignatius, *Epistle to the Ephesians* 15:4; my translation) or Mahāyāna (great vehicle) Buddhism's meditative self-emptying, "emptiness" (*sunyata*), or "nonattachment" (not nihilism) and "dependent co-arising" with Christ. Thus for Asians living according to Paul's in-Christ teaching, "I live, now not I, but Christ lives in me" (Gal 2:20, my translation), this reality is a direct mystical experience of God that grants them freedom and eternal life.

### Decolonial Christ, the Womanist, and the Ecojustice Lord

The decolonial Christ critiques and resists any colonial interpretation of Jesus's death and suffering that legitimizes the subjugated obedience of the colonized to colonizers from the West or the East. The Asian decolonial Christ is complex because of the region's patriarchal, dominating societies, intra- and intercountry colonization, and militarism compounded by greed and corruption.

Oceanian faces of Jesus resemble the Oceanian world, those islands that are often unknown and passed by or passed over. If those airplanes and ships make a stop, the visitors or settlers are prone to dominate. Almost all indigenous Pacific languages are given spelling systems (orthography) by European missionaries. Asian companies, also colonizers and settlers, have similarly profited from the areas and devastated the ecology there. Jione Havea's Oceanian Jesus is the "ecojustice" Lord and Savior who seeks to restore intrinsic worth, interconnectedness, voice, purpose, mutual custodianship, and resistance for the people and the Earth (Havea 2014b). Oceanian Christians view belonging as an important attribute of Jesus, and they regard Jesus as opalescent, offering to the rest of the world potency of life and lustrous theologico-cultural expressions (Havea 2014a, 12). Siosifa Pole, working among the islander diaspora in New Zealand, uses a Tongan understanding of *vahevahe* (sharing) as a life of discipleship participating in the salvific work of Christ (Pole 2015).

Seeing Mother Earth's body in terms of ecojustice, Asian womanists (e.g. Virginia Fabella and Mary John Mananzan in the Philippines) promote the liberation of Jesus for humankind facing all kinds of oppression and discrimination, whether it is economic, political, or religious or based on gender or race. Kwok Pui-lan's feminist ecological Christology uses nature metaphors and wisdom motifs, and she "accentuates Jesus' teachings about right living, his relation with the natural environment and other human beings, his subversive wisdom on ecojustice, and his promise of God's compassion for all humankind" (Kwok 2000, 93).

### Jesus the Shakti, the Shaman, and the Healer

Spirit Christology in Asia (e.g. Pandipeddi Chenchiah and Swami Abhishiktānanda in India) wears the ancient masks of the Hindu concepts of *atman* (breath or life), *antaryāmin* (indweller), Sakti (energy or power), and *ānanda* (bliss) (see Manohar 2007), as well as that of the Korean woman-priest called *mudang*. A. J. Appasamy uses the *bhakti* tradition of Hindu mysticism in the Bhagavadgita, the feminine principle, as Jesus's embodiment in order to speak of a harmonious relationship between humans and nature, men and women (Manohar 2007). Likewise, K. K. Yeo's "Chinese eco-womanist" Christology is based on the ancient yin-yang philosophy and his interpretation of nature as "inspirited" creation of God in Romans 8 from traditional Daoist wisdom (Yeo 2021). To Asian womanists, the fact that Jesus is a man need not cause hermeneutical suspicion, though there is continuing debate about whether and how maleness is an ontological necessity for Jesus's work of salvation. Being a man in a patriarchal society and colonized territory, Jesus in Palestine could speak just as powerfully of truth to oppression or of love to injustice as women can in many parts of the world.

Korean womanists see Christ as the Priest of *han* (i.e. "oppressive sorrow"; "suffering" or "pain" in biblical semantics) – the feeling of the oppressed with just indignation. To rid such deep sorrow (*han*), female shamans called *mudang* would use dances and rituals to allow the oppressed to participate in the mourning and restorative process of *han-puri* (i.e. "release of sorrow"; "salvation" in biblical semantics), as the priests exorcize *han* for liberation in justice and hope. Won-Don Kang interprets the liberation ritual by Christian shamans as the "master of ecstasy" who is able to mediate with empathy and solidarity with the oppressed in the cycle of suffering, death, and resurrection of Christ (Kang 2018).

Jesus the Liberator saves women from patriarchy, militarism, and poverty, which are the predators of nature, women, and children. Critiquing Nagaland "mascu-surrogacy" and patriarchy, the Christology of natality and the cross of childbearing portrays Jesus as a surrogate-friend sharing Naga women's pain, thus sustaining the women with embrace, respect, and nourishment (Jamir 2014). Pandita Ramabai's womanist theology, which is one of gender equality and empowerment in the context of Indian patriarchal and caste society, intends to save high-caste women as well (see Jamir 2014). Indian Pentecostals understand Jesus as the exorcist and healer in their dire context of poor health care, the caste system, and religious persecution.

### Jesus the Savior in Shame and Honor Culture

The Asian lifeworld to a large extent is still plagued by disease, poverty, pollution, and wars. These are registered as dehumanization and disgrace. Asian eyes turn not to perfunctory forgiveness but strive for human dignity and ecological sustainability. Jesus as God's image, which is truthfully beautiful and honorable (2 Cor 3:18; Rom 13:14; Gal 3:27), is also God's holy wisdom (Prov 8; cf. 1 Cor 1:30; Col 1:15, Heb 1:3). In a culture that values honor, Asian Christians value the expiation work of Christ, which is understood by Yeo as follows:

> [A]s *expiation* traced its theological root to the Hebrew word *kappōret*, i.e., "mercy seat" on the Ark of Covenant in the Holy of Holies, thus seeing "God loved us and sent his Son to be the expiation (*hilasmos*) of our sins" (1 John 4:10). Jesus Christ is "the expiation not only for our sins but also for the sins of the whole world" (1 John 2:2) ... Soteriology is not simply about atoning sacrifice but also offering of love. (Yeo 2017, 10)

In Asian cultures of honor and shame, they consider what Jesus *sets right* (*dikiaōthēsetai*, Rom 3:20–24) as not "judicial justification and imputed righteousness," as many Calvinist scholars would understand. Receptive to theologies of world Christianity, the US Methodist scholar Robert Jewett affirms that God stands with the weak and the oppressed and vindicates them by setting them right (Psalm 82:1–3) in reversing the lowly from shame to honor (Psalm 31:1–2). Consequently, the shameful cross of Jesus in the New Testament *sets right* the distorted value system of shame and glory (Jewett 2007, 281).

## RECEPTION OF JESUS BY ASIANS AND THEIR SELF-UNDERSTANDING

### Identity of Jesus and Asian Christians

We become what we worship; the Asian receptions of Jesus reflect their self-understanding through Christ who appears to each person in a form appropriate to their age and setting. The self-understanding of Asian followers of Jesus involves an existential dialogue between Scripture and the deep imbrication of their contexts, languages, and extrabiblical texts. In Asia, Jesus is the spiritual leader as guru (e.g. Nanak, Buddha, Jnana guru [Ponambalam Ramanathan in India]); Jesus's natures are attributes in the yin-yang paradigm of the divine–human and human–human relationship. Keshub Chunder Sen's Christology portrays the "divine humanity" in whom "God of truth and holiness" dwells (Kärkkäinen 2010, 382); Jesus the Satyagrahi (Truth-clinging) of Gandhi esteems Jesus's suffering not as a punishment but as a truth that clings to the struggle for justice even unto death.

A large section of the Indian population are *dalits* (downtrodden), who in turn make up 60 percent of Indian Christians. Jesus not only identifies with *dalits* as their friend; Jesus the *dalit* himself without a halo comes to liberate them (Luke 7:21–22) (Nirmal 1990) – to use Isaiah's words, he has "marred appearance ... no majesty ... despised and rejected ... a man of suffering and acquainted with infirmity ... afflicted and wounded ... but by his bruises we are healed" (Isa 52:14; 53:2–8). Dalits are the "untouchables" (*panchamas*), thought to be "polluted" by birth and thus not taught Sanskrit; yet despite their not initially having been taught to read, Jesus saves and enables them to find hope and salvation in their learning to read the Bible.

### Crucified Identity, Hiddenness, and Silence

The Jesuits led by Francis Xavier first arrived at Malacca in the Malay empire in the 1550s and then embarked to Japan, where they were warmly received by the feudal lords, *daimyo*. Yet Asian reception of Jesus is not always hospitable. The facial lacerations and deformity of Jesus mirror the crucified bodies and traumatized identity of his followers in Asia. If Asia is Jesus's "hometown," he is still to some extent "a prophet without honor" (Luke 4:24) there.

Christians are the minority in most Asian countries (Central Asian nations as well as Saudi Arabia, Afghanistan, Maldives, Bangladesh, Bhutan, and Cambodia), so marginalization and persecution are rampant. Underground churches in China and North Korea and hidden Christians such as Kakure Kirishitan (the Catholic community around Nagasaki, Japan) are a few examples of Christian anonymity adopted for the sake of survival. The Japanese Roman Catholic novelist Shūsaku Endō reflects on God's silence when Japanese Christians were tortured in order to force them to apostatize and renounce Jesus, especially during the Tokugawa Shogunate in the 1600s. Endō thinks that the crucified people hauntingly become "Christs," in the way of Jesus's sacrifice and agony, with no resurrection in sight (see Sugirtharajah 2018, chap. 9).

Despite the prominent use of affective, neighborly (Sadayandy Batumalai in Malaysia), and friendship semantics in Asian Christologies, Asian Christians in persecuted regions push their faith envelopes to experience God's *apatheia* (equanimity), thus continuing an unsettled debate in the universal church since antiquity regarding divine impassibility and immutability. In the aftermath of atomic bombs being dropped in Japan, Paul Inhwan Kim writes about Kazoh Kitamori's "theology of pain" that has an impact on Jürgen Moltmann's *The Crucified God* (Kim 2011). Kitamore's Christology and the theology of *han* (oppressive sorrow) see Jesus's suffering as divine pathos (passion).

Paul Inhwan Kim argues that the patristic theologian Cyril of Alexandria rightly views *apatheia* as going beyond negative qualification of God's perfect affections to positive certitude of God's *agape* in Jesus's work of salvation (Kim 2011). Because of Christ's *communicatio idiomatum* (on the unity of the divinity and humanity of Jesus, thus with God the Father, and the interaction between God and humanity; cf. John 8:58, 10:30), the ineffable mystery of Asian Christologies allows Christians to reflect and live in the incarnate Word's (Jesus's) impassible suffering as (1) God's transformative love, which not only overcomes powers of sin and death but also restores them to eternal communion with God, and (2) their participation in God's divine nature.

### Visualized Jesus and Asian Arts

Asian aesthetic cultures are conducive to Jesus's self-manifestation (glory). Many Asian churches influenced by Hudson Taylor, for example, adopt patristic christological typology and allegorical interpretation, with some churches encouraging the use of aesthetics and imagination to highlight the Bible's spiritual truths and its spiritual sustenance. Catholics in Asia often use local landscapes, buildings, and artistic expressions in their illustrated texts and visualization of Jesus's life with images. The painting of the Virgin Mary with the child Jesus is similar to the image of Guanyin (bodhisattva of great mercy), emphasizing kinship and a spirit of empathy (cf. Mark 6:34; Luke 15:20).

In times of persecution, and for the aesthetic power of inspiring faith, various art forms are used to portray Jesus. Spiritual literature (*ling xing wen xue* by Shi Tiesheng [1951–2010]) and aspirational literature (*yan zhi wen xue*) underline "divinity within humanity" to let beauty, virtue, and the Spirit lift up Christians' devotion to God. Moreover, literary imagination of Jesus in Asia intends to bring about social impact, and it can be found in various forms such as fiction and poetry. Other arts are also used, such as calligraphy, papercutting, skin shadow puppetry, and dance.

### Christ the People, Jesus the Reconciler

The image of Jesus is seen from the Buddhist perspective as bodhisattva –compassionate, spiritual leader – although Buddhism is limited in shedding light on Jesus the Lord as the Son of God and the Savior of humankind from the powers of sin and death. The Vietnamese Buddhist monk and Zen teacher Thich Nhat Hanh and the Sri Lankan theologian Aloysius Pieris advocate a "double baptism," namely baptism in both "the Jordan of Asian religions" and "the Calvary of Asian poverty" (Pieris 1987: 45–48) – for Jesus has crossed over borders from heaven to earth, and in his baptism constitutes a people of God marked by God's righteousness and grace (Matt 3:15).

Jesus the Reconciler is the basis of cross-cultural Christology. Christ's work of "reconciliation" (*katallagē*, Rom 5:10–11; 2 Cor 5:18–20) is translated as "at-one-ment" (William Tyndale). Asians read Paul's usage of atonement sacrifice (Lev 16; cf. Rom 3:25) in their context and identify with the first-century Roman economic context of converting debt dissymmetry to mutual gift-exchange, and of transforming conflict to mutual friendship and sacrificial love (*agapē*). The contemporary Asian context is riven by conflicts across ethnic, national, and religious lines spinning in pernicious lethal cycles, such as the unrest and enmity between India and Pakistan, the strife of the Maoist insurgency in Nepal, and the bad blood between Christians and Muslims in Indonesia. The effacement of divine presence in Asia desperately calls for Jesus to be the Reconciler.

### Jesus at the Table with Asians

In quoting Deuteronomy 8:3, Jesus's words "one does not live by *bread* alone" (Matt 4:4; emphasis mine) may be misunderstood in Asia (the emphasis is actually "alone"). In Asia, "I am the bread of life" (John 6:41–51) is both a spiritual nourishment *and also* food on the kitchen table. The Chinese saying "People regard food as heaven" reiterates the *social-spiritual unity* of a meal as communion with God *and* among each other. Jesus on the Emmaus Road said to his followers, "How foolish you are, and slow of heart to believe all that the prophets have declared! Were it not necessary that the Messiah [Christ] should suffer and enter into his glory?" (Luke 24:25–26). Luke explains the "last" supper that opens their eyes and lifts their hearts: "When he was at the table with them, he *took* bread, *blessed* and *broke* it, and *gave* it to them. Then their eyes were opened, and they recognized him" (Luke 24:30–32; emphasis mine).

Asian churches, especially the house church movement and cell-group gatherings, often share meals together after worship as an extension of the Communion. The *agapē* meal (love feast) in Asian lands is sometimes celebrated as a fellowship meal in homes or soup kitchens with thanksgiving to God's providence. For the early followers of Jesus in the New Testament, the Lord's Supper (Matt 26:17–29; Mark 14:12–25; Luke 22:7–38; 1 Cor 11:23–25) is amplified into the feeding of the multitudes (Matt 14:13–21, 15:29–39; Mark 6:31–44, 8:1–10; Luke 9:12–17; John 6:1–14) – exegetically supported by the liturgical gestures of "he took, he blessed, he broke, he gave." The Asian celebration of this sacrament ("holy rite" in Chinese) of the Communion or the social meals is to save any space partitioned by the secular/sacred split, thus bringing about the communion between God and humanity – in turn as their thanksgiving ethics of living together in the common well-being of God's *oikonomia* (economy, rule).

## CONCLUSION: DIALOGICAL ART OF ASIAN CHRISTOLOGICAL HERMENEUTICS

An Asian hermeneutic of Jesus constantly negotiates both indigenous texts and worldviews with their ingenious cross-cultural translation, expression, interpretation, and reception of Jesus. Such a quest of Jesus in Asia obscures the exact boundaries of exegesis and eisegesis. Asian Christologies hold biblical texts and Asian cultures in creative tension, thereby displaying the power and dignity and auspiciousness of Jesus Christ in Asia and for world Christianity.

Asian Christians have trailblazed a robust quest for Jesus by being a conscientized community of Christ. This quest of Jesus crystallizes a Christian identity and countenance of Jesus that are contextual *and* ecumenical (see the "universal" characteristic of the churches of Asia Minor in the description "saints from every tribe and language and people and nation" in Rev 5:9; 7:9; 10:11; 11:9; 13:7; 14:6; 17:15) – and precisely this dialogical tension between catholicity and indigeneity makes the church authentic and its mission transformative.

Both the Bible and Asian cultures are passages whereby the "All-in-all" (1 Cor 15:28) God envelops the past and future in "the Beginning and the End" (Rev 1:4–8; cf. Isa 44:6). Therefore, Asian Christians bear witness to almighty God-in-Christ, who is in and beyond their history and cultures. In short, the dialectical process of christological readings by Asians aspires toward mutual readings of the universal gospels and Asian scriptures, of languages biblical and vernacular, of Word and cultures both made unique and powerful.

FURTHER READING

Anderson, Allan and Edmond Tang, eds. 2005. *Asian and Pentecostal: The Charismatic Face of Christianity in Asia*. Oxford: Regnum/APTS Press.

Gene, Green, Steve T. Pardue, and K. K. Yeo, eds. 2020. *Majority World Theology: Christian Doctrine in Global Context*. Downers Grove: IVP Academic.

Kärkkäinen, Veli-Matti. 2010. "Christology in Africa, Asia, and Latin America." In *The Blackwell Companion to Jesus*, edited by Delbert Burkett, 375–93. Oxford: Wiley-Blackwell.

Sugirtharajah, R. S. 2018. *Jesus in Asia*. Cambridge, MA: Harvard University Press.

## 21 Jesus of Africa

### DIANE B. STINTON AND VICTOR I. EZIGBO

"Jesus of Africa" signifies the enduring and enlivening presence of the risen Christ among African Christians from the first century to the twenty-first. Africa is part of the Jesus story from the earliest gospel accounts: Egypt provided protection for the infant Jesus and his parents from Herod's persecution (Matt 2:13–15). Simon from Cyrene, on the northern coast of Libya, carried the cross for Jesus on the way to the crucifixion (Matt 27:32; Mark 15:21; Luke 23:26). Africans from "Egypt and the parts of Libya belonging to Cyrene" were among the Jews and proselytes who were present at Pentecost (Acts 2:10). The Ethiopian eunuch, in his Spirit-led encounter with Philip on the road to Gaza, came to faith in Jesus as the one who fulfills the prophetic Scriptures (Acts 8:26–40). And Lucius from Cyrene, a prophet and teacher in the church in Antioch (Acts 13:1), was among those Jewish believers scattered in persecution who proclaimed Christ not only to Jews but also to Greeks (Acts 11:20). Jewish believers also proclaimed the story of Jesus in Africa according to Coptic Christianity, which traces its origins to the apostle Mark.

Christian communities in North Africa contributed to the discussions on the person and work of Jesus Christ that preceded the christological controversies in the fifth century CE. For example, Clement of Alexandria (d. ca. 210) described Jesus as constituting a "New Song," meaning the mystery of the incarnation or the manifestation of the eternal *Logos* for humanity's salvation and knowledge about God's activity in the world.[1] During the Trinitarian debates and controversies in the fourth century CE, the Libyan presbyter Arius, working in Alexandria, argued that God the Father was the unbegotten being who willed or generated the *logos* that became embodied in Jesus Christ. Therefore, Arius insisted, the title *true* God was appropriate for God the Father alone

---

[1] Clement, *Exhortation to the Greeks* 1. Unless otherwise specified, ancient North African Christian writers are cited according to the Loeb Classical Library.

346

(*Thalia*, in Williams 2002, 65). The ecumenical Council of Nicaea (325 CE) ruled against Arius, noting in its creedal statement that Jesus Christ was consubstantial with God the Father and, as such, was the true God. Athanasius, another prominent African theologian, defended this orthodoxy – the official teaching of the church regarding the Trinity, particularly the relationship between the Father and the Son (Anatolios 2004).

In the fifth century, the Council of Chalcedon grounded its deliberation on the ontological constitution of Jesus Christ in the decision of the Council of Nicaea and subsequent councils. Again, African Christian theologians produced creative christological insights. Cyril of Alexandria argued for one incarnate nature (miaphysite Christology) as the most viable way to understand the union of divine and human natures of Jesus and the impact of his salvific work on humanity (Grillmeier 1975, 473–78) After the christological ruling of the Council of Chalcedon, the Coptic Christians who retained the one incarnate nature Christology suffered persecutions. The Melkites, who enforced the ruling of Chalcedon, ferociously persecuted them, yet Coptic Christians found refuge under the newly established Muslim rule. Subsequent persecution under Muslim rule, however, contributed to the later decline of Coptic Christian communities in Egypt. Yet other Christian communities continued to flourish throughout the medieval period, particularly in Ethiopia.

So, despite misconceptions of Christianity as a Western/white religion imported by Europeans since the fifteenth century, the story of Jesus in Africa reveals that, from the beginning, African believers have received, interpreted, and experienced the presence of Christ, embracing and expressing his significance in their individual lives and communities. The wooden figure of the crucified Christ in St. Benedict's Priory, Nubuamis, Namibia, printed on the cover of this volume, clearly illustrates African Christians' experience of Christ as African within their own identity and culture.

Africa is now a wellspring of world Christianity. With estimates of more than 700 million followers of Jesus, comprising approximately 25 percent of the global population of Christians, it is imperative to consider African believers' understanding and lived experience of Jesus Christ, or in the term coined by the New Testament scholar Larry Hurtado, "Christ-devotion."

Hurtado argues that "Christ-devotion" goes beyond "Christology," which commonly refers to "the beliefs about Jesus ... and the factors that shape them" (Hurtado 1998, viii). This term also encompasses "the wider matters of the role of Jesus in the beliefs and religious life of ... Christians" (Hurtado 1998, viii). Hurtado underlines that it was this religious life that formed the most significant difference between the earliest Christians and other religious adherents. However important the titles and functions these believers ascribed to Christ, of greatest consequence was their devotion, or the "actions which flow from and are determined by religious experience" (Wach 1944, 25 quoted in Hurtado 1998, 99), including the inner sphere of thoughts and feelings and the outer sphere of observable, religious practices. Hurtado outlines early Christian hymns, prayers, invocations, celebrations of the Eucharist, confession, and prophecy, all related directly to Jesus. Social and ethical aspects of following Jesus further shaped early Christian practice, or "christopraxis." Hurtado insists that attention must be paid to the actual religious life of early Jesus-followers, not merely the doctrinal and intellectual developments. He concludes: "Whoever would seek to understand truly the fervent christological discussion of ancient or modern times must first appreciate the religious life that preceded and underlay the ancient development and that continues to inspire sacrificial commitment and intense intellectual effort to this day" (Hurtado 1998, 128).

To relate Hurtado's scholarship to "the fervent christological discussion" in modern Africa, it is salutary to consider the actual religious life of African Christians in relation to Jesus and in relation to first-century Christians' beliefs and practices. We will seek to identify currents of Christ-devotion in the life of the apostolic church reported in Acts and their African ripples in analogous or continuous ways throughout history, focusing primarily upon contemporary African Christianity.

Acts is a theological narrative that continues from the Gospel of Luke's account of "all that Jesus did and taught from the beginning" (Acts 1:1) to "the continued accomplishment of God's saving purposes through the risen Lord Jesus" (Thompson 2011, 22). These continuing acts flow along the lines of expansion, as the resurrected Christ calls the disciples to be his witnesses "in Jerusalem, in all Judea and Samaria, and to the ends of the earth" (Acts 1:8). The swelling currents of the gospel and Christ-devotion also extend along cultural lines, breaching religious barriers from Jews to God-fearers to gentiles, as well as social barriers from presumed "insiders" within God's kingdom to "outsiders" welcomed into the people of God.

Correspondingly, the story of Jesus of Africa recounts the expansion of the gospel throughout Africa and its diffusion into manifold cultures, creating the intricate tributaries of Christ-devotion evident today. This description of Acts could also apply to an account of African Christianity today: "various acts of the Holy Spirit reaching across spiritual, cultural, social, and political boundaries. A missionary document ..., it is not intended to be read as a polished book of doctrines or a systematic theology. ... [It] is theology in action; faith lived out in the trenches of real life" (Hertig and Gallagher 2004, 2). The following four episodes will serve heuristically in surveying Christ-devotion in African Christianity: the resurrection and ascension of Jesus, the martyrdom of Stephen, the birth of a bicultural church, and the Jerusalem Council.

THE RISEN CHRIST

Acts begins (1:1–5) by establishing continuity with the Gospel of Luke and outlining the final instructions the risen Jesus gave the disciples before his ascension (1:6–11). The central theme of the kingdom of God, which sums up Jesus's earthly ministry in proclaiming and demonstrating God's saving purposes (Luke 4:43), is now to continue through the witness of the church. Two aspects of this passage elucidate Christ-devotion in Africa today.

First, within this context of Jesus's post-resurrection appearances, the disciples ask a critical question: Was Jesus about to restore the kingdom to Israel? (1:6). Their question reflects Jewish hopes that God's establishing divine rule would mean Israel's deliverance from her enemies, particularly from Roman oppression. The disciples represent Jewish expectations with only a partial understanding that Jesus's message of the kingdom of God surpassed nationalistic political aspirations. However legitimate their question, Jesus's lack of direct response reveals, or even rebukes, their limited comprehension of his identity and the cross-cultural implications of his ministry.

Just as these Jewish disciples sought to understand how Jesus "fit" in relation to their own prior conceptions, so African believers seek to interpret Jesus in view of their religious consciousness and experience. In an analogous query, John Mbiti, considered the father of modern African theology, asks "how the Person of Jesus Christ fits into African conceptualization of the world, and what points of contact the New Testament portrait of Jesus establishes with the African traditional concepts" (Mbiti 1972, 52). Indeed, christological discourse in Africa concerns how African Christians interpret, understand, and experience Jesus in light of indigenous worldviews, as well as historical and contemporary realities. This is an entirely legitimate quest that has spawned substantial reflection and praxis across Africa. However, hazards of African contextualized Christ-devotion might include parochialism, without due attention to the universal discourse on Christ, and an overemphasis on "solution-oriented" approaches to Jesus grounded in what he can do for personal and communal problems. Victor Ezigbo contends that "an adequate *African contextual Christology* occurs when African Christians (laity and theologians) approach, interpret and appropriate the Christ-Event from their own history and experience and at the same time invite Jesus Christ to probe, shape, [and] interpret their perceptions of humanity ... and God" (Ezigbo 2010, 305; emphasis in original). As Jesus indirectly cautioned his Jewish disciples about their constricted understanding of himself, so Mbiti underscores how Jesus is beyond human categories of conceptualizing him: "The uniqueness of Christianity is in Jesus Christ. He is the stumbling block of all ideologies and religious systems; and even if some of His teaching may overlap with what they teach and proclaim, His own Person is greater than can be contained in a religion or ideology" (Mbiti 1969, 277).

Second, Jesus's post-resurrection appearances culminate in his ascension. In response to the disciples' specific question, Jesus avoids apocalyptic speculation and underlines their immediate task of bearing witness to him from Jerusalem to the ends of the earth. He promises that the Holy Spirit will empower them for this ongoing spread of the gospel, which is fulfilled at Pentecost in Acts 2. Acts alone records the visible ascension of Jesus, although it is attested elsewhere (1 Tim 3:16; 1 Pet 3:21–22) with further explication of his exaltation to the right hand of God (Acts 2:33–35). As I. Howard Marshall explains, "The symbolism of 'ascension' expresses the way in which the physical presence of Jesus departed from this world, to be replaced by his spiritual presence" (Marshall 1980, 60).

If the resurrection and ascension were cardinal to Christ-devotion in the apostolic church, so they are central to Christ-devotion in African Christianity. Mbiti asserts that of all the events of Jesus's life, death, and resurrection, African believers' dominant interest is in the resurrection, for "Jesus is seen as the *Christus Victor* above all other things" (Mbiti 1972, 54). Mbiti explains that Africa has no traditional concepts of promise or hope for redemption or rejuvenation or any "supra-human conqueror of evil." Hailing Jesus as the one who overcame "the forces of the devil, spirits, sickness, hatred, fear, and death itself," Mbiti concludes that "the greatest need among African peoples ... is to see, to know, and to experience Jesus Christ as the victor over the powers and forces from which Africa knows no means of deliverance" (Mbiti 1972, 55).

Christ-devotion in Africa manifests the import of Jesus's resurrection and ascension in diverse ways. Charles Nyamiti, a Tanzanian Catholic theologian, interprets the ministry of Christ within the cultural framework of tribal initiation rites, progressing through the life stages of birth, entry into adulthood, passion, death, resurrection, ascension, and eternal reign in glory. Simon Maimela, from South Africa, questions the credibility of affirming Christ's death and victorious resurrection in contemporary Africa, given the pervasiveness of oppression and suffering across the continent. However, despite the seemingly hopeless situation, Maimela contends that "the triumphant message of the resurrection of Jesus Christ proclaims loudly that in Christ humanity is given the possibility and the power to overcome their perverted, polarised and often conflict-ridden relations on this side of the grave" (Maimela 1992, 36). Christ's redemptive suffering is able to heal, forgive, and transform "the oppressor, the exploiter, and the hopeless murderer" into instruments of divine love and reconciliation, who then work with God to address social injustices. Hence "Christ is the liberator and hope even for the Africans ... [who] groan in the economic, political, and social sphere" (Maimela 1992, 38, 39).

Informal expressions of Christ-devotion also reveal the significance of Jesus's resurrection and ascension to African believers. The renowned eucharistic fresco of the risen, glorified Jesus dominates Hekima College Chapel in Nairobi (Figure 20). Designed by Engelbert Mveng, a Cameroonian Jesuit priest, scholar, and artist, and painted by Sudanese Stephen Lobalu, the exalted Christ surrounded in luminous yellow fills the wall behind the altar. The image presents Jesus as reigning over the cityscape of Nairobi, lending contextual specificity. It also evokes Jesus's triumph over "anthropological poverty," the well-known term Mveng coined to signify the utter impoverishment of Africans not only economically but in identity and intrinsic worth (including culture, history, dignity, etc.) through the European slave trade and colonization. The risen, exalted Christ is further celebrated in church liturgies, indigenous hymns, and prayers, such as the praise song of Afua Kuma, a nonliterate farmer and midwife from Ghana:

> Jesus, the Seer among prophets
> who always speaks the truth.
> Wisest of soothsayers, the resurrected body,
> who raised himself from three days in the grave.
> Storehouse of wisdom!
> Jesus is the one who shouted at Death,
> and Death ran from his face. (Kuma 1981, 29)

Even today, African Christians, like the Jewish disciples who grappled to comprehend the significance of Jesus's death, resurrection, and ascension, continue to decipher and express the momentous import of the risen Christ in their lives.

Figure 20 Engelbert Mveng, eucharistic fresco, Hekima College Chapel, Nairobi. Used with permission from Hekima College. Photo by Diane B. Stinton.

## MARTYRDOM AS WITNESS

The martyrdom of Stephen, a Hellenistic Jew, is a significant episode in the apostolic church that sheds light on Christ-devotion in Africa. Acts recounts Stephen's witness to Jesus leading to his arrest, his lengthy speech before the Sanhedrin – condemned as blasphemous – and his consequent stoning. As he faced execution, Stephen declared that he saw heaven opening and "the Son of Man standing at the right hand of God!" (7:56). Not only does this vision affirm the risen Christ alive and active in the ongoing life of the church, but the title "Son of Man," an unusual reference outside of the Gospels, suggests that Stephen sees Jesus as the one who suffered and whom God vindicated (see Luke 9:22). In like manner, "as a pattern to be followed by Christian martyrs" (Marshall 1980, 148), Stephen suffers persecution yet sees Jesus standing at God's right hand to advocate for him and to welcome him into God's presence. Stephen's arrest and death unmistakably parallel those of Jesus. He is accused of blasphemy, prays for forgiveness for those who kill him, and, significantly, cries out to heaven, yet with one striking difference: Instead of calling out to the Father, Stephen explicitly cries out to "the Lord Jesus" to receive his spirit (7:59). This reveals a high Christology, presenting the risen Christ standing at the right hand of God, being the object of devotion, and sharing in God's work. Stephen thus becomes an exemplary "witness" (*martus* in Greek, hence the English word "martyr"). Just as the resurrected Jesus declares in Acts 1:8 that his followers would be his "witnesses" from Jerusalem to the ends of the earth, so Acts 22:20 specifies Stephen as "your witness" in relation to the ascended Christ. Stephen's martyrdom paves the way for the later ecclesiastical concept of a martyr as one who not only bears witness to the truth of Christ but also suffers for it, to the point of death.

Acts also recounts the story of Stephen as a critical turning point in the expansion of the church, with the persecution of believers in Jerusalem prompting their dispersion throughout Judea, Samaria, and beyond. Martyrdom, as a witness to Christ unto death, has shaped African Christianity over the centuries. The African church father Tertullian, writing from Carthage in 197, penned his famous dictum: "the blood of Christians is seed" (*Apology* 50.13).

Martyrdom is performative Christology as far as it is grounded in Christians' costly witness to their understanding of and identification with the suffering and death of Jesus Christ. Though other acts of christological expression often overshadowed martyrdom, it provided a different avenue for African Christians to demonstrate their understanding of the identity of Jesus Christ, what he has accomplished for them, and their faithfulness to him. In the third century CE, for example, Christians in Carthage (modern-day Tunisia), amid persecution, bore witness to Jesus Christ to their captors, family members, and other Christians by enduring horrendous deaths faithfully. Two such Carthaginian martyrs – Perpetua and Felicitas – exemplified martyrs' perceptions of their own impending death analogously to the death of Jesus Christ. In the early eighteenth century, the Congolese Kimpa Vita's execution highlighted African Christians protesting the superimposition of European Christianity on African communities.

Martyrdom continues to the present-day Africa in regions where anti-Christian sentiments persist. Boko Haram have killed well over 50,000 Christians in Nigeria since 2009, and Coptic Christians in Egypt experience sporadic persecutions and killings by Islamic extremists.

African theologians have also reflected on the theme of martyrdom. In the 1960s, John Pobee conducted research on persecution and martyrdom in Paul's theology, against the backdrop of sociopolitical upheaval in his native Ghana (Pobee 1985). Emmanuel Katongole, a Ugandan scholar distinguished for his narrative methodology integrating theological reflection and African experience, contemplates Christian martyrs in Africa today. Highlighting 2 Corinthians 5:17–18, with its declaration of God's reconciling of believers through Christ and giving them the ministry of reconciliation, Katongole contends "Christian martyrs, in their lives and deaths, provide the most concrete, dynamic, and exemplary case of the journey of reconciliation" (Katongole 2017, 105). Among the martyrs Katongole considers is Chantal Mujjawamaholo, a secondary school student at Nyange in Rwanda. In 1997, three years after the genocide, the Interahamwe militia attacked the school while the students were studying in their classrooms. The rebels demanded the students separate into Tutsi and Hutu, yet the students refused, insisting they were all Rwandans. The rebels fired upon them indiscriminately and threw grenades, killing thirteen students. While the other victims were reclaimed by families for burial, Chantal, who came from a distant place, was buried at the school just a month before her twenty-second birthday. In demonstrating solidarity and friendship exceeding ethnic divisions, Chantal, in Katongole's view, embodies both the call and the gift of reconciliation in Christ. From such lives of witness, Katongole urges the church into "a life of vigil, a life of social struggle, and a new and resurrected community" (Katongole 2017, 105).

## MULTICULTURAL EXPRESSIONS OF CHRIST-DEVOTION

The birth of the church in Antioch marks a crucial episode in Acts, reflective of two key facets of Christ-devotion in Africa. First, proclaiming Jesus in Antioch was prompted by the persecution of believers in Jerusalem after Stephen's death, precipitating their migration elsewhere (8:4; 11:19). Just as Philip traveled to Samaria and to the road south of Jerusalem to evangelize, so these believers traveled "as far as Phoenicia, Cyprus, and Antioch." Yet, whereas earlier events focus on the apostles preaching the gospel, this passage records unnamed, "ordinary believers" witnessing about Jesus.

Second, the gospel proclamation in Antioch diverged significantly both in the selected audience and in translating the message. While believers had previously confined their evangelism to Jews, some daring disciples in Antioch, men from Cyprus and Cyrene, took the momentous step of telling gentiles about "the Lord Jesus" (11:20). Previously, Jesus had been proclaimed as the Messiah (*christos* in Greek, "the anointed one"), with all its richness in Jewish tradition. As Andrew Walls points out, this term required extensive explanation for Greek-speaking gentile peoples who did not necessarily share in Jewish history and belief. Notably, within this context of cross-cultural diffusion, they preached Jesus as "*Kyrios*, the title that Greek pagans used for their cult divinities" (Walls 1996, 34). Acts does not specify whether some of these gentiles were already God-fearers; nonetheless, the process of translating the identity and ultimate significance of Christ into Greek thought meant "a new agenda for Christianity" as the gospel increasingly penetrated Greek and Roman thought (Walls 1996, 53). The scale of gentile evangelization was unprecedented and resulted, significantly, in the first bicultural church that embodied the new humanity in Christ (Eph. 2:15). Christopraxis in Antioch further expressed itself in this church becoming a leading center for the expanding mission, especially among gentiles, and in arranging a famine relief fund for the mother church in Jerusalem.

Once again, these observations about early Christ-devotion in Acts 11 are reflected throughout the history of African Christianity, culminating in the twenty-first century. In fourth-century Egypt, Antony (d. 356) heeded Christ's call from Matthew 19:21 to give his possessions to the poor, moving to the desert where he found others escaping persecution and similarly seeking the kingdom of God. His christopraxis of asceticism and spiritual warfare contributed to "the desert [becoming] a city," in Athanasius's account, with thousands of monks following his example and counsel.[2] His legacy has profoundly influenced monasticism ever since, in Egypt and beyond.

Additionally, the Atlantic slave trade from the sixteenth to the late nineteenth century marks the most colossal migration – with ten to twelve million Africans forcibly moved to other continents – and the costliest in terms of human lives lost and enduring impacts in Africa and in the new world. Astonishingly, this movement gave rise to some of the most vibrant and poignant expressions of Christ-devotion in the Americas, including the new genre of African American spirituals such as "Jesus Sitting on the Waterside" and "Steal Away to Jesus." Like the unnamed disciples who preached the gospel in Antioch as laypersons without religious qualifications, countless Africans over the centuries have witnessed to Jesus. Contrary to common thought about Western missionaries evangelizing Africa, Jehu Hanciles underlines that "in the history of African Christianity, the majority of Africans have heard the

---

[2] Athanasius, *Life of Antony* 14 (ed. Gregg 1980, 42–43).

gospel from other Africans (often catechists, schoolmasters, and traders)" (Hanciles 2008, 218).

Whether through "voluntary" or "forced" resettlement, either within or beyond the continent, African believers are among "the extraordinary tidal waves of human migration" over recent decades (Hanciles 2008, 218). Between 1990 and 1995, Kenya's refugee population rose dramatically from 13,452 to 243,544 due to the brutal conflicts that convulsed the region (Hanciles 2008, 219). In this context, Amani ya Juu ("peace from above" in Swahili) was birthed in Nairobi in 1996 as a holistic ministry of economic empowerment, teaching women to sew African crafts, and offering emotional, social, and spiritual support to those from various nations and ethnicities who had suffered intense violence, loss, and trauma. Regardless of the women's religious backgrounds, devotion to Christ is at the heart of this ministry, expressed in worship, prayer, Bible study and more, including, uniquely, in the central symbol of Amani ya Juu: the "Unity Quilt" adorning their chapel. The quilt comprises twelve squares, ten of which depict indigenous reconciliation rites from their various ethnic communities. The bottom right-hand square displays the continent of Africa, still broken and bleeding despite these restoration rites. Between the squares runs a distinct cross in vibrant red, and the final panel depicts a woman dancing before the cross. As the women explain, "The dancing woman ... is celebrating the work of Christ on the cross which has reconciled us to God and given us a higher, more lasting peace ... that transcends all tribal and cultural differences ... [and allows us] to experience genuine forgiveness and reconciliation with one another" (cited in Stinton 2012, 66). This singular quilt, with what it signifies in the lives of these refugee women, forms but one example of myriad expressions of christopraxis that continue to enrich the lives of African believers across the continent.

Moreover, since "migrants travel with their religion," the unprecedented migrations within and beyond Africa, "more than any other single factor, helped to foment a new epoch of African missionary expansion" (Hanciles 2008, 218). For example, the Redeemed Christian Church of God, founded in Nigeria in 1952, now cites more than 50,000 congregations in 197 countries. At the center of its online homepage, the church broadcasts "Jesus Christ the same yesterday, and today, and forever – Hebrews 13:8."[3] Hence the risen Christ, whose Spirit prompted the dispersion of "ordinary" believers to proclaim the gospel in ways that penetrated Jewish and gentile cultures throughout the

---

[3] See the Redeemed Christian Church of God (RCCG) website, www.rccg.org.

first-century Mediterranean world, still fuels its ongoing transmission across Africa and the world.

As we saw, the second aspect of Acts 11:19–30 highlighted believers in Antioch preaching Jesus as *kyrios*, "Lord," to their gentile audience, illustrating the translation of Christ's identity into Greek thought in this early episode of cross-cultural evangelism. In a similar manner, African believers seek to convey the good news of Jesus Christ, not only employing biblical titles such as Lord, Christ, Savior, and Son of God but also in terms that express Jesus's ultimate significance in African thought-forms and experience. This process, often referred to as inculturation or contextualization, will be discussed further in what follows.

CHRISTOLOGICAL IMAGES

The Jerusalem Council deliberated on whether circumcision, in accordance with the custom of Moses, was a criterion for salvation in Christ. This was a critical issue facing the earliest followers of Jesus Christ: namely, how best (a) to imagine the identity of disciples of Jesus and (b) to disciple non-Jewish people to grasp and also benefit from Jesus's gospel. The deliberations on the relationship between circumcision and salvation highlighted two main perspectives that informed how the early (mostly Jewish) Christian communities viewed Christian identity and discipleship. One view was receptive to the multilingual, multicultural, and multitheological features of Christian communities. The other view indicated the insistence of the believers who wanted the gentile converts to become proselytes. In this context, the Council wanted to set some guidelines for cross-cultural evangelism and Christian discipleship. Their ruling (Acts 15:28–29) was a watershed in the early Jewish Christian leaders' initial attempts to contextualize the gospel message in ways that engage with, adapt to, and critique societal cultural practices.

Like the early Christians, African Christian communities have engaged in the complex task of contextualizing the gospel. We can discern African Christians' attempts to interpret the life and teaching of Jesus Christ in the ways they describe him. For example, one of the foremost images, in both formal and informal expressions of Christ-devotion, is that of Jesus as healer. Cécé Kolié examines Jesus's healing ministry in the Gospels alongside concepts and practices of sickness and healing in Africa. He then elaborates the image of Jesus as healer, integrating biblical and African insights (Kolié 1991). Undoubtedly, Jesus as healer features prominently in the preaching, hymns, indigenous choruses, prayers, and testimonies of African believers, particularly in the African Instituted Churches and Pentecostal churches. Despite profound challenges with claiming Jesus as healer, including the pervasive suffering and death across Africa and the dissonance between missionary and African concepts and practices regarding health, African Christians unequivocally identify Jesus as healer in their understanding and experience. Their interpretation is that Jesus restores life in every dimension, both individual and communal; that he reigns supremely over every evil force, whether manifested physically, emotionally, spiritually, or socially; and consequently, his role as healer is intrinsically related to those of savior, liberator, and redeemer.

A more controversial image is that of Christ as ancestor. While less evident in Christian preaching and practice than that of Jesus as healer, several African theologians from Francophone and Anglophone contexts, including the Catholics Bénézet Bujo, Francois Kabasélé, Charles Nyamiti, and Agbonkhianmeghe Orobator and the Protestants Kwame Bediako and John Pobee, have proposed the ancestor image as a meaningful way for African believers to comprehend Jesus from African worldviews and experience. Akin to Jesus as healer, this proposal seeks to integrate biblical and African concepts through a functional analogy that presents Jesus as fulfilling the roles traditionally played by the African ancestors: as the provider of life, founder of the community, mediator between the divine and human, and ongoing participant in the life of the human community. Not only does Jesus fulfill these roles but he also supersedes the African ancestors on account of his divine status, thus being distinguished by titles such as "Proto-Ancestor" or "Ancestor par Excellence." Bujo points out significant implications for African Christians: "He is the ancestor of all humanity... From now on there is neither black nor white, ... yellow nor red, ... Tutsi nor Hutu, ... Luba nor Munyamwezi nor Chagga nor Agikuyu[,] ... man nor woman, cultivator nor minister of states, *'for all you are only one in Christ Jesus'*" (Bujo 1995, 36–37; emphasis in original). Nonetheless, many African believers – generally evangelicals and Pentecostals – object to this image for various reasons. For example, African ancestors gained negative connotations through missionary denigration of African religions, plus modernization and urbanization have distanced African believers from this aspect of their cultural heritage. However, the most serious objections include contrasting definitions, qualifications, and characteristics of ancestors, consequently compromising the divinity of Christ by aligning him with human ancestors.

A third major image is Jesus as liberator, often associated with Christ-devotion in the context of apartheid South Africa and related to developments in liberation theologies from Latin America. Yet theologians across Africa south of the Sahara likewise call for liberation, not only from political oppression but also from economic injustices, cultural captivity, and social structures that suffer enduring colonialism and neocolonialism. For example, in East Africa, Laurenti Magesa insists presenting Christ as liberator in Africa is more than simply a metaphor; it is "active love-justice" that manifests itself in "the struggle for the integral freedom and well-being of all persons" (Magesa 1989, 83). This alone, in Magesa's view, will convey Jesus in a comprehensible and credible way among the rural and urban poor throughout Africa. In West Africa, the Cameroonian theologian Jean-Marc Éla offers an incisive analysis of urgent problems in contemporary Africa, like the oppressive structures of capitalist-driven globalization. He draws together the historical experience of Jesus's suffering with that of Africans, asserting that *"Africa today is crucified"* and that *"the struggles of our people bring the memory of the Crucified One right into our life and times"* (Éla 1994, 146; emphasis in original). Acknowledging the incarnation and the resurrection as how Christ has conquered death and inaugurated a new world, Éla urges believers to discover the risen Jesus in the slums where the poor and oppressed reside, for this is where Jesus's salvation is made visible.

Jesus as liberator also typifies, though does not exhaust, African women's Christologies. Female and male theologians expose sources of women's oppression within African cultures, mission Christianity, and socioeconomic and political realities, and critique androcentric and patriarchal Christologies. They highlight the liberative dimensions of Jesus's ministry including his deep affirmation of women and his solidarity in their suffering. For example, Ghanaian theologian Mercy Oduyoye integrates biblical and African traditions in explicating a multidimensional portrait of Jesus as savior/liberator/redeemer. She relates the significance of this image to the African context according to the goal of feminist theology, which she identifies to be women and men seeking together to become fully human (Oduyoye 2002). In addition to the formal reflections on Christ – and especially notable – are the "lived Christologies" of African women experiencing and expressing salvation and liberation in their daily lives.

African believers express their Christ-devotion in numerous other images of Jesus, such as chief, elder/brother, master of initiation, guest, warrior, and close friend. One significant contribution is the image of Jesus as mother, promoted by the Kenyan theologian Anne Nasimiyu Wasike, among others. Against the backdrop of endemic violence and other life-diminishing forces in Africa, Nasimiyu Wasike develops an analogy between Jesus's ministry and African concepts of motherhood (Wasike 1989). Like Jesus, African mothers symbolize love, compassion, and mercy, and are said to nurture life in all its dimensions. The image is not tied to gender, for Jesus as mother calls all believers – women and men – to protect and nurture life without discrimination on any grounds, including gender. Nonetheless, some other Christians reject the image on account of the historical Jesus being male, despite acknowledging that Christ's love is analogous to that of a mother. The image of Jesus as mother exemplifies Africans' perceptions of Christ while also illuminating certain feminine aspects of the Triune God that may not be as adequately reflected in Western Christologies.

CONCLUSION

In African Christianity, the question of Christology centers on how best to articulate African Christians' experiences and understandings of Jesus Christ from their own context of life and in dialogue with the expressions of Jesus in other parts of the world. Therefore, a survey of African Christology ought to account for grassroots and formal christological expressions and their uniqueness vis-à-vis the Christologies of non-African Christian communities. Our survey accentuates three related themes that permeate the discussions on Jesus Christ in African Christianity.

First, the term "Christ-devotion," as used in this chapter, captures the essence of the diverse representations of the story of Jesus Christ in African Christianity. Using episodes from Acts as launching pads, we have explored the contours of christological expression in African Christianity, highlighting the role that religious experience plays in African Christians' imagination of Jesus Christ's identity and significance. The "lived Christologies" of African believers have taken on particular import in this regard, as they witness to the risen Christ in daily life across the continent. Indeed, African Christians typically express their varied understandings of the identity of Jesus Christ from the perspective of their encounters with him as his disciples. For example, the expression "Jesus is healer" is not merely a conceptual framework for understanding the mystery of Jesus. Rather, it is an expression of the belief in Jesus Christ's participation in the lives of his disciples and his power to bring about both spiritual and physical healings in Christian communities.

Second, both formal and informal African christologies intentionally address African indigenous religious practices and beliefs. The expression "Jesus is Ancestor," for instance, is indicative of African Christians' attempts to construct a viable relationship between the Christian faith and African indigenous worldviews. These christologies demonstrate the universality of the gospel as it is translated into the thought-forms and contextual realities of multitudinous cultures around the world.

Finally, African Christology has contributed significantly to the repositioning of contextual theologizing at the heart of the discipline of Christian theology and to the emergence of the field of world Christianity. In their Christologies, African theologians engage issues pertinent to African communities, while drawing upon theological insights from other sources of theology such as Scripture, tradition, and reason. All theological reflections on the person, work, and significance of Jesus are inherently contextual because they arise in response to the unique questions and needs of particular Christian communities. Therefore, theologians ought to discern and deal with the theological materials in the life-situation, history, and culture of Christian communities. The exponential growth of Christianity in Africa, without necessarily adopting the theological structures of Western Christianity, has heightened Christian scholars' consciousness of the role indigenous agency has played in the expansion of the Christian faith. Hence studying Christ-devotion in Africa significantly enriches the field of world Christianity.

## FURTHER READING

Atansi, Chukwuemeka A., David M. M. Lewis and Diane B. Stinton. 2023. "Christology." In *Bibliographical Encyclopaedia of African Theology*, https://african.theologyworldwide.com/encyclopaedia/227-christology.

Bediako, Kwame. 2004. *Jesus and the Gospel in Africa: History and Experience*. Maryknoll: Orbis.

Clarke, Clifton R. 2011. *African Christology: Jesus in Post-Missionary African Christianity*. La Vergne: Wipf and Stock Publishers.

Manus, Ukachukwu Chris. 1993. *Christ, the African King: New Testament Christology*. Frankfurt: P. Lang.

Mugambi, J. N. Kanyua and Laurenti Magesa, eds. 1989. *Jesus in African Christianity: Experimentation and Diversity in African Christology*. Nairobi: Initiatives Ltd.

Nyamiti, Charles. 2006. *Studies in African Christian Theology: Jesus Christ, the Ancestor of Humankind – An Essay on African Christology*. Nairobi: CUEA.

Oduyoye, Mercy A. and M. R. A. Kanyoro, eds. 1992. *The Will to Arise: Women, Tradition, and the Church in Africa*. Maryknoll: Orbis Books.

Pobee, John S., ed. 1992. *Exploring Afro-Christology*. Studien zur interkulturellen Geschichte des Christentums 79. Frankfurt: Peter Lang.

Schreiter, Robert J., ed. 1991. *Faces of Jesus in Africa*. Maryknoll: Orbis Books.

Stinton, Diane B. 2004. *Jesus of Africa: Voices of Contemporary African Christology*. Maryknoll: Orbis Books.

# Part V
*Outlook*

## 22 The Future of Jesus of Nazareth

*Yesterday, Today, and Tomorrow*

C. KAVIN ROWE

Jesus Christ is the same yesterday, today, and forever.

Hebrews 13:8

### THE CONDITIONS OF OUR KNOWLEDGE

Strictly speaking, of course, there is no way to write on the future of Jesus of Nazareth from within the epistemic possibilities of normal research. Jesus's future is on the other side of death and the world's final reconciliation – and of that place and time, we have no experience and no native knowledge. All of what we might say, therefore, is conditioned by Jesus's self-disclosure of that future in the midst of human time. This does not mean that there is no knowledge. It means, rather, that the knowledge we do have of Jesus's future has itself been given to us. We cannot reach out and attain it – in principle no more than in fact. We receive it, or we do not know. Once received, such knowledge can generate from its own ground, as it were, true things that we come to know. But to know anything about Jesus's future is already to submit to what we have received from him. This is the meaning of revelation.

In light of these conditions, we may say this: The future of Jesus of Nazareth is himself. The rest of this chapter will interpret this statement – first, in light of the future that has and is to come; and second, in light of the future that is also the past.[1] The New Testament texts make complex claims about Jesus and time, and thinking the complexity without dissolving it is the challenge.

---

[1] Contrast the procedure (and title) of Keck 1981. Though it bears the marks of its time, Keck's book is not only an excellent example of thinking through some of the larger questions raised by the phenomenon "the historical Jesus" but also a reminder that many of those questions remain unanswered even today.

## JESUS OF NAZARETH: THE FUTURE AS DISCLOSURE

This section will elaborate two interconnected claims that emerge from a reading of the New Testament as a whole in light of the topic this chapter addresses. The first is that Jesus's future will disclose the character of current Christian existence to have been one in which hope was not in vain. The behavioral anticipation of the end – the actual modes of Christian existence at its best – and the end itself will turn out to cohere (Rowe 2020; Wright 2010). The second is that Jesus's future will be a validation of the purposes of God in original creation and the bringing about of the reality that God's will is not and cannot be thwarted by the recalcitrance of creation (its groaning) or human dysfunction within it (our sin). The future of Jesus is God's overarching will for the world finally coming to pass.

(1) Jesus's future will entail a disclosure of the fact that following him was really possible as a way of life, that the kingdom of God was here, and that those whose lives moved with its patterns were agents of freedom. According to the Gospels, Jesus's advent and ministry announced in multiple ways what has become a frequent manner of naming his purpose: He was here to inaugurate the reign of God.[2] Whether in relation to the kingdom of God (Mark/Luke) or the kingdom of Heaven (Matthew) or simply as King (John and the synoptics),[3] Jesus burst onto the Judean stage with the claim that God's kingdom was on the way (Matt 4:17 // Mark 1:5; Matt 12:28 // Luke 11:20; Luke 17:20–21). To be around Jesus in his earthly life was to learn that God's kingdom was coming.[4]

Modern scholars have wondered whether Jesus meant that God's kingdom arrived with him or was coming in the future, whether it was tied to his person now or whether he was the prophet of a kingdom to come. But this now or later is ultimately a false alternative, and there is no reason to choose between now and later as if they were strictly and competitively opposed. What it meant to be an "eschatological prophet" was concretized in Jesus's case (cf. Sanders 1985, 1993). As Francis Watson puts it, "Only if 'kingdom of God' referred to some reality apart from Jesus would there be a conflict" between now and then;

---

[2] Modern scholarship: Weiss 1892 (English translation: Weiss 1971), among others.
[3] See, e.g., the use of King(dom) language in John (John 1:49; 3:3, 5; 6:15; 12:13, 15; 18:33, 37–38; 19:14–15, 19) and Luke's addition of "the King" to Ps 118 during Jesus's entry into Jerusalem (Luke 19:38). Inauguration of the Kingdom is the presupposition of the royal language that goes with Messiah.
[4] See Dale C. Allison, Jr.'s chapter in this volume.

but, as Watson continues, "that is not the case" (Watson 1997, 75). Jesus told not only of the coming of God's kingdom but of his current role in bringing it about.[5] "Thy kingdom come on earth as in heaven" was simultaneously a plea and a program, an enactment of the heavenly reign of God through the earthly life of Jesus. Jesus was the Messianic King in the arrival of God's own kingdom. Though Jesus's rule had first to be rejected, it would be established on the eternal foundation of his resurrection. Proleptically, then, God's kingdom was forever present as Jesus arrived.

The apostle Paul was perhaps the first Christian thinker to grasp and then extend the importance of the unity in Jesus between the present and future act of God. Paul saw that the renewing, transformative power of God had been put to work in the current moment, that those who came to confess with their mouths "Jesus is Lord" and believe in their hearts that God raised him from the dead were living in a new reality. In what is perhaps the most compressed version of Paul's theology of transformation, he put it this way: "If anyone is in Christ – new creation! The old has passed away and the new has come" (2 Cor 5:17).[6] There was no need to wait for something in the future to begin the life that was God's kingdom life. Those who served the Lord lived under his rule. Indeed, so powerfully was the Lord present in their new life that Paul began to refer to them as Christ's "body" (1 Cor 12:12–13; Rom 12:4–5). The church, thought Paul, was right now, in this very moment, the living embodiment of God's reign.

And yet, nothing could be plainer than the struggle Paul's congregations had with dysfunction of one sort or another. Sin was, as a Power, ultimately and already defeated, but its effects lingered on. The Corinthian church, for example, could even countenance, or at least tolerate, behavior that was beyond the pale of pagan immorality (1 Cor 5:1: "it is reported that there is immorality among you of the sort that is not even found among the Gentiles"). Such a situation called for nothing less than expulsion from the church, though such expulsion had as its telos the eventual return and full welcome of the expelled (vv. 2–13; see Hays 1997, 80–88). Even one of Paul's favorite communities, the church in the Roman colony of Philippi, whom he praised for many things, was not immune from the risk of sin (e.g. 2:16; 3:2, 16). The body of Christ was truly there, but it clearly was not yet fully what it would become.

---

[5] For an illuminating discussion of a "tensive symbol," see Keck 2000, 70–71.
[6] The *gegonen* is always tough in this verse. The other text that comes close to a summary is Romans 12:2: "be transformed by the renewing of your minds."

E. P. Sanders used to say that he thought Paul was genuinely surprised that his congregations continued to sin. Sanders was smarter and knew more than most, but on this point he may well have misplaced the emphasis of Paul's surprise. What surprised Paul was not so much that sin was still in the midst of even the best of them but rather that some in his congregations did not know that they were free. "For freedom Christ has set us free" (Gal 5:1). The now/not yet dialectic is not, that is, a permanent, almost Manichean war between sin and new creation but a dialectic that moves from freedom to freedom. Jesus has set us free, and our freedom consists now precisely in the freedom to move in the rhythms that extract us from the patterns of sin. It is actually possible, said Augustine, capturing Paul's point, not to sin (*posse non peccare*). Perhaps hardly any, if any at all, grow to refrain from sin for life, but Christians are those who are freely catching up to the way things are in new creation. The Pauline explication of Jesus's kingdom being both here and not yet (finally) here is inseparably intertwined with the reality of Christian freedom. In short, as Paul understands the future of Jesus, that future will turn out to have shown that Christians really can be Christians in the here and now even as they await their final transformation.[7]

The church thus both is and will be the body of Christ: Overcoming the visible/invisible church distinction is finally eschatological. The claim that "wherever the church is, there is the body of Christ" is not one of simple identification. The relation between Jesus and his body on earth in the community of the church is dialectical – in part because at any given moment the church may and may not be the church at one and the same time. Under the right conditions, the Eucharist becomes the body of Christ, but the right conditions are not always and everywhere met (or so the ecumenical disagreements over the Eucharist indicate). Still, the future of Jesus of Nazareth on this earth is bound up with the future of the church.

(2) The future of Jesus of Nazareth is a future of reconciliation, reconstitution, fulfillment, and final unity of God's original creative purpose. His beginning will be completed at the end. The angels who appear to the shepherds announce the type of reign inaugurated by the Messianic Lord. "Glory to God in the highest," and "peace on earth among those in whom he delights" (Luke 2:14).

---

[7] Cf. Barth 1969, 3: "We assume that, even if in great poverty, weakness and contradiction, constantly threatened and in need of renewal, there is such a thing as genuine human faithfulness in relation to God's own faithfulness. To that extent we assume that there is such a thing as the event of the Christian life."

Of course, such peace does not immediately come about in all the glory of God in the highest. After a tumultuous ministry replete with attempts to derail and even destroy his mission, Jesus arrives at Jerusalem as the Messiah. A multitude of disciples cry out, "Peace in heaven and glory in the highest!" (Luke 19:38). But only moments later, Jesus weeps. And his weeping is for Jerusalem and its coming destruction: "would that you knew even on this day the things that make for peace!" (Luke 19:42). Within the world of the story, the present point is clear: Had you, Jerusalem, seen me for who I am, you would lay down your dreams of violent recompense and embrace the peace for which I have come. It is tempting to override the significance of this point with later, narratively external knowledge, the knowledge that Jesus will be crucified, or – if one stays within the story – to oppose the force of the statement with Jesus's sayings about his coming suffering. But this is to render Jesus unserious in his statement and takes the "messiah must suffer" lines to determine the text here in a ham-fisted kind of way. In truth there is no contradiction, and there is no need to downplay Jesus's rebuke as if peace were not a serious possibility for Jerusalem. The peace that would be known is exactly the peace that refuses retaliation and instead accepts unjust death. The cross is the revelation of the peace that Jerusalem rejected at its final hour.

The resurrection of Jesus is God's response to that rejection and the foretaste of the final end in which life will triumph over death and the angels' glorious proclamation reverse Jerusalem's rejection. Paul's famous lines in 1 Corinthians 15:55 put it most succinctly and powerfully: "where O death is your victory, where O death is your sting?" The son of the widow of Nain, Jairus's daughter, Lazarus – though they will die again – all adumbrate the future coming of life that is tied to the future of the resurrected Jesus.

New Testament scholarship has often, and understandably, focused on the Parousia or apocalyptic sayings of Jesus as a way to think about his future.[8] But the theological thinking that goes with a contemplation of the future is better captured by Paul's understanding of Adam and Christ and the vision for God's final restoration. In his most elaborate and interconnected letter, Paul compares Christ to Adam on the way to a larger argument about the totality of humanity as carried both in Adam and in Christ, thereby arguing for the unity between Jew and gentile – a pressing concern in Romans. The Adam/Christ relation comes

---

[8] To take only a tiny number of representative examples, see, e.g., Matt 24:37; or in the Pauline literature, 1 Thess 3:13; 4:15; 5:23; 1 Cor 15:23.

to its most important formulation in Paul's phrase in 5:14, where he says that Adam is a "type" of the one who was to come.

Through the one human being Adam, sin and death and condemnation came to all humans, says Paul, establishing the universal problem. But through the one human being Jesus Christ, acquittal and life will come for all, he continues, articulating the eschatological logic of the comparison. Indeed, "where sin increased, grace abounded all the more so that as sin reigned in death, grace might also reign through righteousness to life eternal through Jesus Christ our Lord" (Rom 5:12–21).[9] A few chapters later, as Paul works through the question of Israel's future, he draws the conclusion from the reasoning of the letter to that point and then breaks into praise and worship: "For God has consigned all humans to disobedience, that he may have mercy upon all. ... O the depth of the riches and wisdom and knowledge of God! How unsearchable are his judgments and how inscrutable his ways! ... For from him and through him and to him are all things. To him be the glory forever! Amen" (Rom 11:32–36; cf. Rowe 2024).

Jesus's future is spoken of in materially similar ways in 2 Corinthians 5:14 where Paul pronounces that if one died on behalf of all, then all have died; and then a few sentences later in verse 19 where God is "reconciling the cosmos" – all that is – "to himself." In 1 Timothy 2:3–6, either Paul or someone who thinks like Paul emphasizes the unity between the one God and the one Mediator, the human being Jesus Christ, and the concomitant unity between Jesus and those he redeemed, that is, "all." And in Philippians 2:9–11, Paul exclaims, "at the name of Jesus every knee should bend – whether in heaven or on earth or under the earth – and every tongue confess that Jesus Christ is Lord to the glory of God the Father."

The Johannine literature is likewise expansive in its understanding of Jesus's future. "God sent the Son ... in order that the cosmos might be saved through him" (John 3:17; 1 John 4:14 and 2:2). And, in fact, Jesus "truly [is] the Savior of the cosmos" (John 4:42; cf. 12:47). "Cosmos" and "Son" are coordinated through "Savior." The Son is the Savior of the World God made. The book of Revelation takes this universal coordination to the radical, and logical, conclusion that if Jesus's resurrection reveals God's identification with him as Life, all death will be destroyed, and there will be no more tears. The Alpha and the Omega touch in eternal life.

---

[9] Or as he puts it in 1 Cor 15:22: "For just as in Adam all die, so also in the Christ all will be given life."

In short, the future of Jesus Christ is the future of the human, of humanity, and of the world. To talk about Jesus's future is to talk about ours. The theological grammar of the New Testament dictates a form of speaking about Jesus's future that means he is not extrinsic to us. We cannot speak, that is, as if Jesus is not also what we are to be.[10] He comes to us from the future and takes up our history into his. His history is our forward history, and his future is our future. There is resurrection from the dead, final liberation from sin and death, and ultimate reconciliation with the Living God.

To see this expansive theological vision as the outworking of the future of Jesus of Nazareth is not, however, to erase the significance of the present moral life, as if his future eliminated the weight of the now. The idea that God's reconciliation of all things lessens the gravity of human freedom and obscures the difference between just/unjust or right/wrong cannot find any material support from the New Testament. From Jesus's preaching onward, the grain of human moral life in the here and now is taken to matter. Caesar Augustus, Herod, Nero, and the rest were not Elizabeth, Zechariah, Stephen, or even Sergius Paulus. Or to put it in our terms: Adolf Hitler and St. Teresa of Calcutta are not the same, and no amount of soteriological vision makes them so. Indeed, human works will be tested – even as if by fire (cf. 1 Cor 3:13–15; 4:5; 1 Pet 1:7; Rev 20:12; cf. 1 Pet 1:17). Our "lowly bodies" will be exposed for what they are, and what we have done. But the end will be the transformation into the "glorious body of Jesus Christ by the power that enables him to subject all things to himself" (Phil 3:21). In short, in the calculus of eternity, of Jesus's future for all, it is still decisively crucial whether one obeys the call to "follow me" or not.

## THE JESUS WHO ALWAYS WAS

Thus far this chapter has for the most part assumed a rather basic thing about its topic, namely that time is linear. It runs from the past through the present to the future; to think about the future of Jesus is therefore to think of him in a time that is not yet here.[11] The problem with this

---

[10] Of course, this should not be taken in any sort of crude way, where Jesus is reduced to a symbol for humanity or where the difference between the Son of God and the sons of God is erased.

[11] Though I will speak about time, I am purposefully avoiding the theoretical debates about certain series (A or B), for example, and other metaphysical questions that appear when time is thematized. Cf. the wisdom of E. M. Forster 1927, 29: "I am trying not to be philosophic about time, for it is (experts assure us) a most dangerous

assumption is not that it is false but that it is too limited or too simple. The best way to see concisely the more complicated understanding of time required by thinking of Jesus's future is to consider briefly the Gospel of John's understanding of Jesus and the implications of this understanding for reading the Old Testament.

It would be hard to overstate the importance of the prologue to the Gospel of John's Christology. Not only does the prologue work carefully with the words *theos* and *logos*, it also goes on to say that there was a movement within the relation of *logos* to *theos* in which the *logos* became flesh (1:14, *kai ho logos sarx egeneto*). That the enfleshed *logos* is Jesus of Nazareth in the Gospel of John is obvious. What is not as obvious is how we are to think about time in relation to the *logos* Jesus.

One long-established way of conceiving the importance of verse 14 is to read it as a description of a simple movement in linear time: There was a Logos who was not flesh and who then became flesh. This reading corresponds to a distinction that has often been made in the history of theological reflection between the *asarkos* Logos (the Logos without flesh) and the *ensarkos* Logos (the enfleshed Logos). On this linear understanding, Jesus, the enfleshed form of the Logos, does not exist prior to the event that verse 14 records and thus has no presence in the Old Testament. The interpretative implication for reading Scripture is that it would be inappropriate, hermeneutically speaking, to read the human Jesus back into the Old Testament. Such a move is literally anachronistic. Jesus is not the unenfleshed Word of God but the enfleshed Word of God.

The distinction between the *asarkos* and *ensarkos* Logos makes a kind of prima facie sense. At the very least, the *egeneto* ("became") of verse 14 must point toward *something* that was new in the life of the Logos. That flesh is this "something new" would be hard to deny. Jesus the fleshly Jew of the first century, the one whose flesh hung on the cross, was not present in just this way in the time of the Old Testament. To take an example of a passage that became important to the early church: To say that Jesus was straightforwardly the fourth, mysterious figure in the fiery furnace with Shadrach, Meshach, and Abednego in the book of Daniel is to diminish or even deny the enfleshing of the Logos spoken of in John 1:14. Attending to the *asarkos/ensarkos* systematic distinction thus helps preserve a real incarnation, an enfleshing

hobby for an outsider, far more fatal than place; and quite eminent metaphysicians have been dethroned through referring to it improperly."

of the Word of God that corresponds exactly to the newness of God's advent in Jesus.[12]

The problem, however, with this way of articulating the relationship between Jesus and the Logos is created by the Gospel of John itself. When teaching in the Temple, Jesus is challenged by his opponents with respect to the greatness of Abraham. Jesus confuses them even more with his initial response, and then says, "Before Abraham was, I am" (*prin Abraam genesthai egō eimi*, 8:58).

Despite the good sense the *asarkos/ensarkos* distinction makes of the prologue taken by itself, it would be exegetically impossible – even bizarre – to attempt to distinguish here between the Jesus who John tells us was speaking ("and *Jesus* said...") and the "I" who said "before Abraham I am." Narratively, of course, it is one and the same character: It is *Jesus* who says "I am." Instead of dividing Jesus from the I who speaks as Jesus, we should rather take the point that the Gospel as a whole seems to make: To understand who Jesus is, we need to think two things simultaneously, which is to say, dialectically: on the one hand, the Logos whose Incarnation he is and, on the other, the human person whose "I" was before Abraham.

If we take seriously the narrative unity between John 1:14 and 8:48, then whenever we think about the Logos, we will always, at every point, have to think about the Logos in relation to Jesus. Following John's Gospel means that the Word of God cannot be thought independently of the figure in the narrative who says before Abraham I am and who was crucified and raised. This does not mean that John projects the Logos's first-century flesh back behind creation, for example, or implies that the Logos existed as the enfleshed Logos from eternity (the *egeneto* ["became"] rules that out). But it does mean that insofar as we can think about the Logos "prior to" the Incarnation we must be willing to give him a Name. Traditionally, of course, the Name that John has been understood to give the Logos is "Son" (Son of God). But if we follow John's narrative logic further and ask who the Son of God is, we will answer with the name of Jesus. In short, we cannot think about the Logos apart from his enfleshing in Jesus. Jesus is before Abraham.

Speaking in this way necessarily complicates a view of time that would take its linear aspect to determine the future of Jesus of Nazareth. If one can say that the name of the Logos, the Son of God, from all eternity is Jesus, then one must already be committed to a view of time that is considerably more complex than that of a strictly linear

---

[12] See Jennie Grillo's chapter in this volume.

progression. If one then says, as John does, that this Jesus Logos was crucified, died, and was raised, one has rendered all simple accounts of time completely inadequate.[13]

To the best of my understanding, the Gospel of John neither offers nor presupposes a specific theory of time. What John does do, however, is pressure its readers to think about the future and the past as interpenetrating realities. Jesus's future contains his past and his past contains his future. Whereas Paul's emphasis may be on bringing Jesus's future into the present, John works to bring Jesus's future into the past. What this means for thinking about the larger question of the future of Jesus is not only that Jesus is the self-same throughout time – he will not be who he was not – but also that our thought about the future has to return to the history of Israel. The Old Testament, as it turns out, is an integral part of how we understand Jesus's future: If we want to know what is coming, we should look to the deep past as much as to the present. As an illustration, we can revisit the fiery furnace. There is space for only a few comments.

When the book of Daniel reports a mysterious fourth figure that accompanies Shadrach, Meshach, and Abednego in the fiery furnace, King Nebuchadnezzar describes this fourth figure as like *bar-elahin* (3:25). What exactly Nebuchadnezzar says is undetermined since in Aramaic the phrase can mean "a son of the gods" or "a son of God" or "the Son of God" all at once. (It is only in English – in this case – that we have to choose between these options in order to translate the passage.) Yet on a literary-historical level "a son of the gods" is exactly what one would expect the character Nebuchadnezzar to say. He is not, after all, a Jew. "A son of the gods" corresponds to Nebuchadnezzar's polytheistic theological scheme. The writer of (this part of) Daniel, in other words, knows how to make his characters speak their part.

The knowledgeable reader, however, knows that the theological vision of Daniel's text is not polytheistic and would thus simultaneously hear the same phrase *bar-elahin* in another theological register: "a/the Son of God" (cf. Theod. 3:92, *huio theou*). At this level Nebuchadnezzar would of course be saying more than he knows, speaking by accident, as it were, the truth about the one God whose Son this fourth figure is.[14] Even on this reading, however, the question about the identity of this Son of God remains.

---

[13] For a stimulating article that sees the crucifixion of the Logos as a serious question in Johannine and Jewish interpretation, see Boyarin 2001.
[14] Daniel, like other biblical authors, works deftly with dramatic irony. For a New Testament example, see the Gospel of Luke as discussed in Rowe 2006.

On the one hand, there have been those who believed that the phrase *bar-elahin* did not refer to *the* Son of God. From antiquity, St. Jerome, for instance, thought that Nebuchadnezzar was not worthy of a vision of *the* Son of God, and thus took the fourth figure to be an angel.[15] And most modern Old Testament scholars do not even entertain the possibility of a christological reading of this figure: He is, rather, understood much more generally or amorphously as a "divine being" or "God's presence" or even the ideal form of Daniel himself.[16]

On the other hand, Irenaeus and Hippolytus, for example, both read the fourth figure directly as the Logos or Son of God (cf. Theodotion/Vulgate). In his exegetical notes on Daniel, Hippolytus in particular assumes a deep continuity in identity between the Logos and Jesus when he comments that the fiery furnace text "foreshadows the Gentiles who would recognize him Incarnate whom, while not Incarnate, Nebuchadnezzar saw and acknowledged as the Son of God."[17] And Augustine is willing to say, in the context of his exegesis of Psalm 91, that it was *Christ* who was present in the furnace with Shadrach, Meshach, and Abednego: "Did not Christ," Augustine asks, "deliver the three from the fire?"[18]

Modern interpreters who both take *bar-elahin* to say "a/the Son of God" and refuse to specify the identity of the Son – naming him as a divine being, for example – operate exegetically with a notion of time that subtly denies the unity of identity between the Son who was to be Incarnate and the Son who was Incarnate, and, in so doing, substitute an understanding of a Son who exists quite apart from his relation to Jesus. Which is to say for these scholars that linear time determines materially the conception of Jesus's identity (and, incidentally, God's being – whether acknowledged or not). But, if the Gospel of John is right, there is of course no such thing as the Son of God, or Logos, in

---

[15] Jerome, *in Dan.* 3 (either angel or God, not Jesus). Cf. OG LXX (angel of God); *Exodus Rabbah* 18:5 (Gabriel); *Midrash Tehillim* 9:21 (God's angel); b. *Pes.* 118a–b (the Lord sends Gabriel to save youths).

[16] See, e.g., Goldingay 2019, 235, 240: Nebuchadnezzar's exclamation classes the fourth figure among gods; to Judahites it would indicate a subordinate heavenly being, a divine aide, "the kind of supernatural being acting on God's behalf and representing God who appears elsewhere in the OT (there is no pointer toward its being a preincarnate appearance of Jesus). It is the divine aide who camps around those who honor God and extricates them from peril (Ps 3:47 [8]) and who here enters the fire" (240). Cf. Seow 2003, 59. An exception is Towner 1984, 56 who sees this as typologically correlated with Jesus Emmanuel – the presence of God with us.

[17] Hippolytus, *Comments on Daniel*, 2.33.

[18] *Enarrat.* 91.19.

general, and linear time is but one aspect of a more complex picture of the God–world relation. The modern line of Christian Old Testament commentary on Daniel has thus given up on John 8:28 and the need for a more complicated understanding of time.

Hippolytus stays closer to the logic of John's Gospel in that he trains us to see that interpreting Nebuchadnezzar's exclamation as referring to the Son of God is necessarily to speak of the one who was to become Incarnate. To read the Old Testament after the advent of Jesus of Nazareth at this point is to grasp that the fourth figure in the furnace can never *be* less than a *direct* anticipation of the Incarnation – which is to say that the identity of the Son of God is the one who was to be enfleshed as the human Jesus. Yet the fourth figure can also never be more than a direct *anticipation* of the Incarnation – which is to say that this is not *the* Incarnation itself and that the figure is not Jesus pure and simple. The fourth figure is, therefore, the real presence of the promise of the Incarnation – which is finally to say that in a fully Christian reading what Shadrach, Meshach, and Abednego encountered was nothing other than the real presence of Jesus. (Eucharistic theology here suggests interpretative possibilities: A space is created for a complex view of time by thinking through what "real presence" would entail.) Reading with Hippolytus enables the interpreter of Daniel to retain the pressure created by keeping John 1:14 and 8:28 together within a more complicated understanding of time. In an important sense, it is the future of Jesus that enables us to see him in the past. Or, to put it in the terms of yet another Johannine source, because Jesus is Omega, he is also Alpha (cf. Rev 1:8).

CONCLUSION

It is now time to be explicit. The overall goal of this chapter has been to think about the future of Jesus without positing time as a larger category in which Jesus can be placed.[19] According to the New Testament, Jesus is he who determines what time is. He is the beginning and the end.

---

[19] I thus differ from Oscar Cullmann, who takes linear time to be the "framework" of the New Testament when it comes to its presentation of redemption. See Cullmann 1964, esp. 12: "The message of the NT is most lucid within the framework of linear time." This affirmation did not entail, however, the elevation of the framework into an article of faith. The framework of linear time, Cullmann continues, is "no more than a framework" (cf. p. 15). *Christ and Time* is a classic work that created a remarkable stir in its day. It is not read as often now as it should be. There are problems with it, such as the sort implied by my treatment of the Gospel of John, but Cullmann's study raises important questions with which to think and pursues

Thinking of the future of Jesus of Nazareth, therefore, is not so much an endeavor to plot him on a timeline – even an indefinite one – as it is the attempt to reconceive time in line with Jesus's pervasive reality. I am not aware that this commits us to a particular theory about time as much as it suggests that all theories of time lag behind the complexity of early Christianity's dialectical affirmations of the time-dwelling-eternity of the first century Jew from Galilee. The interpretative task is to retain the tension generated by saying yes simultaneously to linear time with Jesus as historical figure and to the christological reconfiguration of past/present/future. If saying yes to both of these things commits us to an irreducibly complex and conceptually difficult understanding of time, then we will have followed the New Testament's depiction of the future of Jesus of Nazareth.

## POSTSCRIPT

On any reasonable account, Jesus of Nazareth is the most influential individual in human history. Whether he is more than that is the question that Christianity itself puts to the world. Since there is no perspective that exists outside Christianity that could judge whether it is right to have made of Jesus what it has made of him, the question stands for all time.[20] The future of Jesus is not only his own future but is now and forever inescapably tied to the future of the person he has been taken to be.

## FURTHER READING

Boyarin, Daniel. 2001. "The Gospel of the *Memra*: Jewish Binitarianism and the Prologue to John." *Harvard Theological Review* 94: 243–84.

Cullmann, Oscar. 1964. *Christ and Time: The Primitive Christian Conception of Time and History.* Translated by F. V. Filson. Rev. ed. Philadelphia: Westminster Press.

---

answers with exegetical detail and theological sophistication. It is undeniably the case that the New Testament works with linear time, as does the Old Testament. In fact, as some thinkers such as Gadamer have argued, with its focus upon Jesus of Nazareth, the New Testament itself introduces history and linear time into human consciousness in a new and different way. This is, I take it, quite true, but my point is that this is not *the* "framework" or the only way the New Testament conceives of the determination of time by Jesus.

[20] Acknowledging the existence of a perspective outside of Christianity that could somehow "know" whether Christianity was a true account of Jesus would already be to have decided against the Christian verdict. On this point and its implications for truth claims of a religious/philosophical sort, see Rowe 2016.

Dawson, David. 2002. *Christian Figural Reading and the Fashioning of Identity*. Berkeley: University of California Press.

Keck, Leander E. 1981. *A Future for the Historical Jesus: The Place of Jesus in Preaching and Theology*. Philadelphia: Fortress Press.

Keck, Leander E. 2000. *Who Is Jesus? History in Perfect Tense*. Columbia: University of South Carolina Press.

Rowe, C. Kavin. 2006. *Early Narrative Christology: The Lord in the Gospel of Luke*. Berlin: Walter de Gruyter.

Rowe, C. Kavin. 2016. *One True Life: The Stoics and Early Christians as Rival Traditions*. New Haven: Yale University Press.

Rowe, C. Kavin. 2020. *Christianity's Surprise: A Sure and Certain Hope*. Nashville: Abingdon.

Sanders, E. P. 1985. *Jesus and Judaism*. Philadelphia: Fortress.

Sanders, E. P. 1993. *The Historical Figure of Jesus*. London: Allen Lane/Penguin.

Watson, Francis. 1997. *Text and Truth: Redefining Biblical Theology*. Grand Rapids: Eerdmans.

Weiss, Johannes. 1971. *Jesus' Proclamation of the Kingdom of God*. Philadelphia: Fortress.

Wright, N. T. 2010. *After You Believe: Why Christian Character Matters*. New York: HarperOne.

# Bibliography

Akyol, Mustafa. 2017. *The Islamic Jesus: How the King of the Jews Became a Prophet of the Muslims.* New York: St. Martin's.
Ali, Kecia. 2017. "Destabilizing Gender, Reproducing Maternity: Mary in the Qur'ān." *Journal of the International Qur'anic Studies Association* 2: 89–109.
Alkier, Stefan. 2013. *The Reality of the Resurrection.* Translated by L. A. Huizenga. Waco: Baylor University Press.
Alkire, Sabina. 2005. *Valuing Freedoms: Sen's Capability Approach and Poverty Reduction.* Oxford: Oxford University Press.
Allison, Dale C. 1993. *The New Moses: A Matthean Typology.* Minneapolis: Fortress.
Allison, Dale C. 2005. *Resurrecting Jesus: The Earliest Christian Tradition and Its Interpreters.* New York: T & T Clark.
Allison, Dale C. 2010. *Constructing Jesus: Memory, Imagination, and History.* Grand Rapids: Baker Academic.
Allison, Dale C. 2021. *The Resurrection of Jesus.* London: T & T Clark.
Amaladoss, Michael. 2006. *The Asian Jesus.* Maryknoll: Orbis.
Ameling, Walter and Hannah Cotton, eds. 2010–23. *Corpus Inscriptionum Iudaeae/Palaestinae.* 5 vols. Berlin/New York: De Gruyter.
Amoah, Elizabeth and Mercy Amba Oduyoye. 1989. "The Christ for African Women." In *With Passion and Compassion: Third World Women Doing Theology*, edited by Virginia Fabella and Mercy Amba Oduyoye, 35–46. Maryknoll: Orbis.
Anatolios, Khaled. 2004. "Athanasius: *Orations Against the Arians.*" In *Athanasius*, 178–211. London: Routledge.
Anatolios, Khaled. 2020. *Deification Through the Cross: An Eastern Christian Theology of Salvation.* Grand Rapids: Eerdmans.
Anderson, Allan and Edmond Tang, eds. 2005. *Asian and Pentecostal: The Charismatic Face of Christianity in Asia.* Oxford: Regnum; Baguio City: APTS.
Anderson, Paul N. 2011. "The Origin and Development of the Johannine Egō Eimi Sayings in Cognitive-Critical Perspective." *Journal for the Study of the Historical Jesus* 9: 139–206.
Andrae, Tor. 1987. *In the Garden of Myrtles: Studies in Early Islamic Mysticism.* Translated by Birgitta Sharpe. Albany: State University of New York Press.
Appiah, Anthony. 1992. *In My Father's House: Africa in the Philosophy of Culture.* Oxford: Oxford University Press.

Aquinas, Thomas. 1947. *Summa Theologica*. Translated by Dominicans of the English Province. 3 vols. New York: Benziger.

Astell, Ann W. 2006. *Eating Beauty: The Eucharist and the Spiritual Arts of the Middle Ages*. Ithaca: Cornell University Press.

Atansi, Chukwuemeka A., David M. M. Lewis and Diane B. Stinton. 2023. "Christology." In *Bibliographical Encyclopaedia of African Theology*. https://african.theologyworldwide.com/encyclopaedia/227-christology.

Atkins, J. D. 2019. *The Doubt of the Apostles and the Resurrection Faith of the Early Church*. Tübingen: Mohr Siebeck.

Auerbach, Erich. 1984. "Figura." In *Scenes from the Drama of European Literature*, 11–76. Minneapolis: University of Minnesota Press.

Ayres, Lewis. 2004. *Nicaea and Its Legacy*. Oxford: Oxford University Press.

Baarda, Tjitze. 2019. "The Diatessaron and Its Beginning: A Twofold Statement of Tatian." In *The Gospel of Tatian: Exploring the Nature and Text of the Diatessaron*, edited by Matthew R. Crawford and Nicholas J. Zola, 1–24. London: T & T Clark.

Banawiratma, J. B. 1998. "The Fragile Harmony of Religions in Indonesia." *Exchange* 27: 360–70.

Barth, Karl. 1956, 1969. *Church Dogmatics*. Translated by G. W. Bromiley. Vols. IV/1, IV/4. Edinburgh: Clark.

Barton, John. 1976. "Judaism and Christianity: Prophecy and Fulfilment." *Theology* 79: 260–66.

Barton, Stephen C. 2001. "Many Gospels, One Jesus?" In *The Cambridge Companion to Jesus*, edited by M. Bockmuehl, 170–83. Cambridge: Cambridge University Press.

Bauckham, Richard. 2015. "The Incarnation and the Cosmic Christ." In *Incarnation: On the Scope and Depth of Christology*, edited by N. H. Gregersen, 25–57. Minneapolis: Fortress.

Bauckham, Richard. 2017. *Jesus and the Eyewitnesses: The Gospels as Eyewitness Testimony*. 2nd ed. Grand Rapids: Eerdmans.

Bauckham, Richard. 2018. *Magdala of Galilee: A Jewish City in the Hellenistic and Roman Period*. Waco: Baylor.

Bauckham, Richard. 2023. *Son of Man*. Grand Rapids: Eerdmans.

Bauer, Bruno. 1851–52. *Kritik der Evangelien und Geschichte ihres Ursprungs*. 2nd ed. Berlin: Hempel.

Béchard, Dean P., ed. 2002. *The Scripture Documents: An Anthology of Official Catholic Teachings*. Collegeville: Liturgical.

Becker, Eve-Marie, Helen K. Bond, and Catrin H. Williams, eds. 2021. *John's Transformation of Mark*. London: T & T Clark.

Bediako, Kwame. 2004. *Jesus and the Gospel in Africa: History and Experience*. Maryknoll: Orbis.

Beeley, Christopher A. 2012. *The Unity of Christ: Continuity and Conflict in Patristic Tradition*. New Haven: Yale University Press.

Begbie, Jeremy S. 2007. *Resounding Truth: Christian Wisdom in the World of Music*. Grand Rapids: Baker.

Begbie, Jeremy S. 2020. "Making the Familiar Unfamiliar: Macmillan's *St Luke Passion*." In *James Macmillan Studies*, edited by George Parsons and Robert Sholl, 111–28. Cambridge: Cambridge University Press.

Benedict XVI, Pope. 2009. *Homily of His Holiness Benedict XVI, 24 May 2009.* www.vatican.va/content/benedict-xvi/en/homilies/2009/documents/hf_ben-xvi_hom_20090524_cassino.html.

Benoit, Pierre. 1982. "Préexistence et incarnation." In *Exégèse et théologie,* vol. 4, 11–61. Paris: Cerf.

Bermejo-Rubio, Fernando. 2009. "The Fiction of the 'Three Quests': An Argument for Dismantling a Dubious Historiographical Paradigm." *Journal for the Study of the Historical Jesus* 7: 211–53.

Bernhard, Andrew. 2006. *Other Christian Gospels: A Critical Edition of the Surviving Greek Manuscripts.* London: T & T Clark.

Bettenson, Henry Scowcroft, ed. 1984. *Augustine: City of God.* London: Penguin.

Birch, Jonathan C. 2018. "The Road to Reimarus: Origins of the Quest for the Historical Jesus." In *Holy as Homeland? Models for Constructing the Historic Landscapes of Jesus,* edited by Keith W. Whitelam, 19–47. Sheffield: Sheffield Phoenix.

Blanton, Ward. 2007. *Displacing Christian Origins: Philosophy, Secularity, and the New Testament.* Chicago: University of Chicago Press.

Blenkinsopp, Joseph. 2006. *Opening the Sealed Book: Interpretations of the Book of Isaiah in Late Antiquity.* Grand Rapids: Eerdmans.

Blowers, Paul M. 2013 "The Groaning and Longing of Creation: Variant Patterns of Patristic Interpretation of Romans 8:19–23." *Studia Patristica* 63: 45–54.

Blum, Edward J. and Paul Harvey. 2012. *The Color of Christ: The Son of God and the Saga of Race in America.* Chapel Hill: University of North Carolina Press.

Boakye, Andrew K. 2017. *Death and Life: Resurrection, Restoration, and Rectification in Paul's Letter to the Galatians.* Eugene: Pickwick.

Bockmuehl, Markus. 2003. *Jewish Law in Gentile Churches: Halakhah and the Beginning of Christian Public Ethics.* Grand Rapids: Baker Academic.

Bockmuehl, Markus. 2017. *Ancient Apocryphal Gospels.* Louisville: Westminster John Knox.

Bockmuehl, Markus. 2022. "Being Emmanuel: Matthew's Ever-Present Jesus?" *New Testament Studies* 68: 1–12.

Bond, Helen K., ed. 2020. *The Reception of Jesus in the First Three Centuries, Vol. 1: From Paul to Josephus: Literary Receptions of Jesus in the First Century* CE. London: T & T Clark.

Boyarin, Daniel. 2001. "The Gospel of the *Memra*: Jewish Binitarianism and the Prologue to John." *Harvard Theological Review* 94: 243–84.

Brinner, William M., trans. 2002. *'Arā'is al-Majālis fī Qiṣaṣ al-Anbiyā'* or *"Lives of the Prophets" as Recounted by Abū Isḥāq Aḥmad ibn Muḥammad ibn Ibrāhīm al-Thaʻlabī.* Leiden: Brill.

Brock, Brian. 2019. *Wondrously Wounded: Theology, Disability, and the Body of Christ.* Waco: Baylor University Press.

Brown, Colin. 1984. *Jesus in European Protestant Thought 1778–1860.* Durham, NC: Labyrinth.

Brown, Colin, with Craig A. Evans. 2022. *A History of the Quests for the Historical Jesus.* 2 vols. Grand Rapids: Zondervan Academic.

Brown, Raymond E. 1955. *The Sensus Plenior of Sacred Scripture.* Baltimore: St. Mary's University.

Bryan, Christopher. 2011. *The Resurrection of the Messiah*. New York: Oxford University Press.
Bucur, Bogdan G. 2018. *Scripture Re-Envisioned: Christophanic Exegesis and the Making of a Christian Bible*. Bible in Ancient Christianity 13. Leiden: Brill.
Buell, Denise Kimber. 2010. "Cyborg Memories: An Impure History of Jesus." *Biblical Interpretation* 18: 313–41.
Bühner, Ruben A. 2021. *Messianic High Christology: New Testament Variants of Second Temple Judaism*. Waco: Baylor University Press.
Bujo, Bénézet. 1995. *Christmas: God Becomes Man in Black Africa*. Nairobi: Paulines Publications Africa.
Bultmann, Rudolf. 1934. *Jesus and the Word*. Translated by L. Pettibone Smith and E. Huntress Lantero. New York: Scribner's.
Bultmann, Rudolf. 1948. "Neues Testament und Mythologie." In *Kerygma und Mythos*, edited by Hans Werner Bartsch, 15–53. Hamburg: Reich & Heidrich.
Bultmann, Rudolf. 1953. "New Testament and Mythology." In *Kerygma and Myth*, edited by Hans Werner Bartsch, 1–44. London: SPCK.
Burke, Tony and Brent Landau, eds. 2016–2023. *New Testament Apocrypha: More Noncanonical Scriptures*. 3 vols. Grand Rapids: Eerdmans.
Butt, John. 2011. "George Frederic Handel and *The Messiah*." In *The Oxford Handbook of the Reception History of the Bible*, edited by Michael Lieb, Emma Mason, and Jonathan Roberts, 294–306. Oxford: Oxford University Press.
Butticaz, Simon. 2020. "Early Christian Memories of Jesus: Trajectories and Models of Reception in Early Christianity." *Early Christianity* 11: 297–322.
Bynum, Caroline Walker. 1984. *Jesus as Mother: Studies in the Spirituality of the High Middle Ages*. Berkeley: University of California Press.
Byung-Mu, Ahn. 1983. "Jesus and the Minjung in the Gospel of Mark." In *Minjung Theology: People as the Subjects of History*, edited by The Commission on Theological Concerns of the Christian Conference of Asia, 138–52. London: Zed.
Byung-Mu, Ahn. 2013. "The Transmitters of the Jesus-Event Tradition." In *Reading Minjung Theology in the Twenty-First Century*, edited by Yung Suk Kim and Chin-ho Kim, 49–64. Eugene: Pickwick.
Byung-Mu, Ahn. 2019. *Stories of Minjung Theology*. Edited by Wongi Park, trans. Hanna In. Atlanta: SBL.
Cahill, Lisa Sowle. 2019. *Blessed Are the Peacemakers: Just War, Pacifism, and Peacebuilding*. Minneapolis: Fortress.
Caird, George B. 1994. *New Testament Theology*. Edited by Lincoln D. Hurst. Oxford: Clarendon.
Calvin, Jean. 1960. *Institutes of the Christian Religion*. 2 vols. Philadelphia: Westminster.
Casey, Maurice. 2010. *Jesus of Nazareth*. London: T & T Clark.
Cavell, Stanley. 1979. *The Claim of Reason: Wittgenstein, Skepticism, Morality, and Tragedy*. Oxford/New York: Oxford University Press.
Chestnut, R. Andrew. 2003. "A Preferential Option for the Spirit: The Catholic Charismatic Renewal in Latin America's New Religious Economy." *Latin American Politics and Society* 45.1: 55–85.

Cirafesi, Wally V. 2014. "The Bilingual Character and Liturgical Function of 'Hermeneiai' in Johannine Papyrus Manuscripts: A New Proposal." *Novum Testamentum* 56: 45–67.
Clarke, Clifton R. 2011. *African Christology: Jesus in Post-Missionary African Christianity*. La Vergne: Wipf and Stock Publishers.
Cleage, Albert B. 1968. *The Black Messiah*. New York: Sheed and Ward.
Coakley, Sarah. 1996. "Kenosis and Subversion: On the Repression of 'Vulnerability' in Christian Feminist Writing." In *Swallowing a Fishbone? Feminist Theologians Debate Christianity*, edited by Daphne Hampson, 82–111. London: SPCK.
Coakley, Sarah. 2008. "The Identity of the Risen Jesus: Finding Jesus Christ in the Poor." In *Seeking the Identity of Jesus: A Pilgrimage*, edited by Beverly Roberts Gaventa and Richard B. Hays, 301–22. Grand Rapids: Eerdmans.
Coakley, Sarah. 2013. *God, Sexuality and the Self: An Essay "on the Trinity"*. Cambridge: Cambridge University Press.
Collins, Adela Yarbro. 2007. *Mark: A Commentary*. Hermeneia. Minneapolis: Fortress.
Collins, Billie Jean, ed. 2014. *The SBL Handbook of Style*. 2nd ed. Atlanta: SBL.
Comim, Flavio, Mozaffar Qizilbash and Sabina Alkire, eds. 2008. *The Capability Approach*. Cambridge: Cambridge University Press.
Committee on Migration. 2001. "Asian and Pacific Presence: Harmony in Faith: A Statement by the Committee on Migration." Committee on Migration of the United States Conference of Catholic Bishops (USCCB).
Cone, James. 1997. *God of the Oppressed*. Rev. ed. Maryknoll: Orbis.
Connelly, Mark. 2012. *Christmas:A History*. London: Tauris.
Coogan, Jeremiah. 2018. "Divine Truth, Presence, and Power: Christian Books in Roman North Africa." *Journal of Late Antiquity* 11: 375–95.
Coogan, Jeremiah. 2022. "Misusing Books: Material Texts and Lived Religion in the Roman Mediterranean." *Religion in the Roman Empire* 8: 301–16.
Cook, David. 2002. *Studies in Muslim Apocalyptic*. Princeton: Darwin.
Crossan, John Dominic. 1994. *Jesus: A Revolutionary Biography*. San Francisco: HarperSanFrancisco.
Crossley, James G. 2013. "A 'Very Jewish' Jesus: Perpetuating the Myth of Superiority." *Journal for the Study of the Historical Jesus* 11: 109–29.
Crossley, James G. and Robert J. Myles. 2023. *Jesus: A Life in Class Conflict*. Winchester/Washington: Zero.
Cullmann, Oscar. 1964. *Christ and Time: The Primitive Christian Conception of Time and History*. Translated by F. V. Filson. Rev. ed. Philadelphia: Westminster.
Dahl, Nils Alstrup. 1991. *Jesus the Christ: The Historical Origins of Christological Doctrine*. Edited by Donald H. Juel. Minneapolis: Fortress.
Daley, Brian E. 2018. *God Visible: Patristic Christology Reconsidered*. Oxford: Oxford University Press.
Dalferth, Ingolf U. 2016. *Hoffnung*. Berlin: de Gruyter.
Daniélou, Jean. 1960. *From Shadows to Reality*. Translated by W. Hibberd. London: Burns & Oates.
Davies, W. D. 1948. *Paul and Rabbinic Judaism*. London: SPCK.

Davies, W. D. and Dale C. Allison. 2004. *A Critical and Exegetical Commentary on the Gospel According to Saint Matthew.* Vol. 2. London; New York: T&T Clark.

Dawson, David. 2002. *Christian Figural Reading and the Fashioning of Identity.* Berkeley: University of California Press.

de Boer, Esther A. 2010. "Followers of Mary Magdalene and Contemporary Philosophy: Belief in Jesus according to the Gospel of Mary." In *Jesus in apokryphen Evangelienüberlieferungen*, edited by Jörg Frey and Jens Schröter, 315–38. Tübingen: Mohr Siebeck.

De Bruyn, T. S. 2017. *Making Amulets Christian.* Oxford: Oxford University Press.

De Bruyn, T. S. and J. H. F. Dijkstra. 2011. "Greek Amulets and Formularies from Egypt Containing Christian Elements: A Checklist of Papyri, Parchments, Ostraka, and Tablets." *Bulletin of the American Society of Papyrologists* 48: 163–216.

De Certeau, Michel. 1995. *The Mystic Fable, Vol. 1: The Sixteenth and Seventeenth Centuries.* Translated by Michael B. Smith. Chicago: University of Chicago Press.

De Lubac, Henri. 1950. *Catholicism: A Study of Dogma in Relation to the Corporate Destiny of Mankind.* Translated by Lancelot Capel Sheppard. New York: Sheed & Ward.

De Lubac, Henri. 2006. *Corpus Mysticum: The Eucharist and the Church in the Middle Ages.* Translated by Gemma Simmonds. Edited by Laurence Paul Hemming and Susan Frank Parsons. Faith in Reason. Notre Dame: University of Notre Dame Press.

De Lubac, Henri. 2007. *History and Spirit: The Understanding of Scripture According to Origen.* Translated by Anne Englund Nash. San Francisco: Ignatius.

DelCogliano, Mark. 2022. *Christ: Through the Nestorian Controversy.* The Cambridge Edition of Early Christian Writings 3. Cambridge/New York: Cambridge University Press.

Destro, Adriana and Mauro Pesce. 2012. *Encounters with Jesus: The Man in His Place and Time.* Minneapolis: Fortress.

Deutsch, Celia. 1990. "Wisdom in Matthew: Transformation of a Symbol." *Novum Testamentum* 32 1: 13–47.

Diamond, Cora. 1988. "Throwing Away the Ladder." *Philosophy* 63 243: 5–27.

Dilulio, John, Jr. 1995. "The Coming of the Super-Predators." *The Weekly Standard*, November 27.

Doering, Lutz. 2009. "Marriage and Creation in Mark 10 and CD 4-5." In *Echoes from the Caves: Qumran and the New Testament*, edited by F. García Martínez, 133–63. STDJ 85. Leiden: Brill.

Doering, Lutz and Andrew R. Krause, eds. 2020. *Synagogues in the Hellenistic and Roman Periods: Archaeological Finds, New Methods, New Theories.* Ioudaioi 11. Göttingen: Vandenhoeck & Ruprecht.

Douglas, Kelly Brown. 1994. *The Black Christ.* Maryknoll: Orbis, 1994.

Driedger Hesslein, Kayko. 2015. *Dual Citizenship: Two-Natures Christologies and the Jewish Jesus.* Bloomsbury: T&T Clark.

Dunn, James D. G. 2003. *Christianity in the Making*, Vol. 1: *Jesus Remembered.* Grand Rapids: Eerdmans.

Durand, Emmanuel. 2018. *Jésus contemporain: Christologie brève et actuelle*. Paris: Cerf.
Dyson, R. W., ed. 1998. *Augustine: The City of God Against the Pagans*. Cambridge Texts in the History of Political Thought. Cambridge/New York: Cambridge University Press.
Edwards, Denis. 2019. *Deep Incarnation: God's Redemptive Suffering with Creatures*. Maryknoll: Orbis.
Ehrman, Bart D. and Zlatko Pleše. 2011. *The Apocryphal Gospels: Texts and Translations*. Oxford: Oxford University Press.
Eiesland, Nancy L. 1994. *The Disabled God: Toward a Liberatory Theology of Disability*. Nashville: Abingdon.
Éla, Jean Marc. 1994. "Christianity and Liberation in Africa." In *Paths of African Theology*, edited by Rosino Gibellini, 136–53. Maryknoll: Orbis.
Elledge, C. D. 2017. *Resurrection of the Dead in Early Judaism, 200 BCE–CE 200*. Oxford: Oxford University Press.
Emery, Gilles. 2004. "The Ecclesial Fruit of the Eucharist in St. Thomas Aquinas." *Nova et vetera* 2: 43–60.
Evans, Craig A. 2006. "Assessing Progress in the Third Quest of the Historical Jesus." *Journal for the Study of the Historical Jesus* 4: 35–54.
Ezigbo, Victor I. 2010. *Re-Imagining African Christologies*. Eugene: Pickwick.
Fabella, Virginia. 1989. "A Common Methodology for Diverse Christologies?" In *With Passion and Compassion: Third World Women Doing Theology*, edited by Virginia Fabella and Mercy Amba Oduyoye, 108–17. Maryknoll: Orbis.
Farrow, Douglas. 2011. *Ascension Theology*. London/New York: T & T Clark.
Fernandes, Clemir et al. 2013. "CLADE V Pastoral Letter: Final Declaration of CLADE V." *Journal of Latin American Theology* 8 1: 75–9.
Flannery, Austin, ed. 2004. *Vatican Council II: The Conciliar and Post-Conciliar Documents*. Northport: Costello.
Flusser, David. 2001. *Jesus*. 3rd ed. Jerusalem: Magnes Press, 2001.
Forster, E. M. 1927. *Aspects of a Novel*. Edited by Oliver Stallybrass. Harmondsworth: Penguin.
Fredriksen, Paula. 2017. *Paul, the Pagans' Apostle*. New Haven: Yale University Press.
Fredriksen, Paula. 2021. "Paul, the Perfectly Righteous Pharisee." In *The Pharisees*, edited by Joseph Sievers and Amy-Jill Levine, 112–35. Grand Rapids: Eerdmans.
Freeman, Jennifer Awes. 2022. *The Good Shepherd*. Waco: Baylor University Press.
Frey, Jörg. 2018. *The Glory of the Crucified One: Theology and Christology in the Fourth Gospel*. Translated by Wayne Coppins and Christoph Heilig. Waco: Baylor University Press.
Furstenberg, Yair. 2008. "Defilement Penetrating the Body: A New Understanding of Contamination in Mark 7.15." *New Testament Studies* 54: 176–200.
Gathercole, Simon. 2018. "The Alleged Anonymity of the Canonical Gospels." *The Journal of Theological Studies* 69: 447–76.
Gathercole, Simon. 2021. *The Apocryphal Gospels*. New York: Penguin.
Gathercole, Simon. 2022. *The Gospel and the Gospels: Christian Proclamation and Early Jesus Books*. Grand Rapids: Eerdmans.

Gaventa, Beverly Roberts and Richard B. Hays, eds. 2008. *Seeking the Identity of Jesus: A Pilgrimage*. Grand Rapids: Eerdmans.
Geiler von Kaysersberg, Johannes. 1516. *Das buch Granatapfel: im latein genant Malogranatus ...* Strassburg: Knobloch.
Giambrone, Anthony. 2022. *A Quest for the Historical Christ*. Washington, DC: The Catholic University of America Press.
Gilroy, Paul. 1993. *The Black Atlantic: Modernity and Double Consciousness*. Cambridge, MA: Harvard University Press.
Given, J. Gregory. 2016. "Utility and Variance in Late Antique Witnesses to the Abgar-Jesus Correspondence." *Archiv für Religionsgeschichte* 17: 187–222.
Goldingay, John. 2019. *Daniel*. Word Biblical Commentary 30. Rev. ed. Grand Rapids: Zondervan Academic.
Goodacre, Mark. 2002. *The Case against Q*. Harrisburg: Trinity.
Goodacre, Mark. 2021. "Parallel Traditions or Parallel Gospels? John's Gospel as a Re-Imagining of Mark." In *John's Transformation of Mark*, edited by Eve-Marie Becker et al., 77–90. London: T & T Clark.
Gorman, Michael J. 2021. *Cruciformity: Paul's Narrative Spirituality of the Cross*. 20th anniversary ed. Grand Rapids: Eerdmans.
Green, Gene, Steve T. Pardue, and K. K. Yeo, eds. 2020. *Majority World Theology*. Downers Grove: IVP Academic.
Green, Joel B. 1994. "Good News to Whom?" In *Jesus of Nazareth: Lord and Christ*, edited by Joel B. Green and Max Turner, 59–74. Grand Rapids: Eerdmans.
Greenfield, Jonas C., Michael E. Stone, and Esther Eshel, eds. 2004. *The Aramaic Levi Document: Edition, Translation, Commentary*. Leiden: Brill.
Gregersen, Niels Henrik, ed. 2015. *Incarnation: On the Scope and Depth of Christology*. Minneapolis: Fortress.
Gregg, Robert C., trans. 1980. *Athanasius: The Life of Antony and the Letter to Marcellinus*. The Classics of Western Spirituality. New York: Paulist Press.
Grillmeier, Aloys. 1975. *Christ in Christian Tradition*. 2nd ed. Translated by J. Bowden. Atlanta: John Knox.
Grondona, Mariano. 2000. "A Cultural Typology of Economic Development." In *Culture Matters: How Values Shape Human Progress*, edited by Lawrence E. Harrison and Samuel P. Huntington, 44–55. New York: Basic.
Habermas, Gary R. 2021. *Risen Indeed: A Historical Investigation into the Resurrection of Jesus*. Ashland: Lexham.
Hahne, Harry Alan. 2006. *The Corruption and Redemption of Creation: Nature in Romans 8.19-22 and Jewish Apocalyptic Literature*. London: T&T Clark.
Hanciles, Jehu. 2008. *Beyond Christendom: Globalization, African Migration and the Transformation of the West*. Maryknoll: Orbis.
Harley-McGowan, F. 2020. "The Alexamenos Graffito." In *The Reception of Jesus in the First Three Centuries*, 3 vols, edited by Chris Keith et al, 105–40. London: T&T Clark.
Harries, Richard. 2004. *The Passion in Art*. London: Routledge.
Harvey, Warren Zev. 2012. "Harry Austryn Wolfson on the Jews' reclamation of Jesus." In *Jesus Among the Jews: Representation and Thought*, edited by Neta Stahl, 152–58. New York: Routledge.

Havea, Jione. 2014a. "Engaging Scriptures from Oceania." In *Bible, Borders, Belonging(s)*, edited by Jione Havea, David J. Neville, and Elaine M. Wainwright, 3–19. Atlanta: SBL.

Havea, Jione, ed. 2014b. *Indigenous Australia and the Unfinished Business of Theology: Cross-Cultural Engagement*. New York: Palgrave Macmillan.

Hays, Richard B. 1989. *Echoes of Scripture in the Letters of Paul*. New Haven: Yale University Press.

Hays, Richard B. 1997. *First Corinthians*. Interpretation. Louisville: John Knox.

Heine, Ronald E., trans. 1989. *Origen: Commentary on the Gospel according to John Books 1–10*. FC 80. Washington: Catholic University of America Press.

Hengel, Martin. 1985. "The Titles of the Gospels and the Gospel of Mark." In *Studies in the Gospel of Mark*, 64–84. Translated by John Bowden. London: SCM.

Hengel, Martin. 2000. *The Four Gospels and the One Gospel of Jesus Christ: An Investigation of the Collection and Origin of the Canonical Gospels*. London: SCM.

Hengel, Martin and Anna Maria Schwemer. 2019. *Jesus and Judaism*. Waco: Baylor University Press.

Hengstenberg, E. W. 1836–1839. *Christology of the Old Testament, and a Commentary on the Predictions of the Messiah by the Prophets*. Translated by Keith Reuel. 3 vols. Alexandria: Morrison.

Henrix, Hans Hermann. 2011. "The Son of God Became Human as a Jew: Implications of the Jewishness of Jesus for Christology." In *Christ Jesus and the Jewish People Today*, edited by Philip A. Cunningham et al., 114–43. Grand Rapids: Eerdmans.

Henze, Matthias and David Lincicum, eds. 2023. *Israel's Scriptures in Early Christian Writings: The Use of the Old Testament in the New*. Grand Rapids: Eerdmans.

Hertig, Paul and Robert L. Gallagher. 2004. "Introduction: Background to Acts." In *Mission in Acts*, edited by Robert L. Gallagher and Paul Hertig, 1–17. Maryknoll: Orbis.

Heschel, Susannah. 1998. *Abraham Geiger and the Jewish Jesus*. Chicago: University of Chicago Press.

Heschel, Susannah. 2008. *The Aryan Jesus: Christian Theologians and the Bible in Nazi Germany*. Princeton: Princeton University Press.

Hewitt, J. Thomas. 2020. *Messiah and Scripture: Paul's "In Christ" Idiom in its Ancient Jewish Context*. WUNT 2:522. Tübingen: Mohr Siebeck.

Hillner, Julia. 2022. *Helena Augusta: Mother of the Empire*. Oxford: Oxford University Press.

Holmén, Tom and Stanley E. Porter, eds. 2011. *Handbook for the Study of the Historical Jesus*. 4 vols. Leiden: Brill.

Hooker, Morna D. 1971. "Christology and Methodology." *New Testament Studies* 17: 480–87.

Horner, Al. 2020. "'I Have a Sense of Urgency': Sufjan Stevens Wakes from the American Dream." *The Guardian*, September 25. www.theguardian.com/music/2020/sep/25/sufjan-stevens-interview-the-ascension

Hoskyns, Edwyn Clement and Francis Noel Davey. 1981. *Crucifixion-Resurrection*. Edited by Gordon S. Wakefield. London: SPCK.

Howley, J. A. 2017. "Book-Burning and the Uses of Writing in Ancient Rome: Destructive Practice Between Literature and Document." *Journal of Roman Studies* 107: 1–24.

Humfress, Caroline. 2007. "Judging by the Book: Christian Codices and Late Antique Legal Culture." In *The Early Christian Book*, edited by William E. Klingshirn and Linda Safran, 141–58. Washington: Catholic University of America Press.

Hurtado, Larry W. 1998a. "The Origins of the Nomina Sacra: A Proposal." *Journal of Biblical Literature* 117: 655–73.

Hurtado, Larry W. 1998b. *One God One Lord: Early Christian Devotion and Ancient Jewish Monotheism*. 2nd ed. Philadelphia: Fortress.

Hurtado, Larry W. 2006. *The Earliest Christian Artifacts: Manuscripts and Christian Origins*. Grand Rapids: Eerdmans.

Hurth, Elisabeth. 1988. *In His Name: Comparative Studies in the Quest for the Historical Jesus*. Frankfurt: Lang.

Instone-Brewer, David. 2011. "Jesus of Nazareth's Trial in the Uncensored Talmud." *Tyndale Bulletin* 62.2: 269–94.

Jacobs, Andrew S. 2012. *Christ Circumcised: A Study in Early Christian History and Difference*. Philadelphia: University of Pennsylvania Press.

Jacobs, Andrew S. 2023. *Gospel Thrillers: Conspiracy, Fiction, and the Vulnerable Bible*. Cambridge: Cambridge University Press.

Jamir, Nungshitula. 2014. "Reimagining the Cross of Childbearing: Towards a Naga Constructive Christology of Natality." ProQuest Dissertations Publishing, PhD, Boston University Massachusetts.

Jeffery, Arthur. 1951. "The Descent of Jesus in Muhammadan Eschatology." In *The Joy of Study: Papers on New Testament and Related Subjects Presented to Honor Frederick Clifton Grant*, edited by Sherman E. Johnson, 107–26. New York: Macmillan.

Jensen, Robin M. 2015. "Allusions to Imperial Rituals in Fourth-Century Christian Art." In *The Art of Empire: Christian Art in Its Imperial Contexts*, edited by Lee M. Jefferson and Robin M. Jensen, 13–47. Minneapolis: Fortress.

Jensen, Robin M. 2017. *The Cross: History, Art, and Controversy*. Cambridge, MA: Harvard University Press.

Jensen, Robin M. 2023. "Icons as Relics, Relics as Icons." In *Interacting with Saints in the Late Antique and Medieval Worlds*, edited by Robert Wiśniewski, Raymond Van Dam, and Bryan Ward-Perkins, 17–45. Turnhout: Brepols.

Jewett, Robert. 2007. *Romans*. Hermeneia. Minneapolis: Fortress.

Jipp, Joshua W. 2015. *Christ Is King: Paul's Royal Ideology*. Minneapolis: Fortress.

Jones, B. C. 2014. "A Coptic Fragment of the Gospel of John with *Hermeneiai* (P.CTYBRP. CTYBR Inv. 4641)." *New Testament Studies* 60 2: 202–14.

Juel, Donald H. 1994. *A Master of Surprise: Mark Interpreted*. Minneapolis: Fortress.

Kähler, Martin. 1964. *The So-Called Historical Jesus and the Historic, Biblical Christ*. Translated by Carl E. Braaten. Philadelphia: Fortress.

Kang, Won-Don. 2018. "The Priest of Han as a Theme in the Christian-Shamanist Interfaith Dialogue." *Estudos de Religião* 32: 1–21 http://doi.org/10.15603/2176-1078/er.v32n3p247-267.

Kärkkäinen, Veli-Matti. 2010. "Christology in Africa, Asia, and Latin America." In *The Blackwell Companion to Jesus*, edited by Delbert R. Burkett, 375–93. Oxford: Wiley-Blackwell.
Käsemann, Ernst. 1964. "The Problem of the Historical Jesus." In *Essays on New Testament Themes*, 15–47. London: SCM.
Katongole, Emmanuel. 2017. *The Journey of Reconciliation: Groaning for a New Creation in Africa*. Maryknoll: Orbis.
Keck, Leander E. 1981. *A Future for the Historical Jesus: The Place of Jesus in Preaching and Theology*. Philadelphia: Fortress.
Keck, Leander E. 2000. *Who Is Jesus? History in Perfect Tense*. Columbia: University of South Carolina Press.
Keith, Chris. 2009. *The Pericope Adulterae, The Gospel of John, and the Literacy of Jesus*. Leiden: Brill.
Keith, Chris. 2020. *The Gospel as Manuscript: An Early History of the Jesus Tradition as Material Artifact*. Oxford: Oxford University Press.
Keith, Chris. 2021. "The Gospel Read, Sliced, and Burned: The Material Gospel and the Construction of Christian Identity." *Early Christianity* 12 1: 7–27.
Keith, Chris and Anthony Le Donne, eds. 2012. *Jesus, Criteria, and the Demise of Authenticity*. London: T & T Clark Continuum.
Keith, Chris et al., eds. 2020. *The Reception of Jesus in the First Three Centuries*. 3 vols. London etc.: T & T Clark.
Kelley, Shawn. 2002. *Racializing Jesus: Race, Ideology, and the Formation of Modern Biblical Scholarship*. London: Routledge.
Khalidi, Tarif. 2001. *The Muslim Jesus: Sayings and Stories in Islamic Literature*. Cambridge, MA: Harvard University Press.
Kim, Paul Inhwan. 2011. "Apatheia and Atonement: Grammar of Salvation for Contemporary Christian Theology." ProQuest Dissertations Publishing, PhD, Baylor University, Texas.
King, J. Christopher. 2005. *Origen on the Song of Songs as the Spirit of Scripture: The Bridegroom's Perfect Marriage-Song*. Oxford: Oxford University Press.
King, Martin Luther. 1998. *The Autobiography of Martin Luther King, Jr*. Edited by Clayborne Carson. New York: IPM/Warner.
Klingshirn, William E. and Linda Safran, eds. 2007. *The Early Christian Book*. Washington: Catholic University of America Press.
Kloppenborg, John S. 2014. "A New Synoptic Problem: Mark Goodacre and Simon Gathercole on Thomas." *Journal for the Study of the New Testament* 36: 199–239.
Kloppenborg, John S. 2022. "The Concept of Myth in Historical Jesus Research and the Rise of the Two Source Hypothesis." In *The Jesus Handbook*, edited by Jens Schröter and Christine Jacobi, 46–53. Grand Rapids: Eerdmans.
Knust, Jennifer and Tommy Wasserman. 2018. *To Cast the First Stone: The Transmission of a Gospel Story*. Princeton: Princeton University Press.
Kolié, Cécé. 1991. "Jesus as Healer?" In *Faces of Jesus in Africa*, edited by Robert J. Schreiter, 128–50. Maryknoll: Orbis.
Kramer, Werner R. 1966. *Christ, Lord, Son of God*. Translated by B. Hardy. SBT 50. London: SCM.
Kreps, Anne Starr. 2022. *The Crucified Book: Sacred Writing in the Age of Valentinus*. Philadelphia: University of Pennsylvania Press.

Kuma, Afua. 1981. *Jesus of the Deep Forest: Prayers and Praises of Afua Kuma*. Translated by John Kirby. Accra: Asempa Publishers.

Küster, Volker. 2001. *The Many Faces of Jesus Christ: Intercultural Christology*. Maryknoll: Orbis.

Kwok, Pui-lan. 2000. *Introducing Asian Feminist Theology*. Cleveland: Pilgrim.

Lawson, Todd. 2009. *The Crucifixion and the Qur'an*. London: Oneworld.

Leppin, Volker. 2023. *Medieval Spirituality: An Introduction*. Baylor: University Press.

Levenson, Jon D. 2006. *Resurrection and the Restoration of Israel*. New Haven: Yale University Press.

Levering, Matthew. 2019. *Did Jesus Rise from the Dead? Historical and Theological Reflections*. Oxford/New York: Oxford University Press.

Lévinas, Emmanuel. 1979. *Totality and Infinity: An Essay on Exteriority*. Translated by Alphonso Lingis. The Hague: Martinus Nijhoff Publishers.

Levine, Amy-Jill. 2014. *Short Stories by Jesus: The Enigmatic Parables of a Controversial Rabbi*. New York: Harper Collins.

Leyerle, B. 1996. "Landscape as Cartography in Early Christian Pilgrim Narratives." *Journal of Early Christian Studies* 64: 119–43.

Li, Lahphai Awng. 2014. "The Ethical Aspect of Salvation in Christianity and Theravada Buddhism." In *Theology Under the Bo Tree: Contextual Theologies in Myanmar*, edited by Samuel Ngun Ling, 309–37. Yangon: Myanmar Institute of Theology.

Licona, Mike. 2010. *The Resurrection of Jesus: A New Historiographical Approach*. Downers Grove/Nottingham: IVP Academic/Apollos.

Liu, Boyun. 2021. "Chinese Buddhist Writings and the Bible." In *The Oxford Handbook of the Bible in China*, edited by K. K. Yeo, 235–49. New York: Oxford University Press.

Loader, William. 2018. "Wisdom and Logos Traditions in Judaism and John's Christology." In *Reading the Gospel of John's Christology as Jewish Messianism: Royal, Prophetic, and Divine Messiahs*, edited by Benjamin E. Reynolds and Gabriele Boccaccini, 303–34. Ancient Judaism and Early Christianity. Boston: Brill.

Loewe, Andreas. 2014. *Johann Sebastian Bach's St John Passion (BWV 245): A Theological Commentary*. Leiden/Boston: Brill.

Lohfink, Gerhard. 2012. *Jesus of Nazareth: What He Wanted, Who He Was*. Collegeville: Liturgical.

Lovinfosse, M. de and Emmanuel Durand. 2021. *Naître et devenir: La vie conversante de Jésus selon Matthieu*. Paris: Cerf.

Lowden, J. 2007. "The Word Made Visible: The Exterior of the Early Christian Book as Visual *Argument*." In *The Early Christian Book*, edited by William E. Klingshirn and Linda Safran, 13–47. Washington: Catholic University of America Press.

Luijendijk, AnneMarie. 2014. *Forbidden Oracles? The Gospel of the Lots of Mary*. Studies and Texts in Ancient Christianity 89. Tübingen: Mohr Siebeck.

MacMillan, James. 2014. "Interview about *St Luke Passion*." Boosey & Hawkes. www.boosey.com/cr/news/James-MacMillan-interview-about-new-St-Luke-Passion/100345.

Magesa, Laurenti. 1989. "Christ the Liberator and Africa Today." In *Jesus in African Christianity: Experimentation and Diversity in African Christology*, edited by J. N. Kanyua Mugambi and Laurenti Magesa, 79–92. Nairobi: Initiatives Ltd.

Magnard, P., 2009. "L'homme universel." *Revue de Métaphysique et de Morale* 61: 19–32.

Maimela, Simon S. 1992. "Jesus Christ: The Liberator and Hope of Oppressed Africa." In *Exploring Afro-Christology*, edited by John S. Pobee, 31–41. Frankfurt: Peter Lang.

Manohar, Christina. 2007. "Spirit Christology: An Indian Christian Perspective." ProQuest Dissertations Publishing: PhD Dissertation, University of Gloucestershire.

Manus, Ukachukwu Chris. 1993. *Christ, the African King: New Testament Christology*. Frankfurt: P. Lang.

Maraschi, A. 2017. "Sympathy for the Lord: The Host and Elements of Sympathetic Magic in Late Medieval Exempla." *Journal of Medieval Religious Cultures* 43: 209–30.

Marcus, Joel. 2000. "Mark–Interpreter of Paul." *New Testament Studies* 46: 473–87.

Marissen, Michael. 1998. *Lutheranism, Anti-Judaism, and Bach's St. John Passion: With an Annotated Literal Translation of the Libretto*. Oxford: Oxford University Press.

Markschies, Christoph. 1998. "Kerinth: Wer war er and was lehrte er?" *Jahrbuch für Antike und Christentum* 41: 48–71.

Marquardt, Friedrich-Wilhelm. 1990. *Das christliche Bekenntnis zu Jesus, dem Juden: Eine Christologie*. Vol. 1. Munich: Kaiser.

Marshall, I. Howard. 1980. *The Acts of the Apostles: An Introduction and Commentary*. Leicester/Grand Rapids: Inter-Varsity.

Massey, Brandon. 2023. "The Quest for the Historical Jesus." *Journal for the Study of the Historical Jesus* 21: 75–161.

Mbiti, John S. 1969. *African Religions and Philosophy*. Nairobi: Heinemann.

Mbiti, John S. 1972. "Some African Concepts of Christology." In *Christ and the Younger Churches*, edited by George F. Vicedom, 51–62. London: SPCK.

McCaulley, Esau. 2019. *Sharing in the Son's Inheritance: Davidic Messianism and Paul's Worldwide Interpretation of the Abrahamic Land Promise in Galatians*. LNTS 608. London/New York: T & T Clark.

McFarlan, Emily. 2020. "How an Iconic Painting of Jesus as a White Man Was Distributed around the World." *Washington Post*, June 25.

Meggitt, Justin J. 2019. "'More ingenious than learned?' Examining the Quest for the Non-Historical Jesus." *New Testament Studies* 65: 443–60.

Meier, John P. 1991–2016. *A Marginal Jew: Rethinking the Historical Jesus*. 5 vols. Anchor Bible Reference Library. New Haven: Yale University Press.

Meier, John P. 1999. "The Present State of the 'Third Quest' of the Historical Jesus: Loss and Gain." *Biblica* 80: 459–87.

Melchert, Christoph. 2020. *Before Sufism: Early Islamic Renunciant Piety*. Berlin: De Gruyter.

Mendelssohn, Moses. 1983. *Jerusalem, or On Religious Power and Judaism*. Translated by A. Arkush. Hanover, NH: Brandeis University Press.

Mercator, Gerhard. 1592. *Evangelicae Historiae Quadripartita Monas, sive Harmonia Quatuor Evangelistarum*. Duisburg: n.p.
Metzger, B. M. 1988. "Greek Manuscripts of John's Gospels with 'Hermeneiai'." In *Text and Testimony: Essays on New Testament and Apocryphal Literature in Honour of A. F. J. Klijn*, edited by T. Baarda et al., 162–69. Kampen: Kok.
Meyer, Barbara U. 2011. "The Dogmatic Significance of Christ Being Jewish." In *Christ Jesus and the Jewish People Today: New Explorations of Theological Interrelationships*, edited by Philip A. Cunningham et al., 144–56. Grand Rapids: Eerdmans.
Meyer, Barbara U. 2020. *Jesus the Jew in Christian Memory: Theological and Philosophical Explorations*. Cambridge: Cambridge University Press.
Moberly, Walter. 1988. "Proclaiming Christ Crucified: Some Reflections on the Use and Abuse of the Gospels." *Anvil* 5.1: 31–52.
Moffett, Samuel H. 1998–2005. *A History of Christianity in Asia*. 2 vols. Maryknoll: Orbis.
Moi, Toril. 2017. *Revolution of the Ordinary: Literary Studies After Wittgenstein*. Chicago: University of Chicago Press.
Moltmann, Jürgen. 1996. "The Resurrection of Christ: Hope for the World." In *Resurrection Reconsidered*, edited by Gavin D'Costa, 73–86. Oxford: Oneworld.
Morrissey, Fitzroy. In press. "Jesus in Islamic Mysticism." In *Son of Mary: Jesus in Muslim Tradition*, edited by Stephen R. Burge. Atlanta: SBL.
Moss, Candida R. 2019. *Divine Bodies: Resurrecting Perfection in the New Testament and Early Christianity*. New Haven: Yale University Press.
Mourad, Suleiman A. 2011. "Does the Qurʾān Deny or Assert Jesus's Crucifixion and Death?" In *New Perspectives on the Qurʾān: The Qurʾān in Its Historical Context 2*, edited by Gabriel S. Reynolds, 349–57. Abingdon: Routledge.
Moxnes, Halvor. 2011. *Jesus and the Rise of Nationalism. A New Quest for the Nineteenth-Century Historical Jesus*. London: I. B. Tauris.
Mshana, Rogate R. and Athena Peralta. 2015. *Economy of Life: Linking Poverty, Wealth and Ecology*. Geneva: World Council of Churches.
Mugambi, J. N. Kanyua and Laurenti Magesa, eds. 1989. *Jesus in African Christianity: Experimentation and Diversity in African Christology*. Nairobi: Initiatives Ltd.
Muir, Carolyn Diskant. 2013. *Saintly Bridge and Bridegrooms*. Turnhout: Brepols.
Mulder, Frederik S. 2019. "Gospel Contradictions, Harmonizations, and Historical Truth: Francis Watson and Origen's Comprehensive Paradigm Shift." In *Writing the Gospels: A Dialogue with Francis Watson*, edited by Catherine Sider Hamilton with Joel Willitts, 166–83. London: T&T Clark.
Nation, Hannah and J. D. Tseng. 2022. *Faithful Disobedience: Writings on Church and State from a Chinese House Church Movement*. Downers Grove: IVP Academic.
Nirmal, Arvind P. 1990. *A Reader in Dalit Theology*. Madras: Gurukul Lutheran Theological College.
Norris, Richard A. 1980. *The Christological Controversy*. Philadelphia: Fortress.
Novenson, Matthew V. 2012. *Christ Among the Messiahs: Christ Language in Paul and Messiah Language in Ancient Judaism*. New York: Oxford University Press.

Novenson, Matthew V. 2017. *The Grammar of Messianism: An Ancient Jewish Political Idiom and Its Users*. Oxford/New York: Oxford University Press.

Nurbakhsh, Javad. 2012. *Jesus in the Eyes of the Sufis*. New York: Khaniqahi Nimatullahi Publications (originally published 1983).

Nyamiti, Charles. 2006. *Studies in African Christian Theology: Jesus Christ, the Ancestor of Humankind – An Essay on African Christology*. Nairobi: CUEA.

O'Donovan, Oliver. 1994. *Resurrection and Moral Order*, 2nd ed. Leicester: Apollos.

O'Loughlin, T. 2007. *Adomnán and the Holy Places: The Perceptions of an Insular Monk on the Locations of the Biblical Drama*. London: T&T Clark.

Oduyoye, Mercy Amba. 2002. "Jesus Christ." In *The Cambridge Companion to Feminist Theology*, edited by Susan F. Parsons, 151–70. Cambridge: Cambridge University Press.

Oduyoye, Mercy Amba. 2010. "Jesus Christ." In *Hope Abundant: Third World and Indigenous Women's Theology*, edited by Kwok Pui-lan, 167–85. Maryknoll: Orbis.

Oduyoye, Mercy Amba and Musimbi R. A. Kanyoro, eds. 1992. *The Will to Arise: Women, Tradition, and the Church in Africa*. Maryknoll: Orbis.

Pals, Daniel L. 1982. *The Victorian Lives of Jesus*. San Antonio: Trinity University Press.

Panikkar, Raymundo. 1964. *The Unknown Christ of Hinduism*. London: Darton Longman and Todd.

Park, Wongi. 2017. "The Black Jesus, the Mestizo Jesus, and the Historical Jesus." *Biblical Interpretation* 25: 190–205.

Pelikan, Jaroslav. 1987. *Jesus through the Centuries: His Place in the History of Culture*. New York: Perennial Library.

Pentiuc, Eugen J. 2021. *Hearing the Scriptures: Liturgical Exegesis of the Old Testament in Byzantine Orthodox Hymnography*. Oxford: Oxford University Press.

Perrin, Norman. 1967. *Rediscovering the Teaching of Jesus*. New York: Harper and Row.

Pieris, Aloysius. 1987. "Christianity and Buddhism in Core-to-Core Dialogue." *CrossCurrents* 37 1: 47–75. www.jstor.org/stable/24458991.

Pobee, John S. 1985. *Persecution and Martyrdom in the Theology of Paul*. London: Bloomsbury.

Pobee, John S., ed. 1992. *Exploring Afro-Christology*. Studien zur interkulturellen Geschichte des Christentums 79. Frankfurt: Peter Lang.

Poinsett, Alex. 1969. "The Quest for a Black Christ." *Ebony* 24.2: 170–78.

Pole, Siosifa. 2015. "Vahevahe: A Tongan Concept of Receiving and Using the Bible in Relation to Matthew 4:19 and 28:19." 2015 conference presentation, Oceania Biblical Studies Association (OBSA, 2015). Abstract: https://bit.ly/vahevahe.

Price, Richard. 2012. *The Acts of the Council of Constantinople of 553*. Liverpool: Liverpool University Press.

Radde-Gallwitz, Andrew, ed. 2017. *God*. The Cambridge Edition of Early Christian Writings 1. Cambridge/New York: Cambridge University Press.

Ragg, Lonsdale and Laura Ragg. 1907. *The Gospel of Barnabas*. Oxford: Clarendon.

Rahner, Karl. 1992. *Foundations of Christian Faith: An Introduction to the Idea of Christianity.* New York: Crossroad.

Reddie, Anthony G. 2016. "The Quest for a Radical Black Jesus: An Antidote to Imperial Mission Christianity." In *Albert Cleage Jr. and the Black Madonna and Child*, edited by Jawanza Eric Clark, 285–300. New York: Palgrave Macmillan.

Reinders, Hans. 2008. *Receiving the Gift of Friendship: Profound Disability, Theological Anthropology, and Ethics.* Grand Rapids: Eerdmans.

Renan, Ernest. 1863. *La vie de Jésus.* Paris: Lévy.

Reynolds, Gabriel S. 2009. "The Muslim Jesus: Dead or Alive?" *Bulletin of the School of Oriental and African Studies* 72 2: 237–58.

Ricoeur, Paul. 2001. "Vers une théologie narrative: sa nécessité, ses ressources, ses difficultés." In *L'herméneutique biblique*, edited by François-Xavier Amherdt, 326–42. Paris: Cerf.

Rittgers, Ronald. 2012. *The Reformation of Suffering: Pastoral Theology and Lay Piety in Late Medieval and Early Modern Germany.* New York: Oxford University Press.

Rivera, Mayra. 2009. "Incarnate Words: Images of God and Reading Practices." In *They Were All Together in One Place: Toward Minority Biblical Criticism*, edited by Randall C. Bailey, Tat-siong Benny Liew, and Fernando F. Segovia, 313–20. Semeia Studies 57. Atlanta: Society of Biblical Literature.

Robinson, James M., Paul Hoffmann, and John S. Kloppenborg, eds. 2000. *The Critical Edition of Q: Synopsis Including the Gospels of Matthew and Luke, Mark and Thomas with English, German, and French Translations of Q and Thomas.* Hermeneia. Minneapolis/Leuven: Fortress/Peeters.

Robinson, Neal. 1991. *Christ in Islam and Christianity.* Albany: State University of New York Press.

Robinson, Neal. 2003. "Jesus." In *Encyclopaedia of the Qurʾān*, edited by Jane Dammen McAuliffe, vol. 3, 7–21. Leiden: Brill.

Rodriguez, Jacob A. 2023. *Combining Gospels in Early Christianity: The One, the Many, and the Fourfold.* Tübingen: Mohr Siebeck.

Roth, Dieter. 2015. *The Text of Marcion's Gospel.* Leiden: Brill.

Rowe, C. Kavin. 2002. "Biblical Pressure and Trinitarian Hermeneutics." *Pro ecclesia* 11.3: 295–312.

Rowe, C. Kavin. 2006. *Early Narrative Christology: The Lord in the Gospel of Luke.* BZNW 139. Berlin: Walter de Gruyter.

Rowe, C. Kavin. 2016. *One True Life: The Stoics and Early Christians as Rival Traditions.* New Haven: Yale University Press.

Rowe, C. Kavin. 2020. *Christianity's Surprise: A Sure and Certain Hope.* Nashville: Abingdon.

Rowe, C. Kavin. 2022. "What If It Were True? Why Study the New Testament." *New Testament Studies* 68: 144–55.

Rowe, C. Kavin. 2024. "Romans 10:13: What Is the Name of the Lord?" In *Studies in Luke, Acts, and Paul.* Grand Rapids: Eerdmans.

Rowlands, Jonathan. 2023. *The Metaphysics of Historical Jesus Research. A Prolegomenon to a Future Quest of the Historical Jesus.* London: Routledge.

Samuel, Claude. 1976. *Conversations with Olivier Messiaen.* London: Stainer & Bell.

Sanders, E. P. 1977. *Paul and Palestinian Judaism*. Philadelphia: Fortress.
Sanders, E. P. 1985. *Jesus and Judaism*. London/Philadelphia: SCM/Fortress.
Sanders, E. P. 1990. *The Question of Uniqueness in the Teaching of Jesus*. London: University of London Press.
Sanders, E. P. 1993. *The Historical Figure of Jesus*. London: Allen Lane/Penguin.
Sanneh, Lamin. 1987. "Christian Missions and the Western Guilt Complex." *The Christian Century*, April 8: 331–34.
Sanzo, J. 2014. *Scriptural Incipits on Amulets from Late Antique Egypt: Text, Typology, and Theory*. STAC 84. Tübingen: Mohr Siebeck.
Schäfer, Peter. 2007. *Jesus in the Talmud*. Princeton: Princeton University Press.
Schäfer, Peter, ed. 2011. *Toledot Yeshu ("The Life Story of Jesus") Revisited: A Princeton Conference*. Tübingen: Mohr Siebeck.
Schimmel, Annemarie. 2018. *Jesus und Maria in der islamischen Mystik*. [Xanten]: Chalice Verlag (originally published Munich: Kösel Verlag, 1996).
Schreiter, Robert J, ed. 1991. *Faces of Jesus in Africa*. Maryknoll: Orbis.
Schröter, Jens. 2022. "'Remembered Jesus': Memory as a Historiographical Hermeneutical Paradigm of Research in Jesus." In *The Jesus Handbook*, edited by Jens Schröter and Christine Jacobi, 108–20. Grand Rapids: Eerdmans.
Schröter, Jens and Christine Jacobi, eds. 2022. *The Jesus Handbook*. Grand Rapids: Eerdmans.
Schröter, Jens, Tobias Nicklas, and Joseph Verheyden, eds. 2019. *Gospels and Gospel Reception in the Second Century: Experiments in Reception*. Berlin: De Gruyter.
Schüssler Fiorenza, Elisabeth. 1997. "Jesus and the Politics of Interpretation." *Harvard Theological Review* 90: 343–58.
Schüssler-Fiorenza, Elisabeth. 2000. *Jesus and the Politics of Interpretation*. New York: Continuum.
Schweitzer, Albert. 1931. *The Mysticism of Paul the Apostle*. Translated by W. Montgomery. London: A&C Black.
Schweitzer, Albert. 2000. *The Quest of the Historical Jesus*. London: SCM.
Seitz, Christopher R. 2011. "The Trinity in the Old Testament." In *The Oxford Handbook of the Trinity*, edited by Gilles Emery and Matthew Levering, 28–40. Oxford: Oxford University Press.
Selak, Annie. 2017. "Orthodoxy, Orthopraxis, and Orthopathy: Evaluating the Feminist Kenosis Debate." *Modern Theology* 33: 529–48.
Sen, Amartya. 1983. "Poor, Relatively Speaking." In *Oxford Economic Papers* 35: 153–69.
Sen, Amartya. 2000. *Development as Freedom*. Oxford, etc.: Oxford University Press.
Seow, C. L. 2003. *Daniel*. Westminster Bible Companion. Louisville: Westminster John Knox.
Setzer, Claudia. 2004. *Resurrection of the Body in Early Judaism and Early Christianity: Doctrine, Community, and Self-Definition*. Leiden/Boston: Brill.
Sharma, Samrat and Piyush Aggrawal. 2021. "Income and Debt Account of Indian Farmers: Explained." In *India Today*, 20 November 2021.
Shenton, Andrew. 2010. *Messiaen the Theologian*. Farnham: Ashgate.
Shoemaker, Stephen J. 2003. "Christmas in the Qur'ān: The Qur'ānic Account of Jesus' Nativity and Palestinian Local Tradition." *Jerusalem Studies in Arabic and Islam* 28: 11–39.

Sider-Hamilton, Catherine. 2017. *The Death of Jesus in Matthew: Innocent Blood and the End of Exile*. Cambridge: Cambridge University Press.
Sievers, Joseph and Amy-Jill Levine, eds. 2021. *The Pharisees*. Grand Rapids: Eerdmans.
Siker, Jeffrey. 2007. "Historicizing a Racialized Jesus: Case Studies in the 'Black Christ,' the 'Mestizo Christ,' and White Critique." *Biblical Interpretation* 15: 26–53.
Sobrino, Jon. 1994. *Principle of Mercy: Taking the Crucified People from the Cross*. Maryknoll: Orbis.
Sommer, Benjamin D. 2009. *The Bodies of God and the World of Ancient Israel*. Cambridge: Cambridge University Press.
Song, Choan-Seng. 1982. *The Compassionate God*. Maryknoll: Orbis.
Stassen, Glen. 2012. *A Thicker Jesus: Incarnational Discipleship in a Secular Age*. Louisville, KY: Westminster John Knox.
Stinton, Diane B. 2004. *Jesus of Africa: Voices of Contemporary African Christology*. Maryknoll: Orbis.
Stinton, Diane B. 2012. "*Amani ya Juu* ('A Higher Peace'): African Refugee Women Living Out Reconciliation in Nairobi." *Crux* 48 3 (Fall): 60–71.
Stott, John. 1975. *The Lausanne Covenant: Exposition and Commentary*. Minneapolis: World Wide Publications.
Stowers, Stanley K. 1994. *A Rereading of Romans: Justice, Jews, and Gentiles*. New Haven: Yale University Press.
Strauss, David Friedrich. 1973. *The Life of Jesus Critically Examined*. Edited by Peter C. Hodgson. Translated by George Eliot. London: SCM.
Sugirtharajah, R. S. 2018. *Jesus in Asia*. Cambridge, MA/London: Harvard University Press.
Tanner, Kathryn. 2010. *Christ the Key*. Cambridge: Cambridge University Press.
Tanner, Norman P., ed. 1990. *Decrees of the Ecumenical Councils*. 2 vols. Washington, DC: Georgetown University Press.
Theissen, Gerd and Annette Merz. 1998. *The Historical Jesus: A Comprehensive Guide*. Minneapolis: Fortress.
Theissen, Gerd and Annette Merz. 2023. *Wer war Jesus? Der erinnerte Jesus in historischer Sicht: Ein Lehrbuch*. Göttingen: Vandenhoeck & Ruprecht. (Revised German version of Theissen and Merz 1998.)
Thiessen, Matthew. 2020. *Jesus and the Forces of Death: The Gospels' Portrayal of Ritual Impurity within First-Century Judaism*. Grand Rapids: Baker Academic.
Thompson, Alan J. 2011. *The Acts of the Risen Lord Jesus: Luke's Account of God's Unfolding Plan*. Downers Grove, IL: IVP Academic.
Tillard, Jean Marie Roger. 1967. *The Eucharist: Pasch of God's People*. Translated by D. L. Wienk. Staten Island: Alba House.
Towner, W. Sibley. 1984. *Daniel*. Interpretation. Atlanta: John Knox.
Tran, Jonathan. 2022. *Asian Americans and the Spirit of Racial Capitalism*. Oxford/New York: Oxford University Press.
UNICEF (United Nations International Children's Emergency Fund) and WHO (World Health Organization). 2020. *State of the World's Sanitation: An Urgent Call to Transform Sanitation for Better Health, Environments, Economies and Societies*. New York: UNICEF and WHO.

Van Buren, Paul M. 1988. *A Theology of the Jewish-Christian Reality, Part III: Christ in Context.* San Francisco: Harper & Row.
van Kooten, George. 2019. "John's Counter-Symposium: 'The Continuation of Dialogue' in Christianity – A Contrapuntal Reading of John's Gospel and Plato's Symposium." In *Intolerance, Polemics, and Debate in Antiquity,* edited by George van Kooten and Jacques van Ruiten, 282–357. Leiden: Brill.
Vanhoye, Albert. 2002. *La lettre aux Hébreux: Jésus-Christ, médiateur d'une alliance nouvelle.* Paris: Desclée.
Venard, Olivier-Thomas. 2015. "Christology from the Old Testament to the New." In *The Oxford Handbook of Christology,* edited by Francesca Aran Murphy, 21–38. Oxford Handbooks. Oxford: Oxford University Press.
Verhey, Allen. 2002. *Remembering Jesus: Christian Community, Scripture, and the Moral Life.* Grand Rapids: Eerdmans.
Verkerk, Dorothy. 2020. "'The Quiet Affection in Their Eyes': Bernhard Plockhorst's Jesus as the Good Shepherd." *Religion and the Arts* 24: 353–78.
Vermes, Geza. 1973. *Jesus the Jew: A Historian's Reading of the Gospels.* London: Collins.
Viladesau, Richard. 2020. *The Wisdom and Power of the Cross: The Passion of Christ in Theology and the Arts.* Oxford: Oxford University Press.
Vischer, Wilhelm. 1949. *The Witness of the Old Testament to Christ.* Translated by A. B. Crabtree. London: Lutterworth.
Viviano, Benedict Thomas. 1998. "The Trinity in the Old Testament: From Daniel 7:13–14 to Matt 28:19." *Theologische Zeitschrift* 54.3: 193–209.
Volf, Miroslav and Ryan McAnnally-Linz. 2022. *The Home of God: A Brief Story of Everything.* Grand Rapids: Brazos.
Wach, Joachim. 1944. *Sociology of Religion.* Chicago: University of Chicago Press.
Walls, Andrew F. 1996. *The Missionary Movement in Christian History: Studies in the Transmission of Faith.* Maryknoll, NY: Orbis.
Ward, Benedicta, trans. 1975. *The Sayings of the Desert Fathers.* Kalamazoo: Cistercian Publications.
Wasike, Anne Nasimiyu. 1989. "Christology and an African Woman's Experience." In *Jesus in African Christianity: Experimentation and Diversity in African Christology,* edited by J. N. K. Mugambi and Laurenti Magesa, 123–35. Nairobi: Initiatives Ltd.
Watson, Francis. 1997. *Text and Truth: Redefining Biblical Theology.* Grand Rapids: Eerdmans.
Watson, Francis. 2001. "The Quest for the Real Jesus." In *The Cambridge Companion to Jesus,* edited by Markus Bockmuehl, 156–69. Cambridge: Cambridge University Press.
Watson, Francis. 2013. *Gospel Writing: A Canonical Perspective.* Grand Rapids/Cambridge: Eerdmans.
Watson, Francis. 2022. *What Is a Gospel?* Grand Rapids: Eerdmans.
Watson, Francis and Sarah Parkhouse. 2018. *Connecting Gospels: Beyond the Canonical/Noncanonical Divide.* Oxford: Oxford University Press.
Watson, Rowan. 2007. "Some Non-Textual Uses of Books." In *A Companion to the History of the Book,* edited by Simon Eliot and Jonathan Rose, 480–92. Malden: Blackwell.

Weaver, Walter. 1999. *The Historical Jesus in the Twentieth Century: 1900–1950*. Harrisburg: Trinity Press International.

Webster, John. 2015. "The Place of Christology in Systematic Theology." In *The Oxford Handbook of Christology*, edited by Francesca Aran Murphy, 596–610. Oxford: Oxford University Press.

Weiss, Johannes. 1892. *Die Predigt Jesu vom Reiche Gottes*. Göttingen: Vandenhoeck & Ruprecht.

Weiss, Johannes. 1971. *Jesus' Proclamation of the Kingdom of God*. Philadelphia: Fortress.

White, Thomas Joseph. 2015. *The Incarnate Lord: A Thomistic Study in Christology*. Washington: Catholic University of America Press.

Wickham, Lionel R., ed. 1983. *Cyril of Alexandria: Select Letters*. Oxford Early Christian Texts. Oxford: Clarendon.

Wiese, Christian. 2004. *Challenging Colonial Discourse: Jewish Studies and Protestant Theology in Wilhelmine Germany*. Leiden: Brill.

Wilfong, T. G. and K. P. Sullivan. 2005. "The Reply of Jesus to King Abgar: A Coptic New Testament Apocryphon Reconsidered (P. Mich. Inv. 6213)." *Bulletin of the American Society of Papyrologists* 42: 107–23.

Wilken, Robert Louis. 1984. *The Christians as the Romans Saw Them*. New Haven: Yale University Press.

Wilken, Robert Louis. 2003. *The Spirit of Early Christian Thought: Seeking the Face of God*. New Haven: Yale University Press.

Williams, Rowan. 1982. *Resurrection: Interpreting the Easter Gospel*. London: Darton, Longman & Todd.

Williams, Rowan. 1996. "Between the Cherubim: The Empty Tomb and the Empty Throne." In *Resurrection Reconsidered*, edited by Gavin D'Costa, 87–101. Oxford: Oneworld.

Williams, Rowan. 2002. *Arius: Heresy and Tradition*. Rev. ed. Grand Rapids: Eerdmans.

Williams, Rowan. 2018. *Christ the Heart of Creation*. London: Bloomsbury Continuum.

Williamson, H. G. M. 1994. *The Book Called Isaiah: Deutero-Isaiah's Role in Composition and Redaction*. Oxford: Oxford University Press.

Wilson, Benjamin R. 2016. *The Saving Cross of the Suffering Christ: The Death of Jesus in Lukan Soteriology*. BZNW 223. Boston: De Gruyter.

Wink, Walter. 1992. *Engaging the Powers: Discernment and Resistance in a World of Domination*. Minnesota: Fortress.

Winner, Lauren F. 2011. "Interceding: Standing, Kneeling, and Gender." In *The Blackwell Companion to Christian Ethics*, 2nd ed., edited by Stanley Hauerwas and Samuel Wells, 264–76. Malden: Wiley-Blackwell.

Witte, Markus. 2013. *Jesus Christus im Alten Testament: eine biblisch-theologische Skizze*. Vienna: Lit.

Wittgenstein, Ludwig. 1991. *Remarks on the Foundation of Mathematics*. Edited by G. H. von Wright et al. Oxford: Blackwell.

Wittgenstein, Ludwig. 2009. *Philosophical Investigations*. Edited by P. M. S. Hacker and Joachim Schulte. Malden: Wiley.

Wiyono, Gani. 1999. "Ratu Adil: A Javanese Face of Jesus." *Journal of Asian Mission* 1: 65–79.

Wolfson, Harry Austryn. 1973. "How the Jews Will Reclaim Jesus." Introduction to Joseph Jacobs, *Jesus as Others Saw Him*. New York: Arno.
World Bank. 1993. *World Development Report 1993 Investing in Health*. Oxford: Oxford University Press, Published for the World Bank.
Wrede, William. 1901. *Das Messiasgeheimnis in den Evangelien*. Göttingen: Vandenhoeck & Ruprecht.
Wrede William. 1971. *The Messianic Secret*. Translated by James C. G. Greig. Cambridge: Clarke.
Wright, Brian J. 2017. *Communal Reading in the Time of Jesus: A Window into Christian Reading Practices*. Minneapolis: Fortress.
Wright, N. T. 1991. *The Climax of the Covenant: Christ and the Law in Pauline Theology*. Edinburgh: T & T Clark.
Wright, N. T. 1996. *Jesus and the Victory of God*. Minneapolis: Fortress.
Wright, N. T. 2003. *The Resurrection of the Son of God*. London: SPCK.
Wright, N. T. 2010. *After You Believe: Why Christian Character Matters*. New York: HarperOne.
Wyschogrod, Michael. 1983. *The Body of Faith: God and the People of Israel*. New York: Seabury.
Wyschogrod, Michael. 1993. "Incarnation." *ProEccl* 2.2: 208–15.
Yeo, K. K. 2017. "Introduction." In *So Great a Salvation: Soteriology in the Majority World*, edited by Gene L. Green et al., 1–13. Grand Rapids: Eerdmans.
Yeo, K. K. 2021. "The Logos and Pneuma of Creation: Cross-cultural Reading of Romans 8 and the Inspirited World." In *Spirit Wind: The Doctrine of the Holy Spirit in Global Theology—A Chinese Perspective*, edited by Peter L. H. Tie and Justin T. T. Tan, 147–61. Eugene: Pickwick.
Yewangoe, A. A. 2003. "The Trinity in the Context of Tribal Religion." *Studies in Interreligious Dialogue* 13: 86–105.
Yong, Amos. 2011. *The Bible, Disability, and the Church: A New Vision of the People of God*. Grand Rapids: Eerdmans.
Young, Frances M. 1997. *Biblical Exegesis and the Formation of Christian Culture*. Cambridge: Cambridge University Press.

# Ancient Sources Index

**Hebrew Bible/Old Testament**

Genesis
  1–2, 40
  1.14–19, 263
  1.27, 37
  2.24, 37
  17.12–14, 26
  18, 104
  22, 83
  32, 103
  49.11, 42
Exodus
  1.22, 48
  2–4, 48
  3.14, 335
  3.6, 130
  8.19, 22
  12.1–28, 189
  12.11 LXX, 22
  12.42, 22
  16.4–5, 22
  16.5, 29
  16.5 LXX, 22
  16.22–30, 22
  16.29, 29
  20.7, 17
  20.8–11, 29
  20.12, 16
  24.8, 22, 50
  29.45, 106
  34.21, 29
  35.3, 29
Leviticus
  4–5, 28
  11, 29

  12.2–5, 29
  12.6–8, 28
  13–14, 29
  14.2–32, 28
  15.2–13, 29
  15.16–18, 29
  15.19, 29
  15.25–28, 29
  16, 343
  16.17, 262
  18.5, 128
  19, 16
  19.2, 16
  19.12, 17
  19.15–17, 16
  19.18, 16
  19.19, 37
  21.11–12, 38
  23.11, 30
  23.15–17, 30
  25.10, 51
  27.32, 30
Numbers
  6.6, 38
  15.26–36, 29
  15.37–41, 295
  18.21–28, 30
  19, 30
  28.3–9, 28
  28.9–10, 28
  28.11–29.39, 28
  32.13, 22
Deuteronomy
  1.35, 22
  4.25–31, 15
  5.12–15, 29

5.16, 16
6.4, 40, 286
6.4–5, 16, 27, 295
6.5, 37
6.13, 27
6.16, 27
8.3, 27, 343
8.8, 30
9.10, 49
14.22–27, 30
14.28–29, 30
15.11, 316
18.15, 17, 22, 39, 42, 49
18.18, 17, 22
18.23, 30
19.9–10, 316
21.23, 126
23.15, 106
24.1, 36
24.1–4, 17
26.1–11, 30
26.12–13, 30
30.1–10, 15
32.8 LXX, 68
32.20, 22
1 Samuel
  2.1–10, 51
  16–17, 62
2 Samuel
  7.13–14, 23
  15.30, 115
  23.3–4, 114
1 Kings
  1.33, 336
  18, 17
2 Kings
  19.15, 34
1 Chronicles
  24, 28
Nehemiah
  10.32, 29
  10.36, 30
  13.15–18, 29
  13.19, 29
Job
  28, 106
Psalms
  8.6, 69

22.1, 52
23, 171, 173
31.1–2, 340
31.5, 52
32.1–2, 63
42, 179
47, 34
55.18, 27
69.21, 55
72, 114
78, 110
82.1–3, 340
89.27, 41
91.13, 179
93, 34
96–97, 34
99, 34
103.19, 191
110.1, 47
Proverbs
  8, 116, 340
  8.2–3, 106
  8.15–16, 106
  16.15, 114
Song of Solomon, 180
Isaiah
  2.4, 15
  5.1–7, 49
  6, 110
  6.1 LXX, 54
  6.5, 34
  6–9, 109
  6.9–10, 109
  7.14, 48
  8.16, 109
  9, 114
  11, 62, 114
  11.10, 61
  18.13, 29
  24.21–22, 34
  25.6–8, 14
  25.8, 31
  26.19, 14, 31
  29.11–12, 110
  29.18–19, 14
  30.8, 110
  30.9–10, 110
  33.17, 114

Isaiah (cont.)
  33.22, 114
  35.5–6, 14
  37.16, 34
  40.6, 254
  40.9, 110
  40.11, 172, 175
  42.18, 14
  44.6, 344
  50.4–9, 110
  52.7, 46
  52.13 LXX, 54
  52.14, 341
  53, 83
  53.2–8, 341
  53.7, 191
  53.11–12, 24
  57.18–19, 14
  58.3–10, 223
  58.6–7, 316
  58.8, 14
  58.13, 29
  61, 21, 24
  61.1, 14, 46
  61.1–2, 51
Jeremiah
  7.1–15, 49
  16.1–2, 20
  17.19–27, 29
  30.17, 14
Ezekiel
  1.10, 44
  4.1–17, 20
  34.5, 172
  34.16, 14
  37.24, 114
  39.17–20, 14
Daniel
  3, 106
  3.25, 374
  3.92 Theod., 374
  6.10, 27
  7, 83
  7.13–14, 22–23, 46–47, 50
  7.14, 12, 24
  7.18, 24
  7.21, 24
  7.26, 34
  8–9, 51
  12:1, 14
  12.2–3, 31, 34
  12.6–13, 12
Hosea
  1.2–8, 20
  6.2, 83
  11.1, 48
  11.11, 18
  14.1–3, 15
Joel
  2.12–14, 15
Amos
  2.7, 316
  5.21–24, 223
  8.5–6, 316
  22.22, 317
Jonah
  1.17, 83
Habakkuk
  2.3–4, 15
Zechariah
  1.3, 15
  6.12–13, 23
  9.9, 42
  9.9–10, 336
  12.10–13.1, 83
  14.1–9, 34
  14.21, 39
Malachi
  3.7, 15
  4.6, 15

**Ancient Jewish Sources**
  (in alphabetical order)
1 Enoch
  37–71, 20–21
  54.4–6, 14
  57.1, 18
  90.28–29, 40
  94.6–8, 12
  95.6, 12
  Apocalypse of Weeks, 14
1 Maccabees
  2.40–41, 29
11Q11/11QApocryphal
    Psalms

# ANCIENT SOURCES INDEX 403

ii 2, 42
v 4 – vi 3, 42
11Q17/*Songs of the Sabbath Sacrifice*, 34
11Q*Melchizedek*, 20
11QPs<sup>a</sup>/11Q*Psalms*
  xxvii 9–10, 42
11QT<sup>a</sup>/11Q*Temple*
  29.8–10, 40
1Q28a/1Q*Rule of the Congregation*
  2, 14
1QM/1Q*War Scroll*
  2.1–3, 18
1QpHab/1Q*Pesher to Habakkuk*
  7.10–12, 15
  12 7–9, 39
1QS/1Q*Rule of the Community*
  1.11–13, 32
  3.13–4.1, 32
  4.6–7, 14
  5.1–3, 32
  5.4–7, 39
  6.4–5, 32
  6.13–23, 32
  6.17–20, 32
  6.24–7.25, 32
  7.13, 32
  8.4–11, 39
  9.3–6, 39
  9.11, 22, 39
  11.7–9, 39
1QSa/1Q*Rule of the Congregation*
  2.4, 50
2 Baruch, 15
  73, 13
  85.10, 12
2 Maccabees
  1.27, 18
  2.18, 18
  6–7, 83
  15.13–16, 79
4 Ezra, 65
  4.26, 12
  5.45, 12
  6.24, 14
  7, 67
  7.28–31, 13
  7.28–32, 65

  8.61, 12
4 Maccabees
  6, 83
  17, 83
4Q174/4Q*Florilegium*, 23
  1+2+21 i 2–7, 40
  1+2+21 i 6–7, 39
  1+2+21 i 10–13, 23
4Q175/4Q*Testimonia*, 22, 39
4Q225/4Q*Ps.-Jubilees*<sup>a</sup>, 83
4Q246/4Q*Aramaic Apocalypse*
  2.1, 23
  2 5, 12
4Q300/4Q*Mysteries*<sup>b</sup>
  3, 14
4Q372/4Q*Apocryphon of Joseph*<sup>b</sup>
  1 16, 41
4Q398/4QMMT<sup>e</sup>
  14–17, 15
4Q400–407/4Q*Songs of the Sabbath Sacrifice*, 34
4Q460/4Q*Narrative Work and Prayer*
  9 i 6, 41
4Q503–509, 27
4Q521/4Q*Messianic Apocalypse*
  2 2.7, 12
  2 2.7–13, 14
Apocalypse of Abraham, 14
Aramaic Levi Document
  13.4[88], 26
  13.6[90], 26
  13.15[98], 26
Avot de-Rabbi Natan B
  26, 33
b. *Baba Meṣiʿa*
  59b, 79
b. Bekorot
  47a, 17
b. Berakot
  56b, 83
b. Šabbat
  31a, 33
b. Sukkah
  52a, 83
b. Yebamot
  22a, 17
  90b, 17

## ANCIENT SOURCES INDEX

Baruch
   4.37, 18
   5.5, 18
CD<sup>a</sup>
   6.11, 38
Josephus, *Against Apion*
   2.165, 34
   2.175, 27
   2.201, 18
   2.204, 26
Josephus, *Antiquities*
   4.212, 27
   4.240, 30
   8.45–49, 42
   13.172, 32
   13.297, 31
   14.41, 34
   16.43, 27
   18.9, 23, 32
   18.11–22, 31
   18.17, 31
   18.19, 39
   18.63, 19
   18.64, 25
   18.118, 15
   20.102, 25
Josephus, *Jewish War*
   2.119–161, 32
   2.119–166, 31
   2.154–158, 32
   2.261–63, 20
   6.300–309, 25
Jubilees
   1.15, 15
   1.29, 40
   11.16, 26
   13.25–27, 30
   22–23, 15
   23, 14
   23.26, 15
   23.29, 14
   23.29–30, 14
   32.10–14, 30
   36.4, 16, 33
   47.9, 26
   50.5, 14
Judith
   11.13, 30

Liber Antiquitatum Biblicarum
   22.5–6, 26
m. Berakot
   1–2, 27
m. Giṭṭin
   9.10, 37
m. Kelim
   10.1, 30
m. Sanhedrin
   10.1, 83
m. Soṭah
   9.15, 14
m. Ta'anit
   4.2–3, 28
Mas 1k/*Songs of the Sabbath Sacrifice*, 34
Mekhilta
   *ki tiśśa* 1, 29
Philo, *Decal.*
   19–20, 16
   108–110, 16
   154, 16
Philo, *Hypoth.*
   7.12–13, 27
   7.14, 26
   11.1–18, 32
Philo, *Praem.*
   87–98, 15
   162–70, 15
Philo, *Prob.*
   75–91, 32
Philo, *Spec. leg.*
   1.1, 16
   2.63, 38
*Pirqe R. El.*
   31, 83
Psalms of Solomon
   17, 42, 67
Sibylline Oracles
   3.46–48, 12
   5.422, 23
Sifra
   *Qedoshim* 2, 2, 33
Sirach
   1.10, 106
   1.56, 105
   3.12, 106
   6.27, 106

24.1-2, 105
24.3, 106
24.4-5, 105
24.8, 53
24.10-11, 106
24.15, 106
30.3-4, 26
42.14, 18
51.10, 41
t. Berakot
  6.18, 18
t. Šabbat
  15[16].11-17, 29
Targum
  Exod 12.42 [Fragment], 22
  Exod 12.42 (Neofiti), 22
  Exod 12.42 (Ps.-Jonathan), 22
  Lev 19.18 (Ps.-Jonathan), 16, 33
  Lev 19.19 (Ps.-Jonathan), 38
  Isa 53.5 (Jonathan), 23
Testament of Dan
  5.3, 38
  6.4, 15
Testament of Issachar
  5.1-2, 38
Testament of Judah
  23.3-5, 15
Testament of Levi
  13.2, 26
Testament of Moses, 15
  1.18, 15
  10.1, 12
  10.1-3, 14
Testament of Reuben
  5.1, 18
Testament of Solomon, 42
Tobit
  1.7, 30
  1.7 GII, 30
  1.8, 30
  4.14-15, 16
  4.15, 33
  13.5-6, 15
*Toledot Yeshu*, 134, 267
Wisdom of Solomon
  1.7, 106
  2, 83
  7.20, 42

7.24, 106
8.1, 106
8.8, 106
9.9-10, 105
9.17, 105
10, 106
*Yalquṭ*
  575, 83
  581, 83

**New Testament**

Matthew
  1.1-17, 48-49
  1.16, 26
  1.21, 48
  1.22-23, 49
  1.23, 48, 50, 105
  2.13, 317
  2.13-15, 48, 346
  2.14-15, 49
  2.15, 305
  2.16-18, 48
  2.19-23, 48
  2.23, 26
  3.1, 325
  3.4, 326
  3.7-10, 17
  3.10, 326
  3.15, 343
  4.1-11, 27, 147
  4.4, 343
  4.8-10, 318
  4.17, 366
  4.18-22, 318
  4.23-25, 318
  5.3, 51
  5.3-11, 35
  5.3-12, 13, 21
  5.5, 13
  5.6, 319
  5-7, 48
  5.9, 226
  5.10-12, 14
  5.12, 13
  5.17, 49, 128
  5.18, 16
  5.18-19, 49

Matthew (cont.)
5.20, 13
5.21–30, 38
5.21–48, 22, 49
5.22–24, 221
5.23, 49
5.23–24, 28
5.31–32, 17
5.32, 37
5.33–37, 17, 38
5.38–42, 38
5.38–47, 16
5.38–48, 15, 226
5.44, 16, 38, 191
5.45, 40
6.2, 224
6.2–4, 319
6.5–7, 224
6.9, 41, 225
6.9–13, 56
6.10, 33
6.11, 18, 22
6.12, 225
6.13, 15
6.13a, 225
6.14–15, 225
6.16–18, 224
6.19, 319
6.19–21, 13, 19
6.25–31, 40
6.25–34, 18
6.26, 35, 41
6.32, 35, 41
6.33, 41
7.1–2, 16
7.2, 13
7.12, 16, 33, 38
7.21, 13
7.24–27, 22
7.28–29, 333
7.29, 38
8.4, 37, 127
8.5–13, 36, 333
8.11, 14, 35
8.11–12, 18
8.16, 316, 318
8.18–22, 18

8.20, 11
8.22, 38
9.20, 296
9.22, 318
9.27, 49
9.35, 318
9.35–38, 172
10.1, 333
10.5–6, 12
10.5–16, 18
10.7, 12
10.7–8, 318
10.9, 319
10.23, 12, 14, 49
10.23–25, 21
10.32–33, 13, 22
10.34–36, 13, 15
10.35–36, 19
10.37, 16
10.42, 221
11.2–4, 35
11.2–6, 20–21, 108
11.3–5, 316
11.4–5, 14
11.5, 316, 318
11.8, 325
11.9, 20–21
11.12–13, 14
11.13, 17
11.20–24, 13, 15
11.21, 15
11.21–24, 22
11.23, 12
11.28, 366
11.28–29, 175
11.29, 105
11.30, 311
12.5, 28, 49
12.22–30, 20
12.23, 49
12.25–28, 316
12.27, 19
12.28, 14, 21
12.39–42, 15, 22
12.40, 83
12.41, 15
12.41–42, 13–14, 19

## ANCIENT SOURCES INDEX

12.49, 221
13.10, 110
13.16, 111
13.16–17, 14, 33
13.31–33, 19
13.34–35, 110
13.51–52, 49
14.1–8, 326
14.13–21, 344
15.1–20, 49
15.21–28, 285
15.27–28, 318
15.29–31, 318
15.29–39, 344
16, 111
16.15, 330
16.16, 60
16.16–19, 50
16.17, 111
16.21, 111
17.1–3, 318
17.5, 49
17.17, 15, 22
17.24–27, 318
18.6, 221
18.10–14, 172
18.15–20, 50
18.15–22, 221
18.20, 48, 169
18.21–22, 225
19.4–6, 132
19.8, 17
19.9, 37
19.12, 37
19.16, 127
19.21, 319, 355
19.28, 18, 23, 42, 191
19.29, 13, 319
20.30–31, 49
21.1–11, 192, 336
21.11, 20
21.12–17, 49
21.25, 50
21.28–32, 35
21.33–44, 49
21.46, 20
22.1–14, 35

22.15–22, 318
22.36–40, 217
22.37, 27
22.37–39, 37
23.5, 296
23.8, 221
23.11, 319
23.12, 13
23.23, 16, 31, 49
23.29–37, 24
23.39, 15
24.17–18, 19
24.27, 13
24.37–39, 13
25, 222–23
25.31, 22–23
25.31–46, 13, 221
25.34, 13
25.34–36, 318
25.40, 51, 221
25.45, 221
25.46, 318
26.11, 319
26.17–29, 344
26.26, 164
26.28, 40, 50
26.39, 100
26.39a, 262
26.39b, 262
26.42, 262
26.44, 262
26.47, 50
26.60–61, 54
26.63, 336
26.63–64, 60
27.19, 189
27.24–25, 50
27.32, 346
27.37, 336
27.39–42, 336
27.47, 52
27.51–53, 50
27.51–54, 258
27.52–3, 80
27.54, 50
27.62–66, 50, 81
27.63, 83

Matthew (cont.)
  28, 75, 211
  28.2–3, 75
  28.4, 81
  28.6, 81, 206
  28.7, 317
  28.8, 75
  28.9–10, 19, 50
  28.10, 317
  28.11–15, 75, 81
  28.13, 78
  28.16–20, 50
  28.17, 78
  28.18, 80, 333
  28.18–20, 217
  28.19, 224
  28.20, 48–49, 169, 225, 230
Mark
  1.1, 45
  1.4, 17, 34
  1.4–9, 12
  1.5, 366
  1.9, 26
  1.9–11, 11, 46
  1.12–13, 46
  1.13, 258
  1.14, 11, 35
  1.14–15, 12, 15, 46
  1.15, 33
  1.16–20, 18
  1.17, 18, 36
  1.21, 46, 325
  1.21–2.1, 12
  1.21–34, 46
  1.24, 46
  1.25, 46
  1.27, 46
  1.35, 18
  1.38, 18
  1.40–44, 33
  1.40–45, 46
  1.44, 16, 28, 37, 46
  2.1–12, 20
  2.5–12, 35
  2.8, 46
  2.10, 46
  2.11, 19
  2.13–17, 18

2.14, 261
2.15–17, 33
2.18–3.6, 46
2.18–20, 14
2.20, 15
2.21–22, 17
2.23–3.6, 31
2.23–28, 16
2.27, 36
3.1–5, 36
3.3, 28
3.4, 36
3.7–8, 35
3.13–19, 18, 20, 23, 46
3.14–19, 35
3.22, 12
3.22–27, 19
3.27, 14, 34
4.12, 46
4.30–32, 33
4.39, 258
5.1–17, 35
5.1–20, 12, 317
5.19, 19, 46
5.20, 12
5.25–34, 33, 160
5.34, 318
5.35–41, 79
5.43, 46
6.3, 11
6.4, 20
6.6–11, 20
6.8–11, 18
6.14–16, 79
6.15, 20
6.30–44, 20
6.31–35, 18
6.31–44, 344
6.34, 261, 325, 342
6.45–52, 20
6.50, 54
6.56, 296
7.1, 12
7.1–23, 46, 128
7.3, 31, 33
7.3–6, 31
7.5, 31, 33
7.8–9, 33

7.8–13, 16
7.15, 37
7.19, 29, 45, 49
7.19a, 37
7.19b, 37
7.21, 16
7.24, 35
7.24–29, 36
7.24–30, 12, 285
7.26, 305
7.31, 12
7.36, 46
7.36–50, 20
8.1–10, 344
8.4, 18
8.17, 37
8.22–26, 47
8.26, 19, 46
8.27, 12, 35
8.28, 20, 79
8.29, 47, 60, 330
8.31, 21, 24, 47, 74, 83
8.32, 111
8.34–35, 14
8.38, 15, 22
9.1, 12, 24, 33
9.5, 46
9.9, 74, 83
9.10, 81
9.12, 79
9.17, 316
9.19, 15, 22
9.22, 316
9.28–29, 35
9.31, 24, 74, 83
9.33, 12
9.33–37, 20
9.46–48, 20
9.47, 13
10.1, 12, 35
10.2–12, 17
10.3–6, 36
10.6, 40
10.6–8, 37
10.6–9, 132
10.9, 37
10.11–12, 37
10.14–15, 35

10.15, 13, 17
10.17, 13
10.17–22, 19
10.17–31, 19
10.19, 16
10.24, 13
10.25, 13
10.31, 13
10.33–34, 24
10.34, 74, 83
10.35–40, 22
10.35–45, 23, 47
10.42–44, 12
10.45, 24, 85, 336
10.46–52, 47
10.47–48, 49
11.1, 35
11.1–7, 42
11.1–10, 20
11.1–11, 47, 336
11.9–10, 42
11.12–14, 20
11.15–17, 24, 39
11.15–19, 20, 47
11.16, 39
11.21, 46
12.1–12, 15
12.10–11, 83
12.18–27, 13, 31, 33
12.25, 37, 83
12.26, 130
12.28–31, 33
12.28–34, 16
12.28–40, 41
12.29, 40, 286
12.29–30, 27
12.30, 37
12.31, 37
12.32–34, 33
12.35–37, 47
12.38–40, 325
12.40, 13
12.44, 263
13, 45, 262–63
13.2, 21, 40
13.3–23, 13–14
13.5–37, 21
13.9, 263

Mark (cont.)
   13.9–13, 14
   13.15–16, 19
   13.24–25, 263
   13.26, 13, 83
   13.26–27, 22
   13.27, 18
   13.30, 12
   13.31, 263
   13.34–35, 15
   14.3, 263
   14.7, 15, 313
   14.12–25, 344
   14.17–25, 40, 42
   14.22, 164
   14.22–24, 85
   14.22–25, 21, 47
   14.24, 22, 24, 40
   14.25, 14–15, 33, 83
   14.28, 74, 83
   14.32–42, 24, 42
   14.35–36, 55
   14.36, 41
   14.45, 46
   14.53–65, 25
   14.58, 23–24, 40, 54
   14.61, 336
   14.61–62, 42, 60
   14.62, 13, 22–23, 46, 54
   14.62–63, 47
   15.1–15, 25
   15.2, 23, 47
   15.9, 23, 47
   15.12, 23, 47
   15.17–20, 47
   15.18, 23, 47
   15.21, 47, 55, 346
   15.26, 23, 42, 47, 336
   15.26–27, 47
   15.27, 15
   15.29, 23
   15.29–32, 336
   15.32, 47
   15.34, 52
   15.39, 46–47
   15.40–41, 18
   16.1–8, 19, 74
   16.5–7, 47
   16.7, 46, 169

   16.8, 47, 74–75
   16.9–20, 48, 74–75
   16.12, 78
Luke
   1, 140, 142
   1.1–4, 45
   1.5–38, 140
   1.20, 141
   1.26, 140
   1.26–38, 51, 143
   1.32–33, 142
   1.42, 141
   1.43, 52
   1.46–55, 51, 319
   1.47, 52
   1.52, 52
   1.53, 319
   1.70, 51
   1.78, 105
   2.1–7, 317
   2.10, 52
   2.14, 368
   2.21, 26, 51
   2.22, 128
   2.22–24, 28
   2.23, 128
   2.25, 127
   2.30–32, 51
   2.34, 127
   2.38, 127
   2.41–50, 125
   2.41–52, 27
   3.7–9, 17, 34
   3.23, 26
   4.5–8, 318
   4.8, 341
   4.16, 26, 317
   4.16–20, 130
   4.16–21, 21, 27
   4.18–19, 51, 219, 316
   4.18–21, 317
   4.19, 261
   4.22, 26
   4.24, 341
   4.25–27, 19, 51
   4.42–44, 325
   4.43, 349
   5.1–11, 20
   5.16, 18, 224

# ANCIENT SOURCES INDEX

6.12, 224
6.17, 35
6.20, 51, 222
6.20–21, 318–19
6.20–22, 35
6.20–23, 13, 21
6.21, 14
6.22–23, 14
6.23, 13
6.24–26, 19
6.25, 319
6.27, 16
6.27–35, 16
6.27–36, 15
6.31, 16
6.36, 16
6.37, 13
6.37–38, 16
6.46–49, 22
7.1–10, 51
7.11–16, 79
7.16, 20
7.18–22, 219
7.18–23, 20–21, 108
7.22, 14
7.22–23, 35
7.26, 20–21
7.36–50, 52, 261
7.37, 203
7.47, 203
8.1–3, 18
8.2–3, 52
8.3, 18
8.26–33, 316
8.43–48, 160
8.44, 333
9.1–2, 35
9.12–17, 344
9.20, 60, 330
9.22, 352
9.29, 330
9.41, 15, 22
9.46–48, 319
9.51, 52
9.51–19.44, 52
9.52, 12
9.57–62, 18
9.58, 11
10.1–12, 18

10.9, 12, 35
10.12–15, 13, 15, 22
10.13, 15
10.13–15, 41
10.15, 12
10.18, 14, 34
10.22, 41
10.23–24, 14, 33
10.25, 13
10.25–37, 52, 319
10.27, 27, 37
10.29–37, 16
10.30–37, 38
10.38–42, 203
11.2, 33, 41, 225
11.3, 18, 22
11.4, 15, 225
11.4b, 225
11.9, 225
11.14–23, 20
11.19, 19
11.20, 14, 21, 35, 366
11.29–32, 15, 22, 51
11.31–32, 13–14, 19
11.32, 15
11.42, 16, 31, 319
11.48–51, 24
12.8–9, 13, 22
12.13–21, 319
12.22–32, 18
12.33–34, 13, 19
12.35–38, 22
12.45, 19
12.51–53, 13, 15, 19
12.8–9, 13, 22
13.1–5, 15
13.11–13, 36
13.16, 316
13.18–21, 19
13.28–29, 18
13.29, 14, 35
13.31–35, 52
13.32, 12
13.33, 20
13.33–34, 42
13.34, 24
13.35, 15
14.1–5, 36
14.5, 29

Luke (cont.)
  14.11, 13, 51
  14.12–14, 13
  14.16–24, 35
  14.26, 16
  15.4–10, 19
  15.11–32, 35, 52
  15.20, 342
  16.1–31, 19
  16.10–11, 56
  16.16, 14, 17
  16.17, 16
  16.18, 17, 37
  16.19–22, 327
  16.19–31, 51
  17.3–4, 225
  17.20–21, 13, 366
  17.21, 14
  17.22, 15
  17.24–30, 13
  17.31–32, 19
  18.1, 225
  18.1–8, 226
  18.8, 12
  18.9–14, 33
  18.12, 31
  18.14, 13, 51
  18.15–17, 51
  18.18–19, 52
  18.18–30, 51, 319
  18.22, 326
  19.1, 326
  19.1–10, 19, 51, 253, 317
  19.7, 326
  19.8, 52, 326
  19.28–44, 336
  19.38, 369
  19.41–44, 52
  19.42, 369
  21.1–4, 261
  22.7–38, 344
  22.19, 164
  22.19b, 223
  22.20, 40
  22–23, 186
  22.28–30, 18, 23
  22.30, 42
  22.59, 305

22.67, 60, 336
23.4, 186
23.14, 186
23.15, 186
23.22, 186
23.26, 346
23.28–31, 52
23.34, 52, 190, 225
23.35–37, 336
23.38, 336
23.42, 13
23.43, 52
23.46, 52
23.47, 186
23.55–24.1, 52
24, 104
24.6–7, 83
24.10, 52
24.11, 75
24.12, 75
24.13–33, 75
24.16, 78
24.19, 20
24.21, 73
24.24, 75
24.25, 112
24.25–26, 343
24.25–27, 53
24.27, 113
24.30–31, 53
24.30–32, 344
24.31, 220
24.32, 53
24.36–42, 220
24.36–43, 219
24.39, 80, 84
24.44, 113
24.44–49, 53
24.46, 83
24.50–53, 53
24.51, 75
24.52, 80
24.52–53, 51
John
  1, 146
  1.1, 53, 69
  1.1–3, 95, 105
  1.14, 53, 159, 254, 372–73, 376

1.18, 53
1.28–29, 12
1.29, 54, 189
1.35–52, 20
1.45, 26
1.46, 317
2.6, 30
2.11, 54
2.12, 12
2.13–16, 39
2.13–17, 24
2.13–22, 23, 53
2.16, 39
2.19, 40
2.19–21, 54
2.20–22, 83
2.22, 54, 111
2.23–25, 20
3.3, 17
3.5, 13, 237
3.14, 54
3.16, 55
3.17, 370
3.22–24, 11
3.24, 11
4.4–42, 20
4.11, 333
4.19, 20
4.23, 54
4.25–26, 60
4.26, 54
4.42, 370
4.44, 20
5.17–28, 53
5.25, 54
5.28–29, 13
5.46, 108
6, 112
6.1–14, 344
6.14, 20
6.15, 15, 23, 54
6.17, 12
6.20, 54
6.24, 12
6.35, 54, 164
6.41–51, 343
6.48, 164
6.51, 164

6.53, 249
6.53–55, 237
6.55, 164
6.59, 12
6.68, 309
7.1, 12
7.1–52, 53
7.10–11, 54
7.35, 131
7.40, 20
7.52, 20
7.53–8.11, 130
8.12, 54
8.24, 54
8.28, 376
8.48, 373
8.48–52, 305
8.58, 132, 342, 373
9, 219
9.17, 20
10.11–18, 172
10.18, 55
10.22–39, 53
10.25–30, 53
10.30, 342
10.38, 53
10.40, 12
11.1–44, 149
11.25, 83
11.38–44, 79
11.45–53, 54
12.12–19, 336
12.16, 54, 111
12.20, 131
12.27, 54–55
12.32, 54
12.36–37, 54
12.38–41, 54
12.47, 370
13.1, 54
13.1–30, 42
13.3–17, 228
13.23, 182
13.34–35, 55
14.8–14, 53
14–16, 55
15.13, 55
16.7, 169

John (cont.)
    17.1–5, 53
    17.3, 55
    17.5, 332
    17.11, 53
    18.1, 55
    18.5, 54
    18.5–6, 55
    18.6, 54
    18.8, 54
    18.12–19.16, 25
    18.28, 54
    18.33, 23
    18.36, 318
    18.39, 23
    19.3, 23
    19.5, 55
    19.17, 55
    19.19, 23, 42, 305, 336
    19.21, 23
    19.26, 182
    19.26–27, 55
    19.28–29, 55
    19.30, 55, 176
    19.34, 55
    19.35, 78
    19.41, 55
    20.8, 76
    20.8–9, 111
    20.13, 55, 78
    20.14–15, 78
    20.14–17, 220
    20.14–18, 19
    20.15, 55
    20.17, 76, 169
    20.19, 55
    20.19–20, 220
    20.20, 80
    20.21, 53
    20.22, 55
    20.24–28, 219–20
    20.25, 55, 78
    20.25–28, 84
    20.26, 81
    20.27, 78
    20.28, 53
    20.29, 78
    20.31, 60
    21.1–23, 76
    21.4, 78, 220
    21.7, 220
    21.15–19, 55
    21.24, 78
Acts
    1.1, 348
    1.1–5, 349
    1.3, 75
    1.4, 78
    1.6, 349
    1.6–11, 349
    1–7, 52
    1.8, 217, 348, 353
    1.9, 76
    1.11, 76, 84
    1.21–26, 76
    1.22, 78
    1.25, 78
    2, 350
    2.10, 346
    2.31–36, 80
    2.32, 82
    2.33–35, 350
    2.34–35, 23
    2.36, 60
    2.44–45, 217
    4.32–35, 217
    5.31, 23
    7.55–56, 23
    7.56, 352
    7.59, 353
    8.4, 354
    8.26–40, 346
    8.32, 191
    9.1–6, 331
    9.3–7, 76
    10.38, 252
    10.41, 78
    10.42, 78
    11, 355
    11.19, 354
    11.19–26, 331
    11.19–30, 357
    11.20, 346, 354
    13.1, 346
    13.34–37, 80
    15, 52
    15.4, 46
    15.28–29, 357

16.16, 324
16.16–24, 324
16.19, 325
17, 334
17.3, 60
17.7, 336
17.18, 81
17.28, 332
17.32, 81
20.7, 84
21, 52
22.6–10, 76
22.18, 76
22.20, 353
23.6–8, 81
23.8, 31, 83
26.12–18, 76
26.19, 76
Romans
  1.2–4, 21
  1.3, 45
  1.3–4, 61, 65, 80, 85
  1.4, 80, 86
  1.5, 67
  1.7–8, 21
  1.9, 21
  1.18–32, 67
  3.20–24, 340
  3.25, 343
  4, 63
  4.25, 63, 85
  5.6, 63
  5.8, 63
  5.10–11, 343
  5.12–21, 370
  5.14, 370
  6.3–4, 224, 234
  6.4, 85
  6.7, 64
  6.8, 64, 85
  6.9, 80
  6.11, 85
  8.3–4, 62
  8.21, 258
  8.21–3, 86
  8.32, 63
  8.34, 23, 66
  8.38–39, 68–69
  9.4–5, 67

9.5, 69
9–11, 67
10.6–7, 105
11.28, 67
11.32–36, 370
11.36, 70
12.4–5, 367
12.4–6, 234
13.9, 16
13.11, 12
13.14, 340
14.9, 64
14.14, 45, 62
14.15, 63
14.17, 14, 70
15.3, 24, 45
15.8, 12
15.12, 61
16.25, 109
16.26, 67
1 Corinthians
  1.18, 230
  1.23, 63, 85, 333
  1.30, 340
  1.9, 21
  2.2, 60, 63, 333
  2.8, 25
  3.13–15, 371
  3.22–4.1, 77
  4.5, 371
  4.20, 14, 70
  5.1, 367
  5.2–13, 367
  5.7, 64, 189
  6.3, 68
  6.9–10, 14, 70
  7, 66
  7.10–11, 17, 45, 62
  8.6, 69, 105
  9.1, 76, 78
  9.5, 45
  10.16, 84
  10.16–17, 234, 237, 245
  11.17–22, 223
  11.20–21, 223
  11.23–25, 24, 42, 344
  11.23–26, 45, 62, 223
  11.23–27, 84
  11.24, 164

1 Corinthians (cont.)
  11.24–25, 15
  11.27–34, 223
  11.29–30, 223
  12.12–13, 367
  12.12–27, 234
  12.13, 237
  15.11, 77
  15.17, 72
  15.17–19, 82, 85
  15.19, 72
  15.20, 80
  15.23, 80
  15. 24, 14
  15.24–28, 13, 69
  15.25, 67–68
  15.26, 86
  15.28, 344
  15.3, 63, 83
  15.3–11, 45
  15.32, 72, 82, 85
  15.33, 332
  15.35–49, 220
  15.35–58, 77
  15.3–7, 76–77
  15.3–8, 72
  15.42, 80
  15.42–44, 220
  15.44, 80
  15.47, 105
  15.5, 18, 77
  15.50, 14, 70
  15.55, 369
  15.8, 76
  16.2, 84
  16.22, 21
2 Corinthians
  1.21–22, 252
  3, 108
  3.18, 340
  5.4, 66
  5.14, 64, 370
  5.15, 64
  5.17, 17, 367
  5.17–18, 354
  5.18–20, 343
  5.19, 249, 370
  8.9, 21, 45, 62, 105
  10.1, 15

  11.22–23, 77
  11.5, 77
  12.1, 65
  13.13, 21
Galatians
  1.1, 21, 72
  1.3, 21
  1.4, 24, 63–64
  1.11–19, 77
  1.12, 65
  1.14, 31
  1.16, 65, 76
  1.19, 45
  2.1–10, 77
  2.2, 65
  2.8, 67
  2.20, 24, 64, 66, 338
  3.1, 63
  3.19, 66
  3.24, 66
  3.27, 340
  3.27–28, 224
  4.3–5, 61
  4.4, 21, 105, 299
  4.6, 21
  4.26, 66
  5.1, 368
  5.21, 14, 70
  6.14, 63
  6.15, 17
  6.17, 210
Ephesians
  1.10, 234
  1.17–21, 192
  1.22, 258
  1.22–23, 234
  2.5–6, 85
  2.6, 66
  2.15, 355
  2.16, 234
  3.5, 109
  3.16, 234
  4.4, 234
  4.12, 234
  4.15–16, 234
  4.25, 234
  5.23, 234
  5.30, 234

Philippians
  2, 62
  2.5, 228
  2.5–6, 227
  2.5–7, 95, 104
  2.5–8, 61
  2.5–11, 21
  2.6, 69
  2.6–11, 45
  2.7, 228
  2.8, 15, 24
  2.9–11, 69, 370
  2.10, 67
  2.11, 60
  2.16, 367
  2.19–10, 80
  3.2, 367
  3.10–11, 80
  3.10–12, 85
  3.16, 367
  3.20, 66
  3.21, 86, 371
Colossians
  1.15, 340
  1.16–17, 105
  1.18, 234
  1.20, 258
  1.24, 234
  2.19, 234
  3.1, 23
  3.1–4, 85
  3.15, 234
1 Thessalonians
  1.10, 12, 21, 72
  2.12, 70
  2.14–16, 24
  2.15, 62
  4.2, 62
  4.9, 333
  4.13–18, 12
  4.14, 72
  5.10, 63
1 Timothy
  2.3–6, 370
  3.16, 350
2 Timothy
  2.8, 80
Titus
  1.12, 332

Hebrews
  1.2, 105
  1.3, 95, 340
  1.10, 105
  4.14–16, 262
  5.7, 262
  5.8, 262
  6.18–20, 262
  7.23–27, 262
  10.19–22, 262
  13.8, 356, 365
James
  2.6, 325
1 Peter
  1.3, 74
  1.7, 371
  1.8, 80
  1.17, 371
  1.19–24, 191
  3.21–22, 350
  5.11, 192
  5.13, 45
1 John
  1.1–3, 78
  2.1–2, 237
  2.2, 55, 340, 370
  4.10, 340
  4.14, 370
  4.16, 93
Revelation
  1.4–8, 344
  1.5, 80
  1.8, 376
  4.7, 44
  5.6, 84
  5.9, 344
  5.9–10, 189
  5.13, 258
  7.9, 344
  10.11, 344
  11.9, 344
  11.15, 191
  13.7, 344
  14.6, 344
  17.1, 344
  17.14, 191
  20.12, 371
  21, 191
  22.16, 80

**Early Christian Writings**
(in alphabetical order)

2 Clement
  8.5, 56
Acts of Andrew
  epitome 23, 159
  epitome 28, 159
Acts of Barnabas
  15, 159
Acts of Thomas, 331
Ambrose, *Ob. Theo.*
  46–48, 165
Apocryphon of James, 84, 131
  2.5–20, 129
Apocryphon of John, 126, 132
Arius, *Thalia*, 347
Athanasius, *Life of Antony*, 355
Augustine, *C. litt. Petil.*
  2.11.25, 162
  3.32.72, 162
Augustine, *Civ.*, 243
  399–400, 92
Augustine, *Cons.*, 267
Augustine, *De Trinitate*
  4.3, 204
Augustine, *Doctr. Chr.*
  1.36.40–41, 223
Augustine, *Enarrat.*
  91.19, 375
Augustine, *Ep.*
  55.20, 160
Augustine, *Tract. Jo.*
  7.12.2, 159
Clement of Alexandria, *Protr.*
  1.1, 346
Clement of Alexandria, *Stromata*
  IV, 23, 255
  IV, 150, 255
Cyril of Alexandria, *Second Letter to Nestorius*
  3, 95
Cyril of Alexandria, *Third Letter to Nestorius*
  6–7, 96
Cyril of Jerusalem, *Catechetical Lectures*, 208
Dialogue of Adamantius, 129

Dialogue of the Savior, 131
Didache
  1.2, 16
  8.2, 56
  14.1, 84
Egeria, *Itinerarium*
  17.1, 155
Epiphanius, *Apophthegmata Patrum*
  8, 159
Epistula Apostolorum, 122, 134
  1–2, 129
  4.1–2, 125
Eusebius, *Hist. eccl.*
  1.13.2, 154
  1.13.3, 155
  1.13.5, 22, 155
  2.16.1–2, 45
  3.39.15, 45, 266
  5.1.41, 209
  6.12.1–6, 55
Gospel according to the Hebrews
  fr. 12, 127
Gospel of Barnabas, 135
Gospel of Judas, 131, 133–34
  18, 127
  34, 126
  47, 131
  47–49, 132
  50, 132
  51, 132
Gospel of Mary, 122, 131
  17–19, 133
Gospel of Peter, 55, 73, 122, 126, 132–33
  5.17, 126
Gospel of Ps.-Matthew
  20, 143
Gospel of the Egyptians, 132, 134
Gospel of Thomas, 56, 121, 130, 133
  4, 13
  13, 133
  16, 15
  22, 17
  31, 20
  36, 19
  42, 18–19
  52, 20, 125

53, 126
56, 19
Gospel of Truth, 163
  20.21–39, 159
Gregory Nazianzen, Letters
  101, 259
Gregory of Nyssa, De Anima et
  Resurrectione, 220
Hippolytus, Comm. Dan.
  2.33, 375
Hippolytus, Haer.
  9.27.1, 32
Ignatius of Antioch, Eph.
  20.2, 164
Infancy Gospel of Thomas, 122,
  124–25
  2, 142
  6, 125
Irenaeus, Against Heresies
  1.3.2, 84
  1.20.1, 125
  1.22.3, 259
  1.24.4, 144
  1.30.14, 84
  3.11.8, 44, 56
Irenaeus, Demonstration
  34, 259
Jerome, Comm. Soph.
  preface, 75
Jerome, in Dan.
  3, 375
John Chrysostom, Adv. Iud.
  8, 160
John Chrysostom, Hom. 1 Cor.
  4.4 on 1.25, 79
John Chrysostom, Hom. Jo.
  32, 159
  75.1, 165
John Chrysostom, Hom. Matt.
  72.2, 160
John of Damascus, De Fide
  Orthodoxa
  64, 254
Justin, 1 Apology
  35.9, 155
  48.3, 155
  65–7, 84
  66.3, 56

Justin, Dialogue with Trypho
  88, 11
  103.8, 56
Justinian, Codex
  3.1.14.1, 163
Justinian, Edict on the Right Faith, 98
Letter of Aristeas
  207, 16, 33
Minucius Felix, Octavius
  9, 168
  29, 168
Nestorius, First Sermon Against the
  Theotokos, 94
Optatus of Milevis, App.
  1, 164
Origen, Against Celsus, 134, 266
  1.6, 160
  2.55–8, 80
  5.14, 81
  6.29, 81
Origen, Comm. John
  1.33, 112
P.Mich.inv. 6213, 155
P.Oxy. 840, 128
Protevangelium of James, 56, 122,
  124–25, 142, 199
  7–10, 128
  16, 128
  19, 128
Questions of Bartholomew, 131, 133
Rufinus, Hist. eccl.
  10.7–8, 165
Sophia of Jesus Christ, 122, 131
Sozomen, Hist. eccl.
  6.30.10–11, 163
Syriac/Arabic Infancy Gospel, 198
Teaching of Addai
  6.1–2, 157
Tertullian, Apology
  16, 168
  50.13, 353
Tertullian, Cor.
  3, 168

**Greco-Roman Literature**

Alcinous, Didaskalikos, 130
Chariton, Chaireas and Callirhoë
  Bk. 3, 79

Diodorus Siculus, *Bibliotheca historica*
   40.2, 34
Diogenes, *Lives of Eminent*
   *Philosophers*
   6.2.37, 147
Pliny the Elder, *Nat.*
   5.73, 32
Sallustius, *De diis et mundo*
   1, 86

**Qur'an**

   2.87, 139, 146
   2.154, 145
   2.253, 139, 146
   3, 140, 142
   3.33–63, 139–40
   3.35, 138, 141
   3.36, 141
   3.37, 141
   3.38, 141
   3.39, 140–41, 146
   3.40–41, 141
   3.42, 141
   3.45, 139–41, 145–46
   3.45–47, 143
   3.46, 142, 146
   3.47, 139, 141, 146
   3.48–57, 140
   3.49, 125, 137, 142, 150
   3.50, 142
   3.51, 138
   3.52, 138–39, 143
   3.55, 140, 144
   3.59, 139, 146
   3.169, 145
   3.185, 145
   4.41, 151
   4.155, 144
   4.157, 139, 143–45
   4.158, 144
   4.159, 151
   4.171, 139, 145–46
   4.172, 145

   5.17, 138, 146
   5.46, 142
   5.72, 138, 146
   5.75, 146
   5.110, 125, 142, 146, 150
   5.110–118, 139
   5.111–112, 138
   5.116–117, 138
   5.117, 138
   9.30, 146
   9.31, 146
   10.103, 144
   15.29, 141
   19, 140, 142–43
   19.2, 141
   19.2–40, 140
   19.8–11, 141
   19.16–40, 139
   19.17, 140
   19.17–21, 143
   19.20, 139, 141
   19.22, 141
   19.22–23, 142
   19.23, 142
   19.24–26, 142
   19.27–28, 142
   19.29–33, 142
   19.30, 143
   19.33, 145
   19.34–40, 138, 143
   19.36, 138
   19.41–50, 143
   21.35, 145
   21.69, 145
   21.91, 141, 146
   29.57, 145
   32.9, 141
   38.72, 141
   40.51, 144
   43.64, 139
   58.22, 146
   61.6, 142, 149
   61.14, 138–39, 143
   66.12, 138, 141, 146

# Subject Index

Abgar correspondence, 129, 154–58, 169
almsgiving, 218, 224
Arius, 89–90, 346–47
art, 171–73, 177–83, 187–94, 200, 342–43
ascension, 48, 75–76, 84, 208, 349–51
asceticism, 66, 147, 151, 355
Augustine, 65, 92–93, 234, 249, 260, 368
authority, 3, 11–12, 19, 38, 46, 50, 54, 85, 115, 130, 163, 318, 333

baptism, 11, 46, 62, 64, 85, 199, 224, 234, 237–39
birth narratives, 48, 51, 115, 139–43
birth of Jesus, 11
　virgin birth, 48
Black Theology, 293–94, 300–304
body of Christ, 233–234, 238, 241, 244–46, 368
Bultmann, Rudolf, 72, 272–73, 292

Chalcedon, 97–99, 201, 347
Christianity, African, 348–49, 360
Christianity, Coptic, 347
Christianity, global, 1–2, 347. *See also* church, global
Christology, 20–22, 41–42, 50–52, 295, 321, 353
　African, 349–50, 357–60
　Asian/Indigenous, 332, 334–35, 337–40, 343–45
　Chalcedonian, 94–101
　Islamic, 152
　Pauline, 21

church, 198, 232–33, 245–46, 367–68
church, global, 320. *See also* Christianity, global
*communicatio idiomatum*, 342
compassion, 11, 319
councils, church, 89–90, 97, 100, 199
creation, 258–59, 366
　new creation, 86, 367
creed(s), 88–89
　Nicene, 105
cross, crucifixion, 11, 47, 50, 52, 54–55, 62–64, 72, 78, 84–85, 143–45, 165, 167–68, 201, 217, 222–24, 230, 252, 259, 333, 340, 369, 374

Dead Sea Scrolls, 32, 38, 274. *See also* Qumran
Diatessaron, 127–28, 266
disability, 218–21
disciples, 18–19, 35–36, 46–50, 55, 75, 348

ecology/ecological crisis, 258, 320, 338, 340
Eighteen Benedictions, 27
empty tomb, 47, 50, 74–80
Enlightenment, 287, 305–7
eschatology, 12–15, 39–40, 54, 319
Essenes, 31–33
ethics, 11, 16–17, 198, 211–13, 321, 332
Eucharist, 96, 164–65, 208, 223–24, 234, 237, 239, 241, 244–45, 248, 368
evangelism, 217, 320, 357

*421*

evil, 13–14, 16, 37, 41, 159, 187, 226, 328, 358
exorcism, 19, 20, 19–20, 46, 316

face, 330
faith, 62, 67, 78–79, 254, 318
festivals, 12, 26–29
food laws. *See* kashrut
forgiveness, 17, 63, 217, 225–26
form criticism, 272

gender, 2, 139, 228, 278, 314, 338–39, 360
glory, 53–55, 89, 115, 342
God, 40–41, 53, 69–70, 90–91, 93, 232, 252, 294, 366
Good Shepherd, Jesus as, 171–76
Gospel books, 158–63. *See also* Jesus books
Gospel(s), 45–46, 121
    apocryphal, 55–56, 121–23
    fourfold, 44, 55–57
    John, 53, 76
    Luke, 50–51, 75
    Marcion, 122, 126, 129
    Mark, 45, 74–75
    Matthew, 48, 75
    Peter, 55, 73

harrowing of Hell, 132
healer/healing, 14, 19, 35, 46, 49, 219, 357–58
historical Jesus, 72–73, 76–79, 82–84, 86–87, 265–66, 271, 277–78, 283, 289–90, 294, 301, 305–11
Holy Land, 11–12, 35–36, 165
Holy Spirit, 55, 66–67, 80, 85, 91–94, 101–2, 234, 236, 252, 335, 350
homelessness, 315
    of Jesus, 148
*homoousios*, 89, 97
hope, 70, 86, 260–63, 321, 339
humanity, 101, 151, 235, 254
hymns, 201, 204. *See also* music

iconography, 157–58, 167, 300
identification, 198, 209–11, 222, 230, 303–4, 309, 317

imitation, 197, 211, 229–30
incarnation, 53–54, 61, 92–93, 101, 104–105, 201, 232–33, 252, 254, 256, 258–60, 303, 325, 346, 372–74, 376
indigenization, 330–31
inreligionization, 332. *See also* indigenization
intersectionality, 2
Islamic tradition, 134–35, 137

Jerusalem, 12, 23–24, 27–31, 39–40, 42, 47, 52, 78, 82, 149, 165, 199, 369
Jesus books, 121–22, 135–36. *See also* gospel books
Jesus scholarship, 2, 72–73, 250
*Jingjiao Bei*/Stele, 332
John the Baptist, 11, 17, 34, 138, 140–41, 146, 224, 325–26
Judaism, 26–33, 67–68, 81, 83, 103, 271, 273, 276, 278, 285–87, 290–91, 294
justification, 85, 340

kashrut, 29–30, 297
King and Lord of Lords, 191–96
King of Israel, 22–23, 50, 114–15
kingdom of God, 11, 12–15, 33–35, 58, 69–70, 318, 366–67

liberal theology, 270
liberation, 51, 58, 316, 321, 327, 337, 339, 359, 371
liberation theology, 222–23, 253, 293, 335, 359
liturgy, 154, 201, 209, 248, 253–54, 344
Logos, 105–6, 146, 332, 334, 346, 372–75
Lover, Jesus as, 180–86

martyrdom, 14, 24–25, 352–54
Mary, 48, 51–52, 104, 124, 138–43, 146, 151, 199, 248, 254, 319
Mary Magdalene, 19, 47, 48, 50, 55, 74–77, 146, 203–4

## SUBJECT INDEX

Messiah, 17, 23, 42, 47, 49–50, 53, 58–62, 70–71, 111, 144–45, 252, 336
miracles, 11, 19–20, 150
Mishnah, 288–9, 295
modern theology, 250–51
monotheism, 90, 139, 152
multicultural church, 354–57
music, 173–77, 184–87, 194–96, 201
mystery, 233, 235, 243–44, 346
mystical body, 233–34, 239, 242, 245–48
mystical experiences, 200, 202, 204

nature, 91, 94, 96–97, 100, 201
  human, 98, 100, 236, 254–56
Nestorian Tablet. *See Jingjiao Bei/Stele*
Nicaea, 89–90
Nicene Trinitarian theology, 89–94, 95–96, 101
*nomina sacra*, 158, 167
non-competition with divine, 256

P.Oxy. 840, 128
painting, 201. *See also* art
parables, 11, 33, 46, 49, 52, 110, 221, 291, 297, 319
Parousia, 84, 262–63. *See also* second coming
passion plays, 205–6, 208
Paul, 58, 72, 76–77, 81, 85, 224, 234, 332, 367–68
peacebuilding, 226–27
Pentecostalism, 335, 340, 358
periodisation, 274, 278
Peter, 45–47, 50, 55, 72, 75–78, 133, 146–47
Pharisees, 31–33, 50, 81, 285–86, 289, 292, 295–96
poverty, 11, 51, 147, 211, 217–18, 221–23, 230, 313
  global poor, 313–28
prayer, 27, 217, 224–25
predestination, 32
presence and absence, 85, 154, 158, 168–69, 197, 205, 223, 230, 232
Prophet, Jesus as, 20–21, 46, 108
  like Moses, 22, 39, 48–49

Qumran, 34, 110. *See also* Dead Sea Scrolls
Qur'an, 137–40

race, 2, 228–311, 336, 338
redemption, 15, 58, 252
Reimarus, H. S., 265, 268–69, 273, 277
relics, 154, 164–67, 206–7
resurrection, 13, 47–48, 50, 52–53, 55, 62, 64–67, 69–70, 108, 149–50, 219–20, 230, 248, 252, 259, 350–51, 369, 371, 374

Sabbath, 29, 36
sacraments, 85, 154, 164, 197, 204, 217, 223–24, 234, 237–43, 246, 248, 344
sacrifice, 28, 39, 84, 92, 244
Sadducees, 31–33, 50, 81, 285
Salvation, 26, 34, 51, 88–89, 96, 101, 105, 124, 126–29, 132, 155, 202–3, 211, 246, 252–54, 258, 260–62, 335, 337, 339, 341–42, 346, 357, 359
Satan, 14, 34–35, 147, 318
Schweitzer, Albert, 265, 268, 271
Second Coming, 151. *See also* Parousia
*Sensus Plenior*, 107
Shema Israel, 27, 40, 286, 295
signs, 54
sin, 58, 62–64, 240, 367, 370, 371
social justice, 320
solidarity, 313, 320
Son of God, 47, 53, 60–62, 65–66, 70, 80, 85, 89, 139, 186, 254, 373–76
Son of Man, 13, 20, 23–24, 41–42, 46–47, 352
Strauss, D. F., 269–70
substance, 234, 237, 244, 252
Sufism, 148

Talmud, 134, 288
teacher, Jesus as, 11, 36–39, 46, 48–49, 52, 148, 333
temple, 23, 39–40, 47, 53–54, 76, 106, 149, 286

Theodotus inscription, 27
theology, North African, 346–47
*Theotokos*, 94, 97
Third Quest, 273–74, 290
tithing, 30–31
*Toledot Yeshu*, 134, 267, 284
Torah observance of Jesus, 16–17, 26–31, 36–39, 46, 127–28, 288, 290
transfiguration, 47, 108, 113, 115, 318
Trinity, 88–94, 101, 233, 252, 310

union/participation/identification with Christ, 64, 66–67, 93, 232, 241

Victor, Jesus as, 176–80, 350

Wisdom, 89, 94, 105–6, 332, 335
women, 18–19, 47, 52
  'apostles of the apostles', 75, 77
Word, 53, 88–90, 92–101, 105–106, 112, 235–236, 254–55, 373
worship, 27–29, 197, 217, 340

CAMBRIDGE COMPANIONS TO RELIGION *(continued from page iii)*

FEMINIST THEOLOGY Edited by Susan Frank Parsons
FRANCIS OF ASSISI Edited by Michael J. P. Robson
GENESIS Edited by Bill T. Arnold
THE GOSPELS Edited by Stephen C. Barton
THE GOSPELS, 2nd edition Edited by Stephen C. Barton and Todd Brewer
THE HEBREW BIBLE/OLD TESTAMENT Edited by Stephen B. Chapman and Marvin A. Sweeney
HEBREW BIBLE AND ETHICS Edited by C. L. Crouch
THE JESUITS Edited by Thomas Worcester
JESUS Edited by Markus Bockmuehl
JOSEPH RATZINGER Edited by Daniel Cardó and Uwe Michael Lang
JUDAISM AND LAW Edited by Christine Hayes
LAW IN THE HEBREW BIBLE Edited by Bruce Wells
C. S. LEWIS Edited by Robert MacSwain and Michael Ward
LIBERATION THEOLOGY Edited by Chris Rowland
MARTIN LUTHER Edited by Donald K. McKim
MEDIEVAL JEWISH PHILOSOPHY Edited by Daniel H. Frank and Oliver Leaman
MODERN JEWISH PHILOSOPHY Edited by Michael L. Morgan and Peter Eli Gordon
MUHAMMED Edited by Jonathan E. Brockup
THE NEW CAMBRIDGE COMPANION TO BIBLICAL INTERPRETATION Edited by Ian Boxhall and Bradley C. Gregory
THE NEW CAMBRIDGE COMPANION TO CHRISTIAN DOCTRINE Edited by Michael Allen
THE NEW CAMBRIDGE COMPANION TO JESUS Edited by Markus Bockmuehl
THE NEW CAMBRIDGE COMPANION TO ST. PAUL Edited by Bruce W. Longenecker
NEW RELIGIOUS MOVEMENTS Edited by Olav Hammer and Mikael Rothstein
NEW TESTAMENT Edited by Patrick Gray
PENTECOSTALISM Edited by Cecil M. Robeck, Jr and Amos Yong
POSTMODERN THEOLOGY Edited by Kevin J. Vanhoozer
THE PROBLEM OF EVIL Edited by Chad Meister and Paul K. Moser
PURITANISM Edited by John Coffey and Paul C. H. Lim
QUAKERISM Edited by Stephen W. Angell and Pink Dandelion
THE QUR'AN Edited by Jane Dammen McAuliffe
KARL RAHNER Edited by Declan Marmion and Mary E. Hines
REFORMATION THEOLOGY Edited by David Bagchi and David C. Steinmetz
REFORMED THEOLOGY Edited by Paul T. Nimmo and David A. S. Fergusson

RELIGION AND ARTIFICIAL INTELLIGENCE Edited by Beth Singler and Fraser Watts

RELIGION AND TERRORISM Edited by James R. Lewis

RELIGIOUS EXPERIENCE Edited by Paul K. Moser and Chad Meister

RELIGIOUS STUDIES Edited by Robert A. Orsi

FRIEDRICH SCHLEIERMACHER Edited by Jacqueline Mariña

SCIENCE AND RELIGION Edited by Peter Harrison

ST. PAUL Edited by James D. G. Dunn

SUFISM Edited by Lloyd Ridgeon

THE *SUMMA THEOLOGIAE* Edited by Philip McCosker and Denys Turner

THE TALMUD AND RABBINIC LITERATURE Edited by Charlotte E. Fonrobert and Martin S. Jaffee

THE TRINITY Edited by Peter C. Phan

HANS URS VON BALTHASAR Edited by Edward T. Oakes and David Moss

VATICAN II Edited by Richard R. Gaillardetz

JOHN WESLEY Edited by Randy L. Maddox and Jason E. Vickers

BIBLICAL WISDOM LITERATURE Edited by Katharine J. Dell, Suzanna R. Millar, and Arthur Jan Keefer